Integrating Adult Learning and Technologies for Effective Education: Strategic Approaches

Victor C.X. Wang
California State University at Long Beach, USA

Information Science REFERENCE
INFORMATION SCIENCE REFERENCE
Hershey · New York

Director of Editorial Content: Kristin Klinger
Director of Book Publications: Julia Mosemann
Development Editor: Julia Mosemann
Typesetter: Kurt Smith, Sean Woznicki
Quality control: Jamie Snavely
Cover Design: Lisa Tosheff
Printed at: Yurchak Printing Inc.

Published in the United States of America by
Information Science Reference (an imprint of IGI Global)
701 E. Chocolate Avenue
Hershey PA 17033
Tel: 717-533-8845
Fax: 717-533-8661
E-mail: cust@igi-global.com
Web site: http://www.igi-global.com/reference

Library of Congress Cataloging-in-Publication Data

Integrating adult learning and technologies for effective education : strategic approaches / Victor C.X. Wang, editor.
p. cm.

Includes bibliographical references and index.
Summary: "This book provides relevant theoretical frameworks and the latest empirical research findings in the area of integrating adult learning and technology, exploring different innovative and strategic instructional approaches"--Provided by publisher.

ISBN 978-1-61520-694-0 (hardcover) -- ISBN 978-1-61520-695-7 (ebook) 1. Adult education--Computer-assisted instruction. 2. Internet in education. I. Wang, Victor C. X.
LC5219.I54 2010
374.0028'5--dc22

2009045728

British Cataloguing in Publication Data
A Cataloguing in Publication record for this book is available from the British Library.

List of Reviewers

Royce Ann Collins, *Kansas State University, USA*
Victor Hernandez, *University of South Florida, USA*
Barbara Hinton, *University of Arkansas, Fayetteville, USA*
John Hope, *Auckland University, New Zealand*
Kerry Lee, *University of Auckland, New Zealand*
Judith Parker, *Teachers College/Columbia University, USA*

Table of Contents

Detailed Table of Contents

Andragogy had a very slow beginning over a period of almost one century as a term referring to the theory and practice of adult education. Numerous elements were involved in the seventy years it took to establish its foundation: starting in England and the USA; andragogy and human resource development [HRD]; andragogy and self-directed learning [SDL]; conflict between supporters and detractors; comparing European and USA perspectives; trust in learners' abilities; scientific foundation of andragogy; skepticism and its counter-balance; and, antecedents of andragogy. Trends in usage and considering its possible benefits set the tone for the future of andragogy from 2000 forward.

This chapter explores the use of various learning technologies as tools for facilitating learner-centered teaching. The chapter offers another perspective on the scholarship of teaching with technology – through discussion of various theoretical models of learner-centered teaching, the role of technology on the student/instructor relationships, the impact on technology in different educational settings and contexts, and learners' cultural differences. The chapter concludes with a brief discussion of future trends, cautions, and speculations related to technology use in learner-centered teaching.

Effective teaching with technology in adult education stems from many factors. Technology is only used to enhance learning. Not only are teachers of adult learners required to study the tools related to the use

Online education is becoming an important component of career and technical education (CTE) in teacher preparation and at the graduate level. In the midst of such growth, and in response to questions about quality compared to traditional learning, there is a consensus that online courses and programs should be designed based on the needs of adult learners. However, much of the literature in online CTE lacks implicit connections to emerging notions of adult development and learning. This chapter provides an overview of the status of online education in CTE at the postsecondary level, discusses related issues and current research focus, and highlights adult learning developments and the implications for curriculum design, instruction, and use of technology. The chapter concludes with an outline of emerging trends bridging adult learning and online education relevant to career and technical education.

This chapter provides a conceptual discussion about the interaction between information and communication technologies (ICT) and the learning society. It focuses on the importance of knowledge and social capital building as key stones of the connected learning society, which is built upon online networks. This chapter also highlights the role of lifelong learning in the connected learning society as an instrument which can support flexicurity policies in the labor market. This work follows the common argumentation logic that the introduction of ICT usually leads to a change in lifelong learning opportunities, which are playing an especial role in achieving economic, employment and social goals. In the connected learning society, how technology is being used will ensure the continual adaptability and employability of workers.

As Web 2.0 surfaces as the latest trendy phrase in education and technology discussions, it is imperative that instructors not get caught up in the glamour of the latest technology and loose sight of the required andragogical underpinnings necessary for effective and efficient teaching and learning. This chapter will begin by exploring the major theories and theorists in the field of adult education and the meshing of these theories with technology applications in higher education and global business venues. While Malcolm Knowles is credited with popularizing adult learning theory in the 1970's, Stephen Brookfield, Jack Mezirow, Maxine Greene and Knud Illeris are among those who have moved the field forward over the past decades. Along with this progression in theory, the use of technology has escalated in popularity creating a need to frame its application in the foundational principles of adult education; an "Andragogy 2.0" focus is required. This chapter will expand on this theoretical base by offering short case studies that are linked to the theories as examples of innovative strategic approaches in the use of technology in adult teaching and learning.

Learning style research has informed effective classroom teaching strategies for decades. Technology has allowed faculty and students to move the learning environment from the four-walled classroom to a fluid global virtual space. Knowledge gained through the application of learning style research to the online instruction has enhanced practice; however, research demonstrating the alignment of learning styles with current technological resources has been limited. Learning styles and their interrelationship with technology and adult learners is as important today as initial learning style research was in the six decades after its beginnings in the 1940s. Education today must meet the needs of students who are more comfortable in electronic environments as well as those who need the four-walled classroom. The ability to use learning style research to accomplish both will lead to enhanced student learning and a more productive experience.

Technology incorporation adds another dimension to instructional design because it requires that the adult educator be skilled enough to design and use technology-enhance instruction as well as diagnose learners' skill levels and predispositions. Because each media has its unique combination of features, instructional designers should select and create technology resources carefully to best address the learning task and learner preference. Technology-enhanced communication methods are now available for sophisticated instruction and interactive learning: among students, educators, and resources: Web 2.0, egaming, video conferencing, and course management systems, as examples. Furthermore, technology-based accommodations can address access to resources as well direct instruction for people with disabilities. In any case, technology-infused instruction requires material and moral support by the organization's decision-makers.

This chapter is an examination of the influences involved in the integrating of adults into higher education. The chapter begins with an exploration of the increase in the number of adults in higher education since 1969. Comparing the changes in demographics from 1969 to 2007 shows how little large public

Preface

In the 1970s, Knowles predicted that education in the 21st century would be delivered electronically. His prediction came true as more and more universities in North America have purchased either WebCT or Blackboard programs to deliver their educational programs to students, especially to working adults who cannot come to campuses for the face to face meetings because of their family/work responsibilities. Since its inception in 1833 when the word andragogy was first coined by the German grammar school teacher Alexander Kapp, principles of adult learning have been used in one way or another to guide adult education practices in the field. The field of adult education was formally established in the 1920s in North America. Then, Knowles popularized the concepts of andragogy in North America in the 1970s. Adult learning principles have been critiqued, analyzed and refined. Overall, no better principles or theories can be found in the field for effective education than the principles of adult learning. As adult learners and adult educators pioneered the use of technology in the new century, central attention has focused on the following questions. How can technology improve teaching and learning in the field? What is the best instructional strategy to teach our subjects to our adult students and students in general? Is integrating adult learning and technology the solution to effective education for adult learners? With these questions in mind, this book will revolve around integrating adult learning and technology so that strategic approaches can be derived from this process of integrating adult learning and technology. Without strategic approaches, teaching and learning cannot be effective.

OBJECTIVE OF THE BOOK

This book will aim to provide relevant theoretical frameworks and the latest empirical research findings in the area of integrating adult learning and technology. Different innovative and strategic instructional approaches will be explored. It will be written for professionals who want to improve their instructional/training strategies revolving around integrating adult learning and technology. These professionals come from a variety of settings such as universities, community colleges, vocational/technical institutes, business and industries, correctional institutions, churches, museums, libraries, voluntary organizations, community action agencies, armed forces, and plethora of other settings. For those who seek teaching credentials in adult education and career and technical education, this book will provide pertinent information.

TARGET AUDIENCE

The target audience of this book will be composed of professionals and researchers working in the field of adult/higher education, career and technical education and instructional technology. Naturally, these professionals and researchers come from universities, community colleges, vocational/technical institutes, adult schools, public schools, business and industries, correctional institutions, churches, museums, libraries, voluntary organizations, community action agencies, armed forces, and a plethora of other settings. Moreover, the book will provide insights and support executives concerned with using principles of adult learning and technology to educate and train today's traditional age and non-traditional age students in the information age.

ACKNOWLEDGMENT

To ensure quality of books, editors/authors have their books go through the double blind review process so that their books will become refereed books in the field. This book is no exception. As my proposal to publish such a book was approved by IGI Global, I began to collect chapter proposals. All proposals were carefully reviewed by the editor in light of their suitability, the researcher's records of similar work in the area of the proposed topics, and the best proposal for topics with multiple proposals. The goal was to assemble the best minds in the adult education and technology fields from all over the world to contribute entries to this cutting edge book. Upon receipt, each full entry submission was forwarded to expert external reviewers on a double-blind basis. Only submissions with strong and favorable reviews were chosen as entries for this book. In many cases, submissions were sent back for several revisions prior to final acceptance. As a result, this book includes more than 10 entries highlighting current concepts, issues and emerging technologies in the field of adult learning. All entries are written by knowledgeable, distinguished scholars from many prominent research institutions around the world. Many of the reviewers happened to be authors who contributed chapters to this book. They were invited to be reviewers based on their sustained scholarship in this field. Also, they are highly respected teachers/scholars in their fields. Therefore, I extend a huge thank you to the following reviewers/authors:

- Royce Ann Collins, Kansas State University, USA
- Victor Hernandez, University of South Florida, USA
- Barbara Hinton, University of Arkansas, Fayetteville, USA
- John Hope, Auckland University, New Zealand
- Kerry Lee, University of Auckland, New Zealand
- Judith Parker, Teachers College/Columbia University, USA

Last but not least, I wish to thank my fellow authors and IGI Global for their contribution to this book. Without their contribution, this book would not be a reality. This book is designed for the teacher-practitioner and is written from both a scholar's and a practitioner's perspective. Because of the rich information provided by this book, individual chapters can be selected according to readers' specific needs and interests.

Victor C. X. Wang, Ed.D.
Associate Professor of CTE and Adult Education
California State University, Long Beach
Long Beach, California
May 28, 2009

Chapter 1
Beginnings of the History and Philosophy of Andragogy, 1833-2000

John A. Henschke
Lindenwood University, USA

ABSTRACT

Andragogy had a very slow beginning over a period of almost one century as a term referring to the theory and practice of adult education. Numerous elements were involved in the seventy years it took to establish its foundation: starting in England and the USA; andragogy and human resource development [HRD]; andragogy and self-directed learning [SDL]; conflict between supporters and detractors; comparing European and USA perspectives; trust in learners' abilities; scientific foundation of andragogy; skepticism and its counter-balance; and, antecedents of andragogy. Trends in usage and considering its possible benefits set the tone for the future of andragogy from 2000 forward.

INTRODUCTION

History and philosophy of andragogy was chosen as the topic to be addressed rather than history and philosophy of adult education. The reason for this is that there are already numerous published volumes of the history of adult education: M. S. Knowles – *History of the adult education movement in the United States;* Stubbelfield, H. W., and Keane, P. – *Adult Education in the American Experience: From the Colonial Period to the Present;* Kett, J. F. – *The pursuit of knowledge under difficulties: From self-improvement to adult education in America, 1750-1990;* and, Fieldhouse, R. and Associates – *A history of modern British adult education.* These are a few of the excellent published volumes on the history of adult education. There is one strong volume that is now in its third edition on the philosophy of adult education: Elias, J. and Merriam, S. B. – *Philosophical foundations of adult education.*

This chapter is mainly limited [with a few exceptions] to a chronological history and the accompanying philosophy of andragogy during the initial 167 years, in line with when the English language documents were published.

DOI: 10.4018/978-1-61520-694-0.ch001

BACKGROUND OF NEARLY A CENTURY: 1833-1927

The term 'andragogy', as far as we know, was first authored by Alexander Kapp (1833), a German high school teacher. In the book entitled 'Platon's Erziehungslehre' (Plato's Educational Ideas) he describes the lifelong necessity to learn. He begins the book with a discussion on childhood. However, from page 241 to 300 he turns attention to adulthood – Andragogy or Education in the man's age [a replica of the document is available at http://www.andragogy.net]. Kapp argues that education, self-reflection, and educating the character are the first values in human life. He then refers to vocational education of the healing profession, soldier, educator, orator, ruler, and men as the family father. Here we find patterns which repeatedly can be found in the ongoing history of andragogy: Included and combined are the education of inner, subjective personality ('character'); outer, objective competencies (what later is discussed under 'education vs. training'); and, that learning happens not only through teachers, but also through self-reflection and life experience, which makes it more than 'teaching adults'.

The term andragogy lay fallow for many decades, perhaps because adult education was being conducted without a specific name to designate what it was. Nonetheless, in the 1920s Germany became a place for building theory and another German resurrected the term. Rosenstock-Huessy (1925) posed andragogy as the only method for the German people and Germany, despirited and degenerated in 1918 after World War I, to regenerate themselves and their country. He suggested that all adult education (andragogy), if it is to achieve anything original that shapes man, which arises from the depths of time, would have to proceed from the suffering which the lost war brought them. Historical thinking is a fundamental dimension of andragogy, in that historical events are to be analyzed for what can be learned from them so that past failures might not be repeated. In this way the past becomes unified with the present and future – history past becomes unified with present knowledge and action for moving us toward the future. In andragogy, theory becomes practical deed, in the responsible word, in the crucible of necessity; however, practical deeds become the stuff of theory. Andragogy is not merely 'better' as an educational method for this purpose; it is a necessity.

About the same time, Lindeman (1926a) from the USA traveled to Germany and became acquainted with the Workers Education Movement. He was the first to bring the concept to America. Although he clearly stated that andragogy was the method for teaching adults, the term did not take hold in the new land until many years later. Lindeman presented an interesting piece on the method for teaching adults. Basically he asserted (1926a) in his first use of the word andragogy, that the method for teaching adults is discussion, which he says is different from the teaching of children. Moreover, in his classic book *The Meaning of Adult Education* (1926b), he never uses the term andragogy, but does include a chapter entitled, 'In terms of method'. A thorough analysis of this chapter reveals that he extensively explores, describes and explains the discussion method. Consequently, it seems safe to assume that he laid the earliest groundwork in the USA for a major practical application of andragogy as the method for teaching adults. In addition, Anderson and Lindeman (1927) reiterated the concept as it was brought to the new land of America.

ESTABLISHING THE FOUNDATION OF ANDRAGOGY: 1964-1980

England and the USA 1964-1970

Another extensive period of time elapsed until the term andragogy was used again in published literature. This time, it appeared in Great Britain. Simpson (1964) proposed that andragogy could serve as a title for an attempt to identify a body of knowledge relevant to the training of those concerned with Adult Education. He posited that the main strands could be parallel to what already existed in child education. The four main strands were the study of adult education, the study of adults, educational psychology of adults, and generalized andragogical methods for teaching adults. He issued a call for adult education to do this.

Knowles (1968a) presented his first published iteration of andragogy [a new label and a new approach] as being a major technological breakthrough in the field of adult education. For him this breakthrough was the conceptualization that adults learn differently from children. This breakthrough came as a result of a Yugoslavian adult educator, Dusan Savicevic, introducing him to the term with Knowles attaching his own special philosophy and meaning.

Knowles, (1968b) a short time after he published his first article on andragogy, was already applying andragogy in leadership training with the Girl Scouts. Although it was a new approach, it was enthusiastically embraced in that organization.

Knowles (1969) was also applying andragogy in his adult education graduate courses at Boston University. He used the approach of group self-directed learning as the means for implementing andragogy. Thus, he helped groups of students take responsibility for learning as much as they were able concerning a part of the subject matter of the course. Next, the various groups engaged the remainder of the class to actively learning that section of the course content. This was the way all the contents of the course were studied by the students.

Knowles (1970) indicated that he acquired the term in 1967 from Dusan Savicevic. [It was actually in 1966]. However, after becoming acquainted with the term, Knowles infused it with much of his own meaning garnered from his already extensive experience in adult education. He then combined his expanding practice around the world, his university teaching of budding adult educators, and quite broadly fleshed out his ideas on andragogy through the publication of *The Modern Practice of Adult Education: Andragogy vs. Pedagogy.* He originally saw pedagogy as being for children and andragogy being for adults. This American version of andragogy became popularized as a result following 1970. The main structure of his andragogical expression took the form of a process design instead of a content design, with assumptions and processes. The assumptions about adult learners at that time were: (1) they are self-directing, (2) their experience is a learning resource, (3) their learning needs are focused on their social roles, (4) their time perspective is one of immediate application. The learning processes adults want to be actively and interactively involved in are: establishing a climate conducive to learning, planning cooperatively, diagnosing their needs, setting objectives, designing the sequence, conducting the activities, and evaluating learner progress.

Andragogy and Human Resource Development (HRD) 1971-1973

Furter (1971), from France, proposed that universities recognize a science for the training of man to be called andragogy. The purpose would be to focus, not on children and adolescents, but on man throughout his life.

Ingalls (1972) provided the first handbook as a guide to using andragogy in helping adult educators [referred to as 'trainers'] become more systematic and consistent in their engaging learners in the learning process. This was developed and tested in a branch of the U.S. Government.

In the same year, Knowles (1972) declared that there was a growing interest of many industrial corporations in the andragogical education process, with managers functioning as teachers (or facilitators of learning), and that andragogy offers great potential for improving both interpersonal relationships and task effectiveness. Knowles (n.d.) also suggested that andragogy applies to any form of adult learning and has been used extensively in the design of organizational training programs, especially for 'soft skill' domains such as management development. An example he provided on this is for the design of personal computer training.

A series of doctoral dissertations over a number of years, focusing on the work of Malcolm S. Knowles, placed him squarely in the center of helping to expand and further develop the concept and philosophy of andragogy. In the first one, Henschke (1973) saw Knowles as a 'field builder' in adult education with his ideas on andragogy becoming a central core of his contributions to the theory and practice of the adult education field.

Knowles (1973) focused a full application of his conception of andragogy toward the Human Resource Development (HRD) Movement. He worked vigorously in the corporate sector and thus saw the importance of testing and relating andragogy within it. Then Knowles divided the listing of numerous learning theorists into the categories of mechanistic and organismic. His identifying andragogy as being in the organismic category helped cast, clarify and nudge the philosophy toward a more humane frame.

Andragogy and Self-Directed Learning (SDL) 1975-1981

Knowles (1975) published his guidebook for learners and teachers on the topic of Self-Directed Learning. This was the first time that he labeled pedagogical as 'teacher-directed' learning and andragogy as 'self-directed' learning. Previously, pedagogy was for children and andragogy was for adults. Now his perspective was that where new, unfamiliar content was involved with children and adults, pedagogy was appropriate; and, where adults or children had some background in the content, andragogy was appropriate. Andragogy was the underlying philosophy, and self-directed learning was the way andragogy was to be implemented. He also presented the nine competencies of self-directed learning, as follows.

1. An understanding of the differences in assumptions about learners and the skills required for learning under teacher-directed learning and self-directed learning, and the ability to explain these differences to others
2. A concept of [*the learner*] myself (sic) as being a non-dependent and a self-directing person
3. The ability to relate to peers collaboratively, to see them as resources for diagnosing needs, planning [*the learner's*] my (sic) learning, and learning; and to give help to them and receive help from them
4. The ability to diagnose my own learning needs realistically, with help from teachers and peers
5. The ability to translate learning needs into learning objectives in a form that makes it possible for their accomplishment to be assessed
6. The ability to relate to teachers as facilitators, helpers, or consultants, and to take the initiative in making use of their resources
7. The ability to identify human and material resources appropriate to different kinds of learning objectives
8. The ability to select effective strategies for making use of learning resources and to perform these strategies skillfully and with initiative
9. The ability to collect and validate evidence of the accomplishment of various kinds of learning objectives (p. 61)

Hadley (1975) in his Doctoral Dissertation at Boston University developed and validated an instrument of 60 items [30 andragogical and 30 pedagogical] that could help in assessing an adult educator's orientation with respect to the constructs of andragogy and pedagogy. The instrument was labeled as the Education Orientation Questionnaire (EOQ). The 60 items were developed from a pool of more than 600 statements illustrating how pedagogical or andragogical attitudes and beliefs about education, teaching practices and learning were obtained.

Ingalls (1976) added to the idea of using andragogy in corporate settings, in which he identified nine dimensions that the manager needs to function as a person who helps his workers learn and keep up-to-date in their various fields. The nine dimensions are: (1) creating a social climate in which subordinates feel respected; (2) treating mistakes as opportunities for learning and growth; (3) helping subordinates discover what they need to learn; (4) assisting the staff to extract learning from practical work situations and experiences; (5) letting staff members take responsibility for designing and carrying out their own learning experiences; (6) engaging staff members in self-appraisal and personal planning for performance improvement; (7) permitting or encouraging innovation and experiments to change the accepted way of doing things if the plan proposed appears possible; (8) being aware of the developmental tasks and readiness-to-learn issues that concern his staff; and, (9) trying to implement a joint problem-finding and problem-solving strategy to involve his staff in dealing with day-to-day problems and longer-range issues.

Kabuga (1977), an adult educator from Africa, broke ranks with strict adult education processes and advocated using highly participative teaching/learning techniques with children as well as adults in his native Africa. He was quite committed to and convinced of the value of the andragogical idea in all education, despite the fact that he had not tested those andragogical techniques with other than adults.

The second in the series of doctoral dissertation focusing on the work of Malcolm S. Knowles, came from Eskridge (1978). He looked long range from that present time in 1978 into the future, viewing Knowles' wholehearted commitment to the concept of andragogy as being the proper vehicle for the promotion of adult learning.

Knowles (1978), in this second edition of *The Adult Learner*, updated and added to his application of andragogy in HRD. He continued to be involved very much with corporate adult education and added some information that helped to clarify what was then the current situation.

Hoffman (1980), very much a practitioner, emphasized the differences between children and grown-ups (adults), with 'schooling' being for children and 'learning' being for adults. He affirmed his successful use of active learning techniques in working with more than 600,000 adult participants.

Knowles (1980) revised and updated his classic work on *The modern practice of adult education*, thus changing the subtitle from 'andragogy vs. pedagogy' to 'from pedagogy to andragogy'. In addition he added the fifth assumption – adults are motivated more intrinsically *(internally)* than extrinsically *(externally)*. He also added up-to-date illustrations from the field, thus supporting some progression and advances in the practice of andragogy. This revision and slight change in perspective was based on friends' who were in K-12 education, commenting that andragogy also worked for them in their classrooms.

Mezirow (1981), adding to the discussion on andragogy, developed a critical theory of adult learning and education, and laid the groundwork for what he called a charter for andragogy that included twelve core concepts that would help with an organized and sustained effort to assist adults to learn in a way that enhances their capability to function as self-directed learners. The core concepts are:

1. Progressively decreases the learner's dependency on the educator
2. Help the learner understand how to use learning resources–especially the experience of others, including the educator, and

how to engage others in reciprocal learning relationships

3. Assist the learner to define his/her learning needs–both in terms of immediate awareness and understanding the cultural and psychological assumptions influencing his/her perceptions of needs
4. Assist learners to assume increasing responsibility for defining their learning objectives, planning their own learning program and evaluating their program
5. Organize what is to be learned in relationship to his/her current personal problems, concerns and levels of understanding
6. Foster learner decision making–select learner-relevant learning experiences which require choosing, expand the learner's range of options, facilitate taking the perspectives of others who have alternative ways of understanding
7. Encourage the use of criteria for judging which are increasingly inclusive and differentiating in awareness, self-reflexive and integrative of experience
8. Foster a self-corrective reflexive approach to learning–to typifying and labeling, to perspective taking and choosing, and to habits of learning and learning relationships (sic)
9. Facilitate problem posing and problem solving, including problems associated with the implementation of individual and collective action; recognition of relationship between personal problems and public issues
10. Reinforce the self-concept of the learner as a learner and doer by providing for progressive mastery; a supportive climate with feedback to encourage provisional efforts to change and to take risks; avoidance of competitive judgment of performance; appropriate use of mutual support groups
11. Emphasize experiential, participative and projective instructional methods; appropriate use of modeling and learning contracts
12. Make the moral distinction between helping the learner understand his/her full range of choices and how to improve the quality of choosing vs encouraging the learner to make a specific choice (pp. 21-22)

Suanmali (1981), a doctoral student of Mezirow, focuses his dissertation research on the agreement he found that 174 adult educators, including professors and practitioners, had on ten of those twelve core concepts of Mezirow (1981) that all related to self-direction in learning. All items except numbers eight and twelve were included. The major theme that came out of his research was that to assist adults to enhance their capability to function as self-directed learners, the educator must: decrease learner dependency, help learners use learning resources, help learners define his/her learning needs, help learners take responsibility for learning, organize learning that is relevant, foster learner decision-making and choices, encourage learner judgment and integration, facilitate problem-posing and problem-solving, provide a supportive learning climate, and emphasize experiential methods.

CONFLICT BETWEEN SUPPORTERS AND DETRACTORS 1981-1984

Zemke and Zemke (1981) selected at least thirty ideas/concepts/techniques that they thought they knew for sure about adult learning/andragogy. These ideas lend themselves to three divisions: motivating to learn, designing curriculum for adults, and working with adults in the classroom. They asserted that if it is our job to train adults – whether they want to be trained or not – these ideas can give insight and practical help toward accomplishing that job.

Christian (1982) provided the perspective of assessing the Student's Orientation Questionnaire (SOQ). This instrument is similar in arrangement to and based upon 25 pedagogical and 25 andragogical items from Hadley's (1975) Educational Orientation Questionnaire (EOQ).

Allman (1983) regarded the connection between brain plasticity (fluid intelligence) and adult development. She asserted that this concept and research coupled with Mezirow's (1981) and Knowles' (1970, 1980) understanding of andragogy could be linked with her ideas on group learning and then merged into a more comprehensive theory of andragogy.

Both the Nottingham Andragogy Group (1983) and, Allman and Mackie (1983) addressed their beliefs about adults and adults' abilities to think creatively and critically in learning settings. They describe methods, several features of a teaching and learning process, and some stages of course development centered on their notions about critical thinking. Section one deals with adult development; section two with the empirical and theoretical foundations for a theory of andragogy; and section three purposes a model and theory. The perspective is clearly driven by research in adult development through life phases. They also reported a belief that Alexander Kapp, a German teacher, first used the word andragogy in 1833 to describe the educational theory of Plato.

Brockett (1983) substantiated that andragogy is being used to help hard-to-reach adults become more self-directed in learning to improve their lives. Brockett (n.d.) also affirmed that the principles of andragogy have been applied successfully in a wide range of settings. These include business, government, colleges and universities, continuing professional education, religious education, adult basic education, and even elementary/secondary settings. Moreover, Brockett (1984) also indicated that an andragogical approach works in using a proactive approach for developing written materials.

Eitington (1984) promoted pro-active engagement of andragogy with adult learners in most every situation throughout a book containing 21 chapters, 600 pages, and 100 handouts.

Nevertheless, some lack of enthusiasm about Knowles' andragogy concept was reflected by Hartree's (1984) feeling that Knowles' andragogy did not live up to what she interpreted as his desire for its becoming a comprehensive learning theory for adult education She also asserted that if viewed from the psychological standpoint, Knowles' theory of andragogy fails to make good its claims to stand as unified theory because it lacks coherent discussion of the different dimensions of learning; and, equally, if viewed as philosophy, it falls short because it does not incorporate an epistemology – an explanation for a way of knowing what one knows.

Jarvis (1984) wrote that the theory of andragogy had moved into the status of an established doctrine in adult education, but without being grounded in sufficient empirical research to justify its dominant position. Thus, andragogy was best understood in curriculum terms as an expression of the romantic, was launched into a romantic philosophy, similar to it and receptive to it. So it would seem that andragogy emerged at a time when its romantic philosophical structures reflected the romantic structures of the wider society. He also viewed andragogy as having been connected with a sign of the times when romantic curriculums were dominant, and with that passing, andragogy was losing much of its appeal.

Despite the hesitancy that some had about Knowles involvement in andragogy, Knowles (1984a) third edition of *The Adult Learner* relating to HRD appeared at this time. He was still actively engaged in the field, although he had retired from his professorship some years earlier in 1978. Knowles updated and added to his application of andragogy to HRD in this third edition. He continued to be involved very much with corporate adult education and added some more information.

Not to be deterred at this point, Knowles (1984b) presented the first book in which he cites thirty-six extensive case examples of applying andragogy in practice, revealing what worked and what did not, and summarizing the lessons that could be learned from experience in the effectiveness of andragogy in various settings. This wide ranging array of connections with various groups included applications of andragogy in these settings: Business, Industry, and Government; colleges and universities; education for the professions; continuing education for the health professions; religious education; elementary and secondary education; and remedial education.

COMPARING THE EUROPEAN AND USA PERSPECTIVES 1985-1988

Young (1985) perceived the European concept of andragogy as being more comprehensive than the American conception, even though he considered that Europeans do not use the terms andragogy and adult education synonymously. In addition, the primary critical element in European andragogy is that an adult accompanies or assists one or more adults to become a more refined and competent adult, and that there should be differences in the aims of andragogy and pedagogy (assisting a child to become an adult). Likewise, there should be differences in the relationship between a teacher and adult pupils and the relationship between a teacher and children.

Taylor (1986) offered a very strong and articulate research based model that reflected the andragogical process of transition into learning for self-direction in the classroom. This is from the learners' point of view and has eight stations on a cycle of what may be characterized as a cultural journey. The process alternates between phases and transitions. The critical points are: (1) equilibrium phase; (2) disconfirmation transition; (3) disorientation phase; (4) naming the problem transition; (5) exploration phase; (6) reflection transition; (7) reorientation phase; (8) sharing the discovery transition; and the next step is to come back to equilibrium.

Brookfield (1986) claimed that with andragogy (most probably as exemplified by Knowles) not being a proven theory, adult educators should be hesitant to adopt it as a badge of identity or calling themselves *andragogues* with the attendant belief that it represents a professionally accurate summary of the unique characteristics of adult education practice. Nevertheless, he suggested that in Andragogy, facilitating learning is a transactional encounter in which learner desires and educator priorities will inevitably interact with and influence each other.

Ross (1987) connected the concept of andragogy and its value with some of the research on teacher effectiveness. He believed that teachers' behavior relate to student achievement regarding such things as: Clarity, variability, enthusiasm, task-oriented behavior, use of student ideas, types of questions asked, probing, and levels of difficulty of instruction.

Henschke (1987) posed an andragogical model for conducting preparation of new and seasoned adult educators to ready them for engaging adults in active learning. The five building blocks of this model are: Beliefs and notions about adult learners; perceptions concerning qualities of effective teachers; phases and sequences of the learning process; teaching tips and learning techniques; and, implementing the prepared plan.

Davenport (1987) presented a case for questioning the theoretical and practical efficacy of Knowles' theory of andragogy, growing out of his research and perspective, perhaps adding to the confusion with his paradoxical definitions of andragogy and pedagogy and with his assumptions that lack clarity and solid empirical support. Davenport finished with his argument that some adult educators strongly urge that field would simply be better off to drop the word from its lexicon.

Burge (1988) said that one reason for distance educators to look at andragogy is the concept of quality. She asks the question: Would an andragogical learner-centered approach contribute to or undermine academic rigour? She believed that a closer examination of the key implications of andragogy and a learner-centered view within the new classrooms of distance education will contribute to academic rigour. It will also expand the definitions of helping adults learn to include more of the subtle qualitative aspects of learning. The quality of counseling and tutoring, as distinct from quality of course content, is another professional issue that benefits from a closer look at andragogy.

Pratt's (1988) stance appeared to question the value of andragogy as a relational construct. He had supported it previously, but grew more skeptical of it as time progressed. He suggested that further debate of it presents tension between freedom and authority, between human agency and social structures, thus seeming to stall the consideration of the usefulness of Knowles' conception of andragogy.

TRUST IN LEARNERS' ABILITIES 1989-1991

Eitington (1989) continued to promote pro-active engagement of adult learners through andragogy in most every situation throughout this second edition of his book. He thought andragogy had very practical use and was well received in the situations where he conducted adult education workshops.

Henschke (1989) developed an andragogical assessment instrument entitled, Instructional Perspectives Inventory (IPI) that included the following seven dimensions: Teacher empathy with learners, teacher trust of learners, planning and delivery of instruction, accommodating learner uniqueness, teacher insensitivity toward learners, learner-centered learning processes, and teacher-centered learning processes. The central and strongest major core of this instrument was originally and still is a focus on the teacher trust of learners. There are 11 items that teachers exemplify trust of learners:

1. Purposefully communicating to learners that they are each uniquely important
2. Believing learners know what their goals, dreams and realities are like
3. Expressing confidence that learners will develop the skills they need
4. Prizing the learners to learn what is needed
5. Feeling learners' need to be aware of and communicate their thoughts and feelings
6. Enabling learners to evaluate their own progress in learning
7. Hearing learners indicate what their learning needs are
8. Engaging learners in clarifying their own aspirations
9. Developing a supportive relationship with learners
10. Experiences unconditional positive regard for learners
11. Respecting the dignity and integrity of learners (pp. 4-5.)

Warren (1989) makes a clear connection between andragogy and the assumptions N. F. S. Grundtvig makes about adult learners and learning. He indicates that Grundtvig's assumptions drawn from his collected papers between 1832 and 1855 include: (1) students should bloom according to their individual capacity and not be crushed into conformity by externally-derived ideals; (2) subject matter is not important, but study should be chosen according to interests and should be geared toward personal growth rather than scholarship; (3) reciprocal teaching is the ideal learning process engaged through the living word; and, (4) the ultimate reason for learning is enlightenment of life – the gaps of religious/historical/poetic knowledge of one's world, and thus of one's self, integrated through both freedom and fellowship.

Imel (1989) mainly concentrated on answering the question 'is teaching adults different' by answering 'yes' and 'no' regarding the use of the andragogical model. She said that it mainly comes down to the following emerging considerations for practice. Determine the purpose of the teaching-learning situation, the context, the goals of the learners, and the material to be covered. Provide opportunities for teachers to practice learner-centered methods, by engaging teachers in learning technuiques especially suitable for adult students, such as small-group discussion methods, and effective use of non-traditional room arrangements. Select teachers on the basis of their potential to provide learner-centered instructional settings.

Knowles (1989a, successfully tested and refined this theory and design of andragogy on a broad spectrum in numerous settings: corporate, workplace, business, industry, healthcare, government, higher education, professions, religious education, and elementary, secondary, and remedial education.

In another work at this time Knowles (1989b) provided a clue about a major ingredient necessary and quite obviously present in everything he did and everyone he touched deeply. In his development and revision of his theory he considered both pedagogical and andragogical assumptions as valid and appropriate in certain varying situations (to the delight of some, and to the dismay of others). The pitfall and problem he discovered with this approach is that ideological pedagogues will do everything they can to keep learners dependent on them, because this is their main psychic reward in teaching. However, on the other hand, Knowles saw that andragogues will accept dependency when it clearly is the reality and will meet the dependency needs through didactic instruction until the learners have built up a foundation of knowledge about the content area sufficient for them to gain enough confidence about taking responsibility for planning and carrying out their own learning projects. Even pedagogues, when they experience being treated like an adult learner, experience greater psychic rewards when learners become excited with learning, and began experimenting with andragogy.

Nadler (1989) stated that HRD is based in learning, and every HRD practitioner should have an understanding of the theories of Adult Learning. This was a crucial observation, because many in HRD have overlooked that consideration.

Krajinc (1989) in echoing some others provides the most succinct and pointed definition of andragogy to that date, and perhaps one of the most beneficial definition, as she states, "Andragogy has been defined as...'the art and science of helping adults learn and the study of adult education theory, processes, and technology to that end' " (p. 19).

Knowles (1990) came out with the fourth edition and strongest edition of *The adult learner* book. In it he added the sixth assumption that adults need to know a reason that makes sense to them as to why they should learn some particular thing. In addition, he underscored the crucial importance of equalness, openness, democratic, realness, genuineness, prizing, acceptance, and empathic understanding or adult learners on the part of the andragogue. The andragogical teacher/facilitator accepts each participant (student) as a person of worth, respects his feelings and ideas, and seeks to build relationships of mutual trust and exposes his own feelings regarding the relationship between the teacher and adult learner.

From a very practical standpoint, Carroll (1990) supported the andragogical point of view. She vowed that adults need to know why and the importance of learning something, to learn experientially, to learn problem-solving, and that they learn best when the topic is of immediate value to them.

Heimstra and Sisco (1990) made what could be considered an extensive addition to the theory, research, and definition of andragogy. They provided annotations on 97 works related to andragogy, thus contributing to its international foundation. Heimstra said that applied correctly, the andragogical approach to teaching and learning in the hands of a skilled and dedicated facilitator can make a positive impact on the adult learner. He also suggested a situation that gave rise to the emergence of andragogy as an alternative model of instruction to improve the teaching of adults. They asserted that mature adults become increasingly independent and responsible for their own actions. Thus, those adults are often motivated to learn by a sincere desire to solve immediate problems in their lives, and have an increasing need to be self-directing. In many ways the pedagogical model does not account for such developmental changes on the part of adults, and thus produces tension, resentment, and resistance. Consequently, the growth and development of andragogy is a way to remedy this situation and help adults to learn.

Mazhindu (1990) established a foundational link between andragogy and contract learning. Thus, he asserted that contract learning (with its foundation in andragogy) may well help to facilitate continuous, meaningful and relevant learning throughout the nurse's career. Andragogy (contract learning) is suggested as one effective alternative to traditional nurse education.

Robb (1990) believed that South African andragogics can enable the improvement of understanding between Continental European and American adult educationists. However, for this improvement to take place, he saw the need for three further studies: whether andragogy terminology is necessary; whether adult educationists are scientists; and, where adult educationists differ in America and Continental Europe that could pave the way for a more adequate description of what andragogy is.

Knowles (1991) shares his dream of lifelong learning. In it he presents the eight skills of self-directed learning (SDL) and the competencies of performing life roles, as he tell how he conceives this kind of a learning system operating in the 21st century. The life roles he offers are: learner, being a unique person, friend, citizen, family member, worker, and leisure-time user. The Skills of Self-Directed Learning presented here were different from the ones presented in his 1975 *Self-Directed Learning* book.

1. The ability to develop and be in touch with curiosities. Perhaps another way to describe this skill would be 'the ability to engage in divergent thinking'. [This is the most striking skill of SDL].
2. The ability to perceive one's self objectively and accept feedback about one's performance non-defensively
3. The ability to diagnose one's learning needs in the light of models of competencies required for performing life roles
4. The ability to formulate learning objectives in terms that describe performance outcomes
5. The ability to identify human, material, and experiential resources for accomplishing various kinds of learning objectives
6. The ability to design a plan of strategies for making use of appropriate learning resources effectively
7. The ability to carry out a learning plan systematically an sequentially. This skill is the beginning of the ability to engage in convergent thinking.
8. The ability to collect evidence of the accomplishment of learning objectives and have it validated through performance (p. 1)

Peters and Jarvis (1991) call Malcolm S. Knowles one of the best-known and most respected adult educators of all time. They had him provide an epilogue to their book, which addressed an andragogical vision of the future of the adult education field.

Long (1991) speculated that although Knowles' form of andragogy is weak in empirical confirmation there are five reasons it has survived the criticism leveled against it: (a) The humanistic ideas underlying andragogy appeal to adult educators in general; (b) The limited empirical refutation of andragogy has not been strongly convincing; (c) Knowles' reaction to criticism was flexible and encouraging, which permitted him to incorporate some of the criticism in his later revision of the concept; (d) Knowles is a leader in the field and is widely respected for other contributions; and, (e) The inclusion of Knowles' concept of andragogy into the adult education knowledge base, has provided a framework for integrating several potentially useful ideas about adult learners, including self-directed learning.

Griffith (1991) credited Knowles as being the best-known American adult educator. He has made numerous contributions to the literature of the field, with an orientation toward practice that makes them attractive to teachers of adults in diverse settings and very likely has resulted in increasing the effectiveness of these teachers. In addition, his commonsense approach in his primarily descriptive rather than analytical writing has a wide appeal. Griffith concluded by saying that Knowles'

concept of andragogy has undoubtedly inspired countless practicing adult educators to adopt the term, to embark upon graduate study in the field, and to profess allegiance to their perception of the concept. Knowles has also stimulated a great deal of interest in the self-directed learner and the use of learning contracts (p. 105).

Lieb (1991) was involved in health services. His perspective on andragogy is that adults are autonomous and self-directed, have accumulated a foundation of life experiences and knowledge, and are goal-oriented, relevancy-oriented, and practical. He focuses on what motivates adult learners, learning tips for effective instruction in motivation, reinforcement, retention, transference, and insists that we 'treat learners like adults'.

Scientific Foundation of Andragogy 1991-1995

Savicevic (1991) provided a critical consideration of andragogical concepts in ten European Countries – five western (German, French, Dutch, British, Finnish), and five eastern (Soviet, Czech-Slovak, Polish, Hungarian, Yugoslav). This comparison showed common roots but results in five varying schools of thought: (1) Whether andragogy is parallel to or subsumed under pedagogy in the general science of education; (2) Whether agology (instead of andragogy) is understood as a sort of integrative science which not only studied the process of education and learning but also other forms of guidance and orientation; (3) whether andragogy prescribes how teachers and students should behave in educational and learning situations; (4) the possibility of founding andragogy as a science is refuted; and, (5) that endeavors have been made to found andragogy as a fairly independent scientific discipline. Moreover, he clearly aligned himself with the fifth school of thought in that the kind of research he was conducting aims toward establishing the origin and development of andragogy as a discipline, the subject of which is the study of education and learning of adults in all its forms of expression.

Savicevic (1991) also suggested that Socrates, Plato, Aristotle, the Sophists, Ancient Rome, the epochs of humanism and the renaissance, all reflect thoughts and views about the need of learning throughout life, about the particularities and manners of acquiring knowledge in different phases of life, and about the moral and aesthetic impact. He also credited J. A. Comenius in the 17th century with being regarded the founder of andragogy with his primary wish to provide comprehensive education and learning for one and all to the full degree of humaneness, and urging the establishment of special institutions, forms, means, methods and teachers to work with adults. In addition, he theorized that the institutional basis for adult education actually formed in the late eighteenth and early nineteenth centuries in Britain and other countries with the emergence of Mechanics' Institutes, workers' colleges & educational associations, university extensions, Boarding schools for adult instruction, correspondence education, and people's universities.

At this time, there was again strong criticism of American andragogy coming from Candy (1991) in Australia At the time Knowles articulated andragogy, self-expression and personal development were in vogue. Thus, self-directed learning and andragogy were gaining some prominence in becoming known as autonomous learning.

In addition, a third doctoral dissertation focusing on Malcolm Knowles involvement in andragogy was done by Muller (1992). She misinterpreted Knowles in that she critiqued his andragogical ideas from the philosophical perspective of progressivism rather than understanding his concept of andragogy from his predominately humanistic philosophical perspective.

Houle (1992) in contrast, emphasized the impact of Knowles on American andragogy, and how he worked this out in practice especially in non-school settings and the workplace. He went on to indicate that scholars and theorists may find great value in Knowles' discussion of the development of learning theories in the educational literature, and his exploration of the roots of his own thinking about theorizing. He also spoke about Knowles' work being practical and providing concrete examples and in depth case studies of how learning activities are planned, structured, and executed.

The struggle regarding andragogy and Knowles involvement in it was still heating up. Pratt's (1993) perception that after 25 years, Knowles' approach to andragogy did not fulfill a promise of being somewhat of a panacea for a teaching approach in all adult education. Pratt had become somewhat guarded about his earlier involvement in the andragogical approach.

Bragar & Johnson (1993) in addressing andragogy/adult learning in the business environment indicated that their research has identified five principles. They are as follows: Learning is a transformation that takes place over time; learning follows a continuous cycle of action and reflection; learning is most effective when it addresses issues relevant to the learner; learning is most effective when people learn with others; and, learning occurs best in a supportive and challenging environment.

Morrall (1993) raised the question of whether andragogy may flourish outside of a sustained, concentrated time period, in a part-time, short-term course. Although some evaluations suggest that it may, the critical component contributing to its success appeared to be in the residential aspect of the program that was involved in enabling the implementation of andragogy.

Ellis (n.d., circa, 1993) focuses on an application of andragogy to a graduate-level web technologies course comprised of working professional students. Both student feedback and instructor opinion on the application of Knowles' theory of andragogy to this course have been strongly positive. In seeking to bring numerous factors together in online learning,

Newman (1993) asserts that "to appeal morally-cognitively to adult inmates, in at least a somewhat context and in study of their membership in the human community, is to entail the principles of andragogy (the learning of adults, as opposed to the teaching of children, as elaborated by Knowles" (p. 49).

Kaminsky (1993) suggested that whether we have knowledge for naming something academically or not, we may still be practicing pedagogy, andragogy, or any other 'gogy' or 'ism'. This is the reason she selected that idea from hooks. She finds Ferro's (1997) remarks snobbish and exclusionary sounding as it appears that he does not want anyone, other than 'linguists', to try and name the world, or even to make up new ways of naming things. She argues that he wants that job to belong to the expert name-makers, who, it seems, can never be adult educators, let alone people who have never seen the inside of a college or high school.

hooks (1994) said "the possession of a term does not bring a process or practice into being: concurrently one may practice theorizing without ever knowing/possessing the term..." (p. 61). It is sometimes later that this kind of practice is given a label that comes into common use.

Poggeler (1994) listed ten trends which he hopes will be helpful for future development of European andragogical research, including: international knowledge, comparative understanding, political influences, a clear picture of *adult* as the 'subject' of adult education, concentration on the thirty to fifty age group, explaining the *social structure* of the clientele, "development-andragogy" of the Third World, criteria for successful learning and teaching, understanding the "lifeworlds" of the participants, and new types and alternatives of adult education. Some of these may also be applicable to the USA.

Zmeyov (1994) clearly in support of andragogy, stated that the most important trend in adult education in Russia is the application and further development of Knowles' (1970, 1980) theory of adult learning, or andragogy, in the process of education. Zmeyov further stated that Knowles' concept of andragogy [the art and science of helping adults learn]

which scientifically founds the activity of the learners and of the teachers in the process of the determination of goals and tasks, of content, forms and methods, of organization, technology and realization of learning, is considered now in Russia by many scholars and teachers as a fundamental theoretical base for adult education. The main scientific and practical problem for the adult educators consists in finding out the most appropriate combination of pedagogical and andragogical models of learning for obtaining assigned objectives of learning for a learner in an actual situation (pp. 36-37).

Wartenberg (1994) shows two seemingly disparate concepts of andragogy (the study of how adults learn) and whole language are compatible and should be considered by planners and implementers of adult literacy programs.

Delahaye et al. (1994) measured student's orientation to andragogy and pedagogy by using the Student's Orientation Questionaire (EOQ) developed by Christian (1982), and found them represented as being orthogonal or at right angles to each other. This relationship reflects some of the complexities involved in adult learning. Basically, he conceived the maturity of the adult learner as moving from lower to higher through the four stages of learning, as follows: 1) low andragogy / high pedagogy; 2) high andragogy / high pedagogy; 3) high andragogy / low pedagogy; and, 4) low andragogy / low pedagogy.

The fourth doctoral dissertation focusing on Knowles' view of andragogy was Cooke (1994) who observed Knowles in personal human terms and he thought it quite appropriate to designate him as the 'father of American andragogy', Perhaps, however, he considered that it would be better to just call him 'Malcolm' as he so many times referred to himself.

Knowles (1995) provided the most articulate expression and most complete understanding of andragogy from the American perspective. The structure of the theory is comprised of two conceptual foundations: The learning theory and the design theory. The learning theory is based upon adult and their desire to become and/or to express themselves as capable human beings and has six components: (a) Adults need to know a reason that makes sense to them, for whatever they need to learn, (b) They have a deep need to be self-directing and take responsibility for themselves, (c) Adults enter a learning activity with a quality and volume of experience that is as resource for their own and others' learning, (d)They are ready to learn when they experience a need to know, or be able to do, something to perform more effectively in some aspect of their life, (e) Adults' orientation to learning is around life situations that are task, issue- or problem centered, for which they seek solutions, (f)Adults are motivated much more internally that externally.

Knowles' (1995) conceptual foundation of the design theory is based in a process, and is not dependent upon a body of content, but helps the learner acquire whatever content is needed. There are eight components of the design process: (a) Preparing the learners for the program; (b) setting a climate that is conducive to learning (physically comfortable and inviting; and psychologically – mutually respectful, collaborative, mutually trustful, supportive, open and authentic, pleasurable and human); (c) involving learners in mutual planning; (d) involving learners in diagnosing their learning needs; (e) involving learners in forming their learning objectives; (f) involving learners in designing learning plans; (g) helping learners carry out their learning plans; and, (g) involving learners in evaluating their learning outcomes. Active involvement seems to be the watchword of Knowles' (thus American) version of andragogy, and each step of the andragogical learning process.

Milligan (1995) scientifically investigated andragogy. He conceptualizes his summary of it as the facilitation of adult learning that can best be achieved through a student centered approach that, in a developmental manner, enhances the student's self-concept, promotes autonomy, self-direction and critical thinking. However, despite some questions being raised, and lingering doubts, he believed that problem-based learning, most notably used in nursing education, has elements of andragogy within it.

Henschke (1995) focused on the description of a dozen different episodes with groups in various settings. In these, he showed results he considered successful in using the andragogical approach with the participants.

Skepticism and its Counter-Balance 1995-1998

Welton (1995) leveled one of the most vigorous assertions against andragogy and Knowles's influence in it, that,

the 'andragogical consensus' (anchoring the study of adult education in methods of teaching and understanding the individual adult learner), formulated by the custodians of orthodoxy in the American Commission of Professors in the 1950s and solidified by Malcolm Knowles and others in the 1960s and 1970s, has unraveled at the seams (p. 5).

Welton went on to express that the fundamental accusations expressed are that because of this perspective, adult education has abandoned its once vital role in fostering democratic social action, is on a shaky foundation, works to the advantage of large-scale organizations, and is conceptually inadequate to serve the interests of the disenfranchised in North American society.

Eitington (1996) was continuing to revise his book *The winning trainer* and use his andragogical approach with great success with many audiences. The contrasting perspectives made for some cogent debate in the field.

Zhang (1996) told about how andragogy was used in a major way to help the People's Republic of China move from a traditional planned economy toward the socialist market economy system. He told that in the discussing educational theories in the development of andragogy, Deng XiaoPing pointed to adult education/andragogy as the key to developing human potential, skills, technology, talent and knowledge. This would be accomplished through a job training system, continuing education, adult basic education system, and adult higher and middle school education system.

Van Gent (1996) asserted that andragogy has been used to designate the education of adults, an approach to teaching adults, social work, management, and community organization. He considered that its future lies only as a generic term for adult education and as a complement to pedagogy, which has been used mainly to focus on the art and science of teaching children.

Hanson (1996) from the other side of the discussion, called for adult educators not to search for a separate theory of adult learning [andragogy], but rather that we remove many of the unsubstantiated assumptions based on almost utopian beliefs about the education and training of adults linked to un-contextualized views of learning and empowerment.

Smith (1996) provided a brief history of the use of the term andragogy. He then limited himself to presenting Malcolm Knowles' major andragogical assumptions, and addresses some general issues with Knowles' approach by exploring the assumptions including the surrounding, continuing debate.

Also, Mynen (n.d., circa, 1996) offered a personal statement on andragogy's meaning to himself by focusing only on Knowles' (1996) assumptions. He sought to address where andragogy came from, what it involves, and how one actually does it. He asserted his belief that andragogy may also be applicable to everyone including children, and considered the possibility that the distinction between adult and child learners may not be relevant anymore, but that the two may need to be merged into one.

Zemke (1996) updated his ideas about andragogy / adult learning. He more strongly emphasized learning designs being: problem-centered learning, having pre-program assessment, integrating information, containing true case studies, orienting toward various learning styles, supporting growth and changing values, and including transfer strategies.

Houle (1996), in talking about Knowles' work in andragogy said that it remains the most learner centered of all patterns of adult educational programming. He also added a number of other things. Knowles kept evolving, enlarging, and revising his point of view and therefore became something of a moving target, particularly since he was intimately involved with numerous projects at every level of magnitude in both customary and unusual settings all over the world. He could bring to discussions and debates a wealth of experience that his opponents could not match. In addition, some of his followers developed variant conceptions of andragogy, thereby enlarging the discourse. Knowles idea on andragogy had application to a wide variety of settings. Houle concluded by saying,

Those who wish to do so can wholly contain their practice in the ideas expressed by Knowles and others, establishing appropriate physical and psychological climates for learning and carrying forward all of its processes collaboratively. Far more significantly, andragogy influences every other system. Even leaders who guide learning chiefly in terms of the mastery of subject matter, the acquisition of skills, the facing of a social problem, or some other goal know that they should involve learners in as many aspects of their education as possible and in the creation of a climate in which they can most fruitfully learn (p. 30).

Most dictionaries previous to 1996 have not included andragogy. However, the Webster Encyclopedic Unabridged Dictionary (1996), showing some recent recognition of the term in modern vocabulary, includes the definition of andragogy as, "the methods or techniques used to teach adults" (p. 77). However, this was a definition that did not exactly coincide with various definitions from the adult education field. As an illustration of using words that may be unclear or do not have one precise definition, Webster (1996) included 179 definitions of the word 'run'. However, we have not given up use of that term in our vocabulary because of the multiplicity of definitions. This would seem to give impetus that andragogy could still be appropriately used in adult education, despite there was no common agreement on a single definition.

However, Ferro (1997) insists that use of the term andragogy is not encouraged because of its being an unclear term. He charged that the use and meaning of the term, *andragogy,* has spawned a debate on the term and fostered the creation of additional unclear terms intended to define aspects of adult education; but he made a plea for adult educators instead to concentrate on what they know best, the planning and delivery of learning opportunities for adults.

Conner (1997) strongly declared that andragogy refers to learner-focused education for people. Thus, in the information age, the implications of a move from teacher-centered to learner-centered education are staggering. Postponing or suppressing this move will slow our ability to learn new technology and gain competitive advantage. She also depicted andragogy's major focus as understanding and adjusting our experiences and beliefs in relationship with the world we face on a daily basis. She questioned how we can expect to analyze and synthesize the extensive information with which we come in contact if we allow others to determine what should be learned, how it will be learned, and when it will be learned. She insisted that in order to succeed, we must unlearn our teacher-reliance.

Milligan (1997) continued to support his original investigation of andragogy (1995) in which he conceptualized his summary of it as the facilitation of adult learning that can best be achieved through a student centered approach.

Rostad (1998) outlined the library of the Nordic Folk Academy as a meeting place and an information center specialized in non-formal adult education, adult learning and andragogy. It possesses 20,000 volumes of books and 250 periodicals. It applies andragogy to make certain that people with low education, elderly people or people from sparsely populated areas avoid being marginalized.

In a very practical way, Billington (1998) found that the andragogical process of self-directed learning used in a doctoral program positively influenced a number of things. These were: The ego growth in doctoral students, their intrinsic motivation, the time they spent in the program, their desire for stimulation, their embracing challenge, and their ability in high level of complexity relating to pacing.

Jorgensen (1998) combined ideas of Knowles, Rogers, Jarvis and Ellen White into a comprehensive andragogical process. He suggested this for engaging Seventh-Day Adventist college students to think through their faith and what it means to them.

ANTECEDENTS OF ANDRAGOGY 1998-2000

Henschke (1998a) asserted that long before the term andragogy appeared in published form in 1833, ancient Greek and Hebrew educators, if not others, used words that although they were antecedents to andragogy, included elements of the concept that has come to be understood as some of the various meanings and definitions of andragogy. He attempted a descriptive definition of andragogy that moved in the direction of calling it a scientific discipline of study. This he posed in contrast to what others considered to be a fading influence of andragogy. He went back earlier in history and claimed that the language of the Hebrew prophets, before and concurrent with the time of Jesus Christ, along with the meaning of various Hebrew words and their Greek counterparts -- learn, teach, instruct, guide, lead, and example/way/model -- provide an especially rich and fertile resource to interpret andragogy. He expected that by combining a probe of these words and elements with other writings, a more comprehensive definition of andragogy may evolve.

Zmeyov (1998) aptly defined andragogy differently from others. He said that andragogy is "the theory of adult learning that sets out the fundamentals of the activities of learners and teachers in planning, realizing, evaluating and correcting adult learning" (p. 106).

Draper (1998) in providing an extensive, world-wide background on andragogy, reflected on and presented an overview of the historical forces influencing the origin and use of the term andragogy: The humanistic social philosophy of the 1700s & 1800s, the early twentieth century labor movement in Germany and USA, international expansion of adult education since World War II, commonalities of different terminologies, the debate in North America, the progressive philosophy underlying andragogy in North America, stimulation of critical discussion and research, and the viability of andragogy as a theory. He concluded, "Tracing the metamorphoses of andragogy/adult education is important to the field's search for identity. The search for meaning has also been an attempt to humanize and understand the educational process" (p. 24).

Baden (1998) developed and outlined twenty-seven different themes with accompanying interactive techniques that he perceives as being extremely useful in the process of helping association executives become more effective in fulfilling their responsibilities. Knowles et al. (1998) presented this revised fifth edition, but it was much changed from the previous four editions, thus moving andragogy into what was a somewhat different direction from the earlier editions.

Green (1998) comments on some important andragogical factors he suggests need to be considered in online learning. These factors include that in andragogy: (1) teachers need to guide learners to their own knowledge rather than supplying them with facts; (2) learners must balance life responsibilities with the demands of learning; (3) learners need to connect their tremendous amount of life experiences to their knowledge base and recognize the value of the learning; (4) learners are goal oriented and know the purpose for their learning new information; and, (5). learning is largely self-initiated and tends to last a long time.

Henschke (1998b) also emphasized that in preparing educators of adults, andragogy becomes a way of being or an attitude of mind, and needs to be modeled/exemplified by the professor. Otherwise, if we are not modeling what we are teaching, we are teaching something else.

Further, Hoods Woods (1998) perceived andragogy, as related to wilderness teaching, being based on four environmental influences active in every being. They are: external (physical); internal (physical); external (spiritual); and, internal (spiritual). These four influences interact with one another to determine how successfully we will be able to face survival challenges in any environment.

The most comprehensive of all the publications on andragogy is a book that includes thirty of Savicevic's (1999b) publications within a twenty-six year period. His work has addressed how andragogy has and will shape the literacy, the work place, universities, training and research, the humanistic philosophies, the evolution and future of andragogy and the practice of adult education. He also provided a number of descriptions and definitions of andragogy.

Boucouvalas (1999) insisted that although refined methodological or epistemological tools and indicators are critical for sound research in comparative andragogy, the role and influence of the 'self' of the researcher in the research process, is an equally critical element to be considered.

Additionally, Milligan (1999) added more support to his scientifically investigated andragogy (1995, 1997). More evidence agreed that the facilitation of adult learning can best be achieved through a student- centered adult learner approach.

Dewar (1999) articulated what she deems to be important principles of andragogy/adult learning for consideration when facilitaiing adult learning online. Increasing and maintaining ones sense of self-esteem and pleasure are strong secondary motivators for engaging in learning experiences. New knowledge has to be integrated with previous knowledge; that means active learner participation. Adult learning must be problem and experience centered. Effective adult learning entails an active search for meaning in which new tasks are somehow related to earlier activities. A certain degree of arousal is necessary for learning to occur. Stress acts as a major block to learning. Collaborative modes of teaching and learning will enhance the self-concepts of those involved and result in more meaningful and effective learning. Adults will generally learn best in an atmosphere that is nonthreatening and supportive of experimentation and in which different learning styles are recognized. Adults experience anxiety and ambivalence in their orientation to learning. Adult learning is facilitated when: The learner's representation and interpretation of his/her own experience are accepted as valid, acknowledged as an essential aspect influencing change, and respected as a potential resource for learning; the teacher can give up some control over teaching processes and planning activities and can share these with learners; teaching activities do not demand finalized, correct answers and closure; teaching activities express a tolerance for uncertainty, inconsistency, and diversity; and, teaching activities promote both question-asking and –answering, problem-finding and problem-solving. Adult skill learning is facilitated when individual learners can assess their own skills and strategies to discover inadequacies or limitations for themselves.

Savicevic (1999b) however, indicated that Knowles was inconsistent in determining andragogy and thus had caused much confusion and misunderstanding. He identified six mistakes of Knowles regarding his perspective on andragogy. First, Knowles defined andragogy as 'science and art' following in the footsteps of Dewey in doing the same thing with pedagogy. Second, he defined andragogy as the science and art of 'helping adults to learn' thus reducing it to a prescription or a recipe for how a teacher needs to behave in educating adults. Third, he declared andragogy as a 'model' for teaching even in pre-school, thus moving it away from just applying to adults. Fourth, he directed andragogy only toward problems of learning, thus neglecting social and philosophical dimensions of adults. Fifth, he emphasized an individualistic approach to learning and education with no link to adults' existing circumstances, education level, and other factors relating to learning. Sixth, Knowles' lack of historical awareness prompted him to think he was the first to use andragogy in the American adult education literature.

Mihall and Belletti (1999) provide an example of a one hour training program. It includes: objectives, a contrast of children and adults as learners, comparing the assumptions of pedagogy and andragogy, adult learning principles, current training methods' advantages and drawbacks with appropriate application, participants giving feedback, and a quiz.

It has been suggested by Savicevic (1999b) that andragogy is defined as a scientific discipline, which deals with problems relating to HRD and Adult Education and learning in all of its manifestations and expressions, whether formal or informal, organized or self-guided, with its scope of research covering the greater part of a person's life. It is linked with advancing culture and performing: professional roles and tasks, family responsibilities, social or community functions, and leisure time use. All of these areas are part of the working domain of the practice of HRD and Adult Education. It could be said that a clear connection is established from the research to practice of andragogy, with andragogy being the art and science of helping adults to learn and the study of HRD and Adult Education theory, processes, and technology relating to that end.

Reischmann (1999) saw andragogy at the academic level as the science of the education of adults. However, in Germany most scholars in andragogy still have direct connections to selected segments of the adult education providers and practitioners working in the field.

Clark (1999) considered that two books written in the 1920s began to change the term "adult learning" – Thorndike's *Adult Learning,* and Lindeman's *The Meaning of Adult Education.* In the 1950s, European educators started using the term 'andragogy', from the Greek word 'anere' for adult, and 'agogus', the art and science of helping students to learn. They wanted to be able to discuss the growing body of knowledge about adult learners in parallel with pedagogy. In contrast to pedagogy – transmitting content in a logical sequence; andragogy seeks to design and manage a process for facilitating the acquisition of content by the learners.

Thorpe (1999) developed a 24 slide Power Point presentation addressing the question of how to put the pieces together: learner, institution, and technology. He also focuses on: (1) who the learner is, (2) the fact that andragogy must be learned, (3) designed to fit the learner, and, (4) to incorporate technology positively.

Osborn (1999) declared that andragogy has the potential to play an important role in distance learning. However, she found that students need to be coached in the principles of the approach so they understand the teacher's expectations. Most students have been trained to rely on their teachers for leadership. Some need to be shown how to take responsibility for their own learning and become self-directing.

Similarly, Ovesni (1999) supported the idea that andragogy is to generate its own knowledge and is able to offer something to other sciences in scientific cooperation. Andragogy does not belong to any other science no matter what that other science is called. It is simply an integral part of a family of sciences studying education and is neither superior nor subordinate to any other science. Andragogy thus retains its independence from other sciences.

Merriam (1999) asserted that andragogy is one of the major ideas in adult education that was derived from the practice of the adult education field or discipline. rather than being informed by research and knowledge from other disciplines, especially psychology.

Henschke (1999) explored the gap between 'learning' and 'performance' within the andragogy concept relating to Adult Education and HRD. Considering some of the literature in both areas within the Academy of Human Resource Development [AHRD] led him to indicate that the two distinct terms together are different sides of the 'same coin'; and their close relationship is the key to HRD.

Savicevic (2000) also explored various antecedents to and backgrounds of andragogy before the term came into publication. In this he added another component to the scientific foundation and design of andragogy in this book. It is in the Serb language, but he has provided a summary in English. The summary indicates this study as dedicated to search for the roots of andragogical ideas starting from the antique civilizations up to the present time. We understand the term andragogical ideas as thoughts and concepts of persons about education and learning of adults, system of andragogical institutions that appeared in certain civilizations, as well as andragogical practice in which such ideas were realized. The structure of the study is made of several chapters that interconnected and logically linked, and is divided into the following five parts. 1. Conceptual and methodological frames of research includes: The nature and characteristics of research of andragogical ideas; and, methodological frame of researches. 2. Searching for the roots of andragogical ideas includes: Adult learning before literacy; Ancient Greek civilization; activity of sophists; Socrates; Plato; Aristotle; diffusion of Greek culture and science; Ancient Rome; Jewish cultural heritage; Middle ages; and, reversal which brings New Century. 3. Andragogical ideas in the international context includes: The work of Jan Amos Komensky; ideas of Gruntdvig and their practical realization, thoughts of E. N. Medinsky;

view of E. C. Lindemann; Thorndike's comprehension; and, thoughts of Friere. 4. Andragogical ideas in Yugoslav frame and context includes: Practical realization in Yugoslav cultural space; social philosophy of Svetozar Markovic; Radovan Dragovic; Dimitrije Tucovic; Dusan Popovic; Filip Filipovic; activities of the Serbian social democrats in practice; and, thoughts of Vicentije Rakicc. 5. Andragogical comparisons and conclusions included a final general discussion.

Ovesni (2000) proposed three concepts and models of andragogues' professional preparation, based upon scientific research in andragogy. They area model of professional preparation of andragogical personnel of general profile; a model with viable tendency toward distinction; and, models of diversification with respect to the field of the system of adult education, i.e. the scope of the system and with respect to institutions and associations within which the process of education is performed.

Further, Monts (2000) suggested that various research issues regarding andragogy need to be explored, such as the effect of instruction of students in self-directed learning has upon academic success. There is also the necessity of instructors and students needing training in andragogical teaching and learning in order to break away from the pedagogical mentality, and gain a greater effectiveness in the utilization of the andragogical model.

Reischmann (2000) indicated that in 1994 he changed the Otto Freiderick University, Bamberg, Germany, 'Chair of Adult Education' to 'Chair of Andragogy'. His understanding differentiates 'andragogy as the research' and 'adult education as the practice' in the education and learning of adults.

Johnson (2000) saw andragogy as an approach to learning that includes a focus primarily on the needs of the learner in every aspect of his/her life. He also asserted that given most, if not all definitions in the social science literature, andragogy could qualify as a theory or at least an emergent theory. He also believed that built into andragogy is a method for engaging learners in the discovery of meaning for them in their personal and professional lives. During his forty years in the field [much of that time he worked in some capacity with Malcolm Knowles], in a wide variety of settings he successfully tested and applied this andragogical method with many participants affirming the results.

TRENDS OF RESEARCH

Some trends which may be helpful for future development of both qualitative (i.e. phenomenology) and quantative (i.e. empirical) research in andragogy, could include: International knowledge, comparative understanding, political influences, a clear picture of *adult* as the 'subject' of adult education, concentration on the thirty to fifty age group, explaining the *social structure* of the clientele, 'development-andragogy' of the Third World, criteria for successful learning and teaching, understanding the 'life-worlds' of the participants, and new types and alternatives of adult education. Even a bit more specific may be some empirical evidence to clarify whether andragogy provides better results from learning that other approaches that emphasize teaching or facilitating adult learning.

CONCLUSION

Andragogy was first authored by Alexander Kapp (1833) a German high school teacher. He asserted andragogy as education at the man's age including self-reflection, and educating the character are the first values in human life. Patterns in andragogy encompassed the inner, subjective personality, and outer, objective competencies, that learning happens not only through teachers, but also through self-reflection and life experience, which makes it more than teaching adults.

Lindeman (1926) brought andragogy to the USA from the Workers Education Movement in Germany. He laid the earliest groundwork in the USA for a major practical application of andragogy as the method for teaching adults. Although the term lay fallow for many years, Knowles (1970) helped establish the foundation for it in the USA. The foundation was initially based on assumptions and processes as follows. The assumptions were the self-directedness of adults, their experience being a resource for learning, learning needs grew out of their social role tasks, and immediate application of learning was one of its hallmarks. The process elements were setting a climate conducive to learning, mutual planning of learning by teachers and learners, self-diagnosis of learning needs, learning objectives growing out of needs, designing a pattern of learning experiences, conducting the activities, and evaluating the progress made in learning.

Hadley (1975) developed and validated an instrument entitled Educational Orientation Questionnaire of 60 items that could help in assessing and adult educator's orientation with respect to the contructs of andragogy and pedagogy. Knowles (1975) provided a self-directed guide for learners and teachers including a list of required skills of self-directed learning. Mezirow (1981) provided a charter for andragogy, with Suanmali (1981) undergirding it with his research in the field, that solidly established self-directed learning as the cardinal principle and major approach for implementing andragogy. The Nottingham [UK] Andragogy Group (1983) added critical thinking to the andragogy equation, with much attention directed to research in adult development through life phaes.

Among other things, Hartree (1984) felt that Knowles' andragogy did not live up to what she interpreted as his desire for its becoming a comprehensive learning theory for adult education. In addition, Jarvis (1984) estimated that the theory of andragogy had moved into the status of an established doctrine, but without geing grounded in sufficient empirical research to justify its dominate position. Moreover, Jarvis thought that andragogy had been connected with a sign of the times when romantic curriculums were dominant, and with that passing, andragogy was losing much of its appeal.

Not to be deterred at this point, Knowles (1984b) presented the first book in which he cites 36 extensive case examples of applying andragogy working in practice within various groups: Business, industry, government, colleges, universities, education for the professions, continuing education in the health professions, religious education, elementary and secondary education, and remedial education. Taylor (1986) offered a very strong and articulate research based model, for the andragogical process of transition into learning for self-direction in the classroom. The phases and transitions are: equiibrium, disconfirmation, disorientation, naming (sic) the problem, exploration, reflection, reorientation, sharing (sic) the discovery, and back to equilibrium. Nonetheless, Davenport (1987) asserted that because of the lack of clarity and solid empirical support, that adult educaton would simply better of to drop the work andragogy from its lexicon.

Henschke (1989) developed an andragogical assessment instrument entitled Instructional Perspective Inventory which was later validated. The central and strongest core element in it which includes 11 items is the teacher trust of learners and the learners trust in their own ability to learn. Knowles (1991) added a crucial dimension to the skills of self-directed learning – the ability to develop and be in touch with curiosities. Savicevic (1991) provided a critical consideration of the scientific foundation of andragogical concepts in ten European Countries: Five western – German, French, Dutch, British, Finnish; and, five eastern – Soviet, Czeck-Slovak, Polish, Hungarian, Yugoslavian. Moreover, he aligned himself with the endeavors to found andragogy as a fairly independent scientific discipline, the subject of which is the study of education and learning of adults in all its forms of expression. Poggler (1994) listed ten trends which he hops will be helpful for development of European andragogical research, including: International, comparative, political, adult as a subject, 30 to 50 age group, social structure, development-andragogy in the 3rd World, criteria for successful teaching and learning, understanding participant 'lifeworlds', and new adult education types and alternatives.

Welton, (1995) expressed that the fundamental accusations against the andragogical consensus is that adult education has abandoned its once vital role in fostering democratic social action. Thus, it is on a shaky founjdation, which works to the advantage of large-scale organizations, and is conceptually inadquate to serve the interests of the disenfranchised in North American society. However, counter to this point of view, Houle (1996) said that Knowles' work in andragogy remains the most learner-centered of all patterns of adult educational programming. He states that andragogy influences every other system, with the leaders knowing that they should involve learners in as many aspectsw of their education as possible and in the creation of a climate inwhich they can most fruitfully learn.

Henschke (1998) asserted that long before the term andragogy appeared in published form in 1833, ancient Greek and Hebrew educators, if not others, used words that although they were antecedents to andragogy, included elements of he concept that has come tgo be understood as some of the various meanings of andragogy. He attempted a descriptive definition of andragogy that moved in the direction of calling it a scientific discipline of study, in contrast to what others considered to be a fading influence of andragogy. Draper (1998) in providing an extensive worlk-wide background on andragogy, reflecte on and presented an overview of tghe historical fordces influencing the origin and use of the term andragogy. He closed by saying that tracing the metamorphoses of andragogy / adult education is important to the field's search for identity, and the search for meaning has also been an attempt to humanize and understand the educational process.

In a very timely manner, the most comprehensive of all the publications on andragogy is a book that included 30 of Savicevic's (1999b) publications within a 26 year period. He claimed that andragogy is defined as a scientific discipline, which deals with problems relating to Human Resource Development and Adult Education and learning in all of its manifestations and expressions, whether formal or informal, organized or self-guided, with its scope of research covering the greater part of a person's life. However, in this work he also criticized Knowles as being inconsistent in determining andragogy and thus had caused much confusion and misunderstanding. He identified six mistakes of Knowles regarding his perspective on andragogy: Defined andragogy as 'science and art'; defined andragogy as the science and art of 'helping adults to learn' thus reducing it to a perscription how a teacher needs to behave in educating adults; declared andragogy as a 'model' for teaching even in pre-school; directed andragogy only toward problems of learning, thus neglecting social and philosophical dimensions of adults; emphasized an individualistic approach to learning and education; and, lacked historical awareness of the first use of andragogy in the USA.

Savicevic (2000) also explored various antecedents to and background of andraogy before the term came into publication. The study is dedicated to search for the roots of andragogical ideas start from the antique civilizations up to the present time. Billington (2000) found that with 60 men and women ages 37 to 48, a number of key factors relating to andragogy that helped them to grow, or if absent made them regress and not grow. Among all of the andragogical factors, self-directed learning is one of the most prominent and important.

REFERENCES

A philosophy of adult education (n.d.).

Allman, P. (1983). The nature and process of adult development. In M. Tight (Ed.), *Education for adults: Adult learning and education* (vol. 1, pp. 107-123). London: Croom Helm & The Open University.

Allman, P., & Mackie, K. J. (Eds.). (1983). *Towards a developmental theory of andragogy.* Nottingham, UK: The University of Nottingham, Department of Adult Education.

Anderson, M. L., & Lindeman, E. C. (1927). *Education through experience: An interpretation of the methods of the academy of labor*, Frankfurt-am-Main, Germany, (Workers' Education Research Series, Monograph no. 1). New York: Workers Education Bureau Press, Inc.

Baden, C. (1998). *Adult learning in associations: Models for good practice*. New York: American Society of Association Executives.

Billington, D. D. (1988). Ego development and adult education, (Doctoral Dissertation, The Fielding Institute). *Dissertation Abstracts International, 49*(7), University Microfilms no. 88–16, 275.

Billington, D. D. (2000). *Seven characteristics of highly effective adult learning programs*. Seattle: New Horizons. Retrieved June 3, 2009 from http://www.newhorizons.org

Boucouvalas, M. (1999). Comparative thinking and the structures of adult cognition: An epistemologica and methodological challenge for comparative adult education. In J. Reischmann, A. Jelenc & M. Bron (Eds.), *Comparative adult education: The contributions of the international society for comparative adult education [ISCAE] to an emerging field of study*, (pp. 65-76). Ljubljana, Slovenia: Slovenian Institute for Adult Education and ISCAE.

Brager, J., & Johnson, K. (1993). *Adult learning: New research on continuous learning in the business environment.* Atlanta, GA: American Society for Training and Development Annual Conference.

Brockett, R. G. (1983, April). Self-directed learning and the hard-to-reach adult. *Lifelong Learning: An Omnibus of Practice and Research, 6*(8), 16–18.

Brockett, R. G. (1984, February). Developing written learning materials: A proactive approach. *Lifelong Learning: An Omnibus of Practice and Research, 7*(5)16–18, 28.

Brockett, R. G. (n.d.), *Humanism as an instructional paradigm.* Retrieved June 6, 2009, from http://www-distance.syr.edu/romira1&html

Brookfield, S. D. (1986). *Understanding and facilitating adult learning.* San Francisco: Jossey-Bass.

Burge, L. (1988). Beyond andragogy: Some explorations for distance learning design. *Journal of Distance Education, 3*(1), 5–23.

Candy, P. (1991). *Self-direction for lifelong learning: A comprehensive guide to theory and practice.* San Francisco: Jossey-Bass.

Carroll, J. M. (1990). *Learner characteristics: When working adults sit down to learn.* Retrieved May 4, 2009, from www.spsu.edu/htc/hughes/com

Christian, A. C. (1982). *A comparative study of the andragogical-pedagogical orientation of military and civilian personnel.* Unpublished doctoral dissertation, Oklahoma State University, Stillwater, OK.

Clark, D. (1999). *Andragogy.* Retrieved October 10, 2002, from http://www.nwlink.com/~donclark/hrd/history/history.html

Conner, M. L. (1997). Andragogy + pedagogy. *Ageless Learner.* Retrieved October 22, 2007, from Internet

Cooke, J. C. (1994). *Malcolm Shepherd Knowles, the father of American andragogy: A biographical study.* University of North Texas, Denton, TX, Unpublished Doctor of Philosophy Dissertation.

Davenport, J. III. (1987). Is there a way out of the andragogy morass? *Lifelong Learning: An Omnibus of Practice and Research, 11*(3), 17–20.

Delahaye, B. L., Limerick, D. C., & Hearn, G. (1994). The relationship between andragogical and pedagogical orientations and the implications for adult learning. *Adult Education Quarterly, 44*(4), 187–200. doi:10.1177/074171369404400401

Dewar, T. (1999). *Adult learning principles (a selection).* Retrieved October 22, 2009, from Internet

Draper, J. A. (1998). The metamorphoses of andragogy. *The Canadian Journal for the Study of Adult Education, 12*(1), 3–26.

East Lansing, MI: Michigan State University.

Eitington, J. E. (1989). *The winning trainer, instructor, facilitator, teacher, conference leader, etc.* (3rd ed.) Houston, TX: Gulf Publishing Company.

Ellis, H. J. C. (c. 1993). *Andragogy in a web technologies course.* Hartford, CT: Rensselaer at Hartford, Department of Engineering and Science.

Eskridge, R. C. (1978). *The literary contributions of Malcolm Shepherd Knowles to the process of adult education.* St. Louis University, Missouri, Unpublished Doctor of Philosophy Dissertation.

Ferro, T. R. (1997). The linguistics of andragogy and its offspring. In J. Levine, (Ed.), *Proceedings of the Midwest research-to-practice conference in adult, continuing and community education* (pp. 29-34).

Furter, P. (1971). Grandeur et misere de la pedagogie. University of Neuchatel. In E. Faure (Ed.), *Learning to be: The world of education today and tomorrow,* (p. 116). Paris: UNESCO.

Gehring, T. (2000). A compendium of material on the pedagogy-andragogy issue. *Journal of Continuing Education, 51*(1), 151–163.

Green, J. (1998), *Andragogy: Teaching adults.* In B. Hoffman (Ed.), *Encyclopedia of educational technology.*

Griffith, W. S. (1991). The impact of intellectual leadership. In J.M. Peters & P. Jarvis (Eds.), *Adult education: Evolution and achievements in a developing field of study* (pp. 97-120). San Francisco: Jossey-Bass.

Hadley, H. N. (1975). *Development of an instrument to determine adult educator's orientation as andragogical and pedagogical.* Unpublished doctoral dissertation, Boston University School of Education, Boston, MA.

Hanson, A. (1996). The search for a separate theory of adult learning: Does anyone really need andragogy? In R. Edwards, A. Hanson, & P. Raggatt (Eds.), *Adult learners, education and training 1* (pp. 99-108). London: Routledge and The Open University.

Hartree, A. (1984). Malcolm Knowles's theory of andragogy: A critique. *International Journal of Lifelong Education, 3,* 203–210. doi:10.1080/0260137840030304

Henschke, J., & Cooper, M. (2007a). Additions toward a thorough understanding of the international foundations of andragogy in HRD and Adult Education. An. Inst.de Ins. "G.Barit" din Cluj-Napoca, Series umanistica, tom. V, 2007, pp. 7-54. [This is the 2007 Yearbook of the Romanian Institute of Adult Education.]

Henschke, J. A. (1973). *Malcolm S. Knowles: His contributions to the theory and practice of adult education*. Boston University, Unpublished Doctor of Education Dissertation. Retrieved June 3, 2009, from http://www.umsl.edu/~henschke

Henschke, J. A. (1987). Training teachers of adults. In C. Klevins (Ed.), *Materials and methods in adult and continuing education: International – illiteracy* (pp. 414-422). Los Angeles: Klevens Publications.

Henschke, J. A. (1989). Identifying appropriate adult educator practices: Beliefs, feelings and behaviors. In C. Jeffries, (Ed.), *Proceedings of the eighth annual Midwest research-to-practice conference in adult, continuing and community education* (pp. 89-95). St. Louis, MO: University of Missouri.

Henschke, J. A. (1995). Theory and practice on preparing human resource development professionals. In *Proceedings of Academy of Human Resource Development Research Conference* (pp. 1-11). St. Louis: University of Missouri.

Henschke, J. A. (1998a). *Historical antecedents shaping conceptions of andragogy: A comparison of sources and roots*. Paper presented at the International Conference on Research in Comparative Andragogy, Radovljica, Slovenia, September 10-13, 1998.

Henschke, J. A. (1998b). Modeling the preparation of adult educators. *Adult Learning, 9*(3), 11–14.

Henschke, J. A. (1999). Historical antecedents shaping the terms performance and learning in human resource development: An exploratory study." In K. P. Kuchinke (Ed.), *Proceedings of the Academy of Human Resource Development Research Conference*, Alexandria, VA. (pp 611-619).

Henschke, J. A. (2000-ff.). *Andragogy*. Retrieved June 1, 2009, from http://www.umsl.edu/~henschke/andragogy/

Hoffman, F. (1980*). How to teach grown-ups.* Calabasas, CA: Practical Management Associates, Inc.

Hooks, B. (1994). *Theory as liberatory practice,* (from *Teaching to Transgress – as quoted by Kaminsky, Sherrie in "Comparing Pedagogy and Andragogy for Both Common and Dissimilar Meanings").* Retrieved June 4, 2009, from http://www.usm.maine.edu/~dlarson/ kaminsky2.htm

Houle, C. O. (1992). *The literature of adult education: A bibliographic essay*. San Francisco: Jossey-Bass.

Houle, C. O. (1996). *The design of education* (2nd ed.). San Francisco: Jossey-Bass.

Hugo, J. (2003). *A comparison of and characteristics of educational multi-media.* Uganda: Naledi3Dfactory and UNE.

Imel, S. (1989). Teaching adults: Is it different? *ERIC Digest, 82*(ED 305495).

Ingalls, J. D. (1972). *A trainers guide to andragogy.* Washington, DC: United State Department of Health, Education and Welfare.

Ingalls, J. D. (1976). *Human energy: The critical factor for individuals and organizations*. Reading, MA: Addison-Wesley Publishing Company.

Jarvis, P. (1984). Andragogy: A sign of the times. *Studies in the Education of Adults, 16*, 32–38.

Jorgensen, H. K. (1998), *Adult learning theories andreligious educationfor seventh-DayAdventist college students: From theory to practice.* Presented for the 22nd Faith and Learning Seminar held at Seminar Schlossbogenhofen St. Peter Am Hart, Austria, August 9–21.

Kabuga, C. (1977). Why andragogy in developing countries? *Adult Education and Development: Journal for Adult Education in Africa, Asia, and Latin America.*

Kajee, L. (n.d.). *Making waves, not just surfing the net: ICT and learning in the ESL classroom.* Unpublished paper, University of the Witwatersrand, Johannesburg, South Africa. Kamansky, S. (n.d.). *Comparing pedagogy and andragogy for both common and dissimilar meanings.* Retrieved July 18, 2004, from http://www.usm.maine.edu/!dlarson/kaminsky2.htm

Kapp, A. (1833). *Die andragogik ober bildung im mannlichen alter. Platons Erziehungslehre, als Padagogik fur die Einzelnen und als Staatspadagogik.* Germany: Minden und Leipzig.

Knowles, M. S. (1968a). Androgogy, not pedagogy. *Adult Leadership, 16,* 350–352.

Knowles, M. S. (1968b). How andragogy works in leadership training in the Girl Scouts. *Adult Leadership, 17,* 160–162.

Knowles, M. S. (1969). An experiment with group self-directed learning: The learning teaching team. In p. Runkel, R. Harrison, & M. Runkel (Eds.), *The Changing College Classroom.* San Francisco: Jossey-Bass.

Knowles, M. S. (1970). *The modern practice of adult education: Andragogy vs. Pedagogy.* New York: Association Press.

Knowles, M. S. (1972). The manager as educator. *Journal of Continuing Education and Training,* 2(2), 97–105.

Knowles, M. S. (1973). *The adult Learner: A neglected species.* Houston: Gulf Publishing Company.

Knowles, M. S. (1975). *Self-drected learning: A guide for learners and teachers.* New York: Association Press.

Knowles, M. S. (1978). *The adult learner: A neglected species* (2nd ed.). Houston, TX: Gulf Publishing Company.

Knowles, M. S. (1980). *The modern practice of adult education: From pedagogy to andragogy,*(Rev. ed.). New York: Cambridge Book Publishers.

Knowles, M. S. (1984a). *The adult learner: A neglected species* (3rd ed.). Houston: Gulf Publishing Company.

Knowles, M. S. (1984b). *Andragogy in action: Applying modern principles of adult learning.* San Francisco: Jossey-Bass.

Knowles, M. S. (1989a). Adult learning: Theory & practice. In L. Nadler & A. Nadler (Eds.), *The handbook of human resource development* (2d ed.) (pp. 6.1 -- 6.23). New York: John Wiley & Sons.

Knowles, M. S. (1989b). *The making of an adult educator: An autobiographical journey.* San Francisco: Jossey-Bass Publishers.

Knowles, M. S. (1990). *The adult learner: A neglected species* (4th ed.). Houston, TX: Gulf Publishing Company.

Knowles, M. S. (1991). *Lifelong learning: A dream.* Retrieved June 3, 2009, from http://www.newhorizons.org/future/Creating_the_Furure/crfut_knowles.html

Knowles, M. S. (1995). *Designs for adult learning: Practical resources, exercises, and course outlines from the father of adult learning.* Alexandria, VA: American Society for Training and Development.

Knowles, M. S. (1996). *Adult learning*. In R. L. Craig (Ed.), *ASTD training & development handbook: A guide to human resource development* (4th ed.) (pp. 254-265). New York: McGraw Hill.

Knowles, M. S., Holton, E. F., III, & Swanson, R. A. (1998). *The adult learner* (5th ed.). Houston: Gulf Publishing.

Krajinc, A. (1989). Andragogy. In C. J. Titmus (Ed.), *Lifelong education for adults: An international handbook* (pp. 19-21). Oxford, UK: Pergamon.

Lieb, S. (1991). *Principles of adult learning*. Phoenix, AZ: Vision – South Mountain Community College. Retrieved May 26, 2009, from http://honolulu.hawaii.edu/intranet/committees/FacDevCom/ guidebk/teachtip/adults-2.htm

Lindeman, E. C. (1926a). Andragogik: The method of teaching adults. *Workers' . Education, 4*, 38.

Lindeman, E. C. (1926b, 1961*). The meaning of adult education*. Montreal: Harvest House.

Long, H. B. (1991). Evolution of a formal knowledge base. In J.M. Peters & P. Jarvis (Eds.), *Adult education: volution and achievements in a develping field of study* (pp. 66-96). San Francisco: Jossey-Bass Publishers.

Maehl, W. (2000). *Lifelong learning at its best: Innovative practices in adult credit programs*. San Francisco: Jossey-Bass Inc., Publishers.

Mazhindu, G. N. (1990). Contract learning reconsidered: A critical examination of the implications for application in nursing education. *Journal of Advanced Nursing, 15*, 101–109. doi:10.1111/j.1365-2648.1990.tb01678.x

Merriam, S. B. (1999). The development of the discipline of adult education in the United States. *Andragogy Today: Interdisciplinary Journal of Adult and Continuing Education, 2*(3), 31–49.

Mezirow, J. (1981, Fall). A critical theory of adult learning and education. *Adult Education, 32*(1), 3–24. doi:10.1177/074171368103200101

Mezirow, J. (1991), *Transformative dimensions of adult learning* (pp. 198-201). San Francisco: Jossey Bass.

Mihall, J., & Belletti, H. (1999). *Adult learning styles and training methods. Forget those 13,000 hours*. FDIC ADR.

Milligan, F. (1995). In defence of andragogy. *Nurse Education Today, 15*, 22–27. doi:10.1016/S0260-6917(95)80074-3

Milligan, F. (1997). In defence of andragogy, Part 2: An educational process consistent with modern nursing aims. *Nurse Education Today, 17*, 487–493. doi:10.1016/S0260-6917(97)80010-X

Milligan, F. (1999). Beyond the rhetoric of problem-based learning: Emancipatory limits and links with andragogy. *Nurse Education Today, 19*, 548–555. doi:10.1054/nedt.1999.0368

Moore, M. (1986). Self-directed learning and distance education. *Journal of Distance Education. "Revue de L'enseignmenta a Distance", 1-15*. Retrieved December 28, 2004, http://cade.athabascau.ca/voll.l/moore.html

Morrall, P. (1993, September-October). The beginning of the end of andragogy. *Senior Nurse, 13*(5), 42–44.

Muller, L. H. (1992). *Progressivism and U. S. adult education: A critique of mainstream theory as embodied in the work of Malcolm Knowles*. New York: Teachers College, Columbia University.

Mynen, M. (C. 1997). *What andragogy means to me*. Retrieved December 3, 2003, from http://www.instructordiploma.com/ core/102%20b/victoria/mynen.htm.

Nadler, L., & Nadler, Z. (Eds.). (1989). *The handbook of human resource development* (2d ed.). New York: John Wiley & Sons.

Newman, A. P. (1993). *Prison Literacy: Implications for Program and Assessment Policy*. Bloomington, IN: ERIC Clearinghouse on Reading and Communication Skills. ED 363 729 (pp. 49). Unpublished Doctor of Philosophy Dissertation.

Nottingham Andragogy Group. (1983). Towards a developmental theory of andragogy. *Adults: Psychological and Educational Perspective, 9*. Nottingham, UK: University of Nottingham Department of Adult Education.

Osborn, S. (1999). *Andragogy*. Belgrade, Yugoslavia: Faculty of Philosophy. Retrieved May 23, 2009, from http://ifets.gmd.de/

Ovesni, K. (1999). *Andragogy as an integral part of educational sciences*. Belgrade, Yugoslavia: Faculty of Philosophy. Retrieved April 23, 2009, from http://ifets.gmd.de/

Peters, J. M., & Jarvis, P. (1991). *Adult education: Evolution and achievements in a developing field of study*. San Francisco: Jossey-Bass.

Poggeler, F. (1994). Introduction – Trends of andragogical research in Europe. In P. Jarvis & F. Poggeler (Eds.), *Developments in the education of adults in Europe, 21*(9-15). Frankfurt am Main: Peter Lang, Studies in Pedagogy, Andragogy and Gerontology.

Pratt, D. D. (1984). Andragogical assumptions: Some counter-intuitive logic. In *Proceedings of the Adult Education Research Conference*, (no. 25). Raleigh, NC: North Carolina State University.

Pratt, D. D. (1988, Spring). Andragogy as a relational construct. *Adult Education Quarterly, 38*(3), 160–172. doi:10.1177/0001848188038003004

Pratt, D. D. (1993, Spring). *Andragogy after twenty-five years*. In S. Merriam (Ed.), *New directions for adult and continuing education: An update on adult learning theory, 57*(15–24). San Francisco: Jossey-Bass.

Rachal, J. (2000). *Effectiveness of andragogy.* Concurrent session presentation. American Association for Adult and Continuing Education Conference, Providence, RI, November, 2000.

Reischmann, J. (1999). Adult education in Germany: Roots, status, mainstreams, changes. *Andragogy Today: Interdisciplinary Journal of Adult and Continuing Education, 2*(3), 1–29.

Robb, W. M. (1990). *Can South African andragogics improve understanding between Anglo-American and Continental European adult educationists?* In *Toward 1992 – Education of Adults in the New Europe. Proceedings of the 20th SCUTREA* Conference (pp. 71-77), West Sheffield, UK.

Rosenstock-Huessy, E. (1925). *Andragogy – 1925*, Retrieved October 26, 2005, from Internet

Ross, B. E. (1987). Integrating Andragogy with Current Research on Teaching Effectiveness. In *Proceedings of the Lifelong Learning Research Conference* (pp. 29–33). College Park, MD: University of Maryland.

Rostad, S. (1998). *Nordic Folk Academy Socrates project entitled 'The public and the library'*. Nordic Council of Ministers, St. Strandstraede 18, DK-1225 Copenhagen K, Denmark. Retrieved June 1, 2009, from http://x-stream.fortunecity.com/melrose/81/sweden.htm

Savicevic, D. (1991). Modern conceptions of andragogy: A European framework. *Studies in the Education of Adults, 23*(3), 179–201.

Savicevic, D. (1999a). Adult education: From practice to theory building. In F. Poggeler (Ed.), *Studies in pedagogy, andragogy, and gerontagogy,* (pp. 1-275). Frankfurt am Main: Peter Lang.

Savicevic, D. (1999b). Understanding andragogy in Europe and America: Comparing and contrasting. In J. Reischmann, Z. Jelenc, & M. Bron (Eds.), *Comparative adult education 1998: The contribution of ISCAE to an emerging field of study* (pp. 97-119). Bamburg, Germany: ISCAE Proceedings.

Simpson, J. A. (1964). Andragogy. *Adult Education, 37*(4), 186–194.

Smith, M. K. (1996). Andragogy: The history and current use of the term plus an annotated Bibliography. In *The Encyclopedia of Informal Education*. Retrieved April 12, 2009, from http://www.infed.org/lifelonglearning/b-andra.htm

Suanmali, C. (1981). *The core concepts of andragogy*. Doctoral Dissertation, Columbia University Teachers College, New York City, Dissertation Abstracts International, University Microfilms no. 8207343.

Taylor, K., Marienau, C., & Fiddler, M. (2000). *Developing adult learners: Strategies for teachers and trainers.* San Francisco: Jossey-Bass.

Taylor, M. (1986). Learning for self-direction in the classroom: The pattern of a transition process. *Studies in Higher Education, 11*(1), 1986.

Thorpe, Dr. E. (1999). *Andragogy and technology*. Dissertations and Theses: A&I database, Publication No. AAT 3194155.

VanGent, B. (1996). Andragogy. In A. C. Tuijnman (Ed.), *The international encyclopedia of adult education and training* (pp. 114-117). Oxford, UK: Pergamon.

Warren, C. (1989). Andragogy and N. F. S. Grundtvig: A critical Link. *Adult Education Quarterly, 39*(4), 211–223. doi:10.1177/0001848189039004003

Wartenberg, A. D. (1994). *Andragogy and whole language*. Paper presented at the Annual Meeting of the Deleware Valley Reading Association, Merion, PA, 3/15/94. ERIC Documentation Reproduction Service No. ED 365958.

Webster's Encyclopedic Unabridged Dictionary of the English Language – Updated Revised Deluxe Edition. (1996). New York: Random House Value Publishing, Inc.

Welton, M. R. (1995). *In defense of lifeworld.* Albany, NY: SUNY Press.

Woods, H. (1998). *Andragogy: The act, process, or art of imparting knowledge and skill to adults*. Retrieved October 23, 2007, from http://www.survival.com/gogy.htm

Young, G. (1985). Andragogy and pedagogy: Two ways of accompaniment. *Adult Education Quarterly, 35*(3), 160–167. doi:10.1177/0001848185035003005

Zemke, R., & Zemke, S. (1981). Thirty things we know for sure about adult learning. In P. G. Jones (Ed.), *Adult learning in your classroom,* (pp. 115-118). Minneapolis: Lakewood Publications.

Zemke, R., & Zemke, S. (1996). *Adult learning: What do we know for sure*? In D. Zielinski (Ed.), *The new training library: Adult learning in your classroom* (pp. 71-74). Minneapolis: Lakewood Books.

Zhang, W. (1996). *Adult education in China*. In W. Zhang (Ed.), *International/global comparative education in adult education* (pp. 99-119). Beijing: Industrial Publishers.

Zmeyov, S. I. (1994). Perspectives of adult education in Russia. In P. Jarvis & F. Poggeler (Eds.), *Developments in the education of adults in Europe* (pp. 35–42). Bern, Switzerland: Peter Lang.

Zmeyov, S. I. (1998). Andragogy: Origins, developments and trends. *International Review of Education, 44*(1), 103–108. doi:10.1023/A:1003107931006

Chapter 2
Learner-Centered Teaching and the Use of Technology

Annette Greer
East Carolina University, USA

Vivian W. Mott
East Carolina University, USA

ABSTRACT

This article explores the use of various learning technologies as tools for facilitating learner-centered teaching. The article offers another perspective on the scholarship of teaching with technology—through discussion of various theoretical models of learner-centered teaching, the role of technology on the student/instructor relationships, the impact on technology in different educational settings and contexts, and learners' cultural differences. The article concludes with a brief discussion of future trends, cautions, and speculations related to technology use in learner-centered teaching.

INTRODUCTION

A mere mention the word "technology" often renders anxiety in instructors and students alike. However, the term "technology" can represent the simplest of tools to aid the learning process. For instance, a pencil with an eraser on the end, a chalk board and chalk, or even a Chinese abacus are instrumental technologies that we have used across time to facilitate the learning process. Relative to technology in the 21st century, the difference is the speed at which we are experiencing growth in both hardware (the pencil vs. computer) and software (writing vs. applications) in technological tools (Saba, 2001).

Where do we find these technological tools in use in higher education? Kennedy, Judd, Churchward, Gray, and Krause (2008) found that individuals who embrace emerging technologies in everyday life were more apt to be early adopters, using those same technologies in educational settings. In higher education, we find technological tools inside the traditional classroom and among various created virtual learning environments generated by the technology itself—in a place we often call *cyberspace*. Technology permeates our global environment, offering tools that assist us in economic, social, and political dimensions. Technological tools are one of many elements that can aid communications and application, in education. A closer look at the elements of education will help us in understanding the positive and negative value of technology as an educational resource and sometimes as the environment of learning. The purposes of this article are threefold: first, to explore critical educational elements and the role educational technologies play in these elements; second, to consider how key theoretical models of learning are impacted by technology; and, third, to examine how instructors and learners variously respond to educational technologies and the impact of technological use on both instructor/learner relationships and learning. Ultimately, the article seeks to add to the scholarship of teaching through an evidence-based review of the contextual influence of technology in education.

BACKGROUND: EDUCATIONAL ELEMENTS

There are many elements to be considered in any educational environment: instructors, learners, content, delivery, application, context, environment, and resources. Not only are the elements essential to understand; further, the interaction of these elements, within the context of time and the roles that each of these elements play, have varied across historical time as higher education has evolved as well. The relationship between the elements of education changes rapidly as the elements themselves have transformed with time and as knowledge has both become obsolete and expanded exponentially (Billings & Halstead, 2005; Mott, 2009). It is the changing relationship among the educational elements of instructors, students, content, environment, all influenced by the application of technology resources, that have stimulated this article.

Demonstration of technological competencies is central to the ability of instructors to meet the diverse learning needs of students. Technological competencies are based on the same continuum as the technology itself from simple to complex according to the International Society for Technology in Education (ISTE, 2008). ISTE has set national technology competency standards for instructors and students. As early as 1995, ISTE commissioned a white paper regarding the technological literacy skills needed for the 21st century (Thomas & Knezek, 1995). Technological literacy includes: (a) understanding math and science concepts underlying technological systems, (b) operability relative to various systems, (c) utilization and evaluation of diverse applications, (d) ability to innovate technology to solve emerging science problems, (e) awareness of the role of technology to any given career, (f) responsiveness to critical factors that lend success to any given career, and (g) appreciation of the role technology has on the various cultures of our global society.

As with any competency, technological competency can be considered as three distinct skill areas: basic, professional, and application of technology in instruction. Basic technological skills include the introductory level of function that is the operation of applications for personal communications. These applications can include e-mail, basic blogs, word processing, spreadsheets for home use, and simple presentations, for example. Professional technological skills include higher, intermediate levels for professional communications. E-mails, for example, used professionally require knowledge of embedded applications such as certified signature use, timed release, tracking delivery and opened status, and automation of e-mail rules for organization and management. Another example would be use of the word processing at the professional level to track changes, merge documents, insert citations and references, automate a table of contents, and import from other applications into the word processor. At the advanced competency level, professionals using technology to teach would have evolved from basic to professional intermediate, and are poised to expand and transfer existing skills into instructional design. It is at the advanced applied level that innovation in educational design occurs, when technological competency of instructors approximates or matches the progression of the technological tools created.

Innovative use of technology facilitates the development of instructor-student relationships to promote positive learning outcomes and thus the scholarship of teaching. Boyer (1990) noted the following examples of teaching scholarship: innovative curricula (organization of disciplinary content), teaching methods that engage students in learning, collaborative interactions among instructors, students, and peers, and exploration of the efficacy of learning. The relationship between instructors and student is at the core students' engaged learning; as such, technology should augment—not inhibit—the formation of that valuable relationship. Mentoring, cultural influence, effective communication, and feedback are primary to relationship building and professional socialization. When used effectively, any number of instructional technologies can facilitate processes of communication, and so enhance the development of learning relationships.

Assessment of the students' technological skills is essential to determining if the curricular design allows for variability in skills and learner styles that will be found in most learning environments. The technological literacy level and the technological competency of students will vary widely and may be inconsistent with the level of the instructor designing the curriculum and learning environment. Hence, if the student is at an advanced level and the instructor at a basic level, the design may cause students to become bored and distracted. If the instructor designs the learner environment only for advanced users and assumes a high level of resource availability—when student resources are low and skills are basic—the student is greatly disadvantaged in terms of access and achievement. In either of these cases, the instructor-learner relationship is encumbered and learning jeopardized.

THEORETICAL LEARNING MODELS IN EDUCATION

There are a multitude of theoretical models that focus on teaching and learning. This section will explore only a few of those, models which deal primarily with learners' increased responsibility for, and even control of, their learning processes and outcomes.

Self-Directed Learning Theory

Self-directed learning or the individual pursuit of learning based upon independent motivation supports the selection of advanced distributed learning technologies. O'Lawrence (2007) reported that self-directed learning was a key factor in the selection of distance education environments. The flexibility offered to adult learners in distance education environments was the motivator that allowed them to make adaptations to balance family, career, and transportation further facilitating completion of higher education programs. Various technological tools, such as discussion groups can provide a forum for self-directed learners to self-assess, to highlight the value of the individual contributions to the learning community, and provide a means to reflect on the meaning of the learning experienced (Kayler & Weller, 2007). Du and Wagner (2005), as well, studied outcomes of self-directed learners' use of weblogs as a learning reflection aid. Weblogs are a form of journaling that are published online as Web pages. Their research outcomes suggested a positive predictive association between the use of weblog journaling and improved course outcomes that could not be accounted for through traditional coursework. Bonk, Wisher, and Lee (2004) maintained that Web-based technologies allow for increased learner responsibility and control with meaningful engagement activities, which is not only attractive to self-directed learners, but aids in transfer of learning as well. Self-directed and responsible learners become peer instructors, emerge as leaders in the educational process, and facilitate self-learning and critical reflection through teaching. Technologies seem to impact the manner in which leadership emerges with text facilitating task-orientation and video-audio conferencing facilitating a relationship orientation. A shared learning process is established that allows for self, peer, and instructor reflection and assessment driving self-directed learning to higher levels of development. Derntl and Motschnig-Pitrik (2004) found that blended or hybrid learning environments (face-to-face and Web-based combination) help to establish patterns for alternating the teaching strategies and technologies that are applied to enhance the processes of learning, further advancing self-directed learning.

Knowledge management also becomes more powerful, organized, and expansive using the technological tools such as blogs, wikis, and management systems for concept mapping. Further, integration applications offered through various software companies promotes organizational knowledge building and transfer. This knowledge control shift further places the learner at the center of the learning process. Technology, then, helps bring about a shift in educational philosophy, one that is learner-centered and can maximize the benefit to both learner and stake-holders (Schaffert, Bischof, Bürger, Gruber, Hilzensauer, & Schaffert, 2006).

A Learner-Centered Framework and Technology

The American Psychological Association's Board of Educational Affairs work group, after a thorough systematic review of existing research, first published fourteen distinct learner-centered principles in 1993 (1997). Publication of these principles significantly influenced educational agendas at the end of the twentieth century and resulted in defining a new *learning paradigm,* one that is learner-centered (Barr & Tagg, 1995). Previous to the publication of these principles, the paradigm for education was an *instruction paradigm,* and reflected an instructor-centered and content approach to education. McCombs and Vakili (2005) proposed that learner-centered approaches can serve as a theoretical or conceptual framework for educators using distance education technologies. Implementation of learner-centered approaches that use technology includes: (a) building an environment that connects learners' need for interpersonal relationships, (b) using strategies that meets diverse learner styles, (c) tailoring strategies that allow for learners' enhanced control over learning, and (d) assessing technological efficacy to meet needs of individual learners and community of learners. Instructors need to be provided with the skills to create effective learner-centered environments that offer both context and opportunities for inquiry and collaboration (McCombs & Lauer, 1997).

Among the most well-cited and utilized learner-centered framework was that offered by Weimer (2002). Her efforts to advance instructors' effectiveness in the various educational settings was proposed in a seminal book that recommended five concepts, or "key changes to practice" (p. xvii) needed for instructors to transition to a learner-centered approach to teaching. Weimer's *key changes* are based on research and theory, both formal theory and theories-in-use, and include "action learning, self-directed learning, constructivism, critical and feminist pedagogies, and reflective practice" (Mott, 2004, p. 244). Weimer's five key concepts include: (a) balance of power, (b) function of content, (c) role of instructors, (d) responsibility for learning, and (e) purposes and processes of evaluation.

Power

One learner-centered value is that of shared power between instructors and learners. Technology and the level of skills required to use technology as a tool for learning can alter the balance of power in an educational setting. According to the Commonwealth of Learning (Farrell, 2001) there are several global forces that generate a sense of exigency to adopt new technologies, among them the impetus of the "post-industrial information age and the explosive growth and distributed nature of new knowledge" (p. 10). It is this explosive change that generates a level of anxiety that can often result in rushing to include technologies that may not fit a curriculum. The dynamics of technological change can position both learners and instructors to share the experience of learning technology, an upgrade in a course management software mid-semester, for example. Krichen (2004) suggested that technical support systems for instructors and students should be learning platforms that offer 24-7 availability to resolve technological issues. Further, that these support systems should offer ongoing training for instructors and students to meet the cycle of evolutions in hardware and software.

The vulnerability shared by instructors and learners can stabilize power differentials in learning environments. Diekelmann, Schuster, and Nosek (1998) researched new pedagogies, particularly ways online technologies may change the relationship between instructors/student. They found that some pedagogies can reverses the power and expertise fields for learning. This places the instructors in a position of learner in order to remain current with the technology used by younger, often more technologically proficient learners. Pettitt (2002) studied the possession and negotiation of power in an online undergraduate business management course. The structure of an online course was found to be just as important as flexibility in providing stability in organizing time and setting routines. Routines were a positive factor in the relational system needed to maneuver the variable roles of worker, spouse, parent, family member, and student/peer learner. Distance education provided the learners power, or control over time, space, and proximity of learning, and allowed learners a negotiation tool within their relational systems. Thus, the power differential can shift from content- or instruction-centered to student-centered when students request that instructor availability match the asynchronous flexibility of the course's right of entry.

Issues with power and access regarding the implementation of technology as a teaching and learning tool can also produce disparities among students that are economically or otherwise disadvantaged. Magjuka, Shi, and Bonk, (2005) noted that there is a wide range of cost both to the educational institution and to the students based on administrative decisions for commercial or open source (freeware) systems of course delivery. Administrators and educators should take into consideration the simplest and most cost-effective measures of technology that will serve to empower rather than to oppress diverse student populations. Essential to the balance of power in the learning context is institutional support for instructors and students that creates equity in knowledge and skills in operating the technology used in or as the learning environment. From a learner-centered philosophy, this balance of shared power must be based on relationship (Cornelius-White, 2007). Technology should serve to ease the development of educator-learner relationship, not impede it.

Function of Content and Technology

According to Weimer (2002), with one's move to greater learner-centeredness, content becomes less important than the process of learning. Reynard (2009) reinforced the value of process versus content-driven design, noting that the focus for learning should be on *how, why*, as well as emerging disciplinary trends rather than on *what, when*, and current practices. The learner has to be prepared to function in a knowledge economy that is in dynamic change and be able to relate existing knowledge to new and emerging knowledge.

Novak (2003) noted that learners are searching for relationships between their current knowledge and the generation of new knowledge. Educators promote meaningful learning by using learner-centered strategies that actively engage learners with the content. Technology has proven a useful tool to providing a venue for learner engagement. Concept maps created online in a collaborative team manner augment engagement with knowledge/content for learning (Novak). Thus, learners become active participants in co-constructing higher order thinking skills and increase cognitive, affective, and psychomotor abilities. Discussion threads found in variable applications allow for multiple reflections that merge diverse cultural knowledge perspectives. Content then is in constant flux and the process of learning gains greater importance.

The pathway for learning content when using technologies such as concept mapping may become more non-linear, less systematic (Hartley & Bendixen, 2001). Open systems of learning that are technology-based support construction of learner knowledge. Content accessibility is heightened with the ever-present World Wide Web where emerging knowledge is immediately available versus the delayed accessibility of print. These open content systems of accessibility do present issues of reliability and validity of knowledge, however. This issue is compounded as knowledge is hyperlinked to exponentially expanding and integrated knowledge bases. Content is generated rapidly as new knowledge is constructed, but often without older information integrated, corrected, or removed. Hartley and Bendixen noted that learners' beliefs about the nature of knowledge are linked to cognitive processes and comprehension. Learners have to be taught how to ascertain the accuracy of the information they access, or risk a compromised or erroneous knowledge base. Weimer's (2002) learner-centered framework emphasizes the role of the instructor to provide a learning design that will assist the learner in gaining discriminate skills to advance their autonomy and their ability to maneuver 21st century open-ended learning environments.

Role of the Instructor

In an online learning environment, it is the responsibility of the instructor to select the types and patterns of technology use that are consistent with the content/context for learning. O'Lawrence (2007) noted that, "instructional strategies are what really make a difference in how adults learn online, not technology" (p.¶ 437). Hence, it is the use of the instructor's selection of the types of technology that make the learning interesting and meaningful to the learner. Technology (the tool) should augment an assignment with the flexibility that allows the learner comfort at the level and in the style that is consistent with individual development. In a learner-centered framework, the role of the instructor is to facilitate learning as an open system that supports learner autonomy (Weimer, 2002).

Koper and Olivier (2004) noted that electronic, or e-learning is a learner-centered, non-linear, and self-directed personalized approach to education that requires intentional learning design. Educators designing online educational opportunities have to consider the variability within a diverse set of learners without making assumptions regarding technological skill levels. In fact, Hartley and

Bendixen (2001) noted that too much flexibility offered to learners in online environments can be counter-productive to successful learning when the learners' belief systems are based on simple knowledge and the educational design is complex with multiple levels of links to definitions, graphs, and readings. Designs that do not provide a direct pathway from the facts needed to facilitate learning are seen by learners as pointless and unnecessary. Thus, the role of the instructors is to keep the designs as simple as possible with technologies that complement the content of the course with consideration of learner styles.

Kolb's learning style (1984) has been linked to computer mediated instruction in numerous studies (Lu, Jia, Gong, & Clark, 2007) since the advent of instructional technologies. Various recommendations have included the need for more research in the application of design and development of appropriate instructional strategies and virtual materials, but in created educational environments as well. Researchers have also noted that more work is needed in determining what educational strategies and instructional methods would best match learning styles, and the necessity of advocating for learner assessments using Kolb's learning style inventories and other assessments. All of these recommendations are aimed at the increased attention to learners' visual, auditory, kinesthetic and tactual learning styles in virtual learning environments. With these critical considerations, computer mediated education and training venues can become fluid environments that can be adapted to the learner, providing opportunities for beneficial interaction and engagement (Kolb, 1984; Lu et al., 2007; Quinsee & Hurst, 2005).

Koehler and Mishra (2005a,b) found that the issues surrounding design of technological based learning environments serve as the context for instructors' continuing professional education. They offered seminars for instructors that focused on the design of online courses which actively engaged instructors in the process of inquiry and design using collaborative learning groups. Participants' learning outcomes were technological designs for use in online courses: Web sites, syllabi, and adapted teaching approaches/strategies (Koehler & Mishra, 2005a,b). The design process is anything but static, as the technology evolves, as Web links expire, as upgrades are implemented for specific applications, or as new courseware is adopted by institutions, for example. Therefore, the role of the instructors is to seek professional development on a continuous basis, regularly solicit feedback on their instruction, and to revise curricula as warranted. As an additional benefit, the instructors' modeling of behavior and self-directedness as learners is another way to prepare student learners to be accountable and self-directed in their learning (Weimer, 2002).

Responsibility for Learning

Learners must also self-assess their own technological readiness and resources for learning. Criteria for required technology should be included in the syllabus to allow learners to access, plan for, and learn to use the needed learning resources. Many higher education institutions publish these criteria prior to student enrollment and offer funding through financial aid to cover costs, assist with loan programs, or offer computer labs with the needed resources for use during a given semester.

Once the technology is accessible, learners must also assume responsibility for acquiring and maintaining skills to support learning. Communication with the instructor, tutorials, and institutional "help desks" are imperative when any technological issues arise that conflict with the ability to learn. Learners have to be their own advocates at times to insure the instructor or computer lab technician are alerted when technologies are not functional or available. Huang (2002) noted that learners can learn to self-assess the quality and authenticity of the learning in a more rigorous manner when using online environments.

Many online designs incorporate high levels of peer learner interaction, which if not facilitated appropriately by the instructors, may lead to misinformation that deters authentic learning. Hence, learners must learn how to assess the accuracy of exchanges when shared peer learning is used as an online teaching strategy.

Purpose of Evaluation

Fundamental to Weimer's (2002) learner-centered values is how evaluation can be used to expand and reinforce learning. Online learning environments offer strategies that balance these values. Barrett (2007) discusses the use of portfolios as a strategy of evaluation that is both a measure of learner outcomes and a means by which deeper learning can occur through reflection based on the learning journey. In the traditional classroom, portfolios can be created with computer software and placed on CD-ROM, Flash-drives, DVD, or can be text, photographs, or video-audio productions. These same portfolios can be published to online environments, such as a blog, a Wiki, or a personalized Web page. Permissions can be restricted for privacy or can be published with open access for social networking. The advantages of using more sophisticated levels of technology for portfolio development include the ability to archive, to link, and to publish (Barrett, 2007).

TECHNOLOGY'S INFLUENCE ON INSTRUCTOR / STUDENT RELATIONSHIPS

The influence of the instructor/student relationship is profound in the socialization process of a personal and professional becoming. MacIntosh wrote that "professional socialization is the process whereby individuals acquire and integrate into their lives the expected knowledge, behaviors, skills, attitudes, values, roles, and norms" (2003, p. 725) of their discipline. Socialization has benefits in that it perpetuates the historical values and norms of a profession (Kenny, Potin, & Moore, 2004; MacIntosh, 2003). Instructors should serve to model the essence of their disciplines in a myriad of activities that contribute to learning experiences. Often, this modeling is done through either classical or instructional mentoring.

Gender, socioeconomic, and cultural attributes influence characteristics of both instructors and students. These attributes blend in any given individual to make them unique in their approach to teaching or learning. This instructors/student diversity is further complicated by the preference for learning styles (Kolb, 1984). Kolb describes four major types of learners: accommodators, divergers, assimilators, and convergers. These types are based on the learning modes that are preferred by individuals, best portrayed in a humanistic frame as feeling, watching, thinking, and doing, respectively. These modes are influenced by the cultural phenomena of communication, personal space, social organization, time, environmental control, and biological variation (Bastable, 2003; Merriam, Caffarella, & Baumgartner, 2007; Mott, 2009). Each factor can also be mediated by technology and impact the ability of instructors to relate to students in the learning context.

One reason for the inability to relate to students may pivot on generational issues. Oblinger and Oblinger (2005) defined the generational variability within the academic arena among instructors. She stated that most instructors in the university institutions are usually *Baby Boomers*—optimistic workaholics who assume that responsibility is an element of their work ethic and can-do attitude. They disdain laziness and fear aging. *Boomers*, born between 1946 and 1964, are usually administrated by *Traditionals* (born between 1920 and 1945) who represent control and self-sacrifice. *Traditionals* are focused on family, community, and respect for authority. And, while typically thought to dislike technology, we cannot "assume that older [*Traditionals*] are uniformly anxious, resistant, or under-skilled where e-learning is concerned" (Mott, 2009, p. 785).

Current students, on the other hand, may yield from several generations including later *Baby Boomers, Generation Xers* (born between 1965 and roughly 1985), or the *Millennials* (birth years beyond the mid- to late-1980s). These later generations are thought to be more liberal in values, flexible to change, open to technology, and more prone to consumerism. However, as Mott noted elsewhere:

It is perhaps misguided to assume that younger learners are all comfortable with e-learning. Most Generation-X and Millennial learners have grown up with information and communication technologies; many would, in fact, be lost without their iPhones™ and Blackberries™.... More learners of every age have grown accustomed to the presence and even necessity of technology in their lives and readily embrace its use in their continued learning, both on and off the job. (Mott, 2009, p. 785)

The divergence in values, ideas, ethics and cultural phenomena makes the establishment of relationship between instructors/students more difficult across generations increasing the complexity of learning potentials (Johnson & Romanello, 2005). Instructors are called to become adept at recognizing generational differences and value them to broaden learning opportunities.

Further research in instructor/student relationship was conducted by Gillespie (2005). She concluded that the instructor/student relationship was so imperative to student learning that it raised implications for the preparation and evaluation of educators and educational practice. The research of Johnson and Romanello (2005) resulted in the development of an educational activities model that represents a cross-generation framework designed to assist relational development between instructors, students, and peers. Their work, like that of Gillespie encourages educators to consider personal beliefs, actions, and influences that are exerted on relationships with students through the educational process. The connection of instructors and student acting in relationship is influenced by the manner in which technology is applied.

The technological connection between instructors and students must be transparent (Krichen, 2004). Technology should not impede development of the relational system between instructors and students, nor among students, but should enhance its progress. Russo and Benson (2005) found that the instructors' presence in online teaching environments was positively correlated to students' satisfaction levels and to their affective learning outcomes. They also determined that students' self perception relative to cognitive learning was positively correlated to grade performance and self-evaluation of learning progress (Russo & Benson, 2005). Their findings reinforce the concept that it is not the technology, but the dynamic social interaction among the instructors and students and the engagement of the students with the knowledge that enhance the learning outcomes.

One technology that allows for synchronous relational presence among instructors and students is an online "chat." Chats allow for real time online dialogue between instructors and students, and student to student. Use of chats to supplement and add clarity to learning through the use of text is realized through the process of reciprocity (Kreijns, Kirschner, Jochems, & Van Buuren, 2004). In this reciprocal process, the learning interaction between instructors and students includes clarifying, questioning, predicting, and summarizing in a collaborative learning manner based on the cognitive development level of students (Kreijns et al., 2004). A relational presence is experienced in the collaborative interaction of reciprocity during use of synchronous chats and serves to sustain virtual learning genres, which are complex media that allow for similar collaborative interactions for learning.

Mikropoulos and Strouboulis (2004) defined factors that influence presence in educational virtual environments. Using six different input devices with 29 adolescents they were able to produce three distinct kinds of presence: personal, social, and environmental. Presence is strongly tied to identity and establishing an identity in a traditional classroom or online environment and can be facilitated by technology (Flores, 1998). Identity is established as a result of physical attributes, pattern of behaviors, and adherence to commitments all of which can be represented in realistic or symbolic ways using technology (Flores, 1998). Identity and learning styles can be masked or less transparent based upon educators technological designs for the learning setting and environment.

TECHNOLOGY'S INFLUENCE ON EDUCATIONAL ENVIRONMENTS

As previously discussed, instructors must take into account the readiness level of students to learn, as well as their learning styles. Information alone does not insure learning; rather it is the manipulation of the learning environment by the educator that provides an opportunity for interaction with the affective, cognitive, and behavioral domains of learning (Bastable, 2003). Traditional instructional settings have been classroom, internship or field work in industry of the discipline, and in laboratory settings. The curriculum design and the instructional methods are adapted to the setting or environment. The setting/environment determines the instructional strategies and materials for learning based on impacting factors or elements (Bastable, 2003). Impacting factors include, but are not limited to, organizational or administrative structures, time and resource constraints, collegial and clientele support for participation in the educational process, and environmental or structural confines. Pervasive in all educational settings is the escalation of technology for the delivery of education. Comparisons of traditional classrooms and online learning environments yield student satisfaction levels that are analogous one to the other when controlled for instructor and content (Cooper, Taft, & Thelen, 2004; Schoech & Helton, 2002). Examination of the technological factors that affect student outcomes of learning as well as satisfaction levels requires greater scrutiny.

The biological stimulus that occurs in virtual environments (physical imagery, sight, and sound) add realistic attributes to the learning environment that mimic real life stimulating brain responses (Mikropoulos & Strouboulis, 2004). One could compare this level of technological complexity to a child playing with a cardboard box (simple technology) versus playing with an elaborately made dollhouse or tree house. We have not yet researched using matched controls to compare the value of learning outcomes when applying the simple technology to the complex technology. Therefore, we cannot make assumptions at this point that virtual multimedia environments are better than (say for example), synchronous chat using text. We can say, however, that technological generated virtual environments are different while achieving the desired outcomes for learning.

Another virtual technology that is used increasingly in traditional learning settings is achieved through simulators. Simulators are used in the classroom, training laboratories, and other traditional settings. Simulators in health care are life size mannequins realistically representing the biology of human form and equipped with sensors that provide computer feedback to stimulators as programmed scenarios. In the military and airline industry, simulators are the monitors and indicators of a given aircraft to train pilots before an actual flight occurs. Simulators are most often used in health care, disaster training for service personnel, or in safety training in industry, among others (Holcomb, Dumire, Crommett, Stamateris, Fagert, & Cleveland, 2002). Thus, the range for interaction either at an individual level of learning or for collaborative shared learning can be augmented in virtual or traditional learning environments. Environments for use of technologies can be traditional, blended (a combination of Web-based virtual and traditional face-to-face), or Web-based virtual online.

Research has also been conducted that provided insights into the rapid expansion of technology as a platform for learning. Allen and Seaman (2003) reported that in public institutions of higher education, approximately 97% offered one course fully online or blended, and 49% offered a complete degree program online. Further, 67% of the higher education institutions surveyed projected that online education is a long-term strategy for educational delivery. The survey noted that an additional critical issue was the readiness of the instructors to deliver online education. Another noteworthy aspect found was that only 59.6% reported that instructors accepted the value and legitimacy of online education. In an updated survey report in 2008, Allen and Seaman suggested that enrollment in online programs continues to grow at rates that exceeds traditional higher education programs. They maintain that enrollment will increase even during economic downturns as more unemployed seek to develop and enhance job skills through online education. Bourne and Moore (2004) cited that most students will be educated in a blended model of learning using a mix of technologies and educational activities, and where learning is focused from a systems thinking approach.

TECHNOLOGIES FOR LEARNERS

The technologies that are currently employed in higher education range from smart boards in traditional classrooms to virtual learning environments like *Second Life*™. Smart boards replace the traditional blackboard and are integrated with computer programming to applications used by the instructors, such as Excel, PowerPoint, or Word. For instance, a power point presentation designed by the instructor is projected on the smart board and then concepts are outlined or highlighted as a lesson progresses. The changes are then saved and electronically distributed to learners in hard copy, note format.

Interactive "clicker" systems engage the students in responding silently and simultaneously to the instructor in an electronic manner that synchronously displays the results in a graphed manner. Instructors review learner understanding and redirect misconceptions reinforcing accuracy in learning. These systems are often costly; thus some educators have taken advantage of the common use of cell phones integrated to an internet site to achieve the same end as the clicker system. *Ipod*™ and MP3 player technologies, universally used by many for listening to music, have now been adapted to include auditory learning sessions such as lectures and can now accommodate video lectures. These learning sessions can be posted and distributed through *YouTube*™ or *Itunes*™ for immediate download by learners creating the ultimate in mobile learning.

Course management software such as Web CT™ or Blackboard™ offer complex, yet sophisticated and highly adaptable learning systems. These programs have embedded applications that integrate with external sources for linking learning objects and others which expand learning strategies. Blogs, wikis, audio-video applications such as *Centra*™ and *Elluminate*™ increase the ability of course management software to facilitate learning socialization. These learning systems are taking a rapid leap forward as Web 3.0 approaches.

Communications software that extends the use of technology such as *SKYPE*™ allows a computer to serve as a videophone connecting to anywhere in the world. Use of this phone system and other communication tools could allow instructors to have virtual office hours with distributed learners. Social Web applications like *Facebook*™ and *My Space*™ are being integrated in learning environments for learner interaction, portfolio development, and social networking for job opportunities (Batson, 2009).

Campus Technology featured East Carolina University's (ECU) use of *Second Life*™, a virtual world economy (Harrison, 2009). Land is purchased; campuses, towns, and business are set up. The currency of exchange is *linden* dollars. Classes are conducted using *avitars*, digitized images designed to allow for human-like mobility. At East Carolina University, ten classes are on-going and other services for library, bookstore, career services, and undergraduate support can be accessed via *Second Life*™. Some of the disciplines offering classes include interior design, computer management, counseling, business management, and business information technology education. Some like interior design meet both in a traditional classroom and in *Second Life*™ while others, like business management only hold class within *Second Life* ™. *Second Life*™ can facilitate lecture formats but also allows for auditory exchange between the instructors and learners. Use of these technologies provides learners with skills that will be used as they leave an academic environment to progress into the work environment.

Learning currently available and emerging technology is crucial for the preparation of tomorrow's workforce. Organizational consultants note that since 2004, our virtual workforce has increased by 800% (Gargiulo, 2009). Gargiulo predicted that in 2011 the mobile workforce will comprise 73% of the total U.S. workforce (2009). This means that workers must be competent in working from various locations while maintaining relationships for collaborative workflow and management to deliver the work required. E-mail, instant text messaging, Web-conferencing enable communications for virtual team functions. Word documents, spreadsheets, and other software applications become the tools indispensable for collaboration. In 2006, small to medium enterprises were using Web-conferencing 41% of the time to include persons who could not previously attend, enable meeting not previously held, and to solve problems they were unable to address without the collaborative input (Nilssen & Greenberg, 2006). Technology is fundamental to small to medium businesses for customer presentations, demonstrations, training/e-learning, and internal/external team function. The rationale for use of Web-conferencing includes economic savings, improved time management, scheduling flexibility, increased personnel productivity, and advance work flow (Nilssen & Greenberg, 2006). Thus, teaching with technology is not just an option, but is vital to preparing workers who have the skills to compete in current work environments.

FUTURE TRENDS

One can barely imagine what future educational technologies may eventually be commonplace in our daily lives, much less in education. We will surely employ more realistic virtual environments such as *Second Life*™, more educational materials on demand via our ever smaller and faster personal digital assistants, increased virtual networking and communications, and even holographic models on which to apply the theories and concepts learned. These possibilities are already present in our laboratories and think tanks today, if not yet readily available to us as instructors and learners. But, might we also explore more direct means of transfer of knowledge in – and out – of our minds, similar to the ways in which PET scans and EEG now monitor our brain waves in medical diagnoses. We are already on the edge of enhanced understanding of the incredible power of our sleep and unconscious mental states in learning. We will surely continue this exploration of ways to maximize these alternative states of consciousness in knowledge capture and transfer. What other instructional technologies are already budding in the minds of our youngest learners? The possibilities of next generation technological tools that await us as educators and learners are virtually unimaginable.

Other future trends that await us will surely be impacted by increasingly complex global economies, changing political pressures, environmental concerns, and ever changing demographics. We may see continued interest in a single worldwide language, for instance, at least for business and educational transactions. Technologies will surely support improved multicultural understanding and perhaps somehow ease international communications and travel among people of the world, hopefully while protecting both our individual cultural selves and the environment. And, the demographic realities of longer, healthier working lives will undoubtedly influence not only what we learn, but how instructional technologies can facilitate that learning and application to our future workplaces. Other demographic and cultural attributes will also impact the use of various instructional technologies, as we consider not just race, gender, and age, but other critical issues such as language, abilities, and other aspects of culture.

But, given the focus of this article on the use of educational technologies in learner-centered instruction, we must also continue to consider the impact of these future trends and emerging technologies on both learning processes and outcomes. How will educators ensure that future instructional technologies narrow, instead of widen the access and achievement gap of learners? How might the technologies of the future continue to balance the power dynamic in our learning environments? Can learners continue to develop self-directed capacity and autonomy so that the technologies in place help us *learn how to learn*, and so capture ever increasing and necessary knowledge available? Can the instructional technologies aid instructors in alternative and improved ways to consider content and evaluation in service of learning. The inevitable growing knowledge obsolescence, expansion, and development of the future demand that instructors and learners alike be able to develop and master instructional technologies. By doing so, we may continue to empower learners toward greater personal autonomy, critical thinking and reflection, and self-actualization.

CONCLUSION

Instructional technologies, as tools for learning in the classroom and as generators of created environments, are artifacts of human existence (Bruce, Feng, Nishizawaumiko, Palulis, Russel, & Worthing 2003). Technology holds meaning within the educational experience and via interaction to facilitate the acquisition of knowledge, to share knowledge, and to create new knowledge. Throughout history, we have come to know the meaning of many cultures through the technologies used to depict drawing on cave walls and symbols on stone tablets. The technologies of the 21st century will, at some point in the future, be viewed as primitive as those ancient cultures that came before us. Neal and Winnipeg (1995) noted that technology becomes the way a culture expresses itself and is a reflection of its societal values. Future societies may also judge our educational use of technology in the same way. Technological tools of learning must allow for tone and emotion, human connection, and presence to transmit contextual meaning—especially as they relate to the further development of learner-centered instruction. It is important that we document the legacy of current learning technologies and continue to study the most effective use of these evolutions of time.

REFERENCES

Allen, I. E., & Seaman, J. (2003). *Sizing the opportunity: The quality and extent of online education in the United States*. Needham, MA: Sloan & Sloan Center for Online Education (SCOLE).

Allen, I. E., & Seaman, J. (2008). *Staying the course: Online education in the United States,*

2008. Needham, MA: Babson Survey Research Group, The Sloan Consortium.

American Psychological Association. (1997). *Learner-centered psychological principles: A framework for school redesign and reform*. Retrieved April 20, 2009, http://www.apa.org/ed/lcp.html

Barr, R. B., & Tagg, J. (1995). From teaching to learning—a new paradigm for undergraduate education. *Change*, *27*(6), 12–25.

Barrett, H. C. (2007). Researching electronic portfolios and learner engagement: The REFLECT initiative. *Journal of Adolescent & Adult Literacy*, *50*(6), 436–449. doi:10.1598/JAAL.50.6.2

Bastable, S. B. (2003). *Nurse as educator: Principles of teaching and learning for nursing practice* (2nd ed.). Sudbury, MA: Jones & Bartlett.

Billings, D. M., & Halstead, J. A. (2005). *Teaching in nursing: A guide for instructors* (2nd ed.). St. Louis, MO: Elsevier Saunders.

Bonk, C. J., Wisher, R. A., & Lee, J. Y. (2004). Moderating learner-centered e-learning: Problems and solutions, benefits and implications. In T. S. Roberts (Ed.), *Online collaborative learning: Theory and practice* (pp. 54-85). Hershey, PA: IGI Global.

Bourne, J., & Moore, J. (2004). *Elements of quality online education: Into the mainstream*. Needham, MA: Sloan Consortium.

Boyer, E. (1990). *Scholarship reconsidered: Priorities for the professoriate*. Princeton, NJ: The Carnegie Foundation for the Advancement of Teaching.

Bruce, A., Feng, F., Nishizawaumiko, S., Palulis, P., Russel, B. D., & Worthing, C. (2003). Provoking signs: Un/canny moments as curriculum theorizing. *Educational Insights*, *8*(2), 1–20.

Cooper, C., Taft, L. B., & Thelen, M. (2004). Examining the role of technology in learning: An evaluation of online clinical conferencing. *Journal of Professional Nursing*, *20*(3), 160–166. doi:10.1016/j.profnurs.2004.04.003

Cornelius-White, J. (2007). Learner-centered instructors-student relationships are effective: A meta-analysis. *Review of Educational Research*, *77*(1), 113. doi:10.3102/003465430298563

Derntl, M., & Motschnig-Pitrik, R. (2004, March 14-17). Patterns for blended, person-centered learning: Strategy, concepts, experiences, and evaluation. In *Proceedings of the 2004 ACM Symposium on Applied Computing*, Nicosia, Cyprus (pp. 916-923). ACM Publishing.

Diekelmann, N., Schuster, R., & Nosek, C. (1998). *Creating new pedagogies at the millennium: The common experiences of University of Wisconsin-Madison instructors using distance education technologies* (commissioned final report to University System of Wisconsin no. 1). Madison, WI: University of Wisconsin.

Du, H., & Wagner, C. (2005). Learning with weblogs: An empirical investigation. In *Proceedings of the 38th Annual Hawaii International Conference on System Sciences (HICSS'05)*, Big Island, Hawaii (pp. 7). IEEE.

Farrell, G. M. (2001). *The changing faces of virtual education*. London: Commonwealth of Learning.

Flores, F. (1998). Information technology and the institution of identity. *Information Technology & People*, *11*(4), 351–372. doi:10.1108/09593849810246156

Gargiulo, T. L. (2009). *The top ten strategies for managers of mobile workers*. Retrieved April 10, 2009, from http://makingstories.net

Gillespie, M. (2005). Student-instructors connection: A place of possibility. *Journal of Advanced Nursing*, *52*(2), 211–219. doi:10.1111/j.1365-2648.2005.03581.x

Harrison, D. (2009). *Engaging students in virtual learning.* Retrieved April 23, 2009, from http://campustechnology.com/Articles/2009/04/22/Engaging-Students-in-Virtual-Learning

Hartley, K., & Bendixen, L. D. (2001). Educational research in the Internet age: Examining the role of individual characteristics. *Educational Researcher, 30*(9), 22. doi:10.3102/0013189X030009022

Holcomb, J. B., Dumire, R. D., Crommett, J. W., Stamateris, C. E., Fagert, M. A., & Cleveland, J. A. (2002). Evaluation of trauma team performance using an advanced human patient simulator for resuscitation training. *The Journal of Trauma Injury Infection and Critical Care, 52*(6), 1078. doi:10.1097/00005373-200206000-00009

Huang, U. (2002). Toward constructivism for adult learners in online learning environments. *British Journal of Educational Technology, 33*(1), 27–37. doi:10.1111/1467-8535.00236

Johnson, S. A., & Romanello, M. L. (2005). Generational diversity: Teaching and learning approaches. *Nurse Educator, 30*(5), 212–216. doi:10.1097/00006223-200509000-00009

Kayler, M., & Weller, K. (2007). Pedagogy, self-assessment, and online discussion groups. *Journal of Educational Technology & Society, 10*(1), 136.

Kennedy, G. E., Judd, T. S., Churchward, A., Gray, K., & Krause, K. L. (2008). First year students' experiences with technology: Are they really digital natives. *Australasian Journal of Educational Technology, 24*(1), 108–122.

Kenny, G., Pontin, D., & Moore, L. (2004). Negotiating socialisation: The journey of novice nurse academics into higher education. *Nurse Education Today, 24*(8), 629–637.

Koehler, M. J., & Mishra, P. (2005a). Instructors learning technology by design. *Journal of Computing in Instructors Education, 21*(3), 94–102.

Koehler, M. J., & Mishra, P. (2005b). What happens when instructors design educational technology? The development of technological pedagogical content knowledge. *Journal of Educational Computing Research, 32*(2), 131–152. doi:10.2190/0EW7-01WB-BKHL-QDYV

Kolb, D. A. (1984). *Experiential learning: Experience as the source of learning and development.* Englewood Cliffs, NJ: Prentice-Hall.

Koper, R. (2004). Use of the semantic web to solve some basic problems in education. *Journal of Interactive Media in Education, 6*, 1–23.

Koper, R., & Olivier, B. (2004). Representing the learning design of units of learning. *Journal of Educational Technology & Society, 7*, 97–111.

Koper, R., & Tattersall, C. (2004). New directions for lifelong learning using network technologies. *British Journal of Educational Technology, 35*(6), 689–700. doi:10.1111/j.1467-8535.2004.00427.x

Kreijns, K., Kirschner, P. A., Jochems, W., & Van Buuren, H. (2004). Determining sociability, social space, and social presence in (a) synchronous collaborative groups. *Cyber-psychology & Behavior: The Impact of the Internet . Multimedia and Virtual Reality on Behavior and Society,* 7(2), 155–172.

Krichen, J. P. (2004). *Online university administration: Impacts on instructors' management and course delivery.* Retrieved from http://www.decadeconsulting.com/decade/images/Jkrichen.pdf

Lu, H., Jia, L., Gong, S., & Clark, B. (2007). The relationship of Kolb Learning Styles, online learning behaviors, and learning outcomes. *Educational Technology & Society, 10*(4), 187–196.

MacIntosh, J. (2003). Reworking professional nursing identity. *Western Journal of Nursing Research, 25*(6), 725–741. doi:10.1177/0193945903252419

Magjuka, R. J., Shi, M., & Bonk, C. J. (2005). Critical design and administrative issues in online education. *Online Journal of Distance Learning Administration, 8*(4), Article 4. Retrieved April 28, 2009, from http://www.westga.edu/~distance/ojdla/winter84/magjuka84.htm

McCombs, B. L., & Lauer, P. A. (1997). Development and validation of the learner-centered battery: Self-assessment tools for teacher reflection and professional development. *Professional Educator, 20*(1), 1–21.

McCombs, B. L., & Vakili, D. (2005). A learner-centered framework for e-learning. *Teachers College Record, 107*(8), 1582–1600. doi:10.1111/j.1467-9620.2005.00534.x

Merriam, S., Caffarella, R., & Baumgartner, L. (2007). *Learning in adulthood: A comprehensive guide* (3rd ed.). San Francisco: Jossey-Bass.

Mikropoulos, T. A., & Strouboulis, V. (2004). Factors that influence presence in educational virtual environments. *Cyberpsychology & Behavior, 7*(5), 582–591.

Mott, V. W. (2004). Book review: Learner-centered teaching: Five key changes to practice. *Adult Education Quarterly, 54*(3), 244–245. doi:10.1177/0741713604263058

Mott, V. W. (2009). Evolution of adult education: Is our future in e-learning? In V. C. X. Wang (Ed.), *Handbook of research on e-learning applications for career and technical education: Technologies for technical training* (pp. 778-791). Hershey, PA: IGI Global.

Neal, A., & Winnipeg, M. (1995). Group apraxia: The phenomenology of acculturalism. *The Canadian Journal of Native Studies, 10*(2), 219–242.

Nilssen, A., & Greenberg, A. (July 2006). *The vital role of web conferencing in small and medium enterprises.* Live Oak, FL: Wainwright Research.

Novak, J. D. (2003). The promise of new ideas and new technology for improving teaching and learning. *Life Sciences Education, 2*(2), 122–132.

O'Lawrence, H. (2007). An overview of the influences of distance learning on adult learners. *Journal of Education and Human Development, 1*(1), 7. Retrieved March 12, 2009, from http://www.scientificjournals.org/journals2007/articles/1041.htm

Oblinger, D., & Oblinger, J. (2005). *Educating the net generation* (1st ed.). Retrieved from http://www.educause.edu/educatingthenetgen

Pettitt, J. M. (2002). *Power relationships in two web-based courses.* Raleigh, NC: North Carolina State University. (ERIC Document Reproduction Service No. ED471832)

Quinsee, S., & Hurst, J. (2005). *Blurring the boundaries? Supporting students and staff within an online learning environment* (ERIC Document Reproduction Service No. ED494786). Retrieved on April 28, 2009, from http://www.eric.ed.gov/ERICWebPortal/Home.portal?_nfpb=true&_pageLabel=basic&Clearme=true

Reynard, R. (2009). *Can we gauge technology's impact on learning outcomes?* Retrieved April 23, 2009, from http://campustechnology.com/Articles/2009/03/25/Does-Technology-Improve-Learning

Russo, T., & Benson, S. (2005). Learning with invisible others: Perceptions of online presence and their relationship to cognitive and affective learning. *Educational Technology & Society, 8*(1), 54–62.

Saba, V. K. (2001). Nursing informatics: Yesterday, today and tomorrow. *International Nursing Review, 48*(3), 177–187. doi:10.1046/j.1466-7657.2001.00064.x

Schaffert, S., Bischof, D., Bürger, T., Gruber, A., Hilzensauer, W., & Schaffert, S. (2006, June 11-14). *Learning with semantic wikis.* Paper presented at the 1st Workshop on From Wiki to Semantics, 3rd Annual European Semantic Web Conference (ESWC), Budva, Montenegro. Retrieved April

29, 2009, from http://www.salzburgresearch.at/research/gfx/semantic_wiki_elearning.pdf

Schoech, D., & Helton, D. (2002). Qualitative and quantitative analysis of a course taught via classroom and internet chatroom. *Qualitative Social Work*, *1*(1), 111–124. doi:10.1177/147332500200100174 8

Task Force on Distance Education and Training in Professional Psychology American Psychological Association. (2002). *Principals of good practice in distance education and their application to professional education and training in psychology*. Washington, DC: American Psychological Association, Task Force on Distance Education.

Thomas, L., & Knezek, D. (1995). *Technology literacy for the nation and for its citizens*. Retrieved April 28, 2009, from http://www.iste.org/AM/PrinterTemplate.cfm?Section=Technology_Literacy

Weimer, M. (2002). *Learner centered teaching* (1st ed.). San Francisco: Jossey-Bass.

This work was previously published in the International Journal of Web-Based Learning and Teaching Technologies, Vol. 4, Issue 4, edited by E. M. W. Ng, N. Karacapilidis, and M. S. Raisinghani , pp. 1-16, copyright 2009 by IGI Publishing (an imprint of IGI Global).

Chapter 3
Effective Teaching with Technology in Adult Education

Victor C. X. Wang
California State University at Long Beach, USA

ABSTRACT

Effective teaching with technology in adult education stems from many factors. Technology is only used to enhance learning. Not only are teachers of adult learners required to study the tools related to the use of technology, but are also required to study the nature of knowledge, the nature of learning, constructivism and various kinds of teaching philosophies. Without thorough knowledge of these factors, effective teaching with technology cannot occur in adult education, let alone other educational fields. This article is comprehensive concerning effective teaching with technology in adult education because it also addresses the interrelationships between the use of technologies and the teaching and learning process.

INTRODUCTION

Using technology for education and training of adult learners offers many challenges. However, the greatest challenge is to focus not on technology itself but on the learner and learning (Olgren, 2000). Olgren argues that technology invites a tools-first emphasis, but technology is only as good as our knowledge of how to use it to enhance learning (p. 7). Her point is well taken in the field of adult education whose focus is placed on the education and training of adult learners in the 21st century. One of the characteristics of adult learners is that they have multiple work/family responsibilities (Wang, 2008). Because of this characteristic, adult learners find it hard to attend face-to-face meetings in a traditional classroom on a physical campus at the end of a week day or on a weekend. Universities and colleges have seized this great opportunity to accommodate the needs of adult learning by moving their courses onto computer screens, hence the issue of effective teaching with technology in adult education. Knowles, the father of adult education, predicted in the early 1970s that education, especially the education of adults in the 21st century would be delivered electronically. His predication came true as universities and colleges began to address adult learning by using WebCT or Blackboard programs. These educational programs were purchased in the late 1990s. Adult learners have been taking advantage of these educational programs by taking courses online to meet their needs of upgrading their work skills, getting a college degree/diploma/credentials or simply satisfying their sheer joy of learning. Giant online universities, such as the University of Phoenix, have emerged to launch massive online educational programs to address the learning needs of adult learners. Bash (2003) noted, "In 2002, the University of Phoenix, part of the Apollo Group, saw its enrollment surpass 100,000 students—making it the largest institution of higher learning in the United States" (p. 50). No doubt, this enrollment can be much higher especially when universities and colleges have the need to do more with less. As our student numbers are expected to grow, our budgets continually are shorn. It is a not a matter of whether faculty enjoy teaching with technology. Gone are the days when faculty could argue that they are philosophically against teaching with technology. Currently, faculty is required to embrace with open arms the biggest change in their lives to integrate at least some measure of teaching with technology in their practice. It is not surprising when we hear that a certain university has put one third of its courses online. Teaching with technology has emerged as a new trend in this new century. As Brookfield (2006) noted, "These days no college teacher can avoid teaching in a hybrid manner, combining electronic and face-to-face communication. The only question remaining is the degree to which electronic communication is integrated into course activities" (p. 191). As I write, I am teaching over 100 adult learners in four different classes via either hybrid format or entire online format. Here, I am not trying to say that face-to-face education with adult learners would be marginalized with the advent of Internet technology. Rather, teaching with technology like regular teaching in university settings seems to treat learning as a commodity, turning it into an external object marketed for a hefty price to save cash-strapped programs trying to stay afloat (Brookfield, 2006, p. 192). Perhaps this is where pragmatism comes into play. Where there is learning with technology, there is teaching with technology. After all, programmed instruction with computers was popularized even in the 1960s by behaviorists. Pedagogically, faculty is worried about the fact that teaching with technology would take the personal dimension out of teaching, or remove the relational element. The fundamental question that can be asked is how can students always trust someone they have never seen in person or spoken to directly? Or another question can be asked is can students learn with technology in an isolated environment?

To address such pedagogical questions, let's turn to the advantages of teaching with technology as summarized by Brookfield (2006):

- Teaching with technology is not necessarily qualitatively different from its face-to-face counterpart. Indeed, various introductory guides to e-teaching explore many of the exact same problems (how to engage students, respond to racial differences, take account of different learning styles, and so on) that engage the attention of teachers in face-to-face classrooms (Conrad & Donaldson, 2004; Palloff & Pratt, 1999, 2003).
- In asynchronous discussion learners would have the time to think through their responses without the pressure to come up with an impromptu contribution or response to a teacher's question that would make them look good in class.
- Students who struggled with language, who were introverts, or who needed time to process information and create meaning, as well as those who were intimidated by the theater of the classroom (particularly having to play the role of the smart, capable,

committed student), would all benefit from learning with technology's privacy.

- Learning with technology also placed a greater degree of control into the students' hands over when and how fast learning happened, something Piskurich (2003) argues increases both retention and self-directed learning.
- Finally, in learning with technology, students stressed the importance of feeling a member of some type of learning community in exactly the way that students in face-to-face classrooms did.

Although a case can be made about the benefits of teaching/learning with technology, there are potential problems associated with teaching with technology that equally deserve our attention. The first issue is the learner's physical isolation which may pose problems with learning. How can a teacher evaluate the learner's learning? Will the learner do the learning on his or her own in an isolated environment? The second issue is teaching with technology is time consuming. The time spent in giving extensive feedback is considerable. The third issue is impossible for teachers to read and give visual and tonal cues when teaching with technology. Although smiley faces, exclamation points, dots for pauses, boldface and capitals can be used to express importance, the possibility for misunderstanding does exist. There is a delay between the individual typing the words he/she wants to convey and all other chat participants seeing the words projected on the computer screen. The similar delay also exists when students try to communicate with each via microphones. Finally, as Brookfield points out that students from cultures in which collective decision making is the norm, will find it hard to sit by themselves, stare at their screen, and respond to words typed by others at a different time and in a different place (2006, p. 195).

While acknowledging the benefits and problems of teaching with technology, the purpose of this article is to show our readers how we can capitalize on the known benefits and address the problems associated with teaching with technology so that effective teaching with technology in adult education will occur. Teaching with technology should enable users to exercise maximum control and freedom to create or do what they intend. Helping adults learn with the use of technology involves innovative approaches such as adopting useful teaching philosophies, problem-solving models, constructivist model or critical thinking skills. It is these innovative approaches or instructional methods that will enhance adult teaching and learning with the use of technology. As technology is used to enhance learning, it must be used to with innovative approaches. Otherwise, effective teaching with technology in adult education would not occur. Next, I will provide broad definitions and discussions of this article that will incorporate view of others regarding our topic under discussion.

BACKGROUND

Burge (2000) defines technology as any tool that requires informed design and appropriate use in order to enhance an adult's ability to learn; that is, to enhance the use of various information processing strategies and learning activities alone, with peers, and with appropriate advisers and educators (p. 1). Teaching with technology is characterized by a physical separation between learner and instructor and by the use of media for communications and content resources. These characteristics have important effects on the learner. First, teachers have the responsibility for carrying out the teaching process. Second, teachers must be able to use technology to access resources and communicate with others. Third, teachers need to find ways to motivate learners to learn in an isolated setting. Since we mentioned media and technology here, it is necessary for us to make a distinction between the two. According to Bates and Poole

(2003), speech, writing, drama, radio and television programming, computer programming, and Web-based courses are all media, or more strictly, symbol systems that uniquely define specific media. Classrooms, books, theaters, cinemas, radio sets and transmitters, cable, satellites, television monitors, computers, computer software, and computer networks are all technologies (2003, p. 48). In addition, they indicate that technologies are physical things whereas media are means of communication. In our everyday use of the term media, we usually refer to the whole organization of a communications industry, such as television, newspapers, publishing, and the Internet.

The role of technology in education goes back to 25 centuries ago. For the ancient Greeks, oratory and speech were the means by which people learned and passed on learning. Likewise, the ancient Chinese learned and passed on learning by the means of Confucius's analects. People in the past learned basically by listening, not by reading or writing. People learned by recitation (Bates & Poole, 2003). After paper and printing were invented, books emerged as early as the fifth century B. C. Later, people realized although writing would not help memory, it would act as a reminder. To the Chinese, teaching embraces twin goals: to teach books and to teach people (Wang, 2007). Naturally, teaching through a computer is not the same as teaching from a book or teaching from a lecture. These activities are all different forms of teaching and each results in a slightly different way of students' learning about something. Deep understanding occurs when all forms of knowing developed by a learner are internally reconciled and integrated by the learner (Bates & Poole, 2003). Therefore, we need to focus on how media can be used to facilitate knowledge-construction and meaning-making on the part of the learner (Cranton, 1994; Mezirow, 1985, 1990, 1991, 2000; King, 2005; Wang & King, 2006, 2007).

The goal of teaching with technology is to facilitate learning, not to inhibit learning on the part of adult learners, and learning leads to knowing. Bates and Poole (2003) argue that teaching with technology is not necessarily better or worse than face-to-face education; it is, though, different. They further argue that once we come to accept that different is not necessarily better or worse, we change the nature of the argument about teaching technologies. The fundamental question then is not are they better or worse, but in what contexts and for what purposes are technologies best used? I agree with Bates and Poole on their insights regarding the use of technology as these two scholars have been keeping up with the latest development of technology. Technology should be used as a tool for effective education to maximize learning on the part of learners although doing more with less should be just the by product of teaching with technology. Having defined technology, we want to know: what exactly are technologies that can be used in teaching adult learners and learners of any kind? Bates and Poole indicate that five media represent different clusters of symbol systems and ways of mediating and interpreting knowledge and these five primary education media are listed below:

- Direct face-to-face contact
- Text (including still graphics)
- (Analogue) audio
- (Analogue) video
- Digital multimedia

To educators of adults, the distinction between synchronous and asynchronous technologies is important. While synchronous technologies require all participants to participate at the same time. Asynchronous technologies allow participants to access the technology at any time of their choosing. While bringing everyone together for an educational event can create a sense of community, asynchronous technologies provide flexibility and convenience for both teachers and learners. As I write this article and this book, I have found that most adult learner prefer the asynchronous technologies to synchronous technologies simply because their family and work responsibilities do not allow them to be brought together for an educational event. Below, I have modified Bates and Poole's 2003 table to illustrate when to teach with technology to maximize learning. The questions that are worth asking can be:

1. When can we use technology to replace direct personal contact without educational loss or with educational gain?
2. When can we combine face-to-face with technology based teaching for the best results?
3. When can we teach with technology alone?

It can be seen that various technologies differ significantly on key structural characteristics that are of potential importance for educational purposes. The challenge is to decide when to use which technology for what educational purposes. The strength of technology comes from the combination of different media. No single medium is likely to be sufficient for any university-level subject (Bates & Poole, 2003). Poorly-designed applications of multimedia can frustrate learners. Well-designed applications of multimedia can, according to Bates and Poole (2003):

- Enable learners to come to understandings more quickly than through more conventional verbal or textual media.
- Help students develop and practice skills.
- Change how we come to know or to understand and hence what we know and understand. In other words, through the use of multimedia, a learner may have an image or a mental construction that is far richer than an abstract verbal understanding.
- Enable a learner to move from concrete, specific examples to more general abstractions, and vice versa.

Without knowing some background information about technology and media, how technology has evolved, the difference between technology

Table 1. A classification of educational technologies by structural characteristics

Technologies				
	Broadcast (one-way) Applications		Communication (two-way) Applications	
Media	Synchronous	Asynchronous	Synchronous	Asynchronous
Face-to-face	Lectures	Lecture notes	Seminars	
Text		Books		Mail
Audio	Radio	Audio-cassettes	Telephone tutoring Audio-Conferencing	
Video	Broadcast TV Cable TV Satellite TV	Video-cassettes	Videoconferencing	
Digital multimedia	Webcasting Audio-Streaming Video-Streaming	Web sites CD-ROMs DVDs Learning objects Multimedia clips	Chat MUDs Web-conferencing	E-mail Discussion forums

Adopted from Bates and Poole (2003, p. 55)

and media, and a detailed classification of technologies, teachers cannot help adult learners learn effectively. The goal of teaching with technology is to facilitate learning, not to inhibit learning. To know some background information about technology and media is just the first step towards teaching effectively with technology. Our next section will address issues such as the nature of knowledge, the nature of learning, and one's teaching philosophies, all of which will contribute to teaching effectively with technology. Teaching with technology requires teachers to know something about the nature of knowledge. The nature of knowledge focuses on the question of how we know what we know. Epistemology is a branch of philosophy concerned with the nature and justification of knowledge (Hofer & Pintrich, 1997). In our previous articles, we indicated that adults and children learn differently. This distinction was made by the father of adult education, Malcolm Knowles in the early 1970s (Knowles, 1975). This distinction alone will require teachers to use technology differently. It is natural that one's teaching philosophies predetermine one's teaching methods including the use of technology. Our next section will specifically address the nature of knowledge, the nature of learning and teacher's teaching philosophies. More importantly, we will address how these elements influence the use of technology, particularly, the effective use of technology so that the goal of teaching with technology can be achieved. If the use of technology can not be justified, then, technology should be abandoned.

THE NATURE OF KNOWLEDGE CONCERNING ADULT LEARNING

An important part of adult education is aimed at developing students' understanding, within this academic discipline, of the criteria and values that underpin academic study of this discipline. These criteria and values include questions of what constitutes valid knowledge in this subject area. Valid knowledge in adult education consists of not only instructional strategies, but also content of the field. For these two kinds of knowledge bases, instructional strategies and content of the field, both teachers and adult students are required to know the nature of knowledge in the field. Do adults approach their knowledge differently from children? How can technology be used to help adults approach their knowledge? These are the first two questions teachers should ask themselves before delving into the nature of knowledge.

Two dominant epistemological positions that exist today are worth discussing for our purpose—objectivism and constructivism. First objectivists believe that there exists an objective and reliable set of facts, principles, and theories that either have been or will be discovered and delineated over the course of time. Bates and Poole write in 2003,

> This position is linked to the belief that truth exists outside the human mind or independently of what an individual may or may not believe. The laws of physics are thus constant, although our knowledge of them may evolve as we discover the "truth" out there (p. 28)

Do teachers of adults view themselves as objectivists in the field of adult education? In fact, a large number of teachers of adults are labeled as objectivists who still believe that a course must present a core body of knowledge to be learned on the part of adult students. Their courses may consist of formulas, terminology, theories, and the like. The effective transmission of this core body of knowledge becomes of central importance. Instructors prefer lectures and standardized textbooks to discussions. Their courses are well organized and clear and instructors like to be considered as authoritative figures in the field (Wang, 2007-2008). Course assignments and exams require students to find the right answers and justify them. When it comes to using technology to teach courses to adult students, these objectivist instructors normally set ground rules regarding online discussions. Their online course may be well laid out, mapped out, and well designed. Exams are usually timed. Course instructors grade students' work according to rubrics. I am not saying this approach to teaching adults is wrong. Rather, it is predetermined by multiple factors. Often times, instructors have no choice but to follow objectivist approaches to teaching and to teaching with technology. First and foremost, if instructors believe that there exists an objective and reliable set of facts, principles, and theories that either have been or will be discovered and delineated over the course of time, they are bound to use objectivist approaches including objectivist approaches to using technology. Also, the nature of course may determine such approaches to teaching. For example, in adult basic education, students do not have the basic knowledge, skills or attitudes in the field. Instructors have to use this approach. One more factor that needs our attention is the fact that some institutions may require instructors to conform to objectivist approaches to teaching even adult learners. What if you have a department chair who has an advanced degree obtained from the field of K-12 education and who is so comfortable with approaches of teaching children? If this chair requires that the objectivist approaches be the main instructional methods in the department, teachers of adults would have no other choices but to follow this norm. If you read books by Knowles, Holton, and Swanson (2005), they would probably tell you that it depends on your learners' experience with a subject matter. They would say, "Use objectivist approaches if you believe your adult learners are inexperienced with a subject matter and if they depend on instructors for speed and convenience." Is there a better approach than the objectivist approach to teaching with technology in the field of adult education?

The answer lies in a different epistemology, that is, constructivism in adult education. Constructivists believe that knowledge is essentially subjective in nature, constructed from our perceptions and mutually agreed upon conventions. Bates and Poole (2003) explain this epistemology as follows:

> *We construct new knowledge rather than simply acquire it via memorization or through transmission from those who know to those who did not know. We construct meaning by assimilating information, relating it to our existing knowledge, and cognitively processing it (that is, thinking about it). Social constructivists believe that this process works best through discussion and social interaction, allowing us to test and challenge our own understanding with those of others. For a constructivist, even physical laws exist because they have been constructed by people from evidence, observation, and deductive or intuitive thinking and, most important, because certain communities of people (in our example, scientists) have mutually agreed what constitutes valid knowledge.* (p. 28)

Constructivism falls squarely in line with one of the principles of adult learning, namely, adult learners' rich reservoir of experience. Knowles (1990, p. 45) stated, "as adults mature, they accumulate an increasing reservoir of experience that becomes an increasingly rich resource for learning." Without prior experience, adult learners can not construct meaning by assimilating information, relating it to their existing knowledge, and cognitively processing it. Mott (2008) takes prior experience a step further by linking it to instruction. She indicates that our experience is important not only as a basis for greater and more meaningful learning, but also because such experience provides links and connections that teachers can use in instruction. When using technology to teach adult learners, definitely instructors can create an online discussion forum where adult learners' rich experience is included. Discussion topics can revolve around adult learners' prior experience. By discussing learners' prior experience, new knowledge can be generated regarding a certain subject in adult education. For example, for a course titled *Curriculum Development for Auto Mechanics*, instructors can arrange for students (auto mechanics) to discuss their prior experience and make a summary of their prior experience. This rich reservoir of experience can be translated into task analysis which may serve as an important part of curriculum development for auto mechanics. And video clips showing how these auto mechanics repair vehicles on a day to day basis will help students learn via learning with technology. Video clips on CD-ROMs and DVDs will also help students learn according to their individualized learning pace. Constructivism also works with Mezirow's (1985, 1990, 1991, 2000) theory or transformative learning as discussed in our previous articles. The central theme of transformative learning theory is change of adult learners' perspectives by giving meaning to their prior experience. In other words, adult learners need to make sense of their own prior experience. Again, we can give meaning to our experience by assimilating information, relating it to our existing knowledge, and cognitively processing it (i.e., thinking about it).

Translated into instructional approaches, constructivism requires instructors to ask their students to read about the experience of other people in the field and relate these experiences to their own. Students are asked to work in small groups to identify common themes, and important differences, within the experiences of both the subjects of their required readings and those studying in each group. Students then report back to the whole group, which provides feedback and discussion on each individual group's report. Later, students are asked to summarize their own feelings and opinions on what they have read and discussed. Then, instructors may check whether this learning experience can lead to change in their perspectives. Such is the constructivist approach to teaching if instructors have adopted a constructivist view on epistemology.

Another important principle of adult learning is self-directedness. Knowles (1990, p. 45) posits that adults approach their learning in a more independent and self-directed manner as opposed to being dependent on a teacher for one's learning, resources, strategies, and evaluation of outcomes. Knowles went on to explain that self-directedness is always present on a continuum—that all learners, children and adults alike, are more or less self-directed depending on maturity, preexisting knowledge, motivation, and risk involved in the learning experience. If we take into consideration this prominent adult learning principle, we must admit that students can automatically construct knowledge through argument and discussion with their peers and through self-directed study (Laurillard, 1993; Tough, 1967, 1971). Then the role of the teacher is to help students understand not just the facts or concepts of a subject discipline, but also the rules and conventions for acquiring and validating knowledge within that subject discipline. According to Bates and Poole (2003), the notion of academic knowledge requiring mediation has major significance for the use of technology. They further argue that language (i.e., reading and speaking) is only one channel for mediating knowledge. Media such as video, audio, and computing can provide teachers with alternative channels of mediation.

In summary, one's epistemological positions predetermine one's teaching approaches, especially one's use of technology. As an objectivist approach works with adult learners in the field based on different factors, constructivist approaches enhanced by adult learning principles and Mezirow's theory of transformative learning work even better with adult learners when it comes to teaching with technology. In the final analysis, Bates and Poole (2003) remind us that technology can accommodate a wide variety of epistemological positions. Because a teacher's preferred epistemology has such an influence on the design not just of technology-based teaching but all forms of teaching, we need to illustrate how technology design can accommodate different epistemological positions.

THE NATURE OF LEARNING

There has been a great deal of research into how adults learn in the field of adult education. One of the principles of adult learning is internal motivation as popularized by Knowles in the 1970s. According to Knowles (1990), adults are more often internally or intrinsically motivated to learn. Even though virtually all of formal education includes some external motivation in the form of grades, better jobs, or higher salaries, adults are more likely to focus on the knowledge gained, the experience itself, rather than any extrinsic reward that accrues. That is, even when learning is problem-focused or performance-centered, adults understand that learning is valuable and often its own reward, that the learning will add value to their lives, and that it will improve their tomorrows. Because of this well reasoned principle stated by Knowles, does this mean that behaviorism has nothing to do with adult learners? If you read further books by Knowles and his associates, you will find out that he and his associates indicated it was okay to switch from an andragogical model of teaching to the pedagogical model of teaching (embraced by behaviorism) if your students are inexperienced with a subject matter and would like to depend on their instructors for a course content because of speed and convenience or learning styles. The reason I raised this issue of behaviorism here is that programmed instruction became such a norm as early as the 1960s in North America. Whenever talking about teaching technology, both scholars and practitioners will address programmed instruction. In fact, behaviorism has led to the creation of programmed instruction in teaching and learning in any academic field. As we know, behaviorist psychology arose in the 1920s and 1930s from an attempt to model the study of human behavior on the methods of the physical sciences. At the heart of behaviorism is the idea that certain behavioral responses become associated in mechanistic and invariant way with specific stimuli. It is obvious that a certain stimulus will evoke a particular response. According to behaviorists (Skinner, 1968; Watson, 1960-1961, 1967), it is possible to reinforce through reward or punishment the association between any particular stimulus or event and a particular event. Bates and Poole (2003) explains that:

The bond formed between a stimulus and response will depend on the existence of an appropriate means of reinforcement at the time of association between stimulus and response. Behavior therefore can be modified or controlled by appropriately reinforcing random behavior (trial and error) as it occurs. (p. 31)

Underlying behaviorism is the belief that human behavior is predicable and controllable. Behaviorism stems from a strongly objectivist epistemological position as discussed earlier in this article. Clearly, behaviorism has led to programmed instruction, such as observable and measurable learning objectives, and computer-assisted instruction. Although there has been a strong movement away from behaviorist approaches to teaching in adult education, the reality is a large number of adult educators still use behaviorist approaches in teaching. Influenced by behaviorism, Tyler (1950) developed a definitive model of teaching which has been adopted by adult educators in the field of adult education. It must be pointed out that Tyler's model is still in print even to this day. Based on Tyler's model, teaching and evaluation revolve around four basic issues: identifying objectives, selecting the means for attaining those objectives, organizing those means, and evaluating the outcomes. Specifically, Tyler advocated that:

In the syllabus, the question that must be answered is "What educational purposes should the school seek to attain?" these educational objectives can first be identified by examining three sources: studies of the learners themselves, studies of contemporary life outside of school, and suggestions from subject specialists.

The second question is "How can learning experiences be selected that are likely to be useful in attaining these experiences?" Here he argued for several general principles that should guide teachers in selecting objectives.

The third question is, "How can learning experiences be organized for effective instruction?" In making determinations about the organization of experiences, teachers should consider three criteria: continuity, sequence, and integration.

The final question is, "How can the effectiveness of learning experiences be evaluated?" Valid and reliable tests should be developed and the results used to improve the teaching (Glatthorn, Boschee, & Whitehead, 2006, p. 43)

Although there has been a movement away from behaviorism in adult education, there is no way adult learners can say goodbye to this approach to teaching permanently. It is so common sense that adult learners do respond to external stimuli such as economic crisis, family crises, downsizing at work and critical incidents in life (Brookfield, 2005). When these situations occur, adult learners turn to learning. As I write this article, I can tell for sure that every time we have an economic recession, we have more adult learners seeking teaching credentials to teach their occupations to others as some of them are laid off from their employment in both public and private industries. When our economy recovers, we will have less adult learners seeking state certification.

On the contrary, cognitivists believe otherwise. They insist that there are mental processes—internal and conscious representations of the world—that are essential for human learning. To behaviorists, learning is determined by external environmental structures that lead to reinforcement of behavior. Fontana (1981, p. 148) explains cognitive approach as follows:

The cognitive approach... holds that if we are to understand learning, we cannot confine ourselves to observable behavior, but must also concern ourselves with the learner's ability mentally to reorganize his psychological field (i.e., his inner world of concepts, memories, etc.) in response to experience. This latter approach therefore lays stress not only on the environment, but upon the way in which the individual interprets and tries to make sense of the environment. It sees the individual not as the somewhat mechanical product of his environment, but as an active agent in the learning process, deliberately trying to process and categorize the stream of information fed into him by the external world.

Clearly, instructors who place emphasis on learners' developing personal meaning through reflection, analysis, and construction of knowledge through conscience mental processing rely on the constructivist epistemological position. On the other hand, instructors who place emphasis on artificial intelligence to provide mechanical, electronic, and physical representations of mental process via the use of computer technology would depend on an objectivist or behaviorist epistemological position. I would suggest for effective adult education to occur, use a combination of a behaviorist and constructivist approaches. Although adults are basically internally motivated to learn, they are also externally motivated to learn. There is no denying that external structures such as economic crises, critical incidents trigger new learning of any kind.

RELATIONSHIP BETWEEN ONE'S PHILOSOPHIES AND THE USE OF TECHNOLOGY

To teach effectively with technology requires teachers to adopt the right teaching philosophies. The aim of philosophy is, after all, to explain, to make sense of the world (Merriam & Brockett, 2007, p. 28). Above all, teaching philosophies teachers adopt and adapt influence their decisions regarding the use of technology to facilitate adult learning. Based on Elias and Merriam's original framework (1995, 2005), it consists of six orientations of liberal education, progressivism, humanism, behaviorism, radicalism, and philosophical analysis. Later, they added another philosophical orientation, which is post modern philosophy. While liberal adult education values the acquisition of knowledge, the development of a rational perspective, and the ability to analyze critically, the progressive adult education places more value in knowledge derived from observation and experience than from tradition and authority. When it comes to teaching with technology, we can conclude that liberal adult educators involve heavy use of lectures via online teaching. Instructors may arrange more audio clips, text-based lectures, and assigned readings. On the other hand, progressive instructors may arrange online discussion forums where participants can discuss their prior experience or other people's experience related to their subject under study.

As discussed earlier in this article, behaviorists believe that human actions are the result of prior conditioning and the way in which a person's external environment is arranged. To humanistic adult educators, their focus is on developing the potential of the learner. Further, their education is learner-centered and the role of the instructors is that of a learning facilitator. No need to repeat here that behaviorist will arrange artificial intelligence for their teaching with technology. Humanistic adult educators would serve as facilitators, linking their students to learning resources. They don't believe in being treated by their students as authority figures. Students are considered by humanistic adult educators as capable of teaching themselves given their rich reservoir of prior experience and internal motivation. Independent study via CD-ROMs and DVDs is not a bad idea for humanistic adult educators. Asynchronous teaching is another channel humanistic adult educators can use to post pertinent information for adult learners so that students may access it anywhere, any time.

To Freire (1970), the role of adult education is, through dialogue with learners, to facilitate acquisition of critical consciousness. Once learners become conscience of the forces that control their lives, they become empowered, and empowerment leads to action (p. 47). As Newman (2006) explains this philosophy, he advocates that we should teach defiance. As to analytic philosophy, Elias and Merriam (1995, 2005) posit that analytic teachers seek to clarify concepts, arguments, and policy statements used in adult education. Finally, they explain post modern philosophy as questioning such fundamental concepts as truth, theory, reality, knowledge and power.

The fundamental question that needs to be asked is "What is the relationship between one's philosophies and the use of technology?" As discussed in this section, teachers' philosophical positions determine their teaching approaches and the use of technology.

FUTURE TRENDS

Although adult education has tended to distance itself from K-12 and higher education (Merriam & Brockett, 2007), it has pioneered the use of technology to deliver instructional programs to students. From the University of Phoenix to all other traditional universities and colleges in North America, they all have used technology to teach even their traditional age students. Brilliant or outstanding teaching is in your face-to-face context, faculty is required to do more with less. It is not a matter of whether faculty like teaching with technology. Teaching in the new century has become a matter of whether faculty is able to teach effectively with technology. Teaching requires many things on the part of the faculty. Mastery of the subject matter, skill, hard work and practice are just not enough. Effective technology-based teaching is particularly demanding as more and more adult learners juggle between school and employment.

WebCT and Blackboard will continue to dominate the educational settings as these two learning resource management systems allow for the loading and storing of content in the form of text, graphics, or multimedia objects, the design of asynchronous discussion forms, online testing and the use of some course management tools (Bates & Poole, 2003). As soon as Elluminate. Com launched its service to provide synchronous interaction between faculty and students in 2007, many universities purchased an unlimited license.

Regarding the Internet, it will continue to spread at a rapid rate around the world. Wideband access has already replaced narrow-band access. As universities and colleges in developed countries are teaching more than one third of all their courses with technology, this trend will sooner or later spread to developing countries that are still undecided as to whether they would deliver instructional programs via technology. Once they overcome their prejudice against technology, they will start to deliver teaching via technology by leaps and bounds as their student population is formidable. I agree with Bates and Poole on their insights regarding whether technology can change face-to-face formats or vice versa. Their argument has been technology does not really transform the traditional formats of face-to-face teaching. Rather, face-to-face formats transfer very easily to technology. In addition, they projected that as a result of technology, we may see a shift in the future to more project work and problem-based learning, the creation by students of multimedia projects and assignments, and more student choice in learning and curriculum. Indeed, innovative teachers will discover new ways or formats that will exploit the potential of technology.

In adult education, faculty is concerned with whether there is enough technology available to support their methods of teaching because methods of teaching ultimately affect student learning outcomes. The answer is there is more than enough technology to support any methods of teaching in the field. Adult learning principles and methods are not just something only adult educational professionals know and practice. Instructional designers, librarians, university administrators and even software engineers are familiar with these principles and methods. Design teams are aware of academic goals for a university that will enhance the following:

- Learner-centered teaching
- Problem-based learning
- Collaborative learning
- Use of departmental research in undergraduate teaching
- Teaching linked to the community
- Lifelong learning
- Use of information technology in teaching (Bates & Poole, 2003, p. 271)

If we take a closer look at these academic goals, we know that they are derived from adult learning principles and methods. The next question can be: will technology refine the principles of adult learning, that is, andragogical assumptions about adult learners? As adult learning professional apply andragogical assumptions in practice, they may find that technology when used carefully and thoughtfully by university and college teachers can not only facilitate the development of academic rigor, rational thinking, and evidence-based research, but can also help learners apply their learning to real-world contexts, understand more deeply and more quickly complex ideas, and construct new personal meanings (Bates & Poole, 2003, p. 274). This may mean that principles of adult learning cannot become more powerful without the proper use of technology. As we talk about self-directed learning in adult education, technology can provide this mode of learning by providing self-controlled activities. Future research may answer the question of what asynchronous learning can be considered as self-controlled activities. As lifelong learners, part time students enjoy access and flexibility that technology can provide; traditional age students will find it more beneficial to learn with technology in the future.

CONCLUSION

I have made an attempt to illustrate that technology cannot replace face-to-face teaching. Rather, it does drive change. When used carefully and thoughtfully, technology will increase not only access and flexibility, but also facilitate and make the learning process more efficient and more effective. The reason is simple: technology can provide more opportunities for practice and access to a wider range of materials. I still remember how I learned to drive a manual vehicle in Kansas when I attended a university there in the late 1990s as a graduate student. I was also teaching the Chinese language to American students as a visiting scholar at a Foreign Language Department. Two students offered me verbal instructions and helped me practice driving on a university parking lot. After two hours of practice, I still failed to learn to drive a manual vehicle. Then one student took me to a computer game in a local mall. He told me the importance of practicing to drive with computer games in order to get the right feel. I did what I was told and the next day, I did learn how to drive a manual vehicle. Also technology enables teachers to offer alternative approaches to learning that suit the needs of different kinds of learners. When we talk about linking students to learning resources because of an adult learning principle, technology is the one that can offer access to resources that would not otherwise be available in a traditional classroom. To access an online library from an online class, this is just a mouse click away. Technology will save your money and trips to a physical university library. Indeed, technology can add value to the process of teaching and learning by creating richer or more authentic learning environments (Bates & Poole, 2003). When we think of benefits and disadvantages of teaching with technology, benefits will definitely outweigh disadvantages. Bates and Poole made a summary of the benefits that technology can bring to both faculty and students:

Technology provides teachers and students with opportunities to organize their teaching and learning in radically different ways. Neither teachers nor students have to be (always) present in the classroom. They can be freed from the requirement to be at a specific place at a specific time in order to teach or study. Technology allows for access to materials that would otherwise not be available in a classroom, and allows teachers and students to structure learning materials in a variety of ways. Technology enables various preferences for learning to be more easily accommodated, and makes it easier for part-time or working students to access learning. In particular, technology provides lifelong learners with a flexible and convenient way to continue to study and learn throughout their lives (p. 269-270)

This article has also demonstrated that deciding to use educational technologies can be challenging. Effective teaching with technology in adult education is even more challenging. Effective teaching with technology requires faculty to adopt and adapt not only their epistemological positions, but also their teaching philosophies. These factors and others such as nature of learning may predetermine one's instructional approaches, especially approaches to using technology. Although an objectivist (behaviorist) epistemological position works well with artificial intelligence, a combination of this approach with a constructivist approach may further facilitate learning on the part of students. After all, technology may enhance one dimension of learning, effective learning occurs when faculty are innovative with instructional approaches.

REFERENCES

Bash, L. (2003). *Adult learners in the academy.* Bolton, MA: Anker Publishing.

Bates, A. W., & Poole, G. (2003). *Effective teaching with technology in higher education: Foundations for success.* San Francisco: Jossey-Bass.

Brookfield, S. D. (2006). *The skillful teacher: On techniques, trust, and responsiveness in the classroom* (2nd ed.). San Francisco: Jossey-Bass.

Burge, E. J. (2000). Editor's notes. In E. J. Burge (Ed.), *The strategic use of learning technologies: New directions for adult continuing education, no. 88* (pp. 1-5). San Francisco: Jossey-Bass.

Conrad, R. M., & Donaldson, J. A. (2004). *Engaging the online learner: Activities and resources for creative instruction.* San Francisco: Jossey-Bass.

Cranton, P. (1994). *Understanding and promoting transformative learning.* San Francisco: Jossey-Bass.

Elias, J. L., & Merriam, S. B. (1995). *Philosophical foundations of adult education.* Malabar, FL: Krieger Publishing Company.

Elias, J. L., & Merriam, S. B. (2005). *Philosophical foundations of adult education* (3rd ed.). Malabar, FL: Krieger Publishing Company.

Fontana, D. (1981). *Psychology for teachers.* London: Macmillan/British Psychological Society.

Freire, P. (1970). *Pedagogy of the oppressed.* New York: Seabury Press.

Glatthorn, A. A., Boschee, F., & Whitehead, B. M. (2006). *Curriculum leadership: Development and implementation.* Thousand Oaks, CA: SAGE Publications.

Hofer, B., & Pintrich, P. (1997). The development of epistemological theories: Beliefs about knowledge and knowing and their relation to learning. *Review of Educational Research, 67*(1), 88–140.

King, K. P. (2005). *Bringing transformative learning to life.* Malabar, FL: Krieger Publishing Company.

Knowles, M. S. (1975). *Self-directed learning: A guide for learners and teachers.* New York: Association Press.

Knowles, M. S. (1990). *The modern practice of adult education: From pedagogy to andragogy.* New York: Cambridge.

Knowles, M. S., Holton, E., & Swanson, A. (2005). *The adult learner* (6th ed.). Boston: Elsevier Butterworth Heinemann.

Laurillard, D. (1993). *Rethinking university teaching: A framework for the effective use of educational technology.* London: Routledge.

Merriam, S. B., & Brockett, R. G. (2007). *The profession and practice of adult education: An introduction.* San Francisco: Jossey-Bass.

Mezirow, J. (1985). A critical theory of self-directed learning. In S. Brookfield (Ed.), *Self-directed learning: From theory to practice: New directions for continuing education, no. 25.* San Francisco: Jossey-Bass.

Mezirow, J. (1990). *Fostering critical reflection in adulthood: A guide to transformative and emancipatory learning.* San Francisco: Jossey-Bass.

Mezirow, J. (1991). *Transformative dimensions of adult learning.* San Francisco: Jossey-Bass.

Mezirow, J. (Ed.). (2000). *Learning as transformation: Critical perspectives on a theory in progress.* San Francisco: Jossey-Bass.

Mott, V. W. (2008). Learner-derived curriculum development. In V. C. X. Wang (Ed.), *Curriculum development for adult learners in the global community volume I: Strategic approaches* (pp. 58-78). Malabar, FL: Krieger Publishing Company.

Newman, M. (2006). *Teaching defiance*. San Francisco: Jossey-Bass.

Olgren, C. H. (2000). Learning strategies for learning technologies. In E. J. Burge (Ed.), *The strategic use of learning technologies: New directions for adult continuing education, no. 88* (pp. 7-16). San Francisco: Jossey-Bass.

Palloff, R. M., & Pratt, K. (1999). *Building learning communities in cyberspace*. San Francisco: Jossey-Bass.

Palloff, R. M., & Pratt, K. (2003). *The virtual student: A profile and guide to working with online learners*. San Francisco: Jossey-Bass.

Piskurich, G. M. (Ed.). (2003). *Preparing learners for e-learning*. San Francisco: Jossey-Bass.

Skinner, B. F. (1968). *The technology of teaching*. New York: Appleton-Century-Crofts.

Tough, A. (1967). *Learning without a teacher. Educational research series, no. 3*. Toronto, Ontario, Canada: Ontario Institute for Studies in Education.

Tough, A. (1971). *The adult's learning project*. Toronto, Ontario, Canada: Ontario Institute for Studies in Education.

Tyler, R. W. (1950). *Basic principles of curriculum and instruction*. Chicago: University of Chicago Press.

Wang, V. C. X. (2007). Chinese knowledge transmitters or western learning facilitators adult teaching methods compared. In K. P. King & V. C. X. Wang (Eds.), *Comparative adult education around the globe* (pp. 113-1370). Hangzhou, China: Zhejiang University Press.

Wang, V. C. X. (2007-2008). Chinese knowledge transmitters or western learning facilitators adult teaching methods compared. *Perspectives: The New York Journal of Adult Learning, 6*(2), 15–40.

Wang, V. C. X. (2008). *Facilitating adult learning: A comprehensive guide for successful instruction*. Boston: Pearson Education.

Wang, V. C. X., & King, K. P. (2006). Understanding Mezirow's theory of reflectivity from Confucian perspectives: A model and perspective. *Radical Pedagogy, 8*(1), 1–17.

Wang, V. C. X., & King, K. P. (2007). Confucius and Mezirow—understanding Mezirow's theory of reflectivity from Confucian perspectives: A model and perspective. In K. P. King & V. C. X. Wang (Eds.), *Comparative adult education around the globe* (pp. 253-275). Hangzhou, China: Zhejiang University Press.

Watson, G. (1960-1961). What do we know about learning? *Teachers College Record*, 253–257.

Watson, G. (Ed.). (1967). *Concepts for social change*. Washington, DC: National Training Laboratories Institute for Applied Behavioral Science, NEA.

This work was previously published in the International Journal of Web-Based Learning and Teaching Technologies, Vol. 4, Issue 4, edited by E. M. W. Ng, N. Karacapilidis, and M. S. Raisinghani, pp. 17-31, copyright 2009 by IGI Publishing (an imprint of IGI Global).

Chapter 4
From Pedagogy to Andragogy: Transitioning Teaching and Learning in the Information Technology Classroom

Steven. W. Schmidt
East Carolina University, USA

Jeremy Dickerson
East Carolina University, USA

Eric Kisling
East Carolina University, USA

ABSTRACT

It is generally accepted that there are differences in the way children and adults learn. Pedagogical philosophies and practices about classroom instruction, activities, and the roles of both the educator and learner are typically associated with primary and secondary education. The concept of andragogy, however, deals with the art and science of the adult learner. The andragogical classroom looks quite different than the pedagogical, and features more student-centered instruction, self-directed learning, and emphasis on the needs of the individual learner. Many adult learners are familiar with the pedagogical approaches used in primary and secondary education. Those learners may find principles of pedagogy employed in higher education as well, which may not be effective. Is a pedagogical approach appropriate in higher education? What role does content play in pedagogical versus andragogical decisions? Most importantly, what approach results in student learning? Using the information technology classroom as an example, pedagogical and andragogical approaches to instruction are compared, and strategies for transitioning from pedagogical to andragogical approaches are illustrated. An empirical research study on preferred ways of learning is also included in this chapter. While the examples discussed in this chapter relate to the information technology classroom, the material presented is applicable in a variety of learning situations.

DOI: 10.4018/978-1-61520-694-0.ch004

INTRODUCTION

"How does one learn?" This is a question around which books and articles are written, theories are developed, research studies are conducted, discussions and debates are held, and courses at colleges and universities are facilitated. Especially for those in the education field, this question has been pondered for years, and as of right now, there have been no definite, fool-proof conclusions made. While we may not know exactly how people learned, we do know that learning depends on a variety of factors, including the age and experience of the learner. We also know that because of factors like age and experience, adults learn differently than children. These differences are represented in the concepts of pedagogy and andragogy, which are, respectively, theories about how children learn and about how adults learn.

This chapter will begin with a discussion of pedagogy and andragogy. Each will be introduced, and comparisons will be made. An empirical study on teaching methods will be presented in this chapter as well. This study brings the voice of the learner into the discussion of pedagogy versus andragogy. Conclusions regarding both pedagogical and andragogical approaches in the teaching of adult learners follows that study. To set the stage for this discussion, background information on important variables that form the foundations of the chapter follow.

There are several variables that must be explained in order to more clearly frame both the study presented in this chapter, and the chapter conclusions. Because the type of course to be examined is the post-secondary information technology (IT) classroom, a description of IT education (ITE) is presented. The mission and goals of primary/secondary and post-secondary education are compared and contrasted, as are differences in child and adult learners. Characteristics of the pedagogical and andragogical ITE classrooms are also presented.

It is easy to make claims about the merits of andragogy versus pedagogy in a chapter such as this one without firm evidence of the benefits of doing so. This chapter is different in that it contains an actual empirical research study on student opinions regarding the teaching of IT courses. Students were asked for their opinions about aspects of pedagogy and andragogy, along with their preferred methods for learning IT-related topics. The study will be described in this chapter, and findings will be discussed. As the title of this chapter suggests, a great deal of research suggests that transitioning from pedagogy to andragogy is appropriate in the teaching of adults. Based on this research and on the results of the empirical study described in this chapter, recommendations will be made and examples of ways to make the transformation from pedagogy to andragogy will be presented.

BACKGROUND

A History of Pedagogy

The concept of pedagogy has evolved over time. Over a century ago, Compayre and Payne (1885) define pedagogy as "the art or practice of education" (p. vii). Pedagogy, they believed, was associated with "the doctrines and the methods of educators" (p. xi) and included "the premeditated action which the will of one man exercises over other men in order to instruct them or train them" (p. xi). As evidenced in this quote, a characteristic of pedagogy is the idea that the teacher instructs or transmits information to the learner, who absorbs or learns it. From the start, pedagogy was teacher-directed learning, and that concept hasn't changed. Characteristics of pedagogy today include the idea that the instructor is in charge, and is responsible for all aspects of the teaching process, including needs assessment, planning, goal-setting, teaching, and evaluation (Robinson, 1995).

When the concept was conceived, pedagogy was associated with the teaching of students of all ages. That philosophy remained in place for quite some time, as pedagogical approaches were used in the teaching of children, and adults. Around the turn of the century, education became a field of study onto itself, and institutes of higher education became involved in the training of educators. Departments and schools of pedagogy began appearing in colleges and universities in the mid-1890's (Lagemann, 2002). However, even the earliest proponents of pedagogy realized that there were differences in child learners and adult learners. In Compayre and Payne's *The History of Pedagogy*, published in 1885, the authors note that in addition to "proper education", which "is given in schools and which proceeds from the direct action of teachers" (p. ix), there are other forces in place that shape one's learning. "Upon that delicate and variable composition known as the human soul, how many forces which we do not suspect have left their imprint! (p. ix). In addition to formal educational experiences, they believed learning was shaped by "innumerable agents, besides personal effort and what is produced by the original energy of the individual" (p. ix). In other words, even early researchers on pedagogy noted the importance of factors we know today as individual experience and informal learning in the development of the individual as that individual grows and progresses through adulthood.

Fast forward more than a century and today pedagogical approaches are still used in education; most often associated with the teaching of children. Factors identified many years ago as important in the learning process, such as the role of an adult's experience and the process of informal learning, have become more prominently recognized as influencers of adult learning. These factors, among others, have become tenants of andragogy; a term coined to denote the teaching of adult learners.

The Introduction of Andragogy

In the late 1960's, and based on European concepts of adult learning, Malcolm Knowles proposed the concept of andragogy, or "the art and science of helping adults learn" (Merriam, Caffarella & Baumgartner, 2007, p. 84). Key in the concept of andragogy are several assumptions about adult learners. Adult learners, Knowles posited, are self-directed. They collect experiences throughout their lives which they bring to each new learning situation. They are ready to learn when they perceive a need to learn, and are more problem-centered than subject-centered in their learning. Knowles also believed that adult learners are internally rather than externally motivated to learn, and that they need to understand why they need to learn something (Merriam, et. al., 2007). As opposed to the pedagogical approach, which is instructor-directed and formal in climate, andragogical approaches center on the learner and that learner's needs. Because those needs may be different for each learner in a classroom, the andragogical approach is flexible enough to allow for those different needs to be met, while still staying within a general framework of course topic.

Pedagogy and Andragogy in the Classroom

As noted above, the concepts of pedagogy and andragogy are fairly different in their focus and scope. How does this translate to the classroom? An examination of the pedagogical classroom compared to the andragogical classroom highlights the differences one might find in each.

The pedagogical classroom is defined by its focus on teacher-directed learning, as the teacher is the authority figure in the classroom. In the pedagogical classroom, the teacher presents information in a formal manner and the students take in that information. Lectures, presentations, and demonstrations conducted by the instructor, and designed to transmit information to the student, are characteristic of this approach. Assigned readings are also common. The instructor determines all aspects of course structure, including diagnosis of needs, setting of goals, and the design of lesson plans. Units or lessons are structured sequentially, and order is maintained. In the end, evaluation of what has been learned is also conducted by the instructor, and is based on goals set by that instructor (Robinson, 1995).

The andragogical classroom features a much different approach. In this type of classroom, the focus is on the learner, and all activities are designed to center around the needs of the learner. The classroom atmosphere is informal, collaborative and supportive, and the instructor and the learner work together to determine that learner's needs. Based on those needs, the instructor and learner again collaborate on the setting of goals and the designing of methodologies to attain those goals. Activities consist of learning projects, inquiry projects, independent study, and experimental techniques. Unlike the pedagogical classroom, there are no set steps to follow to get to the formal "end" of the lesson. Content is sequenced based on the needs and readiness of the learner. Learning activities could take the learner anywhere, and it is the job of the instructor to support and guide the learner as they work through the learning process. Evaluation may be conducted by the teacher and the learner, but much of the evaluation is self-assessment on the part of the learner (Robinson, 1995).

In reviewing the characteristics of the andragogical and pedagogical classrooms, you probably saw some characteristics of each with which you were familiar. Now consider how you were taught in different educational settings. It is likely that the pedagogical approach most closely relates to how you were taught in primary and secondary education. Perhaps you were taught as an adult using a more andragogical approach, although it is likely that you have encountered characteristics of the pedagogical approach in adult learning situations as well. This comparison may have resulted in even more questions about andragogy versus pedagogy. In order to examine these types of issues most effectively, it is best to look at them in the context of an actual educational setting. In this chapter, we will look pedagogy versus andragogy in post-secondary information technology education.

Information Technology Education

Information technology (IT) education can be defined as an academic discipline that "focuses on meeting the needs of users in an organizational and societal context through the selection, creation, application, integration, and administration of computer technologies" (Reichgelt, Lunt, Ashford, Phelps, Slazinski & Willis, 2004, p. 21). In short, students in IT courses learn about the use of computer systems, programs, and applications. The Society for Information Technology Education (SITE) has compiled a list of skills and capabilities for IT graduates. They include the use and application of current technological concepts and practices in computer programming, networking, hardware, databases, web technologies, and in human/computer interaction. They also address the analysis of IT-based needs, the identification of effective solutions, the development and implementation of project plans, and the ongoing integration of IT in organizations (Reichgelt, et. al., 2004).

Educational Mission and Goals

In order to examine the appropriateness of andragogy and pedagogy in the teaching of IT skills to adult learners, it is beneficial to look at the differences between primary/secondary and post-secondary information technology education. Major differences include educational mission and goals, as well as differences in students and classroom structure. These differences will be examined in this section using aspects of andragogy and pedagogy discussed in the introduction.

Differences in the missions and goals of secondary versus post-secondary education can call for the use of different approaches in the teaching at those two different levels. Broad goals of secondary education are often related to proficiency in a subject matter judged against some type of standard. The development of proficiency in subjects such as English, reading or math is an important life skill that allows the learner to continue to learn throughout his or her life. Other goals include the development of the learner's personality, talents and abilities, the development of respect others, and the preparation of the student for life (Cohen, 2006). In the IT classroom, these missions and goals may translate to the basic understanding of the capabilities of various programs and systems. It may also include proficiency in basic features of computer applications. Exposure to a variety of programs is also important, as are basic skills, such as keyboarding, that will serve the learner in multiple ways.

Goals for adult learners can change over time, and are most often related to situations the adult encounters. As stated in the tenants of andragogy, adults are typically motivated to learn when they encounter a new situation or problem or when they are making long-term plan for their futures. Learning is specifically related to goals, and in that, the adult learner is motivated to succeed. With regard to subject matter, courses can be more focused and more specific, but goals are typically broader. This allows for the learner to clearly understand course content (in order to make sure the correct course is chosen), while determine his or her own specific goals based on that content.

The Level of the Learner

Differences in the mission and goals of secondary and post-secondary education are directly related to the age, maturity level, and needs of the student. There are several differences between secondary students and adult learners that should be examined when comparing approaches to teaching and learning. As learners mature, they shift from "the here and now orientation of a child to the future orientation" (Bee & Bjorkland, 2004, p. 34). Reasons for a more teacher-centered or pedagogical approach are related to the development level and motivation of the secondary students themselves. Secondary students may be allowed limited choices in the classroom, "only when those choices are perceived as equal or structured in such a way that the child's choice is guided by interest and not by an intent to minimize effort, protect feelings of self-worth, or avoid failure" (Ames, 1992, p. 266). Without some type of structure, students of this age may produce meaningless work, and without some assistance in the selection and planning of learning strategies, the learning process may be hindered rather than enhanced (Ames, 1992).

Adults, on the other hand, approach learning situations differently. They have specific reasons for participation which may be short or long-term in nature. They have goals to attain and problems to solve and want to learn in order to attain their goals or solve their problems. Their identities as adults are more clearly developed, and unlike secondary students, their participation in educational activities is voluntary rather than mandatory. An andragogical approach allows for the student to tailor their learning to meet their own needs. Choices and options are important in the learning process, and the instructor acts more like a guide; helping the learner to work through the problem to be solved or issue to be addressed. Learning situations must be flexible, as sometimes learners find themselves taking paths they never expected. Adult learners would first choose the IT course that best meets their needs. They would probably arrive at the course with some type of agenda, and with goals to accomplish. They might have done some preliminary self-directed learning on the subject in order to be better prepared in class. They would also have predetermined benchmarks for success, or at least some idea of how they might evaluate their own success in the course. Throughout this process, they would see the instructor as a guide who would provide them with feedback, offer advice and assistance when needed, and overall, help them to reach their goals.

The Pedagogical and Andragogical IT Classroom

Differences in pedagogy versus andragogy are also evident in examining the classroom structure. Classroom structure can be defined to include materials, assignments, and evaluation. In the traditional secondary-school classroom, a pedagogical approach is taken with regard to these structural elements. The teacher sets goals for the student, develops materials and assignments that are designed to help the student learn the content and meet the predetermined goals. Assignments for all students are the same, and success is determined by whether or not the students can follow the directions and arrive at the instructor's desired conclusion. In IT training, this may mean using a computer application to create a spreadsheet or flowchart.

An andragogical approach to assignments may also involve a computer application and the creation of documents like spreadsheets or flowcharts. However, guidelines for the assignment would be broad enough for learners to choose from several options. The assignment itself may not be presented as simply "Create a spreadsheet using XYZ computer program". Rather, assignments may be worded as such: "Develop a solution for the management of 1000 pieces of data, and use an appropriate computer program to show the solution you've developed". The learner may further modify the assignment based on his or her own needs and interests.

Summary

In order to effectively examine the concepts of andragogy and pedagogy in ITE, it is important to frame that discussion with information on ITE, goals of primary and secondary education versus adult education; differences in adult and child learners, and examples of andragogical and pedagogical approaches to education in general, and in the ITE classroom. Based on the terms and definitions covered in this introduction, what type of approach do you think would work best in the IT classroom? To some of you, it might seem natural that an andragogical approach would be used in the teaching of adult learners. Others might think a pedagogical approach would be best – perhaps based on the content rather than the learner. Considering how a course is taught leads to a myriad of questions in decisions regarding the use of pedagogy or andragogy. When is it appropriate to take a more andragogical approach to teaching? What role does content play in decisions about approach? Does the age and maturity level of the students matter? Are there situations in which an andragogical approach is not effective in the teaching of adults, and a pedagogical approach, or some combination of both approaches, is more appropriate? In cases in which the instructor is the expert, is a more teacher-centered approach is called for? One might make that argument in the teaching of IT courses. Adult learners typically take IT courses to learn how to use computer systems and software. They are very familiar with receiving instruction in pedagogical style, most likely having experienced this approach through their primary and secondary educations. Furthermore, instructors are typically experts on the software they teach. This seems to indicate that a pedagogical approach is called for. But is that the case, and is it the best way for adult learners to learn? This chapter will continue by examining learner preferences regarding the use of both pedagogical and andragogical approaches in the teaching of IT courses. It will examine how students actually learn in the IT classroom as a reason behind the shift from pedagogy to andragogy in the effective teaching of these courses to adult learners.

ISSUES, CONTROVERSIES, PROBLEMS

As noted above, taking a pedagogical approach in the IT classroom is very different than taking an andragogical approach. There are many questions that result when a move of this nature is to be considered. Think about the courses you have taken in the area of computer technology. Were those courses taught using a pedagogical or andragogical approach? Most often, IT courses for children and adults are taught the same way; featuring a pedagogical approach. Is that approach taken because it is the most effective way for learners to learn the subject? Or is it more based on tradition, and "that's the way we've always done it"? It may be because some IT instructors are not familiar with the tenants of andragogy. Perhaps those teachers were taught using a pedagogical approach, so they teach as they were taught.

Understanding how students attempt to learn in the post-secondary information technology classroom is critical to planning effective teaching methods for learning to occur. Students in the post-secondary classroom come from very diverse backgrounds and enter the classroom with very diverse IT skill sets. Some students come with no formal education in the area of information technologies and others come with a high degree of training or instruction in the area. All of these students enter the classroom with the same expectation, which is to actually use information technology in the course (Lukow & Ross, 2003; Rickman & Grudzinski, 2000). They expect to see IT used to teach them and for them to use IT to complete their class work. Having this IT use expectation coming into the class, how do these students learn new software applications? In order to address these questions, the authors of this chapter conducted a research study to understand how students set out to learn topics covered in the IT classroom.

A survey-based research methodology was use to collect data concerning post-secondary student strategies in learning new software applications. The convenience sample consisted of students enrolled in an introductory computer literacy course at a large university located in the southeastern region of the United States. The course is required for all education and nursing majors at the university, but any university student may enroll in the course. Only four students in the sample were not education or nursing majors. Students for whom this is a requirement have the opportunity to try to test-out of the course prior to taking the course. They are given one chance to pass the test, and if they do not pass they must enroll in the course. Test-outs are administered nine times a year. Two are offered at the beginning of each semester; fall, spring, and summer. One is offered at the mid-point of each semester.

Survey questions consisted of fill-in-the-blank, check-box and radio-button selection questions. The questions were developed based on reviews on the literature on andragogy and pedagogy, and on the teaching of IT-related subjects. The authors' own experiences in these areas were also used in question development. The survey was developed and administered through the Perseus Survey Solutions (PSS) system over the World Wide Web. The questions addressed the students' personal strategies for learning new software applications and how they had been instructed in IT classes in the past when learning new software applications. Students were asked three demographics questions consisting of gender, age, and class standing. The following questions concerning the learning of new software applications were then posed:

- How many computer courses have you taken in your education career? (1; 2; 3; 4; 5; more than 5)
- Please describe your strategy for learning to use a new software application (open-ended)
- Please describe the best method of instruction you have had with regard to learning a new software application (open-ended)

Table 1. Age

AGE	MALE	FEMALE	TOTAL
17-22	15 14.0%	88 82.2%	103 96.3%
23-30	2 1.8%	2 1.9%	4 3.7%
TOTAL	17 15.9%	90 84.1%	107 100.0%

- Please describe how most of your technology courses have been taught to you (open-ended)
- Please choose the methods you have used to learn a new software application (Tutorials; Computer Based Training; Self-study Guides; Trial and Error (Using the program until you have figured it out))
- Please choose the method you personally use the most to learn a new software application (Tutorials; Computer Based Training; Self-study Guides; Trial and Error)
- Please choose the instructional delivery methods you have had in the technology courses you have taken. You may choose more than one. (Lecture; Discussion; Hands-on Laboratory; Step-by-step Instruction; Project Based)
- Please choose the instructional delivery method that was most effective for you in learning a new software application (Lecture; Discussion; Hands-on Laboratory; Step-by-step Instruction; Project Based)

With regard to sample size for studies of this nature, Lincoln and Guba (1985) note that sample size should be large enough to provide informational redundancy. Patton (1990) added that sample size is dependent upon many factors including "what is useful, what will have credibility and what can be done with available time and resources" (p. 184). The challenge is to make sense of all the findings of the study, keep bias in check, and to record for the reader what has been found (Patton, 1990, p. 371-372; Denzin & Lincoln, 2000). A total of 152 post-secondary students enrolled in an introductory computer literacy course were asked to participate in the survey. Of that number, 108 surveys were submitted with 107 completed and usable, for a response rate of 70 percent. That response rate is adequate for drawing conclusions regarding survey variables. For open-ended questions, individual responses were imported into Microsoft Excel and themes, keywords, and phrases related to study topics were identified and categorized.

Results

Table 1, Table 2 and Table 3 display respondents' demographic information and number of computer courses taken in their education careers. The respondents to the survey were predominantly female (84.1%) between the age of 17 and 22 (82.2%) and the majority were members of the freshman class (57%).

When students were asked the open ended questions, trends appeared concerning their self-selected strategies, their best experience being taught in the IT classroom, and how their IT courses have been taught. The resulting trends show that a majority use trial and error (55.14%) for their learning strategy, want to be taught through demonstration/modeling (55.14%), and have been taught

Table 2. Class standing

CLASS	MALE	FEMALE	TOTAL
Freshman	8 7.5%	53 49.5%	61 57.0%
Sophomore	4 3.7%	25 23.4%	29 27.1%
Junior	4 3.7%	8 7.5%	12 11.2%
Senior	1 0.9%	4 3.7%	5 4.7%
Graduate	0 0.0%	0 0.0%	0 0.0%
Non-degree	0 0.0%	0 0.0%	0 0.0%
TOTAL	17 15.9%	90 84.1%	107 100.0%

via demonstration/modeling (57.0%) the majority of the time. Table 4, Table 5 and Table 6 show the resulting themes expressed by the respondents to the three open-ended questions.

After the respondents finished their open-ended questions, the survey moved to the check boxes and radio button questions. The respondents did not see these questions until after they completed the previous three questions and once they moved to the next page of the survey, they had no ability to go back. This was to prevent these questions from biasing the respondents' answers to the previous questions. The following four questions were asked of the respondents:

- Please choose the methods you have used to learn a new software application (Tutorials; Computer Based Training; Self-study Guides; Trial and Error (Using the program until you have figured it out))
- Please choose the method you personally use the most to learn a new software

Table 3. Number of computer courses taken

CLASS	MALE	FEMALE	TOTAL
1	7 6.5%	36 33.6%	43 40.2%
2	2 1.9%	19 17.8%	21 19.6%
3	5 4.7%	12 11.2%	17 15.9%
4	2 1.9%	20 18.7%	22 20.6%
5	0 0.0%	2 1.9%	2 1.9%
more than 5	1 0.9%	1 0.9%	2 1.9%
TOTAL	17 15.9%	90 84.1%	107 100.0%

Table 4. Learning strategy

Themes From, Please describe your strategy for learning a new software application N=107		
Theme	**N**	**%**
Hands-on, Practice it, Repetition, Trial and Error	59	55.1%
Read about the software	20	18.7%
Obtain help from the teacher	12	11.2%
Online Tutorials & Training	6	5.6%
Learn in class	4	3.7%
Google for help	3	2.8%
Use the application's Help menu	3	2.8%
Totals	107	100.0%

Table 5. Best method of instruction

Themes From, Please describe the best method of instruction you have had with regard to learning a new software application N=107		
Theme	**N**	**%**
Demonstration/Modeling	59	55.1%
Exploration of application, Hands-on	26	24.3%
Training	13	12.1%
Read the instructions	4	3.7%
Study	3	2.8%
Discussion	2	1.9%
Totals	107	100.0%

Table 6. How are most IT courses taught

Themes From, Please describe how most of your technology courses have been taught to you N=107		
Theme	**N**	**%**
Demonstration/Modeling	61	57.0%
Lecture	23	21.5%
Hands-on	15	14.0%
Reading a Book on the Application	8	7.5%
Totals	107	100.0%

Table 7. Methods you used to learn new software

Response	Frequency	Count
Tutorials	53.3%	57
Computer Based Training	73.8%	79
Self-study Guides	43.0%	46
Trial and Error (Using the program until you have figured it out)	74.8%	80
Total Responses		**107**

Table 8. Method used most often to learn new software

Response	Frequency	Count
Tutorials	19.6%	21
Computer Based Training	25.2%	27
Self-study Guides	1.9%	2
Trial and Error	53.3%	57
Total Responses		**107**

application (Tutorials; Computer Based Training; Self-study Guides; Trial and Error)

- Please choose the instructional delivery methods you have had in the technology courses you have taken. You may choose more than one. (Lecture; Discussion; Hands-on Laboratory; Step-by-step Instruction; Project Based)
- Please choose the instructional delivery method that was most effective for you in learning a new software application (Lecture; Discussion; Hands-on Laboratory; Step-by-step Instruction; Project Based)

Respondents expressed that computer based training (73.8%) and trial and error (74.8%) were the most frequent methods used to learn new software applications, but trial and error (53.3%) was their personal learning method. The respondents also expressed that hands-on laboratories (95.3%) and step-by-step instructions (87.9%) were the most common instructional methods used in their IT classrooms, while hands-on laboratories (57.9%) was their most preferred instructional method. Table 7, Table 8, Table 9 and Table 10 display below the results of the respondents' answers to the four questions.

Discussion

The results of the survey show that most of the post-secondary students surveyed in IT courses benefit from having demonstrations and hands-on activities to assist them in learning new software applications. This is in line with their preferred method of learning software applications. These findings are consistent with respondents' answers to the open-ended questions. It is also apparent that male students prefer an andragogical approach (88.2%) for learning new software while female students prefer a pedagogical approach (65.5%). However, when all the respondents are considered, a majority (59.8%) preferred an andragogical approach to learning a new software application.

Knowing that students have a desire to explore applications, try out software on their own, and

Table 9. Instructional delivery methods used in IT classes

Response	Frequency	Count
Lecture	68.2%	73
Discussion	39.3%	42
Hands-on Laboratory	95.3%	102
Step-by-step Instruction	87.9%	94
Project Based	44.9%	48
Total Responses		**107**

Table 10. Most effective delivery method used in the IT classroom

Response	Frequency	Count
Lecture	2.8%	3
Discussion	1.9%	2
Hands-on Laboratory	57.9%	62
Step-by-step Instruction	35.5%	38
Project Based	1.9%	2
Total Responses		**107**

once stumped ask an instructor for assistance will allow IT course instructor to develop appropriate course materials for enabling students to learn new applications. Some students will want to see demonstrations, while the majority of their peers just want to start trying out the software. Having this knowledge will enable new instructional strategies to be considered when teaching in the IT classroom. These strategies should foster both life long learning skills and critical thinking skills. The respondents to the study indicated that they prefer an andragogical approach to be used in the classroom, but some aspects of pedagogy are also helpful.

Instructors can look at ways to incorporate critical thinking and problem solving into the curriculum while giving the students the freedom to learn the material using their own preferred methods. This freedom will enable those who prefer hands-on exploration the independence to pursue the outcomes of the lesson on their own, while others may prefer the instructor perform a demonstration before they venture to complete the assignment. This blended approach will allow all students to benefit. The ultimate concern for the IT classroom instructor will be when or if a blended approach should be incorporated into the classroom. Addressing this question means that instructors who typically use pedagogical-type approaches will need to consider incorporating elements of andragogy into their classrooms.

The ways learners interact with a discipline beyond the walls of formal educational institutions has a distinct impact on what occurs within the classroom. Students seem to naturally gravitate toward andragogical methods of learning because of their individual interest and personal needs for using information technologies. Unlike many other disciplines, people all over the world are interacting daily with new technologies in informal ways. Most secondary or post secondary educators of disciplines such as biology, history and engineering do not have to be concerned about the entry level knowledge or the amount of self-teaching and exposure students have had about their content outside of class. The perpetual "self-direction" and pursuit of new learning and use of IT by students puts IT educators at a disadvantage and should cause them to examine and reflect on what they are doing in their classrooms to counter students' independent explorations of IT knowledge and skills. Information technology educators can and should begin to re-envision themselves and their roles as instructors. It is practically impossible for IT educators to stay ahead of the knowledge bases and skill sets of all of their students over time. The days of being the "sage on the stage" may be coming to an end for IT education.

If indeed the time of the "sage on the stage" is over in IT education, then what should it be replaced with? The philosophy, abilities and perspectives of the instructor sets the tone within every classroom. The way an instructor sees him/herself teaching and leading students through their curriculum can influence the teacher's effectiveness and the student's short and long term uses of the content. Perhaps this is the prime opportunity for IT educators to begin to reinvent themselves as a "guide on the side" – a facilitator of natural inquiry who uses student skills, abilities and dispositions to focus and direct learning. This is the stance of an instructor who works within the andragogical classroom. Instead of standing at the front of class in a teacher-centered manner, IT educators should begin to move toward student-centered approaches. A student-centered approach allows the learner to take responsibility for their own learning and builds off of the notion that the learner is ready and motivated to learn. For many instructors (IT or otherwise) this can be an uncomfortable scenario. Typically, instructors model themselves from the teachers they have had in their pasts. For many of us, this is rooted into our formative years in elementary, middle and high schools. Unfortunately, as children and young adults, most of us were not psychologically or emotionally mature enough to respond appropriately to a student-centered approach, thus we received a teacher-centered approach and in turn, we as well become teacher-centered as instructors today – even in higher education settings. How does one change their instructional philosophy? How does one adapt their classrooms around the concept of andragogy? This is explored in the following section.

SOLUTIONS AND RECOMMENDATIONS: TRANSITIONING TO AN ANDRAGOGICAL PERSPECTIVE IN INFORMATION TECHNOLOGY EDUCATION

Why and when should an information technology educator adopt and implement an andragogical approach in the courses they teach? Information technology education (ITE) is often misconstrued or inaccurately described as "computer skill training" or the practice of specific computer skill recitation and memorization. Molynuex (1986) states that the learner generally wants to learn a specific or particular piece of technology and may consider the bigger parts irrelevant. However, we now know that when the learner is taught how to use a specific technology through the lens of problem solving, they retain more and feel better about their abilities to keep learning. The results of the research project described earlier in this chapter are in keeping with this philosophy. Adult ITE learners want to have that background information that allows them to solve problems rather than simply follow directions.

Benbunan-Fich (2002) states that there is a lack of systemic models to successfully guide the use of IT in educational settings. McCormick and Scrimshaw (2001) suggest that more attention be given to the methods of teaching and learning of information and communication technologies in schools. From an academic perspective, the ITE field is focused on the development of problem solving capabilities within the context of computer systems and information/communication technologies. This is similar to the mission of engineering education which Holvikivi (2007) suggests as being to develop capable of adapting to technological advances. Kirkwood and Price (2005) discuss teaching not only the *what*, but also the *why* in order to ensure higher level learning is occurring in ITE courses. The field of ITE is thick with courses, curricula, programs and even entire institutions which base their operations and conceptual frameworks around the mastery of skills (what) within specific computer hardware and software as opposed to the how and why of the technology and the future abilities of the learner. Problem-solving sometimes inadvertently includes memorization-based activities, but is never the aim or goal of the activity. ITE instructors should design, develop and deliver content and materials from a problem-solving perspective if they are to teach student to "learn how to learn" so that they may be successful in future situations using information technologies. Learning how to learn is essential for ITE because of the speed at which information technologies changes. Andragogy is a philosophy which naturally fits into the landscape of ITE. As stated earlier in the chapter, andragogy works when the self directed, intrinsically motivated learner encounters a new problem and understands the learning task is related to their futures. ITE programs who espouse problem-solving as a foundation are well poised to shift from pedagogy to andragogy and will experience many benefits and challenges. The benefits of shifting to an andragogical approach in ITE include the development of learners who are poised to be successful as adults in schools and the workplace, less reliance on product-specific curricula and a classroom which is easily adaptable for curricular changes. Challenges of shifting from pedagogy to andragogy in ITE includes moving away from teacher-centered approaches, designing authentic problem-based lessons and assignments and requiring students to be more self-motivated in order to be successful.

General characteristics of both the pedagogical and andragogical ITE classrooms were presented earlier in this chapter. More detailed methods on transforming from pedagogy to andragogy are described here. Adapting instruction from pedagogy to andragogy in college classes requires specific instructor behaviors in order for a true transformation to occur. First, instructors must begin from the assumption that their students are adults. Too often, college students are treated like high school students and are thought of as lacking the aptitudes and abilities of adult learners. Given the common perception that young people are generally interested and have some level of knowledge and skills with computer technologies, ITE is as well-poised as any discipline to work from the stance that students are adult learners. How an instructor designs syllabi, selects course materials, designs assignments, provides feedback and conducts class are all components of restructuring a class around andragogy.

ITE instructors who intend to implement an andragogical philosophy in their courses should begin with their syllabi. By clearly stating their expectations and acknowledging their students as adult learners in the syllabus, the instructor is able to set the tone of the semester. Instructors should look to have an "overview" or some sort of introduction in their syllabus so that they can discuss their philosophy and their expectations. This is a good area to address students as adults and to set the tone of the semester. Knowles (1995) describes the andragogical approach in the context of process elements such as learner preparation and climate. This include the preparation of learners by providing information, preparing them for participation, helping them develop realistic expectations while beginning to think about course content. An example of this type of introductory andragogical language found in a syllabus might be written as the following for a "Computer Systems 101" course;

Computer Systems 101 is designed to help the learner develop knowledge and skills with basic office productivity software in the areas of desktop publishing, electronic spreadsheets, databases and multimedia presentations. Students are expected to conduct themselves as adult learners and strive to get the most out of this course by actively engaging in the content and exercises to the best of their ability, given their entry-level knowledge and skills. The instructor has prepared problem-based activities based around real-world applications which will allow each learner to grow to their own optimum levels, recognizing each student's individual abilities and potential.

The following syllabi introduction is written from a more pedagogical perspective;

Computer Systems 101 is designed to build specific skills in the areas of Microsoft PowerPoint®, Excel®, Word® and Access®. Students will receive training and will be measured on their abilities to complete tasks in these software programs. Students will be assessed on a mastery level and must accurately demonstrate skill proficiency at 90% or above with each skill set. All assignments must be accomplished in a computer lab to ensure authenticity via proctor.

As you can see, these two course overviews have very different tones and communicate very different messages to the learners. The andragogical approach invites the learner into the learning environment with open-ended ideas and potential whereas the second overview (pedagogical) is teacher centered and specifies exact actions, products and authority.

ITE instructors who are designing an andragogical course should also take time to select course materials which lend themselves to the core principles of andragogy. Many of the books and software products in the information technology education market are designed from a pedagogical, teacher-centered approach. It is popular to find text books which have step-by-step instructions for using technologies with minimal background, theory or discussion about practical real-world applications. Such materials are often supported with assessments which require the student to replicate an assignment by following specific steps or actions. Ultimately, with these types of assessments usually end with students creating identical projects. Course texts and materials which are more andragogically based have less emphasis on step-by-step skill building or at least have an equal amount of information on theory and practical application in real world settings.

Perhaps the most critical differences between the andragogical and pedagogical texts are the design and nature of assignments. Andragogically designed assignments are problem based and do not duplicate or replicate activities in a one-size fits all style typical of pedagogical assignments. According to Bridges and Hallinger (1995), problem based learning involves both knowing and doing and should resemble the context in which it will subsequently be used. Andragogically based assignments in present a problem or scenario which allows learners to demonstrate their understanding of content and course material in their own way, at their own levels with their own evaluation system in mind. Imagine an ITE instructor teaching a unit on electronic spreadsheets. An example of an andragogically based assignment may resemble the following;

Prepare an electronic spreadsheet with a high level of professional appearance and qualities based on our lessons in this course. Using data from a reliable source on the Internet, select a city in North America, then enter the data for the monthly high and low temperatures during the past five years. Using this data, make an estimate for the average monthly temperatures for each month for the up coming year. Design a graphical chart which you believe best displays this data, and then have a peer perform an evaluation and discuss their findings with them prior to submission.

Alternatively, a pedagogically-based assignment may look more like the following;

Research temperature data on the city of San Francisco using the National Oceanographic and Atmospheric Administration (NOAA) website. Using Microsoft Excel, create a spreadsheet with each month as a column heading and the average high and low monthly temperature as row headings. Using the AVG function, calculate the average yearly high and low temperature, then design a chart using the bar chart displaying the data.

As you can see from these basic examples, the pedagogically centered assignment is more strict in design, calls for less creativity and requires less critical thinking and problem solving than does the andragogically centered example above.

Another component of the andragogical ITE classroom is the actual behaviors of the instructor. It is common (and convenient) for ITE instructors to model the uses and specifics of any particular technology. The problematic issue with this style of classroom presentation is that it tends to encourage students to "watch and mimic" instead of learning how to discover and solve problems. ITE instructors should be careful of the amount of time spent actually demonstrating technologies. It is a good practice to give brief demonstrations then use well designed assignments to engage learners through the learning objectives. After students begin work on their assignments, instructors then can facilitate or guide students through problems they encounter with their assignments as opposed to pointing out the answers. It is beneficial for ITE instructors to learn how to use questions so that they may guide students to discovering the correct answers to their questions. Additionally, ITE instructors attempting to shift towards an andragogical approach should learn to use student mistakes as learning opportunities. Being a considered traditionally a "hard science," with difficult learning objectives, ITE instructors should reconsider how to use errors and mistakes on assignments as opportunities for student growth and direction.

THE FUTURE OF ANDRAGOGY IN INFORMATION TECHNOLOGY EDUCATION

What does the future hold for ITE in terms of philosophical approaches to instruction? As more students become distance education students, there will be a continued reliance on andragogical practices and principles because of the obvious limitations and requirements of distance education students. Successful distance education students must have many of the same qualities as adult learners; the must move from dependency to self-directedness, use experiences as a platform for learning, and understand the immediacy in their learning as a way to improve their performance. Distance education is a pivotal and critical area of growth in all areas of education, especially ITE. Distance education instructors and students typically interact more asynchronously than synchronously, therefore requiring the student to be a self starter and self-regulator – both elements of andragogy and adult learning in general. This said, it behooves the ITE instructor to embrace andragogy and to design their courses around the principles of adult learner. ITE classes which remain transactional and pedagogical in nature will look less dynamic, interesting and useful to students at a distance, thus making the program of study look stale and unattractive. With so many core similarities between andragogy and the attributes of successful distance education students, ITE instructors who teach online should find it both simple as well as a good investment of time to design their courses with an andragogical approach.

Andragogy can also be seen as having both relevance and potential in terms of workforce development. At the time of this publication (2009), society has come to the common understanding that we are indeed a global economy. In fact, we are a global economy which is struggling to succeed and prosper. Perhaps now more than ever, people need to be taught to be self-directed, self regulating, intrinsically motivated problem solvers who learn from their mistakes. These are the types of people the global workforce needs as opposed to the opposite–extrinsically motivated, stepwise learners who need someone to direct and regulate their every move. The global economy is broken and needs workers who have andragogical philosophies towards not only formal education, but their jobs and the problems which they encounter on a daily basis. Specifically, information technology workers during the next five to ten years will need an andragogical mindset perhaps as much as the members of any workforce. The information technology industry has several major obstacles which makes andragogy applicable and suitable for today's classrooms. First, the information technology industry is changing too rapidly for workers to learn within a pedagogical perspective. The pace of which information technology changes requires workers to be self directed and motivated problem solvers who can take it upon themselves to learn, invent and devise creative solutions to problems. Secondly, the information technology industry is over crowded and inundated with workers. In this market, only the best, most self-directed, self motivated problem solvers will survive the lay-offs and reductions of this economy.

CONCLUSION

Information technology education is a dynamic, ever-changing academic field. Flecknoe (2002) suggests that information and communication technologies are currently being used to assist students learn and make teaching more effective. The literature suggests that the use of information technologies can/will revolutionize areas such as health care education (Downing, 2001), and second language education (Potts, 2005), workforce re-education for the unemployed (Shananhan, 1992) and even theological education (Delamarter, 2006). Learners in ITE settings should understand that unlike many other subject areas, ITE is as much or more about the future as it is the past. While it is important to understand the historical perspective (past) and the technologies of today (present), perhaps the most important piece of wisdom which can be imparted to an ITE student are the skills and abilities to be a life long learner (future). In order to develop life longer learners who are prepared for the challenges of the 21st century, ITE instructors must often forego the drill and practice ways in which they themselves were taught and seek alternative teaching methodologies. Andragogy is one philosophy which can help ITE instructors look beyond their own classroom experiences so that they may create unique and transformational educational environments which are needed today.

REFERENCES

Ames, C. (1992). Classrooms: Goals, structures and student motivations. *Journal of Educational Psychology*, *84*(3), 261–271. doi:10.1037/0022-0663.84.3.261

Bee, H. L., & Bjorkland, B. J. (2004). *The journey of adulthood.* Upper Saddle River, NJ: Pearson.

Benbunan-Fich, R. (2002). Improving education and training with IT. *Communications of the ACM*, *45*(6), 94–99. doi:10.1145/508448.508454

Bridges, E., & Hallinger, P. (1995). *Implementing problem based learning in leadership development.* Eugene, OR: Eric Clearinghouse on Educational Management.

Cohen, J. E. (2006). Goals of universal basic and secondary education. *Prospects*, *36*(3), 247–269. doi:10.1007/s11125-006-0016-1

Compayre, G., & Payne, W. H. (1885). *The history of pedagogy*. Boston: J. S. Cushing & Co.

Delamarter, S. (2006). Strategic planning to enhance teaching and learning with technology. *Teaching Theology and Religion*, *9*(1), 9–23. doi:10.1111/j.1467-9647.2006.00256.x

Denzin, N. K., & Lincoln, Y. S. (2000). The discipline and practice of qualitative research. In N. K. Denzin & Y. S. Lincoln (Eds.), *Handbook of qualitative research* (2nd ed., pp. 1-28). Thousand Oaks, CA: SAGE Publications, Inc.

Downing, K. (2001). Information technology education and health care: Constructivism in the 21st century. *Educational Studies*, *27*(3), 229–235. doi:10.1080/03055690120076510

Flecknoe, M. (2002). How can ICT help us to improve education? *Innovations in Education and Teaching International*, *39*(4), 271–279. doi:10.1080/13558000210161061

Holvikivi, J. (2007). Learning styles in engineering education: the quest to improve didactic practices. *European Journal of Engineering Education*, *32*(4), 401–408. doi:10.1080/03043790701332909

Kirkwood, A., & Price, L. (2005). Learners and learning in the 21st century: What do we know about students' attitudes towards and experiences of information and communication technologies that will help us design courses? *Studies in Higher Education*, *30*(3), 257–274. doi:10.1080/03075070500095689

Knowles, M. (1995). *Designs for Adult Learning*. Alexandria, VA: American Society for Training and Development.

Lagemann, E. C. (2002). *An elusive science: The troubling history of education research*. Chicago: University of Chicago Press.

Lincoln, Y. S., & Guba, E. G. (1985). *Naturalistic inquiry*. Newbury Park, CA: SAGE Publications, Inc.

Lukow, J., & Ross, C. M. (2003). How learning styles affect student attitudes toward technology. *Schole: A Journal of Leisure Studies and Recreation Education, 18*, 67-80.

McCormick, R., & Scrimshaw, P. (2001). Information and communications technology, knowledge and pedagogy. *Education Communication and Information*, *1*(1), 2001.

Merriam, S. B., Caffarella, R. S., & Baumgartner, L. M. (2007). *Learning in Adulthood: A Comprehensive Guide*. San Francisco: John Wiley & Sons Inc.

Molyneux, E. (1986). Information technology education in industry. *Journal of Information Technology*, *1*(2), 30–31. doi:10.1057/jit.1986.20

Patton, M. Q. (1990). *Qualitative evaluation and research methods,* (2nd ed.). Newbury Park, CA: SAGE Publications, Inc.

Potts, D. (2005). Pedagogy, purpose and the second language learner in online communities. *Canadian Modern Language Review*, *62*(1), 137–160.

Reichgelt, H., Lunt, B., Ashford, T., Phelps, A., Slazinski, E., & Willis, C. (2004). A comparison of baccalaureate programs in information technology with baccalaureate programs in computer science and information systems. *Journal of Information Technology Education*, *3*, 19–34.

Rickman, J., & Grudzinski, M. (2000). Student expectations of information technology use in the classroom. *EDUCAUSE Quarterly*, *23*(1), 24–30.

Robinson, R. D. (1995). *Helping adults learn and change*. West Bend, WI: Omnibook.

Shananhan, P. (1992). Towards a knowledge democracy? University adult education, information technology and unemployed persons. *Studies in the Education of Adults*, *24*(1), 57–68.

ADDITIONAL READING

Bridges, E. (1992). *Problem based learning for administrators*. Eugene, Oregon: Eric Clearinghouse on Educational Management.

Isenberg, S. (2007). *Applying andragogical principles to Internet learning*. Cambria Press.

Keirns, J. (1999). *Designs for self-instruction*. Needham Heights, MA: Allyn and Bacon.

Knowles, M. S., & Elwood, F. Holton, E. F., & Swanson, R. A. (1998). *The Adult Learner: The Definitive Classic in Adult Education and Human Resource Development (Managing cultural differences)*. Houston, TX: Gulf Publishing.

Posner, G., & Rudnitsky, A. (2001). *Course design: A guide to curriculum development for teachers*. New York, NY: Longman.

Swanson, R., & Holton, E., III. (2001). *Foundations of human resource development*. San Francisco, CA: Berrett-Koehler.

Werner, J., & DeSimone, R. (2009). *Human resource development*. Mason, OH: South-Western Cengage Learning.

Chapter 5
Adult Learners and Their Development in the Information Society

Lesley Farmer
California State University at Long Beach, USA

ABSTRACT

In a digital world where the amount of information doubles every two years, adults need to evaluate resources carefully and determine how to use relevant information to solve problems and make wise decisions. This changing informational environment affects adult education, and also emphasizes the need for lifelong education and learning organizations, and the intersection of technology and globalization has led to more intense and pluralistic interactions across societies. Because information's meaning and impact are contextualized, shared knowledge and understanding can be harder to achieve. Therefore, information literacy and knowledge management are needed in order to fully realize one's self-potential and an organization's vision. Emerging trends that impact adult learning are discussed: equity, culturally-sensitive information, and information cross-fertilization. A model of adult learning and information interaction is provided.

INTRODUCTION

The need for critical use of information is more important than ever. As early as1991, the SCANS report noted information location and manipulation as vital skills for contemporary employees. In a digital world where the amount of information doubles every two years, adults need to evaluate resources carefully and determine how to use relevant information to solve problems and make wise decisions.

Furthermore, it is no longer principally an issue ofgetting information: it's getting the right information at the right time to do things right and to do the right things. Economic and social activities rely on information and communication technologies. Knowledge is ever-flowing, and social interactions seem web-like (Daniel, 2007). As the world seems to grow smaller, due to increased communication and population transience, the global scene reflects

DOI: 10.4018/978-1-61520-694-0.ch005

a more interactive mode relative to information. Even when a nation appears to act alone to seem isolationist, it cannot survive in that manner because the world is so interdependent. This changing informational environment affects adult education, and also emphasizes the need for lifelong education to prepare today's workforce to deal with an uncertain tomorrow.

If the underlying message is "things change," then the inevitable question is: "What should adult education look like in an information society?" If traditional adult education could be compared to Theory X businesses where employees are told what to do in a highly hierarchical bureaucracy, then contemporary adult education could be compared to Theory Y businesses where participatory management is the name of the game. Learning communities would compare to Theory Z organizations where highly- autonomous networks of teams have replaced hierarchy. In any case, adult education needs to address these changes constructively.

BACKGROUND

To understand the problem and contributing factors, an overview of the information society and adult education is needed.

The Information Society

At the 2003 world summit on the Information Society, governments and world leaders "made a strong commitment towards building a people-centred, inclusive and development-oriented Information Society for all, where everyone can access, utilise and share information and knowledge" (United Nations, 2006, p. 6). What constitutes an information society? Fundamentally, an information society is one in which information replaces material goods as the chief driver of socio-economics. Human intellectual capital has higher currency than material capital, or at least intellect is needed to optimize the use of material resources.

Since information and material have always been needed, what particularizes the recent notion of an information (or knowledge) society? New information and technology have vastly increased the speed, access, and interconnectedness of information worldwide. Simultaneously, information and communication have converged, such as telecommunications and broadcasting, giving rise to informational industries. At this point in history, telecommunications and media constitute one-sixth of the U. S. economy, and 30 percent of all economic growth between 1996 and 2000 was attributed to enhanced productivity based on information technology (Wilhelm, 2004). The cost of technology has dropped precipitously so that the majority of people can access it, thereby reinforcing mass media and other information entities. As a result, new forms of organization and social interaction have emerged (Webster, 2002).

This information society impacts existing institutions and cultures. The speed and globalization of information leads to constant change, which can be hard to digest and manage. The majority of jobs now involve technology and other related new skills, so that the idea of a "terminal" degree or a static skill set is becoming an outdated paradigm. Rather, adults often need to "retool" themselves throughout their work lives. Particularly for adults who are largely digital immigrants, this new world of information, especially in electronic form, can be puzzling and overwhelming. Do they have enough background information to understand and use the *new* information?

Using Technology to Manage the Information Society

The attitude about information has changed because of technology; Rutenbeck (2000) identified several challenges of the digital information age: information's malleability and vulnerability, the under-value of print information and the possible over-value of digital information, and the rise of exclusivity because of inequitable access based on economics and the added need for digital literacy. The nature of technology also impacts how people communicate the information they find; in effect, technology-enhanced communication itself becomes a new literacy that people have to learn (Coiro, Klein & Walpole, 2006).

How does technology help adults cope with all this information? Certainly, technology has interconnected the world's information. Knowledge is every flowing, and social interaction seems weblike (Daniel, 2007). That same web can be hard to evaluate and manage, though. The constant bombardment of information can negatively impact productivity; Spira and Feintuch (2005) calculated the loss of productive hours to total $588 billion in one year. Even information technology (IT) organizations seek more effective ways to manage technology; while some organizations hire professional technicians to deal with change, the prevailing strategy is education and training (Benamati & Lederer, 2001).

Technology impacts such adult learning. It has been found to aid literacy instruction and learning both in academic and non-academic settings (Coiro, Klein & Walpole, 2006). However, technology itself must be learned as well as the information it conveys. As much as the term information overload is bandied about, the term technostress is even more prevalent. Thus, the very tool to help manage changing information itself requires change on the part of adults. Adults have to change and learn in order to manage change.

Information Literacy Within the Information Society

More specifically, international stakeholders at the World Summit on the Information Society stated their shared values of information literacy:

Information Literacy lies at the core of lifelong learning. It empowers people in all walks of life to seek, evaluate, use and create information effectively to achieve their personal, social, occupational and educational goals. It is a basic human right in a digital world and promotes social inclusion of all nations (Garner, 2005, 3).

Although it sometimes seems as if librarians created information literacy and its need, current key decision makers recognize the importance of information literacy. As early as the 1991 SCANS (Secretary's Commission on Achieving Necessary Skills) report, governmental agencies have noted the need for employees who can: locate, interpret and organize information; communicate information; create documents; solve problems; work with a variety of technology; and know how to acquire new knowledge.

In a landmark study of CEOs from 28 countries, Rosen (2000) documented four global literacies need in today's business world: personal literacy (self-knowledge and self-esteem), social literacy, business literacy, and cultural literacy. As businesses increasingly realize the importance of intellectual capital, knowledge management has become a key ingredient for success. In 1995, G-7 leadership agreed that a global information society needed to be built, providing infrastructure and applications as they impact societies and cultures. Particularly since one of the main reasons for education is to prepare its students to contribute to society's economic well-being, it makes sense to incorporate information literacy into the curriculum.

UNESCO Bangkok has identified communication and information as a major program, with information literacy constituting a major thread within that initiative. This international organization asserts:

Information literacy enhances the pursuit of knowledge by equipping individuals with the skills and abilities for critical reception, assessment and use of information in their professional and personal lives. For the society to have informa-

tion literate adults, information literacy education needs to start as early as possible (¶1).

UNESCO as a whole has embraced information and communication technology, and is facilitating global discussion and efforts.

Everyone should be offered the opportunity to acquire the necessary skills in order to understand, participate actively in, and benefit fully from, the Information Society and the knowledge economy. Given the wide range of ICT [information and communication technology] specialists required at all levels, building the institutional capacities to collect, organize, store and share information and knowledge deserves special attention. Governments should develop comprehensive and forward-looking strategies to respond to the new human capacity needs, including the creation of an environment that supports information literacy, ICT literacy and life-long learning for the general public (p. 6)

Even beyond economics, information literacy is needed in order to fully realize one's self-potential and to be a responsible and participatory citizen. On a more profound level, information literacy is imperative for a democratic, open society (U. S. Department of Education, 2004).

The intersection of technology and globalization has led to more intense and pluralistic interactions across societies. Because information's meaning and impact is contextualized, shared knowledge and understanding can be harder to achieve. In a world scarred with political turmoil and terrorism, information literacy has never been so important. Adult educators, in collaboration with librarians and other information professionals, should be discussing strategies to promote the value of information literacy – and ways to optimize its attainment by global citizens -- through initiatives facilitated via private and public entities.

Lifelong Learning and the Learning Society

The concept of lifelong learning seems self-evident. As long as one is alive, one is likely to encounter new situations that need to be resolved; each of those encounters is a potential learning moment. Nevertheless, because today's information society drives change in so many aspects of life, lifelong learning takes on new and explicit meaning. People consciously have to pay attention to the world around themselves, and decide if they want to change – and what they need to do in order to accommodate those changes. In this respect, the information society has sometimes been called the learning society to emphasize the dynamic nature of social change throughout people's lives (Field, 2006).

It must be first acknowledged that many adults do not feel that the information society affects them significantly. Nor do all adults think of themselves as lifelong learners. To some adults, lifelong learning is equated with going back to school: book learning. These individuals may well be learning skills, such as dealing with water shortages or adjusting to personal ailments or figuring out how to work with a new boss, but they might not *label* these adaptations as learning per se. Such learning characterizes most people's daily lives. Adult educators must also acknowledge the validity of such learning approaches. Nevertheless, the implications of a learning society lead to a more systematic approach to adult education rather than trial and error on a personal basis (Livingstone, 2001; Selwyn, Gorard & Furlong, 2006).

The idea of a learning society that affects adult education has a fairly short history. Global war forced people to develop new skills and assume new roles, which led to social changes such as women's emancipation. World War II brought with it technology advances that had far-ranging implications. During and after both war times, massive adult training quickly prepared people for new and different jobs.

The new information society has led to ongoing change rather than event-specific change so it might be posited that widespread adult education would result. Evidence supports that assumption; about 46 percent of the U. S. population participated in adult education activities in 1999 (Westat & Creighton, 2000). Although non-vocational training dropped between 1997 and 2002 in Great Britain, a rise in self-directed learning and vocational training balanced the overall picture of an increase of 60 percent since 1985 (Fitzgerald, Taylor & La Valle, 2003). Nevertheless, a forced government-based adult education initiative, such as proposed in Great Britain (Istance, Schuetze & Schuller, 2002), would be likely to fail if for no other reason than adult learners need to feel control about their learning experience, choosing if and how to participate. Rather, the conditions for adult learning need to be provided widely and systemically so that adults have opportunities for meaningful learning.

Adult Education Premises

As a review, adult learning or andragogy builds on the experiences and needs of adult. Knowles (1990) identified factors that need to be considered when designing instruction for this population. The following list addresses the realities of the information society.

- **Self-direction:** Adults want to be treated as responsible, self-directed learners. They want to be in control of their use of information. Therefore, instructors should develop a learning environment that provides adults choices in how they identify, access, and use information according to their needs.
- **Experience:** Adults have extensive and diverse experiences, which influence how they construct meaning from their engagement with information. Instructors should help adult learners identify what they already know and then build on that knowledge. Instructors should also realize that adult learners might have little access to digital information so explicit instruction on technological use is necessary.
- **Motivation:** Adults are motivated internally: by job needs, personal desire, and self-esteem. Whenever possible, instruction should be developed in response to adult interests and needs. For instance, adults may want information in order to improve their economic statues or to solve personal health problems. In these scenarios, adults are willing, committed learners, thus offering a positive atmosphere.
- **Readiness:** Adults learn when they see a need to learn in order to cope with their lives or improve them. As with motivation, readiness should dictate the creation of learning opportunities. Additionally, learning activities should be contextualized so adults see how they fit into their daily experience. It should also be noted that instructors need to incorporate methods of dealing with change since that aspect of learning may be unexpected and uncomfortable. Particularly when new information contradicts adults' existing knowledge base, the most likely outcome is rejection of the new information, especially if it impacts adults' livelihood or established values.
- **Need to know:** Adults need to know what they are going to learn and why they are learning it before they commit to the learning. An information need determined by adult learners offers an ideal opportunity for instructors should leverage the opportunity to design and introduce learning activities.
- **Timing:** Adults have many demands for their time, so they need to fit learning within the framework of the rest of their lives. Instructors need to schedule learning activities to best fit existing schedule demands,

and they should offer options for self-pacing. Instructors may need to remind adult learners about deadlines since other priorities may overtake learners' time. Need for timely information can foster engagement with meaningful learning.

- **Practicality:** Adults appreciate immediate and close transfer of learning and practical instruction. Hands-on, concrete learning activities that address needed information work well with adults, especially if adults can apply that information to their lives immediately.
- **Socialization:** Adults want their social needs to be met as well as their informational needs. Moreover, adults learn through shared knowledge construction. Instructors should provide opportunities for adult learners to share information, and build in networking time. By offering these outlets, instructors find that learners are more satisfied with the session and learn more as well.

Additionally, adults develop cognitively and psychologically throughout their lives. This factor becomes critical in professional development where an entire faculty or professional group is participating. Illustrative examples need to cross generational experiences.

Information Factors Driving Adult Education

What is driving change in adult education? Most of the factors are external to the educational environment. Changing demographics probably tops the list. Particularly with NAFTA (North American Free Trade Agreement), business has become increasingly international. Information, materials and labor cross national borders constantly. Downturns in economies and worldwide political upheaval have resulted in growing migration. Outsourcing offered a means to get low-cost labor, although recent economic downturns have lessened that practice as domestic unemployment demands that in-country personnel be used first. However, such domestic employees oftentimes have to be retooled to gain the knowledge base and accompanying skills to be productive in a new career. Increasingly, their ability to learn how to learn, to integrate and apply new information appropriately, is their key to financial survival. In any case, the message is clear that adult education functions within and as a part of global economic realities (Friedman, 2006).

Another major factor facilitating – or forcing – change in the information world is technology. More households have televisions than bathrooms. Digital storage and data manipulation has transformed business practices, aiding collaboration and streamlining supply and demand processes. Technology has the potential to collapse space and time, disseminating information and documentation at an incredible speed. It has also democratized communication to some degree, bypassing traditional selection and filtering processes to share all kinds of information and misinformation. Technology can also "flatten" communication if it relies only on text; people do not have sound and visual cues to contextualize a message. Therefore, one needs to communicate more clearly and unambiguously. Technology also introduces another dimension in group learning: the need to know the technical aspects of communicating. Thus, contributions may be a factor more of software and hardware availability and protocol than of subject expertise. However, these same advances have also given rise to the Digital Divide; a direct positive correlation exists between household income and household computer ownership.

More recently, the Digital Divide has been applied to age differentials, where millennial youth outperform older adults in their use of information technology. Interactive Web 2.0 furthers distinguishes adults and youth. Over two-thirds of adults use email while minors are more likely to text message. A little more than a third of adults constitute 'power' online users in contrast to almost two-thirds for youth. In addition, youth are generally twice as likely to use Web 2.0 tools and mobile technology than adults (Drago, 2008; Li, 2007). Adults are learning from youngsters rather than the other way around, which upsets the 'natural' order of education whereby adults transfer knowledge to younger ones.

DEVELOPMENT OF ADULT LEARNERS IN AN INFORMATION SOCIETY

In optimizing adult learning in an information society, educators need to incorporate the concept of change, information literacy, and social learning.

The Nature of Change and Its Adoption

Change is hard. Most people prefer the status quo to change. Generally, adults have to be motivated to make an effort to change, to learn. Adult educators can rightly be called change agents because they can serve as catalysts for learning. Not only do they design instruction to optimize learning, but they also try to help learners contextualize their learning and incorporate into their daily lives. In effect, adult educators try to provide the conditions for effective and sustainable change on the part of their clientele.

While adults exhibit varying degrees of comfort with learning, they tend to display overarching attitudes about new knowledge integration as a guiding principle. The Center for Research and Development in Teaching at the University of Texas at Austin developed a seven-step model that identifies the issues that concern learners as they progress from unawareness to full integration. The developers assert that adult educators need to modify instruction to align with each person's stage of concern. Interestingly, this model aligns well with Bloom's Affective Domain taxonomy of: Receiving, Responding, Valuing, Organization, and Value Complex (1964). Such an approach works best for homogeneous groups, obviously. However, when educators are sensitive to their learners' varying stages, they can try to include ideas and activities that may be addressed at different levels.

1. **Awareness:** Learners start from a point of ignorance: no knowledge of a situation or mental set. Adult educators first need to let people realize that something is happening; they have to get the learners' attention. A supervisor may make a comment in a corporate meeting that gets the employee's attention; a human resource development officer might contact employees about retooling training as a follow-up memo.
2. **Information (Receiving):** Learners receive information, but they do not have to give any feedback; this step constitutes one-way communication. Adult educators start by giving objective information through documents, telecommunications, or presentations. A new set of nursing standards might be explained; an online database might be introduced.
3. **Personal (Responding):** Learners then react; communication is now two-way. Usually, learners respond in a personal manner, so adult educators need to help them feel comfortable. Adult educators can optimize learning at this stage by showing the immediate benefits of the new information for the learner. As much as possible, adult educators should provide just-in-time training based on learners' perceived needs. A gradebook software program might resonate for the disorganized teacher; e-mail "broadcasting" might help an administrator; PowerPoint presentations might enliven a sales presentation. Often at this stage, learners focus on a learning tool rather than on educational content outcome. At this stage, also, learners need

to know that support is available: coaching, manuals, Web tutorials, etc.

4. **Management:** Learners try to fit new information into their practice at this stage. The more that instructors can help learners identify appropriate application of the new information within their present practice, the more likely that learners will take related intellectual risks and value that information. Some activities at this point might include: reviewing workflow, developing a Web page, or developing an exercise regime.
5. **Consequence (Valuing):** Learners may question the return on their investment of time and effort at this stage. They fine-tune their use of new information, embracing it when it results in significant adult learning or it increases their own productivity, and abandoning it if it does not improve their lives. Adult educators should applaud this critical analysis and suggest alternative strategies when appropriate. For instance, a database might be a more robust way to keep track of insurance policies than a spreadsheet because files can be sorted and merged; a current practice might be more useful than a new one if the client is uncomfortable with technology.
6. **Collaboration (Organization):** Learners want to optimize new information integration at this stage, and they may work with others to leverage impact. Adult educators should encourage learners to support each other and share best practices through establishing networks that foster communities of practice. Examples of activities at this stage include: program reviews, department Web pages, and repositories.
7. **Re-focus (Value Complex):** At this stage, learners become pro-active experts who work to sustain and institutionalize change for the entire organization. They become instructors and engage in efforts such as strategic planning and policy development.

Typically, each person progresses through each stage but may take different amounts of time to transition from one stage to another. As noted above, the stage of concern may vary by the nature of information or situation. Still, adult educators should conduct ongoing needs assessment to determine the stage of relevant learners and design activities accordingly. This process can result in differentiated instruction to fit the needs of each group of potential participants. In this manner, those individuals further along the process can engage in activities when they need it. However, if a major educational initiative is being started at a site, adult educators would do well to develop learning experiences that progress along those same stages in order to maximize participation and integration.

Impact of Information Literacy on Adult Learning

Lifelong learning often implies that the learner knows *how* to learn as well as identifies *what* to learn. The ability to identify an information task, locate and access resources, comprehend and evaluate those resources, and manipulate them to accomplish the task comprise the essential elements of information literacy. At one time, these competencies were typically labeled "library skills" or "research process skills" but they now encompass much more than a physical library, incorporate many more formats of information, and address the issues of generating new knowledge as much as verifying and applying existing knowledge. Particularly with the advent of electronic information, information literacy also deals with social learning and responsibility. Technology also makes information literacy more complex so that adult education needs to consider information literacy as an underlying principle of lifelong learning. While information transcends technology, as evidenced when individuals interview experts, technology certainly impacts information literacy.

To jumpstart adult learner knowledge building, adult educators should investigate their current instructional design efforts to identify possible examples of information literacy, which they might not have formally "named" accordingly. By linking learning goals to information literacy standards, adult educators can then identify those skills and resources they need to incorporate into instruction. By blending information literacy into instructional design, adult educators can optimize professional development sessions because adults are not only gaining subject-specific knowledge but they are also gaining lifelong learning skills. A core learning competence is, in effect, updated and expanded into the realm of a community of practice.

Adult education that addresses information literacy tends to focus on assessment, instructional design, and management. Technology can inform this process. Representative activities follow.

1. Assess learner needs and choose appropriate resources to meet those needs
   - Use software and online diagnostic tests
   - Videotape learner performances and analyze them
   - Use a spreadsheet to record and analyze learner performance
   - Read reviews of resources
   - Locate and develop rubrics
2. Develop and implement learning activities that meet learner needs
   - Locate and develop self-paced tutorials
   - Locate and develop documents and directions
   - Develop presentation templates
   - Schedule an educational videoconference
   - Plan a field trip
3. Manage the learning environment
   - Include social breaks for learners to process new information
   - Use network supervision software to monitor learner use of computers
   - Create learning stations
   - Produce a class Web site that includes assignments, exemplars, and resources
   - Create a wiki for learners to share information

Specifically during the delivery of adult educational learning opportunities, several activities can be incorporated to foster understanding and practice of information literacy:

- Highlight information literacy standards that are explicitly addressed in learner projects
- Have adults generate concept maps (either manually or with graphic organizer applications) about information literacy before and after a professional development session
- Starting with learner outcomes, identify associated literacies
- Trace the instructional design process and incorporate information literacy accordingly
- Pair adults in two different disciplines to compare information literacy overlap and transference
- Lead a discussion with administrators or supervisors about the impact of information literacy on workplace mission, production outcomes, and employee evaluation. The SCANS report could be referenced.

The Learning Organization

With the advent of the information society has come the concept of the learning society and more specifically the learning organization. In the information age, companies realize the importance of their intellectual capital or assets, and they are couching enterprises within a framework of a learning organization. The enterprise has a vision, identifies the gaps between reality and that vision, and sets about ways to bridge those gaps (Laiken, 2001). Senge (1990) defined learning organizations as:

organizations where people continually expand their capacity to create the results they truly desire, where new and expansive patterns of thinking are nurtured, where collective aspiration is set free, and where people are continually learning to see the whole together (p. 3).

This approach to entrepreneurial practice is particularly important in an information age where both internal and external change is constant. Entities have to keep nimble and flexible in response to changing external environmental factors such as changing clientele demographics, technological advances, economic turns, and political priorities of the moment. Change comes from within the organization as much as from without; for example, the concept of company loyalty is less valued among young workers. Therefore, enterprises need to manage knowledge efficiently so that new employees can get up to speed quickly, and exiting employees can transfer their knowledge to their successors in order for the enterprise as a whole to keep operating smoothly between human resource transitions. Both individual and organizational learning is needed to keep a competitive edge.

The basic tenet of knowledge management holds that organizations have tacit and explicit information, which may be otherwise designated as informal and formal information. To optimize learning, efficient sharing of that information is needed. Tacit information is made explicit through social channels, and explicit information is internalized by newer members of the organization. At the site level, knowledge management helps to acclimate new employees and facilitates consistency within a unit. Typically, this is accomplished through mentoring and the sharing of function-specific documents (Nonaka & Takeuchi, 1995).

The explicit focus on a learning organization transcends these informal and arbitrary practices to provide a predictable and sustainable system of knowledge sharing. Senge (1990) identified five principles within this framework: personal mastery, mental models, shared vision, team learning, and systems thinking. Adult education can play a key role at each stage.

- **Systems thinking** needs to frame adult learning within the organization in order to allocate and manage the necessary resources to support such learning. Especially since organizations are comprised of interdependent functions, those relationships need to be examined as a whole in order to optimize results. For instance, if accounting learns how to track workflow more efficiently using technology, they may find that certain departments are not using their time efficiently and may call them to task – and suggest that they learn more effective ways to conduct business. Adult educators, in this case, probably human resource developers (HRD), need to be informed of this development, and help impacted departments understand the consequences and gain the knowledge needed in order to improve their practice. In collaboration with the affected units and the management, the HRD office needs to calculate the costs and resources needed to provide timely training.
- **Personal mastery** connotes an ongoing process of self-assessment and self-improvement. While individuals can choose to learn or not learn, their attitude and actions impact the overall organization as a whole, particularly if they share their new knowledge. HRD can provide the conditions for learning by announcing learning opportunities within the organization and

beyond, linking learners to experts, locating resources that can provide desired information, documenting the learning effort, and facilitating the public recognition of gained knowledge.

- **Mental models** impact individual and group learning in that they codify the organization's assumptions and expectations. If, for instance, the mental model of *statis* permeates the organization, then learning that leads to innovation will probably not be supported or encouraged. If, on the other hand, a mental model of mutual support and encouragement exists, then shared learning is more likely to blossom. Generally, a corporate attitude of open dialogue and positive problem-solving tend to support the principles of a learning organization. HRD needs to recognize the organization's mental models in order to frame their own work and support. Even in a static organization, if the corporate culture is not too dictatorial, HRD can support individual learning if for no other reason than to enable new employees to gain the knowledge needed to maintain the status quo.
- **Shared vision** offers a touchstone to anchor the learning organization. Adults can determine whether their learning efforts contribute and manifest the vision – or detract from it. Usually, shared vision also demonstrates a commitment to long-range planning and innovation that mark a learning organization. Having a shared vision certainly helps HRD frame their functionality, and enables them determine what resources and service are needed to actualize the shared vision through efficient learning within the organization.
- **Team learning** acknowledges the social aspect of adult education. Individuals want to check their understanding to confirm their learning or make needed changes. More importantly, team learning appreciates the unique skill sets of each person, and builds on those individualities to produce a significant product that no one person could do independently. HRD can help individuals gain expertise in collaboration: building mutual respect and trust, communicating and negotiating effectively, understanding group interaction and dynamics, sharing control, assessing efforts and progress, and making adjustment to optimize results (Greenberg & Baron, 2002).

Knowledge Management

As a vehicle for documenting information, knowledge management has gained attention in adult learning communities. What is the more effective way to gather, organize, and store information in order to optimize its retrieval and use? Traditionally, librarians have served as information managers. In general, librarians have gathered information from outside an organization in order to inform the organization and support organizational learning and operations, although they might well archive internal documents. Knowledge management tends to focus on the information generated *within* the organization, which can run the gamut from policies and manuals to informal memos and personal guide sheets, from architectural blueprints to party snapshots, from Dictaphone tapes to podcasts, from code books to spreadsheet templates. Additionally, knowledge management is likely to use a decentralized model where information could be stored in several physical and virtual spaces. Centralization occurs in the identification, description and classification of the information; a portal is usually developed as a means to link and relate the various informational sources (McElroy, 2006). Librarians can still serve as knowledge managers, although some companies label such experts as chief information officers.

Adult educators are most likely to keep documentation about their own operations and instructional design and training resources. They would benefit from working with librarians to standardize their own documentation practices as well as identify information that could be collected in order to facilitate learning within the organization. Adult educators can also inform librarians about appropriate ways to categorize information to better reflect the organization's operations. By having more effective access to an organization's knowledge base, adult educators can design more accurate and encompassing instruction that will benefit all of the organization's members.

A CASE STUDY OF ADULT LEARNING TO ADVANCE THE INFORMATION SOCIETY

A need exists to increase economic work force capability in the information society, particularly in the fields of mathematics, science, engineering, and technology. Unfortunately, the percentage of students enrolling in mathematics and sciences in higher education is decreasing, partly because students rarely experience the applications of scientific and mathematical knowledge in real life. The problem becomes critical as females and under-served populations are under-represented in associated coursework and careers. Since technology and content standards have been established, mathematics teachers need to provide students with positive role models to help "prime the pipeline" for the future work force.

To address this need, the California State University Long Beach (CSULB) built on their partnership with Cerritos College and the Long Beach Unified School District to develop and administer a federal education grant: Preparing Tomorrow's Teachers to Use Technology (PT3). The consortium's ultimate goal was K-12 student success, including meeting ISTE technology standards, which were dependent on:

- Teacher candidate success, including the California Commission on Teacher Credentialing (CCTC) technology standards, which depended on
- CSULB and CCC faculty infusing technology across the curriculum, which depended on
- CSULB and CCC faculty technology competence and support

To achieve these goals, the PT3 grant had three priorities:

- **Faculty development:** Developing and implementing technology competencies for students and faculty through assessment, adult education, and integrating technology into student-centered classrooms
- **Curriculum development:** Developing coherent cumulative technology infusion throughout basic teacher preparation programs and related undergraduate programs with student benchmarks
- **Infrastructure:** Expanding computer success, supporting communication and planning, and coordination articulation and collaboration among Consortium members.

Particularly since technology has the potential to transform teaching and learning, it demanded a change in the academic culture as well as in best practice. Counterintuitively, change that involves technology requires significant psychological support and increased collaboration. The grant research conducted at California State University Long Beach, examined how technology raise negative responses, and determined how those obstacles could be addressed positively to facilitate technology integration, and incorporating information literacy collaboratively.

Bloom's Affective Domain and the Organization

In the final analysis, the incorporation of technology is about change, not about technology. It's about people and organizational behavior, not machines. While the lack of technology is a barrier to change, the presence of technology does not guarantee change. Most teachers prefer the status quo, and do not want to stray from their comfort zone. Thus, when confronted with technology that is foreign to their experience – or if teachers have had negative encounter with technology – they are not likely to change their behavior.

Bloom's 1964 taxonomy of the affective domain posits five stages:

- **Receiving:** Getting and holding one's attention relative to technology issues
- **Responding:** Active participation and satisfaction in learning about technology
- **Valuing:** Commitment to the underlying value of technology-infused education
- **Organization:** Integration of possibly conflicting values to support technology
- **Value Complex:** Pervasive and consistent incorporation of technology

Typically, each stage needs to be addressed before the next stage can occur. Thus, adult education efforts started by focusing on the initial stage of awareness and receiving. The grant director gave presentations about the project and its benefits. To establish a technology baseline, the director had all College of Education faculty members identify how they used technology presently, and what they wanted to accomplish that could be facilitated through technology. This same approach was used in individual coaching as educational technology coaches worked with individual mathematics teachers. By valuing the present level of technology comfort and willingness to risk change and learn, the coaches helped individuals feel more relaxed and open to developing a trusting relationship with the coach. The math teachers also felt that they could control their learning focus and pacing.

At this point, the grant director and coaches worked with the faculty to identify areas *in student achievement* that demanded attention. Perhaps more communication with students was needed. Maybe students had a hard time understanding a mathematical concept – or how to teach it to K-12 students. Where might technology provide a solution? By showing a simple use of email as an ersatz threaded discussion or sharing appropriate interactive Web sites, coaches provided a non-threatening technology tool that teachers could use immediately to help their own students succeed academically. This focus on student work helped faculty advance to the next stage in Bloom's affective domain: responding.

Because math teachers were then motivated to engage in activities that incorporated technology to improve student learning, they were open to using electronic resources such as graphing calculators, software programs such as Geometry Sketchpad, and Internet web sites. They also saw the use of tools-based workshops to learn courseware and spreadsheets, for instance. They also appreciated demonstrations given by other mathematics teachers who learned how to leverage a technology tool to help students learn. Of particular value have been web-support systems such as the Apple Learning Interchange (http://ali.apple.com), where streaming video clips of technology-enhanced mathematical instruction provided realistic models for pre-service teachers. The California Learning Resource Network (http://www.clrn.org) also provided valuable information: online state math content standards, evaluations of technological resources in K-12 mathematics, and a lesson builder template – and peer-reviewed lessons – that incorporated technology.

By this point, faculty began to value technology (Bloom's third stage within the affective domain), and sought ways to manage their learning and technology incorporation. To insure that faculty controlled their own technology development, the PT3 project offered mini-grants to individuals who had concrete plans to improve their curriculum through technology integration. Grantees received individual coaching and a $1000 stipend or equivalent amount of technology resources (i.e., software, mathematics manipulatives) to facilitate course review and implementation of technology enhancements. Typically, math teachers focused on courseware and faculty web site development. They also examined electronic resources to help teach math concepts. They were also encouraged to share their experiences with their colleagues. It should be noted that most teachers started with technology that helped their own teaching; afterwards, they could feel more relaxed about using technology as a learning tool with their students. They also valued developing a concrete *product* as a means to demonstrate authentic results. Throughout the process, the emphasis was on close transfer of learning, not generic technology tools but math-specific applications. Technology coaches had to show that they knew mathematics as well as technology in order to gain credibility with their mentees. As in the earlier stage, the intended goal was student learning, so participating faculty had their students self-assess their own technology competence through a state-wide online assessment tool (http://ctap2.iassessment.org). Faculty could use pre-test results to help diagnose student needs and craft instruction accordingly. Post-tests helped demonstrate their own effectiveness in instructional design and delivery as well as student learning over the semester.

These efforts led to the next stage in Bloom's taxonomy: organization. It also signaled readiness for collaborative learning. Second-year mini-grants required at least two math teachers and aimed for program-wide curriculum review and modification. Typical projects included programmatic Web sites, rubrics, e-portfolio development, and streaming video instruction, all of which fostered consistent teaching and assessment.

Serendipitously, the university began a BeachBoard (BlackBoard-based courseware managed system) Users Group, which has been attended by math faculty. This effort facilitated the top stage in Bloom's taxonomy: value complex. By the end of the second year, the college's teacher credential programs needed to revise their curriculum to meet new state standards. In the process, technology could be woven in naturally. Faculty also sought outside funding to sustain their technology efforts, which again demonstrated their long-term commitment to technology infusion.

Findings

This complex approach to technology incorporation into mathematics instruction through adult education mirrors the complexity of changing attitudes.

Researching one specific technology tool, teacher-preparation faculty use of the university's course management system, BeachBoard (based on BlackBoard), the grant director noted the following adult learning benefits:

- Increased frequency and quality of out-of-class, student-to-student dialogue (e.g., collaboration on assignments and projects; peer review of work, etc.) via email, online 'chat' and discussion group facilities
- Increased opportunity for faculty-student communication through individual and group email
- Ability of instructors to evaluate efficiently the quality of student work by means of online quizzes and exams and to monitor student effort and engagement in the subject matter on a more frequent and regular through the use of online discussion groups
- Mutual reinforcement of out-of-class and in-class student interaction;
- Increased student confidence in their ability to use facilities such as email, chat rooms, discussion boards

Overall, the following adult education strategies were derived from successful efforts to improve teacher technology competency and incorporation that would impact K-12 student learning.

- Start with the volunteers
- Aim for a critical mass and then push for inclusion
- Base first steps on existing structures and programs
- Use feasible, available low-end technology
- Focus on relationships
- Do personal coaching, and then buddy up
- Be responsive; empower faculty to shape their own development
- Have faculty share their successes
- Give incentives and recognitions

In sum, faculty learning and technology incorporation were needed to provide a seamless articulation of technology-rich learning so K-12 students would be successful. This shared vision was a deeply-felt value that underlied the effort to change attitudes toward technology and gain technical expertise. By addressing such belief systems in training adults, learning coordinators and curriculum leaders modelled and facilitated deep mathematical learning.

FUTURE TRENDS

While changing issues mark the information society, three significant emerging trends are worth investigating because of their potential impact on adult learning: equity, culturally-sensitive information, and information cross-fertilization.

Equity of Access

Equity has been a long-standing issue in adult education. If people are unaware of educational opportunities or have limited access to such opportunities, then they cannot benefit from such adult education. Now the stakes are higher in an information society where timely and efficient access to information can determine one's earning power as well as their physical health.

When technology first entered the adult education "door," a Digital Divide blocked that doorway. As noted previously, lower-income adults could not afford the technology, and non-English readers had difficulty comprehending the largely textual Internet. Now the prices for technology have dropped, English now constitutes only a third of text languages (and translation programs are improving in quality), and web-based information incorporates images and sound. Smart phones and other mobile devices offer a comparably low-cost mechanism potentially to enable people around the world to access information to support adult learning.

Nevertheless, access issues remain. The principles of adult education that support self-determined adult learning still threaten the social norms of some cultures. Several governments have tight controls on Internet access, and block websites that might contradict or discount those governmental values. Economic and political instability and crisis also impact access to and sustainability of adult education.

Even with physical access to information, its surfeit can actually compound the difficulty adults have in locating and evaluating the usefulness of resources and opportunities for their professional and personal development. Especially if adults lack background knowledge about information, they are less likely to comprehend and make use of that information. As people move between cultures, they are less apt to know the cultural context of information, which then hampers their learning.

Thus, adult educators need to continue to address the equitable physical and intellectual access to information. The former probably needs to involve government entities, particularly in terms of infrastructure. The latter reinforces the need for explicit information literacy instruction.

Culturally-Sensitive Information

Paradoxically to the trend of globalization, the nature of information has become more culturally-sensitive. Information by its nature gains meaning through context; it does not exist separately from its social environment. Historically, information was transferred from one generation to another in order to maintain and sustain society; learning was a matter of internalizing and duplicating existing knowledge. When people encountered a different culture, they had to learn that culture's information in order to survive (McElroy, 2002).

With the move to globalization in the workplace, the cultural framework of information is the organization itself. The organization's employees have to learn and internalize the corporate culture. When the organizational culture contradicts the daily societal culture, employees have to confront those differences and decide how to resolve them: accepting one culture and rejecting another, or reconciling the differences. Additionally, in international companies, their employees also encounter the societal cultures of one another, which forces still another round of negotiation of meaning and possible consequences. As a survival technique, some employees may compartmentalize their private culture and their workplace culture, interacting with their professional colleagues only within the corporate culture. Unfortunately, that approach leads to shallower relationships and less authentic learning, which lessens the benefits of a learning community (McMahon & Bruce, 2002).

As a result, adult education has to incorporate cultural training in order to be aware of the cultural connotations of information, understand and respect those cultural differences, and leverage those unique culturally-sensitive characteristics of information to create deeper and more nuanced knowledge.

Information Cross-Fertilization

Technology, transportation, and globalization have also led to more cross-fertilization of adult learning. International organizations have existed for centuries as adults have reached out to other like-minded individuals around the globe. Indeed, institutions such as the Catholic Church influenced governments significantly in the Middle Ages, providing a consistent set of values and accepted norms of behavior across ethnicities in the face of political instability.

With the rapid pace of information and consequential change, adults need to constantly learn in order to maintain their professional "edge." Those individuals working in relative isolation, particularly in highly-specialized professions, may have difficulty keeping current. While journals publish new research and practice, they may lag in timeliness, and they provide only passive connectedness for the reader. Fortunately, with today's instant telecommunications, international organizations and other entities have risen in number, and can significantly impact adult learning. Web-based communities of practice can exist anywhere, crossing national borders almost seamlessly.

A variety of communication methods facilitate collaborative adult learning. Digitized documents can be quickly created, stored, accessed and retrieved in remote servers. Adults can email, instant message, and phone one another at any time via the Internet. For group synchronous interaction, adults can use chat rooms, webcasting, and video conferencing. In short, a number of technology-based tools enable adults to experience learning communities and apply the latest research, even if each person is the sole expert at his or her workplace.

Adult educators should comprise part of those borderless organizations to optimize learning. They can design the conditions for learning by helping those organizations conduct needs assessments, define appropriate learning goals, locate or develop relevant learning resources, design activi-

Table 1.

Element	Adult Learners	Information	Adult Educator Facilitation
Pre-engagement:	Background, knowledge, capabilities, situation	What are its characteristics? What are the characteristics of the environment in general and at that moment?	Knowledge, role, situation
Origin of Need:	Personal, professional	Producer wants to influence or gain power	Standards, Needs assessment
Task determinator:	Self-determined or other-determined (e.g., employer)	Format parameters	Instructional design
First contact:	Attention (may choose to ignore it)	Physical access issues (equipment, availability)	Introduction
Comprehension/ Intellectual Access:	Decoding (e.g., visuals, sound, linguistics, language); Understanding content (e.g., vocabulary, semiotics, concepts, context)	Layout, cues to understanding, glossary, dual coding	Language instruction; oral reading; simplification; deconstruction; contextualization
Evaluation:	Agreement/ rejection/ incorporation of ideas (based on cognitive, affective, behavioral); Determination of use; Task or need change	Comparative information; peer review	Criteria lists, rubrics; critical thinking / information literacy skills instruction
Manipulation of Information:	Interpretation; Organization; Synthesis; Re-Formatting; Changing; Relating or Combining with other information	Characteristics of information and its representation; malleability	Analytical and manipulation skills instruction; Provision of tools
Application/ Use:	Problem-solving; Learning; Self/ group change; Adding to knowledge base	Generation of new information; Change in environment; Change in power	Assessment; Providing venue for implementation; Knowledge management

(adapted from Farmer, *Librarians, Literacy and the Promotion of Gender Equity.* McFarland, 2005, p. 166)

ties that optimize learning and application, and assess efforts. Adult educators also appreciate the context of learning, and can help adults negotiate change within their workplace and daily life.

CONCLUSION

The information society is only as strong as the information generated within it – and the extent to which that information is used to contribute to society. As change permeates society, adult learners constantly encounter new information occur throughout their public and private lives. Each time they have to decide how to handle this information, which can be stressful and complex.

Adult learning must also change with the times, leveraging technology and social trends to provide meaningful learning opportunities that address global, cultural, and individual information needs. Information literacy offers one way to provide a series of processes that can help deal with information and facilitate lifelong learning. At the very least, adult education needs to leverage its principles of participatory learning to include effective ways that learners can participate in instructional design. The social aspects of adult learning also resonate in today's information society, so adult educators should serve as vanguards in fostering and optimizing adult learning communities.

Adult educators have more physical and intellectual tools than ever to insure that *all* adults have equitable access to quality adult education so that each person can choose what to learn, when to learn, and how to learn. Both individualized and collaborative learning is possible more than ever, and systematic approaches to adult learning can optimize impact. Together, adult learners can contribute to and take advantage of the information society.

The following chart (Table 1) provides a conceptual model to visualize how adults interact with information, and show how adult educators can facilitate learning in an information society.

REFERENCES

Bangkok, U. N. E. S. C. O. (n.d.). Information Literacy. *Communication and Information.* Retrieved March 15, 2009, from http://www.unescobkk.org/index.php?id=1897

Benamati, J., & Lederer, A. (2001). Rapid information technology change, coping mechanisms, and the emerging technologies group. *Journal of Management Information Systems, 17*(4), 183–202.

Bloom, B., Mesia, B., & Krathwohl, D. (1964). *Taxonomy of educational objectives.* New York: David McKay.

Coiro, J., Klein, R., & Walpole, S. (2006). Critically evaluating educational technologies for literacy learning: Current trends and new paradigms. In M. McKenna, L. Lobbo, R. Kieffer, & D. Reinking (Eds.), *International handbook of literacy and technology* (pp. 145-162). New York: Routledge.

Daniel, G. (2007, October 9). Elearning in K-12 education. *WWWtools for Education.* Retrieved May 14, 2009, from http://www.getmail.com.au/wwwtools/viewpage.aspx?rid=37767

Daniel, G. (2007, September). Elearning trends in K-12 education. *WWWtools for Education.* Retrieved March 15, 2009, from http://www.getmail.com.au/wwwtools/viewpage.aspx?rid=37767

Drago, V. (2009). *How generations view the mobile Internet.* Boston: Forrester Research. Retrieved March 15, 2009, from http://www.forrester.com/Research/Document/Excerpt/0,7211,47296,00.html

Farmer, L. (2005). *Librarians, literacy and the promotion of gender equity.* Jefferson, NC: McFarland.

Field, J. (2006). *Lifelong learning and the new educational order.* Sterling, VA: Trentham Books.

Fitzgerald, R., Taylor, R., & La Valle, I. (2003). *National Adult Learning Survey (NALS) 2002.* Nottingham, UK: Department for Education and Skills.

Friedman, T. (2006). *The world is flat* (updated and expanded). New York: Farrar, Straus and Giroux. *G-7 Ministerial Conference on the Information Society: Cooperation on applications and testbeds.* (1995, January 12). Brussels. Retrieved March 15, 2009, from www.ifla.org/documents/infopol/intl/g7/g7-113qa.txt

Garner, S. (2005). *High-level colloquium on information literacy and lifelong learning.* Alexandria, Egypt: International Federal of Library Associations.

Greenberg, J., & Baron, R. (2002). *Behavior in organizations* (10th ed.). Englewood Cliffs, NJ: Prentice Hall.

Istance, D., Schuetze, H., & Schuller, T. (Eds.). (2002). *International perspectives on lifelong learning: Form recurrent education to the knowledge society.* Berkshire, UK: Open University Press.

JISC & SCONUL. (2008). *Library Management Systems Study.* Sheffield, UK: Sero Consulting.

Laiken, M. (2001). *Models of organizational learning: Paradoxes and best practices in the post industrial workplace.* Toronto: University of Toronto.

Li, C. (2007). *How consumers use social networks.* Boston: Forrester Research. Retrieved March 15, 2009, from http://www.forrester.com/Research/Document/Excerpt/0,7211,41626,00.html

Livingstone, D. (2001). *Adults' information learning: Definitions, findings, gaps and future research.* Toronto: University of Toronto Centre for the Study of Education and Work.

Maness, J. (2006). Library 2.0 theory: Web 2.0 and its implications for libraries. *Webology, 3*(2).

McElroy, M. (2006). *The new knowledge management: Complexity, learning and sustainable innovation.* Boston: Elsevier Science.

McMahon, C., & Bruce, C. (2002). Information literacy needs of local staff in cross-cultural development projects. *Journal of International Development, 14*(1), 113–127. doi:10.1002/jid.864

Nonaka, I., & Takeuchi, H. (1995). *The knowledge creating company.* Cambridge, MA: Oxford University Press.

Rosen, R., et al. (2000). *Global literacies.* New York: Simon and Schuster.

Rutenbeck, J. (2000). The 5 great challenges of the digital age. *Netconnet,* (Fall), 30-33.

Selwyn, N., Gorard, S., & Forlong, J. (2006). *Adult learning in the digital age: Information technology and the learning society.* New York: Routledge.

Senge, P. (1990). *The fifth discipline: The art and practice of the learning organization.* New York: Doubleday.

Spira, J., & Fientuch, J. (2005). *The cost of not paying attention: How interruptions impact knowledge worker productivity.* New York: Basex.

United Nations. (2003). *Declaration of principles. Building the information society: A global challenge in the new millennium.* The Hague: United Nations.

United Nations. (2006). *World information society report.* Paris: United Nations.

United States Department of Education. (2004). *Toward a golden age in American education.* Washington, DC: U. S. Department of Education. Retrieved May 14, 2009, from http://www.ed.gov/about/offices/os/technology/plan/2004/index.html

United States Department of Labor. (1991). *Secretary's Commission on Achieving Necessary Skills (SCANS).* Washington, DC: Government Printing Office.

Webster, F. (2002). *Theories of the information society,* (2nd ed.). London: Routledge.

Westat, K., & Creighton, S. (2000). *Participation in adult education in the United States: 1998-1999.* Washington, DC: U. S. Department of Education.

Wilhelm, A. (2004). *Digital nation: Toward an inclusive information society.* Cambridge, MA: MIT Press.

Chapter 6 Teaching Adult Learners in Online Career and Technical Education

Victor M. Hernández-Gantes
University of South Florida, USA

ABSTRACT

Online education is becoming an important component of career and technical education (CTE) in teacher preparation and at the graduate level. In the midst of such growth, and in response to questions about quality compared with traditional learning, there is a consensus that online courses and programs should be designed based on the needs of adult learners. However, much of the literature in online CTE lacks implicit connections to emerging notions of adult development and learning. This article provides an overview of the status of online education in CTE at the postsecondary level, discusses related issues and current research focus, and highlights adult learning developments and the implications for curriculum design, instruction, and use of technology. The article concludes with an outline of emerging trends bridging adult learning and online education relevant to career and technical education.

INTRODUCTION

Online education enrollments in higher education over the past decade are revealing. The online instructional delivery system is no longer an afterthought for postsecondary institutions as students are enrolling in related programs at higher rates compared to enrollments in traditional education. Practically all institutions of higher education now offer online education opportunities to meet the demand from students seeking alternatives to traditional on campus instruction (Allen & Seaman, 2008). Career and technical education (CTE) is no exception to this trend as the field has experienced similar growth at the undergraduate and graduate education level including doctoral programs (Flowers & Baltzer, 2006b; Havice & Havice, 2005). However, as online education continues to grow, there are lingering concerns about the quality of curriculum and instruction, student experiences, and use of technology (Hernandez, Kirby, & McGee, 2004; Flowers, 2001; Kim & Bonk, 2006).

Furthermore, although the adult population is the target audience for CTE in teacher preparation and graduate degree programs, there is limited literature examining the connections to adult development and learning principles. Much of the literature focuses on demand for online education, related curriculum and program development, and perceptions about quality and barriers and opportunities for adoption (Flowers, 2005; Flowers & Baltzer, 2006b; Schmidt & Gallegos, 2001). As such, there is a need for an examination of adult learning principles in the context of online education and the implications for curriculum development, teaching, and use of technology. To this end, the objectives of this article are to: First, review the status of online education with an emphasis in career and technical education and related issues for adoption; second, highlight adult learning developments with potential to inform curriculum design and instruction; third, outline implications on the use of instructional technology; and fourth, point out emerging trends bridging adult learning and online education relevant to CTE efforts in this area.

BACKGROUND

Online education is often used interchangeable with other terms such as distance education, virtual learning, Web-based learning, distributed learning and other variations associated with teaching and learning whereby instructors and students are not interacting in the same location in real time. In this context, distance education represents a larger umbrella including a wide array of formal and informal strategies bridging physical separation between instructors and students (King, 2008). In turn, online education represents a formal asynchronous instructional system offered by educational institutions through courses and entire programs. Online education is characterized by the use of communication networks building upon varying combinations of online technology such as the Internet, electronic libraries, Web-based conferencing, virtual discussions, and e-mail communication. Typically, the delivery of online education is organized through a Web-based management system (e.g., Blackboard, WebCT) with many variations in delivery and support services depending on institutional resources and the nature of individual courses (e.g., size of student enrollment) (Aragon, 2003; Conrad, 2008; Paloff & Pratt, 2001).

Formal online education opportunities for adults are offered in higher education, often referred to as post-secondary or tertiary education, and may be available in formal and informal settings after high school. Although the term "higher education" is often associated with universities and colleges, it is in fact a broader term including formal programs leading to credentialing at community colleges as well as baccalaureate and graduate degrees granted by private and public universities (Clark, 1983). Similarly, while career and technical education (CTE) is often associated with programs at the secondary education level, it is also a prominent component of higher education. At the post-secondary level, CTE contributes with programs and services designed to help adult students promote their career development and transition into specific occupations or further education. Informal programs are also available in community and corporate settings for technical training and re-training purposes. Teacher preparation programs and opportunities for professional advancement through master's degrees and doctoral programs are available at universities, while technical preparation and entry-level occupational credentialing are offered at two-year colleges (Athanasou, 2008; Hernández-Gantes & Blank,

2009; Johnson & Benson, 2003). Thus, the focus of this article is on reviewing issues relevant to teaching adult learners in online CTE programs in higher education.

CURRENT ISSUES AND RESEARCH FOCUS

As online education continues to grow, it is important to review online learning trends and issues related to adoption in CTE, bridging adult learning developments with curriculum design and instruction, and implications for using instructional technology.

Online Education Growth

The formal beginnings of distance education date back to the late 1800s, born out of the necessity to overcome geographical distances and provide educational access to rural students (Banas & Emory, 1998). Initially rooted in programmed instruction through correspondence courses, distance education experienced a booming renewal with the advent of computers and the Internet. Today, while correspondence methods still remain in use, contemporary distance education has shifted to more extensive use of instructional technology to develop and deliver courses and programs in a variety of formats from text to virtual interactive activities (Johnson & Benson, 2003). In the past two decades, the development of related instructional technologies has been dramatic and the demand for distance learning has consistently increased during this period as people seek flexible learning opportunities (Allen & Seaman, 2008; Havice & Havice, 2005; National Center for Education Statistics, 2000). Under the umbrella of distance education, online learning emerged based on the prominent use of computer technologies and the Internet. As such, online education is also referred to electronic learning (or e-learning), Web-based instruction, and virtual learning. At the core of online education is the fact that students can have access to instructional resources anytime, anywhere, and engage with the material at their convenience (Conrad, 2008; Lorenzetti, 2003). These underlying features of "online" learning have appealed to young and older adults seeking professional advancement through flexible educational opportunities in higher education, CTE included (Flowers, 2005; National Center for Education Statistics, 2002).

In general, compared to student enrollment in traditional programs, online student enrollments have continued to grow substantially in recent years. The sixth report of the Sloan Consortium on the status of online learning in higher education indicated that about 20% of all higher education students were enrolled in at least one online course in the fall of 2006. This figure represents over a 12% increase compared to 1.2% increase in the overall higher education student population (Allen & Seaman, 2008). This dramatic growth has been well documented also noting the increase in the number of programs offered by postsecondary institutions with growth as high as 70% in a single year reported in the 1990s (National Center for Education Statistics, 2000). Although the growth in higher education, as a whole, has been steady, 2-year colleges have shown greater growth rates in online education compared to baccalaureate institutions. Overall, the demand for online education is expected to continue growing, though at a less dramatic pace, as current efforts are expanded and new institutions respond to related demand (Allen & Seaman, 2008).

Although comprehensive data is not available to gauge the full extent of enrollments in CTE, there is emerging evidence of growth mirroring that of national trends (Flowers, 2005; Johnson & Benson, 2003). Community colleges have shown an increase in enrollments due to the expansion of distance learning programs in various occupational areas (Johnson & Benson, 2003). Similar growth has been reported in the broader field of career and technical education including teacher preparation programs and in graduate education including doctoral level programs (Baltzer, Lazaros, & Flowers, 2007; Flowers, 2005; Flowers & Baltzer, 2006a, 2006b). In general, it has been reported that at the master's degree level, face-to-face enrollments have tended to decrease as new online courses have begun to attract many more students (Blank & Hernandez, 2008; Flowers, 2005). In turn, at the doctoral level, online courses are available and entire programs may become available in the future. At this time about a third of doctoral programs in the field have indicated the possibility of evolving into online models or are already in their way to do so (Baltzer et al., 2007; Blank & Hernandez, 2008; Flowers & Baltzer, 2006b).

The demand for online education has been fueled by individuals seeking professional advancement who are most likely to be married, have dependents, and are employed full-time. These students are also most likely to seek flexible programs on a part-time basis (National Center for Education Statistics, 2002). For such students the flexibility of online education is the only way to earn a degree as they factor in issues of time, physical location, family, and work demands. These trends are also reported in graduate programs in CTE (see Blank & Hernandez, 2008; Flowers, 2005).

Lingering Issues

As online learning continues to grow at all levels in higher education, CTE included, there are still some lingering issues about overall quality, instructor-related factors, use of technology, and nature of online learning experiences compared to traditional education (Kim & Bonk, 2006). The first issue persistently cited in the literature is the perception that online education, compared to traditional instruction, is of inferior quality. This perception ranges from traditional views on education regarding classroom instruction as the only appropriate setting for teaching and learning, to legitimate questions about the quality of online instructional approaches (Baltzer et al., 2007; Bower, 2001). In CTE such perceptions have elicited a warning to program graduates about how potential employers may perceive a degree earned primarily online (Flowers & Baltzer, 2006b). In some cases such concerns may be reinforced by the limited evidence of online student performance compared to counterparts in equivalent traditional courses (Ryan, 2000). To be sure, there is positive evidence of impact on higher engagement and motivation, increased collaboration, and extended access to students who may have not otherwise enrolled or completed a program of study. Some reports have indicated that student performance is relatively equivalent when comparing technology-mediated and classroom instruction, although the nature of related research has raised questions about the generalizations of the findings (Johnson & Benson, 2003; Kim & Bonk, 2006; Phipps & Merisotis, 1999; Ryan, 2000; Zirkle, 2002).

Albeit the inconclusiveness of available data, emerging evidence appears to suggest that the general quality of online education is really a secondary issue. What matters is the quality of specific instructional strategies and materials, much like in traditional education, pointing to design and development issues (Stilborne & Williams, 1996). During the rush to join the bandwagon of online education, there has been widespread variability in the quality of courses and programs available online. The pressure to develop courses and programs in a short period of time regardless of the unique design and development requirements may contribute to the varying quality of online courses as well (Aragon, 2003; Zirkle, 2002). To ensure quality of online courses, participating instructors need sufficient time for design and development of online courses and programs, and sometimes such accommodations are not in place (Lorenzetti, 2003). This, in turn, brings instructor-related factors into the discussion as institutions ask faculty to convert courses online even though they may not be well prepared or—worse yet—may not believe in the value of online education to participate effectively in related efforts (Flowers & Baltzer, 2006a). Since every institution is bound to have instructors resisting participation in online education for related reasons, resentment and low morale are often the results of forced participation. This situation has prompted calls to rethink faculty supports and reassess how to consider participation in online instructional efforts for tenure and promotion evaluations given the unique demands of such work (Baltzer et al., 2007; Bower, 2001; Hernandez et al., 2004; Flowers, 2005).

Another issue stemming perhaps from the push to put courses online, compounded by concerns about appropriate instructors' preparation, is reliance on design and development strategies building upon sets of documents, lectures, and PowerPoint presentations void of interactive or meaningful connecting activities (Bower, 2001; Stilborne & Williams, 1996). At the other extreme are courses featuring all the "bells and whistles" of technology without regard to practical and pedagogical considerations. In both cases, the limited use of technology in the former case and the over-use in the latter case, the facilitation of learning may be hindered in the absence of explicit pedagogical connections and further complicated by technology compatibility issues or distracting technical glitches (Palloff & Pratt, 2001; Partlow & Gibbs, 2003). At the core of this issue is the tendency to focus more on the selection and management of resources and use of technology to teach online, rather than the actual design of instructional strategies appropriate for online delivery (Flowers, 2005). Thus, another lingering issue has been the challenge to facilitate productive interactions among students and between students and instructors. Traditional instructors have argued that such interactions, often taken for granted in the traditional classroom, are difficult to reproduce in an online environment. Critics are also quick to note that students may be left wandering in online courses under the so-called premises of self-paced learning (Kirschner, Sweller, & Clark, 2006; Rovai, 2001; Schmidt & Gallegos, 2001).

Research Focus in Online CTE

In the midst of the steady growth of online education and the lingering issues noted above, available research in CTE has been limited in relation to the general body of knowledge in other fields (Zirkle, 2002). Much of the research focus in CTE contexts has been on descriptive studies of institutional efforts to promote and develop online programs. This includes studies on barriers for placing programs online, instructor-related research looking into issues of participation in design and implementation efforts, and assessments of student satisfaction in higher education programs at both undergraduate and graduate level (Flowers, 2005; Sloan-C, 2009; Zirkle, 2002). As such, some researchers have suggested it is time to shift from an emphasis on institutional factors and online course development and management to the study of pedagogical strategies and student experiences that maximize online learning. As online education continues to grow in CTE, the quality of online pedagogical strategies appropriate to adult learners in higher education is a critical issue that needs to be addressed. While, there is evidence dispelling the perceived lack of interactions in online education as well as questions about self-regulated learning (Kirschner et al., 2006; Rovai, 2001; Schmidt & Gallegos, 2001), researchers agreed that it is imperative to study new ways of designing learning experiences that are appropriate for online delivery (Aragon, 2003; Flowers, 2001; Hirumi, 2002).

Another important component of the suggested shift in research focus is the apparent void in the literature bridging adult education principles and online learning. While there is research exploring the connections between adult learning principles and online pedagogical strategies stemming from adult education, related literature and focus has yet to be integrated into parallel lines of research in CTE contexts. The bulk of the literature in online CTE contexts does not make explicit connections to adult education principles, which appears to be taken for granted. For the most part, current literature reflects an emphasis on the management of learning experiences and mediation of delivery through technology (Flowers, 2001, 2005; Zirkle, 2002).

BRIDGING ADULT LEARNING AND ONLINE CTE

Promising theoretical conceptions of how people learn including transformative learning, contextual teaching and learning principles and holistic views on adult development and learning have emerged over the past decade (Hoare, 2006; Merriam, 2001b, 2008). The challenge for instructors is to bridge emerging theoretical conceptions of adult teaching and learning and online instructional environments. A brief description of recent developments in adult learning is presented in this section along with implications for curriculum design and development, instructional strategies, and use of technology with potential to inform online CTE.

Emerging Developments in Adult Learning Theory

Historically, adult development and learning have coexisted as separate, albeit complementary, fields of study. The development dimension has been typically treated under the field of psychology, while learning has been usually addressed in educational research (Hoare, 2006). This artificial divide may stem from the traditional view of adult development as progressive age stages, which in turn is associated with the development of experience (i.e., ways of knowing). Under this worldview to understanding how adults develop and learn, andragogy has been a prominent learning theory used in adult education based on the premise of stages of development and noting the unique characteristics of adults compared to children (Knowles, 1980; Merriam, 2001a). Over the past two decades, however, emerging developments in related theoretical and practical teaching and learning conceptions have noted the inclusive interface of adult development and learning (Hoare, 2006; Merriam, 2008). Building upon notions of how people learn, it is becoming clear the relationship between adult development and learning must be understood and taken into consideration when designing teaching and learning strategies. To this end, contextual learning, self-directed learning, and transformational learning have been consistently highlighted in adult education as promising conceptions of teaching and learning with potential to inform online curriculum development and instruction (Partlow & Gibbs, 2003; Roschelle, 1999; Taylor, 2007).

Andragogy as an Initial Frame of Reference

Andragogy is a theory of adult education advocating a learner-centered approach to teaching introduced in the 1970s underlined by five major premises. At the core of the andragogy is the idea of adult learners as mature individuals with a clear identity of who they are and capable of self-regulated learning (Knowles, 1980; Merriam, 2001a). The premise is that adults have moved from a younger stage of development where extrinsic motivation and guided learning were the norm. The challenge for instructors is to promote autonomous learning while recognizing individual differences and stages of development (Cercone, 2008; Cooper & Henschke, 2003; Knowles, 1980). Another important premise is the role of prior knowledge in adult learning suggesting that students learn best when they are provided the opportunity to build on what they know and can do (Fidishun, 2000). Andragogy also relies on the premise that adults are more likely to be goal oriented and will perform better when content relevancy is high and clearly aligned with personal goals. In this case, the instructor's goal should be to ensure relevant meaning and connections between new concepts and students' frame of reference (Cercone, 2008; Merriam, 2001a). Further, andragogy assumes that adult learners will respond better to instruction that is designed to provide practical applications as a means to reinforce the above premises (Fidishun, 2000; Knowles, 1980). Finally, intrinsic motivation to learn is recognized as the driving force in adults who will respond better when they feel their individual needs are met and it is safe to participate in group discourse and collaborate with others (Cercone, 2008; Taylor, King, Pinsent-Johnson, & Lothian, 2003).

Although useful in many ways, some researchers argued that the premises underlying andragogy represent a model for teaching adults rather than a theory (Hoare, 2006; Merriam, 2001a). A key limitation of andragogy is that it overlooks the role of the learning context and the interface with background variables such as culture, gender, and experience beyond the mere fact of being classified as an adult. Thus, it does not consider multiple ways of knowing and learning and the important role for critical reflection as part of the adult learning process (Taylor, 2007; Tsao, Takahasi, Olusesu, & Jain, 2006). With all its limitations, andragogy clearly defined what makes adult learners different and served as the root for useful concepts such as student-centered learning, prior learning, and content relevancy as factors that matter for adult learners (Cooper & Henschke, 2003; Fidishun, 2000; Merriam, 2001a). In this context, and building upon such concepts, emerging literature in adult development and learning suggests promising implications of constructivist strategies for teaching and learning in online environments.

Rethinking Adult Development and Learning

Recognizing the complexity of adult learning, everyone agrees that there is no such thing as a comprehensive adult learning theory that can be applied to all learning situations (Hoare, 2006, Merriam, 2008; Taylor, 2007). Thus, constructivist theoretical conceptions have received greater attention in recent years given their emphasis on both the learners' characteristics and their worldviews facilitated through contextual and self-regulated instructional strategies. Experiential learning, contextual teaching and learning, self-regulated learning, and transformational learning appear to carry promising implications for online adult learning (Cercone, 2008; Merriam, 2008). For instance, experiential learning suggests that when teaching adults, learning is a product of meaningful connections between new concepts and what the learners already know (i.e., experience) (Itin, 1999). Thus, experiential learning emphasizes clear identification of new knowledge and information, connections to relevant prior knowledge, and critical analysis of learning experiences. In turn, contextual teaching and learning stems from the body of knowledge on the role of context as a meaning-making factor in the learning process. When learners engage in activities featuring real-world situations they can relate to by virtue of their prior knowledge and experience, culture, and other personal and professional variables, expertise is reinforced and further developed (Bransford, Brown, & Cocking, 2000; Itin, 1999; Kolb, 1984). Consequently, contextual teaching and learning emphasizes teaching for understanding through relevant tasks requiring active learning (Bransford et al., 2000, Hernández-Gantes & Blank, 2009; Perkins, 1993).

Self-directed learning has also emerged as another important theoretical concept when teaching adult learners. At the root of this concept is the idea that learning should be intrinsically motivated and as such, adult learners should take responsibility for their own learning although some may require different levels of external assistance (Merriam, 2008; Taylor, 2006). Self-directed learning is typically associated with goal-oriented strategies which in the past had been mostly relegated to informal learning. Today, the concept of self-regulated learning offers promising applications in online learning environments where independent learning is promoted and expected of adult learners. Self-directed learning is at the core of lifelong learning bridging ways of knowing, experience, and intrinsic motivation to learn in adult development (Taylor, 2006). In turn, transformational learning takes learning one step beyond and promotes change in ways of knowing and doing (Hoare, 2006; Tsao et al., 2006). In essence, transformational learning allows adult learners to develop deep understandings through critical analysis as the basis for the generation of their own knowledge (Palloff & Pratt, 2001). Critical reflection underlines transformational learning, especially when learners are confronted with learning experiences requiring unique meaning-making relevant only to them based on their individual frame of reference and goals. As such, transformation learning incorporates elements of constructivist conceptions noted above while reinforcing the notion of learning as personal change (Hoare, 2006; Merriam, 2008).

Based on the surmised highlights of emerging constructivist theoretical strands it is clear that, given their complementary nature and shared premises, it is not possible to identify a "grand theory" of adult learning. However, emerging theoretical concepts may contribute to our understanding of the adult learning process and can inform curriculum design and development, online learning, and related use of technology (Cercone, 2008; Hoare, 2006; Merriam, 2008).

Implications for Curriculum Design and Development

Considering theoretical conceptions of adult learning, it is clear that instructors should gauge the unique needs and goals of adult learners when designing curriculum and instruction. This is even more relevant for design and development efforts in online education (Ausburn, 2004; Cercone, 2008; Partlow & Gibbs, 2003). To this end, the use of andragogy and more recent developments in adult learning can be integrated when teaching with technology. Online education provides flexible access for adult learners and the opportunity to work on instructional materials in a self-directed mode. At issue is the adaptation and organization of instructional content and resources through interactive designs that are learner-centered, contextually relevant, and most likely to promote independent learning. In this context, three approaches are highlighted to illustrate efforts to connect learning principles and online curriculum design and development including the use of Bloom's taxonomy, the "backward design" concept, and online blended learning designs.

Revisiting the Use of Bloom's Taxonomy

A model for online curriculum development commonly used in higher education uses Bloom's Taxonomy as a frame of reference to guide the identification of objectives, content, and learning process. This approach focuses on stages of learning including knowledge, comprehension, application, analysis, synthesis and evaluation. The premise behind the use of Bloom's Taxonomy is that students learn through the mastery of important content, opportunities to demonstrate what they know; allowances to apply concepts and skills through problem-based activities, and the use of reflective strategies to foster deep understandings. As such, this approach may use a blend of direct instruction to promote mastery learning complemented with constructivist strategies to engage students in active learning and critical thinking (Anderson & Krathwohl, 2001).

Some critics, however, argued that Bloom's Taxonomy has become outdated and view its contemporary relevance and application as limited. However, recent adaptations have made the use of Bloom's Taxonomy appealing for today's applications to curriculum development (Anderson & Krathwohl, 2001; Clark, 2002). Such adaptations are now being used at the college level as well, as a means to promote active learning. For example, Puzziferro & Shelton (2008) reported that all online courses at Colorado State University are developed following an adaptation of Bloom's work featuring structures for students to check content knowledge, demonstrate what they know and can do through "mastery" activities as well as through application and analytical tasks including reflection components (e.g., discussion forums). Courses also include capstone projects designed to further reinforce individual relevance and reflection. Similar examples are reported at institutions such as Penn State University's World Campus (Thompson & McGrath, 1999) and Georgia Southern University (Center for Online Learning, 2009) to name a few. The common denominator for using Bloom's work for curriculum development is the desire to align objectives with teaching and learning, and with assessment outcomes.

Backward Design: From Outcomes to Objectives

The "backward design" for curriculum development follows an approach counter to Bloom's suggested objectives-teaching strategies-outcomes sequence. In the backward design, instructors identify assessment outcomes first, think about teaching/learning activities second, and then decide on core objectives. This design approach to curriculum development focuses on three stages including the articulation of student competencies, identification of evidence that demonstrates mastery of competencies, and design of appropriate instructional activities (McTighe & Wiggins, 1999).

Identifying expected student competencies sits at the core of the backward design process and aligns with theoretical principles of adult learning related to making learning relevant (Hoare, 2006; Merriam, 2008). This notion predicates that learners will be more motivated to learn when they know what is expected of them up front. However, rather than emphasizing content coverage through a typical list of expected competencies, backward design requires the identification of essential understandings (or "big ideas") underlying curriculum development. That is, it forces instructors to "chunk" important content into a few identifiable expectations serving as the guide for a course. Stemming from research in cognition and how memory works, the concept of "chunking" has been helpful in explaining how people with different levels of expertise process information (Collins, Brown, & Newman, 1989). Essentially, "chunking" represents a cognitive system comprised of a few "chunks", each carrying a number of related informational items for easier retrieval and "big-picture" understandings when put together (Conlon, 2002; Gobet et al., 2001). Chunking has been at the core of information mapping approaches to help instructors organize large amounts of information into a reduced number of blocks (or chunks) to facilitate learning and quick retrieval of needed information In this regard, chunking has been used in a variety of contexts related to human learning and the underlying mechanism can be applied to online curriculum design and development (Ferry, Hedberg, & Harper, 1998; Hirumi, 2002; Janicki & Liegle, 2001). The implications are clear: appropriate curricular chunks need to be developed to promote expertise and understanding in a given domain.

For instructional design purposes, the chunking of essential understandings allows for the alignment between assessment outcomes (i.e., goals), content, and instructional strategies. Using this idea as the point of departure, the backward design also builds upon the concept of cognitive apprenticeship for teaching and learning suggesting that novice learners can develop progressive expertise through experiential strategies, such as modeling, coaching, and scaffolding (Bransford et al., 2000; Collins et al., 1989), and through reflective activities designed to promote understanding and knowledge production (McTighe & Wiggins, 1999; Perkins, 1993). For online curriculum development these ideas can translate into a reduced but optimal number of units or modules, each addressing essential understandings appealing to adult learners. In turn, instructional strategies may emphasize tutorials to model target skills, feedback for scaffolding purposes, and structures for individual and collective analyses. The key emphasis in the backward design is the promotion of understanding through the use of strategies appropriate for the content and the learner (McTighe & Wiggins, 1999).

Blending the Best of Both Worlds?

Blended education, also referred to as hybrid education, has been used in distance learning for a number of years (Dziuban, Hartman, & Moskal, 2004). The use of the Internet for online delivery has reinforced the notion of blended learning as a viable instructional alternative integrating face-to-face and online activities. In this case, there is a general agreement that blended education typically features 30 to 70% of online delivery in single courses, while the rest is complemented with face-to-face instruction. Courses using online instruction at the lower end (less than 30%) are often referred to as Web-enhanced. Although instructors may opt for a blended design seeking the advantages of traditional and online instruction, such courses are still loosely defined and the optimal balance remains in question (Allen, Seaman, & Garrett, 2007; Dziuban et al., 2004). As a result, the implications for curriculum design and development are also fuzzy.

To be sure, blended designs build upon the benefits of traditional instruction drawing from the socialization factors of face-to-face activities. In turn, this approach may also benefit from active learning, asynchronous collaboration, and independent learning made possible by online activities (Ausburn, 2004). Thus, instructors should think of related design development as opportunities to emphasize constructivist strategies (e.g., experiential, contextual, self-regulated, active learning) as part of the entire course independent of the mode of delivery (Aragon, 2003; Partlow & Gibbs, 2003). The design of blended courses should also allow instructors to maximize the opportunities for productive interactions among students and between the students and the instructor. As the face-to-face component is retained, some instructors feel more comfortable embracing the online component and may use blended courses as the springboard for further involvement in online learning. In fact, some reports have indicated high levels of student and instructor satisfaction and student performance surpassing that of counterparts in traditional and fully online instruction (Allen et al., 2007; Ausburn, 2004). The advantages of blended designs may be attributed to the combined support and interactions shared through the two instructional channels. To this end, the design features of blended courses often emphasize learner-centered strategies featuring active learning and relevant content facilitated reinforce through discussion groups and other forms of electronic interactions (Aragon, 2003; Ausburn, 2004; Rovai, 2001).

Blended instruction can be appealing for instructors and institutions given the perceived higher level of comfort for student and faculty participation. Thus, it is possible to expect the blended design to be a popular approach to online learning. A national survey of online learning reported a slightly higher percentage of blended designs compared to fully online programs across disciplines. In general, the survey also reported that students in higher education were more likely to experience a blended course than a fully online course (Allen et al., 2007). This trend suggests that online education may be undergoing a transformation whereby the divide between face-to-face and online instruction is becoming relatively unimportant. As blended learning continues to evolve, it is clear that, if anything, closer attention must be paid to the use of appropriate curriculum development approaches and delivery mode to ensure the needs of adult learners are met.

Implications for Online Teaching and Learning

The instructors' capacity to teach online is critical for making curriculum design and development work as expected. The starting point is to recognize the unique differences of adult learners compared to traditional college students. For example, adult learners in CTE programs seeking certification or graduate degrees—like in many other higher education programs—have to balance family and full-time work while pursuing further education (Cercone, 2008; Blank & Hernandez, 2008; Flowers & Baltzer, 2006b). As such, this type of adult learners represents a goal-oriented group albeit one requiring special considerations to meet special needs processing information brought about by middle age (Clark, 1999). In this context, as suggested by adult learning principles, online instructors should make a shift from lecture-driven and teacher-centered strategies to constructivist approaches to facilitate, rather than manage learning (Fidishun, 2000; Reynolds, 1997).

To be sure, pedagogical knowledge is considered the top requirement for effective participation in online education followed by technical expertise. Reports on online teaching and learning strategies have consistently suggested the ability to facilitate learning is emerging as one of the most important pedagogical skills for online learning (Hirumi, 2002; Kim & Bonk, 2006). Further, the shift to constructivist instructional strategies is requiring the capacity to promote online collaboration, independent learning, problem-based learning and case-based learning to make instruction relevant, engaging, and meaningful for goal-oriented learners (Kim & Bonk, 2006; Partlow & Gibbs, 2003). This is in direct alignment with student-centered learning rooted in andragogy, experiential learning, contextual instruction, and self-regulated learning (Hoare, 2006; Merriam, 2008).

Project-based learning, problem-based learning, and inquiry-based are concepts often used interchangeable as they share principles rooted in information processing theory and aligned with contextual, experiential, and self-directed learning (Bransford et al., 2000; Kirschner et al., 2006; Roschelle, 1999). These instructional approaches have been found helpful in online environments designed to emphasize rich learning experiences. At the core of these strategies is the idea of posing a problem requiring students to produce their own learning (Hmelo-Silver, 2004). For example, problem-based learning (PBL) is an instructional approach that has been used for several decades and stems from project-based learning advocated by Dewey in the early 1900s (Roschelle, 1999). The purpose of PBL is to allow learners to experience and apply knowledge and skills they are learning. Variations of PBL include task-based learning and project-based learning and are sometimes used interchangeable with PBL. What separates PBL from other approaches is the focus on authentic problem situations for which more than one solution can be justified (Ellis, 2003; Ertmer, Lehman, Park, Cramer, & Grove, 2003; Hmelo-Silver, Duncan, & Chinn, 2007). Thus, PBL can be designed as an independent or group activity that can be easily used as part of online learning. In turn, project-based learning is typically associated with cooperative investigations as a means to keep teams of students on task requiring them to follow their own procedures and produce their own knowledge (Hmelo-Silver, 2004; Miflin, 2004). On the other hand, inquiry-based learning is usually connected to individual work whereby students follow specific discipline-based methods requiring the application of reasoning skills in the completion of research activities (Hmelo-Silver et al., 2007).

Common to these strategies is the use of driving questions to guide the understanding of a problem and the design and completion of an investigation or a project. Further, a shared assumption is that these strategies can be implemented with limited assistance from the instructor based on self-directed notions of learning. In this regard, some researchers argued that these strategies are bound to be ineffective if instructors do not account for the role of cognitive processing requiring timely feedback and scaffolding supports (Hmelo-Silver et al., 2007; Kirschner et al., 2006; Taylor et al., 2003). This is particularly relevant given the fact that even though there is a consensus on the importance of constructivist strategies, the extent of use of related pedagogical practices in online education remains limited and uneven in terms of quality (Kim & Bonk, 2006).

Use of Technology

Given the underlying use of technology in online education, instructors have to understand and consider the role of technology in adult learning. In this regard, instructors face the challenge of developing expertise in using instructional technology and striking the right balance when using it to facilitate online learning. Specifically, instructors have to consider the role and use of technology in curriculum development, delivery systems, and as instructional tools (Havice & Havice, 2005; Hirumi, 2002).

Studies describing online curriculum development efforts have noted that instructors tend to focus initially on the technology tools for online teaching and realize in the process that the primary goal should be related to design factors (Flowers, 2001, 2005). Drawing from constructivist theory advocating the facilitation of active knowledge production, it is then crucial for instructors to think about identifying sets of knowledge structures following an appropriate approach (e.g., backward design). One way to accomplish this is to use technology that allows information mapping (e.g., Inspiration). Information mapping technology does not involve a steep learning curve for instructors and can be used in the selection and development of essential understandings for particular courses (Conlon, 2002; Ferry et al., 1998). Another consideration is the use of online lesson building technology such as SoftChalk, NTeQ, CAST Universal Design for Learning, and other commercially available programs and services. These online curriculum builders ease the learning curve for instructors as they typically rely on intuitive interfaces involving the use of word-processing platforms and curriculum templates. The use of this technology should ease concerns from institutions and instructors about the time-consuming process for curriculum development and need for technology expertise as a requirement to participate effectively in online education (Hirumi, 2002; Janicki & Liegle, 2001; Thompso & McGrath, 1999).

Instructors also need to understand the role and use of specific delivery systems used for online education such as Blackboard, Angel Learning, WebCT, and others. As institutions embrace online education, a course management and delivery system has to be adopted and instructors have to learn the system and work within its constraints and opportunities (Harrington, Staffo, & Wright, 2006; Kraemer, 2003). The most popular systems used in higher education today are WebCT or Blackboard (Carnevale, 2005). The use of a course management system represents an additional layer of technology that may hinder or facilitate faculty participation and, in turn, adult learning. In this regard, instructors are forced to assume additional roles when using course management systems including management, facilitation, and evaluation of learning. Not surprisingly, wide differences are observed between novice and experienced instructors in the way they interact and use course management technology (Harrington et al., 2006; Kraemer, 2003). Clearly, as online education continues to grow, the need to evaluate the effectiveness of course management systems from the instructors' perspective will become more important.

The basic premise and appeal of online education is the flexible access to the learners any time, anywhere, at their convenience. In the case of adult learners, it is assumed they are goal-oriented and motivated to learn on their own. Thus, there is false expectation that adult learners will be able to sort out online instructional materials and resources independently (Kirschner et al., 2006). However, despite the popularity of online education, participation in such courses or programs may be frustrating for some students leading to higher drop out rates compared to students in traditional courses. Common reasons for dropping out include limited instructor's assistance, time demands, and difficulty handling the underlying technology (Paloff & Pratt, 2001; Zirkle, 2002). This finding is a reminder that technology should be used as the means to facilitate learning rather than a distraction for learning. This is consistent with reports indicating that in online programs, the way in which technology is used is more important than whether the technology is "cutting edge" or not (Johnson & Benson, 2003; Phipps & Merisotis, 1999).

To ensure that adult learners succeed in online programs, instructors should provide opportunities to acquire relevant technological skills, mediate technical support, and recognize differences in self-directed learning (Fidishun, 2000). Used as an instructional tool, technology should facilitate online spaces for collaborative learning, provide access to resources, allow for information processing, and include multiple representations of ideas to address different learning styles. Given the emerging range of choices made possible by the Internet, instructors can tap into videoconferencing, electronic messaging, real-time conferencing, and other communication tools for online learning (Stilborne & Williams, 1996). Obviously, this is quite a challenge for instructors who may be limited by their own capacity and commitment to using technology and, in many ways, this is a transformational process for instructors as well (Imel, 1998; Tsao et al., 2006).

Recognizing that instructors are by default asked to bear the responsibility of curriculum design, development, online management and delivery, and selection and use of instructional technology, some institutions are promoting a team approach to ensure the quality of online curriculum and instruction. In such cases, instructors are required to partner with librarians and instructional designers for participation in online education to ensure appropriate support (Aragon, 2003; Flowers, 2005; Hernandez et al., 2004). These emerging efforts underscore the need for faculty training and holistic support to help them make a successful shift to online teaching and learning and meet the needs of adult learners effectively (Cercone, 2008; Kim & Bonk, 2006).

EMERGING TRENDS AND NEEDS

Based on the review of enrollment trends in online education and issues related to adult teaching and learning in the context of career and technical education, the following trends and needs are emerging. First, online education should continue to grow at the community college and university level as CTE programs respond to the demand for flexible teacher re-certification and professional development programs, and for advanced degrees including doctoral preparation (Flowers & Baltzer, 2006b; Johnson & Benson, 2003). At the community college level, online CTE education growth is expected to continue with primary focus on course offerings (Aragon, 2003; Johnson & Benson, 2003). In teacher preparation and graduate programs at the university level, similar growth should be expected to address the demand for alternative delivery systems At the graduate level, in particular, the growth may be in the conversion of existing programs catering to the increasing number of part-time professionals seeking to continue working full-time while pursuing advanced degrees (Blank & Hernandez, 2008; Flowers & Baltzer, 2006b). Second, as online CTE continues to grow, the issue of quality should become more critical as prospective students empowered by the online premise of "anytime-anywhere" learning become more discerning when choosing a program without regard to geographical location (Flowers, 2001, 2005). The relative advantage of pioneering programs should be leveraged as others join the market, unless program quality is ensured.

Third, blended learning should continue to grow in popularity compared to fully online courses and programs. There appears to be a consistent trickle of evidence noting an increased preference for this format by both students and instructors (Allen et al., 2007; Aragon, 2003). In this context, the issue of faculty participation in online education and related supports will become more prominent given the complex demands embodied in related work compared to traditional teaching assignments (Flowers, 2005; Kim & Bonk, 2006). In turn, the need to rethink the value of participation in online education for tenure and promotion will be more openly discussed as a strategic measure to ensure the quality of future participation (Bower, 2001; Hernandez et al., 2004).

Fourth, given the growth of online learning, understanding teaching and learning in online environments should become a top research priority in higher education, CTE included. Considering the narrow focus of current research, it will be imperative to explore the connections between adult learning developments in online CTE contexts from teaching and learning perspectives (Aragon, 2003; Hoare, 2006; Merriam, 2008; Reynolds, 1997). For example, what constructivist instructional strategies work best with adult learners in CTE and under what conditions? What approaches and technologies facilitate social networking and critical reflection? What are the long-term strategies and supports needed for successful participation in graduate programs? Are there interactions between certain groups of adult learners and particular types of online instructional strategies? These are but a hint of questions that need to be addressed as online education becomes more prominent in CTE in the future.

Finally, the continuous evolution of instructional technology will demand closer study of discrete technologies used to facilitate online curriculum development, course management systems, and delivery issues. The use of technology to facilitate social interactions, virtual meetings, and collaborative activities appropriate for adult learning and consistent with adult learning theory should also emerge as an important issue to be researched in online CTE in the future (Kim & Bonk, 2006; Partlow & Gibbs, 2003; Schmidt & Gallegos, 2001).

CONCLUSION

Trends in online enrollments suggest a growing share of the education market at the postsecondary level. Similar trends have been reported in CTE in response to demands for alternative delivery formats and to maximize dwindling faculty capacity in the field. At the graduate level, CTE programs appear to be embracing online education, especially in teacher preparation programs and at the master's degree level, while doctoral programs are more cautiously joining the online movement. As online education becomes more prominent in the field, issues related to quality, impact, and connections to adult learning principles have emerged. However, a review of research in CTE revealed that much of the contemporary focus is on institutional and faculty efforts to put courses and programs online. Thus, it is imperative that we bridge emerging developments in adult learning in the context of online teaching and learning in CTE contexts. Recent contributions to the literature on adult learning highlighted in this article provide a promising framework for informing online CTE. At the same time, they underscore the need to rethink online curriculum development, delivery systems, instruction, and use of instructional technology. Further, it is clear that online education is not a fad and will continue to grow in the future, perhaps in some form of blended modes, thus requiring a focus on teaching and learning in online contexts placing the needs of adult learners at the center of the research agenda.

REFERENCES

Allen, I. E., & Seaman, J. (2008). *Staying the course: Online education in the United States, 2008.* Needham, MA: The Sloan Consortium.

Allen, I. E., Seaman, J., & Garrett, R. (2007). *Blending in: The extent and promise of blended education in the United States.* Needham, MA: The Sloan Consortium.

Anderson, L. W., & Krathwohl, D. R. (Eds.). (2001). *A taxonomy of learning, teaching, and assessment: A revision of Bloom's taxonomy of educational objectives.* New York: Longman.

Aragon, S. (Ed.). (2003). *Facilitating learning in online environments: New directions for adult and continuing education, vol. 100.* San Francisco: Jossey-Bass.

Athanasou, J. (2008). Career education. In L. M. English (Ed.), *International encyclopedia of adult education* (pp. 90-92). New York: Palgrave Mcmillan.

Ausburn, L. J. (2004). Course design elements most valued by adult learners in blended online education environments: An American perspective. *Educational Media International, 41*(4), 327–337. doi:10.1080/0952398042000314820

Baltzer, H., Lazaros, E., & Flowers, J. C. (2007). Review of doctoral programs in technical education. *Journal of Industrial Teacher Education, 44*(2), 37–59.

Banas, E. J., & Emory, W. F. (1998). History and issues of distance learning. *Public Administration Quarterly, 22*(3), 365–383.

Blank, W., & Hernandez, V. (2008). Preparing CTE leaders online. *Techniques, January Issue.* Association of Career and Technical Education (ACTE).

Bower, B. (2001). Distance education: Facing the faculty challenge. *Journal of Distance Learning Administration, IV*(II). Retrieved February 25, 2009, from http://www.westga.edu/~distance/ojdla/summer42/bower42.html

Bransford, J. D., Brown, A. L., & Cocking, R. R. (2000). *How people learn: Brain, mind, experience, and school.* Washington, DC: National Academy Press.

Carnevale, D. (2005). Government's request for data may delay Blackboard's purchase

Center for Online Learning. (2009). *Online course design: Bloom's taxonomy.* Statesboro, GA: Georgia Southern University. Retrieved on March 15, 2009, from http://academics.georgiasouthern.edu/col/id/bloom.php

Cercone, K. (2008). Characteristics of adult learners with implications for online learning design. *Advancement of Computing in Education Journal, 16*(2), 137–159.

Clark, B. (1983). *The higher education system.* Berkeley, CA: University of California Press.

Clark, B. (2002). *Growing up gifted: Developing the potential of children at home and at school.* Upper Saddle River, NJ: Merrill Prentice Hall.

Collins, A., Brown, J., & Newman, S. (1989). Cognitive apprenticeship: Teaching the crafts of reading, writing, and mathematics. In L. Resnick

(Ed.), *Knowing, learning and instructing: Essays in honor of Robert Glaser* (pp.453-494). Hillsdale, NJ: Lawrence Erlbaum.

Conlon, T. (2002). Information mapping as support for learning and teaching. *Computers & Education, 106*, 6–14.

Conrad, D. (2008). Online learning. In L. M. English (Ed.), *International encyclopedia of adult education* (pp. 442-447). New York: Palgrave Macmillan.

Cooper, M. K., & Henschke, J. A. (2003, November). *An update on andragogy: The international foundation for its research, theory and practice.* Paper presented at the Commission of Professors of Adult Education (CPAE) Conference, Detroit, MI.

Dziuban, C. D., Hartman, J. L., & Moskal, P. D. (2004). Blended learning. *EDUCAUSE Center for Applied Research . Research Bulletin (Sun Chiwawitthaya Thang Thale Phuket), 2004*(7).

Ellis, R. (2003). *Task-based language learning and teaching.* Oxford, UK: Oxford University Press.

Ertmer, P. A., Lehman, J., Park, S. H., Cramer, J., & Grove, K. (2003, March). Barriers to teachers' adoption and use of technology in problem-based learning. In *Proceedings of the Association for the Advancement of Computing in Education (AACE) Society for Information Technology and Teacher Education (SITE) International Conference*, Albuquerque, NM (pp. 1761-1766). Chesapeake, VA: AACE.

Ferry, B., Hedberg, J., & Harper, B. (1998). How do preservice teachers use concept maps to organise their curriculum knowledge? *Journal of Interactive Learning Research, 9*(1), 83–104.

Fidishun, D. (2000). *Andragogy and technology: Integrating adult learning theory as we teach with technology.* Retrieved on January 27, 2009, from http://frank.mtsu.edu/~itconf/proceed00/fidishun.htm

Flowers, J. (2001). Online learning in technology education. *Journal of Technology Education, 13*(1), 17–30.

Flowers, J. (2005). The effect of online delivery on graduate enrollment. *Journal of Industrial Teacher Education, 42*(4), 7–24.

Flowers, J., & Baltzer, H. (2006a). Hiring technical education faculty: Vacancies, criteria, and attitudes toward online doctoral programs. *Journal of Industrial Teacher Education, 43*(3), 29–44.

Flowers, J., & Baltzer, H. (2006b). Perceived demand for online and hybrid doctoral programs in technical education. *Journal of Industrial Teacher Education, 43*(4), 39–56.

Gobet, F., Lane, P. C. R., Croker, S., Cheng, P. C.-H., Jones, G., & Oliver, I. (2001). Chunking mechanisms in human learning. *Trends in Cognitive Sciences, 5*, 236–243. doi:10.1016/S1364-6613(00)01662-4

Harrington, T., Staffo, M., & Wright, V. H. (2006). Faculty uses of and attitudes toward a course management system in improving instruction. *Journal of Interactive Online Learning, 5*(2), 178–190.

Havice, W. L., & Havice, P. A. (Eds.). (2005). *Distance and distributed learning environments: Perspectives and strategies: 54th yearbook of the Council on Technology Teacher Education.* New York: Glencoe McGraw-Hill.

Hernandez, V., Kirby, J., & McGee, S. (2004). *Competency assessment in distributed education.* Washington, DC: Association of Jesuit Colleges and Universities.

Hernández-Gantes, V. M., & Blank, W. (2009). *Teaching English language learners in career and technical education programs.* New York: Routledge.

Hirumi, A. (2002). A framework for analyzing, designing, and sequencing planned e-learning interactions. *The Quarterly Review of Distance Education, 3*(2), 141–160.

Hmelo-Silver, C. E. (2004). Problem-based learning: What and how do students learn? *Educational Psychology Review, 16*(3), 235–266. doi:10.1023/B:EDPR.0000034022.16470.f3

Hmelo-Silver, C. E., Duncan, R. G., & Chinn, C. A. (2007). Scaffolding and achievement in problem-based and inquiry learning: A response to Kirschner, Sweller, and Clark (2006). *Educational Psychologist, 42*(2), 99–107.

Hoare, C. (Ed.). (2006). *Handbook of adult development and learning.* New York: Oxford.

Imel, S. (1998). *Technology and adult learning: Current perspectives.* Columbus, OH: ERIC Clearinghouse on Adult, Career and Vocational Education. (ERIC Document Reproduction Service No. 197).

Itin, C. M. (1999). Reasserting the philosophy of experiential education as a vehicle for change in the 21st century. *Journal of Experiential Education, 22*(2), 91–98.

Janicki, T., & Liegle, J. O. (2001). Development and evaluation of a framework for creating Web-based learning modules: A pedagogical and systems approach. *Journal of Asynchronous Learning Networks, 5*(1).

Johnson, S. D., & Benson, A. D. (2003). *Distance learning in postsecondary career and technical education.* St. Paul, MN: National Research Center for Career and Technical Education.

Kim, K., & Bonk, C. J. (2006). The future of online teaching and learning in higher education: The survey says… . *EDUCAUSE Quarterly, 29*(4).

King, K. P. (2008). Distance education. In L. M. English (Ed.), *International encyclopedia of adult education* (pp. 192-199). New York: Palgrave Macmillan.

Kirschner, P. A., Sweller, J., & Clark, R. E. (2006). Why minimal guidance during instruction does not work: An analysis of the failure of constructivist, discovery, problem-based, experiential, and inquiry-based teaching. *Educational Psychologist, 41*(2), 75–86. doi:10.1207/s15326985ep4102_1

Knowles, M. S. (1980). *The modern practice of adult education: From andragogy to pedagogy.* Englewood Cliffs, NJ: Cambridge Adult Education.

Kolb, D. A. (1984). *Experiential learning: Experience as the source of learning and development.* Upper Saddle River, NJ: Prentice-Hall.

Kraemer, E. W. (2003). Developing the online learning environment: The pros and cons of using WebCT. *Information Technologies and Libraries, 22*(2), 87–92.

Lorenzetti, J. P. (2003). Thirty-two distance education trends. *Distance Education Report, 7*(21), 1–6.

McTighe, J., & Wiggins, G. (1999). *The understanding by design.* Alexandria, VA: Association for Supervision and Curriculum Development.

Merriam, S. B. (2001a). Andragogy and self-directed learning: Pillars of adult learning theory. *New Directions for Adult and Continuing Education, 89,* 3–13. doi:10.1002/ace.3

Merriam, S. B. (Ed.). (2001b). *The new update on adult learning theory. New directions for adult and continuing education.* San Fransisco: Jossey-Bass.

Merriam, S. B. (Ed.). (2008). *Third update on adult learning theory: New directions for adult and continuing education, vol. 119.* San Francisco: Jossey-Bass.

Miflin, B. (2004). Adult learning, self-directed learning and problem-based learning: Deconstructing the connections. *The entity from which ERIC acquires the content, including journal, organization, and conference names, or by means of online submission from the author. Teaching in Higher Education, 9*(1), 43–53. doi:10.1080/1356251032000155821

National Center for Education Statistics. (2000). *Distance education at postsecondary education institutions: 1997-1998* (NCES Publication No. 2003-013). Washington, DC: U.S. Government Printing Office.

National Center for Education Statistics. (2002). *A profile of participation in distance education: 1999-2000* (NCES Publication No. 2003-154). Washington, DC: U.S. Government Printing Office.

Paloff, R. M., & Pratt, K. (2001). *Lessons from the cyberspace classroom: The realities of online teaching.* San Francisco: Jossey-Bass.

Partlow, K. M., & Gibbs, W. J. (2003). Indicators of constructivist principles in Internet-based courses. *Journal of Computing in Higher Education, 14*(2), 68–97. doi:10.1007/BF02940939

Perkins, D. (1993). Teaching for understanding. *American Educator, 17*(3), 28–35.

Phipps, R., & Merisotis, J. (1999). *What's the difference? A review of contemporary research on the effectiveness of distance learning in higher education.* Washington, DC: The Institute for Higher Education Policy.

Puzziferro, M., & Shelton, K. (2008). A model for developing high-quality online courses: Integrating a systems approach with learning theory. *Journal of Asynchronous Learning Environment Learning Networks, 12*(3). Retrieved on February 15, 2009, from http://sloanconsortium.org/node/1409

Reynolds, K. C. (1997, March). *The name assigned to the document by the author. This field may also contain sub-titles, series names, and report numbers.Postsecondary education in cohort groups: Does familiarity breed learning?* Additional information about the document that does not fit in any of the other fields; not used after 2004.Paper presented at the Annual Meeting of the American Educational Research Association, Chicago.

Roschelle, J. (1999). Transitioning to professional practice: A Deweyan view of five analyses of problem-based learning. *Discourse Processes: A Multidisicplinary Journal, 27*(2), 231-240.

Rovai, A. P. (2001). Building classroom community at a distance: A case study. *Educational Technology Research and Development Journal, 49*(4), 33–48. doi:10.1007/BF02504946

Ryan, R. C. (2000). Student assessment comparison of lecture and online construction equipment and methods classes. *T.H.E. Journal, 27*(6), 76–83.

Schmidt, E. K., & Gallegos, A. (2001). Distance learning: Issues and concerns of distance learners. *Journal of Industrial Technology, 17*(3). Retrieved on February 22, 2009, from http://nait.org/jit/Articles/schmidt041801.pdf

Sloan-C. (2009). *NASULGC-Sloan national commission on online learning benchmarking study: Preliminary findings.* Retrieved on March 3, 2009, from http://www.sloan-c.org/publications/survey/nasulgc_prelim

Stilborne, L., & Williams, L. (1996). *Meeting the needs of adult learners in developing courses for the Internet.* Retrieved on January 15, 2009, from https://www.isoc.org/inet96/proceedings/c4/ca_2.htm

Taylor, E. W. (2007). An update of transformative a critical review of the empirical research (1999-

2005). *International Journal of Lifelong Education, 26*(2), 173–191. doi:10.1080/02601370701219475

Taylor, K. (2006). Autonomy and self-directed learning: A developmental journey. In C. Hoare (Ed.), *Handbook of adult development and learning*. New York: Oxford.

Taylor, M., King, J., Pinsent-Johnson, C., & Lothian, T. (2003). Collaborative practices in adult literacy programs. *Adult Basic Education, 13*(2), 81–99.

Thompson, M. M., & McGrath, J. W. (1999). Using LNs to support a complete educational experience. *Journal of Asynchronous Learning Environment Learning Networks, 3*(2). Retrieved on March 17, 2009, from http://www.sloan-c.org/publications/jaln/v3n2/v3n2_thompson.asp

Tsao, J., Takahashi, K., Olusesu, J., & Jain, S. (2006). Transformative learning. In M. Orey (Ed.), *Emerging perspectives on learning, teaching, and technology*. Retrieved March 10, 2009, from http://projects.coe.uga.edu/epltt

WebCT. *Chronicle of Higher Education, 52*(16), A29. Retrieved January, 22, 2009, from http://chronicle.com/weekly/v52/i16/16a02901.htm

Zirkle, C. (2002). Identification of distance education barriers for trade and industrial teacher education. *Journal of Industrial Education, 40*(1), 20–44.

This work was previously published in the International Journal of Web-Based Learning and Teaching Technologies, Vol. 4, Issue 4, edited by E. M. W. Ng, N. Karacapilidis, and M. S. Raisinghani, pp. 32-49, copyright 2009 by IGI Publishing (an imprint of IGI Global).

Chapter 7
Information Technology and the Learning Society:
Supporting Lifelong Learning and Flexicurity Policies

Teresa Torres-Coronas
Universitat Rovira i Virgili, Spain

Mario Arias-Oliva
Universitat Rovira i Virgili, Spain

M. Arántzazu Vidal-Blasco
Universitat Rovira i Virgili, Spain

ABSTRACT

This chapter provides a conceptual discussion about the interaction between information and communication technologies (ICT) and the learning society. It focuses on the importance of knowledge and social capital building as key stones of the connected learning society, which is built upon online networks. This chapter also highlights the role of lifelong learning in the connected learning society as an instrument which can support flexicurity policies in the labor market. This work follows the common argumentation logic that the introduction of ICT usually leads to a change in lifelong learning opportunities, which are playing an especial role in achieving economic, employment and social goals. In the connected learning society, how technology is being used will ensure the continual adaptability and employability of workers.

INTRODUCTION

Learning has always been essential for humans through information transfer, collaboration and social capital building. In today's world, the continuing-education demands of a changing workforce and the accelerated pace of technological change have increased demands for continuing education and lifelong learning (LLL), a concept that has be defined as "the process of intellectual and professional renewal that leads to both personal enrichment and occupational growth" (Kellogg Commission, 1999, p. 23) or as "all learning activity undertaken throughout life, with the aim of improving knowl-

DOI: 10.4018/978-1-61520-694-0.ch007

edge, skills and competences within a personal, civic, social and/or employment related perspective" (European Commission, 2001, p. 9).

Lifelong learning is also seen as one of the central means of challenging the exclusion of people with learning difficulties (Riddel, Baron, & Wilson, 2001) and, as a tool for improving labor force mobility, both between jobs (job mobility) and within and between countries (geographic mobility). As population ages, Bork (2001) pointed out that "lifelong learning, including adult learning, will be the tail that wags the dog" (p. 195). Nowadays, the need for economic development fosters the importance of LLL in political institutions, firms and workers agendas. The Action Plan for Skills and Mobility, adopted by the EC in February 2002 and endorsed by the Barcelona European Council in March 2002 was principally designed as a contribution to achieving the Lisbon objective of more and better jobs, greater social cohesion and a dynamic knowledge-based economy.

In the 90s, lifelong learning established itself in Europe as a public policy in response to the problems of increased unemployment (Žiljak, 2005). Due to our current economic crisis, the worst financial crisis since the Great Depression, some economists expect the economy to undergo painful structural transformations. In that sense, this last economic crisis should be seen as an opportunity to think afresh about technology and the learning society. More than ever, we need a global learning society with learning available to all. Information Communication Technology (ICT) will play an important role in supporting the future of the learning society.

Investment in education and training is defined as essential to increase human and social capital. From the point of view of the Human Capital Theory, the benefits of investment in human capital are set out (Schultz, 1961): where returns to other forms of capital are constant or decreasing, the development of human capital, primarily through education and training, will constitute the prime source of economic growth. But, today, the current global economic meltdown is affecting national education budgets and firms' investment in training and human capital development. Although the full impact is yet to be determined, one thing is clear: LLL is an increasingly crucial factor both for the competitiveness of nations and firms and, for the long-term employability of workers because LLL strengths a country's workforce and its economic productiveness (Gorard & Selwyn, 1999). These ideas are supported by the Employment in Europe Report 2006 (European Commission, 2006), which clearly states that "high participation in lifelong learning is positively associated with high employment and low (long-term) unemployment." (p. 108).

In a context of labor market changes and growing threats for the working population, the term *flexicurity* is gaining acceptance, especially among European countries. *Flexicurity* can be defined as an integrated strategy to enhance, at the same time, flexibility and security in the labor market. Flexibility, on the one hand, is about successful moves ("transitions") during one's life course. The dimension of (income) security is related to the various features of unemployment benefit systems and their interaction with active labor market policies. So, *flexicurity* can be implemented across four policy components: 1) flexible and reliable contractual arrangements; 2) effective active labor market policies, 3) social security systems and, 4) comprehensive lifelong learning (LLL) strategies to ensure the continual adaptability and employability of workers.

In a context in which workers need to remain employable throughout their careers to cope with labor market changes, unemployment threats and transitions to new jobs, everyone needs to be in continuous learning processes. Everyone can learn, but not everyone learns in the same way and, of course, people can learn almost everywhere through formal and informal learning. Each individual has a learning profile with three core constituents: cognitive style, learning style, and personality type. These three components interact in ways which produce individual and personalized approaches to learning and e-learning. For Webster and Sudweeks (2006) "developing an understanding of the range of possible learner profiles via accessing and reflecting on their own profile can help academics to facilitate more effective e-learning practices" (p. 635). In 2006, 19% of Europeans declared that they used Internet for educational purposes, although only 8% used it for formalized educational activities (source Eurostat, quoted in Ala-Mutka, Punie & Redecker, 2008, p. 4).

With the acceleration of ICT, we find ourselves living and working in an increasingly information society. Professionals are beginning to consider how ICT will influence the way in which we learn together whether it will enhance or hinder learning effectiveness. In that sense, the work of Selwyn, Gorard and Furlong (2006) sheds light on the ways in which adults interact with technology in different learning environments. Based on one large-scale academic research project, the authors invite debate on what makes a lifelong learner and on the wider social, economic, cultural and political realities of the information age and the learning society.

Technology has created new ways of learning, including opening up new opportunities in LLL that have not been possible before. Every day, technology is easier-to-use through social software development and web 2.0 technologies. Social software encompasses a range of software systems that allow users to interact and share data. This computer-mediated communication has become very popular with social sites like MySpace and Facebook, media sites like Flickr and YouTube, and commercial sites like Amazon.com and eBay. Many of these applications share characteristics like open APIs, service oriented design, and the ability to upload data and media. The terms Web 2.0 and (for large-business applications) Enterprise 2.0 are also used to describe this style of software. (Retrieved March 10, from http://en.wikipedia.org/wiki/Social_software). So, opportunities for a growing learning society are now a reality.

Drawing on these ideas, this chapter reviews relevant writings to address how technology encourages LLL in the learning society through knowledge sharing and social capital building and how ICT through online communities can help us to produce lifelong learners as a factor that influence employability in the information society. Exploring these issues are the major aims of this chapter.

To provide an adequate framework of terms and ideas, we start by looking at currently discussed concepts of knowledge and social capital in the learning society. Next, we discuss about the connected learning society and the role ICT is playing in building social capital through online communities. Following this discussion, we connect ICT and the development of the connected learning society with flexicurity policies. Although this last idea should be further investigated, we do really believe that technology will impact LLL performance, thus helping workers' employability. The chapter concludes by considering the implications of this study for the future role of technology in the learning society as an essential tool to achieve economic growth and competitiveness, social inclusion, and active citizenship.

BACKGROUND

Knowledge and Social Capital: The Keystones of the Learning Society

We are living in a society where knowledge is the key to prosperity for the economy and for individuals (Council of the European Union, 2001; OECD, 2004). With no doubt, knowledge has become the key economic resource and the dominant source of comparative advantage (Drucker, 1994).

In the 90s, Lundvall and Johnson (1994) divided knowledge into four categories:

- *Know-what* or knowledge about facts
- *Know-why* or knowledge about principles and laws of motion in nature, in the human mind and in society
- *Know-how* or the skills and the ability to do something
- *Know-who,* which refers to who knows what and who knows what to do and it also refers to a combination of information and social relationships

The central role of information and knowledge in building the learning society has been widely accepted. Coffield (1996) argued that a learning society would be one that offered high quality learning opportunities equitably and would encourage a collective responsibility from individuals, employers and institutions for the content and organization of continuing education. Within the context of the learning society, *know-who* has become increasingly important as it involves the social ability to co-operate and collaborate (OECD, 2000). As the OECD (2000) states "the concepts of "knowledge economy" and "knowledge worker" are based on the view that information and knowledge are at the centre of economic development. The ability to produce and use information effectively is thus a vital source of skills for many individuals". The idea that knowledge can emerge from the collective activities of individuals is not new. In the digital era, blogs, wikis and other social software encourage knowledge sharing and creation. This social interaction connects knowledge with the concept of social capital.

Social capital has a variety of definitions in multiple fields (Adler & Kwon, 2002). The most common distinction established when discussing social capital is between bridging, bonding and linking. Putman (2000, p. 19) differentiates between bridging and bonding by suggesting that "bonding social capital constitutes a kind of sociological super glue, whereas bridging social capital provides a sociological WD 40" (p. 19). Bonding social capital refers to the value assigned to social networks among homogeneous groups of people. Bridging social capital refers to the value assigned to social networks among socially heterogeneous groups of people. Finally, linking social capital refers to relations between individuals and groups in different social strata in a hierarchy where power, social status and wealth are accessed by different groups (Cote & Healy, 2001, p. 42). According to Nahapiet and Ghoshal (1998), social capital can be defined as "the sum of the actual and potential resources embedded within, available through, and derived from the network of relationships possessed by and individual or social unit" (p. 243). In a different context, Putnam (1995) describes social capital as the "features of social organization such as networks, norms, and social trust that facilitate coordination and cooperation for mutual benefit" (p. 66).

Other authors, such as Bourdieu and Wacquant (1992) define social capital as "the sum of the resources, actual or virtual, that accrue to an individual or a group by virtue of possessing a durable network of more or less institutionalized relationships of mutual acquaintance and recognition" (p. 14). For Cohen and Prusak (2001) social capital is also "a stock of active connections among people: the trust, mutual understanding, and shared values and behaviors that bind people as members of human networks and communities" (p. 4). In the above definitions, we can look at the generation of social capital as the result of continuing interactions and as the cause of continuing interactions.

All interactions create new knowledge by externalization (tacit to explicit), internalization (explicit to tacit) and combination (explicit to explicit) of knowledge (Nonaka, 1994). It has been shown that communities high in social capital tend to have higher levels of knowledge and ideas (Putman, 2000). Learning and knowledge creation may be threatened if social capital creation is undermined. And this is why one fundamental characteristics of the learning economy should be the development of knowledge-based networks such as collaborative learning communities. The knowledge economy will not be a reality without knowledge citizens being able to develop their knowledge in autonomous and different ways (such as formal education and training, work experience, networking or self learning).

In the area of collaborative learning communities, social interactions among members lead to the creation of social capital, which is linked to the creation, acquisition, exchange, transfer and combination of knowledge (Adler & Kwon, 2002). Social capital is accumulated when people value relationships among each other, interact, collaborate, learn and share ideas (Daniel, McCalla & Schwier, 2001) and, through the exchange of information within (online) groups (Blanchard & Horan, 2000). In these communities, social capital is tied to trust and trust is created through (virtual) storytelling.

Organizational learning was introduced to the field of organizational studies in the early work of March and Simon (1958). In the literature on this topic there is a harsh debate about how an entity like an organization actually learns. One way of understanding the process is to define organizational learning as individuals' acquisition of information and knowledge, and analytical and communicative skills (March & Simon, 1958). In organizational settings, and from the point of view of the learning organization, social capital represents the stock created when a network of organizations develops the ability to work in collaboration to promote mutual productive gain and innovation (Fountain & Atkinson, 1998). According to Cohen and Prusak (2001), social capital enables knowledge to flow in communities of practices, which come into existence when people with a shared practice feel a need to share what they know and to learn from others (Wenger, 1999). People are willing to cooperate, share, help, and support with their views, opinions, feedback, and experience because they and trust each other and believe in the common cause. Community of practices contributes to the knowledge management cycle for organizational learning (Secundo, Elia & Taurino, 2006) and they serve as a vehicle for building social capital. In our current technological landscape a new typology of communities has emerged: the virtual communities of practices, which enable an efficient and effective process of knowledge creation in the digital era.

Knowledge and social capital linked to LLL are the key stones of the economic development. In the learning economy "the success of individuals, firms, regions and countries will reflect, more than anything else, their ability to learn" (OECD, 2000, p. 29).

Online Communities, Social Capital and the Connected Learning Society

To advance the concept of the learning society "we need to move beyond the currently dominant theories of learning and of economic behavior which are individualistic in nature" (Coffield, 1997, p. 454). This supports the idea of thinking of learning by a collectivity as opposed to an individual. The technologies of the Internet and the World Wide Web have come to support an infrastructure that promotes virtual communities or social networks who are trying to achieve common goals and interest through the use of technology. In the connected learning society people interact primarily through computer-mediated communication, particularly in a Web environment.

An important feature of virtual communities is "the ability to search for other who share specific interests and, thus, for communities of interests" (Blanchard & Horan, 1998, p. 297). Describing the experience of participating in on-line communities Rheingold (1993) notes that "people in virtual communities...exchange pleasantries and argue, engage in intellectual discourse, conduct commerce, exchange knowledge, share emotional support, make plans, brainstorm, gossip, feud, fall in love, find friend and lose them, play games, flirt, create a little high art and a lot of idle talk" (p. 3). Online communities rise in popularity by bringing people together to socialize, work together, learn, and communicate. Online communities encourage massive interaction through a variety of means such as chat rooms, asynchronous discussion lists, web logs, or web-based collaboration systems (such as wikis). In the academic world, linking in academic weblogs links are now used for distribution of information and collaborative construction of knowledge (Luzón, 2009). As the world become increasingly shaped by web 2.0 technologies and social software, our learning experience is transformed and this transformation leads us to build new social capital. Technology is ideally suited to creating social capital (Resnick, 2002) or Socio Technical Capital in Resnick's words.

Daniel, Schwier and McCalla, (2003) define social capital in virtual communities as "common social resource that facilitates information exchange, knowledge sharing, and knowledge construction through continuous interaction, built on trust and maintained through shared understanding." Individuals share knowledge with the expectation of helping the virtual community to accumulate its knowledge, continue its operation, and grow (Kolekofski & Heminger, 2003).

In the connected learning society is important to understand the role of (virtual) social capital in connection to digital networking. Charlton-Laing and Bailey (2007) assesses the components of social capital and their impact on knowledge sharing in virtual learning communities. Fountain (1997) argues that social capital increases the ability to build and use informational capital because trustful relationships increase information flows. Researchers interested in understanding the motivations prompting people to share knowledge or participate in virtual communities have shown the importance of social influences. Wellman and Wortley (1990) reported that strong community ties could provide important environmental conditions for knowledge exchange while trust has been defined as a key element in fostering the level of participation or knowledge sharing in virtual communities. Other studies found that a sense of community (Hars & Ou, 2002) and social identity (Dholakia, Bagozzi & Pearo, 2004) enhance the likelihood of members' contribution and participation in virtual communities.

A positive correlation between community network use and social capital has been observed (Wellman et al., 1996). The primary reason for this is that Internet use enhances social relationships (Kraut et al., 2002). The research work of McNally et al. (2005) has also showed that there is a link between online community networks usage and social capital.

As Hopkins and Thomas (2002) argue the distinction between bridging capital (weak ties between numerous people) and bonding capital (strong ties within small groups) is very important in the context of electronic networks: "At first glance, online relationships would seem more likely to contribute to the relatively weak ties that constitute "bridging" capital than to the strong, multifaceted, and highly personal relationships which underpin "bonding" capital. But they may also contribute to bonding capital, not only in situations where families and communities are divided by distance, but also when particular media, for instance instant messaging, make a useful and economical addition to people's existing repertoire of communications channels." The article of Ellison, Steinfield and Lampe (2007) examines the relationship between use of Facebook© as an online social network site, and the formation and maintenance of social capital. These authors found correlations between greater "bridging" and "bonding" social capital with greater usage of Facebook© on a college campus, meaning that the ties to one's immediate and extended friends are stronger with greater use of social software such as Facebook©. ICT can be a tool that fosters social capital to support faster innovation and economic growth. Encouraging participation and engagement in online communities is a key issue for creating social capital. When engaging with virtual community a person is involved in social activities so, in the connected society, virtual social capital "supplements "real" social capital (Rafaeli, Ravid & Soroka, 2004).

In summary, both virtual communities and physically based communities have the potential to increase social capital through knowledge sharing. As ICT supply supplementary services to the formal education system the effects of ICT in building a new learning society needs to be further explore.

Technology and Connectivism as Tools for Supporting Lifelong Learning

The e-Learning initiative part of the e-Europe Action Plan, seeks to promote a digital culture and wider use of ICT in education and training. In the connected learning society the use of ICT will facilitate easy access to LLL for all. In that sense, ICT has been described as a significant educational tool in the professional life for LLL (Maddux, 1994) as it reduces, among others, barriers to participate in formal education. Promoting LLL opportunities, especially through the use of ICTs, is the only means of overcoming existing barriers to participation, particularly barriers of 'time, space and pace' (European Commission, 2001)

Online communities (or e-communities) are designed to provide users with a range of tools for personal development. E-communities use web technology and social software to help members pursue new ways of learning and also, as stated by Ala-Mutka, Punie and Redecker (2008), e-communities enhance learning outcomes by:

1. Supporting different senses with multimedia visualizations and representations.
2. Supporting collaboration with new online production and networking tools.
3. Supporting diversity by supplying a wide variety of methodological tools.
4. Empowering learners to personalize their learning process through interaction, combining formal, non-formal and informal learning.

In these communities, the main characteristics of technology for community support include (van der Spek, Mulder, de Poot & Moelaert, 2002):

1. Technology as a promoting factor for social relations.
2. Technology as a coordinating factor (e.g. meeting support agent).
3. Technology as a means of communication (virtual gathering, electronic bulletin boards or virtual shared open spaces).

Collaborative development and sharing of media content (e.g. blogging, podcasting, Wikipedia, Flickr®, YouTube™) and social networking (e.g. MySpace™, Facebook®, SecondLife®) are transforming knowledge sharing, social capital and the learning society.

As learners have different background and competences several different learning approaches are needed. This implies that the skills needed and the most adequate learning styles will vary with professions and industries (Kolb, 1984). Thus, for instance, Oblinger and Oblinger (2005) characterize Net generation ("N-gen") students as digitally literate, always connected via networked media, used to immediate responses, preferring experiential learning, highly social, preferring to work in teams, oriented toward inductive discovery, feeling more comfortable in image-rich environments than with text and, having a preference "for structure rather than ambiguity". This means that there is a growing need to stimulate the creation of successful strategies for lifelong learning. Information technologies, including interactive and multimedia technologies, are tools for building up such strategies and enriching learning. Modern technology not only makes learning a daily need for people but also makes it easier to learn. The Net generation, the workers of the future, are ready for connectivism as a new learning paradigm.

In the present landscape of technological change there is a growing shift on the need to support the acquisition of knowledge and competencies to continue learning throughout life. "With respect to ICT, we are witnessing the rapid expansion and proliferation of technologies that are less about "narrowcasting", and more focussed on creating communities in which people come together to collaborate, learn and build knowledge" (McLoughlin & Lee, 2007, p. 664). So, constructivist approaches have grown to include social constructivism, which refers "to learning as the result of active participation in a "community" where new meanings are co-constructed." (Brown, 2006, p. 111). Different learning strategies have been designed based on a community supported constructionist approach in which constructionism strategy is situated in a supportive community context (Bruckman, 1998). This approach emphasizes the importance of social aspect of learning environment. The construction of new knowledge and social capital is the aim of the constructivism.

But beyond constructivism and social constructivism new paradigm are emerging. Brown (2006) focus on navigationism as a learning paradigm shift. In this new learning paradigm the emphasis will be on knowledge navigation. Learning will take place when learners solve contextual real life problems through active engagement in problem-solving activities, and networking and collaboration. Siemens' principles of connectivism (Siemens, 2004) provides a summary of the connectivist learning skills required within a navigationist learning paradigm:

- Learning is a process of connecting specialized nodes or information sources.
- Capacity to know more is more critical than what is currently known.
- Nurturing and maintaining connections is needed to facilitate continual learning.
- Ability to see connections between fields, ideas, and concepts is a core skill.
- Currency (accurate, up-to-date knowledge) is the intent of all connectivist learning activities.
- Decision making is itself a learning process.

Connectivist learning skills are required to learn within a navigationist learning paradigm. And this is why Brown (2006) states that "connectivism is part and parcel of navigationism," (p. 117) a learning paradigm that needs further development. The main practical implication of Brown's work is that teachers and trainers should become coaches and mentors within the knowledge era and learners should acquire navigating skills for a navigationist learning paradigm. To enhance learning in the connected learning society, it is vital to integrate learning experiences with ICT tools as the key solution to equipping people with the evolving knowledge and skills that will be needed to adapt to the continuously changing nature of the learning society.

FLEXICURITY, ICT AND THE LEARNING SOCIETY

As we have previously stated, a key to the learning society is the need for individuals and institutions to adapt to their changing environment throughout their lives. Contemporary society is described as a knowledge society based on the extensive penetration of all its spheres of life and institutions by scientific and technological knowledge. In a knowledge-based economy, a high-skilled and adaptable workforce is essential for growth. What is needed is a whole set of core competencies that allow individuals to seek and capitalize on opportunities: the ability to be creative, to (e-)communicate, to make judgments, to (e-)learn, to analyze, to assess (e-)information critically, to solve problems and to work in (virtual) teams.

Based upon previous research, Coffield (1997, p. 451) pointed out that a learning society would be one in which:

- Learning is accepted as a continuing activity throughout life
- Learners take responsibility for their own progress
- Assessment confirms progress rather than brands failure capability, personal and shared values, and team working are recognized equally with the pursuit of knowledge
- Learning is a partnership between students, parents, teachers, employers and the community, who all work together to improve performance
- Everyone accepts some responsibility for the learning of others
- Men, women, the disabled and minority groups have equal access to learning opportunities
- Learning is seen as creative, rewarding and enjoyable
- Learning is outward looking, mind opening and promotes tolerance, respect and understanding of other cultures, creeds, races and traditions
- Learning is frequently celebrated individually, in families, in the community and in the wider world

Thus, the objectives of the learning society are perfectly linked to workers' employability and to fulfill the requirements of the changing shape of work and patterns of employment. "As people change jobs more frequently than in the past and as the life of particular skills gets shorter and shorter, education and training is needed in the workplace to complement formal educational provision" (OECD, 2000, p. 68). In our current economic landscape future expectations are very pessimistic. The largest segment of European public opinion, for example, believes that the national employment and economic situation, as well as the world economy and the EU economy will deteriorate (European Commission, 2008, p. 12). In this context, ICT can offer the degree of flexibility and adaptability to the individuals' needs not in reach for the conventional education and training and therefore ICT will play a dominant role in any policy towards high quality LLL. Learning is fundamentally social, and technology development should focus on providing powerful social and virtual contexts for learning.

From the point of view of the learning organization, networks are seen as the best tool to facilitate enhanced learning. "Actors in a collaborative network learn interactively. They learn of new technologies, opportunities, challenges, and the outcome of transactions more quickly because of the density of interaction within the network. Learning is of a higher quality because it is subject to discussion and debate among counterparts whose perspectives and backgrounds may differ" (Fountain & Atkinson, 1998). Findings from the American Society for Training & Development (ASTD) and the Institute for Corporate Productivity research (see Paradise, 2008) established the presence of informal learning in almost all organizations. Workers are clearly accessing knowledge through channels besides official company platforms. Many of the best practices identified by survey respondents fell into two classes at opposite extremes: embracing new technology for information exchange and creating time for face-to-face interactions. Workers are often encouraged to compile information through any technological platform –such as intranets, social networking or internal wikis- that proves useful.

The above poses great challenges for the learning society and its organizations. OECD (2000, p. 30) summarize them as:

1. People should be prepared for a professional life where learning by doing and learning in interaction with others is crucial for economic success and social cohesion

Table 1. External and internal flexibility

External flexibility	Internal flexibility
External-numerical flexibility or numerical adjustment of the workforce.	Internal-numerical flexibility or temporal adjustment of the volume of work with the help of working time accounts and employment-protecting working time reductions.
External-functional flexibility or workforce's ability to adjust to the external labor market in the case of structural change	Internal-functional flexibility or adjustment of work organization as well as suitably well-qualified employees.

Source: Keller and Seifert (2004)

2. Those who may be slow learners must receive a better foundation for taking part in social and economic activities
3. Adult training as part of LLL is a key element of the learning economy
4. The ethical dimension and the contribution to the formation of social capital are increasingly important
5. The rapid growth of knowledge production and knowledge mediation in the private sector may call for a new division of labor and collaboration between schools and other places of learning

Within this context, ICT can support workers' employability by supporting LLL and flexicurity strategies. As previously stated, the normative idea of the flexicurity's concept is to encourage flexible labor markets and ensure high levels of security. Following up this idea, the concept of flexicurity has been associated with four fundamental elements:

1. A legal framework for internal and external flexibility which allows companies to make the necessary human capital adjustments when market opportunities arise, and thereby promotes employment growth
2. An effective and efficient labor market policy to reduce unemployed and to achieve rapid labor market integration
3. Sustainable social security systems which offer workers basic protection
4. Modern and lifelong forms of training to promote companies' competitiveness and workers' employability

The core argument in favor of labor market flexibility is two-fold (Boyer, 2006). On one side, in response to economic and technological shocks, the labor force has to be shifted from one firm to another and across sectors. On the other side, when technological change is speeding up an intensive shift of workers has to take place from the mature to the sunrise industries. In the labor market we can differentiate between external and internal flexibility (see Table 1 for a definition of these concepts). External-functional flexibility possibilities can include further training and learning directed towards the external labor market and structural adjustments while internal flexibility is more likely to provide solutions for cyclical problems. Flexicurity is about generating opportunities to replace a job with a new one (external flexibility). In addition to strengthening external flexibility, flexicurity also involves mobility within an existing work relationship in order to address the threat of job losses. This approach relies less on the safeguarding of a given workplace (job security) than on individual employment capabilities in both internal and external labor markets.

In a knowledge-based society qualification and skills became a key feature of knowledge-based work so workers need to adapt themselves to the new demands of the labor markets. The challenge for knowledge-based work is that the employees should have easy access to complex knowledge in order to make decisions. They are in a continuous learning process. At the same time, the importance of knowledge as a precondition of economic progress has led governments, firms and educational institutions to take a greater interest in the formation of a highly skilled work force. Due to these factors, internal and external flexibility modes have changed the acquisition of the required skills towards a demand for higher qualifications in nearly all sectors.

In the connected learning society, the encouragement of ICT in order to improve the "employability" of the workers seems one important strategy which should be embedded into the contextual framework of LLL strategies and flexicurity policies.

FUTURE TRENDS

Researchers are starting to investigate the complex relationships between technology and the learning society. Further research is needed to study the importance of examining the learning society from both an online and physical point of view. According to McClelland (1994): "Rather than providing a replacement for the crumbling public realm, virtual communities are actually contributing to its decline. They are another thing keeping people indoors and off the streets. Just as TV produces couch potatoes, so on on-line culture creates mouse potatoes, people who hide from real life and spend their whole life goofing off in cyberspace." (p. 10). Though, other researchers (see Hamman, 1998) have reported that the use of ICT serves as a complement to face-to-face interaction, rather than a substitute. So, empirical research is needed to clarify this important first controversy.

More research is also needed for finding evidence on how technology can enhance learning and LLL. Together, tool developers and educational researchers should study and develop models for embedding new learning paradigm such as connectivism in teaching and learning approaches. In the world of connectivism, the role of mobile devices in transforming the learning society should be deeply analyzed. According to Bleeker (2006), mobile devices are social devices "in the degree to which they mediate social relationships, social networks and manage the circulation of culture that sustains such networks". Social networking applications developed for mobile phones would leverage both existing technology usage patterns and information seeking patterns in the developing world (Kolko, Johnson & Rose, 2007). The expectation of anytime, anywhere access to learn is just beginning to growing up.

The Internet leads to new forms of social capital that cannot be easily captured with existing forms of measurement. Thus, to assess the full impact of the Internet on social capital and economic development, researchers need to develop new forms of measurement that complement existing ones. But, researchers need also think about other relevant questions:

- What knowledge and social capital are likely to be needed and by whom in the connected learning society?
- How can technology help us in producing and disseminating such knowledge?
- What technological infrastructure might be needed to support the connected learning society?
- How can ICT ensure that LLL systems are efficient and effective for workers' employability?
- Are people really ready to learn independently and in a range of contexts (work, leisure, home) other than formal educational institutions? Is ICT is producing more participation in LLL strategies linked to flexicurity policies?
- Is there any evidence of the impact of social capital on employability?

ICT has opened new learning opportunities, but maybe it has not extended enough the number of learners, nor the range of contents available for adult learners. Technologies, tools, and practices related to collaborative learning networks can create a fruitful context for developing a global connected learning society.

CONCLUSION

As Peter Drucker (1994) pointed out "The great majority of the new jobs require qualifications the industrial worker does not possess and is poorly equipped to acquire. They require a good deal of formal education and the ability to acquire and to apply theoretical and analytical knowledge. They require a different approach to work and a different mind-set. Above all, they require a habit of continuous learning". At the very least (workers) have to change their basic attitudes, values, and beliefs" (p. 62). In this context, LLL is about:

- Acquiring and updating all kinds of abilities, interests and knowledge from the pre-school years to post-retirement in order to promote the development of knowledge and competences that will enable each citizen to adapt to the knowledge-based society
- Valuing all forms of learning, including: formal learning (university's degrees); non-formal learning (such as vocational skills acquired at the workplace); and informal learning (such as inter-generational learning)

Drawing on these ideas, this chapter has reviewed writings that address how ICT can encourage social capital building as the key factor that influence the development of the connected learning society. The literature review highlights online communities as both a source and a tool that enhance learning. In an age where education and training policies promote the need for higher levels of knowledge creation to achieve economy prosperity, learning can be conceived as a direct route into economic growth and employment at the individual level. The employability of people, which depends upon ICT and LLL strategies, is vital to build a competitive and dynamic knowledge-based society.

But, a learning society is about much more than economics. It also promotes the goals and ambitions of every country to become more inclusive, tolerant and democratic. A learning society is about building a better society. So now, it is time for perfectly matching technology with people's learning capacities.

REFERENCES

Adler, P. S., & Kwon, S. (2002). Social capital: Prospects for a new concept. *Academy of Management Review*, *27*(1), 17–40. doi:10.2307/4134367

Ala-Mutka, K., Punie, Y., & Redecker, C. (2008). *ICT for learning, innovation and creativity*. European Commission, Joint Research Centre, Institute for Prospective Technological Studies. Retrieved 15 February, 2009, from http://ipts.jrc.ec.europa.eu

Blanchard, A., & Horan, T. (2000). Virtual communities and social capital. In E. L. Lesser (Ed.), *Knowledge and social capital: Foundations and applications* (pp. 159-178). Woburn, MA: Butterworth-Heinemann.

Bleecker, J. (2006, May). *What's your social doing in my mobile? Design patterns for mobile social software*. Paper presented at the WWW2006 Workshop MobEA IV-Empowering the Mobile Web. Edinburgh, Scotland.

Bork, A. (2001). Adult education, lifelong learning, and the future. *Campus-Wide Information Systems, 18*(5), 195–203. doi:10.1108/EUM0000000006266

Bourdieu, P., & Wacquant, L. (1992). *An invitation to reflexive sociology*. Chicago, IL: University of Chicago Press.

Boyer, R. (2006). *Employment and decent work in the era of 'flexicurity'*. DESA Working Paper No. 32. United Nations, Department of Economic and Social Affairs, New York.

Brown, T. H. (2006). Beyond constructivism: Navigationism in the knowledge era. *Horizon, 14*(3), 108–120. doi:10.1108/10748120610690681

Bruckman, A. (1998). Community support for constructionist learning. *Computer Supported Cooperative Work: The Journal of Collaborative Computing, 7*, 47–86. doi:10.1023/A:1008684120893

Charlton-Laing, C., & Bailey, A. (2007, April). The effects of social capital on knowledge sharing within a virtual collaborative learning community. In *Proceedings of the 6th Annual ISOnEworld Conference*, Las Vegas, NV. Retrieved 15 February, 2009, from http://www.isoneworld.org

Clayton-Pedersen, A. R., & O'Neill, N. (2005). Curricula designed to meet 21st-Century expectations. In D. Oblinger & J. Obligner (Eds.), *Educating the Net generation* (pp. 9.1-9.16). Educause. Retrieved February 15, 2009, from http://www.educause.edu/educatingthenetgen/5989?time=1236850547

Coffield, F. (1996, November). *A tale of three little pigs: Building the learning society with straw*. Paper presented at the European Union Conference on Lifelong Learning, University of Newcastle upon Tyne, UK.

Coffield, F. (1997). Introduction and overview: Attempts to reclaim the concept of the learning society. *Journal of Education Policy, 12*(6), 449–455. doi:10.1080/0268093970120601

Cohen, D., & Prusak, L. (2001). *In good company. How social capital makes organizations work*. Boston: Harvard Business School Press.

Commission of the European Communities. (2006). *Towards common principles of flexicurity: More and better jobs through flexibility and security*. Retrieved February 15, 2009, from http://ec.europa.eu/employment_social/news/2007/jun/flexicurity_en.pdf

Cote, S., & Healy, T. (2001). *The well-being of nations. The role of human and social capital*. Organization for Economic Co-operation and Development, Paris.

Council of the European Union. (2001). *Report from the education council to the European Council: The concrete future objectives of education and training systems*. Retrieved 15 February, from http://ec.europa.eu/education/policies/2010/doc/concrete-future-objectives_en.pdf

Daniel, B., McCalla, G., & Schwier, R. (2001, December). *A process model for building social capital in virtual learning communities*. Paper presented at the International Conference on Computers in Education (ICCE'02), Auckland, New Zealand.

Daniel, B., Schwier, R., & McCalla, G. (2003). Social capital in virtual learning communities and distributed communities of practice. *Canadian Journal of Learning and Technology, 29*(3), 113–139.

Dholakia, U. M., Bagozzi, R., & Pearo, L. K. (2004). A social influence model of consumer participation in network- and small-group-based virtual communities. *International Journal of Research in Marketing, 21*(3), 241–263. doi:10.1016/j.ijresmar.2003.12.004

Drucker, P. F. (1994, November). The age of social transformation. *Atlantic Monthly, 274*(5), 53–80.

Ellison, N. B., Steinfield, C., & Lampe, C. (2007). The benefits of Facebook friends: Social capital and college students. Use of online social network sites. *Journal of Computer-Mediated Communication, 12*(4), 1143–1168. doi:10.1111/j.1083-6101.2007.00367.x

European Commission. (2001, November). *Making a European area of lifelong learning a reality*. Retrieved February 15, 2009, from http://eur-lex.europa.eu/LexUriServ/LexUriServ.do?uri=COM:2001:0678:FIN:EN:PDF

European Commission. (2006, October). *Employment in Europe 2006 report*. Retrieved February 15, 2009, from http://ec.europa.eu/employment_social/employment_analysis/employ_2006_en.htm

European Commission. (2007, November). *Employment in Europe 2007 report*. Retrieved February 15, 2009, from http://ec.europa.eu/employment_social/employment_analysis/employ_2007_en.htm

European Commission. (2008, December). *Eurobarometer 70*. Public opinion in the European Union. Retrieved February 1, 2009, from http://ec.europa.eu/public_opinion/standard_en.htm

Fountain, J. (1997). Social capital: A key enabler of innovation in science and technology. In L. M. Branscomb & J. Keller (Eds.), *Investing in innovation: Toward a consensus strategy for federal technology policy* (pp. 84-111). Cambridge, MA: The MIT Press.

Fountain, J. E., & Atkinson, R. D. (1999, July). *Innovation, social capital and the New Economy: New federal policies to support collaborative research*. Progressive Policy Institute, Technology Policy Library. Retrieved January 15, 2009, from http://www.ppionline.org/ppi_ci.cfm?cp=1&knlgAreaID=140&subsecid=293&contentid=1371

Gorard, S., & Selwyn, N. (1999). Switching on the learning society? Questioning the role of technology in widening participation in lifelong learning. *Journal of Education Policy, 14*(5), 523–534. doi:10.1080/026809399286198

Hamman, R. B. (1998). *The online/offline dichotomy: Debunking some myths about AOL users and the effects of their being online upon offline friendships and offline community*. Unpublished doctoral dissertation, University of Liverpool. Retrieved March 20, 2009, from http://www.cybersoc.com/mphil

Hars, A., & Ou, S. (2002). Working for free? Motivations for participating in open source projects. *International Journal of Electronic Commerce, 6*(3), 301–311.

Hopkins, L., & Thomas, J. (2002). *E-social capital: building community through electronic networks*. Retrieved 20 March, 2009, from http://www.sisr.net/publications/nd_hopkins_2.pdf

Keller, B., & Seifert, H. (2004). Flexicurity. The German trajectory. *European Review of Labor and Research, 10*(2), 226–247.

Kellogg Commission (1999, September). *Returning to our roots: A learning society. Fourth Report*. Kellogg Commission on the Future of State and Land-Grant Universities.

Kolb, D. A. (1984). *Experiential learning*. Englewood Cliffs: Prentice Hall.

Kolekofski, K. E., & Heminger, A. R. (2003). Beliefs and attitudes affecting intentions to share information in an organizational setting. *Information & Management, 40*, 521–532. doi:10.1016/S0378-7206(02)00068-X

Kolko, B. E., Johnson, E., & Rose, E. (2007, July). *Mobile social software for the developing world*. Paper presented at the 2nd International Conference, OCSC 2007, Held as part of HCI International 2007, Beijing, China, (pp. 385-394).

Kraut, R., Kiesler, S., Boneva, B., Cummings, J., Helgeson, V., & Crawford, A. (2002). Internet paradox revisited. *The Journal of Social Issues*, *58*, 49–74. doi:10.1111/1540-4560.00248

Luzón, M. J. (2009). Scholarly hyperwriting: The function of links in academic weblogs. *Journal of the American Society for Information Science and Technology*, *60*(1), 75–89. doi:10.1002/asi.20937

Maddux, C. D. (1994). The Internet: Educational prospects and problems. *Educational Technology*, *34*(9), 37–42.

March, J., & Simon, H. A. (1958). *Organizations*. New York: Wiley.

McClelland, J. (1994, February 13). Netsurfers. *The Observer*.

McLoughlin, C., & Lee, M. J. W. (2007, December). Social software and participatory learning: Pedagogical choices with technology affordances in the Web 2.0 era. In *ICT: Providing choices for learners and learning. Proceedings ASCILITE*, (pp. 664-675), Singapore. Retrieved September 15, 2008, from http://www.ascilite.org.au/conferences/singapore07/procs/mcloughlin.pdf

McNally, M., Bannon, M., Greaney, J., Hickey, A., McDonnell, M., & Riordan, M. (2005, September). *The effects of a wireless on-line community network on social capital*. Paper presented at MobileHCI'05, Salzburg, Austria, (pp. 215-218).

Nahapiet, J., & Goshal, S. (1998). Social capital, intellectual capital, and the organizational advantage. *Academy of Management Review*, *23*(2), 242–266. doi:10.2307/259373

Nonaka, I. (1994). Dynamic theory of organizational knowledge creation. *Organization Science*, *5*(1), 14–37. doi:10.1287/orsc.5.1.14

Oblinger, D., & Oblinger, J. (2005). Is it age or IT: First steps toward understanding the net generation. In Oblinger, D. & Oblinger, J. (Eds.), *Educating the Net Generation, Educause*. Retrieved 15 February, 2009, from http://www.educause.edu/educatingthenetgen/5989?time=1236850547

OECD. (2000). Knowledge management in the learning society. *Education and skills*. OECD Publications Service, Paris.

OECD. (2004). OECD education. Retrieved 15 February, from http://www.oecd.org/document/7/0,3343,en_2649_39263238_33712135_1_1_1_1,00.html

Paradise, A. (2008, July). Informal learning: Overlooked or overhyped? *T+D*, 52-53.

Putnam, R. D. (1995). Bowling alone: America's declining social capital. *Journal of Democracy*, *6*, 65–78. doi:10.1353/jod.1995.0002

Putnam, R. D. (2000). *Bowling alone, the collapse and revival of American community*. New York: Simon and Schuster.

Rafaeli, S., Ravid, G., & Soroka, V. (2004). Delurking in virtual communities: A social communication network approach to measuring the effects of social and cultural capital. In *Proceedings of the 37th Annual Hawaii International Conference on System Sciences (HICSS '04)*-(Track 7-Vol. 7), Big Island, Hawaii.

Resnick, P. (2002). Beyond bowling together: Socio technical capital. In J. M. Carroll (Ed), *HCI in the New Millennium* (pp. 247-272). Reading, MA: Addison-Wesley.

Rheingold, H. (1993). *The virtual community*. Reading, MA: Addison-Wesley. Retrieved January 6, 2009, from http://www.rheingold.com/vc/book/intro.html/

Riddel, S., Baron, S., & Wilson, A. (2001). *The learning society and people with learning difficulties*. Bristol, UK: The Policy Press Publishing.

Schultz, T. W. (1961). Investment in human capital. *The American Economic Review*, *51*(1), 1–17.

Secundo, G., Elia, G., & Taurino, C. (2006). A process-oriented and technology-based model of virtual communities of practices: Evidence from a case study in Higher Education, Paper presented at the IV International Conference on Multimedia and ICTs in Education (m-ICTE2006), Seville, Spain. In *Current Developments in Technology-Assisted Education*, (pp. 1032-1036).

Selwyn, N., Gorard, S., & Furlong, J. (2006). *Adult Learning in the Digital Age: Information Technology and the Learning Society*. London: Routledge

Siemens, G. (2004). *Connectivism: A learning theory for the digital age*. Retrieved September 15, 2008, from http://www.elearnspace.org/Articles/connectivism.htm

van der Spek, J., I. Mulder, de Poot, H., & moelaert, F. (2002). *A Comparative Study on Social Capital in Communities in Three Sectors*. Presented to the Research workshop on social capital and IT, held on 27-28 May 2002. https://doc.telin.nl/dscgi/ds.py/Get/File-23047/social_capital_gigac-scw_final.pdf

Webster, R., & Sudweeks, F. (2006). *Teaching for e-learning in the knowledge society: Promoting conceptual change in academics' approaches to teaching*. Current Developments in Technology-Assisted Education. Retrieved January 10, 2009, from http://www.formatex.org/micte2006/pdf/631-635.pdf

Wellman, B., Salaff, J., Dimitrova, D., Garton, L., Gulia, M., & Haythornthwaite, C. (1996). Computer networks as social networks: Collaborative work, telework and virtual community. *Annual Review of Sociology*, *22*, 213–238. doi:10.1146/annurev.soc.22.1.213

Wellman, B., & Wortley, S. (1990). Different strokes from different folks. *American Journal of Sociology*, *96*(3), 558–588. doi:10.1086/229572

Wenger, E. (1999). *Communities of practice, learning means and identity*. Cambridge, MA: Cambridge University Press.

Žiljak, T. (2005). Lifelong learning policies in the European Union and Croatia . *Political Education*, *1*(1), 67–95.

Chapter 8
Adult Learning Principles as the Foundation for Innovative Technology Applications in Business and Higher Education Venues

Judith Parker
Teachers College/Columbia University, USA

ABSTRACT

As Web 2.0 surfaces as the latest trendy phrase in education and technology discussions, it is imperative that instructors not get caught up in the glamour of the latest technology and loose sight of the required andragogical underpinnings necessary for effective and efficient teaching and learning. This chapter will begin by exploring the major theories and theorists in the field of adult education and the meshing of these theories with technology applications in higher education and global business venues. While Malcolm Knowles is credited with popularizing adult learning theory in the 1970's, Stephen Brookfield, Jack Mezirow, Maxine Greene and Knud Illeris are among those who have moved the field forward over the past decades. Along with this progression in theory, the use of technology has escalated in popularity creating a need to frame its application in the foundational principles of adult education; an "Andragogy 2.0" focus is required. This chapter will expand on this theoretical base by offering short case studies that are linked to the theories as examples of innovative strategic approaches in the use of technology in adult teaching and learning.

INTRODUCTION

As Web 2.0 surfaces as the latest trendy phrase in education and technology discussions, it is easy for instructors to get caught up in the glamour of the latest technology and loose sight of the required andragogical underpinnings necessary for effective and efficient teaching and learning. Online social networks are in. Wiki's and blogs are the norm. But what do these add to the learning process? Some universities offer space behind password-protected firewalls, while others advocate the use

DOI: 10.4018/978-1-61520-694-0.ch008

of public spaces for these online collaborations. What impact does this have on confidentiality and intellectual property issues for students and faculty? A plethora of questions begin to emerge and answers are only beginning to follow.

This chapter will begin by exploring the major theories and theorists in the field of adult education and the meshing of these theories with technology applications in higher education and global business venues. While Malcolm Knowles is credited with popularizing adult learning theory in the 1970's, Stephen Brookfield, Jack Mezirow, Victoria Marsick and Knud Illeris are among those who have moved the field forward over the past decades. Along with this progression in theory, the use of technology has escalated in popularity creating a need to frame its application in the foundational principles of adult education; an "Andragogy 2.0" focus is required. This chapter will then expand on this theoretical base by offering short case studies that are linked to the theories as examples of innovative strategic approaches in the use of technology in adult teaching and learning. These case studies may serve as examples for professionals who might want to adapt them to their own venues or use them as a springboard for new innovations in the field. This chapter will then explore the possibilities of utilizing Web 2.0 to generate even more effective and efficient learning 2.0. If I were to create a lighthearted subtitle to this chapter, it would be "Andragogy meets Web 2.0".

BACKGROUND

The need for theory as a foundation of practice is articulated by Elias and Merriam (2005). "Theory without practice leads to empty idealism and action without philosophical reflection leads to a mindless activism" (p. 4). In Malcolm Knowles' (2005) classic text "The Adult Learner" he provides the historical development of learning theories in a summary of propounders and interpreters of learning theory from Thorndike and Dewey of the early 1900's to Brookfield and Mezirow today. His list includes 61 propounders and 33 interpreters who have influenced the development of learning theories over the past 130 years. Only a few individuals from this extensive list will be profiled in this chapter. Dewey believed that experience was always the starting point of an educational process, not the end result. Thorndike believed that 3 laws governed the learning of animals and human beings: the law of readiness for learning, the law of exercise which connects learning to practice, the law of effect which is dependent on the consequences of learning. In stark comparison Knowles refers to his own ideas of separating humans into adults and children.

In his autobiography, Knowles (1989) credits a seminar led by Cyril Houle at the University of Chicago with initiating his own interests in the historical foundations of adult education. He notes that many great teachers of ancient China, Rome and Greece taught adults, not children, and "invented techniques for engaging learners in active inquiry" (p.61). He noted the continuing importance of adult education throughout and on history and described himself as being "part of a long and significant historical movement" (p.72) He cited examples in the citizen involvement initiatives in the American colonies and during the Civil War and the "compulsion for knowledge" (p.64) instigated by the industrial revolution. Building on Houle's classic "The Inquiring Mind" in 1961, Tough's seminal publications in "Learning Without a Teacher" (1967) and later in "The Adult's Learning Projects" (1979) introduced the idea of self-directed learning and further influenced Knowles andragogical model. Tough (1979) discovery that adults were more successful learners if they knew the benefits from their learning and the negative consequences of not learning became one of Knowles assumptions about adult learners. Knowles (2005) articulated his 6 core andragogical principles as "the learner's need to know, self-directed learning, prior experience of the learner, readiness to learn, orientation to learning and problem solving, and motivation to learn" (p.183). While a great deal of discussion around these principles continues in the field of adult learning, they provide a foundation for new theories and a guide for practice. These principles will be examined in the context of technology, especially on-line learning, later in this chapter.

Stephen Brookfield (1986) was among those who commented on Knowles work. He questioned the principles of self-directedness, the assumption of relating learning to particular social roles and the focus on the need for immediate application. Brookfield (2005) continues to develop his own focus on critical thinking and critical theory. Critical thinking or critical reflection is "reflecting on the assumptions underlying our and others' ideas and actions, and contemplating alternative ways of thinking and living" (Brookfield, 1986, p.x). Brookfield (2005) further suggests that we might explore the way critical theory applies the critical reflection on assumptions – often claimed to be a distinctive characteristic both of adult learning and of adult education practice-on itself" (p.30).

Mezirow uses Habermas's idea of "reflective discourse" as a condition for his own transformative learning theory. Mezirow defines transformative learning as a process by which our taken-for-granted frames of references are transformed by making them more "inclusive, discriminating, open, emotionally capable of change, and reflective" (Merriam, 2006, p.255).

Transformational learning has had a long standing impact on adult education. As Sharan Merriam (2008) reflects on the changes in emphasis in adult learning theory, she cites a chapter on transformational learning as the only constant across three updates of New Directions for Adult and Continuing Education. However she notes important differences in emphasis across the 15 years that these chapters span. The 1993 edition was mostly Mezirow's description of the theory. In 2001 the chapter had a base of empirical research. Finally, in the 2008 update, the empirical research continued but included diverse theoretical perspectives.

Brookfield offers a connection between transformative learning and critical reflection. He states that "although critical reflection is an ineradicable element of transformative learning, it is not a synonym for it. It is a necessary but not sufficient condition of transformative learning;... transformative learning cannot happen without critical reflection but critical reflection can happen without an accompanying transformation in perspective" (Brookfield in Mezirow, 2000, p.125). If one accepts the notion that critical thinking is "reflecting on the assumptions underlying our and others' ideas and actions, and contemplating alternative ways of thinking and living" (Brookfield, 1986, p.x), then it becomes obvious that critical reflection is not a process that is accomplished in a few minutes but might take hours or days or weeks. This chapter will examine the role of technology in facilitating critical reflection over time. For example, a classroom discussion relies on students' instant insights and reactions. In contrast, an asynchronous discussion online affords students the opportunity to read another student's comment, reflect on it, then return to the discussion at a later time with a thoughtful comment as the result of critical reflection creating a foundation for transformative learning.

From a Danish perspective, Illeris (2004) comments on Brookfield's and Mezirow's ideas on critical reflection as he develops his theory that considers adult learning to comprise three different dimensions: cognitive, emotional and social. Illeris's inverted triangle model places the two psychological poles, Piaget's cognition and Freud's emotion, at the two corners at the top of the model and society at the lower vertex but he stresses that "all three dimensions are always integrated parts of the learning process and in practice do not exist as separate functions"(p.20). Applying this model to online learning would seem to particularly emphasize the emotional and social dimensions. The author's experience with adult learners attempting an online course for the first time is that they approach it with a great deal of emotion and often judge its effectiveness as much on how they felt about the experience as how much content they learned. The emerging application of social networks such as wiki's and blogs speaks to Illeris' social dimensions.

Merriam (2008) suggests that as we move into the twenty-first century, we should consider the past shifts in the focus of adult learning in order to prepare for those of the future. She feels that there have been two main shifts in the focus of adult learning. One shift is from the individual learner to the learner within the various contexts in which learning takes place. This new perspective considers "learning as part of the system's cultural and historical norms…(and) how physical space and spatiality encourages or inhibits learning" (p.94). The second shift is from learning as a purely cognitive activity to a multidimensional phenomenon. This is often considered to be a more holistic approach in which "learning is construed as a much broader activity involving the body, the emotions, and the spirit as well as the mind"(p.95).

Fenwick (2008) lists 4 emerging trends in adult learning in the areas of definitions, an increased emphasis on practice-based learning, the importance of identity and literacy and power and politics. Learning is now defined as a process not just an outcome and is "understood to involve not just human change but interconnections of humans and their actions with rules, tools and texts, cultural, and material environments" (p.19). The emphasis on practice-based learning is consistent with Merriam's note on the increasing emphasis on the contests in which learning takes place. It also has been increasing in importance as Senge (2006) proposed his concept of the learning organization in the early 1990's and Wenger's (1998) communities of practice model emerged in the late 1990's. This was also evidenced by the growing popularity of Ravens (1982) Action Learning methodology which will be discussed in more detail in a case study to follow. Fenwick suggests that "people's sense of their own knowledge in work and the knowledge valued by the group to which they see themselves belonging form a critical element of their sense of identity" (p.22) and there are "fundamental tensions related to what knowledge counts most and who says so (p.24). Finally, the traditional organizational power and politics are taking new forms in the virtual organizations and transnational work sites.

Much of the work of these theorists has been developed through the lens of the practioner. As theories developed, practice changed. Sometimes a tension resulted but often the available tools and technology that facilitated the change were welcomed. For example, Malcolm Knowles (2005) sees technology as providing learning opportunities in the "andragogical tradition" (p.237) and as consistent with the adult learning idea of self-directedness. Nilson's (2003) observation that students learn best when they are actively engaged, when learning evokes emotional not just intellectual involvement is consistent with one of Illeris's three dimensions of learning. Cranton (2006) emphasizes the importance of empowering the student by interactions in the learning environment and being aware of power relationships. "The creation of a learning community supports and encourages knowledge acquisition. It creates a sense of excitement about learning together and renews the passion involved with exploring new realms in education" (Palloff and Pratt, 1999, p.163). Yiu and Parker (2005) provided a strategic model which integrated numerous distance learning elements (electronic forums, video/phone conference meetings, email, and even a virtual graduation) into an action learning model program on leadership. As Kasworm and Londoner (2000) advise, "the challenge for adult education is to accept and embrace the possibilities of technology(p.225).

While numerous examples of theories that inform practice could be elucidated here, this chapter will focus on examples of a few select theories/principles of adult learning and Knowles andragogical principles as "the learner's need to know, self-directed learning, prior experience of the learner, readiness to learn, orientation to learning and problem solving, and motivation to learn"(2005, p.183). Jochems, Merrienboer and Koper (2004) stress the importance of addressing the pedagogical, technological and organizational aspects in order for online learning to be successful(p.199).

PRINCIPLES APPLIED TO TECHNOLOGY IN PRACTICE

Technology in Practice

While the case studies to follow will focus on more recent technology, it is useful to reflect on the development of various forms of technology and their usefulness in teaching and learning. In the courses at Teachers College referred to in this chapter, the author often divides the class into groups and assigns each group a decade in history. She then presents the scenario that the students have just been invited to attend a workshop on the latest technology impacting their practice. They are asked to identify what technologies they will expect to be presented at the workshop and how those technologies likely impacted educational practice at that time. With so much focus on computers and learning it is always informative for students to realize that this is not the first time that educators have had to adapt to technological changes in their practice. Whether it was the printing press, telephone, copying machine or computer, educators have always been challenged to use new technology for effective teaching and learning.

Since many applications of technology in learning have the students working alone and learning independently, Knowles' self-directedness is essential. But these virtual classrooms are modeled after the familiar classroom. For example, in physical dimensions, the virtual classroom is really thousands of miles wide by thousands of miles long by thousands of miles high. The physical distance is further amplified by time difference. The challenge is how to foster a sense of "community" among the participants without the comfort of physical proximity. The traditional whiteboard and flip charts are replaced by fax machines, computer files, email, telephones, and video conferencing facilities. The instantaneous feedback between a teacher and a student are broken when using a communication medium other than a telephone or a video conferencing facility. The challenge is to sustain individual learner's willingness to participate. With competing personal and professional priorities participants' attention is often diverted from the learning process. Conditions can also differ from location to location in terms of telecommunication infrastructure. This divergence can affect the choice of technical options which vary from simple text to more sophisticated attached files with graphic design, from voice exchanges to full visual images. It also affects the possibilities of setting up conference calls to allow for more than two parties to be on line at once. The challenges are to present the information in an engaging manner and to accommodate the logistical constraints faced by different participants.

Sitting in the classroom is replaced by typing on a computer keyboard, reading a computer screen, listening to voices on the phone, or watching a monitor" The sensory inputs were reduced to the transmission on one's monitor in isolation. Instead of feeling the presence of other learners, participants are learning in front of their monitors and hence are often distracted by other more pressing daily tasks. With the exception of pre-arranged audio and video conferencing, the participants need to direct their own learning just as they would in regard to their day-to-day responsibility. They decide on the timing and frequency of entering into the "classroom" and leave notices for others to act or to react. The teachers'communications are limited to writing and reading, but much less speaking; facilitating and group maintaining become essential skills. Course participants enter the virtual classroom on their schedule that may not coincide with the schedule of their classmates and from that of the teacher-facilitators. In cyberspace, besides occasional person-to-person meetings, individual actors move on their own orbit in the pursuit of learning.

Transformative Learning in Higher Education

This section will examine how technology has significantly enhanced the transformative learning that occurred in two academic institutions. It will address how integrating technology into courses and offering courses in an online and blended format can facilitate the expansion and transformation of the course and its participants to be more inclusive, discriminating, open, emotionally capable of change, and reflective.

While transformative learning is a very personal experience and technology can initially appear to be a cold and distant tool, this presentation will examine how the process of transforming can be enhanced using technology. It will also offer two examples: one at Teachers College, Columbia University in New York and the other at Moravian Theological Seminary in Bethlehem, Pennsylvania.

Teachers College prepares its students to educate others in business, higher education, K-12, and non-profits. Moravian Seminary prepares its students for ministry to others in religious organizations. The two organizations' shared values include the importance of reflection on learning and the importance of community building. They share the idealism of "thinking of things as if they could be otherwise" (Greene, 2001, p.127). These students are the dreamers and innovators; those most open to transformation.

This example from Teachers College/Columbia University utilizes the situation where the same instructor, with the same syllabus, is teaching two courses, Staff Development and Introduction to Adult and Continuing Education, both on campus and on line. Both require the student to apply principles of adult learning and examine the application of that theory in practice. Although the core of the Staff Development course is the development of a staff training module and students arrive with very pragmatic expectations, comments at the end of the course suggest that transformative learning has occurred.

Using technology in an education course offers a unique advantage. In most courses technology is utilized as a course delivery system. In an education course, the course objectives facilitate the inclusion of an analysis of the effectiveness of the use of technology. Students are continually required to reflect on and discuss the learning advantages and disadvantages of technology as they participate in the learning. Course assignments that utilize technology enhance this learning. The qualitative comments from the end of course survey and reflection assignments will be examined with regard to students' reflections on the experience and their learning.

Teachers College uses Blackboard software as a platform for their distance learning classes. Two particular functions of Blackboard, the Discussion Forum and the Virtual Classroom have been most mentioned by students in commenting on elements of transformative learning. The use of the asynchronous Discussion Board where students post their own ideas and comments then reply to other students' ideas was seen to facilitate critical reflection. Following are a few representative student comments:

The discussion conducted here is very involving; everybody could get a chance to express his own ideas. Moreover, the discussion board online gives us a further opportunity to share ideas with all of the class. It has been developed into a real learning forum. Everybody chose their favorite articles about learning and training in their fields, and then shared their own ideas on the "blackboard", thus evokes a real open discussion. This learning style makes me feel that I can learn anytime anywhere from so many people of diverse fields.. By posting, reading, and replying online, our learning location has burst out of the limited classroom and lecture time boundary, thus it has given us an authentic flexibility and motivation to learn.

It is a medium that does promote student engagement in discourse without the normal bias of face-to-face communication (because our appearance is reduced to letters in a computer screen). And although we have the opportunity to influence and suggest tone, etc. by the use of color, sizes, etc. the initial barriers to traditional communication are somehow diminished. The use of discussion boards allows for a lot of reflection prior to committing to opinions. The student has the time and the resources to build a message that will convey every idea that s/he wants to communicate.

The process of responding to skilled questions posed by co-group members allowed me to consider and deeply reflect on my actions with respect to learning and how it is applied at the workplace.

The methodology used for this course integrates technology with a pedagogy practice that supports the deeper, more reflective self-directed activity thus, emphasizing on constructivist teaching.

The Virtual Classroom (chat room) was considered to particularly foster the transformative learning characteristics of inclusion and openness in addition to reflection. The class was divided into smaller groups in order to make the discussion logistics manageable. Following are a few representative student comments:

The conversations were not superficial interactions but purposeful, focused and useful. The instructions preceding the chat in terms of reading position papers, preparing questions followed by chat on each paper allowed all group members an equal opportunity to have their "voices" heard, making the chat more effective. Setting up small groups of 4 students, rather than a whole class, allowed each one the time and opportunity to participate and understand each other's situations more closely and attentively. The archived feature of the chat that automatically creates transcripts of discussions make it useful for rereading and future reference.

I was enamored with the power of this medium. In my opinion, the on-line synchronous communication came closest to simulating a traditional classroom context within the distance-learning framework. It gave me a sense of jointly occupying a temporary space (similar to a class room) and created the illusion of physical proximity and group cohesion through spontaneous conversation and sharing. At the same time it eliminated space restrictions—all four of us gathered from numerous locations, Carol from as far as the UK, to meet and discuss the topic in a real-time environment.

A community emerged during the chat session as the group members experienced a sense of personal relatedness.

Since my partner is from different culture, industry and gender from mine, I learnt a lot of new perspectives.

The chat session personalized e-learning, which can sometimes seem cold and robotic. It provided an interactive, personal channel through which numerous learning and experiences could be shared.

The best part lies in my realization toward the end of the chat that a synchronous professional discussion isn't too difficult a thing for me. This is my first time to do a real one with international professionals. As a non-native speaker, I was very self-conscious and afraid I'd loose face before this highly learned group who seem to have a better and deeper understanding of all the theories we're learning. But the 2-hour went by fast and I felt more and more comfortable, even not nervous when it's my turn.

Moravian Theological Seminary is unique in its small size and ecumenical nature. A grant from the Lilly Foundation provided the funds for the seminary to build a videoconference classroom at its seminary in Bethlehem, Pennsylvania and a similar room on the campus of Salem College in Winston Salem, NC where there is a large Moravian population with an interest in participating in Moravian Seminary courses. The mechanics were being put in place and the faculty mindset was enthusiastic about the grant and the possibilities that it offered. However the success of the program necessitated the transformative learning on the part of both the faculty and students. Their taken-for-granted frames of references about space and collocation needed to be transformed into ones that were more inclusive, discriminating, open, emotionally capable of change, and reflective. They were apprehensive about their personal role as distance learning faculty members. There was a strong commitment to the philosophy that everyone needed to be in the same room or at least on the same campus to build community. And building a strong faith community was a significant part of the seminary education. In the chapter, "The Passion of Pluralism", Maxine Greene (1995) comments about community: "We are in search of what John Dewey called 'the Great Community" but at the same time, we are challenged as never before to confront plurality and multiplicity" (p.155). "To open up our experience to existential possibilities of multiple kinds is to extend and deepen what each of us thinks of when he or she speaks of a community" (p.161).

To help bridge the gap between the two campuses, the faculty of the videoconferenced classes traveled to Winston-Salem once a semester and taught the course from that location back to Bethlehem. "Learning to look through multiple perspectives, young people may be helped to build bridges among themselves; attending to a range of human stories, they may be provoked to heal and to transform. Of course there will be difficulties in at once affirming plurality and difference and working to create community" (Greene, 1995, p.167).

Blackboard software was initially used to support these courses offered at distance. After 3 years, every faculty member had taught at least one course using videoconferencing and Blackboard software is now an integral part of most courses taught on campus. A transformation on the part of both the faculty and students had taken place. Faculty are requesting use of the videoconference room and students are depending on the technology for class presentations and projects for many classes. The technology has become an integral and expected part of the class – not a frustrating add on. One might argue that this is simply adapting not transforming. But a review of the process in the past three years gives evidence of this being a transformative experience. The faculty and staff's past "taken-for-granted frames of reference" was that students would travel to the seminary for education and community building lead by resident faculty who would provide on site face-to-face education. The past 3 years have been filled with critical reflection about the inclusion of this new technology and students in a new venue. An educational technology committee was established to champion the discussions and reflections as the technology was integrated into the curriculum. A program committee of church leaders was established to critically reflect on the role of this technology in the education of their new leaders. This was not using technology for the sake of technology but a critically reflective process by which these bodies lead the transformation in a thoughtful, purposeful way into a new paradigm of seminary education.

Another transformative application of technology was lead by a paraplegic student who relies on technology for her self-sufficiency. She has become a champion in the use of the Virtual Classroom in Blackboard. She requests a "group" within Blackboard be set up for each of her classes. It is her study group. Since the computer is her only voice, she brings students to her world by using the Virtual Classroom for her study group sessions. While technology has expanded her world, it has transformed her fellow students' thinking about communication and forming community. It has brought her fellow students to the brink of being "emotionally capable of change".

In both examples, many elements of transformative learning and adult learning theory are evident. "The learning organization is a living, breathing organism that creates the space that enables people and systems to learn, to grow, and to endure"(Marsick & Watkins, 1999, p.210). As seen in the above comments, the use of threaded discussions in Blackboard facilitates critical reflection. The asynchronous nature of this Discussion Board offers students the opportunity to take the time necessary for reflection in order to generate more thoughtful responses. Unlike classroom discussions where the discussions focus on thoughts from that moment, the threaded discussions can be well thought out ideas and facilitate continual discussion on the topic. The worldview is enhanced during the online format and videoconference classes by making it possible for students from another location with differing views to participate in the course. Elements of transformative learning and adult learning theory in action are evidenced in the comments and actions of participants in technology enhanced learning cited above.

Action Learning in Global Leadership Training

Action learning, pioneered by Rag Ravens (1982), involves working on real work opportunities, problems, tasks and projects. It encompasses a learning cycle of action, reflection, theorization and application. Mezirow (1990) delineates three essential components of action learning: action, critical reflection, and the building of one's own theories. In the past two decades, numerous practitioners and theorists have added their comments on the process. Mumford (1997) notes that learners are expected to try out new behaviors, to reflect critically on their experiences, to distil some generalizable principles and to try it out in other similar contexts. He cites "recognized ignorance not programmed knowledge is the key to Action Learning; people start to learn with and from each other only when they discover that no one knows the answer but all are obliged to find it"(p.3). He cites people who accept responsibility, real issues and colleagues who support and challenge each other as essential to the process. Marsick (1999) describes action learning as a process in which "people take action while they are learning, and bring the results of their experiments to the group for discussion, as would happen in an action research project. Unlike action research, however, equal (and sometimes more) attention is paid to the personal learning than to problem solving"(p. 120).

The venue for the action learning project was a Fortune 500 company founded in Minnesota over 100 years ago and currently operating in 63 countries worldwide. Rapid expansion in the Asia region initiated the need for effective leadership among the country nationals managing the country technical centers. The 12 participants of this learning forum were the technical managers heading various technical centers and laboratories in China, Hong Kong, India, Philippines, Singapore, South Korea, Taiwan, Thailand and the regional technical managers from the regional headquarters of 3M in Asia. Geographically, the participants and facilitators were separately located in three continents, 10 countries and 5 time zones. The greatest time difference between two locations was 14 hours while the smallest time difference was 1 hour. In addition to the geographically dispersed locations of 3M, the participants represented culturally diverse groups.

While training is one of the often-used solutions for rapidly strengthening management capacities within local subsidiaries, to carry out traditional training in a non-western context has its inherent difficulties. Transfer of management know-how to a non-western business environment has proven to be difficult (Hofstede, 2001; Kanungo & Mendonca, 1996; Saner & Yiu, 1994). Training capacity can oftentimes be stretched to the limit. As a result, technology-based learning has become a source to deliver training across geographic boundaries.

This case example reports on how a regional management development program in Asia was used to illustrate how technology was an enabler for management development across national boundaries. The objective of the learning process was to enhance management and leadership competencies of the technical managerial team in the Asia region. The function of these technical laboratories was to support the business plans at country and regional levels. Instead of an event-driven learning process, i.e., workshop based learning, an action learning (AL) based learning process was adopted to ensure successful learning transfer and adequate organizational level change impact as described by Kirkpatrick (1976). The total learning process lasted for 15 months and was carried out primarily in cyberspace. Participants met mostly through intra-net and through audio and video conferencing.

Three concentric Learning processes were woven throughout the process: Organization, Teams and Individual Levels. Organization learning and on-going adaptation, require changes of mental models and behavioral responses (Senge, 2006). However, such changes cannot be accomplished through managerial decisions only. Rather they have to be rooted in individual learning processes with are based on acquiring task-relevant information, carrying out critical reflection and initiating appropriate actions. Edmondson & Moingeon (1998) suggest that innovation and organization learning have to be an on-going process that requires individual cognition and supports organizational adaptiveness. Figure 1 below depicts this on-going learning process and the inter-relations between individual learning and organizational adaptiveness. In this conceptual frame, the learning was perceived as a social process where learning groups formed the basic unit for management development intervention. In a learning team, individuals were better supported in acquiring new information, checking out underlying assumptions, testing solutions and forming new routines. In addition, the team meetings themselves became vehicles for significant interpersonal learning.

The training program was designed so that each participant belonged to 2 small groups, a project group and a learning group. In total, there were three project groups consisting of one site manager (client) and three consultants. Learning groups were determined by the individual learning styles. Based on the results of their learning styles inventory, participants were assigned to learning groups #1, #2 or #3. The managers of the project sites comprised their own learning group #4.

Participants worked on projects pertaining to organizational and/or managerial issues that were close to their actual work and of significant importance to the corporation. Support from the regional technical director was enlisted from the identification of potential projects to the recommendation and implementation. Feedback loops would be established at the country, regional and corporate level to facilitate exchanges and action.

In the context of this Asia Technical Managers' Learning Forum (ATMLF), the linkages between action and reflection were explicit. Managers were asked to work in peer groups on a real management related project and to formulate recommendations based on research and data analysis (action research). This data and recommendations would

Figure 1. Inter-relations between individual and global organizational learning

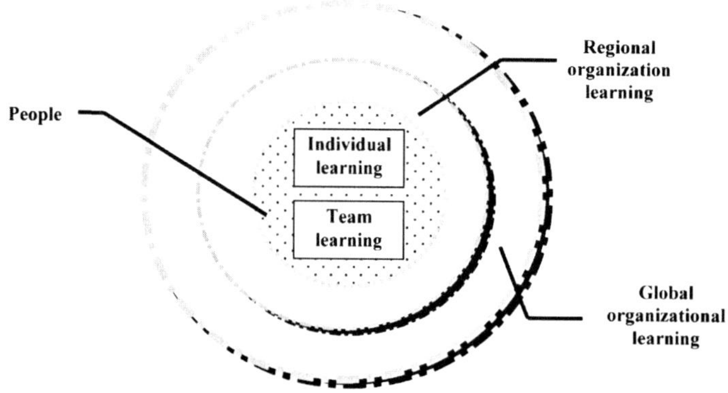

be subsequently utilized in the second phase of the ATMLF. The selected learning projects were placed within the context of other development activities of 3M in the region so that business benefits could also be obtained in addition to the development of people.

The course objectives were to provide

- Education and training relevant to all country subsidiaries and unique for the managing of a laboratory
- A learning experience that would serve to develop a cohesive technical manager's team with multi-cultural characteristics in the Asian region
- A vehicle to foster inter-country and intra-regional synergy within the Asian technical community

Being on-line, the task of the teachers was less of providing content input, but primarily of structuring the learning process and of motivating the trainees to stay engaged and contribute. They needed to spend more of their energy in sustaining the group cohesion, to nudge the group moving forward and to conjure when social loafing taking place.

The entire development, delivery, and management of the learning experience took 3 months to prepare and 15 months to implement. The whole learning process consisted of the following components:

- Outlining of the learning activities consistent with Raven's (1982) action-learning model
- Identifying and selecting the relevant domains for action learning projects in consultation with the Technical Director for the Asia region
- Soliciting 3M volunteer sites for the identified project domains from the participating managers
- Deciding on the learning projects and preparing project brief together with the clients
- Sending prework to participants including self-assessment questions and learning styles inventory
- Conducting a 3-day off-site workshop with training inputs and project planning exercises
- Creating computer forums for each project group and learning group
- Holding video/phone conference learning group meetings
- Conducting site visits by the facilitator-instructor team
- Organizing a wrap-up workshop at the corporate headquarters to debrief

- Documenting all project reports into a compendium for discussion with the respective Managing Directors and for general dissemination
- Commencing a virtual graduation ceremony with top executives of the technical community present

Participants were engaged in the process beginning with the actual planning. Four months before the workshop, each participant received an invitation to the course by the Asia Technical Director. Six weeks before the workshop, each participant received an email from the instructors. It welcomed them to their Asia Technical Managers Learning Forum and outlined the first stage of this 14-month learning experience. They received the pre-work assignment, information on the workshop session to be held at the Hotel Shilla at Cheju Island, Korea beginning on Tuesday, March 18 at 17:30 and ending by 12:00 on Saturday, March 22. They were informed about the expectations for the small group sessions to be held between April and February of the following year and the future classroom session to be held the week before and in the same location as the next year's Asia Technical Managers' Meeting. The message of the email was that the instructors had developed this learning experience based on feedback from many sources including their technical director. Conveying the support of their management was considered to be a key motivator. The message further emphasized that the instructors intended for the learning to be both informational and experiential so they will be able to learn new skills and practice them on a real life issue. They were presented with a list of issues compiled from their own volunteering of issues within the region and with confirmation of the regional technical director. They were asked to review the suggested list of issues and to consider their country as a possible site to be studied for the project. They were told that this was an opportunity for them to address a real issue, be provided with free consulting and advice, and to have concrete recommendations for their management on resolving the issue. They were informed that the hope was to publish the educational experience and results to the region so that they and their site might become a role model for education and problem solving to the global 3M technical community.

Results obtained from the three project groups and four learning groups differed depending on their own self-directedness as well as multiple factors such as time and energy invested, willingness to tackle at times difficult problems and issues, and different perceptions and expectations regarding the benefits resulting from these action learning projects. Knowles' six principles were clearly evident. Most importantly, results differed according to the team's ability to manage its project and the respective team's dynamics in cyberspace. All things considered, most of the results were outstanding. ATMLF represented an innovative management development process. It pioneered a potential prototype for large-scale application with the corporation.

Key results were achieved in all three domains: individual learning, development of a regional team, support of business related results. Results in individual learning included:

- In-depth knowledge of other subsidiaries in the region, especially of China, India and Taiwan where in-depth Action Research projects were conducted
- Exchange of information, expertise and suggestions regarding common interests and concerns
- Learning the methodology of starting a project and getting people and resources together
- Gaining better insight into establishing a productive client-consultant relationship
- Practicing problem analysis and handling time consuming and demanding tasks

Results in the development of a regional team included:

- Acquisition of better knowledge of colleagues and form informal ties
- Better appreciation of each other's strengths and weaknesses and of ways to achieve synergy
- learning how to respect each other's ideas and opinions and how to handle differences
- Building of relationships to work together and to share ideas and experiences
- Recognition that remote location was not necessarily an excuse for poor communication
- Gaining better knowledge and skills in managing virtual teams through scheduled meetings, setting timeline, assigning task, leading meetings, and taking minutes
- Getting experienced in running a "remote" project with available technology

Results in the support of business-related results included:

- How to capitalize business opportunities through organization development in China and India
- How to build up a higher-level technological development center in Taiwan
- The development of decision-making models for the technical communities

Train-the-Trainer Instructional Model

Growth in the Asia region resulted in a second project in that region but this one involving the technical service engineers in the country technical centers. Each country technical center had a large numbers of recent college graduates in their centers functioning as technical service engineers. A large part of the job of technical service is to train customers, salespeople, etc on the technical aspects of new products. A relatively new employee base in Asia produced the need for a course to train technical service employees on how to do better product training. These employees are located throughout the Asia region from as far north as Shanghai and Korea to as far south as Singapore and Malaysia. While some technical service employees travel throughout the region, most travel only in their own country.

One option that was explored was to bring in a traveling consultant. However, this would not only be extremely expensive but with a 25% growth rate, the continual influx of new employees would continue to create a need for additional sections of the course. It also failed to build any sustainable expertise within the country and region itself. Therefore the decision was made to develop the expertise to deliver a train-the-trainer course within the technical community itself in each country. This would establish a master trainer in each country who would be available to conduct future courses and continuing support for the technical service engineers themselves. The regional technical manager selected a group of experienced technical service professionals from countries across the region to be trained to deliver the course. An instructor from Scotland who had been successfully teaching a course on how to be a better trainer to technical service professionals in Germany was identified as the subject matter expert. She and the Technical Education manager from the corporate headquarters met in Europe to develop and to plan the delivery of a course that would teach these technical service professionals how to teach the course she had been teaching for seven years. They also developed a series of steps for instructor certification.

Each of the 14 new trainers was required to attend a week-long training class, co-teach a class under the supervision of the two instructors, teach or co-teach the class in their home country, participate in a follow-up audio or videoconference with one of the instructors. Only at the completion of all the steps were they awarded a plaque as a certified instructor. This model was only possible by integrating the use of technology into the course design itself. Similar to the previous case study involving management training, the course was positioned to start with the first email contact from the instructors outlining the course expectations and was not completed until the last follow-up feedback/reflection connection between the instructor and the trainer. The onsite learning experience in Singapore was the focal point of the training. For the first ½ of the first week of onsite training, the course content was taught to the new trainers by the two instructors. During the second ½ of that week they were taught the methodology of how to teach the course that they had just participated in.

During the next week, actual classes of employees at the Singapore technical center were scheduled. The new trainers were grouped to co-train these classes under the supervision of the two instructors. An hour feedback session was scheduled at the end of each day for new trainers to receive feedback from their peer trainers and observers. It was an opportunity to critically reflect on their previous assumptions about training and being a trainer and compare them with their new experiences. Since the participants had been selected for this training as a tribute to their experience and the confidence that their country technical manager had in them, there was a high level of motivation to succeed.

The instructors encouraged the participants to adapt or integrate any country/culture specific activities as they prepared to deliver the course in their home country. Participants also shared difficulties in translating some theoretical terms into meaningful words in their own language. Upon returning to their home technical center, the new trainers scheduled their own classes. After completing their first training, the new trainers who were in locations with videoconference facilities, used them for their follow-up conference with the instructor. Other locations used audio-conferences. While technology played an important part in the design of the program, there was the continuing assessment of what countries had what technologies available and adapting the process to be inclusive as possible for everyone.

After the completion of each class, instructors fax attendance sheets to the company headquarters. A personalized certificate with the student's name, the instructor's signature for that class and the Global Technical Education Manager's signature is prepared and sent to the technical manager at the country site. At the original Singapore training class, the signatures of every new instructor were collected so they could be scanned and inserted in the certificates. This final step served several purposes. It ensured the continuing contact between the country trainers and the instructor/technical manager at company headquarters who was available for any consultation about the courses and who could keep statistics on the attendees and courses held in each country. It also provided a consistent and personalized certificate from the headquarters to the student's manager to be awarded to the student at an appropriate time. It kept a constant link between headquarters, the technical manager in the country, the technical service employee, and the country trainer. Since it had the signature of the country trainer on it, it was meant to showcase his/her expertise as a trainer at that location.

FUTURE DIRECTIONS

The geographic distance encompassed by organizational learning communities will demand more use of technology as the major vehicle for training. Technology will also increasingly enhance traditional face-to-face seminars and allow for the expansion of the course before and after the seminar. There is yet a lot to learn in order to be effective in a virtual classroom. A lot still needs to be discovered as to the limitation, shortcomings and optimal utility of technology-enhanced and technology delivered learning. Professional educators are poised at the doorstep of an exciting new journey. But there is a great need for researchers to delve into the many questions surrounding this methodology. The exploration of this new learning landscape in the literature and online venues will likely continue. Researchers and practitioners alike have only scratched the surface of possibilities.

In particular, some of the personal connections in the previous examples seemed clumsy at best. New online social networks would improve on this. While this chapter connects decades old learning theories to today's technology rich classrooms, the concept of learning community in the world of adult learning is only a few decades old. Yet technology in the form of Web 2.0 is providing exciting options for enhancing and expanding learning communities across space and time. Truly the time has come for andragogy to meet Web 2.0 technology. Welcome to the world of Andragogy where Malcolm Knowles six principles of adult learning exist in cyberspace.

CONCLUSION

Examining many of the theories and methodologies mentioned earlier in this chapter will reveal many learning models with geometric shapes. Some appear to have closed circular orbits such as Kolb's or the Action Learning Cycle while others are triangular like Illeris' three dimensions of learning. While we seem to continually experiment with new methodologies in practice, it might be useful to experiment with new geometries as well. An image of fractals might be an appropriate one for the new social online networks that are emerging. The interconnectedness that is displayed is neither linear nor circular nor triangular but the similarity in shapes is reproduced on various scales. While fractals seem to have an apparent randomness in their design, closer examination reveals the reproductions and mirrors of the original shapes. Fractals might prove to be an appropriate model for the emerging learning communities in Andragogy 2.0.

REFERENCES

Brookfield, S. (1986). *Understanding and facilitating adult learning*. San Francisco: Jossey-Bass.

Brookfield, S. (2005). *The power of critical theory: liberating adult learning and teaching*. San Francisco: Jossey-Bass.

Cranton, P. (2006). *Understanding and promoting transformative learning*. San Francisco: John Wiley & Sons.

Edmondson, A., & Moingeon, B. (1998). From Organizational Learning to the Learning Organisation. *Management Learning*, *29*(1), 5–20. doi:10.1177/1350507698291001

Elias, J. L., & Merriam, S. B. (2005). *Philosophical foundations of adult education*. Malabar, FL: Krieger Publishing Company.

Fenwick, T. (Fall, 2008). Workplace learning: emerging trends and new perspectives in *New directions for adult and continuing education*, *119*, 17-26.

Greene, M. (1995). *Releasing the imagination*. San Francisco: Jossey-Bass.

Greene, M. (2001). *Variations on a blue guitar*. New York: Teachers College Press.

Hofstede, G. (2001). *Culture's Consequence: Comparing values, behaviors, institutions and organizations across nations*. London: Sage Publication.

Houle, C. O. (1961). *The Inquiring Mind*. Madison, WI: University of Wisconsin Press.

Illeris, K. (2004). *The three dimensions of learning*. Malabar, FL: Krieger.

Jochems, W., von Merrienboer, J., & Koper, R. (2004). *Integrated e-learning: implications for pedagogy, technology and organization*. New York: RoutledgeFalmer

Kanungo, R. N., & Mendonca, M. (1996). Cultural Contingencies and Leadership in Developing Countries. In P.A.Banberger, M. Erez, & S.B. Bacharach, S.B. (Eds.), *Research in the Sociology of Organizations*, (vol. 14, pp. 263-295). Greenwich, CT: Jai Press.

Kasworm, C. D., & Londoner, C. A. (2000). Adult learning and technology. In A.L. Wilson & E. Hayes, (Ed.), *Handbook of adult and continuing education*, (pp.224-42). San Francisco, CA: John Wiley & Sons.

Kirkpatrick, D. L. (1976). Evaluation of Training. In R.L. Craig. (Ed.) *Training & Development Handbook: A Guide to Human Resource Development* (2nd Ed.). New York: McGraw-Hill.

Knowles, M. (1989). *The making of an adult educator.* San Francisco, CA: Jossey-Bass.

Knowles, M., Holton, E., & Swanson, R. (2005). *The adult learner*. Burlington, MA: Elsevier.

Marsick, V., & Watkins, K. (1999). *Facilitating Learning Organizations*. Brookfield, VT: Gower.

Merriam, S., Caffarella, R., & Baumgartner, L. (2006). *Learning in adulthood: A comprehensive guide*. San Francisco, CA: John Wiley & Sons.

Merriam, S. B. (2008, Fall). Adult learning theory for the twenty-first century. *New Directions for Adult and Continuing Education*, *119*, 93–98. doi:10.1002/ace.309

Mezirow, J., & Associates. (2000). *Learning as transformation*. San Francisco: Jossey-Bass.

Mumford, A. (1997). Action Learning as a Vehicle for Learning. In A. Mumford (Ed.) *Action Learning at Work*. Hampshire, UK: Gower.

Nilson, L. B. (2003). *Teaching at its best*. San Francisco, CA: Anker Publishing.

Palloff, R., & Pratt, K. (1999). *Building learning communities in cyberspace*. San Francisco, CA: Jossey-Bass.

Ravens, R. (1982). *The Origin and Growth of Action Learning*. London: Chartwell Bratt.

Saner, R., & Yiu, L. (1994). European And Asian Resistance to the Use of the American Case Method in Management Training: Possible Cultural and Systemic Incongruencies. *International Journal of Human Resource Management*, *5*(4), 953–976.

Senge, P. M. (2006). *The Fifth Discipline: the Art and Practice of the Learning Organization*. New York: Doubleday Currency.

Tough, A. (1967). *Learning without a teacher.* Toronto: Institute for Studies in Education.

Tough, A. (1979). *The adult's learning project*. Toronto: Institute for Studies in Education.

Wenger, E. (1998). *Communities of practice: learning, meaning and identity.* Cambridge, UK: Cambridge University Press.

Yiu, L., & Parker, J. (2005) Cyber action learning and virtual project teams for leadership and management development. In R.L. Jacobs & A.M. Osman-Gani(Ed.), *Workplace training & learning: cases from cross-cultural perspectives,* (pp. 1-14). NY: Pearson/Prentice Hall.

ADDITIONAL READING

Barab, S., Kling, R., & Gray, J. (2004). Designing for virtual communities in the service *of learning*. Cambridge, UK: Cambridge University Press.

Brookfield, S. (1987). Developing critical thinkers. San Francisco: Jossey-Bass.

Brookfield, S. (2006). The skillful teacher. San Francisco, CA: John Wiley & Sons.

Carr, P. B., & Ponton, M. K. (2003). The e-learning instructor. In Piskurich, G. *Preparing learners for e-learning* (pp. 139-154). San Francisco, CA: John Wiley & Sons

Conrad, R., & Donaldson, J. (2004). *Engaging the online learner.* San Francisco, CA: John Wiley & Sons

Jeong, A., & Lee, J. M. (2008). The effects of active versus reflective learning style on the processes of critical discourse in computer-supported collaborative argumentation. *British Journal of Educational Technology*, *39*(4), 651–665. doi:10.1111/j.1467-8535.2007.00762.x

Li, C., & Irby, B. (2008). An overview of online education: attractiveness, benefits, challenges, concerns and recommendations. *College Student Journal*, *42*(2), 449–458.

Meyers, S. A. (2008, Fall). Using transformative pedagogy when teaching online. *College Teaching*, *56*(4), 219–224. doi:10.3200/CTCH.56.4.219-224

O'Lawrence, H. (2006). The influences of distance learning on adult learners. *Techniques*, *81*(5), 47–49.

Parker, J. (1992). *Employees pursuing technical baccalaureate degrees: Success factors.* NY: Teachers College/Columbia University.

Parker, J. (1996). Integrating technology into delivery methods for global technical education. *Compendium on uses of distance learning technologies in engineering education.* American Society for Engineering Education.

Parker, J. (2003). Transformative learning enhanced with technology. *Proceedings: transformative learning conference.* NY: Teachers College/Columbia University.

Parker, J., & Yiu, L. (2000). Action learning in cyberspace: a case example of a technology-supported laboratory management development program. *Compendium on uses of distance learning technologies in engineering education.* American Society for Engineering Education

Piskurich, G. (2006). *Rapid instructional design.* San Francisco, CA: John Wiley & Sons.

Sandman, L. R., Reischmann, J., & Kim, Y. S. (2007). Emerging adult educators' experiences in an international on-line forum. *Convergence*, *40*(1/2), 25–40.

Schlenker, B. (2008). Conversation 2.0. *c>training*, 45(7), 32.

Taylor, E. W. (Fall 2008). Transformative learning theory in New directions for adult and continuing education no. 119 p. 5-15.

White, B. A., & Bridwell, C. (2004). Distance learning techniques. In Galbraith, M. (Ed.) *Adult learning methods: a guide for effective instruction.* (pp. 273-288). Malabar, FL: Krieger

Chapter 9
The Role of Learning Styles and Technology

Royce Ann Collins
Kansas State University, USA

ABSTRACT

Learning style research has informed effective classroom teaching strategies for decades. Technology has allowed faculty and students to move the learning environment from the four-walled classroom to a fluid global virtual space. Knowledge gained through the application of learning style research to the online instruction has enhanced practice; however, research demonstrating the alignment of learning styles with current technological resources has been limited. Learning styles and their interrelationship with technology and adult learners is as important today as initial learning style research was in the six decades after its beginnings in the 1940s. Education today must meet the needs of students who are more comfortable in electronic environments as well as those who need the four-walled classroom. The ability to use learning style research to accomplish both will lead to enhanced student learning and a more productive experience.

INTRODUCTION

New technology has changed the way adults receive and solicit information. No longer do adults have to go to a book, journal or newspaper to gain information on a topic; they just 'Google it'. To think a few years ago, that phrase would have never been written and understood by those who read it. The irony of the situation is this chapter is being written for a book (static) about technology (fluid).

Wireless connections and mobile technologies have changed the flow of information. The new learning spaces on the Internet and online course delivery systems have created a fluid nature to learning. Have these devices and new ways of processing changed our learning styles? What is the impact of technology on the way adults absorb and process information?

DOI: 10.4018/978-1-61520-694-0.ch009

There is a variety of technological approaches to education that can be incorporated into online and face-to-face courses. Some face-to-face courses have become web-enhanced, meaning items for the course are placed in an online environment. These items could include the syllabus, PowerPoint slides, links to websites, or group presentations. The hybrid or blended learning format was developed by combining the face-to-face with 30% to 79% of the course time in the online environment (Allen & Seaman, 2007). Entirely online learning is making a significant impact on U.S. colleges and universities with just the number of courses offered in this format. The number of students enrolling in online courses has steadily increased over the past few years according to the Sloan Consortium series on online learning (Allen & Seaman, 2007). In the fall 2007 semester, over 20 percent of students were enrolled in an online course (Allen & Seaman, 2008). Technology has entered the educational system and is here to stay.

In order to offer more convenient, flexible course options to adult students, instructors engage in converting their courses to an electronic environment, examining how they teach, researching the technological capabilities available, implementing the best possible tools for the learning objectives and re-thinking how they approach the educational setting. What is the effectiveness of using CD-ROM, videotapes, Internet, discussion forums, Web 2.0 technologies in higher educational courses? "The challenge for educators is to utilize this technology in ways that facilitate the highest level of learning outcomes" (Cox, 2008, p.1). While some institutions may give assistance to the faculty to enhance courses with the aid of an instructional designer, other institutions may not provide such assistance, so it is up to the individual instructor to create the learning situation with more technological opportunities. How does an instructor create an online learning experience that uses technology appropriately and enhances the learning possibilities for students?

One way in which education has been enhanced historically is through application of learning style research. This research and the development of assessment inventories have been influencing the entire education system since the 1940s. An online search for 'learning styles' using Google Scholar received 1,480,000 hits. Numerous studies concerning learning styles have been conducted on K-12 students as well as undergraduate and graduate students (Butler & Pinto-Zipp, 2006). Kolb (1984) found that students' learning styles made a significant impact on their learning preferences and choices; however, "individual styles of learning are complex and not easily reducible into simple typologies" (Kolb, 1984, p. 66). This is important to keep in mind when reading this chapter which will include several different learning style inventories and research. Although researchers may distill their ideas down to a simple model to grasp the complex reality of learning, this phenomenon is multi-faceted. Each learning style author has his/her own lens for examining learning styles and it is too complex to ever expect that one instrument can assess all aspects.

As early as 1991, Verduin and Clark stated that "those designing distance education should, moreover, pay attention to differences among adults—in individual learning styles, preferences for acquiring new knowledge and skills, and levels of maturity or ways of responding to new learning situations" (p.32). While learning styles complicate the course design process, they must be taken into consideration if an instructor truly desires to create an environment that will enhance the learning for each student (DuCharme-Hansen & Dupin-Bryant, 2004).

In this chapter, learning styles will be discussed first to give the reader a brief background of several instruments. The research on learning styles and online courses will be aligned with the learning style instruments discussed previously. Finally, the interrelationship of learning styles and technology will be discussed including some instructional strategies which coincide with the learning styles described by the Gregorc Style Delineator and the VARK instruments.

LEARNING STYLES

What is a learning style? Unfortunately, there is a plethora of definitions to accompany each researcher's lens from learning preferences to multiple intelligences. Grasha (1996) defined learning style as the participant's preferred way of learning. Cranton (2005) defines learning styles as "preferences for certain conditions or ways of learning, where learning means the development of meanings, values, skills, and strategies" (p.362). Although researchers cannot agree on one definition of learning styles, most believe that learning style is the way students process, internalize, and remember information (Dunn & Griggs, 2000). Every person has a learning style; however, styles can be influenced by experience and environment. Most people have a learning style preference, but even within a single preference there is great diversity among learners. "The researcher or practitioner entering the areas of learning style may well do so with some sense of trepidation given the volume, diversity, and apparent dissociation of writing, theory, and empiricism in the field" (Cassidy, 2004, p.440). Learning style and cognitive style are often used interchangeably by authors, while other authors define the terms distinctly. The term cognitive style came from cognitive psychologists and usually limits its discussion to the processing of information (Cranton, 2005). Some researchers made a distinction between learning styles and learning modalities. They defined learning modalities as sensory (i.e., visual, auditory, kinesthetic) ways to take in information. To keep the confusion to a minimum, this chapter will just use the term learning style and limit the scope to those authors using this term.

On the first day of a course, the instructor encounters extraverts, introverts, visual learners, auditory learners, concrete learners and abstract learners, just to name a few. The diversity alone can be overwhelming. When working with an array of adults, knowledge of learning styles can foster effective teaching techniques.

For years, educational specialists have identified that students in a face-to-face classroom learn more if the learning activities are directed at their different learning styles (Dunn, Honigsfeld, & Doolan, 2009; Merriam, Caffarella, & Baumgartner, 2007). Building on adult education literature, Cranton (2005) lists six approaches to addressing learning styles: "1) experiential, 2) social interaction, 3) personality, 4) multiple intelligences and emotional intelligence, 5) perceptions, and 6) conditions or needs" (p. 362). Because of the diverse learning style typologies, Cranton's framework will be used to organize and focus this discussion of learning styles. The instruments described here will be used in the following discussion of research on learning styles and online courses.

The first category, experiential approaches, encompasses learning styles which incorporate making meaning from the learner's experiences. The most popular and most researched experiential learning style inventory was developed by David Kolb (1984). His model has been adapted to classroom instruction where students are taken through the four stages of a learning cycle (concrete experience, reflective observation, abstract conceptualization, and active experimentation) in order to touch on the strengths of each student. Kolb's Learning Style Inventory (LSI) rates learners on a bipolar scale, which indicates the learner's preference for active experimentation (doing) versus reflective observation (reflecting) and concrete experience (experiencing) versus abstract conceptualization (thinking). Learners fall into one of four quadrants: Diverger, Converger, Assimilator or Accommodator. Each of these learning styles appreciates a different learning experience. Convergers need action which is driven by their understanding of the abstract concepts.

They use logic and a scientific approach with the preference to actively experiment with the information and need to be able to immediately apply the material to a practical situation. They are unemotional in their approach to learning and prefer to work alone. Converger and Assimilator types share a preference for abstract conceptualization. Assimilators combine their strength for abstract concepts with reflective reasoning. They can distill information down to a more logical form and are more interested in abstract thoughts than people. Assimilators like to spend time refining theories. Diverger and Accommodators learn through the concrete experience (hands-on activity) instead of abstract conceptualization. Accommodators combine concrete experiences with a preference for active experimentation, which means they dive in and learn by trial and error. Divergers prefer a concrete experience with time for reflections and observation. They look at the information from many different angles and can become overwhelmed with the volume of information. Divergers are creative learners who consider multiple potential strategies for learning and problem-solving. The LSI was the predominant instrument utilized in studies reviewed later in this chapter.

In the experiential category, another popular learning style indicator with adult students is Gregorc Style Delineator (Gregorc, 1982). This instrument measures a person's perceptual and ordering abilities. Perception is the means by which a learner grasps information on a continuum of abstractness and concreteness. The abstractness qualities enable the learner to grasp information using intuition and feelings. The concreteness qualities enable the learner to grasp the information via the five senses. The ordering abilities are ways in which learners organize, arrange, and reference information on continuum from sequential to random. The learner with a sequential preference will organize information in a step-by-step fashion, logically, and methodically. Those with a random preference will organize information nonlinearly, in leaps or large chunks at a time. These qualities are grouped together in four distinct patterns: concrete sequential, abstract sequential, abstract random and concrete random. A critical difference between Kolb's LSI and the Gregorc Style Delineator is the ordering dimension, which notes whether a student likes a sequential approach to the learning or a random approach to topics (Miller, 2005). This is an important consideration in selecting a learning style instrument for research.

Cranton's (2005) second category, the social interaction approach, focuses on the engagement of students with others during the learning process. With the emphasis in most adult education classrooms on collaboration and discussion, this approach might not be as neutral as some of the other assessments. Grasha-Riechmann Student Learning Style Scale (Grasha, 1996) measures the social interaction preferences of a learner. Although developed for college age students, this instrument has adult norms available and has been rated with strong reliability (James & Blank, 1993). The Grasha-Riechmann Student Learning Style Scale addresses six dimensions: 1) competitive, where students try to outperform others, 2) collaborative, where students like to share ideas and discuss, 3) avoidant, where students do not like to participate in class activities or attend class, 4) participative, where students take responsibility and like to be active in the learning environment, 5) dependent, where students rely on the instructor for information and requirements, and 6) independent, where students are self-directed and learn on their own. All learners possess all six of these categories to a certain extent; however, most learners will show a stronger preference toward one or two categories.

The third learning style category described by Cranton (2005) was the personality models, which give a much broader description of the person than just a learning style inventory. One of the popular instruments, Myers-Briggs Type Indicator (MBTI), builds on Carl Jung's theories

(Myers, 1993). Personality is a much broader concept and gives a more comprehensive picture of the student. Learning characteristics are derived from the psychological type preference. It places a significant role in what grabs a learner's attention. The theory is that if the instructor can teach in a manner that is in sync with the student, then that student will attend to the lesson and the possibility of learning increases. The Myers Briggs is based on the fact that there is a logical reason for the differences among people. "Psychological type theory is based on two attitudes towards the world and four functions of living" (Cranton, 2005, p.364). MBTI delineates these differences down to how a person perceives (the process of becoming aware) and judges (the conclusions made about these perceptions) each encounter. The introvert gains energy within, focusing on self, while the extravert gains energy from and focuses on the external world. The thinking function is demonstrated by persons approaching the topic logically and analytically. The feeling function is demonstrated when people take others and values into consideration. The sensing function is demonstrated when people take in information from the world through their five senses. When persons perceive the world through intuition, possibilities, and imagination, they are using the intuitive function determined by the MBTI. These elements are combined to create 16 different personality types. Examples of the learning characteristics derived from personality type are persons using introverted thinking are reflective and critical as they approach the topic, while extraverted thinkers learn through organized planned experiences (Myers, 1993).

The fourth category encompasses multiple intelligences and emotional intelligence. While Cranton (2005) states that these are not learning styles, it is her perspective that they inform adult educators understanding of learning styles. Howard Gardner (1999) brought the idea of multiple intelligences to the education community. He argued for the existence of relatively autonomous human intellectual competencies: linguistic, logical-mathematical, musical, spatial, bodily-kinesthetic, interpersonal, intrapersonal, naturalist, spiritual, and existential. Linguistic and logical mathematical have traditionally been the most recognized intelligences in the educational systems. Those people with linguistic intelligence are sensitive to the written or spoken word. People whose strength is the logical mathematical intelligence analyze information logically and scientifically. According to Gardner, people with musical intelligence excel at musical performance and composition. Those who possess spatial intelligence exhibit the potential to see and manipulate patterns, have depth perception, and work in three-dimensional space, such as artists or surgeons. The intelligence demonstrated by dancers and athletes is bodily-kinesthetic, which involves the potential to use the entire body to create.. Individuals who work effectively with others and understand their desires and motivations are expressing the interpersonal intelligence. Intrapersonal intelligence involves understanding oneself and regulating ones performance and emotions. Persons who display the naturalist intelligence understand living things (plants and animal). The gift for mysticism, religion, or spiritual feeling is associated with spiritual intelligence. Existential intelligence is revealed by persons who have an aptitude for transcendence and understanding the meaning of life and death. Daniel Goleman (1998) popularized the theory of emotional intelligence, which includes understanding, knowing and managing one's emotions and handling relationships with others. Emotional intelligence closely aligns with intrapersonal and interpersonal intelligences.

Perception models, the fifth category listed by Cranton, primarily deal with the observable traits or instructional preferences of visual, auditory, tactile or kinesthetic. Physiological styles are sensory-based. Some researchers refer to these as learning modalities. A simple example is when people ask for directions to a new location. Would they rather have the person draw a map (visual) or just listen to the directions (auditory)? Perhaps, they prefer to have the person tell them the directions while they draw the map (tactile). Do they listen to the person and physically move their body to make the turns as indicated (kinesthetic)? A popular physiological style inventory is the VARK. VARK is an acronym for visual, auditory, read/write, and kinesthetic (Fleming, n.d.). Visual learners prefer information presented using mind maps, concept maps, models, patterns, or graphs. Auditory learners prefer to hear the information, so lectures, podcasts, chat rooms, mobile phones, and discussing the material are all ways to tap into their strengths. The read/write learners prefer information displayed in print, so textbooks, PowerPoint, and websites work well. Kinesthetic learners prefer information demonstrated and like to interact with the topic, write notes, highlight, and touch it. An instructor could use simulations, videos, and documentary films with these learners. Most learners possess all these modalities and will mix them as the context deems appropriate.

Cranton's sixth category described was conditions and needs. These include the environmental condition and physical needs for students to learn. Environmental conditions include such elements as amount of light, background sound, temperature of the room, and location of learning space. Physical needs takes into consideration the time of day, extent of mobility and quantity and type of foodstuff. The most popular model in this category is Dunn and Dunn Learning Style Model. This sociological approach takes into consideration the environment (sound, light, temperature, learning space), emotions (motivation, persistence, responsibility, structure), sociological (working alone, in pairs, with peers, with a team, with an instructor, or varied), physiological (perceptual, intake, time, mobility), and psychological (global, analytic, impulsive, reflective) processing (Dunn & Griggs, 2000). The learner can use these simultaneously or successively.

As demonstrated above, "the construct of learning style is a complicated issue and cannot be defined in simple terms" (James & Maher, 2004, p.123). Many of the learning styles discussed are based on Western culture, which tends to emphasize individuality and competition. A more holistic, collaborative environment may be learning style strength for persons from other cultures. While knowledge of learning styles can facilitate guiding the activities for learning experiences, instructors cannot focus on just one. An understanding of the diverse learning style research is a good foundation for designing learning experiences in any format (face-to-face, hybrid, or online). The diversity of learning style research also significantly impacts the information gleaned from researching online course experiences.

LEARNING STYLES AND ONLINE COURSE STUDIES

As online learning gained momentum, research studies followed suit. There have been numerous studies conducted concerning online learning and learning styles on K-12 learners and undergraduate students. Fewer studies have focused on graduate students and adult students. Even fewer studies have looked at the impact of learning styles, online learning and adult students. These particular research studies were chosen because their population included what has been classified as adult students (25 years or older) and they addressed one of the instruments described in the experiential, social interaction and perception categories. The personality and multiple intelligences categories were excluded because as described earlier they do not include learning style inventories, but learning characteristics were derived from their models. The condition and need category was excluded because no research was found investigating online learning or online instructional strategies.

Diaz and Cartnal (1999) questioned if there was a difference between the learning styles of students who choose a face-to-face format and those who choose to take the course in the online format. Their research compared student learning styles in a face-to-face and an online health education course at a community college. There were students over the age of 26 in both formats. Thirty-six percent of the online students were over the age of 26 compared to only six percent of the students in the face-to-face format. Diaz and Cartnal (1999) observed the lack of social interaction in the online format during their investigation and chose to use the Grasha-Reichmann Student Learning Style Scales (GRSLSS). The researchers based their decision on the fact the GRSLSS was created for use with college students and it focuses on interactions between students, instructor and learning in general. As briefly described earlier, the GRSLSS measures learning styles across six categories: independent learners, dependent learners, competitive learners, collaborative learners, avoidant learners, and participant learners. Using correlation analysis, their findings indicated that the online learners showed a negative relationship between the independent learning style and the collaborative and dependent styles. This means they preferred more independent study, working alone on assignments, and a self-paced approach to instruction. Students in the face-to-face environment had a significant positive correlation between collaborative and competitive and participant learning styles. This group demonstrated a preference for working collaboratively with students and instructor, a drive to perform better than their classmates, and a need for direction from the instructor. While some may see collaboration and competition as direct opposites, these students were working on group projects (collaborative), but wanted their group project to be better than other groups in the course (competitive). There was also a positive correlation between competitive and participant, which means they were willing to do what the instructor wanted them to do. The conclusion that Diaz and Cartnel (1999) generated from their research was that online learning must emphasize the independent nature of the learning and limit group work. By giving students choices over their learning projects, instructors can tap into the independent nature of these learners. From this research, instructors can glean the learning style type (independent and self-regulating) that may self select the online course environment.

Terrell and Dringus (1999) studied the effect of learning styles on student performance in an online master's level course. Using Kolb's Learning Style Inventory (LSI), they found out of 98 graduate students, seventy-five percent fell into the Converger and Assimilator categories. Kolb's (1984) studies demonstrated there were "reasonable indications of the learning style orientations that characterize the different professions" (p. 88). The Converger and Assimilator indicated an association with technical, information processing, and scientific careers. The learning style that had the lowest completion rate was the Accommodator category. Accommodators value hands-on concrete experiences and people. Terrell and Dringus (1999) hypothesized that perhaps it was the Accommodators need for working with people, relying on people to gather information, needing to affect change or do something, and drawing on intuition that caused them to be unsuccessful in the online course environment. Being a person who likes to be immersed in the learning situation and collaborate with others, Accommodators may find the distance between instructor and other learners a determent to their ability to maximize their learning. This research leads to the question as to whether the online course environment is suited for all types of learners. Once again, the implication is that certain learning styles will self-select online courses because they are better suited to succeed with the technology and remoteness of the instructor.

In another study using Kolb's Learning Style Inventory, Simpson and Du (2004) looked at the relationship between learning style and enjoyment level in an online course for graduate students. Their findings revealed that Convergers liked the online experience the most, while Assimilators liked the online experience the least. Simpson and Du (2004) classified participation as "hits," "reads," and "posts." A "hit" was when a student accessed an online course page or course tool. A "read" was when a student accessed a posting in the mail or discussion area of the course. A "post" was when a student composed a message either in the mail or discussion area. Divergers made the most "hits" and "reads," and Assimilators made the least "posts" even though students knew that participation counted toward their final grade. As courses are designed, instructors need to look at ways to incorporate electronic activities that appeal to the observing and doing strength of one student and the reflecting and theorizing strength of another student. Simpson and Du (2004) concluded it was "good practice for online instructors to incorporate students' learning styles into the pedagogical design of their courses to maximize their students' success" (p.133). It also demonstrates research that documents which learning style has a more positive attitude toward online learning.

Butler and Pinto-Zipp (2006) was the one study found that broke down the online experience into instructional strategies used in the online environment with a population of adult students. They used the Gregorc Learning Styles Delineator to assess the learning styles of 96 graduate students with an age range of 23 to 83. Approximately 72 percent of the population was female, and 83 percent stated that they had taken at least three online courses. Fifty-six percent of the respondents exhibited a dual learning style rather than a single style, with the 25 percent reporting a combination of concrete random and abstract random and 18 percent a combination of concrete sequential and abstract sequential. The percentage of single learning styles reported was concrete sequential (14%), concrete random (14%), abstract random (9%), and abstract sequential (5%). They also had students rank a variety of instructional methods on a scale of most helpful to least helpful in learning the material. Several positive correlations were found between learning styles and online instructional method. The concrete sequential style and email had a positive correlation ($r = .562, p < .05$). A strong positive correlation (r = 994, $p < .01$) was reported between abstract sequential type and computer simulations. The abstract random learning style was positively correlated with mandated number of assignments ($r = .787, p < .05$) and email (($r = .787, p < .05$). Although these may not seem to correlate according to the learning style descriptors for an abstract random learner, these strategies assisted the learners in staying on track with the course. Negative correlations were found between concrete random and online exams ($r = -.743, p < .01$) and abstract sequential with e-journals ($r = -.918, p < .05$), use of multimedia ($r = -.984, p < .01$), and video clips ($r = -.976, p < .01$). There were four positive correlations between the combination concrete sequential and abstract sequential with self-assessment quizzes ($r = .712, p < .01$), video clips ($r = .596, p < .05$), chat rooms ($r = .556, p < .05$), and group activities ($r = .485, p < .05$). Butler and Pinto-Zipp (2006) caution the reader about making cause and effect relations based on these correlations. Another point to keep in mind is that adult population in the Butler and Pinto-Zipp (2006) study was very experienced with online learning and very satisfied with their current experiences. "The instructional methods that emphasized interactions and convenience were rated highly by the subjects as most beneficial to online learning" (Butler & Pinto-Zipp, 2006, p. 213). With working adults, convenience and flexibility are hallmarks whether the course is delivered face-to-face or online. A good mix of discussion, sharing ideas, debating, and fostering a learning community are important to adult students in any forum (Collins & Zacharakis, 2009). However, it does demonstrate the variety of learning elements needed in an online course and how different learning styles prefer different forms of electronic learning. In a classroom setting, instructors should make the same accommodations to the different learning styles. This knowledge can now be transferred to the electronic tools available.

While Gaytan and McEwen (2007) studied effective online instructional strategies, their research only included one statement concerning learning styles. Out of 332 students, 67 percent of the students surveyed were over the age of 23. They compared the perceptions of faculty and students in online courses. One of the quality indicators of online instruction was "a variety of instructional strategies (e.g., visual, audio, kinesthetic) are being used to address various learning styles of students" (Gaytan & McEwen, 2007, p.124). Seventy-two percent of the faculty agreed or strongly agreed with this statement. Interestingly, only 42 percent of the entire student population agreed or strongly agreed with it. While Gaytan and McEwen (2007) recommend that instructors review the literature on learning style preferences and develop a variety of teaching strategies, there is not much data in their research study to support it.

These are just a few of the rich studies that are published researching learning styles and online learning. Most of the studies as represented above are concerning learning style preferences and students' choice for online instruction or face-to-face instruction. The researchers all chose their learning style instrument deliberately for its measure of certain learning characteristics or traits with a majority choosing Kolb's Learning Style Indicator. While this type of research informs the questions of which learning styles seem to assist the learner in having a more positive experience in an online environment, they do not assist the instructor in developing teaching strategies to address multiple learning styles. One study examined the technological instructional strategies and learning style with adult students. Ultimately, knowledge of learning styles should impact the teaching strategies used in the course.

USING TECHNOLOGY INFORMED BY LEARNING STYLES

From the research discussed in this chapter, we know that learning styles are important for instructors to understand and that just as certain learning styles prefer certain approaches in a face-to-face classroom, similarly certain learning styles will prefer certain technological approaches to learning. The question for the instructor is how to design a course using the technology appropriately informed by the learning style research. Much of the literature focuses on online learning and technology; however, technology can equally be incorporated into a face-to-face environment as well.

Further, from the research, instructors could be led to believe that students with a certain learning style will self-select to enroll in online courses, but instructors can never take for granted the student population's learning styles. Therefore, instructors need to design learning experiences that touch on the variety of learning styles. Kolb (1984) even stated that exposing learners to different approaches to the learning material increased the students' adaptability and strengthened their non-dominant learning styles. The learning style researchers consistently state that learners possess all the traits measured by the instrument, but that learners prefer or are dominate in one or two traits over the others. When instructors create a course and develop the myriad of approaches to the content, a mix of all the styles can be incorporated into the learning activities. The goal is to use the technology appropriately for the learning style.

What electronic tools are available to assist instructors in meeting the learning style preferences of all learners? Since the information about learning styles is incredibly diverse and the descriptions of learners various, to demonstrate the application of technology with learning styles, this section will narrow the focus to some Web 2.0 tools which can enhance learning and the electronic tools aligned with the learning style physiological category represented by the VARK approach (visual, auditory, read/write, and kinesthetic) and the experiential category represented by the Gregorc Style Delineator (concrete sequential, abstract sequential, abstract random and concrete random). This section is informed by the research studies as well as information gathered from discussions with adult students in higher education courses concerning their learning styles according to the VARK approach and the Gregorc Style Delineator. The experience of these adult learners with electronic mediums varied; some only had experience with a few of the electronic tools in one course, while others had experience with several in up to 50 courses.

IMPACT OF WEB 2.0

While practitioners have incorporated many of these tools into educating and training the adult population, researchers are just now beginning to consider some of the Web 2.0 functions currently available. The new technologies include web logs, wikis, podcasting and video casting, photo galleries, such as Flickr, and virtual multiplayer games (e.g., Second Life). These are innovative technologies for all educators to grapple with and come to some understanding of how they can be used to improve the learning of students (Richardson, 2009). While this section will not describe how to create some of these, it will link the technologies with learning style research.

Web logs, commonly known by the shortened name of blogs, have become very popular. They are simply websites that individuals easily update and contain conversations or reflections (Richardson, 2009). Blogs are dynamic learning sites which allow readers to exchange ideas, links, and questions. In addition, blogs can include graphics, photos, audio and video files. The learner, who needs interaction with other people and active products, would find blogging a great technique to enhance their learning. For instance, one use with adult students would be assigning a blog instead of a typewritten or handwritten reflective journal. Blogs can be open to fellow students or closed to just a few people. Blogs can be public on the Internet or private to just course participants or small group within the course. Students can explore other blogs on the web and link to contradictory and supporting opinions. "Posting to a Weblog can take many forms. Students can write about personal reactions to topics covered in class, post links, write reflectively, and summarize and annotate reading" (Richardson, 2009, p. 28). Blogs can even be combined with a research activity such as web site evaluations. Students would link to the sites, analyze and critic each site within the blog format.

Another use of blogs is to structure a student portfolio. Portfolios have been used in programs to demonstrate student learning throughout a degree program. These allow students to collect and present the best work to demonstrate their learning aligning with program outcomes or rubrics created by the faculty of the program. Traditionally, students have submitted massive notebooks or the institution may have specialized software they purchased to allow for electronic submissions. Unfortunately at this time, special software may be too expensive for an institution. An alternative submission format, using the electronic medium, is to create a blog electronic portfolio. Students just upload or link to their work, write their reflections on the learning experience and examine their own progress through the degree program. Instructors have permissions to view student blogs and evaluate them online, allowing for feedback to be given expediently.

Wikis are another electronic tool that supports fluid interaction. From the constructivist mindset, knowledge is not created in isolation, and a wiki provides a great collaborative site for knowledge to be shared. Wikipedia is an example of a group created and edited encyclopedia (Richardson, 2009). In a course, students could be assigned to find information on Wikipedia that conflicted with information the students had learned through their own research and update the Wikipedia site. Wikis are a great way for students to create an online text for a course. Students learn to evaluate and analyze the work of others as they are responsible for the content collected on the Wiki. If students are reviewing separate books on a subject, instead of just writing a book critique for the instructor, these could be placed on a wiki and available to all the students in the course. The learning community is enlarged from one-to-one to one-to-many. From year-to-year, the wikis become increasingly more dynamic as each section of the course access the book's wiki page and add to the site. Now the learning community is expanded from just the students enrolled this semester or for this course to students from year to year. The collaborative world of wikis really "demonstrates how knowledge and information is becoming more and more a group effort" (Richardson, 2009, p.69). Wikis definitely appeal to learning styles that enjoy collaborating with others and generating a creative product.

Podcasting or audio streaming is already being used by instructors to record lectures and make available to students with great success (Evans, 2008; Richardson, 2009). Podcasts are audio material which can be downloaded to a mobile listening device (e.g., iPOD, iPhone, Blackberry) or to a computer. Students listen at a time that is convenient for them. In reverse flow, the students could also digitally record material, such as an interview and upload the file for everyone to hear.

Digital cameras are very popular, providing a wonderful electronic tool for the educational environment. They enable instructors and learners to create a video and upload to the course management system. It also gives students the means to creatively complete an assignment. For example, in a course on group dynamics, the instructor could give students different scenarios and record the small group interactions. The digital recordings could then be played back, so all students review and analyze the group dynamics displayed. Digitally recording a graduate of the program and playing it the first night of a class or making it available for students to download and view at their convenience, allows students to see and hear a testimonial without having to be physically present with the graduate. Smartphones or cell phones are other digital recording devices used to capture digital photos. On the web there are numerous places to publish these photographs and videos. Flickr is one such place which educators have been using in their classrooms (Richardson, 2009). Flickr allows annotations to be created and comments to be posted, allowing for conversations to develop.

Multiuser virtual environment was once isolated to the digital gaming community. However, Second Life has moved into the education and corporate environment (Vossen & Hagemann, 2007). Second Life provides a three-dimensional virtual world where participants own a place or an island. Several institutions have islands where prospective students can take a tour of the campus. Through the use of an avatar, students are able to virtually walk across campus. Classrooms are constructed and instructors can lecture in a virtual world. Second Life is also being used by instructors to create real life professional scenarios students will encounter in the world. Instead of just reading a case study, an instructor could create a hotel and conference center. In groups, students have to market and host an event at the center with all the aspects of catering, signage, and audiovisual equipment at a fraction of the cost to experience such an event as at a real world hotel or conference center.

Web 2.0 features are being used by K-12 teachers and are being integrated into adult and higher education quickly. While more research needs to be conducted as to how these support different learning styles, the alignment of electronic educational tools with learning styles in the following section is informed by adult student experiences.

LEARNING STYLES AND INSTRUCTIONAL STRATEGIES

"I learn best by hands on and interaction with peers;" an adult student responded when asked if he/she preferred face-to-face or online learning. To this student the only way to experience learning in this manner was for it to be presented in a face-to-face format. The challenge for educators is to create a hands-on and interactive learning experience even if the format is not face-to-face. Creating a learning experience with learning styles in mind is one way to approach this student's needs. What learning style aligns with different electronic mediums at the disposal of the instructor? We will look first at the physiological model as described by VARK learning styles (visual, auditory, read/write, and kinesthetic), which was explained earlier.

According to VARK, the visual learners need images (Fleming, n.d.). The best learning strategies to incorporate into a course include graphics, pictures, flow charts, and graphs. Video streaming a lecture where students can see the instructor's facial expressions and gestures is a wonderful way to enhance the learning with electronic medium. Many instructors may get stage fright as they are being recorded. It is important to be as animated on the video as in the classroom. To appeal to this learning style, instructors need to use color and lots of it. Examples include highlighting portions of the announcements or emails and writing messages in different colors. Another excellent tool to use with these learners is to create a mind map of the course structure and assignment due dates. Instructors can begin linking with this learning style by brainstorming all the ways a course can be enhanced with color and visual representations.

Auditory learners need to listen to the message and verbally process it with another person. This learner will attend face-to-face classes, because they need to hear and discuss with others the ideas presented. To enhance these learners' experience using electronic medium the course format will include downloadable audio versions of lectures and PowerPoint slides. These learners enjoy the experience of hearing authors read their own book or present their own concepts. With many course management systems, it is possible to make an audio recording of announcements and any lectures created through PowerPoint. Instructors can describe the graphs and upload the recording along with the PowerPoint slide. This is a great way to enhance the learning experience for auditory learners. The facilitator can create Podcasts of interviews or lectures with authors or link to podcasts already created on the Internet. To appeal to the auditory learner, podcasts and audio streaming are great electronic tools to incorporate into any course. Many instructors are already digitally recording lectures and placing them on websites for students to download to their iPod, computer, or other listening device. This allows the auditory learner to review a lecture in the learning format that is their strength. It also allows for students who are at distance or unable to attend to have access to the information in a verbal format instead of just reading an instructor's or classmates notes. These learners would also benefit from a synchronous session where they connect with the instructor using visual software, such as Skype. For instance, Skype users make telephone and video connections through the Internet using their computer and Skype software. This gives the learner and instructor the opportunity to see and hear each other in real time. Another possibility is the use of Webinar (web-based seminar) software where again the students and instructor can connect using their telephone and computer. Participants can all hear each other as they view the same document on their computer screens; however, most software does not allow them to see each other. This is a tool to deliver a lecture, presentation, or seminar. It is very interactive with the participants able to discuss and engage each other.

The third learning style documented by VARK is read/write. The read/write learner has a strong preference for reading and writing as a way to learn. Textbook assignments, readings, lecture notes, and manuals are important learning tools for these students (Fleming, n.d.). These learners like to turn graphs and flow charts into words. Links to e-journals and electronic databases align with this learners need to read. The message board or discussion board also assists these students in learning the material. Assignments which tap into the read/write learners strengths include writing and posting papers, and peer evaluation of assignments. These students often enjoy blogging and wikis. As described earlier, blogging could be in the form of an electronic reflective journaling activity which allows for comments to be made by other students; whereas wikis are platforms for the creation of group papers and online collaboration.

The kinesthetic learner needs to incorporate all their senses into the learning situation. They need hands-on experiences, field trips, and laboratory experiences where they can see, touch, smell, hear and taste the concepts. Even distance learners can be sent out into their community to experience a concept and then share that experience in a pictorial and written format in an electronic format. Digital cameras are one option to capture the experience, but another is just a cell phone with a camera or a smartphone. Instructors can create videos of real life experiences (i.e., capturing a video of a face-to-face adult learning experience), upload the videos and have students work in groups to evaluate the example. Flickr is a tool that allows instructors to upload photos and annotate parts of the picture. Group discussions can result as students add their comments and questions under the picture. These tools address the kinesthetic learner need to "do" things to learn. Virtual gaming technology is another electronic tool to be used with the kinesthetic learner. In a community such as Second Life, the kinesthetic learner could immerse themselves into a learning situation, such as planning a conference as illustrated earlier.

While physiological category is important to consider, the experiential approaches inform instructors of the ways adults make meaning of the information. The next learning styles types, which will be discussed in alignment with suggested technological tools to enhance their learning, are the Gregorc's concrete sequential, abstract sequential, abstract random, and concrete random.

The concrete sequential learner has a preference for step-by-step directions, concrete examples, and specificity (Gregorc, 1982). Learning tools appealing to this style which can be incorporated into a face-to-face environment or an online environment include: checklists, mandated number of assignments, mandated number of posts on the message board, self-assessment quizzes, textbook readings, CD-ROM tutorials, video clips with step-by-step instructions or explanation, threaded discussion about current trends with application to their workplace or life, and online examinations.

The abstract sequential learner has a preference to analyze, compare, contrast, and evaluate (Gregorc, 1982). A person with this learning style prefers to work alone and needs recognition of their personal effort. Learning tools appealing to this style which can be incorporated into a face-to-face environment or an online environment include: individual assignments, textbook readings, webquest (read, analyze, and synthesize material contained on the web), threaded debate, blogs, case studies, problem-based assignments, online tutorials, and computer simulations.

The abstract random learner has a preference for subjective, abstract material (Gregorc, 1982). This learner likes to collaborate with others and demonstrate learning through creative artifacts (e.g. art, music, prose, film). Learning tools appealing to this style which can be incorporated into a face-to-face environment or an online environment include: wikis, blogs, student lounge on the message board, synchronous discussions, post bios and pictures, collaborative opportunities, group projects, audio conferencing, video conferencing, video clips, movies/films, using emoticons, and express emotions in posts. A possible assignment is to have the students create a webpage introducing themselves to the group. If a webpage is not an option, the course management systems may have the capability for learners to post their bios and pictures. In the online environment, many students, and especially those who are abstract random (Gregorc), find it difficult because their strength is reading body language and they feel disconnected from the learning environment without the physical presence of classmates and the instructor. To build a learning community, it is important to give students time to become acquainted; it does not matter whether the environment is face-to-face or online.

The concrete random learner prefers to create new ideas, products, or approaches (Gregorc, 1982). This learner begins with the big picture, is naturally curious, competitive, inventive, and explores. Learning tools appealing to this style which can be incorporated into a face-to-face environment or an online environment include: individual assignments with creative products, video clips, multimedia, computer simulations, virtual multi-player games (e.g. Second Life), threaded discussions, chat rooms, graphics, audio and video lectures, self-assessment quizzes, online examinations, and CD-ROM or online tutorials.

Technology has provided the opportunity for instructors to include multiple learning experiences into their courses. Manner (2005) recommended that instructors incorporate redundancy and reciprocity into their online course design and delivery. Redundancy involves giving multiple ways for students to access information in navigation opportunities, formats (audio and visual files), and descriptions of material. There is not one way to access information online which aligns with the multiple learning preferences discussed earlier. Instructors need to take this into consideration when designing a course and provide links to the same material in multiple locations. In its early generations, online learning relied heavily on print to instruct. It seemed instructors took correspondence courses and merely transferred them to a different type of technology. Today, there are numerous alternatives from audio files (i.e., podcasts) of instructor lectures, audio and video files of others, and websites that convey the same information found in a textbook. Just as instructors vary examples in a face-to-face classroom, the online environment needs numerous examples. Reciprocity can be achieved by keeping in mind that some students need the forest (the big picture) and others need the trees (the details and steps). Instructors need to approach the learning from all directions in order to create a learning environment for all learning types. By providing a summary of information, instructors provide for students who need to start with the big picture and then move to the details and as well as providing for students who start with the details a way to capture the overall picture at the end. For instance, in addition to the narrative discussion which appeals to abstract random, instructors can create templates with assignments for the concrete sequential.

Synchronous learning options are necessary for some learning styles, as described earlier. One student responded, "The instant response to my questions and the information from fellow students is useful in my learning effectiveness". Real time chats and video conferencing can assist these students in achieving their learning goals.

These are just a few examples on how to align technological enhancements in the learning environment with learning styles for adult students. More research needs to be conducted with an adult student population concerning learning styles and online instructional strategies.

FUTURE RESEARCH RECOMMENDATIONS

Where do we go from here? Many of the studies have been reviewing learning styles and online learning. They have noted which learning styles are successful in the electronic environment. Few studies have analyzed the instructional devices or Web 2.0 features aligning them with learning styles with adult learners.

In addition to adult learners in the Western culture, researchers need to explore the link between learning styles and adult students from different cultures. With online courses, the possibility of students from different cultures and regions of the world enrolling in a course anywhere is very high. The holistic approach to learning found in more collaborative cultures may affect how the learning styles and electronic tools align.

Students have commented that their analysis of learning in an online environment was tainted by whether they value their online course experiences as good or bad. If the experience was bad, then no electronic instructional strategies appeal to them or seem to be effective. If students perceived the experience in a positive light, then many of the learning approaches were perceived to be very effective. However, the real reason some students may have perceived the experience as "bad" was because the instructor did not give them enough feedback. This issue has nothing to do with learning styles and effective learning techniques. First, conduct a course created to include technology-enhanced learning experiences for all learning types. Then study the students' perception of the learning and the effectiveness of the electronic instructional tools.

Research with learning styles and technology needs to also take into consideration whether the adult learner is a digital native (born with technology and very familiar with the electronic world) or digital immigrant (relearning how to do things with technology). How familiar a person is with the medium will impact how easy it is to navigate and accomplish tasks. How does learning style affect the advanced user in contrast to the inexperienced user of technology?

CONCLUSION

With the current economic situation of rising gas prices and laying off more workers, Allen and Seaman (2008) predict adults will be seeking viable ways to increase their knowledge base and diversify their skills in order to find employment opportunities. Historically, in economic down turns adult students have been a major source for increased enrollments. According to Allen & Seaman (2008), there is widespread conviction that adults will opt for the online course. For example, adults may need to save money on fuel and need the flexible time schedule in order to complete their education anytime and anywhere. Instructors of online courses must improve their understanding of students and how this medium influences learning.

There is a range of offerings that different institutions classify as online learning. Online courses began as text-only using just PowerPoint slides and instructor notes. Most courses may still be at this point as instructors new to using technology join the ranks of experienced online facilitators. There are more tools available now for online courses, from blogs to wikis to webquests, which have the potential to enhance the learning and engage the learner in new and different ways. Some institutions may also offer online courses using an avatar and the third dimensional world, such as Second Life. Instructors need not limit the incorporation of technology to just online course formats. These tools can greatly enhance the learning in a face-to-face environment as well.

While instructors cannot be all things to all learners, the knowledge of learning styles can assist instructors in making deliberate decisions about what technologies to incorporate in courses. Web 2.0 features should be given serious consideration. Multitasking is moving to a new level. Learning is fluid and students move easily from synchronous events to asynchronous explorations. There are new learning spaces, such as blogs, wikis, and Flickr, which appeal to multiple learning preferences. Students and faculty can post a comment while walking to lunch with the mobile wireless devices available. Learning styles can still inform instructors and learners as they move from the walled learning environment to dynamic, fluid, mobile, and global knowledge exploration.

REFERENCES

Allen, I., & Seaman, J. (March, 2007). *Online nation: Five years of growth in online learning.* Needham, MA: Sloan Consortium. Retrieved April 22, 2009, from http://www.sloan-c.org/publications/survey/pdf/online_nation.pdf

Allen, I., & Seaman, J. (November, 2008). *Staying the Course*. Needham, MA: Sloan Consortium. Retrieved April 22, 2009, from http://www.sloanconsortium.org/publications/survey/pdf/staying_the_course.pdf

Butler, T., & Pinto-Zipp, G. (2006). Students' learning styles and their preferences for online instructional methods. *Journal of Educational Technology Systems*, *34*(2), 199–221. doi:10.2190/8UD2-BHFU-4PXV-7ALW

Cassidy, S. (2004). Learning studies: An overview of theories, models, and measures. *Educational Psychology*, *24*(4), 419–444. doi:10.1080/0144341042000228834

Collins, R. A., & Zacharakis, J. (2009). Impact of e-learning on adult education: A changing postmodern approach. In V. Wang (Ed.), *Handbook of research on E-learning applications for career and technical education: Technologies for vocational training,* (pp. 286-296). Hershey, PA: IGI Global.

Cox, T. (2008). Learning styles and students' attitudes toward the use of technology in higher and adult education classes. *Institute for Learning Styles Journal, 1*(Fall), 1-13. Retrieved February 13, 2009, from http://www.auburn.edu/~witteje/ilsrj/latestissue.htm

Cranton, P. (2005). Learning styles. In L. English (Ed.), *International encyclopedia of adult education* (pp. 362-366). New York: Palgrave McMillan.

Diaz, D., & Cartnal, R. (1999). Students' learning styles in two classes: online distance learning and equivalent on-campus. *College Teaching*, *47*(4), 130–135. doi:10.1080/87567559909595802

DuCharme-Hansen, B. A., & Dupin-Bryant, P. A. (2004). *Web-based distance education for adults.* Malabar, FL: Krieger Publishing.

Dunn, R., & Griggs, S. A. (Eds.). (2000). *Practical approaches to using learning styles in higher education.* Westport, CT: Bergin & Garvey.

Dunn, R., Honingsfeld, A., & Doolan, L. (2009, January/February). Impact of learning-style instructional strategies on students' achievement and attitudes: Perceptions of educators in diverse institutions. *Clearing House (Menasha, Wis.)*, *82*(3), 135–140. doi:10.3200/TCHS.82.3.135-140

Evans, C. (2008). The effectiveness of m-learning in the form of podcast revision lectures in higher education. *Computers & Education*, *50*(2), 491–498. doi:10.1016/j.compedu.2007.09.016

Fleming, N. (n.d.). *VARK: A guide to learning styles.* Retrieved March 16, 2009, from http://www.vark-learn.com/english/page.asp?p=categories

Gardner, H. (1999). *Intelligence reframed: Multiple intelligences for the 21st century*. New York: Basic Books.

Gaytan, J., & McEwen, B. (2007). Effective online instructional and assessment strategies. *American Journal of Distance Education, 21*(3), 117–132. doi:10.1080/08923640701341653

Goleman, D. (1998). *Working with emotional intelligence.* New York: Bantam Books.

Grasha, A. (1996). *Teaching with style: A practical guide to enhancing learning by understanding teaching and learning styles*. Pittsburgh, PA: International Alliance of Teaching Scholars.

Gregorc, A. F. (1982). *An adult's guide to style.* Columbia, CT: Gregorc Associates, Inc.

James, W., & Blank, W. (1993). Review and critique of available learning style instruments for adults. *New Directions for Adult and Continuing Education, 59.* San Francisco: Jossey Bass.

James, W., & Maher, P. (2004). Understanding and using learning styles. In M.Galbraith (Ed.), *Adult Learning Methods: A guide for effective instruction,* (3rd Ed.) (pp. 119-139). Malabar, FL: Krieger Publishing.

Kolb, D. A. (1984). *Experiential learning.* Englewood Cliffs, NJ: Prentice Hall.

Manner, J. (2005). Accommodating diverse learning styles with online course enhancements. *Journal of Interactive instruction . Development, 17*(4), 19–21.

Merriam, S. B., Caffarella, R. S., & Baumgartner, L. M. (2007). *Learning in adulthood: A comprehensive guide* (3rd Ed.). San Francisco: Jossey Bass.

Miller, L. (2005). Using learning styles to evaluate computer-based instruction. *Computers in Human Behavior, 21*(2), 287–306. doi:10.1016/j.chb.2004.02.011

Myers, I. B. (1993). *Gifts differing: Understanding personality type.* Palo Alto, CA: CPP Books.

Richardson, W. (2009). *Blogs, wikis, podcasts, and other powerful web tools for classrooms.* Thousand Oaks, CA: Corwin Press.

Simpson, C., & Du, Y. (2004). Effects of learning styles and class participation on students' enjoyments level in distributed learning environments. *Journal of Education for Library and Information Science, 45*(2), 123–136.

Terrell, S., & Dringus, L. (1999). An investigation of the effect of learning style on student success in an online learning environment. *Journal of Educational Technology Systems, 28*(3), 231–236.

Verduin, J. R., & Clark, T. (1991). *Distance Education: The foundations of effective practice.* San Francisco: Jossey-Bass.

Vossen, G., & Hagemann, S. (2007). *Unleashing Web 2.0 from concepts to creativity.* Burlington, MA: Morgan Kaufmann Publishers.

Chapter 10
Innovative Instructional Strategies with the Use of Technology for Adult Learners

Lesley Farmer
California State University at Long Beach, USA

ABSTRACT

Technology incorporation adds another dimension to instructional design because it requires that the adult educator be skilled enough to design and use technology-enhance instruction as well as diagnose learners' skill levels and predispositions. Because each media has its unique combination of features, instructional designers should select and create technology resources carefully to best address the learning task and learner preference. Technology-enhanced communication methods are now available for sophisticated instruction and interactive learning among students, educators, and resources: Web 2.0, egaming, video conferencing, and course management systems, as examples. Furthermore, technology-based accommodations can address access to resources as well direct instruction for people with disabilities. In any case, technology-infused instruction requires material and moral support by the organization's decision-makers.

INTRODUCTION

The world is changing faster than ever because of social and economic factors, which have been significantly impacted by technology. The world seems smaller as technology has connected people globally; resultantly, economic entities are increasingly interdependent, and cultures may clash more often.

DOI: 10.4018/978-1-61520-694-0.ch010

As individuals and entities try to manage change from the outside, they need to retool themselves. Adults can expect to change jobs and even careers several times in their lifetimes. Since their daily lives are also impacted by changing environments, adults will need to also adjust personal behaviors as well. Formal and informal education is needed now more than ever.

Since 85 percent of twenty-first century jobs will involve technology, it makes sense to incorporate technology in adult instruction. The intrinsic properties of technology obviously impact learning with its potential combinations of text, image, sound, and movement. These elements enable learners with varying learning style preferences to engage meaningfully with different aspects of information. In addition, the hyperlink feature of the web, electronic resources, and tools enable users to control their learning as they choose whether to explore those links or to access information in a nonlinear fashion. Indeed, technology-infused instructional design fosters learner-centered experiences; instructional designers basically create the environment or structure for optimal learning.

THE CONTEXT OF INTEGRATING TECHNOLOGY INTO INSTRUCTION

The instructional design process itself exists within the context of the organizational entity that is sponsoring the learning experience. Therefore, for technology to be incorporated effectively into adult education, organizational leadership needs to have a shared vision for technology integration and the means to allocate resources (such as material, facilities, infrastructure, and technical support) to that end. Policies also need to be put in place that support technology-enhanced adult education; aspects might include acceptable use, skills baselines, professional development and incentives, hardware specifications and refresh cycles, and equity issues. In short, the entire enterprise needs to have the motivation and the capacity to incorporate technology into its system (Roblyer & Doering, 2009).

The organization also needs to be realize that learning *about* technology differs from learning *with* technology; the former views technology as an end in itself while the latter views technology as a means. With technology as an end, systems and organizational goals are the central concern, and advanced project management skills are needed; the entire enterprise is changing. When technology supports learning, job performance is the focus, and the training department controls the process to the large extent; the organization as a whole is not in flux (Main, 2000).

Most adult education incorporates technology for the latter reason. Nevertheless, too often technology is added on top of existing instruction, like icing on the cake, rather than transforming instructional design. Some of the changed elements include: the locus of control from teacher to learner, just-in-time learning, emphasis on resource-rich inquiry, and heightened interaction. In fact, one of the first questions in the instructional design process that needs to be answered is: "Should technology be used?" The following lists contrasts deciding factors.

Incorporating technology is appropriate when:

- Accessing remote digital resources
- Addressing sensory modes via simulations and other knowledge representations
- Building on or repurposing existing digital resources or instruction
- Encouraging repeated practice (e.g., drills for rote learning)
- Supporting anytime/anywhere learning
- Recording and archiving communication and effort

Incorporating technology is not beneficial when:

- Focusing on in-house, non-technical resources
- Face-to-face personal contact is important
- Providing one-time customized training
- Other resources and means are more effective

A good rule of thumb is to employ the most stable, low-tech format applicable to the concept being taught. Once the decision to use technology is made, regardless of the type of technology used, instructional designers need to acknowledge and take advantage of these media.

It should be noted that the choice and implementation of instructional strategies need to be addressed in light of the entire instructional design process. Throughout the instructional design process, instructors need to determine which technologies will be used – and to what extent. In fact, technology-infused instructional design often requires the use of several technologies. At the very minimum, instructors need to determine whether technology will be used as a tool to deliver instruction, as a learning aid, or as the outcome itself. Even the instructional focus, whether to emphasize a technology tool or educational task, requires careful consideration. The decision-making process itself may well involve technology, particularly when gathering data (e.g., online surveys, PDA observation templates, web counters) and analyzing it (e.g., spreadsheets, databases, content analysis software). Technology-based choices apply at each step in designing instruction, as shown here.

- **Assess needs:** Online survey, video capture of behavior, analysis of website "hits"
- **Identify learners:** Online solicitations, RSS feed subscriptions, organizational lists
- **Identify outcomes:** Technology standards, online content standards, online education syllabi
- **Identify indicators:** Technology rubrics, technology products, electronic Delphi method (i.e., getting experts to come to consensus on key points)
- **Identify prerequisite skills:** Web-based assessment, performance observation, content analysis of sample work
- **Identify content:** Online training documents, electronic journal articles, virtual chat
- **Identify the instructional format:**
  - Resources (Internet, DVDs, e-books)
  - Instructor (technician, instruction designer, remote-site expert)
  - Methods (web tutorial, hands-on instruction, video presentation)
  - Timeframe (self-paced, real-time, just-in-time)
  - Location (computer lab, classroom, home)
  - Grouping (individual, online group, work unit)
  - Individualization (programmed instruction, choice of technology, coaching)
  - Affective domain (wiki, threaded discussion, virtual chat)
- **Contextualize instruction:** Web page within work website, professional development database, digital images of applications
- **Implement the plan:** Project planning software program, web page development, video conferencing
- **Assess the plan:** PDA (personal digital assistant) questionnaire, videotape, online survey

Each type of technology tool lends itself to specific learning approaches. Whenever possible, the unique properties of each tool should be exploited to optimize these experiences. An illustration of how these choices impact instructional strategies follows. A local Leche group meets monthly to support pregnant mothers. The group's facilitator wants to make sure that the women maintain a healthy lifestyle, so she shows them a free online personalized health plan website that generates an appropriate exercise regimen and nutritional guide based on each woman's situation. She prints out the website front screen and URL, and reminds the attendees that the local public library has Internet computers that they can use in case they do not have other access to the Internet. The facilitator also volunteers to help individuals set up their free account after class. A couple of women do not speak English well, so the facilitator locates a good website that includes information in Spanish. The women have already paired for other Leche activities, so the facilitator has them pair up for this health plan project as well, making sure that at least one person in each pairing is comfortable with the Internet. In this way, the pairs can support each other during the week.

STAGES OF TECHNOLOGY ADAPTATION AND INSTRUCTION

As adult educators design instruction, they need to ascertain their learners' prerequisite skills. When incorporating technology, adult educators have to consider the added dimension of technology, determining adults' predisposition toward and comfort with that technology. Yet even if adults get their hands on the equipment, they might not be able to take advantage of the information resources themselves. Adult educators need to make sure that adults have opportunities to learn how to:

- Operate computer and other technological systems (i.e., open and close an application, save a document, print, use a mouse, use a menu and navigation bar, etc.)
- Use productivity tools
- Navigate the Internet (i.e., use browsers and search engines, use email, etc.)
- Evaluate information critically

The learning environment should foster learner engagement, learning, and application, and technology has the potential to enable learners to access, navigate, and explore course material according to their own needs and abilities. If learners can see the overall structure and rationale of the course, they are more likely to see its relevance to their own work. However, if adults are stymied by the technology, they will not be able to concentrate on the content matter that they are supposed to master. Thus, a central issue is prior technology skill or at least comfort. To address this issue, adult educators need to assess learners' current technology knowledge base, and frontload instruction with opportunities for technology-challenged learners to get acquainted with the technology needed to engage in the desired content.

The Center for Research and Development in Teaching at the University of Texas at Austin developed a seven-step Technology Adoption Model (TAM) that takes into account individual's emotional and social states (Konana & Balasubramanian, 2005). Instructional designers can then match the appropriate learning activity with the learner's level of technology adoption, which can then facilitate the learner's progress to the next level. It should be noted that when new content or skills are being introduced, learners should perform at their comfort level of technology so they can focus on the new subject matter.

1. **Awareness:** Learners have no knowledge of technology. "What technology?" The adult educator needs to get the learner's attention through a technology demonstration or an impactful tech product. A survey is an easy way to point out novel information.
2. **Information:** Learners receive objective information about technology but do not contribute ideas. "So that is technology." This one-way communication can be in the form of handouts, presentations, or digital document. Sample technology might include technology standards, online database, or library portal.
3. **Personal:** Learners respond personally to the technology. "Cool technology!" To optimize the response, adult educators should find out what motivates the targeted learners, and set up the learning environment to ease the learner. Just-in-time training works well at this level. Examples of appropriate

technology include a grading program for a disorganized teacher, a simple income tax preparation software program, and an online photo album. In general, tool-based technology that solves an immediate problem is favored at this point.

4. **Management:** Learners try to fit technology into their practice. "I can use technology." Adult educators help learners use technology appropriate to their work. Using subscription databases for research, creating online quizzes that do automatic grading, and blogging constitute typical applications at this stage. Adult educators can demonstrate the critical features of the technology, allowing learners to get started successfully and to explore advanced functions as needed.
5. **Consequence:** Learners examine technology in terms of investment of time to insure it has a sufficient payoff value. "Is this valuable technology?" At this point, learners determine which technology is the most effective for the identified task. For instance, learners might choose between a blog and a wiki, or between a database and a spreadsheet, depending on the desired result. Adult educators help learners compare technology features and their relative costs and benefits.
6. **Collaboration:** Learners want to optimize technology's integration so they work with others to advance group knowledge or develop larger-scale projects. "Let's work with technology." Learners may want to create organizational portals, repositories, or podcast collections. Adult educators help learners plan collaboratively and manage projects using technology.
7. **Re-focus:** Learners want to sustain and institutionalize technology throughout the organization. "Tech R Us." Example project include knowledge management systems, organizational technology policies and procedures, and hiring/training/promotional practices based on technology expertise. Adult educators help learners assess their organizations using technology tools, and help them research technology-based organizational change.

In assessing technology competence, instructional designers are reminded that today's adults include people in their twenties who constitute the first generation of adult learners who had the opportunity to grow up with digital technology; these individuals are being called "digital natives." Indeed, the adult population also includes digital "immigrants" who first learned about technology from their digital native descendants. Depending on the work situation, some employees have incorporated technology into their practice for decades while others are just now using computer technology as a productivity tool to aid in record-keeping or communication. In some cases, younger adults may have used technology more in their personal life rather than in work settings, so while they may be expert bloggers, these beginning employees might not know how to manage a dozen computer systems within a work unit. This complex mix of experiences requires instructional finesse, particularly to later technology adopters who may feel embarrassed or singled out by their lack of knowledge. Providing a safe environment, offering buddy coaching, and finding ways to enable such learners to practice on their own time can ameliorate the situation.

TECHNOLOGY-BASED RESOURCES FOR INSTRUCTIONAL STRATEGIES

Once the learning outcome is determined, and learners have been assessed, other instructional design principles come into play, which need to consider technology:

- **Cognitive tools to organize and externalize knowledge:** Teaching learners how to use utility software applications (such as spreadsheets and databases), hypermedia and graphic organizers to structure knowledge linearly and non-linearly; incorporating simulations and other models to represent knowledge

- **Scaffolding:** Using hypermedia with branching options to enable learners to decide what content to access; providing shared learning spaces for peer tutoring
- **Expertise development:** Providing simulations and other interactive models to test and practice content knowledge
- **Social construction of knowledge:** Including web 2.0 social networking features; assigning tasks that require collaboration utilizing technology
- **Integrating face-to-face and online delivery:** Supplementing class time activity with online resources; following up in-class discussion with online chat (Tynjala & Hakkinen, 2005)

All of these instruction strategy decision points include selecting appropriate resources to incorporate. Two major categories are content-centric resources and production-centric resources. While applications are emphasized here, it should be mentioned that digital resources need equipment in order to use them, so instructors need to check their availability and ease of operability before choosing dependent digital resources. In terms of physical access to technology, adult educators need to consider several factors.

- **Site access:** Is technology available to classes and individuals throughout the day and evening to accommodate adult working hours?
- **Remote access:** Can learners get to technology resources from home or public buildings?
- **Equipment circulation:** Does the site lend computers to learners or families? These days, a variety of options are feasible: low-end word-processors and Internet devices; mobile devices; older donated computer systems that can be checked out for the year in a fashion similar to textbook circulation.
- **Physical accommodations:** Does the site have computers with larger monitors for visually impaired users, trackballs for physically limited motion, scanners to read text, adjustable desks to accommodate wheelchairs or other seating?

Nevertheless, equipment is not the end. Rather, hardware is merely the mechanism for adult learners to access and use information. What content-rich resources drive instruction?

Content-Centric Resources

Content-rich resources include subject-specific software, DVDs, audiotapes, podcasts, and Internet files, particularly online databases. Digital access tools include library catalogs, indices, telecommunications, Internet directories, and search engines. The advantages of these technology tools include: combination of media, currency, multiple access points, user control, and capability to be repurposed. These features are particularly useful to meet the needs of learners with different learning styles and English language barriers. Additionally, when instructors transmit their information via content-rich tools, they facilitate learning anytime and anywhere in a standardized way, which can provide large-scale instruction.

Learners can access these resources independently or as part of face-to-face classroom course delivery. In the latter situation, technology resources provide immediate exploration of relevant information. For instance, the instructor might talk about copyright and then have learners take an online copyright test; afterwards, the class can discuss the answers and implications. A class may talk about finding real world connections to geometry; they can use cell phones to capture those images.

Discrete portions of resources may be selected and edited to demonstrate one specific concept or insight. That individual learning object may be used for another course for another purpose. For example, a video clip of a lung surgery detail may be used in an anatomy class as well as in a drug-prevention course. When well indexed and incorporated into a database for easy access and retrieval, these learning modules provide an effective way to optimize electronic resources. They can be easily inserted into multimedia and online presentations to offer a quick, clear explanation or to serve as an open-ended, generative learning prompt.

Whatever technology resources are used, instructors need to make sure that learners *do* something with them; the learning needs to be interactive rather than passive. To facilitate critical viewing, the instructor should provide guiding questions. Having an activity based on the resources helps reinforce and build on learning, so providing information about that project *before* viewing the resource optimizes transfer of learning.

Probably the most interactive web-based instruction format is a WebQuest. In this model, a meaningful task is presented. The WebQuest creator provides the learner with links to appropriate web-based documents in order to complete the task. Often collaborative roles are incorporated into the WebQuest to promote human interaction as well as interaction with resources. WebQuests blend information access, manipulation, and presentation.

Production-Centric Resources

Other digital resources facilitate content manipulation and presentation, which are detailed here. Application suites such as MicroSoft Office and Google Docs enable individuals to transform digital information from one format to another easily.

- **Word processing/desktop publishing:** Easy to use and repurpose, and other applications can often be inserted. Instructors can create learning guide sheets, and learners can present and share their findings
- **Spreadsheet:** Helps organize data and facilitates numerical analysis. Instructors can locate data sets for analysis; learners can test hypotheses about data
- **Database:** Helps sort and links data sets. A newer form of databases is social networking websites, as exemplified by delicious, Flickr, and Facebook. Instructors can locate data sets for analysis; learners can test hypotheses about existing data and collaboratively create their own social sharing database
- **Authoring/presentation:** Combines media to present content sequentially or in other structured order locally and online. Instructors and learners can present content, and reorder or combine presentations
- **Audio files/podcasting:** Presents aural information such as voice and music. Instructors and learners can record and archive explanations and sound clips for later use
- **Graphic programs:** Represents knowledge visually; some programs require hours of training. Instructors can diagnose learner knowledge as they create content concept maps; instructors and learners can explain concepts with images
- **Video editing:** Realistic, multimedia format for presenting concepts, particularly processes and persuading audiences; requires some training and equipment. Instructors and learners can demonstrate how the selection and sequencing of video information can impact perception.

For most content areas, a variety of technologies may be incorporated for successful instructional strategies. By examining all of the instructional design factors, optimum technologies can be chosen with confidence.

Task-Specific Resources

To demonstrate how the choice of resource impacts instructional strategies, the following outline of content matter to teach information literacy incorporates technology at each step.

1: Identify the need for information
   a. **Video:** Learners brainstorm information needs for a Middle East peace summit simulation
   b. **Web activity:** Concept mapping and other educational techniques to help learners identify information needs
2. Access information effectively
   a. **Video:** Learners identify various search strategies to locate information, such as generating key words and using library catalogs and indexes
   b. **Web activity:** Tutorial on use of online databases and university catalog; use of bibliographies, etc.; locate educational research and lesson plans
3. Evaluate and select information
   a. **Video:** Learners use web evaluation criteria
   b. **Web activity:** WebQuest that explains use of rubrics and other tools to evaluate materials; evaluate educational research and learning activities
4. Manipulate information to accomplish a specific purpose
   a. **Video:** Learners create spreadsheets and timelines to organize information
   b. **Web activity:** Instructional design process
5. Communicate product or performance
   a. **Video:** Learners create a PowerPoint presentation
   b. **Web activity:** Tutorial on presentation software
6. Evaluate process and product
   a. **Video:** Learners use rubrics to evaluate their learning experience
   b. **Web activity:** Locate and evaluate assessment and standards websites; WebQuest on copyright and other legal issues

Rapid Proto-Typing and Adult Learning

While technology resources that support instructional strategies abound, adult educators may need to create customized digital resources to address the specific learning objectives and learner needs. This situation happens most frequently in workplace training about proprietary content or tools. Rapid proto-typing is a technology design process that quickly facilitates high-quality, responsive implementation.

To start with, the design team of the stakeholders (usually the supervisor, content expert, adult educator, and technician) meets to identify the learning objective and the target audience; at this programming phase the planning timetable is set, and the program is approved by management. At the schematic phase, the design team determines the training parameters, design criteria, technical requirements, and the cost; a user group reviews the plan as does management. At the design development phase, potential materials are reviewed and chosen, and development documents are created taking into account design principles and technology architecture, with feedback given from the user group again. The actual documents are prepared and reviewed at the construction documentation phase. At the integration and administration phase, on-site staff are prepared for the product and observe it; the materials are given a final inspection and integrated into the system.

By working with the stakeholders throughout the process, adult educators get organizational buy-in, and the final resource is more likely to be accepted and used in training and application. Moreover, as adult learners constitute the user focus group, their learning experiences inform the development and deployment of the resource so that they, in essence, co-constructing knowledge (Beguin, 2003).

DELIVERY OF INSTRUCTION

Probably the most effective instructional strategy is one that most closely resembles the situation in which learners apply their new knowledge and skills. For this reason, apprenticeships continue as a popular method for learning a skill. However, such one-on-one or small group training is labor- and time-intensive, and does not scale up well. Additionally, when the consequences of poor performance by novices, such as neophyte surgeons and pilots, are costly, simulations provide approximate experiences without the dangers. Access to instruction can also pose problems and lead to educational inequalities. Fortunately, technology offers many tools for cost-effective, equitable instructional delivery. Several technology-based current delivery methods are detailed below.

It should be noted that all of these strategies involve both cognitive and social aspects, which mark effective adult learning principles. Particularly with the incorporation of technology, instructional strategies have to address learners' fears so that adult will find pleasure in learning with technology. As learners get involved with technology, they also need opportunities to use technology when communicating with each other, which activities abound in the following strategies. Additionally, ways need to be found to ensure equitable access to these technologies.

Web 2.0

Web 2.0 is the term given to express the idea of interactivity that now marks some web-based collaborative tools such as wikis and blogs. Rather than one-way communication, web 2.0 applications enable people to participate in two-way active communication to create information. In studying information management systems, JISC and SCONUL (2008) noted the impact of web 2.0 in: 1) concentrating the aggregation of information; and 2) diffusing the dissemination and reuse of content. The comparatively easy access of the Internet further broadens the base of participation.

Wikis exemplify participatory web 2.0 practice. Wikis (based on the Hawaiian term "wiki wiki," which means "fast") are web pages that can be generated without markup language knowledge. Wikis are probably best known because of Wikipedia, a user-built web-based encyclopedia. The underlying concept of Wikipedia is that experts around the world can contribute to the body of knowledge; the ability of individuals editing each other's works result in higher quality information. While some people may dispute Wikipedia's veracity, the concept of collaboratively edited content holds valid potential. Furthermore, most wikis have a feature that allows participants to see the page's history, so that contributions can be tracked accurately. These two features, collaborative editing and tracking, make wikis a useful adult learning tool.

Just as web 2.0 acknowledges and builds on each person's knowledge base, so too does adult education. Especially in today's web 2.0 world, adult education should incorporate interactivity options and social networking features, such as push technology RRS feeds, comment/messaging options, incorporation of learning community repositories, enterprise mash-ups, and user-customizable folksonomy "shells."

Maness (2006) identified four essential elements that are applicable to adult education 2.0:

- **User-centered:** Dynamic consumption and creation of content between user and librarians
- **Multimedia experience**
- **Socially rich:** Adult educators and learners communicate synchronously and asynchronously
- **Communally innovative:** Adult educators and learners change each other.

Examples of adult education 2.0 include chat-based learning sessions, streaming media tutorials with interactive databases, and social networking applications. Adult education could become a participatory network, enabling learners to access information and each other. Adult instructional design then would provide a coordinated framework for participatory adult learning. Adult educators could provide a personalized social network with individual learning spaces. This learning network would include structured information and instruction provider by educators and learners, as well as permit social tagging for customizable access to these resources and learning activities.

Egaming

Egaming constitutes a new form of instructional strategy that enables learners to explore issues within a prescribed virtual environment, often interacting with other players. In terms of gaining knowledge, egames can introduce learners to technology through motivating activities. Indeed, one predictor of college success is computer gaming (Wilson, 2002). Increased practice with video games improves spatial skills, and collaborative work in computer games improves mathematics problem-solving (Agosto, 2004). Foster (2008) asserted that gaming can develop individual interest in science as players experience the relevance of scientific concepts and applications. Social gaming can lead to positive identity assets: self-esteem, self-employment, personal sense of purpose, and personal positive future orientation (Helmrich & Neiberger, 2007). Many studies have been conducted using games that address historical content, such as Civilization, Revolution, and Age of Mythology. These games proved intellectually engaging, highly challenging, and complex learning activities (De Kanter, 2005; Gee, 2007; Squire & Jenkins, 2003), perhaps making them best suited to the university settings in which the studies were conducted.

Many egames meld educational and recreational components (Nicholson, 2008), and it is important to note that in order to be engaging to learners, games should be both fun and interactive (Amory, 1999). Particularly for females and older adults, the egaming protocols need to be easy and intuitive so that the focus is on the content rather than on navigation through a virtual space. Halverson (2005) distinguished between exogenous games (which use technology to organize information) and endogenous games (which drive the content via the technological environment). The latter typology facilitates exploration more. Halverson also identified four learning environments for egames: learner-centered to help users to apply knowledge, assessment-centered, knowledge-centered to help users learn, and community-centered to build social skills.

In sum, games, particularly role playing games, offer a rich learning environment in which to explore and achieve specific goals. What characteristics of gaming inform instruction?

- Use of fixed, equitable rules
- Clear roles and expectations
- Internally-consistent environment where everything is possible
- Clear goals within a rich context that gives goals personal meaning and relevance
- Opportunities to explore identities
- Cognitive and affective engagement
- (Usually) multiple ways to achieve them through constructivist strategies
- Specific, timely feedback

- Sense of control and personal investment
- Situated learning
- Sense of reward for effort, including trial and error
- Structured interaction between players, and between players and the game
- Blend of cooperation and competition (DeKanter, 2005; Deubel, 2006; Gee, 2007; Simpson, 2005; Squire, 2006; Lee & Young, 2008)

As with other technology-based instructional strategies, the affective domain needs to be addressed. In that respect, participants may perceive that they are having fun rather than learning. For instance, in a study of adult learning in a computer simulation game about science, learners thought that the game interfered with their explicit learning of scientific principles. However, test scores indicated that they learned those principles tacitly through their game playing (Rieber & Noah, 2008). Especially if adults have little prior experience learning academically through gaming, they might assume that gaming is strictly a leisure activity. Therefore, adult educators might consider explaining to adults how games offer beneficial learning experiences, and stating explicitly how specific egames were chosen for an identified learning objective.

Video Conferencing

Video is making a comeback because of its multimedia and archival features. Particularly with the advent of digital camcorders and easy-to-use editing software, video has regained its reputation as a viable educational tool for adult education since video is an appropriate vehicle for training, knowledge management, systems analysis, and public relations.

Video conferencing, in particular, links video equipment and telecommunications to enable people to converse fully in real time. At this point, lag time is practically non-existent, and other input devices such as document stands and whiteboards enrich the experience. Being able to see and interpret body language as well as view other artifacts help to overcome the abstraction experience in sensory-reduced online communities that communicate only by text or sound. As an instructional strategy, video conferencing is especially effective for virtual field trips and other interactions with remote experts.

The process for setting up a video conference has become simpler over the years. At its simplest, video conference can be done with two Internet-connected desktop computers with web cams and microphones. A software program such as Net Meeting enables the two systems to communicate. Nevertheless, more technical preplanning is required for virtual meetings than for face-to-face events. Furthermore, each site should have its own facilitator, so roles need to be negotiated. The following procedures need to be addressed, for instance:

- Identifying and contacting stakeholders, such as employers, associations, agencies
- Identifying and contacting existing online communities of practice
- Identifying and coordinating available video technology systems (hopefully free)
- Setting up processes and protocols
- Identifying and training group "anchors"
- Facilitating video conferencing scheduling and registration

Even with good technology, instruction via video conferencing has its challenges. Individuals in the back of the room may feel less engaged, so microphones should be placed around the room to facilitate wide participation; in addition, the video conference should be held in a shallow room rather than a long narrow one, particularly if the video camera can pan. Talk is more task-oriented, so instructors need to explicitly build in opportunities for socializing, such as introductions and ice-breaker activities. A pecking order may emerge, with each side considering itself more worthy than the other, so instructors should give each group a unique task to perform, which can display each unique contribution (Anderson, McEwan & Carletta, 2007).

Video conferencing as a one-time event is fine if the intent is to get remote expert opinion or to see a remote facility, but it is more powerful if done on a regular basis with a consistent set of people. In that way groups can form communities that can advance their practice through mutual support and accountability. These long-term commitments need to be reinforced between video sessions through telecommunications and online archiving and sharing of documents (Weinfan & Davis, 2004).

Course Management Systems

Increasingly, adult education is incorporating online course management systems (CMS) as part of their educational delivery system. This method facilitates distance learning as well as offers increased interaction. However, care must be taken to make good use of its features in designing and implementing courses. Six proven instructional strategies that incorporate CMS in support of adult education are detailed below.

Online instructional packaging business has increased dramatically in correlation to the drive for distributed education. Particularly as the Internet becomes ubiquitous, web-based products can facilitate asynchronous learning and address issues of space constraints in adult education. For most instructors, courseware offers easy one-stop access to resources and telecommunications. Particularly with robust programs, learners can consider the courseware as a learning space that gives them individual control of their learning. CMS also offer non-linear learning experiences that respond to learner's immediate needs. Its hyperlink features provide another dimension to learning as learners self-identify the amount of detail they need in their learning journey. Additionally, hyperlinks facilitate access to resources worldwide, and help address copyright and duplication issues since the original file remains on the creator's server. Most courseware also provides real-time conversation (chats) as well as asynchronous sharing of reflective learning. On the instructor's part, most courseware includes grading, calendaring, and monitoring features that help one manage the course. Representative CMS products include commercial packages such as BlackBoard and Desire2Learn, and Open Source packages such as Moodle and Sakai.

In reviewing effective instructional strategies in web-based learning, Kanuka (2005) identified seven principles and associated technology-enhanced practices:

- **Engagement with abstracted phenomena:** Concept mapping, role-play
- **Presentation of multiple perspectives:** Multiple readings, WebQuests, online debates
- **Relevant content:** Online remote experts and case studies
- **Diverse ways of knowing:** WebQuests, problem-based learning
- **Learner responsibility:** Group projects, learner presentations
- **Building meaning:** Threaded discussion, joint course building
- **Expanding world view:** Brainstorming, heterogeneous groupings

To concretize these principles, representative instructional strategies using CMS are detailed below.

- **Resources:** Besides the course syllabus and general information, the CMS structure facilitates instruction through its resource manager function. The instructor –and learners – can post readings, lecture notes, and presentation stacks. To increase learning, the instructor can provide learner access to online tutorials, simulations and WebQuests. Not only can a document be posted, but hotlinks to online sources are possible in CMS, which streamline course content and insures compliance with copyright law. With the virtual classroom feature, learners can contact online experts in real time. On a more mundane, but equally useful level, CMS typically include learner and instructor courseware help.

- **Communication:** CMS offer a central telecommunications mechanism that can act in both a one-way and two-way delivery system. Upfront announcements facilitate timely changes. Instructors can email individuals, groups or the entire class. Most threaded discussions can be sorted according to date, author or topic for easy analysis. Learners can share documents via the real-time virtual classroom (i.e., textual and graphical chat) and within instructor-designated groups. Indeed, with the group feature, discussion remains closed to anyone outside the group – except for the instructor. With guest privileges, outside experts can communicate with the class synchronously or asynchronously. Learners can communicate their own interests via their personal online home page within the course, and they can submit their work to the instructor via a drop-off box feature. It has been found the communication can increase with CMS; learners who might sit passively in the back row now become equal participants, and English learners have the time to think and find the right words to better demonstrate their own knowledge.
- **Learner engagement:** With the variety of communications means as well as the modular design of the typcial CMS, learners can increase their engagement with resources, peers and their instructor. The act of using CMS helps kinesthetic learners. Learners appreciate the sense of an interactive and open-ended learning environment that is theirs to explore according to their own time and needs parameters. Online activities such as WebQuests and simulations foster interactivity and reflective learning. Discussion forums and virtual classroom expand communication opportunities, and also enable learners to initiate their own threads. Learners learn more about their peers through personal home pages, and they work more easily with the group pages. Instructors can use quizzes and surveys to help learners self-assess their own progress, and learners appreciate the faster feedback of online grading throughout the course period.
- **Collaboration:** The communication and engagement approach certainly fosters collaborative learning activities. As already mentioned, threaded discussion forms, chats and grouped projects expand traditional means of collaborating. Tele-based experts offer a link between the classroom and the professional world. On a very real level, CMS facilitate knowledge management as shared learning ramps up the class's own expertise.
- **Dynamic course building:** Instead of a pre-determined and static course, CMS-enhanced courses can be ongoing, responsive learning "journeys." Some of the means to develop and hone a course during the time period include:
    - Creating a database of learner responses
    - Developing course topics and content based on diagnosis of learner needs
    - Adding links and reading based on class action
    - Archiving learner projects
    - Providing feedback on learner work
    - Developing discussion forums based on learner needs and wants

Here are more tips for optimizing instructional strategies using CMS:

- Explore the software's features and potential
- Clarify all instructions, assignments and feedback
- Work offline and upload content
- Test layout and content conversion
- Train learners in navigating the course-work, and have veteran learners coach their peers
- Check for understanding: never assign a resource without requiring some kind of learner action
- Warn learners if the site will be dynamic (that is, content will change)
- Distribute instructional responsibility: have learner take lecture notes, create study guides, locate good readings

THE OTHER DIGITAL DIVIDE

Most instructional designers try to address the issue of the Digital Divide: that is, inequities in access to information, with a focus on technology. However, most effort seems to think in terms of socio-economic terms. Yet a significant population is sometimes overlooked: individuals with physical disabilities. While the congenitally visually impaired or wheelchair-bound might be the first images that come to mind, adult educators need to remember that an aging population brings a greater need for physical accommodations. In designing instructional strategies for these groups' varied demands, adult educators need to think about hardware and software as well as at communications and instructional issues.

Only one-third of adults with disabilities are working at any point, and women with disabilities have far less chance of being hired then their male counterparts. Moreover, women, African Americans, and Latinos with disabilities earn less per hour than their Anglo peers. Ironically, of those adults with disabilities who *are* employed, 69% asserted that they did not need special accommodations to work effectively (Greene & Kochhar-Bryant, 2003). When the issue of technology arises, these same populations tend to have less access and less knowledge than other populations; since so many jobs require technical skill, it is imperative that adults with disabilities get technical training so they will have a better chance for economic success. It should be noted that much of the training success depends as much on the potential employer as on the adult; perceptions can impact learner efforts and success significantly. Indeed, technology can play a role in most adult training and placement for these populations.

Assistive technology is usually the first consideration for providing learning accommodations. It may be defined as "any aid, device or tool, compensatory strategy, used in different environments, information and referral, evaluation and recommendation, resources for funding, designing, fabricating, repairing and filling, training, support and follow-through service that improves a person's functional capacity." (http://www.ihdi.uky.edu/projects/EmployAT/ComputerAccessHTML/atdefinition.htm) This list of physical differences and supportive assistive technology provides a beginning point for planning instructional strategies:

- **Visual differences:** Larger view font on monitors, change in background color on monitors, audiotapes, screen reading software (including SimpleText on Macs and Narrative option in PCs), scanners, oral-input devices
- **Hearing differences:** Closed caption materials, transcriptions
- **Mobility differences:** Seating options, trackballs and joysticks, digital controls (switches, scanning), oral-input devices

Another major element in accessibility is universal design: designing strategies that incorporate resources for everyone's use to the greatest extent possible without need for adaptation. Thus, when selecting materials or thinking about instruction, the following principles should be considered:

- **Flexible use**
- **Simple, intuitive use:** Regardless of experience or language
- **Tolerance of error:** Compensating for accidental or unintended action
- **Low physical effort:** Does not fatigue the user
- **Size and space for approach and use:** Regardless of body size, posture, mobility (http://www.design.ncsu.eduL8120/cud/univ_design/princ_overview.htm)

With the passage of new government and industry guidelines regulating web accessibility for disabled users, public educators need to comply with Section 508 of the Rehabilitation Act (http://www.section508.gov) and priority one standards of the World Wide Web Consortium's Web Content Accessibility Guidelines (http://www.w3.org/WAI). When incorporating the Web into instruction and learning, be it in using websites or creating them, adult educators need to make sure that the following elements are considered to insure that websites are accessible.

- Caption or use the ALT attribute to describe images and functions
- Summarize or use a LONGDESC attribute for graphs and charts. Make tables readable line by line
- Label hyperlinks so the user can understand them out of context (avoid "click here")
- Use consistent layout features and headings. Avoid frames, or create a non-frame version of the website. In case applets or plug-ins are not supported by visually-impairment "reader" software, provide alternative content
- Check accessibility through technology-based guidelines: http://www.w3.org/TR/WCAG and http://www.cast.org/buddy

Adults with disabilities should be given opportunities to practice learning, so as adult educators plan instructional strategies, they should consider incorporating technology resources that can help learners develop skills, such as educational computer programs, videos, podcasts, telecommunications, and relevant websites. One-on-one coaching can provide the focused structure that these adults need and can help adults learn how to use these resources collaboratively and independently. Probably the two greatest motivators are a sense of self-control and the acceptance as a participant in a meaningful social activity. The diagnostic and interactive features of high-quality relevant digital programs also provide the immediate feedback and structure that can benefit these populations. By providing technologies that help adult *produce* knowledge, adult educators are enabling these individuals to contribute meaningfully to society.

Fortunately, educators have been working on access issues for decades, so the technology aspects can build on solid foundations. Cornell's website on disability laws discusses the rights of people with disabilities (http://www.law.cornell.edu/topics/disability.html). State services for the blind and visually impaired are well known. WestEd in San Francisco lists several good web sites on assess and equity, with particular attention to assistive technology; this is a good starting point: http://rtecexchange.edgateway.net/cs/rtecp/view/rtec_str/2. California State University at Northridge offers an Assistive Technology Applications Certificate program (http://www.csun.edu/cod). The University of Illinois at Urbana-Champaign's Center for Disability Resources and Educational Services offers technology-related instructional strategies that are disability-specific (http://www.disability.uiuc.edu/page.php?id=38). Other organizations that focus on instruction to these populations include the Association for Persons in Supported Employment (http://apse.org), Learning Disabilities Association of America (http://www.ldaamerica.org), and the University of Washington's DO-IT website (http://www.washington.edu/doit/). With information from these and other experts, adult educators can develop instructional strategies that can be accessed by *all* populations.

TRENDS

With the convergence and miniaturization of technology, adult education instructional strategies can leverage emerging technologies that have caught the attention of the public. Indeed, leveraging those technologies that adults already use makes the learning curve flatter, and also affirms adults' technology habits.

Podcasting and **videocasting** basically compress audio and video files for portable, flexible consumption. Increasingly, instructors are recording their lectures, and uploading them onto online 'casting databases such as iTunes, iUniverse, and Open Courseware Database. Learners can download the 'casts onto their portable digital media player, the cost of which has dropped down to as little as $10, to play them at their convenience. In a study of podcast lectures, Evans (2007) found that adult learners thought podcasts were more useful than textbooks or notetaking for reinforcing learning. English language learners and learners with disabilities find 'casts especially attractive because they can review the 'casts repeatedly until the information is well comprehended. Instructors are also designing learning activities that require learners to create their own 'casts to share with their peers or other authentic audiences.

Another popular technology tool affecting adult instructional strategies is **mobile learning,** or **m-learning**. Starting with portable digital assistants (PDA), instructors have used these handheld devices to help collection observation data and to facilitate quick in-class quizzes to check for understanding. The ability of PDAs to "beam" data wirelessly enables instructors to disseminate short documents throughout the class, or create learning stations at which learners can download information for just-in-time learning. Stripped down application programs such as word processing and concept mapping enable learners to brainstorm and journal their learning experiences easily, and then share those ideas with their peers.

Mobile devices such as **"smart" phones**, particularly the iPhone, has ratcheted up m-learning and associated instructional strategies because of their many features: two-way communication, text messaging, photo capture, calendaring, calculating, Internet access, application downloading and operating options, geographic information system (GIS) or global positioning system (GPS) functions, and language support. Clough, Jones, McAndrew, and Scanlon (2008) developed a framework for m-learning instructional suggestions, which these examples concretize.

- **Referential:** Instructors can ask learners to access reference sources and ebooks online
- **Interactive:** Hundreds of micro-programs are available for free or low cost that can reinforce in-class learning; instructors should be aware of these programs in order to recommend them to their learners
- **Microworlds:** Instructors can ask learners to experience models of downloadable micro world domains as seen in the phone screen
- **Location aware:** Instructors can ask learners to take photos that demonstrate training concepts, and identify their locating using the device's GIS/GIP function. That data can also be used to create class "mash-ups" of maps and photo info

- **Data collection:** Instructors can give learners observation templates to use to collect observational data out in the field
- **Collaborative:** Learners can collectively build a database of information, or play educational egames online

On a grander scale, **virtual worlds** enable learners to experience situated learning in three dimensions, or a facsimile thereof. Visual immersion systems, from head-mounted visual systems to 3D "caves," enable learners to experience a visual simulated environment. These systems can sense the learners' movements, and adjust the visual components accordingly. Individuals with physical limitations can approximate movement in real situations (Roblyer & Doering, 2009).

CONCLUSION

Adult education instructional strategies have to meld learning goals, be they individual or organizational, with learners' abilities and dispositions. Technology incorporation adds another dimension to instructional design because it requires that the adult educator be skilled enough to design and use technology-enhance instruction as well as diagnose learners' skill levels and predispositions. Furthermore, technology-infused instruction requires material and moral support by the organization's decision-makers.

In terms of instructional design, technology greatly expands the repertoire of available resources that can be used to gain and apply new knowledge and skills. Because each media has its unique combination of features, instructional designers should select and create technology resources carefully to best address the learning task and learner preference.

The delivery of instruction is also part of the instructional strategy. With today's changing technology, communication methods are now available for sophisticated interactive learning: among students, educators, and resources. Web 2.0, egaming, video conferencing, and course management systems exemplify these delivery systems that incorporate learning activities. Furthermore, technology-based accommodations can address access to resources as well direct instruction for people with disabilities. Instructional designers are also starting to leverage the emerging technologies used by the public to create convenient and exciting instruction: via 'casting, mobile devices, and even virtual realities.

In short, technology constitutes another strand in designing instructional strategies, affecting the entire process from determining learning goals to assessing the impact of learning. Therefore, adult educators need to be technology-savvy in terms of theory and practice at every phase of education. Adult educators also need to be able to state their case about technology-enhanced instructional strategies to their parent organizations in order to get the needed leadership and support required for successful implementation and application.

REFERENCES

Agosto, D. (2004). Girls and gaming: A summary of the research with implications for practice. *Teacher Librarian, 31*(3), 8–14.

Alliance for Technology Access. (n.d.) Retrieved from http://www.ataccess.org

Amory, A. (1999). The use of computer games as an educational tool: identification of appropriate game types and game elements. *British Journal of Educational Technology, 30*, 311–321. doi:10.1111/1467-8535.00121

Anderson, A., McEwan, R., & Carletta, J. (2007). Virtual team meetings: An analysis of communication and context. *Computers in Human Behavior, 23*, 2558–2580. doi:10.1016/j.chb.2007.01.001

Assistive, T. A. P. (n.d.). Retrieved from http://www.resna.org/taproject/at/statecontacts.html

Beguin, P. (2003). Design as a mutual learning process between users and designers. *Interacting with Computers, 15*(5), 709–730. doi:10.1016/S0953-5438(03)00060-2

Clugh, G., Jones, A., McAndrew, P., & Scanlon, E. (2008). Informal learning with PDAs and smartphones. *Journal of Computer Assisted Learning, 24*, 359–371. doi:10.1111/j.1365-2729.2007.00268.x

De Kanter, N. (2005). Gaming redefines interactivity for learning. *TechTrends, 49*(3), 26–31. doi:10.1007/BF02763644

Deubel, P. (2006, Jan.). Game on. *T.H.E. Journal*, 30–41.

Enders, A. (2007). Rates of computer and Internet use: A comparison of urban and rural access by people with disabilities. *Ruralfacts*. Missoula, MT: University of Montana. Equal Access for Software and Information. (n.d.). Retrieved from http://www.rit.edu/~easi

Evans, C. (2007). The effectiveness of m-learning in the form of podcast revision lecturers in high education. *Computers & Education, 50*, 491–498. doi:10.1016/j.compedu.2007.09.016

Federal Access Board. (n.d.). Retrieved from http://access-board.gov

Foster, A. (2008). Games and motivation to learn science: Personal identity, applicability, relevance and meaningfulness. *Journal of Interactive Learning Research, 19*(4), 597–614.

Gee, J. (2007). *What video games have to teacher us about learning and literacy* (2nd ed.). Palgrave, UK: Macmillan.

Greene, G., & Kochbar-Bryand, C. (2003). *Pathways to successful transition for youth with disabilities.* Upper Saddle River, NJ: Merrill.

Halverson, R. (2005). What can K-12 school leaders learn from video games and gaming? *Innovate, 1*(6). Retrieved from http://www.innovateonline.info

Helmrich, E., & Neiburger, E. (2007). Video games as a service: Three years later. *VOYA, 30*(2), 113–115.

Hutchinson, N. (2001, June). Beyond ADA compliance: Redefining accessibility. *American Libraries*, 76–78.

JISC & SCONUL. (2008). *Library management systems study.* Sheffield, UK: Sero Consulting.

Kanuka, H. (2005). An exploration into facilitating higher levels of learning in a text-based Internet learning environment using diverse instructional strategies. *Journal of Computer-Mediated communication, 10*(3). Retrieved from http://jcmc.indiana.edu/vol10/issue3/kanuka.html

Konana, P., & Balasubramanian, S. (2005). The Social–Economic–Psychological model of technology adoption and usage: an application to online investing. *Decision Support Systems, 39*(3), 505–524. doi:10.1016/j.dss.2003.12.003

Lee, J., & Young, C. (2008). Middle level educators and online social gaming. In K. McFerrin, et al, (Eds.), *Proceedings of Society for Information Technology and Teacher Education International Conference 2008* (pp. 1726-1732). Chesapeake, VA: American Association of Computer Education.

Main, R. (2000). Leveraging technology for human performance improvement. In G. Piskurich, P. Becksi, & B. Hall (Eds.), *The ASTD handbook of training design and delivery* (pp. 453-472). New York: McGraw-Hill.

Maness, J. (2006). Library 2.0 theory: Web 2.0 and its implications for libraries. *Webology, 3*(2), 2006.

National Center of Dissemination of Disability Research. (n.d.). Retrieved from http://www.ncddr.org

National Rehabilitation Information Center. (n.d.). Retrieved from http://www.naric.com

Nicholson, S. (2007). *The role of gaming in libraries: Taking the pulse*. Retrieved from http://boardgameswithscott.com/pulse2007.pdf

Rieber, L., & Noah, D. (2008). Games, simulations, and visual metaphors in education: Antagonism between enjoyment and learning. *Educational Media International*, *45*(2), 77–92. doi:10.1080/09523980802107096

Roblyer, M., & Doering, A. (2009). *Integrating educational technology into teaching* (5th ed.). Boston: Allyn & Bacon.

Simpson, E. (2005). Evolution in the classroom: what teachers need to know about the video game generation. *TechTrends*, *49*(5), 17–22. doi:10.1007/BF02763685

Squire, K. (2006). From content to context: Videogames as designed experience. *Educational Researcher*, *35*(8), 19–29. doi:10.3102/0013189X035008019

Tynjala, P., & Hakkinen, P. (2005). E-learning at work: Theoretical underpinnings and pedagogical challenges. *Journal of Workplace Learning*, *17*(5/6), 318–336. doi:10.1108/13665620510606742

Vischeck (for color blindness). (n.d.). Retrieved from http://www.vischeck.com/index.shtml

Wahlstrom, C., Williams, B., & Shea, P. (2003). *The successful distance learning learner.* Belmont, CA: Wadsworth.

Weinfan, L., & Davis, P. (2004). *Challenges in virtual communication: Videoconferencing, audioconferencing, and computer-mediated communications.* Santa Monica, CA: RAND Corporation.

Wilson, B. (2002). A study of actors promoting success in computer science including gender differences. *Computer Science Education*, *12*, 141–164. doi:10.1076/csed.12.1.141.8211

Chapter 11
Integrating Adult Learning and Technology for Effective Education:
Strategic Approaches

Royce Ann Collins
Kansas State University, USA

James B. Martin
U.S. Army Command and General Staff College, USA

ABSTRACT

This chapter is an examination of the influences involved in the integrating of adults into higher education. The chapter begins with an exploration of the increase in the number of adults in higher education since 1969. Comparing the changes in demographics from 1969 to 2007 shows how little large public universities have done to integrate adults into higher education. This examination shows significant participation by three types of institutions; community colleges, small private four year liberal arts institutions, and for-profit institutions created to meet the higher education needs of adults. The chapter defines adult and higher education and discusses how they differ or interact. A discussion of how adult students learn and effective techniques to facilitate learning in adult classrooms follows these definitions. Finally, a discussion identifying how teaching techniques that are effective for adults can be integrated into traditional classrooms in higher education brings the chapter to a close.

INTRODUCTION

Imagine a faculty lounge in a medium sized Midwestern state university where there is a lively discussion taking place concerning the provost's idea to create programs specifically for adult students. Some faculty members think it is a great idea as they will be able to reach students that they could not reach previously and provide them valuable tools. Other professors are worried that this nontraditional move will have negative effects on the intellectual strength of the university, insisting that it is nothing but a money maker and adults should stay in the continuing education programs the institution already offers. Even worse, some faculty members might come to the conclusion that many of the andragogical methods used in adult programs have a place on their traditional campus, while their less flexible peers will cherish their yellowed lecture notes to their graves. This scene could be played out in any number of institutions, with similar but varying results. There is an ongoing debate in higher education as to the place that adults should occupy and whether programs for them are valid intellectual pursuits. Having taught undergraduate and graduate courses to adult students over 20 years, the authors are strong proponents of the application of adult learning theories and methods in a higher education setting.

Adult students have their own styles of learning which may differ from those most familiar to traditional age college students and most comfortable for traditional faculty who teach based on their own time proven pedagogy. Adults take more responsibility for their own education and often become very involved in their programs, to the point of being assertive. Some higher education institutions understand that adults are a unique population and are dedicated to meeting the needs of this demographic group. As a part of that dedication, these institutions create policies where instructors must attend developmental sessions on the principles of teaching adults, incorporating critical thinking and collaborative learning into the classroom, and how to enhance learning in the classroom with technology.

After modeling adult learning theories and methods while teaching adult students in a higher education graduate program, many instructors hear the question: "Why don't all college instructors teach this way? If we know this is how adults learn and I can attest that it works for me, why isn't it a job requirement for all instructors in higher education institutions?" This is an excellent question and one explored throughout this chapter. The goals of this chapter are to discuss the adult student population in U.S. higher education institutions, compare the terms "adult education" and "higher education" and their relationship, highlight how adults learn, and show how adult learning and teaching strategies can be incorporated into higher education institutions.

BACKGROUND

In the mid 1960s, leading educators in the United States sensed a transition in the role and structure, amongst other things, of American higher education. They believed that a revolutionary change was coming which would create a "change in the basic character of the university from an institution primarily serving youth to one serving at least equally adults and community" (Knowles, 1969, p 3). This belief prompted the American Council on Education to study what they referred to as "Adult Higher Education" in the United States. This term is no longer widely used in the adult education community in the United States, but it accurately describes the issues of adult education that this chapter will examine.

These educators perceived that adult education in America was about to make the leap from the world of continuing education, focused on housewives and farmers, to an integral part of our system of higher education. They envisioned adults becoming as important to universities as the younger, traditional age students that they referred to as "youth." They spoke of the concept of Lifelong Learning as a new process emerging from the ashes of World War II and the enormous pressures that the administration and faculties of academic institutions were under to revise their way of thinking when it came to adults in higher education (Knowles, 1969).

Almost 25 years later, Carol Kasworm (1993) looked at the world of adult higher education in an effort to gain an understanding of where this concept stood internationally. She too was very positive about the growth potential for adult higher education, particularly because of the growth in emphasis on lifelong learning being exhibited in developed and developing countries. She admitted that the concept was fraught with definition issues and a range of terms that created significant confusion about adult higher education. Looking back towards Knowles' study, she observed that "In the last thirty years, many forces acting upon higher education and national educational policy have redefined the relationship between the higher education, the adult learner, and the society" (Kasworm, 1993, p.411). Kasworm (1993) goes on from that observation to share much of the same enthusiasm for the future of adult higher education evident in Knowles's study, concluding that "adult participation in higher education has come to symbolize one important aspect of the 'learning society'" (p. 411).

For many of us who have spent time engaged in the world of adult education, this need to revise thinking is still much the same as it was described by Knowles study in 1969. Though Kasworm paints a positive picture of adult higher education, through most of the 1990s large public universities continued the long tradition of believing that if students wanted an education they could come to campus and study what the university had to offer at the times that the university offered it. This tradition is well illuminated by a comparison of enrollment figures from the fall semester of 1987 to the fall semester of 2007. Large, four-year public institutions grew by over 1.7 million students during this twenty-year period. While growth in student enrollment is something to be celebrated, the demographics of this growth indicate how this alienation of large universities from adult students has worsened. Of that 1.7 million student increase, 81 percent of it occurred in the traditional student population while only 19 percent growth in students over 25 years of age was recorded (Knapp, Kelly-Reid, & Ginder, 2009). This trend further excluded large numbers of potential students who worked in full time day jobs from enrolling in these university programs. This model worked fine when the vast majority of college students were traditional undergraduates who focused as much on the university football team as on their academic programs, and by educating them, the university met the nation's needs for a highly skilled workforce. Today and in our future that is not the case and this "build it and they will come" mentality has separated such institutions from the adult student population and opened the market to more flexible educational endeavors by community colleges, for-*profit* institutions, and small private colleges and universities.

IDENTIFICATION OF THE ADULT STUDENT POPULATION IN HIGHER EDUCATION

The Lumina Foundation (2009) reported in their study, *A stronger nation through higher education*, that approximately 39 percent of American adults hold a two or four year college degree. This statistic portrays an adult population that is largely educated at the high school level, with just over a third having some form of college certification. For instance, in 2007, approximately 87 percent of the 25 to 29 year olds held a high school diploma or the equivalent; while only "30 percent had completed a bachelor's degree or higher" (Planty, et al., 2008, p. 40). In the U.S., the workforce demands are changing. "For generations, the American economy has created large numbers of middle-class jobs that required no college-level knowledge or skills" (Lumina Foundation, 2009, p. 1). Because of our global economy, these jobs are disappearing. In the uncertain economic climate facing Americans, obtaining an associate and baccalaureate degree will become even more important than it has been in the past and the attainment of graduate education is required far more often than in the past. Access to middle class jobs is becoming more and more dependent on earning the appropriate level college degree.

How do we, as a nation, solve this gap that appears to be growing between the education needed for jobs and the amount of education our working adults possess? The Lumina study estimates that with the current graduation rates from two and four year institutions, "there will be a shortage of 16 million college educated adults in the American workforce by 2025" (Lumina Foundation, 2009, pp.1-2). One way to make up this shortage could be to enroll greater numbers of traditional age college students, between the ages of 18-24, and graduate them at higher rates than we currently are achieving. Studies have shown that much of the problem is not in enrolling students, particularly those that are considered at risk, but in providing the necessary support network for these students to complete their studies (State Higher Education Executive Officers [SHEEO], 2008). With the growing requirements for higher education to qualify for middle class jobs, older adults (25+ years old) will need to attend colleges and universities at a higher rate than they do currently. Who are these students and who will provide them the education that the Lumina study indicates will be necessary to meet our economy's needs?

Community colleges, for-profit institutions, and the smaller private four-year colleges and universities are emerging as leaders in the field of designing and providing education to adult students in America. These institutions have proven themselves more innovative and flexible in the way they have approached adult education and because of that have seized the largest share of the booming adult student population in adult higher education (Snyder & Hoffman, 1991; Snyder, 2009). Focused on providing educational offerings to adult students when and where they need them, they have realized the importance of needs analysis and sought to modify the traditional educational product to a model that allows the same learning outcomes in shorter time spans or new modes of education.

This growth is not the specific "revolution" that Knowles (1969) described in his book on adult higher education, but it is the sector of the education industry in which one can see the impact of the growing need for further education of adult students. While Knowles and his contemporaries saw the modification of traditional large universities or the provision of higher education by corporations like General Electric, International Business Machines or Minnesota Mining and Manufacturing to their employees, they did not see the forces that would shape adult education in the future they sought to foretell. They paid only scant heed to the role of community colleges, instead believing that the extension departments of large land grant universities would be the platform by which larger adult populations were served in higher education. They did not foresee the creation of corporations that would make adult students their only market segment and reach sizes unheard of in even the latter stages of the 20th century. They did recognize the role that traditional liberal arts colleges were playing in adult education in 1969, but spoke of them as only a small part of the larger 'headwaters" of adult education in America (Knowles, 1969, p 46).

Groups of educators in community colleges, for-profit institutions, and small private universities identified the gap that existed between the needs and desires of potential adult students and what was offered to them by the traditional academy. They examined the gap and began to determine ways that they could meet the educational requirements and maintain the standards necessary to gain or retain regional accreditation for their institutions. This was critical, as without regional accreditation, such institutions could not attract federal financial aid to provide the necessary funding for the adult students they were targeting in their programs. New scheduling models and greater recognition of the need for quality assessment efforts were two of the modifications that these innovative educators seized upon to make their ideas work. The results of their efforts are borne out in the statistics that show the growth in enrollments and graduation rates from these "adult friendly" institutions.

The newest and most controversial of these adult friendly institutions, for-profit private institutions, experienced an enrollment increase in the number of associate's, bachelor's and master's degrees awarded between academic year 1995-1996 and academic year 2005-2006. Planty, el al. (2008) reported that the associate's degrees awarded between 1995-1996 and 2005-2006 at public institutions decreased from 82 percent to 78 percent, while nonprofit private institutions decreased from 9 percent to 7 percent. While the for-profit private institutions documented an increase from 9 percent to 15 percent in bachelor's degrees, small private institutions also experienced an increase from 1 percent to 4 percent. However, the most dramatic shift was the percentage of master's degrees awarded by for-profit private institutions, which increased from 1 percent to 8 percent for the same period (Planty, et al., 2008). It is important to remember that amongst these three groups; nonprofit public institutions, for-profit private institutions, and nonprofit small private institutions, almost all of the growth shown by for-profit institutions in Planty's study was from adult students while the other two categories experienced growth through a mixed population by age. During the ten years under study, the majority of students enrolled in for-profit education were adults, rather than a mixture of adults and traditional age college students.

These statistics are indicative of the growth of for-profit private institutions in the last three decades. They have grown largely as a result of programs focused on serving the adult student demographic mentioned earlier. In the fall 1987, the National Center for Educational Statistics did not even specify the for-profit category in the collection of data (Snyder & Hoffman, 1991). Institutions that would have a dramatic impact in the next two decades, such as the University of Phoenix, were not large enough to be viewed independently of the established categories. With no identification of student enrollment in 1987 statistics, by 2007 this category had grown sufficiently to indicate enrollments of 912,361 students, of which 72.5 percent were over the age of 25 (Knapp, et al., 2009). The number of students by which this enrollment category grew in this twenty year period is significantly less that the larger categories identifying the public and private not for profit institutions with which we are more familiar, but the percentage of increase from 1987 to 2007 is significantly more (Snyder & Hoffman, 1991; Knapp, et al., 2009). These institutions successfully created undergraduate and graduate programs that catered to the needs of adult students and their employers. For example, the University of Phoenix (UOP) enrolled over 38,000 students on its 20th anniversary in 1996 (Apollo Group, Inc., n.d.), but grew so strongly that by December 2008 they reported a total enrollment to their regional accrediting body of 368,442 students (Higher Learning Commission [HLC], n.d.). In this same report to the Higher Learning Commission, UOP indicated that they had granted 57,140 degrees of all types and 26,585 graduate degrees during 2008 (HLC, n.d.). In fact, because of this focus on the growing adult student market, the University of Phoenix has grown to be the largest educational institution in North America. They focus almost exclusively on adult students and provide education through over 200 academic sites across the United States, as well as through their growing online academic presence (UOP, n.d.).

This drive to serve the adult student population has gripped few traditional state universities, because the majority has not seen adults as their primary market segment. In addition, these institutions have received little or no encouragement from a major source of their funding, their own state legislators. Evidence is beginning to surface that this may be changing and that information such as that provided by the Lumina Foundation

(2009) study has begun to move state officials to affect change in the educational planning dynamics in some states. An article published in the *Chronicle of Higher Education* in February 2008 indicated that several states, including Kentucky, Utah, New Mexico, and Ohio have embarked on programs intended to move state schools in the direction of serving that large portion of their adult population, which does not have college degrees (Sanders, 2008). Many of those state or institutional representatives interviewed for the article cited the Lumina study's findings about the number of college-educated adults needed in the coming years to fill out fully the American workforce. In fact, a new program called "Nontraditional No More" began in 2008 as an effort by the Western Interstate Commission for Higher Education to provide $775,100 to identify adult students who are just shy of achieving their degrees and help them complete their academic requirements. This program, funded by a grant from the Lumina Foundation, does what very few have done over the past twenty years in that it explicitly aids adult students in finishing their degrees at state schools (Sanders, 2008).

It is of note that Carol Kasworm's (1993) study, which examined how the U.S. and other countries were handling this issue of growth in adult higher education, missed the growth of for-profit adult higher education. Her study found interesting systems in Sweden, Norway, and China where these governments have created national academic systems specifically to meet the needs of adult learners. It examined the Open University concept popular in Great Britain and India and indicated the significant student populations enrolled at that time. In the U.S., her focus was mainly on state-supported "universities without walls" such as Thomas Edison College and Metropolitan State College or consortiums of traditional universities in enterprises like the National Technological University. Like Knowles (1969), she examined 'corporate colleges' which were providing education to their employees, rather than on the potential for 'college corporations' which would reach students who found more traditional institutions unappealing. This is surprising when one thinks that just three years after the publication of this article, the University of Phoenix reported enrolling 38,000 students. This observation is not meant to detract from the importance of Kasworm's study, but to again point out that as late as 1993 scholars of adult education believed that adult higher education needs in the United States would be met by state supported institutions or corporate colleges rather than the growing for-profit sector of U.S. adult higher education.

Numerous sources from the world of higher education indicate that our workforce must become better educated and grow in the next 15 to 20 years. They search for answers to the question of where U.S. will find enough students and how will U.S. educate them to meet the economic needs. As with all things complex, there will be no easy answer to this problem. It is important, however, that governmental and private leadership recognize the potential that the adult population holds to meet this growing need. Different educational systems and methodologies, just gaining ground when Knowles wrote in 1969, have been practiced and perfected to the point that they can provide adult higher education when and where it is needed and demonstrate the accountability so important in our current environment.

WHAT IS MEANT BY ADULT/HIGHER EDUCATION?

A mere six years after Knowles (1969) published *Higher Adult Education in the United States*, Webster's Collegiate Dictionary included a definition of adult education that indicated that it was "lectures or correspondence courses for adults usually not otherwise engaged in formal study" (Webster's, 1975, p. 17). This definition does not match up with the concepts presented in Knowles' title, let alone the text of his book. Where Knowles viewed at least part of adult education as higher education, the author of Webster's definition seemed to exclude it. The focus was on the extension type educational activities that had been common for many years. This focus still exists in some venues today, as the same definition was found at the Princeton University Wordnet site by simply running a Google search for the definition of adult education.

A different definition, composed more recently, provides a different focus from Webster's and touches on the line of reasoning undertaken by Malcolm Knowles. "Adult education includes formal education activities in which adults participate to upgrade their work skills, to change careers, or to expand personal interests" (Planty, et al., 2008, p. 5). This definition is very specific in identifying that adult education includes "formal education activities" and not just the continuing education and adult basic education classes that many traditional academics have long considered the totality of adult education.

Higher education would seem to be easy enough to define, but it has its own unique set of characteristics identified largely through the eyes of the individual issuing the definition. For our purposes, we will use the definition found on the website of the National Center for Education Statistics (NCES). This organization is the authoritative source for most quantitative information used in higher education circles, so its opinion as to the definition of higher education should be acceptable for our purposes. On their glossary page, NCES opines that higher education is "study beyond secondary school at an institution that offers programs leading to an associate, baccalaureate, or higher degree (or equivalent degrees in other countries). It also is called tertiary or postsecondary education" (NCES, n.d.).

The definition used by NCES focuses almost entirely on an institution that offers educational programs beyond high school that lead to the attainment of undergraduate or graduate degrees. It does not indicate location, size, appropriate teaching style, age of students, fields of study, or research focus. It is centered around postsecondary education as opposed to secondary education and on the ability to grant degrees to students who meet the institutions' requirements. The programs of study described in the previous section which lead to undergraduate or graduate degrees and are designed specifically for adult students meet this definition, though they may differ from traditional higher education as provided on large public university campuses. For this chapter's purpose, the authors chose to use the phrase noted in Knowles' book and more accurately refer to programs designed for adult students and lead to a degree as "adult higher education."

A growing number of programs that offer undergraduate and graduate degrees focus totally on students who are not in the traditional college age range and who need classes offered at a time outside of the "normal" school day (Commission for Accelerated Programs, n.d.). These students work in a wide variety of industries and economic sectors, both blue collar and white collar, but have in common the desire to earn a college degree to better their chances or meet personal goals. They undertake adult higher education programs for many of the same reasons traditional students engage in higher education, but have markedly different needs and requirements. The secret to bringing these students into the world of adult higher education is to provide the right program in the right format; this is the challenge for the educator of adult students (Knapp, et al., 2009).

Often the programs offered for adult students are referred to as accelerated or intensive schedule formats, but these simply represent different scheduling techniques used to make academic programs available to working adults. These scheduling techniques allow students to attend classes in the evenings or on the weekends, so that they can continue to work if necessary. In fact, prior to the current economic challenges, many companies large and small made financial assistance available to adult students who were willing to work a full schedule and then attend college on their own time. This was a positive program for the companies, as they provided an attractive benefit in a competitive job market and grew a workforce that was more educated.

Later in this chapter, we will discuss the many differences in how adult students learn and the corresponding unique methodologies used to effectively help them learn, but to understand how programs can be successful in meeting the needs of adults simply by modifying traditional semester or quarter scheduling models, it is important to understand these students. They are often focused on the when, where, what, and how of education.

Because most adults over 25 years of age need employment, they have limited opportunities to take classes in the middle of the day. While this model can succeed in some environments, the most successful models have provided students classes at the times when they are not working (Kasworm, Polson, & Fishback, 2002). Evening and weekend classes have allowed legions of adult students to pursue programs of study that are more than just "lecture or correspondence courses" and lead to the attainment of a college degree.

Knowles (1969) believed that a learning community would grow up around large universities to serve the adult population, but this has not been the most common case. The three types of institutions that have carried the load in providing adult higher education have identified the need to make education convenient for adult students and have placed educational sites or course meeting spaces in the locations that work for their students. Admittedly, with the growth of distance education, this will become less important, but we are many years away from totally leaving the classroom behind for a virtual university.

The liberal arts, for decades the staple of university life, are normally not the focus of the adult student population. Needing to improve their education to get ahead or gain a new job, they are looking for specific marketable skills to improve their lot in life. Consistently undergraduate adult focused programs have still met the general education requirements that are a standard of U.S. higher education, but very few students major in political science or foreign languages. These students focus on programs in business administration, nursing, marketing, accounting, or education that will aid them in job creation or maintenance.

Finally, the how of adult education as discussed here relates to the ability to fund higher education in whatever form it is undertaken. Federal financial aid programs are designed for traditional students, and adult focused institutions have to take care to smooth the progress of their students in the pursuit of financing (Kasworm, et al., 2002). Unfortunately, very few scholarships or grants are directed at adult students. These hurdles are what makes the employer reimbursement programs mentioned earlier so important for adult learners.

A growing venue for adult education, as with other educational demographic groups in America, is that of distance education. These programs, all of which use technology in some form, allow students who cannot conveniently get to any type of bricks and mortar campus to work towards their degree through an alternative means. This option works well for adults, particularly as more and more of the population grows comfortable with the capabilities of the personal computer and the Internet. The issues of child care or inflexible work schedules become easier to overcome when a student can choose when they work on their studies or answer questions posed by an online instructor. When Thomas Friedman (2007) wrote that the world is flat, he was describing a world where the playing field has been leveled and businesses no longer have to be in a certain spot on a certain schedule to make their ideas work. Technology has allowed a similar "flattening" of the educational world and opened new alternatives for students of all ages regardless of their location or the specific time they need their education (Allen & Seaman, 2008; Friedman, 2007). In essence, this flattening of the adult education world answers the when, where, and what questions asked in the previous paragraphs. With the advent of distance education, not only can institutions plan degree programs specifically for adult students in a specific town, they can plan them for students in different states and different countries.

This issue of adult education and higher education is largely one of semantics and perceptions. If higher education is defined as stated earlier by NCES and adult students are earning graduate degrees from institutions which have regional accreditation, then why must we separate the two ideas? Higher education is not about the age of students or even the scheduling formats used in program planning, but the level of education and critical thinking required to accomplish the learning outcomes successfully that are the hallmark of a specific academic degree. Adult focused programs that offer higher degrees require the same regional accreditation scrutiny as traditional public universities, if not closer scrutiny. Should we judge the level of education an institution provides by the scheduling processes it uses or the location of its classes? Alternatively, should the level of education be judged by the quality of the students and faculty and whether or not they can demonstrate the required competency in their respective academic discipline? If the focus is on the learning outcomes, should we not create the best possible learning situation and apply the knowledge and understanding of how adults learn? The answer appears to be obvious, but in real life, it is not as simple.

HOW DO ADULT STUDENTS LEARN AND ARE THEY DIFFERENT?

While there is not one learning theory for adults, there are numerous studies documenting the characteristics of adult learners. Of course, "adulthood" is diversified and spans a great deal of time, so all aspects need to take into consideration development, maturation, and culture. For instance, some adults may experience a decline in physical or sensory capabilities as they age (i.e., eyesight changes, hearing losses). Learning approaches in one culture may not transfer to another culture. For example, Westerners have a tendency to approach learning analytically while Easterners lean toward a more holistic attitude (Merriam, Caffarella, & Baumgartner, 2007). This section will explore some of the aspects of adult learning documented over the years including Knowles' (1980) assumptions of adult learning, self-directed learning, cognitive development, and cultural and gender differences.

One aspect is that learning environments for adults should be student focused, rather than teacher focused (Knowles, 1980). This means the instructor is moved off center stage and the students are moved to the center. Following a constructivist approach, the knowledge that the instructor has is not as important as the knowledge the students produce because of the learning experiences. Learners actively construct their own knowledge rather than relying solely on the information in the textbook or lectures from the instructor. Students make meaning out of their own experiences (Merriam, et al., 2007).

Knowles (1980) discussed the different approaches to education as being on a continuum from pedagogy to andragogy. These can be applied to any educational situation according to the fit with the learners. One of the assumptions of andragogy is that adult students can be more self-directed in their approach to the learning environment. This means students will regulate their own learning and they need a climate that respects and supports them. The instructor and student are jointly and equally on a road of inquiry.

Researching self-direction as an attribute of the learner, Gerald Grow (1991) explored the idea that higher education, with its focus on teacher-centered approach to the classroom, actually kept learners at a dependent status. According to Grow, self-direction can be taught and facilitated by the instructor's behavior toward the student. By following the staged self-directed learning model, instructors can assist their students in moving from a dependent learner to an independent learner. This means modifying the instructor's approach to the learning setting. The instructor must move from being the authority figure and granter of all knowledge to a discussion guide, where students participate in a directed dialogue. The instructor then can move to a facilitator where the instructor and learners collaborate on the learning goals, and finally to a mentor as students take responsibility for their own learning and learning projects. Grow's model was created from observation of traditional age (18 to 22 years old) college students. He gives many examples and outlines the roles of the student and instructor in each stage. In following Grow's staged self-directed learning model, any instructor can move students from dependency to independency. (It is interesting to note with this chapter's focus on adult/higher education that Allen Tough (1971), an adult education pioneer, created the self-directed learning theory. This is just an example of the development of a theory in the adult education discipline applied to the traditional higher educational setting.)

While Grow (1991) states there is nothing wrong with a dependent learner, the goal of many higher education institutions is to create learners who think critically and analyze information in order for the graduates to become productive members of society. There are several theories that examined cognitive development of adults (Baxter Magolda, 1991; King & Kitchener, 1994; Belenky, Clinchy, Goldberger, & Tarule, 1997; Perry, 1999). The effect of instructor behaviors and style (e.g., lecturer, facilitator of discussion) on adult student's cognitive development was studied. Collins' (2006) investigation demonstrated that the classroom environment where the instructor lectures for hours and the student takes notes actually forces the student to stay at a lower level of cognitive development. In a classroom environment where the instructor approaches the content and the delivery developmentally, students demonstrate growth in their cognitive abilities. An instructor who teaches from a cognitive developmental approach starts with the content material, but quickly moves to asking questions of the students that help them analyze the content, form their own opinions, debate their ideas with others, and apply the information to the current world setting. Thus, the instructor consciously creates situations that develop students' cognitive abilities as well as address the content of the course.

Adults learn through discussing and applying information (Merriam, et al., 2007). They have a wealth of experience, which can greatly enhance the learning experience of everyone in the course. It is through sharing these experiences and hearing experiences of others that adults engage the learning material with reflection. This reflection allows adults to connect past experiences with current experiences and create implications for the future. Instructors of adult students must know the content area extremely well in order to allow the flow of the discussion and assignments to meet the learning outcomes established for the content. Furthermore, adults fully expect to be respected and to voice their opinions freely in class. This is one area where a difference can be seen between the traditional aged college student and the adult student; the amount of experience they have to drawn upon in discussions. However, we would argue that the same observation can be made between a recent high school graduate from an urban area and one from a rural area as well. The various experiences of the learners contribute to making a rich learning environment. Lack of experience simply calls upon the instructor to expose students to new experiences through video, field trips, or vicariously through the sharing of experiences in the course.

Adult students need immediate and frequent feedback as they progress through a course. It is important for adult students to understand if they are fulfilling the requirements to the best of their ability. Many times, they feel immense responsibility to demonstrate to their children such important habits as completing assignments on time and incorporating the feedback received into the work for the next assignment.

Adults are motivated by a variety of factors both internally and externally (Houle, 1961; Brookfield, 1986). Some adults want to learn for learning's sake and are internally motivated to pursue educational situations. Career paths and the potential for increased income motivate other adults; they have a goal. Application of the learning material is coupled with motivation. Adults want to leave a learning experience with something to apply to their work or life. Wlodkowski (2008) stated that adults need to understand the relevance of the information. "For adults to see learning as truly relevant it has to be connected to who they are, what they care about, and how they perceive and know" (Wlodkowski, 2008, p. 214).

Many adults suffer from imposter syndrome or impostership (Brookfield, 2006). Impostership is the belief that one really does not possess the skills or intelligence in order to be successful in an educational pursuit. Ross-Gordon and Brown-Haywood (2000) documented that many adult students suffer from lack of confidence and that self-perception is a key in student persistence. This phenomenon affects students at all levels of educational attainment, cultures, and genders. "They imagine that once this secret is discovered they will be asked to leave whatever program they're enrolled in, covered in a cloud of public shame, humiliation, and embarrassment" (Brookfield, 2006, p. 76). This is a false image, but it feels very real. To take the power away from this phenomenon, it must be discussed in the light. Just by acknowledging the existence, adults who suffer from this issue can see that they are not unique and alone. "Left unnamed it is the elephant in the room, the silent assassin of student engagement and motivation" (Brookfield, 2006, p. 83).

Literature such as Ross-Gordon and Brown-Haywood's (2000) demonstrates the need for the instructor to incorporate culturally relevant and inclusive curriculum and to allow the students to share their personal cultural backgrounds. The literature chosen by the instructor makes a difference. Is only the dominant society voice heard or are the marginalized stories also told? For instance, is the expansion westward told from the point of view of the white heterosexual male or the Native American Indian in U.S. history courses? Black Elk writes "once we were happy in our country and we were seldom hungry, for then the two-leggeds and the four-leggeds lived together like relatives, and there was plenty for them and us (Neihardt, 1979, pp. 8-9). Black Elk continues to say that the Wasichus (word referred to white man) came and they divided everything up into small islands that continued to decrease in size as the flood of Wasichus continued to take over their land. From Black Elk's perspective, his people were just trying to take care of their own and the land in which they had been occupying. Students from different cultural backgrounds need to be able to share their stories and hear the stories of their culture discussed as a part of the course content.

These are just a few of the principles concerning adult learners. There are volumes of material that cannot be addressed in this chapter, such as adult development theories, transformational learning, spirituality, emotional influences, embodied or somatic learning, and non-western perspectives (Merriam, et al., 2007). However, the authors consider the adult learning principles presented in the previous pages as the basic starting point for any instructor wanting to address the learning of adults in an adult or higher education setting.

Adult developmentalists and cognitive developmentalists will argue that there are some differences between the 18 year old and the 35 or

40 year old. Do strict age lines mark those differences? Not always, sometimes it is differences in types and amounts of experience. So, have adult educators been describing and documenting just good teaching practices? Has all the research on "adult" learning really been examining ways to approach a college student? Are these just excellent ways to approach a college classroom with any age group? Perhaps, instructors in any adult or higher education setting should apply what we know from adult learning to the classroom experience.

INCORPORATING ADULT LEARNING AND TEACHING STRATEGIES INTO ADULT/HIGHER EDUCATION

Teaching adults is not for everyone. Instructors who must be the center of the classroom and be seen as the one with all the knowledge directing all the actions of the learners will probably not find teaching adults an enjoyable experience. Instructors who feel the need to pontificate for 30+ minutes in a setting will find teaching adults a challenge. Instructors who cannot change from approaching the educational situation as teacher-centered will find teaching in any adult/higher education setting less rewarding.

Instructors who can approach the learning environment as student-centered will enjoy teaching adults and traditional age (18 to 22 years old) college students. Incorporating adult learning and teaching strategies into any educational situation means primarily a student-centered approach. A student-centered approach means taking into consideration adult learning principles discussed in the previous section and student life schedules.

Adults need structure and flexibility. Adults have very busy schedules with multiple responsibilities from home, family, community, and jobs. In order to squeeze one more activity into their schedules, they need to have clearly defined dates for assignments and topical discussions in courses. Clarify the entire course the first class session for the adult student and only modify the schedule through mutual negotiation. Adult students will many times take the calendar, examine how it fits with family obligations and work commitments, and make adjustments accordingly. They look for conflicts and strategize how to accomplish all the tasks. Many times adult students work ahead, in order to meet all their commitments and deadlines.

On the other hand, adults need flexibility. If a family emergency arises or work suddenly sends them out of town, adult students need to be certain that the instructor of the course will be flexible and work with them on the due dates. Adult students need to know that the instructor will be reasonable with them. Remember adult students have a drive to succeed or they would not be adding one more thing to their plate. Typically, adult students achieve higher grade point averages than the average 18 to 22 years old enrolled in the same course (Kasworm, et al., 2002). Many times their high achievement is linked to motivation for learning and the fact that adult students are typically paying the tuition bill, rather than getting help from parents.

It is important to create an environment where all are welcomed and all voices have the right to be heard. The environment includes the physical set up of the classroom if in a face-to-face environment. Take the tables or chairs out of rows and place them in a circle or U-shape in order to promote discussion. Allow time for everyone to get to know each other. This could be in the form of bios and pictures in an online format or brief introductions in a face-to-face setting. Include icebreaker activities into the first sessions and create an atmosphere of inclusion. The instructor is instrumental in this process. The instructor must model a positive attitude toward all students, be personable and greet each one individually, and express an attitude of trying to create an excellent learning experience for the entire group. Students bring a variety of cultures and knowledge levels to the learning situation. Learning is enhanced when adults feel they belong to the group. Adults will also be more tolerant of opposing opinions and open to dialogue if they have a positive emotional connection to the group (Wlodkowski, 2008). Instructors need to name impostership and discuss it openly in the first class sessions. Once again, students will find a connection with others in the classroom and will not feel isolated.

Instructors must understand why adult students are taking the course. To obtain this information, invite the learners to complete a short questionnaire at the first meeting or module and ask them what they want to get out of the course. There are varieties of questions or open-ended sentences that will help the instructor get to know the students. For instance, ask the students 1) what they enjoy in a learning environment, 2) what irritates them the most in a learning situation, 3) what do they most want to learn in this course, 4) what is the most important thing the student would like the instructor to know about them, and 5) if there are any special difficulties or problems that might impact their performance in this course (i.e. young children, elderly parents). In a recent course, one student shared concerning the most important thing he wanted the instructor to know about was that his father had Alzheimer's and he wanted to improve his mind. Another student stated that his job forced him to travel a great deal. A female stay-at-home mother shared she was glad to be among adults and that she had not been in a formal classroom for almost 20 years. All these statements help create a trust between the students and the instructor. Use the information gained to prompt discussions. In the instance described above, it gave the instructor the opportunity to discuss the fear of coming back to a formal educational situation and impostership. Students have perceptions of courses, and if not clarified, those perceptions can muddy the learning process. For instance, many students enter the first course of a master's degree program on adult education with the expectation that they will learn how to teach. The first course in the program does not focus on that aspect entirely, so during the next class session or in an online format, the instructor reminds the students of the scope of this course and reviews the course objectives. In addition, the instructor highlights the future courses when the topics are covered. Throughout the course, the instructor brings to the students' attention any learning activities experienced which addresses anyone's expectations. Instructors who take the time to gather and respond to the way students learn, their expectations, and special circumstances will improve the learning environment.

Active learning is a necessity. We know that adults learn through discussion, so let them discuss. Instead of approaching the course content with the lecture material in mind, approach the course content with questions. Allow the students to create the lecture by their comments. Give time for students to discuss in pairs or small groups, but always report small group discussions to the larger group. Make sure students have time to move around in the classroom. Sitting for long periods does not help anyone learn material. Combine short lectures with active participation of the learners by the instructor keeping his/her comments to 10 or 15 minutes in length and interjecting questions or small group discussions.

Adult students value instructors who are credible, trustworthy, and authentic (Brookfield, 2006). Instructors who demonstrate that they have experience and expertise in the content area are well respected by adult learners. In addition, instructors need to be able to articulate a sound rationale for their approach to the course content, required assignments, and activities in the classroom. Adult students identify with instructors who are passionate about their subject and demonstrate that enthusiasm in the classroom or online format. Adults need to see that instructors are consistent and fair with each person in the course. They need to know that instructors are genuinely there to assist the learner in grasping the material, not to play "gotcha." Finally, adult students need to know the instructor will be responsive with email replies, phone messages, assignment evaluations and questions during the course. A student wrote, "Thank you for always providing feedback [on assignments]. Essential to growth, knowing I "got" it. I know it takes a lot of time and effort. I appreciate it." They need to know that the instructor respects them as much as they respect the instructor. That may take the shape of canceling another written assignment, because the instructor's schedule was too busy to accomplish grading and writing comments on all their previous papers. Adult students need to know that instructors have lives as well and can use their own life as an example in class, and can admit it when they make a mistake.

Obtain feedback from students. Use a variety of classroom assessment techniques including critical incident questionnaires (Brookfield, 2006) to find out how adult students are experiencing the course and interactions. The critical incident questionnaire allows the instructor find out when students are most engaged and most distanced from the happenings. It also asks students what they found most helpful during that class session, what they found most puzzling, and what surprised them the most. The information an instructor can learn from such activities can significantly affect the course. Some instructors use these every class session, while others use them periodically throughout a course. It is important to gather feedback from the students prior to the end of the course. By gathering data at the end of the course, the instructor only has the possibility of changing for the next group of students. If data are gathered during the course, the instructor has the opportunity to modify activities or approaches and clarify content confusion.

In a recent higher education course with adult students, the instructor asked the students to respond to the critical incident questionnaire at the end of the third class session. (This course meets for four hours a session once a week.) The responses to the question concerning when they felt the most engaged in the course was dominated by references to the discussion (either large group or small group). One stated "instructor lecture with class interjection and participation." Another student responded, "tying in the assumptions and theories to real world applications." The critical incident questionnaires revealed this rich information concerning what students found most helpful during the four-hour class session:

- Instructor validating my feelings
- Instructor very good in putting lessons in context
- Group evaluation and discussion
- A student comment on the content which clarified the topic for me
- DVDs of authors
- Breaking into groups and small group discussion
- Instructor clarification of subject material
- Questions concerning how subject applies to the real world.
- Handouts provide a wrap up of one segment and transition to the next
- Classroom as a whole with individual input and personal experiences
- When various students spoke up bringing in their personal experiences

From the list of comments the instructor can see that the variety of activities in the classroom assist the students in learning the material. These responses also validate that sharing of personal experiences and tying content to real word examples (adult learning theories discussed earlier) assist the students in understanding the concepts.

On the same critical incident questionnaire, responses to the question concerning what action anyone took in class that they found most puzzling included:

- Neighbor won't stop talking. Has a comment for everything throughout class. Very distracting

- Guy beside me comments on Everything!!!
- Presentation of qualitative research
- The videos, repetitive of assigned readings

Over half the students (14) stated there was nothing puzzling. Notice that in the previous critical incident question discussed some students commented that the DVDs or videos were helpful. In this question, the instructor learns that some students found the videos most puzzling or repetitive of the readings, while others found them to be very helpful. Students will not learn from all activities or assignments equally. From the learning style research, we know that each person has a preferential way to process and absorb information. For the visual learner, the videos and DVDs assist them in learning the material. For the kinesthetic person, this activity just makes them sit still and not grasp the information according to their preference. Student comments must always be weighed with knowledge of adult learning.

One instructor collects the information from the critical incident questionnaire and addresses any content confusion the next day in an electronic format (either by email or posting to an online course message board or announcements). She will type up the student responses to each question and read them to the students at the beginning of the next class session. The students see that the instructor takes their feedback seriously and that their comments matter. In this case, it allowed the students to address disruptive behavior issues. It was also an educational tool since it gave the instructor the opportunity to point out the differences between learners and to remember that what appeals to them may not appeal to the person next to them and vice versa.

These are just a few ways to incorporate adult learning strategies into a higher education course. Even though this section has referred to these strategies as being effective with adult students, the literature supports these teaching strategies for any college course. Weimer (2002) discusses using learner-centered teaching with all college students. Student-centered teaching was discussed earlier as one of the ways to teach adults. Even Meyers and Jones (1993) in their book, *Promoting Active Learning: Strategies for the College Classroom*, were discussing active learning strategies that align with the adult learning principles outlined earlier. In his book, *The Skillful Teacher*, referenced earlier in this chapter, Stephen Brookfield (2006) indicates that he is addressing college teaching. He admits that:

I have often been puzzled by the absence of adult educational literature in books on college teaching. After all, college teaching is focused on learners who are partially or fully immersed in adulthood. In this sense, it is part of adult education. (Brookfield, 2006, p. xv)

Perhaps, the terminology is creating the problem. Perhaps, the marginalization of adult education professions at many higher education institutions has caused a disconnection between the research and application. Whatever the reason, there is much to be gained in higher education from the inclusion of theories of adult learning developed by adult educators.

FUTURE RESEARCH DIRECTIONS

Obviously, from the above paragraphs, future research needs to focus on the application of teaching strategies for adult learners and the college classroom. Community colleges would be a great place to focus this study. From all indications, these institutions will see a boom of adult students and traditional aged students in the next few years. The intergenerational student mix in the courses will provide a rich population to improve the research concerning teaching.

Adult students will enroll where their needs are met. Researchers should continue following the enrollment trends of this population and continue to document best practices in providing higher education opportunities for adult learners. These publications should not be limited to the adult education world, but should also be available to the larger higher education community.

CONCLUSION

As we move further into the 21st century, the U.S. must find a way to incorporate more highly educated adults into the workforce. The Lumina Foundation (2009) report states that the population and graduation rates of the 18 to 22 years old will not be enough. More higher education institutions will find the adults over the age of 24 knocking at their doors. It is time for more than just the for-profit institutions to step up and modify their scheduling and teaching approaches to meet the demands of the adult learner. Whether we use the terms adult higher education, adult/higher education, or higher education, instructors should incorporate the adult learning principles into the learning environment. Instructors can expand their understanding of the teaching and learning environment to include many of the adult learning principles already documented in the adult education discipline. The voices of the students speak loudly to their effectiveness. "I've learned a lot, not just from content, but from her methods as well. When will more instructors teach this way?" Good question!

REFERENCES

Allen, I. & Seaman, J. (November 2008). *Staying the course: Online education in the United States, 2008.* Needham, MA: Sloan Consortium. (http://www.sloan-c.org/publications/survey/pdf/staying_the_course.pdf).

Apollo Group, Inc. (n.d.). Retrieved on March 23, 2009. from http://www.fundinguniverse.com/company-histories/Apollo-Group-Inc-Company-History.html

Baxter Magolda, M.B. (1992). *Knowing and reasoning in college.* San Francisco: Jossey-Bass.

Belenky, M.F., Clinchy, B.M., Goldberger, N.R., & Tarule, J.M. (1997). *Women's' ways of knowing* (10th anniversary edition). New York: Basic Books.

Brookfield, S.D. (2006). *The skillful teacher (2nd edition).* San Francisco: Jossey Bass.

Commission for Accelerated Programs. (n.d.) Accelerated Programs by institutions. Retrieved on March 23, 2009 from http://www.capnetwork.org/modules.php?op=modload&name=CAPDatabase&file=index&&letter=All&sortby=institutionname&.

Collins, R.A. (2006). Cognitive development of adult undergraduate students: Cohort and non-cohort settings. *Educational Considerations, 33(2),* 35-41.

Friedman, T. L. (2007). The *world is flat: A brief history of the twenty first century.* Picador, New York: Release 3.0.

Grow, G. (1991). Teaching learners to be self-directed. *Adult Education Quarterly, 41(3),* 125-149.

Higher Learning Commission (n.d.), Affiliated Institutions, University of Phoenix. Retrieved on March 23, 2009, from http://www.ncahlc.org/index.php?option=com_directory&Itemid=192&Action=ShowBasic&instid=1949

Kasworm, C.E., Polson, C.J., & Fishback, S.J. (2002). *Responding to adult learners in higher education.* Malabar, FL: Krieger Publishing.

King, P.M., & Kitchener, K.S. (1994). *Developing reflective judgment.* San Francisco: Jossey-Bass.

Knapp, L.G., Kelly-Reid, J.E., and Ginder, S.A. (2009). *Enrollment in postsecondary institutions, fall 2007; graduation rates, 2001 &2004 cohorts; and financial statistics, fiscal year 2007* (NCES 2009-155). Washington, D. C.: National Center for Education Statistics, Institute of Education Sciences, U.S. Department of Education.

Knowles, M.S. (1969). *Higher adult education in the united states: The current picture, trends, and issues.* Washington, D. C.: Committee on Higher Adult Education, American Council on Education.

Lumina Foundation (February 2009). *A stronger nation through higher education.* Retrieved March 7, 2009, from http://www.luminafoundation.org/publications/A_stronger_nation_through_higher_education.pdf

Merriam, S.B., Caffarella, R.S., & Baumgartner, L.M. (2007). *Learning in adulthood.* (3rd ed.). San Francisco, CA: Jossey Bass.

National Center for Educational Statistics. (n.d.). International Comparisons in Education Glossary. Institute of Education Sciences, U.S. Department of Education, Washington, D.C. Retrieved on March 18, 2009, from http://nces.ed.gov/surveys/international/Intlindicators/glossary.asp#G

Neihardt, J. G. (1979). *Black elk speaks: Being the life story of a holy man of the oglala sioux.* Lincoln, NE: University of Nebraska Press.

Perry, W., Jr. (1999). *Forms of ethical and intellectual development in the college years: A scheme.* San Francisco: Jossey-Bass.

Planty, M., Hussar, W., Snyder, T., Provasnik, S., Kena, G., Dinkes, R., KewalRamani, A., and Kemp, J. (2008). *The condition of education 2008* (NCES 2008-031). Washington, D.C.: National Center for Education Statistics, Institute of Education Sciences, U.S. Department of Education.

Princeton University Wordnet (n.d.), Retrieved on March 7, 2009, from http://wordnetweb.princeton.edu/perl/webwn?s=adult%20education.

Ross-Gordon, J. & Brown-Haywood, F. (2000). Keys to college success as seen through the eyes of african american adult students. *Journal of Continuing Higher Education, 48(3),* 14-23.

Sander, L. (February 2009). Colleges woo adults who have some credits but no degree. *Chronicle of Higher Education, 54(23),* A29.

Snyder, T. (2009). *Mini-Digest of Education Statistics, 2008* (NCES 2009-021). Washington, D.C.: National Center for Education Statistics, Institute of Education Sciences, U.S. Department of Education.

Snyder, T. & Hoffman, C. (1991, February). *Digest of educational statistics 1990.* (NCES 91-660). Washington, D.C.: Office of Educational Research and Improvement, U.S. Department of Education.

State Higher Education Executive Officers (SHEEO). (2008, September-October). Second to none in attainment, discovery, and innovation: The national agenda for higher education. *Change: The Magazine of Higher Learning.* Retrieved March 7, 2009, from http://www.changemag.org/Archives/Back%20Issues/September-October%202008/full-second-to-none.html.

University of Phoenix (n.d.). Retrieved March 23, 2009, from http://www.phoenix.edu/about_us/about_university_of_phoenix.aspx

Webster's New Collegiate Dictionary. (1975). Springfield, MA: G. & C. Merriam Company.

Wlodkowski, R. J. (2008). *Enhancing adult motivation to learn: A comprehensive guide for teaching all adults (3rd edition).* San Francisco: Jossey Bass.

This work was previously published in the Adult Learning in the Digital Age: Respectives on Online Technologies and Outcomes 4, edited by T.T. Kidd and K. Keengwe, pp. 134-147, copyright 2010 by Information Science Reference (an imprint of IGI Global).

Chapter 12
Prevalent Andragogical Instructional Preferences and Technologies

George Maughan
Indiana State University, USA

Davison Mupinga
Kent State University, USA

ABSTRACT

As developed countries face skilled worker shortages and their workforce becomes more diverse, education and training of adults has taken center stage. Changing workforce demographics, global economies, and advances in technology commonly influence what, when, and how to teach adults. This chapter provides an overview of contemporary andragogical instructional techniques and seeks to describe examples of their application through electronic delivery. Due to the emerging body of literature on some adult instructional techniques, efforts will be made to discriminate between techniques solidly grounded in theory, and those which show promise.

INTRODUCTION

The rationale to understand the linkage between adult learning theory, andragogy, and instructional technique is very basic. By understanding the fundamental ways adults learn, and creating or using methods in harmony with those learning styles to investigate content processes and problems in an area of study, one optimizes the teaching/learning process. To use instructional techniques that are not linked to adult learning theory makes the teaching/learning process ineffective and indiscriminate. At best, learning might occur through serendipity.

Learning at work has become an essential part of work (Billett, 2001; Illeris, 2004; Streumer, 2006). Generally speaking, adults learn in the world of the grown-up, primarily at work, self-study, and at play. The issues of when, where, and how adult learning takes place are addressed in the classic work, *Learning in Adulthood* (Merriam, Caffarella & Baumgartner, 2006). Here, the authors identify three dimensions of society that shape the nature of adult learning: 1) demographics, 2) the global economy, and 3) technology. Of course, these dimensions are in a constant state of change due to the dynamics of

DOI: 10.4018/978-1-61520-694-0.ch012

culture. In fact, these three dimensions are more relevant today due to geopolitical and economic inter-connectivity and the broad fluctuations of important attributes.

The chapter provides an overview of contemporary andragogical instructional techniques and describes examples of their application in teaching adults. In addition, the chapter describes the integration of technology with andragogical instructional techniques. The next sections in this chapter outline the changing demographics of today's workforce, influence of global economies, technological changes, and the impact of cultural or class stratification on andragogical instructional preferences. Subsequent sections describe characteristics of adult learning and some prevalent andragogical instructional strategies: transformative learning, collaborative learning, self-directed learning, narrative learning, and e-learning. Lastly, the chapter provides a summary, implications for practice, and useful references on contemporary andragogical instructional techniques.

BACKGROUND

Pedagogy is derived from two words, *paid* meaning "child" and *agogus* meaning "leader of," and literally means the art and science of teaching children (Knowles, 1973). According to Ozuah (2005), the model was founded on several assumptions about learners: 1) dependent personality of the learner (not knowing own learning needs), 2) learning needed to be subject-centered (curricula were organized around subjects), 3) emphasized extrinsic motivation as driving force for learning (the use of rewards and punishments to encourage learning), and 4) prior experience of the learner was irrelevant (blank slate concept or tabula rasa). The pedagogical model is concerned with the transmitting of information and skills (Holmes & Abington-Cooper, 2000), and therefore, the teacher determines what is to be taught and how.

In contrast to pedagogy, andragogy, the process of engaging adult learners in learning experiences (Ozuah, 2005), is viewed as providing procedures and resources for helping learners acquire information and skills. Knowles (1984) describes the field of andragogy as premised on five assumptions about characteristics of adult learners: 1) self-concept (moves from being a dependent to self-directed being), 2) experience (a mature person has experience), 3) readiness to learn (ready to learn developmental tasks of their social roles), 4) orientation to learning (immediacy of application knowledge and problem centeredness), and 5) motivation to learn (internal motivation to learn as opposed to external). These assumptions guide the selection and delivery of adult learning activities, and therefore, in andragogy, the teacher's role is that of a facilitator, change-agent, or consultant with the learners taking part in deciding what is to be taught and how (Holmes and Abington-Cooper, 2000).

While andragogy assumptions provide a means to classify characteristics of adults, the distinctions between andragogy and pedagogy models have been controversial (Elias, 1979; Knudson, 1980), and hence, andragogy has had its share of critics (Davenport, 1993). Even though differences between children and adults are acknowledged, the learning activities for children can be the same as those for adults. Nevertheless, many authors agree there are occasions when andragogy might be used with children and pedagogy with adults (Holmes & Abington-Cooper, 2000). To reduce the confusion and controversy between pedagogy and andragogy, other scholars have proposed the term *humanagogy* as a replacement for both because it is an inclusive term (Knudson, 1980). Whether its pedagogy, andragogy, or *humanagogy*, adults have unique characteristics that must be considered in designing and delivery of instruction. Based on the work by Malcolm Knowles, Billington (2007) describes seven characteristic of adult education: 1) safety for students; 2) intellectual freedom is fostered, and experimentation and creativity are encouraged; 3) faculty treat adult students as peers; 4) self-directed learning is the norm; 5) optimal pacing challenges the learner; 6) learners are actively involved in the learning experience; and 7) availability of regular avenues for feedback from students to faculty. Again, each of these characteristics helps in understanding the adult learner and therefore influences instructional strategies.

Another aspect of adult learning is that a significant amount of learning occurs outside formal education settings, such as schools (Marsick & Watkins, 1991); much of this informal learning may be incidental and not intentional (Smith & Smith, 2008). Generally, informal learning takes place in workplaces and is not part of a program of training or instruction (Dale & Bell, 1999). Furthermore, informal adult education programs attract mainly older adults (Smith & Smith, 2008) and the programs vary in nature and content, from hobbies to workplace skills. Adult education programs also have their share of students with learning disabilities. For instance, it is estimated that 10-50% percent of individuals participating in adult education programs have learning disabilities (Peterson, 2008). All these characteristics impact the delivery of adult education programs.

In addition to characteristics of adults and adult education programs, other factors influencing the demand and delivery of adult education are changing demographics of the workforce, global economies, technological changes, and cultural/ class stratification. Each of these factors is considered in the following paragraphs.

Changing Workforce Demographics

The industrial world's population is aging (Chodacki, 2005) resulting in shortages of skilled workers. This situation, together with increased diversity in the workforces has called for attention on adult education and training programs, primarily to determine how to provide skills to tomorrow's workforce. Over the years, the make-up of the labor force has slowly changed, creating a multigenerational workforce with the fastest growing group being individuals over the age of 65 (DeRocco, 2005). Currently, there are two 'graying' generations in the workforce: "Pre-boomers" or "traditionalists", those born before 1946, and the Baby boomers, born between 1946 and 1964 (Umbrell, 2006). The Baby boomers are expected to turn 65 years old in 2011 and will be the largest group to retire at the same time (DeRocco, 2005). This retirement, voluntary or forced, coupled with an increasing aging workforce, is expected to create serious labor shortages (Clement, 2004). Therefore, there is a big group of older adults that will require educational and training opportunities to remain in gainful or productive employment. Bearing in mind that some 85% of adult Americans have at least a high school degree and 28% have a college degree (Symonds, 2005), the majority of the ageing adults likely to enroll in adult education programs have formal educational experiences.

Besides the demographic changes, the workforce is now diverse in many respects including gender, racial make-up, religious affiliation, sexual orientation, nationality, and ethnic background. For instance, the workforce has seen an increase in minorities and adult women, by approximately 48% in the past few years (Mahmood, 2006). The number of minorities in the workforce, especially Hispanics and Asians is expected to continue to grow and by 2050. Asians are projected to have the highest participation rate (65%) followed by Hispanics (64%) (Toossi, 2002). According to American Decades (2001), men dominated American business before 1970 largely because of social patterns and cultural values, but after World War II, women and minorities slowly started to establish a presence in American business. Consequently, of the net increase of the workforce between 1992 and 2005, women contributed 62% and their number in the workforce is projected to reach 92 million by 2050 (Toossi, 2002). In terms of racial and ethnic composition, based on the US

2000 Census (National Center for Public Policy and Higher Education, 2005), from 1980 to 2020, the white working-age population is projected to decline while the minority portion of the workforce is expected to double. Furthermore, according to America.gov (2004), the U.S. 2000 Census estimates that Hispanics, who comprised about 12.6% of the population in 2000, will almost double (24.4%) their population in 2050. The population of non-Latino whites, presently 75% of all Americans, will shrink to a bare majority by 2050. The other cultural groups in the workforce also report similar demographic trends. The number of African Americans in the workforce is expected to increase 16.8% by 2014, but more Hispanics (33.7%) than African-Americans will enter the workforce during the same period, and make up 15.9% of the workforce by 2014, according to a report on Minorities in the Workforce (American Decades, 2001). Asians and Pacific Islanders are also a fast-growing group in the workforce. The proportion of Asian-Americans in the workforce is expected to increase (32.4%) by 2014, and the Asians and Pacific Islanders are expected to make up 5.1% of the workforce by 2014 (American Decades, 2001).

While there is strong demand for skilled younger workers as the workforce ages (Ramachandran, 2006), employers still consider older adults as good and responsible employees (Mahmood, 2006), and therefore, older employees will remain in demand for the foreseeable future. Furthermore, the adults in the workforce are no longer a homogeneous group culturally, and hence, it is important to understand the needs and characteristics of a diverse workforce. For adult educators and trainers, such diversity means dealing with a whole slew of cultural, language, and financial challenges facing the workers. The changing demographics of the workforce and issues of class as well as global economies and technological changes are covered in the next paragraphs. These factors impact the provision and delivery of adult education and training programs.

Global Economies and Technological Changes

The global economy was characterized by Friedman (2007) and Smick (2008) in their recent books by exposing some startling insight about the global supply chain of raw materials, products, and markets, and the flow of capital and wealth across borders. Global competitiveness, as described by Friedman (2007), is a natural phenomena resulting from integrated information and communications systems, global logistics to move materials and products, and an anywhere/anytime workforce. Production as well as service jobs have flowed from the United States to many parts of the globe. One thing is certain: manual labor, basic materials (steel and plastic), and the production of durable goods is footloose and can occur anywhere a basic infrastructure exists. The difficult to describe "high value" work is considered to be the future growth industry in United States. However, the described high value work will require an agile and robustly trained workforce.

Using Japan as an example, Smick (2008) explains that the policy-making role of a country's central bank influences the availability of loans, interest rates on savings, and the exchange value of currency. When things go wrong, as they did for the Japanese in the early 1990's, medium and small-sized industries take huge losses. This was very painful for 75% of the country's workforce who labored in these industries that depended largely on domestic consumption of their goods and services. On the other hand, large (more global) corporations were able to take advantage of the situation by borrowing and re-investing in new technology, processes, and business restructuring.

The creation, application, transfer, and management of technology are fundamental processes of the global economy. Contemporary manufacturing technology enables many factories to function with high levels of automation. Robotic manipulators move materials and products, and programmable logic controllers help transfer and mix fluids and powders. Product packaging can be accomplished without human touch. In the transportation and energy sectors, large pipeline and electrical distributions are controlled by signals relayed through satellites and computer networks. In addition, products large and small are inventoried, shipped, and identified by universal product codes or radio frequency identification while GPS (Global Positioning System) tracks everything from neighborhood delivery vans to ocean-going cargo ships.

Other industrial sectors have been profoundly changed by technology as well and, like the changes described above, impact training needs and the adult worker. The service sector, information processing/data processing industry and healthcare have seen information technology become a dynamo for change. According to Daniels (2004) the new economy and services have been dramatic shaped by improvements in organization efficiency and worker productivity. Cashiers, bank tellers, order-takers, reservationists, maintenance technicians and middle managers have been eliminated or seriously reduced in numbers by automation and diagnostic systems which perform work in a fast, reliable and more powerful way. Healthcare has been impacted at both the consumer and clinical level. Internet information on consumer health and pharmaceuticals has expanded and become more accurate in recent years as has the integration of information systems connecting patients, service providers and administrators. This integrating technology has caused serious impact of the number and work of aides, technicians and clerks resulting in huge changes in worker training (Landry, Mahesh & Hartman, 2005).

Basic technological changes in computer and communication infrastructures have also impacted adult training. Hardware and software have become more user friendly and capable of producing faster and more powerful functions. For example, tools to create interactive teaching/learning modules with multimedia features enable instructional developers to use text, sound, video or animation to demonstrate processes from brake repair to using a hotel reservation software package. Developers have user-friendly authoring systems to create training packages in hours or days which would have once taken the skills of many specialists many months to complete. The costs of developing these training packages, still somewhat expensive when compared to stand-up group sessions, have fallen sharply. In addition, the distributed nature of high bandwidth computer-based training can provide fast, easy accessible, interactive training that engages the learner through instant feedback and user control.

In these brief examples, it is clear to see that jobs and work are clearly impacted in a wide range of industries by big changes in global technology and economic conditions. Due to the large percentage of adult learning that occurs in the context of work, it is important then to acknowledge that training and re-training needs are accelerated due to global economic and technological changes.

Cultural and Class Stratification Influences

The issue of social class, work, culture, and teaching/learning are sometimes intertwined when considering why, what, and how adult learning situations exist. A form of cultural/class stratification (Griswold, 2008) may influence the development and delivery of teaching/learning modules on so-called "soft-skills" such as customer satisfaction, diversity training, and communication. Other topics covering the nature of industry competiveness, source(s) of profit, and regulatory or environmental controls can be seriously influenced by cultural/class stratification. For example, workers coming from a lower socioeconomic class may respond to a certain rationale for diversity training based on their experiences (a very important characteristic for adult learners) that are quite different from the experiences of workers coming from a higher level socioeconomic class. According to Griswald (2008 p. 87), "social strata differ in the breath of their cultural participation." So too will be the need to include examples, images, and cases spanning training intended for a broad level of employees. Human resource development (HRD) specialists and instructional designers are typically sensitive to these differences. There may be, however, some inherent characteristics of contemporary learning theories that will challenge organizations in bridging any broad gaps in cultural/class stratification. These issues may be less relevant in specific "hard-skills" training.

PREVALENT ANDRAGOGICAL STRATEGIES

In addition to understanding the characteristics and needs of their learners, adult educators need a working knowledge of a variety of instructional strategies to be effective. Adult educators use a number of teaching and learning instructional strategies, among them: transformative learning, collaborative learning, self-directed learning, and narrative learning. The traditional questions of, what to teach, when, and how to teach adults is complicated by information and communication technologies. The next sections describe each of the strategies and the potential influence of information and communication technologies on adult education.

Transformative Learning

Jack Mezirow, the chief architect of transformative learning, defines it as:

A process by which we attempt to justify our beliefs, either by rationally examining assumptions, often in response to intuitively becoming aware that something is wrong with the result of our thought, or challenging its validity through discourse with others of differing viewpoints and arriving at the best informed judgment. (Mezirow, 1995, p. 46)

According to Taylor (2008), adults are known to develop reliable beliefs by exploring and validating what they know; and the informed decisions they make are fundamental to their learning process. The theory of transformative learning, therefore, explains the process by which adults construct new and/or revise interpretations of world experiences (Merriam & Ntseane, 2008). In essence, the theory focuses on providing events that trigger reflection through transformative learning. As situations, assumptions, or events are presented to adults, they will have an opportunity to reflect on them and construct new meaning. For instance, through dialogue or class discussions, students get opportunities to assess, validate, or justify their assumptions. According to Mezirow (2000), this transformative process results in reflective action, making changes to life experiences.

Transformative learning, according to Mezirow (2000), requires a 10-step process: 1) experience a disorienting dilemma, 2) undergo self-examination, 3) conduct a deep assessment of personal role assumptions and alienation created by new roles, 4) share and analyze personal discontent and similar experiences with others, 5) explore options for new ways of acting; 6) build competence and self-confidence in new roles, 7) plan a course of action, 8) acquire knowledge and skills for action, 9) try new roles and assess feedback, and 10) reintegrate into society with a new perspective. This learning theory is considered uniquely adult (Mezirow, 1996) in that, through transformative learning processes, adults critically reflect on their previous assumptions, knowledge, biases, and beliefs to create new or revised interpretation. The new meaning of the experiences is what is believed to guide any future actions. Adults, therefore, need opportunities for this transformation through assignments and activities.

Collaborative Learning

Collaborative learning is a teaching and learning approach in which students team together to explore a significant question (Educational Broadcasting Corporation, 2004). Collaborative learning takes many forms, including cooperative learning which involves primarily small groups of students working together to achieve shared goals. Although these two terms are often used interchangeably, according to Thistlethwaite (1996), learners enter into collaborations at their own free will while cooperative learning is structured by someone other than the learners. Furthermore, in cooperative assignments, each member needs to "give up" something for the good of the group as compared with each person gaining without compromising in collaborations. In both cases, the students work together for a common purpose as opposed to individually and in competition with one another.

In cooperative learning, the students working together in teams do not need to have the same ability levels, but are expected to work through a variety of learning activities to improve their understanding of the material being studied. Each team member is responsible not only for learning what is taught, but also for helping teammates learn. In essence, cooperative learning is hinged on the concept, "we sink or swim together" (Johnson, Johnson & Smith, 1991)–making the instructional technology ideal for people who work in teams to make a living. In cooperative assignments, the students work through assignments until all group members successfully understand and complete the assignment. Because the students are able to teach one another, cooperative learning is believed to improve their achievement and retention of concepts and skills; and this creates more positive relationships among students (Johnson & Johnson, 1997). Furthermore, opportunities to work together allow students to develop social skills such as communication and working with diverse members.

Collaborative learning instructional strategies are ideal for adults, especially those who approach additional education or training with a sense of excitement or anxiety (Clark, n.d.). For instance, through cooperative learning assignments or activities, the adults will soon realize they are not alone in the struggle and that they have other students for encouragement and support. Besides, when adults learn in one another's company, it is considered that they find themselves engaging in challenging, passionate, and creative activities (Brookfield, 1986). This engagement in creative activities compels them to seek higher level learning (Clark, n.d.).

Overall, using collaborative techniques with adults has benefits, especially from the exchange and processing of information occurring in a non-competitive situation (Johnson, Johnson & Holubec, 1991). For further information on cooperative learning, check out the websites: http://teaching.berkeley.edu/bgd/collaborative.html and http://www.wcer.wisc.edu/archive/cl1/CL/doingcl/DCL1.asp

Self-Directed Learning

Self-directed learning typically takes place outside of organization sponsorship and tends to focus on topics chosen by the learner. Informal learning (a confusing but frequently used phrase to describe self-directed learning) tends to be self-paced and uses "books, procedures manuals, audiotapes or video"; "computer-based software tutorials (CD-ROMS or Internet), attendance at brown-bag or informal presentations; and attendance at conferences, trade shows, or conventions . . ." (NCES, 2005, p. 16). This type of learning is estimated to be the most used form of learning in the workplace (Sorohan, 1993).

When motorcycle technicians, accountants, or computer system operators for example engage in self-directed learning, they use similar strategies. This is true also of family members learning how to cope with a health crisis or a young adult learning how to use the newest electronic gadget. According to Marsick and Watkins (1993), these learners learn through questioning, listening, observing, reading, and reflecting. This can occur in the workplace or outside of the workplace, and can occur as individual or collective practice. These techniques have a basis in traditional androgology theory without the more formal directive nature of organization sponsored learning. They do, however, have a strong participatory practice due to self-motivation necessary to direct an individual to learn.

Because self-directed learning is self-motivated, it frequently causes the individual to be vigilant to everyday incidences that connect to the topic(s) of interest. Relatively fast sorting and labeling of new information in unexpected encounters causes the self-directed learner to attempt to accommodate new information into an emerging framework of understanding. This impromptu strategy lacks the progressive, interpretative, or structured exposure of information in organizational-sponsored training and, according to Hamilton (2006), but is not burdened by it either. It should be noted that gender, age, race, and the existence or strength of a labor union can affect the nature of self-directed learning (Livingstone & Sawchuk, 2005). This said, the impact of diversity on learning and training is covered elsewhere in this chapter along with some reference to social class and learning, however, the effects of organized labor are not clear. Certainly the existence of bargaining units or unions has an impact on many aspects of work in those companies where they exist. This sometimes includes the topics, structure, delivery and assessment of training. Because the nature of self-directed learning is based on individual motivation, the concept of the individual as a self-actuated agent may be influenced by the larger unit. More research in this area needs to be done.

Narrative Learning

Narrative learning is both old and new. Ancients used storytelling as a means to relay lessons learned, enrich cultural context, and to preserve history. New applications emphasize the use of narrative to help construct knowledge and make meaning from information and experience. The narrative process can involve writing, hearing, telling, and recognizing (Clark & Rossiter, 2008). At times, narrative learning can involve self-talk, when individuals construct a narrative in their head that enables them to re-examine an experience or connect the dots of a complex situation. Narrative learning as an adult learning strategy involves storytelling in its most basic mode and can range from personal experiences to sophisticated business case studies. Above all, it makes the story human.

The active engagement of the creator or the recipient of the story occurs when a story is told without explanation or concluding moral. This requires those involved to complete the story or fill-in the blanks thereby personalizing the experience and relating it to previous experiences. Both actions are important in adult learning. For example, a Harley Davidson technician revealed to a colleague in a conversation that he "heard voices in his head" while attempting to diagnose a complex electrical problem. After seeing affirming nods of heads and smiles from his audience, he went on to say that he heard his old man reminding him to "check the basics." This, the technician concluded, was how he found an intermittent problem with a loose ground wire.

The idea of narrative learning as storytelling is not totally accurate. Storytelling, about self or others, may be one manifestation of narrative learning but the strategy extends to the learner who is constructing a context for information in which a "story" emerges. For example, one may construct a story around the relationship of electrons, protons, and neutrons in order to gain insight into the behavior of matter. In the case of written stories, some application to adult learning lies in the product of diaries or autobiographies. In formal education settings, written reflections on lessons learned are considered a form of narrative learning.

How adults learn thorough narrative is, at its root, a function of language. Having words with which to think, speak, or listen is essential. Having the correct words makes the process more exact. Anyone who has taken sailing lessons knows this from an instructor or captain who insists that one use the correct name for the boom yang instead of calling it "that pulley thing." Or, when the situation benefits from a more personalized creative process, to begin the story with, "It was a dark and stormy night." Both approaches can be equally effective in making the narrative engaging thus optimizing the learning opportunity.

In a general sense, the engagement, reexamination (reflection), and meaning making thorough narrative instruction is constructivist in nature (Bruner, 2002; Butcher, 2006; Clark & Rossiter, 2008). Good stories or case studies place facts and theories into a human context, which can evolve over time, and within situations that cause those engaged to reflect on their own life experiences and place their thinking in the present. As a learning theory for adults, the attributes, methods, and effectiveness of narrative learning is just emerging and it will likely take much empirical research before a deep understanding is possible.

ADULT EDUCATION AND E-LEARNING

The impact of information and communication technologies (ICT) in today's society cannot be ignored. In education, ICT influences the what, how and when we teach. For instance, ICT plays a crucial role in the delivery of instruction, especially through computer-based and online education, modifying or enhancing traditional (prevalent) instructional strategies. This section presents examples of ICT's and how they can be integrated with prevalent andragogical instructional strategies already described.

Presently, many adult education instructors incorporate technology as part of instruction. The push to incorporate technology as part of instruction comes from the characteristics and needs of today's students, also referred to as Millennials. The students literary live and rely on internet tools and applications for communication and social networking, they prefer to stay connected, and are generally, accustomed to having information at their finger tips. Furthermore, using information and communication technologies that are familiar and preferred by students for instructional purposes provides an opportunity for teachers to meet students in their comfort zones. Incorporating technologies with instruction tends to reduce resistance from students who often find traditional classes boring. Therefore, adult educators are taking an interest in the technologies which keep the students captivated.

Internet Technologies

Among the common internet technologies or applications incorporated with andragogical strategies are: social networks, wikis, email, blogs and podcasts. Though not as popular with adults, social networks, such as Facebook, MySpace and Twitter are slowly being incorporated with instructional strategies, for networking purposes. In the last few years, the number of adults on social networks has been rising. According to Nielsen (2009), Facebook's greatest growth came from people aged 35-49 years of age (+24.1 million), and from December 2007 through December 2008, the social network added about 13.6 million visitors from the 50-64 year old category. Social networks are therefore, one technology that can easily and readily be incorporated with prevalent andragogical strategies. In addition, Wikis such as Wikipedia are a collection of web pages designed to enable anyone with access to contribute, modify or delete content (Wikipedia, 2009). The wikis provide adults with opportunities to work collaboratively with other members anywhere in the world. In collaborative learning, where the students have to work in groups, small groups tasks can be a challenge, especially when students' schedules conflict. Other internet technologies, such as emails, discussion groups and Google Docs which allow exchange of information and transfer of files can easily overcome these challenges. Therefore, a number of internet technologies make collaborative learning easy.

With so much information available on the internet, adult education instructors and students have many resources at their disposal. Technologies such as blogs or online journals and podcasts (digital media files, usually digital audio or video available for download), allow outside experts to be brought into the mix. These tools when integrated with traditional or prevalent instructional strategies allow the students to get information and sometimes direct instruction directly from experts in the field. For example, there are a number of podcasts, available free of charge, on automotive maintenance, medical procedures, cooking, and computer skills done by professionals that can be used to teach adults. These resources can be downloaded from the internet and used by students at their own pace, the technology becomes ideal to support self-directed learning and in some cases, narrative learning.

Technology enhances self–directed learning, especially by allowing adults to learn outside the workplace. However, there is need to structure the learning tasks so that learners stay on task; otherwise a lot of time is wasted on material that has little or no relevance to the intended material. Furthermore, technologies can be incorporated with transformational learning by using a number of internet tools such as search engines and blogs can be used to explore, research, and validate learner beliefs. In addition, the internet tools, such as, online discussions, chats or listservs provide avenues for adults to share ideas, reflect on other learners' input, and eventually make new meaning. These online discussion forums provide excellent avenues for shy adults to post their thoughts without fear of being humiliated.

While teaching and learning from remote sites is certainly not new, the electronic delivery of education and training seems to be the norm these days, in both industry and educational settings. Judging by the number of programs now being delivered online and the impact of information and communication technologies in day-to-day activities, the question is no longer whether there is a place for e-learning in adult education. In addition, recent advances in communication technologies create more avenues to deliver adult education and training programs.

According to Tremblay (2009), not only does electronic delivery enable adults to gain education without disrupting their busy work and social lives, but the kinds of instructional experiences which succeed in distance delivery tend to accord well with the adult's need for instruction which is personally relevant. But, as Martinez (2003) reminds us, e-learning is not ideal for everyone and therefore may cause high attrition rates.

Electronic delivery of instruction used to be despised and regarded as inferior but has now become a popular format for adult education and training programs. Tremblay (2009) suggests that the benefits of electronic delivery have much to do with the fit between adult learning and delivery format, and "can only be realized if the learner is the focus of the instructional transaction." Therefore, instructors using electronic delivery strategies need to focus on the learner and seek out mechanisms to decrease the feeling of isolation perceived by distance education students (Zirkle, 2002).

A concluding remark by Malcolm Knowles in his book *Andragogy in Action* (see, Dickinson, 1991) clearly sums up the role of electronic delivery of adult education:

We are nearing the end of the era of our edifice complex and its basic belief that respectable learning takes place only in buildings and on campuses. Adults are beginning to demand that their learning take place at a time, place, and pace convenient to them. In fact, I feel confident that most educational services by the end of this century (if not decade) will be delivered electronically . . . Our great challenge now is to find ways to maintain the human touch as we learn to use the media in new ways. (About: Malcolm S. Knowles section, para. 1).

While the delivery of adult education electronically is still in its infancy stage, it is destined to grow as computer access increases. Furthermore, e-learning is expected to revolutionize the way adult education programs are delivered, especially as the technologies to incorporate various instructional strategies become readily available.

CONCLUSION

Adults learn more while working than any other aspect of their lives. Whether in formal/directed learning programs or self-directed activities, adults learn better when they are actively engaged with the content or learning process. Passive learning does take place but to a much lesser extent. The demands for new or more efficient work practices drive much of work-related learning; however, the desire to learn about topics more tangential to one's specific job is also influential. Changing products or processes, services, technology, and/or the globalization of the marketplace are also important factors influencing the need for training.

Who, how, and what workers learn is of critical importance to the learner as well as their organization. Many factors, including social class and education, influence who works in certain jobs and therefore the need and opportunity for training.

How individuals learn is influenced by the instructional strategy employed by the workers' organization. Traditional methods tend to employ training room presentations and manuals and videos, some using performance-based learning techniques but many times not. Multimedia and computer-based training is becoming a more common practice in workforce training. In addition, an increasing interest in learning efficiency is beginning to influence the integration of more sophisticated teaching/learning strategies such as transformative learning, collaborative learning, narrative learning, or a more general constructivist approach.

Adults are known to develop reliable beliefs by exploring and validating what they already know. It is through transformative learning processes that they make informed decisions, hence opportunities for adults to make new meanings are essential and therefore should be encouraged.

As in the workplace, adults are accustomed to working collaboratively for the common good of their organizations. Collaborative learning, specifically cooperative learning, allows adults to get support and guidance from teammates. As an instructional strategy, collaborative learning is therefore ideal for adults who are accustomed to working in teams and may be uncertain about adult education learning experiences.

Narrative learning employs both spoken and written descriptions of attributes of content in a human context. Sometimes appearing as a story or a reflection, the narrative learning technique engages learners to 'fill-in' the blanks in the narration thereby personalizing the information and relating it to previous experiences.

Judging by the impact of information and communication technologies in social and educational settings and the proliferation of online courses, ICT is making profound impact in education. E-learning is certainly gaining ground as a instructional delivery format. Convenience is one advantage of e-learning, especially to working adults. E-learning is therefore destined to be a popular and appropriate instructional delivery format, more so in this information age.

IMPLICATIONS FOR PRACTICE

As adult educators build a repertoire of instructional strategies to be effective, there are four areas they need to focus on:

1. Develop and use instructional approaches sensitive to students' preferred learning styles, culture, and geopolitical situations
2. Understand the changing global economies, processes, and technological advances as this influences the what, when, and how to train
3. Train adult educators in e-learning and how to incorporate information and communication technologies in the delivery of adult education and training programs. This suggestion is more appropriate in light of the characteristics of millennial students entering the workforce and as more adults get comfortable with information and communication technologies.
4. The instructional strategies described in this chapter are not the only ideal strategies; they were considered prevalent and can be used in isolation or in combination with other instructional strategies

FUTURE RESEARCH

Many questions remain in the blended field of adult learning strategy and the enhancement of human performance through the electronic delivery of teaching/learning units or performance support systems. In fact, some emerging adult learning theories/strategies are not fully researched. The brief review of information on collaborative learning and narrative learning in this chapter is an example of such. In addition, the evolution of electronic performance support systems will involve much work to establish a theoretical base to learning, information access, and knowledge transfer.

Other areas for future research include: outcomes of cognitive theory and alternative theories of learning with media; variances in the application of adult learning theories delivered by low-level and high-level interactive media (Moreno, 2006); and the comprehension and transferability of new knowledge to the workplace and the effectiveness of scaffolding in electronic performance support systems (Hung & Chao, 2007).

REFERENCES

America.gov. (2004). *Increasing diversity predicted in U.S. population.* Retrieved March 12, 2009 from http://www.america.gov/st/washfile-english/2004/March/20040318124311CMretro P0.4814264.html

American Decades. (2001). *Minorities and women in the workplace.* Retrieved May 20, 2009, from http://www.encyclopedia.com/doc/1G2-3468302607.html

Anonymous. (2006). *Minorities in the labor force: Workforce projections for 2010.* Retrieved May 5, 2009, from http://www.libraryindex.com/pages/2910/Minorities-in-Labor-Force-WORK-FORCE-PROJECTIONS-2010.html

Billett, S. (2001). *Critiquing workplace learning discourses: Participation and continuity at work.* Retrieved March 20, 2009, from http://www.infed.org/archives/e-texts/billett_workplace_learning.htm

Billington, D. (2007). Seven characteristics of adult education. Retrieved March 25, 2009, from http://meetingsnet.com/associationmeetings/mag/meetings_seven_characteristics_adult/

Brookfield, S. D. (1986). *Understanding and facilitating adult learning.* San Francisco: Jossey-Bass.

Bruner, J. (2002). *Making stories.* New York: Farrar, Straus and Giroux.

Butcher, S. E. (2006, September). Narrative as a teaching strategy. *Journal of Correctional Education, 57*(3), 195–208.

Chodacki, J. A. (2005). *The wisdom of the aging workforce: A commodity in crisis.* Unpublished doctoral dissertation, Colorado Technical University. Clark, J. F. (n.d.). *The role of cooperative education in the adult learning environment.* Retrieved March 20, 2009, from http://horizon.unc.edu/conferences/lc/papers/18.html

Clark, M. C., & Rossiter, M. (2008). Narrative learning in adulthood. *New Directions for Adult and Continuing Education, 119*, 61–70. doi:10.1002/ace.306

Clement, D. (2004). *Welcome to retirement: Now back to work.* Retrieved March 10, 2009, from http://www.minneapolisfed.org/publications_papers/pub_display.cfm?id=1676

Dale, M., & Bell, J. (1999). *Informal learning in the workplace. DfEE Research Report 134*, London: Department for Education and Employment.

Daniels, P. W. (2004, Spring). Reflections on the "old" economy, "new" economy, and services. *Growth and Change, 35*(2), 115–138. doi:10.1111/j.0017-4815.2004.00242.x

Davenport, J. (1993). Is there any way out of the Andragogy mess? In M. Thorpe, R. Edwards, & A. Hanson (Eds.), *Culture and processes of adult learning* (pp. 109-117). London: Routledge.

DeRocco, E. (2005). *Older Americans Act.* Speech by Assistant Secretary, Employment and Training Employment and Training Administration. Committee on Senate Health, Education, Labor and Pensions Subcommittee on Retirement Security and Aging. FDCH Congressional Testimony, May 17, 2005.

Dickinson, D. (1991). Creating the future: Perspectives on educational change. *Lifelong learning: A dream.* Retrieved March 30, 2009, from http://www.newhorizons.org/future/Creating_the_Future/crfut_knowles.html

Educational Broadcasting Corporation. (2004). *What are cooperative and collaborative learning?* Retrieved March 25, 2009, from http://www.thirteen.org/edonline/concept2class/coopcollab/index.html

Elias, J. L. (1979). Critique: Andragogy revisited. *Adult Education, 29*(4), 252–256. doi:10.1177/074171367902900404

Friedman, T. L. (2007). *The world is flat: A brief history of the twenty-first century.* New York: Farrar, Straus and Giroux.

Griswold, W. (2008). *Cultures and societies in a changing world* (3rd ed.). Thousand Oaks, CA: Pine Forge Press.

Hamilton, M. (2006). Just do it: Literacies, everyday learning and the irrelevance of pedagogy. *Studies in the Education of Adults, 38*(2), 125–140.

Hill, R. J. (2008). Troubling adult learning in the present time. *New Directions for Adult and Continuing Education, 119*, 83–92. doi:10.1002/ace.308

Holmes, G., & Abington-Cooper, M. (2000). Pedagogy vs. andragogy: A false dichotomy? *The Journal of Technology Studies, 24*(2). Retrieved February 15, 2009, from http://scholar.lib.vt.edu/ejournals/JOTS/Summer-Fall-2000/holmes.html

Hung, W. C., & Chao, C. A. (2007, May). Integrating advance organizers and multidimensional information display in electronic performance systems. *Innovations in Education and Teaching International, 44*(2), 181–198. doi:10.1080/14703290701240986

Illeris, K. (2004). *Adult education and adult learning*. Copenhagen: Roskilde University Press/ Malabar, FL: Krieger Publishing.

Johnson, D. W., & Johnson, F. (1997). *Joining together: Group theory and group skills* (6th ed.). Boston: Allyn & Bacon.

Johnson, D. W., Johnson, R., & Holubec, E. (1990). *Circles of learning: Cooperation in the classroom*. Edina, MN: Interaction Book Company.

Johnson, D. W., Johnson, R. T., & Smith, K. A. (1991). *Cooperative learning: Increasing college faculty instructional productivity*. ASHE-ERIC Higher Education.

Knowles, M. S. (1973). *The adult learner: A neglected species*. Houston, TX: Gulf.

Knowles, M. S. (1984). *Andragogy in action. Applying modern principles of adult Learning*. San Francisco: Jossey-Bass.

Knudson, R. S. (1980). An alternative approach to the andragogy/pedagogy issue. *Lifelong Learning, the Adult Years*, *3*(8), 8–10.

Landry, B. J. L., Mahesh, S., & Hartman, S. J. (2005, Spring). The impact of the pervasive information age on healthcare organizations. *Journal of Health and Human Services Administration*, *27*(4), 444–464.

Livingstone, D. W., & Sawchuk, P. H. (2005, Autumn). Hidden knowledge: Working-class capacity in the "knowledge-based economy." . *Studies in the Education of Adults*, *37*(2), 110–122.

London, J. (1973). Adult education for the 1970's: Promise or illusion? *Adult Education*, *24*(1), 60–70. doi:10.1177/074171367302400105

Mahmood, S. (2006). The employers' view on older adults as staff in early childhood education services. *Journal of Intergenerational Relationships*, *4*(3), 29–48. doi:10.1300/J194v04n03_03

Marsick, V. J., & Watkins, K. E. (1991). *Informal and incidental learning in the workplace*. London: Routledge.

Martinez, M. (2003). High attrition rates in e-Learning: Challenges, predictors, and solutions. *Learning Solutions e-Magazine*. Retrieved June 1, 2009, from http://www.elearningguild.com/articles/abstracts/index.cfm?action=viewonly2&id=5

Merriam, S. B., Caffarella, R. S., & Baumgartner, L. M. (2006). *Learning in adulthood: A comprehensive guide* (3rd ed.). San Francisco: Jossey Bass.

Merriam, S. B., & Ntseane, G. (2008). Transformational learning in Botswana: How culture shapes the process. *Adult Education Quarterly*, *58*(3), 183–197. doi:10.1177/0741713608314087

Mezirow, J. (Ed.). (1995). *Learning as transformation: Critical perspectives on a theory in progress*. San Francisco: Jossey-Bass

Mezirow, J. (1995). Transformation theory of adult learning. In E. W. Taylor (Ed.), *Transformative learning theory* (pp. 5-15), *New Directions for Adult and Continuing Education, 119* (Fall 2008). San Francisco: Jossey-Bass.

Mezirow, J. (1996). Contemporary paradigms of learning. *Adult Education Quarterly*, *46*, 158–172. doi:10.1177/074171369604600303

Mezirow, J. (Ed.). (2000). *Learning as transformation: Critical perspectives on a theory in progress*. San Francisco: Jossey-Bass National Center for Public Policy and Higher Education. (2005). *Fact #1: The U.S. workforce is becoming more diverse*. Retrieved March 25 2009, from http://www.highereducation.org/reports/pa_decline/decline-f1.shtml

Moreno, R. (2006). Learning in high-tech and multimedia environments. *Current Directions in Psychological Science, 15*(2), 63–67. doi:10.1111/j.0963-7214.2006.00408.x

Nielsen, (2009). *Social networking's new global footprint*. Retrieved June 2, 2009, http://blog.nielsen.com/nielsenwire/nielsen-news/social-networking-new-global-footprint/

Ozuah, P. O. (2005). First, there was pedagogy and then came andragogy. *The Einstein Journal of Biology and Medicine; EJBM, 21*, 83–87.

Patterson, M. B. (2008). Learning disability prevalence and adult education program characteristics. *Learning Disabilities Research & Practice, 23*(1), 50–59. doi:10.1111/j.1540-5826.2007.00262.x

Ramachandran, N. (2006). New paths at work. *U.S. News & World Report, 3/20/2006, 140*(10), 46-48.

Sawchuk, P. H. (2003). *Adult learning and technology in working-class life*. New York: Cambridge University Press.

Smick, D. M. (2008). *The world is curved: Hidden dangers to the global economy*. New York: Penguin Group.

Smith, M. C., & Smith, T. J. (2008). Low-education adults' participation in informal learning activities: Relationships with selected demographic characteristics. *Adult Basic Education and Literacy Journal, 2*(2), 67–73.

Sorohan, E. G. (1993). We do, therefore we learn. *Training & Development, 47*, 47–48, 50, 52–55.

Streumer, J. N. (2006). *Work Related Learning*. New York: Springer.

Symonds, W. C. (2005). America the uneducated. *Business Week, 11/21/2005*, (3960).

Taylor, E. W. (2008). Transformative learning theory. *New Directions for Adult and Continuing Education, 119*, 5–15. doi:10.1002/ace.301

Tennant, M. (1996). *Psychology and adult learning*. London: Routledge.

Thistlethwaite, L. (1996). *Five levels of cooperative learning activities for adult learners*. Retrieved March 15, 2009, from http://aeonline.coe.utk.edu/PDFramework/Instructional%20Approaches/Cooperative.pdf

Toossi, M. (2002). A century of change: The U.S. labor force, 1950–2050. *Monthly Labor Review*, (pp. 15-28). Retrieved May 20, 2009, from http://www.bls.gov/opub/mlr/2002/05/art2full.pdf

Tremblay, E. (2009). *Six strategies for helping the adult distance learner succeed*. Retrieved March 25, 2009, from http://www.lib.unb.ca/Texts/Teaching/bin/get4.cgi?directory=SEP99/&filename=tremblay.html

Umbrell, C. (2006). *Generational health and safety: Five generations, one workplace*. Retrieved March 27, 2009, from http://www.aiha.org/Content/AccessInfo/synergist/synergistsampleart1.htm

Wikipedia, (2009). *Wiki*. Retrieved May 5, 2009. from http://en.wikipedia.org/wiki/Wikis

Zirkle, C. (2002). Identification of distance education barriers for trade and industrial teacher education. *Journal of Industrial Teacher Education, 40*(1), 20–44.

Chapter 13
Ultraversity-Integrating Technology in Adult Education

Geraint Lang
Anglia Ruskin University, UK

ABSTRACT

The influence of technology in our daily live grows unabated and exponentially; some see it as a culture in itself. It has been hailed variously as a universal panacea for enabling lifelong learning; a means of opening the doors to knowledge barred by the education gatekeepers. Recent research has revealed that the metaphoric barriers put in place to obstruct the use of the innovative technology tools for the purposes of engaging in lifelong learning, particularly with reference to adult education may not be due to the often perceived intransigence of adult educators, but to potential learners themselves. Recent research into adult uses of technology draw out interesting results, but do not take into account, nor acknowledge recent and successful wholly online undergraduate degree courses, based upon adult experiential learning in the work place. This chapter outlines one such degree course in the United Kingdom, Ultraversity.

ULTRAVERSITY-INTEGRATING TECHNOLOGY IN ADULT EDUCATION

According to research conducted by Google, (BBC, 2006) browsing the Internet ('surfing') has overtaken television as a leisure time pursuit. There are now opportunities for individuals to keep in touch with world affairs, sports results, check tomorrow's weather, keep up to date with their favourite celebrity's latest exploits, undertake research on virtually any subject, and thus engage in continuing learning, all made possible through utilising a plethora of Web-based technology.

Going on vacation no longer means being out of touch. Mobile phone technology has now evolved to the extent that a photograph taken of the Taj Mahal on a camera phone can be viewed within minutes by friends and family on the other side of the world-even to the extent of appearing within a blog (a web log), where visitors to that blog may

DOI: 10.4018/978-1-61520-694-0.ch013

contribute their own comments in response to the Taj Mahal posting.

Multi-function or smart phones not only have the same photographic facility, but also enable their users to surf the Web wirelessly (when the user is in range of a suitable wireless 'hot spot'), as well as conventionally accessing the Web through their mobile phone service providers, also permitting the smart phone user to be able to send and receive email, and navigate using GPS technology built into the phone.

Live outside television news events broadcasted from one corner of the earth to another are now commonplace, and make possible near instant reporting of sporting events. Viewers are also able to interact with such sporting programmes via instant messaging from their mobile phones, as well as watching these events on them. Even listeners to radio can participate in a live broadcast 'phone-in' via their mobile phones. However, the role played by broadcasters in facilitating distance learning and early face to face 'communities of practice' can be traced back to the Farm Forum experiment which took place during the 1930s in Canada, which supported not only the sharing of good agricultural practice amongst its listeners, but also stimulated 'community development activities' (Brookfield, 1986).

Previously prohibitively priced international telephone calls made via landlines can now be avoided via the use of free voice over Internet protocol technology-VOIP. As this software has developed, allied to the availability of increased bandwidth, this same software also permits free, one to one video conferencing.

These advancements in technology have facilitated access to information on an unprecedented scale. Despite this progress, Selwyn, Gorrard, and Furlong (2006) see barriers and hurdles to harnessing this technology within the field of adult education.

They identify one particular cultural issue that needs to be addressed, namely the perceived barrier between the technology on the one hand, and society on the other, an obstacle that needs to be overcome before technology can truly be utilised as a tool for furthering adult educational opportunities.

This chapter will focus mainly upon issues relating to adults re-engaging with part-time learning in higher education, and focus upon a degree awarded by a United Kingdom based university. The chapter will take into account the constantly evolving culture associated with contemporary technology, particularly computer-related information communication technology (ICT), and using the example of the Ultraversity online degree, show how using online computers as vehicles to facilitate the learning process can assist in addressing some of the cultural issues associated with utilising technology within adult education, thus furthering the ideals of lifelong learning.

The emergence of these technological advancements in communication have simultaneously generated associated cultures-particularly amongst teenagers and young people in their twenties, where a must have artefact of that contemporary culture is an up to date mobile phone that enables them at the very least continue their social lives through utilising SMS and MMS technology, and for others the ability to connect directly to their favourite social networking website, where possibly the person who sent the Taj Mahal image discloses in Facebook that they will next be visiting Mumbai, and promises further images. "No contemporary cultural artefact embodies the genius and the disruptive excess of capitalism as clearly as the cell phone" (MIT, 2005).

Using the Ultraversity model as an example, this chapter will demonstrate how information communication technologies can be harnessed to personalise adult learning opportunities, and in so doing provides a model for possibly modifying the culture of adult learning in Higher Education Institutions.

We now see technology as a force that presents both great opportunities for androgogical adult learning, as well as presenting special challenges. (Knowles, Holton, & Swanson, 2005, p. 236).

One of the special challenges that Knowles et al. (2005) allude to is the need for adults engaging in further education to be self-directed learners. They must be inwardly motivated in the first instance in order to engage in the learning process, let alone undertaking a technology-based course. Therefore in attending to the issues associated with introducing aspects of ICT culture into the design of adult education courses, there is a need to understand the components of the culture associated with adult education.

BACKGROUND

Before introducing an example of how online technology has been harnessed by one UK university in order to provide the facility for distance adult learners to engage wholly online in the pursuit of studying for an undergraduate research degree, it is first necessary to provide an overview of the concept of adult education.

At the outset, this chapter differentiates between content based, taught learning, more typical of pedagogical approaches to learning, familiar within the UK schools system, and on the other hand, situational, experiential learning, linked with Knowles' adult learning theory, and the associated term 'andragogy' (Knowles et al., 2005).

At the heart of Knowles' andragogy theory is the notion that adults who engage in further and higher courses of education do so in order to primarily satisfy particular learning needs. These may be at an informal level, such as learning and mastering a new skill for personal and recreational purposes, or via the formal, qualification route (later in this chapter, reference to the Ultraversity model will provide an insight into how experiential, situational and collaborative community learning are at the heart of that particular undergraduate research degree).

Andragogy is any intentional and professionally guided activity that aims at a change in adult persons. (Knowles et al., 2005, p. 60)

Knowles et al. [ibid] stress the importance of differentiating between the learning process and the actual goals achieved by undertaking that process, facilitated by technology, in the Ultraversity model, that brings about that change.

Despite the recent attention of the UK media in continued lifelong learning, particularly in consolidating the basic skills of the workforce (BBC, 2007) Selwyn et al. (2006) in their '*Adult Learning @ Home Research Project*' see adult education as the weakest sector of the lifelong learning process (Selwyn et al., 2006). They attribute this partly to the range of teaching approaches and the range of learning opportunities available, and the fact that adults undertake learning for a variety of reasons, in different settings and utilising a variety of approaches.

However, the work of Selwyn and his colleagues in part alludes to a problem perceived by other writers and authorities on adult education, namely the recognition that there is a lack of clarity and agreement on exactly what is meant by adult education. Malinen (2000) bemoans this, arguing that adult education "suffers from paradigmatic plurality" (p. 12). Her thesis attempts to distil the work of five recognised authorities on adult learning theory; Malcolm Knowles, David Kolb, Jack Mezirow, Reginald Revans and Donald Schön. She undertakes this 'distillation' process in an attempt to produce an understanding of the concept of adult education. This chapter's author is of the opinion that Malinen does in fact create some clarification as to what exactly is meant and understood by the term adult education, but that further work is required to develop a broader understanding of the subject.

Nearly a decade later after Malinen's foundation work, the United Kingdom's graduate careers website (Prospects, 2007) confirms the continued lack of clarity associated with the term 'adult education'. They appear not to associate the term with full-time university education, instead linking it to part time study. In the Ultraversity example to follow later in this chapter, it is designated as a part-time course. However the potential cost saving benefits both to higher education and to full-time students of pursuing online degrees, if not wholly online but in a blended approach to their learning, must merit more than a passing consideration.

During the same year that Malinen (2000) was attempting to derive a general overview of what constitutes adult education, Fenwick (2000) compared five perspectives of adult experiential learning, grouping them as follows:

Constructivist
Psycho-analytical
Situated Cognition
Critical Cultural
Enactivist
[ibid.]

Fenwick (2000) groups the work of Boud and Miller (1996), and Schön's (1983) earlier foundation work on the construction of knowledge through reflection, within the *Constructivist* Perspective. (Boud and Schön's models of reflection are studied during the development of the online Ultraversity degree.)

The identification by Fenwick (2000) of the *Situated Cognition* perspective in relation to adult experiential learning, relates to another concept underpinning the Ultraversity degree. In particular Fenwick (2000) focuses upon the work of Lave and Wenger (1991), who asserted that learning occurs within the particular setting in which the learner participates (such as in their work-setting)-hence it is referred to as *situational learning*. Unlike pedagogical, teacher-directed learning, where knowledge is imparted from teacher to student, and may later be drawn upon by the student in a different context and at a later time, situational learning is here and now learning, directly applied to the learner's current situation. In his later work, Wenger sees learning as transformative (Wenger, 1998) and introduces the concept of Communities of Practice. (*Referring to the Ultraversity online degree here, individual adult learners can utilise technology to 'meet' online so as to share their experiential learning collaboratively, particularly in homogeneous groups from similar working backgrounds, thus communities of practice are established, and are the main fora for constructing learning.*)

Lave and Wenger (1991) see the concept of the community of practice as one of three essential resources that are inextricably combined along with a community member's ability to understand and participate in the learning process. The other two resources identified by them are the activity itself in which the community is engaged, and the tools available to that community of adult learners to enable and facilitate learning. Technology features amongst those tools.

The increased use of ICT technology in our daily lives has led to the assumption that this technology will become an ever present tool that will be utilised by adult learners. However, despite recent research revealing that half the adult population in the UK have access to and use of computers, there is still a general reluctance to utilise them to engage in the processes of adult learning (Selwyn et al., 2006). They deduce that adults who have a clear need and purpose in utilising ICT will in fact embrace the use of computers, and this has been borne out within the Ultraversity project. In the six years that Anglia Ruskin University has been providing this online degree pathway, learning facilitators (lecturers/tutors) have observed an increase in overall student ICT capability compared to the skills and capabilities present amongst the first students who formed Cohort I. Mindful of the need to provide Ultraversity students with a broad outline of the range of technologies that they are required to utilise, and that are also available to them online, the second module within the first year of their course focuses directly upon online communication and technology.

Salmon (2000) cites the work of the Open University here in the UK, who were early exponents of technology use within their distant learning courses, particularly the use of CMC, supported by email. Ultraversity produced its own CMC system-code named Jelly-OS, but this was later superseded by First Class. Conventional email is also used mainly for personal communication between student and facilitator, and as a back up to ensure that formative work as well as summative work for assessment also reaches a designated facilitator. Importantly, that facilitator then anonymises the work, before despatching it to the marker, again electronically. Ultraversity students join the course already familiar with the use of email, word-processing software, Web browsers and search engines, but are then guided in the use of basic HTML, use of digital media, and basic web design. This is to encourage them to make use of a wide range of media in order to creatively present their assignments, while at the same time stretching their knowledge of and their ability to use ICT as broadly as possible. By far the greatest use is made of First Class as the main means of communicating and collaborating online.

TECHNOLOGY USE IN ADULT EDUCATION: THE ULTRAVERSITY EXAMPLE

Ultraversity (Basiel, Terrell, Revill, & Arnold, 2005) is the project name for the fully online BA Honours degree in Learning, Technology Research provided by Anglia Ruskin University. It was the brainchild of Professor Stephen Heppell, who led the team of software developers, programmers and educationalists to Ultraversity's inaugural role out in March 2003. It's first cohort graduated in November 2006, and recruitment for Cohort X1 has already commenced.

Ultraversity's underlying concept is to provide through the use of computer technology and the Internet, the opportunity for adults in the workplace, or in parenting roles to undertake an undergraduate research degree course, based around their working roles.

I always wanted a degree and the course is aimed at people in jobs they enjoy, providing them with an opportunity to research and influence how they work while completing the degree in just three years. (National Health Service Nurse, St Albans, Hertfordshire. Ultraversity First Class (Hons) graduate 2006)

Many of Ultraversity's future students would ordinarily have been denied the chance to pursue a conventional face-to-face degree course, by virtue of family commitments, economics and location (Selwyn et al., 2006). The majority of successful applicants have stated that the flexibility of being able to engage with the course at a time suitable for them, from almost any location via an Internet-connected computer, was one of its main attractions. Students enrolled upon the course must be self-directed learners, and have to accept that the use of technology is essential, as it is the main tool that makes the degree course possible. Online interaction with fellow students is not only a course requirement, but integral to their continuous situational learning, through ongoing peer review of formative work and other collaborative working practices. By regularly interacting with other students through engaging in the online community of practice (Wenger, 1998), students manipulate the technology to enable them to participate in the current learning situation (Lave & Wenger, 1991). Initial feelings of isolation are soon replaced by the fellowship engendered through online participation in their community of practice (also known as learning communities).

There was a lot of interaction between myself and others [online].The course has definitely improved my job. I feel a lot more confident and I know now that I can achieve a lot more than I thought I could. Now I've finished the relief is absolutely amazing. (ICT Director of Studies, Ingatestone, Essex. Ultraversity 2.2 (Hons) graduate July 2006.)

It is not uncommon to see evidence of social as well as scholastic interactions within Ultraversity's online communities -the shared understanding of Schön's (1983) work on learning through reflection may well be interspersed with personal messages of support when a member is unwell or has to take some time out of the course.

How Ultraversity Originated

The team responsible for developing Ultraversity had previously developed a successful record of building online learning spaces. The majority had worked together for the two years leading to the new Millennium on establishing and developing the international schools' online project, SchoolNet 2000. Some of that project team joined Anglia Ruskin University's learning technology research department, Ultralab in 2000, in order to develop the online pilot '*Talking Heads*' project for the then UK Government's Department for Education and Science (DfES). *Talking Heads* was made up of twelve hundred newly appointed head teachers in England. The DfES supplied each head teacher with an Internet-ready laptop, to enable each one to connect to the bespoke *Talking Heads* online space-which had been developed jointly between Oracle and Ultralab. The *Talking Heads* online community of practice was essentially a metamorphosis of the Think.com software that had been developed earlier under the project name of 'Scoop' by both Oracle and Ultralab.

Think.com-the online home of *Talking Heads*-was essentially a content management system (CMS), although arguably it was also a virtual learning environment (VLE). Each community member-either one of the twelve hundred head teachers, or one of the twelve facilitators-had their own personal profile page, including space for storage of Word and PowerPoint documents, and access to specific discussion forums. In order to better manage the discussion areas, head teachers from similar working backgrounds-for example those leading special schools, or head teachers of rural primary schools were enrolled into their own discussion areas. Facilitated wholly online by an experienced, ICT-literate team of twelve senior educationalists, one of the *Talking Heads* main aims was addressed-namely by regularly using that unique online resource, newly appointed head teachers could form mutually supportive groups to share knowledge and information relating to the varied role associated with running a school. By so doing, the isolation often felt by head teachers was reduced, and the very asynchronous nature of online communication afforded by the *Talking Heads* fora meant that the head teachers could access the discussions at a time that was suitable to them. *Talking Heads* provided a further resource to these senior educationalists-supplementing face-to-face and telephone contact, providing access to a potential online audience of over a thousand other practitioners, along with their collective wisdom.

In reality, during the first sixth months of the project, participation levels amongst the pilot group of head teachers varied between 20%-30% of the total number. Each of the twelve-member facilitation team supported a group of one hundred head teachers, with the majority of contact between the facilitator and their group of head teachers being sustained via the Talking Heads online community spaces within the Think.com software, with email and telephone providing supplementary support, in addition to electronic 'post-it' notes that could also be left between facilitator and head teacher within the main *Talking Heads* online community.

Online Facilitation

The following section will provide an insight into the unique background experience in online facilitation that was collectively developed within the Ultralab facilitation team, and which ultimately helped to shape the future approaches to learning facilitation practices for the Ultraversity project.

At the commencement of the project, Professor Heppell emphasised the key role that the facilitation team would play in establishing and growing the *Talking Heads* online community. Gilly Salmon wrote at the time about the role of such facilitators, referring to them as the e-moderators, likening them to 'champions' who could enliven learning when considering online course delivery to students (Salmon, 2000, p. 11). Heppell saw the role of the facilitation team to that of hosts at a party.

Berge (1995) classifies the facilitator's role as pedagogical, (questions/probes and focus); social, (developing human relationships, group cohesiveness, maintaining the group as a unit, helping members work together), managerial (organisational, procedural and administrative i.e. setting agenda/objectives/ timetable/procedural rules/decision making norms), and technical, (making users comfortable with software and system, preferably making it transparent). (Berg, 1995)

Berger (2007) cautions against ignoring the impact of the culture of technology on the culture of teaching adults. Thus the role of the facilitator is paramount in bridging this culture divide.

As with any party, invitations need to be sent out to guests. These were undertaken both via conventional letters accompanying the laptops, and as a verification of having successfully establishing an online connection and accessing the *Talking Heads* online community, participating head teachers were asked to send both a confirmatory email and leave an 'electronic' post-it note on their facilitator's home/profile page in the *Talking Heads* online community. Illustrated guides introducing *Talking Heads* to its users were also developed, and over the four-year duration of the project, several versions were produced, both in hard copy and pdf format, mirroring the development of several versions of the Think.com software. These particular skills in producing guides to software and presenting rich media learning resources have been further developed amongst the learning facilitation team in Ultraversity.

Although *Talking Heads* was not a vehicle for facilitating formal adult education, it evolved to provide distinct learning opportunities through scheduled online hotseats. These were time-limited events, when an expert in a particular field relating to headship and school management would be invited to 'sit' in a facilitated virtual hotseat for a fortnight, in order to answer questions from head teachers on areas related to their subject specialism.

Such experts included senior civil servants such as Michael Barber, Tim Brighouse and Ralph Tabberer. Each expert posted a short paper on an aspect of school management, and subsequently head teachers were invited to respond, thus stimulating debate. This practice continues within Ultraversity, where specific aspects of the course are expanded upon and students are able to ask questions of facilitators, and responses are then shared amongst all the cohort members. The *Talking Heads* facilitation team each informed their respective group of head teachers about that particular hotseat event, and not surprisingly, there was an increase in participation levels within *Talking Heads* as a large number of head teachers were keen to field questions directly to civil servants who were directly responsible for formulating school management policy.

This was a unique opportunity for the head teachers, not just in their collective role as education professionals, but as members of the UK electorate being provided with an opportunity to directly question policy makers. This event (along with others) provided the head teachers with a clear opportunity to negotiate meaning on educational policy, and demonstrated the constructivist perspective associated with experiential learning identified by Vygotski (1978), which along with the work of Schön (1983), Boud and Miller (1996), later became fundamental to the learning experience underpinning Ultraversity.

These learning opportunities afforded by the *Talking Heads* hotseats sowed the seeds of the concept to transfer the UK Government's face-to-face delivered pre-headship qualification, the National Professional Qualification for Headship-NPQH-to a wholly online delivery. Not only would online access to NPQH tutors reduce the need for aspiring head teachers and their tutors to travel to a central location for face-to-face tutorials, but similar to the *Talking Heads* project, a wealth of potential expertise and opportunities to share good professional practice facilitated by Web technology was thus made available online, at any time. Simultaneously, online communities of practice were established, comprising of aspiring head teachers and their NPQH tutors forming supportive groups that would endure into the future.

The *Talking Heads* facilitation team were located remotely throughout the U K, as were their head teachers. This fact alone contributed to the empathy facilitators were able to feel for first time adopters of the technology, and assisted in developing the facilitation team's understanding of the learning and familiarisation process that these new and sometimes reluctant adopters would need to experience, in order to fully benefit from the informal and continuous learning opportunities that were being generated online. The opportune location of some of the facilitation team within Scotland and Wales, and those team members' unique knowledge of the cultures and education systems of both those regions of the UK enabled the transfer of the *Talking Heads* model to both Wales (Davidson, 2002) and Scotland (Russell & Thompson, 2002). Both additional project role-outs built upon the lessons learned from establishing *Talking Heads* in England, which by 2001 was extended to all 24000 head teachers in England. One main difference with the extension of the project to both Scotland and Wales was the opportunity provided to newly appointed head teachers for face-to-face meetings with the facilitation teams responsible for introducing the regional versions of *Talking Heads* to them. In Scotland the project was known as '*Heads Together*', and in Wales, '*Pen-i-Ben*', with the version in Wales mirroring the deliberate use of the Welsh language in particular sub-communities for head teachers of Welsh-medium schools. Another successful development adopted within *Pen-i-Ben*, taken from *Talking Heads* in England was the establishment of 'local working groups'-these were established face-to-face groups of regionally located head teachers, who had already developed working relationships via their local educational authorities, and who supplemented their face-to-face meetings by continuing their dialogue online. Two groups in particular, located in the south of Wales planned, 'met' asynchronously online and discussed their year-long planning and development within the *Pen-i-Ben* online community. Despite the success and popularity of *Pen-i-Ben* amongst its participating head teachers, lack of funding on the part of the regional Welsh Assembly Government saw the closure of that head teachers online community in December 2003 after two years in operation. In Scotland, *Heads Together*, the online community for head teachers in Scotland, continues alongside other professional school-based online communities (Scotland, 2008). Facilitation of *Talking Heads* continued until December 2003 for Anglia Ruskin University's Ultralab team. *Talking Heads* continues under the auspices of the National College for School Leadership's own facilitation team (NCSL).

The key role played by the facilitation teams, and the unique, collective cumulative knowledge that was built up by them in overcoming some of the main cultural barriers associated with introducing professional adult learners to an online environment, would be invaluable in establishing the future Ultraversity online degree.

How Technology Use Has Evolved Within Ultraversity

Ultraversity was already a developing project as the majority of the Ultralab facilitation team handed over online facilitation duties to colleagues at the National College for School Leadership in December 2003. Their facilitation skills were then utilised within the Ultraversity project, guiding new students through three years of online study and collaboration, culminating in the students' graduation with a BA (Honours) degree in Learning, Technology Research. For the majority of Ultraversity students, the graduation ceremony is the first time they meet their fellow students and facilitators in person. That learning journey is made possible initially by utilising computer technology connected to the Internet. For all students enrolled on this degree programme, access to this technology is a basic requirement for course participation. Many are introduced to the need to make back-up copies of their work, and are encouraged to do so utilising their private e-portfolio space within Ultraversity's Plone content management software. Each student also has space to back up files within the First Class online environment, which is also the online space for each cohort's collaborative communities of practice (also known as learning communities), and First Class is the degree programme's main vehicle for communication. Its system of red flag alerts informs users where new messages are located, as do audible alerts when users are already logged into the system. Built–in synchronous text-messaging augments First Class's more widely used asynchronous messaging system.

When students take their first tentative steps into their cohort's online community space in First Class, it is usually in response to their cohort facilitator's welcome email, sent to their personal email address. This email provides essential instructions on how to access both First Class and Plone. Regular online tracking alerts facilitators to any difficulties new students may be experiencing, and triggers an online intervention from the facilitators initially in the form of an email. Due to the improvement in Internet bandwidth over the last few years, coupled with the development of more online technology tools, Ultraversity students are now able to utilise free VOIP technology in order to contact fellow students or their facilitators free of charge, and from most computers connected to the Internet.

Free VOIP technology also permits one-to-one video conferencing, and this is usually accompanied by instant messaging, which also facilitates file transfer, a particularly useful feature when providing text instructions supported by images. Perhaps one of the most innovative developments of late has been the advent of free, animated screen capture software, which quickly enables facilitators to provide progressive, 'live' reproductions of the steps a student needs to take to perform a particular function using a piece of software, for example initiating a search of the university's digital library, or inserting a hyperlink into an electronic document.

Students are introduced to free, online alternatives to proprietary software-for example Open Office, HTML authoring software, digital photo-editing software, presentational websites and educational video sites.

Plone-the content management software (CMS)-is the main online resource where Ultraversity students are able to locate course-related resources, hotseats and store their work within private file areas (their e-portfolio space). For many, Plone provides them with web space for their first opportunity to produce a personal web page, thus creating an online presence that in turn introduces them to their fellow students. This is an integral part of the personalisation process associated with the first steps each student takes in their online learning journey. Within each student's personal web page in Plone, there is a private area accessible only to the student and facilitator-within that private area, known as the assessment folder, completed work is electronically submitted for assessment. Following the assessment process, the mark and feedback relating to the submitted work is then deposited within the same private assessment folder.

The facilitation team use additional CMS software with student groups from other departments within the university, so as to deliver other modules online. These include the aged WebCT system, and the more recent Moodle course management software. Moodle conveniently combines discussion forums and course resources within the same online environment, which has been well received by the student group who use it. This same group continue to use First Class as a back up system along with Plone, but find Moodle provides easier access to course related discussions than First Class. This same student group had already used both Plone and First Class to complete their very first two course modules, and were therefore less inhibited in adapting to using a new CMS-in this case, Moodle. The research conducted by Selwyn et al. (2006) confirmed this, namely that when initially faced with needing to adapt to the use of unfamiliar technology and software, adult learners will persevere, as a means to an end. At the rate at which advancements and modifications are being made to ICT technology, the learners within Ultraversity will no doubt be familiarising themselves with further technological innovations before long. They are part of a lifelong learning culture facilitated by technology.

Perhaps the most potentially influential ICT tool available to Ultraversity is Adobe Connect Pro. This software, once licensed and installed onto one of a university's servers, acts as a main connection hub that permits a whole tutor group to connect via sound and vision to their tutor. It is claimed by the manufacturers that it is able to host up to one hundred participants within one online conference. Initial trials within Ultraversity have connected twenty remotely located staff via audio and text with a campus based faculty meeting. University staff who are located remotely, such as the Ultraversty learning facilitation team, were able to see and hear a live meeting, and participate either by instant messaging, audio, or by using both audio and video. The software has the ability to record such sessions. Academic staff can also pre-record their delivery of a lecture, with Adobe Connect Pro providing the facility to display PowerPoint slides, whilst simultaneously enabling the lecturer to provide those slides with an accompanying video narration by speaking directly to the web cam on their computer. Students can then access the recording, and watch their lecturer addressing them and presenting the slides alongside the webcast, at a time and place convenient to them. Each participant ideally requires a broadband connection.

For many of the adults enrolled within Ultraversity, this is a significant development in terms of meeting the expectations of a learning culture more familiar to the older students-namely returning almost to the lecture room style delivery of learning. Live lectures are also possible, and these too may be recorded. However, the introduction of Adobe Connect Pro could also help to reduce the gap between the learners and the technology culture. The use of this particular software could become a technology tool to assist each course participant to successfully progress through the course. Learning to use the technology would be a means to an end, with the primary focus being the successful completion of the degree course-where that objective is wholly achieved online.

Personalising the Learning Process

As mentioned, this process commences when each student personalises his or her home space in Plone. There is also space provided for this in First Class too, although some rightly argue that duplication is not necessary. However the converse is true-as both these learning platforms are separate, it is preferable to have personalised spaces in each piece of software, particularly if an individual is only utilising one of those online places, and wants to quickly look up a fellow student's résumé.

Having first established an online presence within the course's software spaces, students begin to build a profile of their work setting. This profile is unique to each student, and serves to further enhance their online presence, by providing other members of their online learning community with an insight into each of their workplace settings. This undertaking also provides students with the opportunity to review their workplace's organisational structure, and their unique role within that structure.

Armed with the essential technology tools and a developing understanding of the processes associated with online collaboration in the learning process, Ultraversity students are introduced to the concepts of action research and the use of reflection as a tool for learning in the workplace. Their shared online dialogue between themselves and other students and tutors assists in the development of understanding and meaning (Wenger, 1998):

I think you've woven some personal reflection into this and also included some good stuff from our online discussions.

I think your work on value added is excellent. What extra benefit, over and above your qualifications, can you bring to this company. Good work that. Sound of penny dropping here. I've just realised that I do this all the time when I'm interviewing people. Just didn't know it was called 'value added'. We've got a bloke coming in next week who can play the guitar, for example. It's not a requirement to teach English, obviously, but learning English through song is a bona fide methodology, so the chap who can play the guitar has some value added benefit to us. I'd not actually realised that till I read your piece. (Excerpt from a current 3rd year student who teaches English responding to a request for peer review from another student, who works in ICT support.)

This ongoing dialogue occurring within a cohort's online learning community not only assists in clarifying meaning, but builds in criticality and reflection within the formative process of crafting the final assignment.

The work produced by each student is based upon their own work setting, and their role within it. Despite the fact that the greatest percentage of Ultraversity students work in support roles within UK schools, there is little opportunity for duplication of research and reflection due to the individual and personalised nature of their studies, which are encouraged by their workplace mentors and managers. This personalised focus to the Ultraversity work based approach to learning provides each student with essential ownership of and responsibility for their learning, added to the motivating realisation that their research is at the very least positively impacting upon their own working practices, and in many cases having a direct and beneficial influence within their place of work.

I thought I would share a comment from my 'Professional Development Interview' by my head teacher: 'Denise is continuing an online degree course which is providing many new aspects of developments for the school as well as for Denise.'

It feels good that the impact of this course is seen to be making a difference to my school, it makes it all worthwhile! (Senior Classroom Assistant, Chelmsford, Essex. Ultraversity 2.2 (Hons) graduate July 2007)

The Use of Patchwork Text in Drawing Together the Cultures of Adult Education and Technology

On element of the culture of learning that adults returning to study must re-engage with is that of completing modules of study, punctuated by the submission of an assignment of work for assessment purposes, at the end of a module. For many students this is initially a daunting prospect, and over the period of the three-year course, tutors see a gradual improvement in the development of students' communication and presentation skills. The pioneering work of Winter (2003) in developing 'an alternative to the essay', namely the patchwork text approach to assessment, has assisted this process, and is another example of where the use of technology embedded within the Ultraversity degree concept addresses a fundamental education culture issue faced by adults returning to formal study practices, namely the requirement to produce assignments as part of the continuous assessment process.

In essence, students are encouraged to make use of the patchwork text approach, which comprises of a series of carefully crafted short pieces of writing, which are produced at regular intervals throughout the lifespan of a module. Some of these pieces of writing may be substituted by the use of media-such as digital slide presentations (which are often provided online), used to provide a synopsis of research undertakings and findings, or a .pdf file representing a research report in the genre of a magazine report. Students make effective use of animations or strip cartoon software to illustrate learning events; these have also been presented in the form of short shadow puppet theatre videos. Not only do students actively engage in utilising the technology for presentational purposes, but also they are sufficiently motivated to master previously unfamiliar technology in order to enhance the quality of their final presentations. Much like the lead up to a theatrical performance, in the final year of the degree students exhibit the results and findings of their action research within their workplace settings-in most cases this is a physical exhibition, although some students conduct their exhibitions online. That isn't the final act of the three-year long play-following the exhibition, feedback is then collected from workplace colleagues, and the impact of each student's research within the workplace is then gauged.

I still think this is the best opportunity of higher education I'm ever likely to have and the fact that it ties in with work makes it more interesting and certainly has changed my practice for the better. I find I question situations more and if things aren't working, I feel confident enough to suggest alternatives. (Graphic Designer, Charity, Peterborough, Cambridgeshire. First Class (Hons) July 2006)

Issues

Ultraversity originated as a project six years ago, and following proof of concept, and the graduation of its first cohort of students in November 2006, it continues to recruit its student base mainly from amongst school support staff, and in its early stages from the Health Service. It therefore needs to broaden its appeal, and recruit from other areas of employment.

Despite its innovative nature, and coverage by press and television, particularly at the time of the first graduations, little is known about the degree outside the traditional catchment area of Anglia Ruskin University. Overseas students who have enrolled and successfully graduated discovered the existence of the degree following a search of the Internet.

Adult Education forums and organisations are not fully aware of the successful integration of adult learning and technology through the Ultraversity project, and this concept needs to be replicated in order to provide opportunities for other adult learners.

FUTURE RESEARCH RECOMMENDATIONS

A clear consensus as to what is meant by adult education needs to be defined and agreed. The UK Government's own graduate website (Prospects, 2007) alludes to the lack of clarity and understanding about this vital area of lifelong learning. Prime Minister Brown's former Skills Envoy and previous CBI Chairman Lord Jones of Birmingham highlighted the need to up skill the UK workforce in order for the country to remain commercially competitive (BBC, 2007). The rise in unemployment due to the current recession has made the task of revisiting these issues more urgent. There are existing adult education bodies that need to be brought together in order to achieve this. SCUTREA (Standing Conference on University and Research in the Education of Adults) is one such body in the UK, as is NIACE (The National Institute of Adult Continuing Education). A recent study sponsored by NIACE (2009) highlights the lack of progress in addressing the education provision for adults over twenty five years of age. A first step in addressing the need for understanding of the term 'adult education' would be a commitment by the UK Government to increase adult education provision, not only for the economic benefits of the country, but also for the well-being of those adults participating in continuing education.

A second step would be to look at successful and cost-effective models of provision, particularly harnessing technology as outlined in this chapter, both supporting and promoting the expansion of similar programmes.

In doing this there would be a reduction in the distance between both the cultures of adult education and that of technology. The relative infancy and rarity of online degree pathways such the Ultraversity excluded it from the type of research conducted by Selwyn et al. (2006), such that their claim that ICT use amongst adult learners was more likely to focus on learning to use the technology, and not learning being facilitated by using the technology, as in the Ultraversity example, can be refuted.

Both universities and employers need to be made more aware of the potential that combining online reflective learning with undertaking action research in the workplace can offer traditional degree pathways. Such courses have no need for physical buildings, nor the requirement for staff and students to travel to a central location in order to make learning happen. In addition, those students who have particular learning needs, perhaps due to hospitalisation are not denied the opportunity to continue their online learning experience-it is essentially asynchronous, anytime, anywhere learning, transcending both national boundaries and time zones.

Hopefully research will be obtained from a small pilot initiative with the Ford motor company (currently being undertaken within Ultraversity) which will elicit further information as to the value of integrating work-based learning using technology in order to improve overall effectiveness and efficiency in the work place. (This is ongoing research, and it is anticipated that an interim report will be available in 2010.)

The role of the learning facilitator in the overall adult learning experience needs to be better understood. Further research would achieve this.

CONCLUSION

The ubiquitous evolution of Information Communication Technology impacts upon most aspects of our lives. This has been especially noticeable since the advent of the microcomputer, and this rate of change is manifested by the regular appearance of new, improved and quicker technologies that leave in their wake a trail of redundant and outdated machines. Would it be correct then to assume that this evolving technology is a culture all on its own, based upon the fact that one of the world's leading centres in technology excellence,

MIT, as previously mentioned in this chapter, view communication technology as artefacts of contemporary culture?

A SCUTREA conference in1992 defined culture that is associated with adult education as 'the values, beliefs and activities [that occur] within groups and whole societies as well as its more traditional sense as a means to enlightenment and sensibility' (SCUTREA, 1992). Therefore within youth culture in the UK, as within other developed countries, mobile ICT devices are certainly 'cultural artefacts' (MIT, 2005). The extent to which other familiar ICT devices such as computers are part of that culture could perhaps form the basis of further research. The earlier mention in this chapter of the work of Selwyn et al. (2006), and in particular the '*Adult Learning @ Home Research Project'* [ibid] provided valuable information relating to impact of ICT within the field of adult education, and in particular the statistic that at least half the adult population in the UK had access to and use of a computer. The extent to which computers are becoming essential tools within society is evidence of a culture change. This has been mirrored within Ultraversity, as recently enrolled students are more ICT literate than the very first students who joined the course in 2003. The '*Adult Learning @ Home Research Project'* revealed that 'the key social determinants predicting lifelong participation in learning are time, place, sex, family and initial schooling' (Selwyn et al., 2006, p. 79). Other factors included the year of birth, the type of school attended, and respondents' socio-economic status. For those involved in delivering adult education, the '*Adult Learning @ Home Research Project'* revealed that the early life experiences of some of those interviewed for that research project had been negatively influenced in respect of their initial learning experiences, directly impacting upon on their reluctance to participate in adult education.

I now see learning as lifelong rather than something to get done and out of the way as quickly as possible. I can see how the negative attitude of a small number of teachers when I was at school affected how I learned. Their voices unfortunately drowned out those of their more positive and gifted counterparts. The Ultraversity degree, however, was facilitated in a very positive way and this has left an indelible mark on my own attitude to life and learning. (Classroom Assistant, Preston, Lancashire. 2.1 (Hons) graduate 2007)

The '*Adult Learning @ Home Research Project'* found that there was limited take-up on the adult learning courses examined, despite reductions and subsidies applied to the costs of participation in those courses, and despite the provision by some prospective participants' employers of dedicated time and opportunity for engagement in further learning. Significantly this included courses utilising ICT technology [ibid].

The culture that has been built up around computers, and the belief held by some that it resides strongly amongst the young seems to have been borne out by a study conducted by Selwyn et al. (2006) which revealed that young people aged 16 and above were twice as likely to use ICT in order to pursue further learning than adults aged 21 and over. In summarising their findings, they [ibid] found that in some cases amongst those aged 21 and over there was a positive resistance to utilising computer technology as a tool for learning.

There are clear implications stemming from that research for government here in the UK and in other developed countries concerned with promoting the continuous professional development of its work force, and for those charged with providing adult education provision.

As the personal computer became more mainstream, and a contemporary cultural artefact, perhaps naively ICT was seen as a universal panacea for involving greater numbers of adults in lifelong learning. The reality according to the findings of Selwyn et al. (2006) research was that unless potential future adult learners have a past history of engagement in learning beyond the compulsory education phase, then they were likely to avoid further involvement in learning.

Wenger (1998) suggests that the emphasis on learning should not only be made in the early years of life, but that the process of learning should involve lifetime membership of learning communities-these would foster a sense of belonging, engendering a sense of collegiality, and thus fostering a lifelong learning ethos (Wenger, 1998). The learning derived by students from their online collaboration within the Ultraversity learning communities would corroborate Wenger's views. The development of social capital within those learning communities (previously identified in this chapter as Wenger's 'communities of practice') is based upon peer reviews, and the mutual understanding of the work to be undertaken and completed, along with the exchange of technical know-how amongst all members of the community-students and tutors alike.

Regular participation in the online community's discussions is crucial, akin to attending a face to face class; if a student does not regularly participate in the online community discussions, he/she risks missing vital learning just as they would by skipping or being absent from a lecture. Irrespective of the fact that all community discussions are there to be read at anytime in the near future, the number of new discussions that await the once absent student can be quite overwhelming.

There is a clear purpose within the Ultraversity example for utilising the technology in order to participate fully in the course. Regular tutor (facilitator) engagement in the community is also of paramount importance-metaphorically speaking they can be compared to the hosts at a party. They model online behaviour, clarify intended learning outcomes, and moderate the discussions, amongst some of their duties. One student recently described one role of the facilitator as developing 'socratic dialogue' within the learning community.

The fact that the specific education culture associated with Ultraversity is 'learner-centred' fosters a sense of empowerment amongst the students, and it is this personalised approach to learning that not only reinforces the use of the core elements of reflection and action research within their workplace settings, but it also brings an immediacy to that learning, whereby it is put into practice and honed throughout the three years of the course.

Computer and Internet technology makes the Ultraversity degree course possible. The use of technology is not taught in isolation, instead it is harnessed for clear learning purposes, with specific goals in mind, such as to search for information relating to the students' focus of study, accessing the university's digital library from students' homes, (some located only five miles away from the university, whereas others are five thousand miles away) and for presenting assignments using a variety of media and genre. West (2006) sees this process as the first rays of light heralding the dawn of educational democracy, where learning is no longer in the hands of a select few, who she refers to as the 'gatekeepers of knowledge'.

There is still however a role for the gatekeepers to perform: In much the same way that Wenger (1998) sees education as a transformative catalyst, so there are parallels in Knowles' thinking-that the educator becomes more of a facilitator of learning, rather than the sole purveyor of knowledge (Knowles et al., 2005). It is this partnership in learning that has often occurred in the compulsory school setting, where the pupils-the 'digital natives' are more familiar with ICT than their teachers, and are thus empowered learners. It is this age group, according to Selwyn et al. (2006) who are more likely than any other generation, to harness the learning opportunities afforded by ICT.

Learning online in higher education is not yet mainstream. Tiffin (2003) saw universities as slow to change. "Universities are the same all over the world. Universities hate change. But slowly, like sheep, they'll follow. We shifted from the medieval religion-based university to the modern scientific-based one. The next one will be the global one" (Tiffin, 2003). Prior to his Presidency, Barack Obama urged universities to concentrate less on their buildings, and more on the quality of their teaching, during these times of constant technological change (Obama, 2006, p. 165).

Allied to the need for universities to more widely exploit ICT technology as a vehicle to facilitate and embrace online and distance learning provision for adult learners returning to education, and in addressing this need confront established cultural practices in the provision of adult education, they first should consider the cost benefits of offering online alternatives to the existing provision of full-time, face to face courses. These are particularly expensive for young people currently leaving UK universities, many of whom are burdened with debt, facing the uncertainty of employment during the current global economic recession, and the added worry of having to balance the long term prospect of repaying a student loan, pursue a career and live a life.

Within established cultures, views are not easily changed-the process takes time, but the culture associated with technology is continually evolving. The other culture discussed in this chapter, namely that associated with adult education, is not clearly defined, and needs to take notice of the implications of recent research into the relationship between the use of technology and adult education, alongside examples of practice where technology has been successfully integrated within adult education.

REFERENCES

Basiel, A., Terrell, I., Revill, G., & Arnold, L., (2005). *Innovations in non-written forms of work based learning assessment.*

BBC. (2006). *Super surfers oust couch potatoes.* Retrieved April 1, 2009, from http://news.bbc.co.uk/1/hi/business/4784518.stm

BBC. (2007). *Skills pledge gauntlet to firms.* Retrieved March 27, 2009, from http://news.bbc.co.uk/1/hi/education/6751953.stm

Berge, Z. (1995). Facilitating computer conferencing: Recommendations from the field. *Educational Technology, 35*(1) 22-30. Retrieved March 27, 2009, from http://comparative.edu.ru:9080/PortalWeb/document/show.action?document.id=15659

Berger, J. (2007). *Cultural components of technology and its implications for adult education.* Retrieved March 28, 2009, from http://www.oise.utoronto.ca/CASAE/cnf2007/Proceedings-2007/AERC%20CASAE%20Berger-2007.pdf

Boud, D., & Miller, N. (1996). Animating learning from experience. In D. Boud & N. Miller (Eds), *Working with experience* (pp. 3-13). London: Routledge.

Brookfield, S. D. (1986). *Understanding and facilitating adult learning.* Milton Keynes, UK: Open University Press.

Davidson, J. (2002). *You are not alone, says Jane Davidson.* Welsh Assembly Government. Retrieved March 27, 2009, from http://new.wales.gov.uk/news/archivepress/educationpress/edpress2002/748994/?lang=en

Fenwick, T. J. (2000). *Experiential learning in adult Education: A comparative framework.* Retrieved March 27, 2009, from http://www.ualberta.ca/~tfenwick/ext/pubs/print/aeq.htm

Jones, S, Lang, G., Terrell, I., Thompson, K., Ramondt, L., & ULTRALAB associates (2001). *Establishing online communities for school leaders-an interim report.* Retrieved March 27, 2009, from http://www.ceilidhfolk.co.uk/bera2001th.pdf

Knowles, M. S., Holton, E. F., & Swanson, R. A. (2005). *The adult learner* (6th ed.). Boston: Elsevier.

Lave, J., & Wenger, E. (1991). *Situated learning: Legitimate peripheral participation*. New York: Cambridge Press.

Malinen, A. (2000). *Towards the Essence of Adult Experiential Learning*, Jyväskylä, Finland: SoPHI Academic Press.

MIT. (2005). Cell phone culture. *MIT communications*. Retrieved March 29, 2009, from http://web.mit.edu/comm-forum/forums/cell_phone_culture.htm

NIACE. (2009). *Education promotes well-being – but over 25s excluded*. Retrieved April 4, 2009, from http://www.niace.org.uk/education-promotes-well-being–but-too-many-over-25-excluded

Obama, B. (2006).*The audacity of hope*. Edinburgh, UK: Canongate.

Prospects, (2007). *The UK's official graduate careers website*. Retrieved March 27, 2009, from http://www.prospects.ac.uk/p/types_of_job/adult_education_lecturer_job_description.jsp

Retrieved March 28, 2009, from http://209.85.229.132/search?q=cache:syDJ2FC_ROAJ:www.mdx.ac.uk/wbl/research/research_docs/Basiel-WBL2005.pdf+Lydia+Arnold&cd=17&hl=en&ct=clnk&gl=uk

Russell, A., & Thompson, K. (2002). *Talking heads, It's progress, transfer to Wales and Scotland and relevance to the Republic of Ireland.* Presented to ITTE at Trinity College Dublin July 2002. Retrieved March 27, 2009, from http://www.ceilidhfolk.co.uk/paper2002.pdf

Salmon, G. (2000). *E-moderating: The key to teaching and learning online*. London: Kogan Page.

Schon, D. A. (1983). *The reflective practitioner*. New York: Basic Books.

Scotland, L. T. (2008). *Online Communities*. Retrieved March 27, 2009, from http://www.ltscotland.org.uk/onlinecommunities/login.asp

SCUTREA. (1992). *Changing culture and adult learning.* Papers from the SCUTREA Annual Conference (22nd, Canterbury, England, United Kingdom, July 8-10, 1992). Retrieved March 30, 2009, from http://www.eric.ed.gov:80/ERICWebPortal/custom/portlets/recordDetails/detailmini.jsp?_nfpb=true&_&ERICExtSearch_SearchValue_0=ED358290&ERICExtSearch_SearchType_0=no&accno=ED358290

Selwyn, N., Gorrard, S., & Furlong, J. (2006). *Adult learning in the digital age*. Routledge: Oxford.

Tiffin, J. (2003). *Virtual Reality.* Retrieved April 1, 2009, from http://www.guardian.co.uk/education/2003/aug/06/highereducation.uk3

Vygotsky, L. (1978). *Mind in society.* (M. Cole, Trans). Cambridge, MA: Harvard University Press.

Wenger, E. (1998). *Communities of practice-learning, meaning, and identity*. New York: Cambridge University Press.

West, A. (2006). *Personalised learning: The limits to individualism*. Retrieved April 1, 2009, from http://www.nec.ac.uk/info/category-browse?usca_p=t&category_id=5480

Winter, R. (2003). *Alternative to the essay*. Retrieved April 1, 2009, from http://www.guardian.co.uk/education/2003/jun/10/highereducation.uk

Chapter 14
Comparing the Principles of Adult Learning with Traditional Pedagogical Teaching in Relation to the Use of Technology:
The Tacit Dimension in ICT-Based University Teaching

Manuel Ahedo
Rovira i Virgili University, Spain

ABSTRACT

The traditional principles of adult learning are being subject to critical reconsideration from new adult teaching approaches and a growing use of information and communication technologies (ICTs). ICTs in adult learning have an ambivalent effect. On the one hand, they offer potential improvement in online communicative activities and the transmission of codified or explicit knowledge. On the other hand, they can reduce socially and interactive-mediated tacit teaching and learning. Thus, the crucial criterion for effective and complementary use of ICTs in adult andragogy is whether they enable time and social space for the tacit dimension of teaching and learning. This article analyzes these issues by comparing how two young universities in Spain have dealt with these effects of ICTs in relation to the tacit dimension of learning and teaching.

INTRODUCTION

Until recently adult learning has been rather marginalized in most countries. For many decades, higher education systems were entrusted with providing industrial societies with the qualified professionals they needed. During the second half of the 20th century, increasing numbers of adults attended an expanding offer of tertiary education programs. In this context, then, it became necessary to discuss and analyze the teaching techniques for both young and mature adult learners. With this purpose, in 1980, Knowles proposed the concept and principles of andragogy, targeted at discovering the specificities of the pedagogy of adult learning. Since then Knowles' principles have been revised and developed within a substantial process of social and educational change. Particularly since the 1990s, in many Western societies, continuing adult education began to get both public and academic attention, and emphasis was increasingly placed on skills, training, and competences. In the same period, other structural changes have occurred: for example, increasing use is made of the information and communication technologies (ICTs), and there are new forms of social relations and networks (Castells, 1997; Webster, 1995).

In these past two decades, learning, lifelong learning and the learning society have served as umbrella concepts in most discussions on adults and learning in the emerging knowledge or learning society and economy (Stehr, 1994). These concepts have become a new analytical framework for educational studies (Young, 1998). The notions of lifelong learning and learning society, however, have also been subject to critical analysis and discussions (Barry, 1999; Coffield, 2000). For Fischer (2001) lifelong learning is broader than adult education or training, as it includes such new dimensions as self-directed learning, learning on demand, informal learning, and organizational learning. Jarvis (2000) advocates that the concept of learning society allows for a more comprehensive comparative educational approach, because in the context of globalization, expanding use of ICTs, and new forms of industrialism and post-industrialism, learning takes place in more than educational institutions. As technology and innovation have gained momentum, knowledge and learning have also received more attention from the social and human sciences. International organizations such as the World Bank (2003) and the OECD (2005) have also highlighted the challenges posed to tertiary and university education in the current era of social and technological change. The European Union has undergone a process of harmonization of national higher education during which, the tacit dimension of teaching and learning clearly emerged in the discussions on competences and skills as will be shown below.

Traditional teaching pedagogy was designed to transmit codified or written knowledge to young generations within the paradigm of general standardized industrial production and mass consumption known as Fordism. This codified or formalized knowledge consisted of lists of technical information and facts, the purpose of which was to ensure stable use over time. The aim of teaching and learning was to acquire it. When the Fordism model entered into crisis in the 1970s and 1980s, alternative proposals for teaching different age groups began to be made. Constructivist and pragmatist pedagogy, inspired by Dewey (1933-1986) and others, became more widespread as qualitative and micro social sciences became more prominent, as can be seen by the evolution of the theory of practices (Bourdieu, 1977; Schatzki, Knor-Cetina, & Von Savigny, 2001; Schön, 1983; Searle, 1995). The educational and pedagogical literature began to go beyond the formal teaching of codified knowledge and started considering the more tacit, reflective and informal dimensions of learning (Burbules, 2008). Learning to learn became one of the key competencies by which students can go beyond the individual and collective skill-bases (Jarvis & Parker, 2005; Schön,

1987; Sternberg & Horvath, 1999). In Spain, as in many other European countries, the discussion on educational methodologies and pedagogies took place as a side-debate on the issues of competencies and skills.

The ICTs have been the driving force behind the change in national adult learning systems. Generally, technology, science and knowledge and the corresponding technological determinism have been strongly criticized, and it is now widely argued that society shapes technology (MacKenzie & Wacjman, 1985). Concerned about the use of technology in education, educational organizations began to use ICTs as both the content to be taught and the means by which this content was taught. At first, the focus was on ICTs as content so that the new generations could acquire technological skills and those already active in the labor market could upgrade their existing skills. Subsequently, ICTs were gradually used in education as instruments for teaching and learning. This second phase has been subject to considerable critical discussion and research. The main problem is that teaching and learning involve a certain amount of tacit practice. And because tacit teaching and learning is highly socially-mediated, it depends mainly on face-to-face interaction. This is even more critical in adult teaching, since adults have already completed their basic process of cognitive and relational socialization, and their face-to-face communication is already highly patterned. Adults can always undergo a process of re-socialization, but they have considerable difficulties in doing so. It can be argued, then, that whereas ICTs have so far been generally practical and appropriate tools for education, they also have important limitations for substantial teaching and learning, especially regarding the tacit dimension.

This article aims to discuss these issues by comparing how ICTs have been used by two universities in Spain in their attempts to provide high quality university education. The section below presents the background in three parts. In the first of these parts, the principles of adult learning and traditional pedagogy are discussed and reviewed from the perspective of tacit learning. In the second, the need for new teaching roles in the emerging information and learning society is discussed, again in connection with the idea of tacit teaching. In the third, the relation between ICTs and tacit learning and teaching is analyzed. The next section provides the main arguments and foci of this article and, once again, is divided into three sub-sections. The first sub-section contextualizes the recent changes brought about by the standardization of higher education in the European Union, under the so-called Bologna process. The second summarizes the most important features of higher education and the use of ICTs in Spain. The third analyzes the attempts made by two Spanish Universities to use ICTs effectively. The two universities studied were the Rovira i Virgili University (Universitat Rovira i Virgili - URV), a conventional university in the province of Tarragona, and the Open University of Catalonia (Universitat Oberta de Catalunya - UOC), a public distance and e-learning university. The third major section also suggests future research directions. A final section summarizes the main arguments and conclusions.

BACKGROUND

The Principles of Adult Learning and Traditional Pedagogy with Regard to the Use of ICTs and the Tacit Dimension

ICT in adult and university education need to be used more effective for a variety of reasons (Figure 1). First, there is a need to develop new andragogical principles that are more relevant to the requirements of adults. Second, university teachers and teachers of adults need to design and adopt new teaching roles for transmitting information and knowledge. And finally, the tacit

Figure 1. The relational triangle of the tacit dimension in university teaching and learning with regard to the use of ICTs

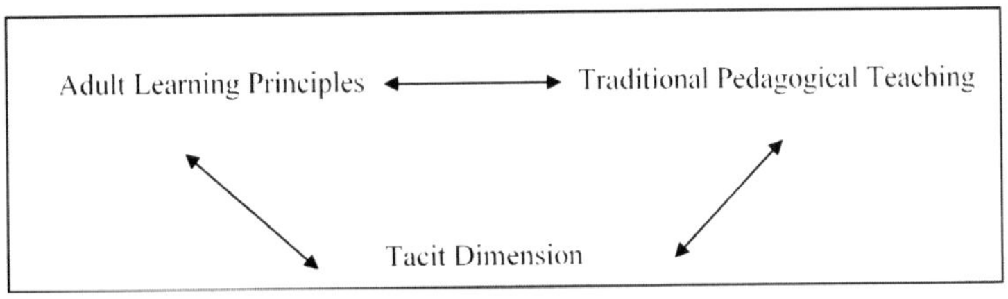

dimension in learning and teaching needs to be operationalized through social face-to-face mediation as a key complementary mechanism for the effective use of ICTs in adult and university education.

Principles of Adult Learning: Toward a New Andragogy

Learning is a complex activity. Learning something new and using it is by no means straightforward, and the complexity of the process can only be grasped by resorting to such traditions as cybernetics, experimentalism and pragmatism. Cybernetics has provided a series of tools for understanding cognitive and information processes (Varela, Thompson, & Rosch, 1993; Von Forrester, 1984). Experimentalism and pragmatism have emphasized reflection and activity. According to Horyp (2006), Dewey regarded reflective thought as an active, persistent and careful consideration of any beliefs or supposed forms of knowledge in the light of the grounds on which they were based and the consequences that they would have. Dewey viewed the process of learning as being similar to the process of scientific knowledge and discovery. Reflection, then, is conceived as the outcome of three main steps: separation, initiation and return. Separation involves inhibiting action, habits and routines first, and then postponing immediate action by controlling impulses, a process that is somewhat similar to un-learning and doubting. Initiation has two sub-steps: learners must first try to define what is wrong, and then formulate an idea to guide the action they take (that's to say, a kind of working hypothesis). Return also involves two sub-activities: firstly, learners must understand what ideas mean in relation to each other (in other words, they test their working hypothesis on their thought process mainly by using memory), and secondly, they must put the idea into action, and observe the feedback. In sum, pragmatism-inspired perspectives regard learning as being similar to discovering scientific knowledge: they aim to ground learning on a firm basis of evidence and rationality, a view that is not far from the cybernetics approach.

Adult learning has specific aspects and features that differentiate it from other types of learning. Knowles (1980) pointed out that adults are autonomous and self-directed individuals, and, therefore, accustomed to participating in equal and mutually respectful adult relationships. They also have life experiences, which are their main source of knowledge. They are goal-oriented, as they know clear objectives are important for saving resources and time, and they are also oriented by relevance and practical application. Adult experience is like a repository of information, consisting of direct experimentation and realities. Although most of these features can be seen as positive assets for learning, this may not to be the case in all respects. Adults' established routines and habits can sometimes hinder reflection. Adults can have difficulty accepting that they lack understanding as they think they have sound knowledge based on life and experience. One of the most critical aspects of adults as learners is motivation. Many adults, already established and safe in family and social routines, need stimulation and incentives.

From the above and the recent literature on learning, adult learning and andragogy (Antonocopoulou, Jarvis, Anderson, Elkjaer, & Hoyrup, 2006; Boud, 2000; Boud, Keogh, & Walker, 1985; Merriam & Cafarella, 1999; Yang, 2003), it is deemed necessary to take a holistic and comprehensive approach to learning in higher education. This holistic process involves three steps: reflection, re-conceptualization and action. First, the initial reflection obliges students to separate themselves from their experiences, and existing knowledge. Second, interactive re-conceptualization enables students to embody and apprehend the new knowledge so that they can overcome the doubts and uncertainties that have arisen in the first step. Third, action allows students to experience how the new knowledge is used or can be used. In fact, in higher education there has been growing interest in applying new knowledge so that it can be seen how it works in reality. To enact all these steps, learners need to undergo a deep and substantial process of questioning, doubting, listening, communicating, interacting and, finally, doing.

Each of these three steps has something to do with the tacit learning process. In particular, two aspects can be highlighted. The first is the importance of the tacit dimension in learning. Tacit learning, as opposed to explicit and codified learning, is an uncertain and undetermined process of learning sophisticated know-how. It can also refer to practical intelligence (Sternberg & Wagner, 1986). After analyzing Wittengstein's experiences of teaching philosophy, Burbules points out: "Tacit knowledge is often related to practical intelligence, 'know-how,' common sense, 'street smarts,' or what Bourdieu calls *habitus*—the experientially grounded capacities that allow us to navigate the choices and activities of everyday life" (Burbules, 2008, p. 669). The second aspect is the importance of organizing inputs and mechanisms to stimulate the learning process, especially in the case of the tacit dimension. After reflecting on some practical and exemplary instances of tacit knowledge, such as how groupware can help to make tacit knowledge more explicit, Durrance (1998) suggests four principles for cultivating the sharing of tacit knowledge among people in an organization: a) watch: observe what your people do and how they do it; b) create an environment of trust, respect, and commitment, beginning with yourself; c) let people learn by doing; and d) in any training exercise, allow time for reflection and interpersonal exchange.

In sum, it has been argued that adult learning in our changing societies is a complex process, which has an important tacit dimension. This process involves developing an updated andragogy, and experimenting with new teaching roles and techniques. In other words, a systematic reflection on tacit teaching is needed. This reflection will be made in the next section.

Traditional Pedagogical Teaching: Toward New Teaching Roles

Traditional pedagogy has long focused on face-to-face guided teaching activities which transmit both information and knowledge. The teaching capacities required for face-to-face communication (both verbal and non-verbal) have been thoroughly discussed. In universities there is a wide range of teaching techniques and options, most of which depend on the instructional form of education (face–to-face, correspondence or distance): for example, seminars (small group teaching), tutorials, research seminars, exercise classes or courses, workshops (classroom-based practical classes), problem-solving sessions, laboratory teaching, demonstrations, placement (internship/traineeship), work-based practice, fieldwork, online/distance or e-learning (which may be paper based or ICT based). University teachers need to adopt all these techniques in their classes, taking into account the subject they are teaching, the age of the students and the size of the group. They should also bear in mind that in democratic societies, adults are increasingly critical and willing to participate actively in learning activities.

Teaching is also better conceived as a process now. Reyes and Zarama (1998) propose a model for learning and teaching that consists of a context with four pre-conditions, and a four-step teaching process. The pre-conditions of the context are: a) the declaration of ignorance (we must accept naturally that we do not know something and that we want to learn it), b) the acceptance of possible cognitive blindness (we must accept that we do not know what we do not know, which brings constructive skepticism and doubt), c) a declaration of trust and authority in the status of the teacher, and d) research into the factors that might hinder learning, so that any self-constraints can be identified, and potentialities and capacities can be exploited. The stages for learning include: a) a break, b) knowing: drawing a distinction by the tools of reflection and language, c) understanding: grounding and embedding the distinction by putting in contexts and historical evolution, and d) learning: embodying the distinction, by practicing and incorporating it. The authority of teachers in our current societies is controversial because it is not taken for granted but needs to be earned.

Therefore, current social, cultural and political changes are challenging the traditional pedagogical principles of teaching adults. In the emerging information and consumption society, adults have increasing access to experience, information and relational networking, which can be a useful tool for learning. Information-oriented technologies stimulate new roles for teachers, such as facilitators, tutors, supervisors, collaborators, guides, etc. They are adopting a role that is more that of assistant and guide, while maintaining the role of knowledge-related authority. Many interesting contributions have been made to the advancement of pedagogy in general (Cochran-Smith, Feiman-Nemser, & McIntyre, 2008), and adult teaching in particular (Apps, 1988; Biggs, 2003; Hillier, 2005; Pratt, 1998; Rogers, 2002). However, the tacit dimension in teaching is still underdeveloped. As Burbules (2008) states,"Tacit teaching refers to the many forms of informal instruction—some intentional, some unintentional, and some difficult to categorize simply as one or the other—by which skills, capacities, and dispositions are passed along within a domain of practice" (p. 668).

In sum, to follow the steps of the learning process described above, processes and mechanisms of information and communication are very important, and it is here that the benefits of ICTs are a clear challenge to traditional pedagogy. In higher education, however, they are limited by their inability to provide the tacit dimension of teaching, which emerges after many face-to-face teaching and communicative situations. Teaching adults in our society means that teachers must adopt the new roles of facilitators, guides, supervisors, tutors, and so forth. This should be kept in mind if ICTs are to be effectively used for appropriate educational purposes.

The Challenge of Integrating ICTs with Tacit Teaching to Adults

The use of technology for educational purposes is not linear: it depends on the social structures in which it is used by individuals and groups (Gorard & Selwyn, 1999). Laurillard (1993) and Pelgrum and Anderson (1999) advocated that technology was a potential means of improving university teaching. Tait and Mills (1999) argue that ICTs and other technologies are important mechanisms through which conventional and distance education can converge. ICTs have been used for educational purposes (Goodman, 2002), and especially for adult and university education, only recently but it is a growing field (Howard, Schenk, & Discenza, 2003; Qvotrup, 2006; Sangrá

& González-Sanmmaned, 2004a, 2004b). Other authors, such as Watson (2001), who focus mainly on primary school education, remain skeptical about the pedagogical potential of ICTs.

The effective use of ICTs for teaching and learning purposes has already been subject to thorough debate. By the end of the 1990s, Katz (1999) had summarized many of the important issues involving ICTs and the challenge they presented to higher education. Higher-education institutions, most of which are public, tend to change slowly in comparison with private organizations. It is necessary to take into account the role that ICT-based codified knowledge plays in the new emerging learning and teaching spaces and processes in higher and adult education. ICTs in adult/higher education have two main functions: a) they are a means by which information can be delivered both before and after face-to-face teaching activity; and b) they make communication possible at various levels (teacher with all students, among students, and teacher with one student). However, how effective can ICTs be for the actual purpose of adult learning in higher education? This is a difficult question. Lundberg, Castillo, and Dahmani (2008), after reviewing a wide range of literature, point out that there is very little to support to the idea that online students perform better than face-to-face students. They also point out that there is considerable disparity in the results of the studies, partly because different methodologies make it difficult for them to be compared.

A particularly important issue is which ICTs are the most appropriate for effective learning and how they should be used for maximum effect. One debate has focused on the advantages of private versus open software resources. The Open Educational Resources (OER) initiatives are a relatively new phenomenon in tertiary education. The open sharing of educational resources means that knowledge is made freely available on non-commercial terms, sometimes in the framework of users and doers communities. In such communities the impact of innovation is greater when it is shared: users freely reveal their knowledge and thus work cooperatively. The financial sustainability of OER initiatives is a key issue. Many initiatives are sponsored by private foundations, public funding or paid for by the institutions themselves. In general, the social value of knowledge and information tools increases to the extent that they can be shared with and used by others. Technically, there are two main software products for secondary and tertiary education: Moodle and Sakai. Both are open software and well tested and developed instruments. The differences between the two have more to do with the logic behind how they function and how they can be improved. It seems that Sakai is more robust technically, as it incorporates several safety and technical criteria of computer science. Moodle, on the contrary, is more pedagogical, as it is more user friendly, and therefore allows more user-based experimentation. In fact, Moodle is most used in secondary education. In many languages, Moodle has user communities that meet regularly and encourage ongoing communication. This system of user communities and communication stimulate interaction between multiple users who strive for intensive experimentation and improvement.

In sum, ICTs have the potential to transform learning and teaching processes, and to provide novel ways of educating and training in conjunction with more traditional teaching. Effective use of ICTs can enable teachers to develop new teaching techniques such as learner-centered guidance, group work and inquiry projects which can result in good skills and competencies. Likewise, interactive forms of e-learning can lead to reflective, deeper and participative learning, learning-by doing, inquiry learning, problem solving and creativity. ICTs provide the means to support personalization, where learners are also regarded as being knowledge builders and creators. Thus, innovative pedagogical and didactic approaches are needed to provide the changing skills and competencies necessary for employment, self-development and participation in a knowledge-based, digital society.

To conclude this section it should be pointed out that ICTs can be very important tools for improving teaching and learning, although it should be borne in mind that they can by no means cover all the depth and complexity of teaching and learning, especially their tacit dimension. Higher education institutions are experimenting with the use of ICTs, and at the same time responding to the challenge of integrating them effectively and discovering the importance of the tacit dimension of learning and teaching.

THE MAIN FOCUS OF THE ARTICLE

This major section will first contextualize the developments of higher education at the European level. Subsequently, it will present the background to Spain's universities and their use of ICTs. Finally, it will analyze how the two Universities selected (URV and UOC) have used and experimented with ICTs, and how they have solved the challenge of the tacit dimension.

European Union: Bologna Process and Harmonizing Competencies

Let us take a look at what has happened in the European Union (EU). The Bologna Process refers to the process of harmonizing higher education, and is to be fully applied in 2010. One of the main issues in this process has been the problem of competencies. It was clear that national scientific and academic traditions were important, and that the convergence process had to take place on a more general and abstract level. Therefore, it was decided that the competencies—the combinations of knowledge and skills—of each degree and subject should be harmonized.

In this integration process, the "Tuning project" (Tuning Educational Structures in Europe) involved one of the leading networks of practitioners and experts who aimed to find common definitions and understandings of learning and competencies. Learning outcomes are statements of what a learner is expected to know, understand and/or be able to demonstrate after the completion of learning. They can refer to a single course unit or a module within a period of study (for example, a first or a second cycle). Learning outcomes specify the requirements students need to satisfy to earn credit. Competencies represent a dynamic combination of knowledge, understanding, skills and abilities. They are developed over various course units and assessed at different stages. The Tuning project distinguishes three types of generic competences: a) instrumental competences: cognitive, methodological, technological and linguistic abilities; b) interpersonal competencies: individual abilities such as social skills (social interaction and co-operation); c) systemic competencies: abilities and skills concerning whole systems (combination of understanding, sensibility and knowledge for which instrumental and interpersonal competencies need to be acquired previously). The Tuning project made a distinction between generic competencies (transferable skills) and specific subject-related competencies, although it is accepted that the key outcomes of university programs are subject-related competences. Finally, three main competencies were identified: knowing and understanding (knowledge skills), knowing how to be (social and interactive skills) and knowing how to act (practical and applied skills). For the discussion about university competences in Spain see Hernández-Pina, Martínez-Clares, Fonseca-Rosario, and Rubio-Espín (2005). The true importance of all this discussion lies in the implications that a competence-based approach has for teaching and learning: which modes of teaching and which learning activities might best foster competencies in terms of knowledge, understanding and skills, and how do we assess these competences? This discussion of competences that centers on the process of harmonizing university education appeals directly for attention to be paid to the tacit dimension of learning, and to the need for a new andragogy of competences.

In Europe, ICTs in higher education are quite widespread. The European Commission's report (2008) shows that practically all universities had Web sites and 9 out of 10 had intranets. By 2004, three out of four EU universities were experiencing high or very high rates of increase in the use of ICT for teaching. By 2005, individual modules, and in some cases whole programs, were being offered online, with a slow shift to more collaborative, problem-based and project-based learning methods. This has changed the role of both students and teachers. One question, however, must be asked: how are ICTs used for adult learning in Europe? The European Commission's report (2008) provides evidence that one out of eight adults outside formal education uses the Internet for formal learning activities, such as research and downloading learning content. Online availability certainly meets the needs of some learners who require formal training, and nearly half of the adult learners consider it a necessary condition. What is more, results seem to be encouraging, because two out of three users are satisfied and five out of six say they would take online courses again. This may reflect the user-focus of ICT-based adult education, which allows individuals to choose appropriate learning paths. Interactive forms of e-learning can lead to more reflective, "deeper" learning and more empowered discussion, better suited to and more motivating for adult learners. E-learning may offer ways of attracting social groups that do not traditionally engage in formal training, such as the 80 million low-skilled workers. Nevertheless, two-thirds of the participants see adult learning as the chance to meet people with similar interests. Home-based e-learning does not satisfy this social need. Moreover, more than half the participants prefer guided learning to self-direction. In sum, there is still considerable ambivalence surrounding e-learning.

ICTs in University Education in Spain

Historically Spain's educational system has been underdeveloped. In the second half of the twentieth century, however, it underwent a rapid and unbalanced growth and in the last two decades it has been modernized and balance has been restored. In university education in Spain, ICT-based technologies have been used for only a short time because Spain embarked rather late on the development of the information society. The European Commission's report (2008) indicates a low level in the use of ICTs for educational and learning purposes. For example, the average percentage of households with access to Internet in 2006 in EU-15 was 54% and in EU-25 51%, whereas in Spain it was only 39%. In EU-25 there were 12.1 computers per 100 pupils in 2006 in the whole of compulsory education (including upper-secondary and vocational levels), whereas in Spain there were 9.5 (the difference was larger in vocational levels: 16.8 in EU-25 and 11 in Spain). Finally, in EU-25 41% of Internet users between 17 and 74 years old used Internet for learning purposes whereas in Spain this figure was 37%. For the population of 16 and 17 year olds, the figures were 25% and 20%, respectively. In university education the picture is rather diverse. Because of complex organizational obstacles and constraints in collective decision-making, large universities tend to work slowly in incorporating ICTs. Medium- and small-sized universities, on the other hand, have been more proactive in adopting ICTs, sometimes through experiments in departments and faculties, which are subsequently extended throughout the university. There are two main e-learning universities: the UNED at the national level and the UOC in the large region of Catalonia.

At the national level, the UNED (National University of Distance Education) was created in 1972. By 2007, the number of students enrolling every year in UNED had reached about 180,000.

It has nine faculties and two graduate technical schools. It offers 33 official degrees, and more than 50 programs in continuing education. It has a teaching staff of about 1,400 university teachers, and close to 7,000 tutors. It has about 60 associated centers, 80 extension centers, and a number of supporting classrooms throughout Spain. Internationally, it has supportive centers in 11 countries, attending more than 2,100 students. Its main objective has been to offer professional opportunities and university education to those who did not have the opportunity in their time (women, for example). In fact, in 1982 UNED elected the first female university dean in Spain. In the 1990s, UNED began to incorporate technologies such as TV, radio, ICTs and multimedia. UNED, then, integrates different technologies and cannot be regarded as a fully Internet-based e-learning university.

At the regional level, the Open University of Catalonia (Universitat Oberta de Catalunya - UOC) is a younger university, created in 1995, with full commitment to ICTs. By 2005 it had over 20,000 students and offered 16 official degrees. Now, in 2009, the UOC is offering more than 250 continuing education courses. The UOC does not offer degrees in technical and experimental sciences, as it is almost impossible to organize the practical dimension in labs and similar infrastructures on line. So, the UOC focuses on human, management, social, law and related sciences, and its format is flexible enough to capture newly emerging niches in the educational and professional market, especially in second and master degrees, and in continuing education. In the region of Catalonia, information society indicators have evolved more rapidly than in the other regions of Spain, because of its advanced industrial and socio-economic structure. In 2008, these indicators were similar to the current EU-25 average, and were particularly high as far as connection to Internet was concerned.

Comparing How Two Universities Cope with the Tacit Dimension in Their Use of ICTs

This section compares the use of ICTs in two Spanish universities: the UOC, a new e-learning-oriented higher education institution; and the URV, a young, conventional university that has experimented with the use of ICTs for teaching purposes.

URV

The URV is a young university, created in the mid-1990s, and it has been proactive in the introduction of ICTs. The use of ICTs for teaching in the URV has undergone a rapid evolution. The Unit for educational resources was created in 2001 for two main reasons. In the pedagogical field, its goal was to help teachers in teaching innovation projects. In the technological field, its goal was to help teachers use the new technologies. Initially, this mainly involved developing specific Web pages for courses, and instructing the teaching staff in basic ICTs, such as e-mail and other software programs. In 2002, the Unit bought some private educational software, the Java Learning Environment (JLE), and began to collaborate with a handful of teachers keen on using ICTs in their teaching. Despite the general interest in using JLE, it had two problems that limited its use. Technically, its interface was rather difficult even for advanced ICT-users. This problem was not eased with a new product, Edustance. Generally speaking, JLE and Edustance were private products so any further development and improvement depended on the company's interest in working with the University. In the academic year 2004-2005, and although Edustance was still the official ICT resource, the Unit decided to experiment with the Moodle program. Moodle, explained above, is a course management system, a free open source software package designed to help educators create online learning communities. Moodle was initially developed by a computer scientist in Australia. Its pedagogical principles are based on constructivist learning and, in this sense, electronic communication between teacher and students and between students is one of the main objectives of the software. The trial year in the URV included a visit to a university in Spain (University of Las Palmas in the Canary Islands) that had already adopted Moodle, and several meetings and discussions, especially with one of the URV's engineering departments that had already used Moodle. The fact that several engineering departments were quick to promote the use of Moodle in their teaching is an indicator of their long pedagogical experience, dating back to the new teaching and andragogical model adopted in the mid-1990s as can be seen below.

In the academic year 2005-2006 Moodle was thus set up officially in the URV and the Unit began a process of diffusion and adaptation of Moodle to the needs and practices of the URV. By the academic year 2008-2009, about 60% of teachers and about 70% of students regularly used Moodle, showing that it has been well accepted and largely adopted. The URV is one of the first three universities in Spain to adopt Moodle, together with the previously cited University of Las Palmas in the Canary Islands and Jaume I University in Castellón. The three Universities are medium-sized with between 10,000 and 15,000 students, which may explain why Moodle was so quickly adopted and implemented. Technicians in the Unit have seen how useful Moodle user communities are for sorting out problems and suggesting improvements. The URV Unit has already identified three challenges for the near future. First, Moodle must be developed and improved, and teachers encouraged to put it to greater use. Second, it must be adapted to the European Higher Educational Area (EEES), which, through the Bologna Process of harmonization of higher education, also involves significant changes in methodology and andragogy. Two examples of this are: a) all course programs now need to be set up in a new software tool, Docnet, the aim of which is to harmonize competences; b) individual tutorials and supervision are central to this European Union process, as is planning courses according to the system of credits (ECTS). Third, the URV needs to integrate new ICT products for video-conference activities and software to identify copying practices by students. The Unit for educational resources is aware that one of the most effective ways of using ICTs in higher education is as information and knowledge depositories, and for teacher-student instructional communication. This use would make high-value time available for more substantial face-to-face teaching and learning activities, thus catering for the tacit dimension of learning. Experimentation with the tacit dimension in the URV can be observed in the cases of the School of Chemical Engineering and the Faculty of Law.

The leading case of combining ICTs and face-to-face interactive teaching and learning can be found in the School of Chemical Engineering (ETSEQ). As stated above, the ETSEQ departments were among the first to use and implement Moodle in their teaching activities. Its current andragogy of chemical engineering was inspired by the methodology of the Harvard School (USA), which was based on practical application of knowledge through teamwork and PBL (problem-based-learning). This methodology was adopted by the ETSEQ in the mid 1990s. After more than 10 years, and despite initial complaints by students because of its demanding nature, this methodology has increasingly been evaluated in positive terms by both students and firms. The American Institute of Chemical Engineers (AICHE), in Ziemlewski (2009), appraised the pedagogical development of URV- ETSEQ in its February bulletin. AICHE is the world's leading organization for chemical engineering professionals, with more than 40,000 members from 93 countries. In this bulletin, URV teachers point out that "Universities have to teach science as well as art, figuring out ways to engage students, and teaching them how to use principles not just apply a procedure to reach a solution" (p. 6). As one of the URV teachers interviewed stated, "In addition to technical knowledge and management competence, chemical engineers need to possess social skills. These skills need to include teamwork, cooperation, creativity, innovation, communication, cultural diversity, leadership, decision-making and organizational development" (p. 6). More interestingly, most of this is achieved through team-based problem-based learning and projects. As the teacher said, "Student teams grow from leader-directed teams in the first academic year to self-directed or empowered teams in the fifth year. Fourth-year students play a key role by acting as facilitative leaders of the first-year and second-year project teams" (p. 8). Students are encouraged to become client-oriented, and to adjust their capacities and skills toward clients' needs. The concept of "integrated project" is important, as it involves both project-based learning and cooperative learning, as a stimulus to learn how to learn, integrating and dispersing knowledge, and developing social skills. The open-ended questions and lack of information force students to understand the principles of different unit operations, to be active in determining the information that is needed to solve a problem and to seek it out. The URV teacher concluded, "Students remember 20% of what we explain, 50% of what they do in the lab, and 100% of the soft skills" (p. 9). Soft skills include know-how and tacit capacities, acquired in face-to-face interaction between teachers and students, and between students.

The Faculty of Law, which also includes several social sciences, has experimented more modestly with ICTs and Moodle. In 2004, a group for pedagogical innovation (Grupo de Innovación Docente - GID) was formally set up to integrate a variety of individual initiatives, one of the aims of which was to apply ICTs to teaching. Since the early 2000s, faculty staff had been investigating various aspects of ICTs (Barrat-Esteve et al., 2007; Giménez-Costa, & González-Bondia, 2007). Considering the specificities of the discipline and its particular tacit dimension, these examples in the Law Sciences are very interesting. Law education has traditionally distinguished three main bodies of knowledge—doctrine, legislation and jurisprudence—each of which has its own rationale of documentation and information. Usually, managing all this information and its sources has been an important part of the teaching of many law subjects. In this respect, several teachers have attempted to use ICTs as repositories and for other information-oriented purposes, such as the creation of wikis, etc., thus making time available to teach the more complex nuances between the three bodies of knowledge. The results have been very interesting. The use of ICTs has meant that information is provided in a more effective way, thus saving time for other more substantial teaching and learning activities. Likewise, teachers have been made more aware of the importance of face-to-face communication for providing instruments and tools to master the three legal rationales in each subject. In sum, the tacit dimension of the teaching and learning of the rationales of law is transmitted best by face-to-face communicative interaction in the classroom. The tacit dimension is gradually coming to the fore, and there is an increasing awareness that it should be made more explicit, as it has been in the new degrees that are to come into effect in autumn 2009.

Several conclusions can be drawn from the URV case. First, the URV has rapidly and substantially incorporated ICTs, and the choice of Moodle seems to have been an effective strategy, especially since it has allowed on-going experimentation and improvement through interactive user communities both inside and outside the URV. Second, university subjects organize teaching and learning in very different ways, so the use of ICTs needs to be adapted to the subject specificities. Third, it was only after a process of experimentation that URV teachers and ICT managers managed to develop appropriate ways of using ICTs and discover the importance of the tacit dimension of learning and teaching, with the subsequent need to incorporate this tacit dimension into teaching practices through more explicit terms.

UOC

As an innovative university, UOC tries to offer a new way of experiencing education (Sangrá, 2002). Building on an intensive use of ICTs, UOC has tried to break through the barriers of space and time by offering an educational model of distance education based on the use of the Internet. From the start, UOC was designed to be an example of a new generation of distance education providers capable of creating cooperative interaction not only between students and professors, students and learning materials, but also among students themselves. To support this goal, the UOC grounds its model on flexibility, co-operation, personalization and interactivity. The UOC has opened out to the world by maintaining contacts with the principal international knowledge networks. Its new strategy is to make students the centre of a completely personalized educational process during which they receive guidance from an accredited teaching team. As a public university in Europe, the UOC has also been involved in changing and organizing competence-based university programs. This has been a critical challenge, since the more social and interactive skills (particularly know how to be and know how to act) seem to be especially difficult to acquire in e-learning processes.

One of the main problems faced by distance universities, and explicitly recognized by the UOC, is the high rate of drop-out among students, mainly because of the difficulties of following a distance teaching system and of maintaining a high level of self-discipline. The high drop-out rate may also be due to a low level of tacit teaching, by which a teacher can better guide a student and learner toward the meaning and purpose of the knowledge taught. In order to solve these problems, the UOC has reorganized the tasks and roles of the various members of the teaching staff. There are a variety of teacher profiles for each course: consultants, supervisors, teachers and teachers in charge. They all play their own role in helping students to complete the course, and in helping them operate within the e-learning system. Recently, two supervisory roles have been experimented with: the initial and follow-up supervisors or tutors. The initial steps have been identified as one of the most critical points in e-learning training. The initial tutor, then, is responsible for assisting students to adapt to the e-learning system. To do so, the tutor must establish some sort of personal relationship with the students, and then help them to design a learning and teaching profile that is compatible with their private and professional life. After completing the initial stage, the follow-up tutor is responsible for assisting students during the course. Students have the right to one face-to-face meeting with each of the two tutors. The problem of the high drop-out suggests that the UOC needs to personalize and foster more proximate and interactive communication with new students. In other words, teachers, tutors and students should have a more face-to-face interactive relation, so that different forms of tacit teaching and learning can be practiced.

To conclude, the UOC was born as an e-learning university, so one of its main goals and one of the main driving forces behind its activity is to make effective use of ICTs. After about 10 years of experience, however, it has opted to improve the personal relations with students through personalized tutors and, in particular, through initial tutors who help students prepare for the e-learning system. This is an example of how face-to-face interaction is needed in communication, teaching and learning, and indirectly to encourage tacit teaching and learning activities.

To sum up, the following conclusions can be drawn about the use of ICTs at the URV and the UOC. First, there is a gradual trend toward convergence in the use of ICTs in the two types of university, the conventional URV and the e-learning UOC. Second, the individual subjects and disciplines affect how ICTs are used: the UOC does not offer some subjects because of clear technological and infrastructure limitations, and at the URV ICTs are being used in different ways in engineering and law studies. Third, in both the universities analyzed, ICTs are used mainly to deliver information and codified knowledge, whereas personal and group interaction has been given the important role of providing more substantial learning, teaching and personal relations, thus ensuring the tacit dimension of the process.

FUTURE RESEARCH DIRECTIONS

In line with the above arguments, three areas are suggested for future research. First, as far as new andragogical principles are concerned, research should be made into how adults' life experiences can be effectively used as a base for the acquisition of different kinds of knowledge (codified, tacit, communicative), and the tacit dimension of learning. Second, if ICTs are to be used effectively to teach adults, teachers need to adopt new teaching roles (e.g., facilitators, guides, supervisors, etc.). Research should also be carried out on how information and communication is managed and delivered, and how these new teaching roles can be combined with the traditional role of knowledge provider. Third, another field for future research is how the effective use of ICTs depends on subjects and disciplines, because the mastery of the essential knowledge of each discipline is tacit rather than explicit, undetermined not planned.

CONCLUSION

Generally, the article has shown the potential and the limitations of using ICTs in adult teaching. On the basis of an analysis of two young universities in Spain, a conventional public University (URV) and an e-learning distance University (UOC), it has been argued that face-to-face interaction and communication is still a very important dimension for adult learning, particularly for the tacit dimension of learning and teaching. The use of ICTs for adult education is in its first stages of development. However as more adult and university educators are experimenting with ICTs, more and more positive complementarities are being found and they are gradually becoming integrated into teaching processes.

The following specific conclusions have been drawn. First, the article has argued that the current technological changes pose important challenges to adult learning principles. In this respect, good management of information and codified knowledge by appropriate ICTs can improve the learning abilities of adults in two main ways: a) the time saved can be used for face-to-face interaction in which adults can show their full capacity for learning; and b) input can be provided to help them reflect upon their life experiences. Second, the article has highlighted various factors that should be taken into account if ICTs are to be strategically used for adult learning (for example, university subjects, distinctions between codified knowledge and tacit knowledge, open versus private educational software). Beyond the general distinction between technical and non-technical sciences, greater efforts should be made to adapt ICTs to specific subjects and disciplines. Third, the increasing use of ICTs by universities has had the positive side-effect of helping to differentiate between information and knowledge. In this respect, it has facilitated the process of making the tacit dimensions of learning and teaching more evident, and thus revealed the need to take the tacit dimension into account in the organization of adult teaching and learning.

REFERENCES

Antonocopoulou, E., Jarvis, P., Andersen, V., Elkjaer, B., & Hoyrup, S. (Eds.). *(2006).* Learning, working and living. *London: Palgrave Macmillan.*

Apps, J. W. *(1988).* Higher education in a learning society. Meeting new demands for education and training. *San Francisco: Jossey-Bass.*

Barrat-Esteve, J., Franquet-Sugrañes, T., Giménez-Costa, A., González-Bondia, A., Jaria i Manzano, J., Marquès i Banqué, M., et al. (2007). El diseño de una comunidad virtual como estrategia de adaptación del profesorado a los postulados docentes del EEES [The design of a virtual community as strategy to adopt teachers to the objectives of the European Higher Educational Space]. In D. García-San José (Ed.), *Innovación docente y calidad en la enseñanza de ciencias jurídicas en el espacio europeo de educación superior [Pedagogy innovation and quality of Law Science teaching in the European Higher Educational Space]* (pp. 171-200). Murcia, Spain: Ediciones Laborum.

Barry, J. H. (1999). Lifelong learning in late modernity: The challenges to society, organizations, and individuals. *Adult Education Quarterly, 49*(2), 79–90. doi:10.1177/074171369904900201

Biggs, J. B. (2003). *Teaching for quality learning at university: what the student does* (2nd ed.). Buckingham, UK: Society for Research into Higher Education.

Boud, D. (2000). Sustainable assessment: rethinking assessment for the learning society. *Studies in Continuing Education, 22*(2), 151–167. doi:10.1080/713695728

Boud, D., Keogh, R., & Walker, D. (Eds.). (1985). *Reflection: Turning experience into learning.* London: Kogan Page.

Bourdieu, P. (1977). *Outline of a theory of practice.* New York: Cambridge University Press.

Burbules, N. C. (2008). Tacit teaching. *Educational Philosophy and Theory, 40*(5), 666–677. doi:10.1111/j.1469-5812.2008.00453.x

Castells, M. (1997). *The rise of the network society.* London: Routledge.

Cochran-Smith, P. M., Feiman-Nemser, S., & McIntyre, D. J. (Eds.). (2008). *Handbook of research on teacher education: Enduring questions in changing contexts.* London: Routledge.

Coffield, F. (2000). *Differing visions of a learning society. Research findings Volume 1.* London: The Policy Press.

Dewey, J. (1986). How we think: A restatement of the relation of reflective thinking to the educative process. In J. A. Boydston (Ed.), *The latter works* (pp. 105-325). Carbondale, IL: Southern Illinois University Press. (Original work published 1933)

Durrance, B. (1998). Some explicit thoughts on tacit learning. *Training & Development, 52*(12), 24–29.

European Commission. (2008). *The use of ICT to support innovation and lifelong learning for all - a report on progress.* Brussels, Belgium: Commission of the European Communities.

Fischer, G. (2001). Lifelong learning and its support with new media. In N. J. Smelser & P. B. Baltes (Eds.), *International encyclopedia of social and behavioral sciences* (pp. 8836-8840). New York: Elsevier.

Giménez-Costa, A., & González-Bondia, A. (2007). Design of a wiki-based collaborative working strategy within the context of legal sciences. *European Journal of Legal Education, 4*(1), 105–114.

Goodman, P. S. (2002). *Technology enhanced learning: Opportunities for change.* Mahwah, NJ: Lawrence Erlbaum Associates.

Gorard, S., & Selwyn, N. (1999). Switching on the learning society? Questioning the role of technology in widening participation in lifelong learning. *Journal of Education Policy*, *14*(5), 523–534. doi:10.1080/026809399286198

Hernández-Pina, F., Martínez-Clares, P., Fonseca-Rosario, P., & Rubio-Espín, M. (2005). *Aprendizaje, competencias y rendimiento en educación superior* [*Learning, competences and performance in higher education*]. Madrid, Spain: La Muralla.

Hillier, Y. *(2005).* Reflective teaching in further and adult education *(2nd ed.). London: Continuum.*

Horyp, S. (2006). Reflection in learning at work. In E. Antonocopoulou, P. Jarvis, V. Andersen, B. Elkjaer, & S. Hoyrup (Eds.), *Learning, working and living* (pp. 85-100). London: Palgrave Macmillan.

Howard, C., Schenk, K., & Discenza, R. (2003). *Distance Learning and university effectiveness: Changing educational paradigms for online learning.* Hershey, PA: IGI Global.

Jarvis, P. (2000). Globalisation, the learning society and comparative education. *Comparative Education*, *36*(23), 343–355. doi:10.1080/713656613

Jarvis, P., & Parker, S. (Eds.). (2005). *Human learning: A holistic approach.* London: Routledge.

Katz, R. N. (Ed.). (1999). *Dancing with the devil: Information technology and the new competition in higher education.* San Francisco: Jossey-Bass Higher and Adult Education Series.

Knowles, M. S. (1980). *The modern practice of adult education: From pedagogy to andragogy* (2nd ed.). New York: Cambridge Books.

Laurillard, P. D. *(1993).* Rethinking university teaching. A framework for the effective use of educational technology. *London: Routledge.*

Lundberg, J., Castillo, D., & Dahmani, M. (2008). Do online students perform better than face-to-face students? Reflections and a short review of some empirical findings. *Revista de Universidad y Sociedad del Conocimiento, 1*(5). Retrieved May 27, 2009, from http://www.uoc.edu/rusc/5/1/dt/eng/lundberg_castillo_dahmani.pdf

MacKenzie, D., & Wacjman, J. (Eds.). (1985). *The social shaping of technology.* London: Open University Press.

Merriam, S. B., & Cafarella, R. S. (1999). *Learning in adulthood: A comprehensive guide* (2nd ed.). San Francisco: Jossey-Bass.

OECD. (2005). *E-learning in tertiary education. Where do we stand?* Paris: Author.

Pelgrum, W. J., & Anderson, R. E. (Eds.). (1999). *ICT and the emerging paradigm for lifelong learning.* Amsterdam, The Netherlands: IEA.

Pratt, D. D. (1998). *Five perspectives on teaching in adult and higher education.* Melbourne, FL: Krieger Publishing.

Qvotrup, L. (2006). *Knowledge, education and learning. E-learning in the knowledge society.* Frederiksberg, Denmark: Samfudsliteratur Roskilde Universitets Forlag.

Reyes, A., & Zarama, A. (1998). The process of embodying distinctions. A re-construction of the process of learning. *Cybernetics & Human Knowing*, *5*(3), 19–33.

Rogers, A. (2002). *Teaching adults* (3rd ed.). London: Open University Press.

Sangrá, A. (2002). A new learning model for the information and knowledge society: The case of the Universitat Oberta de Catalunya (UOC). *The International Review of Research in Open and Distance Learning, 2(2).* Retrieved March 31, 2009, from http://www.irrodl.org/index.php/irrodl/article/view/55/114

Sangrá, A., & González-Sanmamed, M. (Eds.). (2004a). *La transformación de las universidades a través de las TIC: discursos y prácticas* [*University changes through ICTs: discourses and practices*]. Barcelona, Spain: UOC.

Sangrá, A., & González-Sanmamed, M. (2004b). El profesorado universitario y las TIC: Redefinir roles y competencias [University teachers and the ICTs: Redefining roles and competences]. In A. Sangrá & M. González-Sanmamed (Eds.), *La transformación de las universidades a través de las TIC: Discursos y practices* [*University changes through ICTs: Discourses and practices*] (pp. 79-80). Barcelona: UOC.

Schatzki, T. R., Knorr-Cetina, K., & Von Savigny, E. (Eds.). (2001). *The practice turn in contemporary theory.* London: Routledge.

Schön, D. A. (1983). *The reflective practitioner. How professionals think in action.* New York: Basic Books.

Schön, D. A. (1987). *Educating the reflective practitioner. Toward a new design for teaching and learning of professions.* San Francisco: Jossey-Bass.

Searle, J. (1995). *The construction of social reality.* New York: Penguin Books.

Stehr, N. (1994). *Knowledge societies. The Transformation of labor, property and knowledge in contemporary society.* London: Sage

Sternberg, R. J., & Horvath, J. (Eds.). (1999). *Tacit knowledge in professional practice: Researcher and practitioner perspectives.* Mahwah, NJ: Erlbaum.

Sternberg, R. J., & Wagner, R. K. (Eds.). (1986). *Practical intelligence.* Cambridge, UK: Cambridge University Press

Tait, A., & Mills, R. (1999). *The convergence between conventional and distance education.* London: Routledge.

Varela, F., Thompson, E., & Rosch, E. (Eds.). (1993). *The embodied mind.* Cambridge, MA: MIT Press.

Von Forrester, H. (1984). *Observing systems.* Salinas, CA: Intersystems Publications.

Watson, D. (2001). Pedagogy before technology: Re-thinking the relationship between ICT and teaching. *Education and Information Technologies, 6*(4), 266.

Webster, F. (1995). *Theories of the information society.* London: Routledge.

World Bank. (2003). *Constructing knowledge societies: New challenges for tertiary education.* Washington, DC: Author.

Yang, B. (2003). Toward a holistic theory of knowledge and adult learning. *Human Resource Development Review, 2*(2), 106–129. doi:10.1177/1534484303002002002

Young, M. F. D. (1998). *The curriculum of the future. From the "new sociology of education" to a critical theory of learning.* London: Falmer Press.

Ziemlewski, J. (2009, February). Chemical engineering progress. *Bulletin of the American Institute of Chemical Engineers.*

This work was previously published in the International Journal of Web-Based Learning and Teaching Technologies, Vol. 4, Issue 4, edited by E. M. W. Ng, N. Karacapilidis, and M. S. Raisinghani, pp. 66-81, copyright 2009 by IGI Publishing (an imprint of IGI Global).

Chapter 15
Technological Trends in Adult Education:
Past, Present and in the Future

John K. Hope
University of Auckland, New Zealand

ABSTRACT

The purpose of this article is to provide a critical review of the past two decades of technology use in adult education. The article begins with a brief summary of technological trends, such as the introduction of the Internet and the World Wide Web, that have influenced adult education over the past two decades. Political, economic, social, and pedagogical issues that have influenced the use of technology in adult education are also discussed and possible solutions to these issues are outlined. The article concludes with an attempt to extrapolate future technological trends that could influence the direction of adult education in the decade to come.

INTRODUCTION

Knowles 1970s prediction that adult education would be delivered electronically in the 21st century has proved spectacularly accurate. Thirty years later potential adult learners have a bewildering plethora of electronic delivery options available at the touch of a keyboard. Almost all adult educators use distance technology in one form or another and most are either involved with electronic delivery systems, or are contemplating such. Yet traditional face-to-face delivery methods survive alongside the new technological innovations and are likely to continue in the foreseeable future. Just as the invention of the computer and, more latterly, the widespread availability of the Internet, changed the face of the adult education at the end of the 20th century, recent dramatic changes in the political, social, educational and economic systems of the world could stimulate new trends in adult education that will once again change its visible face in directions that as yet, we know not. This article attempts to analyse the past and extrapolate technological trends that will help us plan for an exciting but, uncertain, future in adult education.

BACKGROUND

At the time of completing this article in early 2009, the last two decades encompassed the period from the late 1980s until the present. What significant technological developments influenced adult education during that that time?

Use of new technology (reading glasses) in adult education is mentioned in one of the first recorded books devoted to adult education, that of Thomas Pole who wrote of his 1811 experiences teaching adults to read in England, "when their (adults) attention is gained and fixed, they soon learn: their age makes no great difference, if they are able, by the help of glasses, to see the letters" (Pole, 1968, p. 3). We now jump several generations of technological development in adult education, such as the postal system and ballpoint pen, to the 1980s when most readers of this book will have been involved with education in some form, as either student or teacher. It is likely that most adult educators would recall that use of educational technology in the form of a computer was minimal, being confined to a small group of "early adopters" (Jones, Kirkup, & Kirkwood, 1993) who had access to mainframe computers, or very early purchasers of desktop personal computers mainly used for word processing.

In the late 1980s most adult education was hard copy print based (Bates, 1993). Some institutions were experimenting with live audio and video technology (Isenberg, 2007), television (Bates, 1993) and institutions such as Jutland Open University in Denmark investing hugely in teleconferencing (Jones et al., 1993), but these institutions were the exception rather than the rule (Moore, 1995). Over the last one hundred and seventy years since the recorded inception of adult education, technological innovation was generally limited to print innovations. In 1981 the IBM PC arrived (Olle, 2004), allowing the decentralisation of computer terminals linked to mainframe computers to stand-alone desktop devices. The widespread and extremely rapid of uptake of personal computers in the 1980s and 1990s (Kodama, 2008) was one of the most significant technological developments of that period. Most adult learners, being by definition more mature learners rather than younger computer whiz kids, were not the earliest adopters of the new computer technological aids but the convenience of simplified editing of written text on a personal computer, available in the home, led to rapid growth in computer use by both adult learners and their teachers.

The enhanced convenience of a less significant but, still important technological leap, the invention and mass marketing of the laptop computer, was not lost on adult students either. First developed for the space shuttle programme in 1979 but not mass marketed until Compaq launched their laptop in 1988 and Apple launched the first Mac laptop in 1989 (Roseberry, n.d.), the laptop is today the computing tool of first choice for people on the move. By its portable nature, the laptop computer helped bring home, workplace and tertiary institution together rather than having students limited to using computer laboratories in tertiary institutions. Writing associated with an adult learning programme could continue regardless of location, a major incentive for busy adult learners to trying to pursue their education while working and running a family. Intensive expansion and innovation in adult education e-learning through the late 1980s and 1990s was the result of the PC and later laptop introduction, leading to a subtle but profound paradigm shift in not only the design and delivery of education, but also in the very nature of learning (Harasim, 2006).

Electronic campuses, meaning electronically linked departments via ethernets within one physical institution, were in vogue in the late 1980s and

1990s (Gardner, 1989), but of more significance to this article was the launch of the first totally on-line adult education course in 1981, followed by the launch of the first large scale, on-line learning institution in 1989, the Open University in the United Kingdom (Harasim, 2006). As is often the case with very new technology, the first on-line courses were disasters. There were no pedagogical models to follow and the technical problems associated with using 48K Apple II computers linked to early, slow modems deterred all but the most enthusiastic (Feenberg, 1993).

The most significant new technological development in adult education during the years of the review period must surely be the move from purely experimental use of the Internet up to the late 1980s to its public launch in 1989, use by learning organisations in the early 1990s (Leiner, Cerf, Clark, Kahn, Kleinrock, Lynch, et al., 2003) and its widespread adoption for educative purposes during the past decade. The electronic campus became the virtual campus; geographic proximity no longer limiting the linking of electronic devices. Physical distance barriers to adult education were instantly removed, equity of access to adult education enhanced and the widespread availability of the World Wide Web from its inception in 1990 (Berners-Lee & Mark, 1999) meant that the knowledge of the world became available to any who could purchase and connect to the technology. Such was the impact of this technological leap that use of information and communication technology (ICT) and the more contemporary term e-learning were seen by adult educators in many developed countries as the "technological fix" for adult education (Selwyn, Gorard, & Furlong, 2006).

Explosive growth in the provision of distance education for adult learners (Johnson, 2003) was a predictable outcome from the moment that widespread and cheap electronic communication via the Internet became available. Rather than having the immediate, geographical area as a catchment for recruitment of potential adult learners, or expensive and slow, paper-based mail-out recruitment to more distant areas, educational institutions could inexpensively advertise their programmes almost anywhere on the globe, and they did. The English Open University, one of the "early adopter" universities to offer distance education to adults grew from 70,000 paper-based distance students in the 1980s to more than 180,000 electronically linked students in 2008 (Open University, 2009). The percentage of U.S.-based institutions using Internet-based learning technologies tripled between 1994–5 and 1997–8 (NCES, 2000) and other developed countries rapidly followed suit. Growth of electronic learning is such that in 2009 it would be difficult to find an educational institution in a developed country that did not include at least some Internet-based courses within its adult education offerings. The ultimate expression of the influence of the Internet and World Wide Web in 2009 can be seen by the growing list of virtual universities in first and, more recently, third world countries, many catering for adult students; all distinguishable in that they have no physical campus because all courses are offered on-line.

Explosive growth does not occur without reason. Internet-based technological innovations have been widely adopted within adult education because ICT offers a number of potential advantages for adult educators. Frequently touted advantages include broadening the provision of adult education into new fields, extending participation to more marginalised learners and improving educational outcomes. But these potential benefits have been mitigated by wider issues. These issues will be the focus of the next section of this chapter.

TECHNOLOGICAL TRENDS IN THE FUTURE AND THEIR IMPLICATIONS FOR ADULT EDUCATION

Any academic able to accurately predict technological trends in the future would be unlikely to waste their time writing book chapters, they would be far better employed investing their own money in lucrative technological innovations or, at the least, being first to implement the innovation within their own institution. Future prediction is known to be an inexact science, well demonstrated by the inaccuracy of some future predictions, particularly when new technological inventions are the subject. One example of many that are available from the public school system will suffice. Between 1950 and 1959, television ownership in the United States soared from 10% to 90% (Putnam, 1995), leading to confident 1950s predictions that educational television would be the dominant form of technology used in education. With 50 million dollar backing from the Ford Foundation and Congress, a plane was commissioned to circle above the Midwest beaming educational television to six states. Finding that classroom uptake was only 2–4%, the plane was grounded (Tyack & Cuban, 1995).

There was and, still is, some use of educational television, but the domination of educational television that was so confidently predicted and expensively funded, did not happen. The same can be said for use of radio, film and video in education, limited uptake and no golden bullet solution to educational problems. Unlike its predecessors, the personal computer, and particularly the almost universal availability of the Internet, has fulfilled the touted potential of changing the face of adult education, but their implementation has introduced other problems. Widespread implementation of the Internet has introduced issues such as hacking that were unheard of when earlier educational technology was in use.

Examination of the technologically based issues confronting adult educators today may offer glimpses of potential solutions for the future. A selection of political, economic, social and pedagogical issues that some see as having an influence on adult education will be presented in the next section, followed by an attempt to confront the inexact science of predicting the near future, that of the next decade.

Issues, Controversies, Problems

It is said that optimists see opportunities where pessimists see problems. The next section discusses technologically based issues for adult education but in so doing, also notes the opportunities that may accompany the issue.

Political Issues

Internal, regional and international political issues all have potential to impact on the technological provision of adult education. Western democracies traditionally lurch between left and right over time, often with consequent change to funding and direction for adult education. Examples include national provision of new technology such as high end broadband capability to educational institutions, and policy directives regarding use technology to address the digital divide (enhancing technology-based access to adult education for disadvantaged groups). International examples of governmental policy shifts for adult education oriented technological progress include tax incentives for ICT purchases in Hungary, government funding for the provision of ICT based adult education to targeted groups in Italy, provision of virtual schools in Finland (Pont & Sweet, 2006) and installation of broadband capability for educational institutions in New Zealand.

Evidence of the internationalisation of education can be seen in countries such as China, India and Malaysia that were previously exporters of adult students now becoming or, about to become, net importers of international students. New political forces have emerged, such as the BRIC axis (Brazil, Russia, India, China), where major investment in technological development, often supported by adult education programmes, has generated a new force in world politics. Politically motivated international and domestic terrorism by individuals and groups in countries as diverse as Afghanistan, Iraq and the United States has resulted in reluctance by some to gather in public educational institutions or to travel to providers of adult education in countries deemed unsafe. Politically inspired visa restrictions have also begun to limit physical movement between some countries. The recent emergence of politically inspired censorship of access to the Internet has limited access for some adult students to Web sites deemed a threat to moral standards or the ruling authority and, in turn, has become a threat to wider uptake of electronically mediated adult education.

Economic issues will be discussed in the next section, but protectionism and ultra-nationalism are political issues often arising from economic downturns, as may occur when the global economy confronts a major economic downturn in 2009. Some international markets for adult education by distance may be closed to external providers in such circumstances, but that correspondingly provides an opportunity for domestic providers of adult education to pick up where international providers have been excluded.

Economic Issues

Economic issues have had a major impact on adult education in the past ten years and are likely to have even greater impact in the future. Widespread utilisation of ICT's has increased the rate of globalisation with consequent economic impact, both positive and negative, on many domestic economies. Competition from other countries drives the need for better skilled workers who can compete on a global scale, in turn creating a need for more commercially and internationally oriented adult education programmes. This trend is seen as a potential narrowing of adult education (Selwyn et al., 2006) to vocationally oriented skill training with a consequent reduction in broader adult education provision.

Rapid escalation in oil-based fuel costs has resulted in sky rocketing international fuel surcharges being imposed that can limit the ability of adult international students to travel to other countries to further their education, but also provides a consequent rise in demand for electronic delivery of coursework. Adult educators are not spared either, rising fuel costs encouraging more use of electronic communication for conferences and meetings, in place of face to face gatherings.

Of greater concern for adult education is the so-called credit crunch that at the time of this writing, has the potential to have a greater economic impact than any other issue in the era being addressed in this chapter. Serious budget deficits stop growth, reduce spending, increase unemployment and have the potential to increase protectionism and sharing of economically sensitive information. Adult education, being traditionally seen by some as of lower priority than compulsory schooling, can suffer massive budget cuts or be directed toward outcomes that have immediate commercial application rather than wider educational merit. An alternative view of the outcome of the global "credit crunch" is that it provides an added incentive for the provision of electronically mediated adult education, a view addressed in a later section of this chapter.

Social Issues

Economic issues often create social issues that, in turn, impact on adult education. Social issues that have emerged in the last ten years include increasing limitations on the time available for adult education students to address their continuing education needs. Longer working hours, working spouses and partners, and an increasing emphasis on leisure are social changes that have the potential to limit participation in adult education, but also create an opportunity for electronic delivery methodology to supplant face to face delivery that involves time consuming travel. Those who live within large cities increasingly experience traffic deadlock that can limit the ability to travel relatively short distances to an educational institution in a timely manner. In contrast, longer life spans in many countries create a larger pool of retired workers who have free time and want to continue learning for health, leisure, or social reasons, but also to fulfil life dreams of an education that was thwarted in earlier years for cultural, economic or family reasons. Growth in electronic communication forums dedicated to those more senior in years, such as SeniorNet, have introduced a new generation of learners to electronic communication and, in turn, generated opportunities for Internet-based adult education provision to a group not previously targetted (O'Day, Ito, Adler, Linde, & Mynatt, 2006).

Unemployment can limit the financial capacity of those so affected to enrol in adult education but unemployment, or employment insecurity, can also generate the motivation to obtain better education qualifications that may improve the chance of further employment. Future unemployed workers may look to electronic delivery of courses as a more cost-efficient alternative delivery method and governments may look toward funding targeted adult education programmes to provide a form of work for the unemployed by enhancing workplace skills.

Other rapidly emerging technological trends within adult education include issues related to the conservation movement, sometimes termed "the greening of the adult education academy" (Taylor, 2006). Eco-sensitive adults are more aware of their carbon footprints and may be less inclined to travel overseas to further education, or may want to limit use of paper-based print technologies to save forests, so they turn to electronic delivery mechanisms that are seen as more eco-friendly. In countries emerging from the third world, a new wave of upwardly mobile adults who are ICT literate and have been denied chosen educational opportunities earlier in their lives may also turn to electronic adult education to meet their adult learning needs.

Pedagogical Issues

Pedagogical issues that have, or are likely to impact on adult education in the near future include the emergence of Mandarin to challenge the domination of English as the chosen Internet language of choice in the world. Internet traffic in Mandarin is likely to surpass Internet traffic in English in the near future (Riley, 2008) yet almost all of the adult education research literature is written in English. Electronic translation methodologies offer adult educators possible solutions to this issue, and to the likely emergence of other languages becoming better represented in net traffic, but the translation technology is still in its infancy and is often subject to questionable accuracy of interpretation (Hung, Chen, & Wong, 2006).

In addition to languages other than English having a greater presence in electronic communication, the era under discussion has seen greater awareness of Islamic educational methodologies. On-line adult education is tightly regulated but does exist in Islamic countries, particularly in the moderate Islamic countries such as Malaysia (McCarty, Ibrahim, Sedunov, & Sharma, 2006). Immigration, refugee flows and economic drivers of international mobility have created new pools of potential Islamic adult learners in non-Islamic countries and, in doing so, raised awareness in destination countries of religiously sourced pedagogies different from indigenous pedagogies.

Similarly, greater movement of people from countries with varying Asian pedagogies has created more awareness in destination countries of differing perceptions of appropriate learning styles. Adult students who have received their childhood education using transmitive pedagogies focussed more on direct instruction, and whose only experience of assessment has been examinations with a focus on memorisation and recall, may struggle to adapt to contemporary Western pedagogies often more focussed on critique, synthesis, and formative assessment. A student raised in some Eastern countries may be taught never to challenge their teacher as this would be a mark of disrespect. The same student in a Western educational environment will have difficulty when asked to critique a work by an academic "superior" because it would be a mark of disrespect to criticise. The challenge for adult educators is to bridge this pedagogical gap, with ICT having an important role in providing personal tutorial support to bridge pedagogical differences.

Computer skills are now a critical necessity for students pursuing adult education programmes in most countries, particularly where net-based distance methodologies are utilised. Adult students were most likely to have had some experience with computers if they attended compulsory education in childhood within the last thirty years, so the generations of adult learners who lack computer skills because they engaged in their compulsory education in pre-computer years are becoming smaller every year. Many of those that did not obtain computer skills during their compulsory schooling have gained computer skills through their employment, or from pursuing recreational and personal interests, so the number of adult students who need basic computer skills is reducing every year. Of more pertinence to this discussion is the nature and quality of their computer skills. Many adult students have missing skill sets, searching academic databases being one and learning to discriminate between the qualities of different sources of data being another.

Technical Issues

All users of modern technology know that technical issues can be a problem, often unexpectedly. An example of serendipitous technical issues was found when a New Zealand university set up a distance education adult learning programme in remote farming areas of New Zealand. Adult students studying in their homes in one area were experiencing unexplained, random network crashes that the technical support staff could not solve. The solution was found to be voltage drops caused by sheep farmers turning on electric fences in a remote area where mains power supply was tenuous at best. Technical problems such as these are accentuated in less developed countries with non-existent or uncertain electricity supplies, where technical support is often unavailable and the technology in use is of earlier vintage.

A technical issue that annoys most adult learners is unsolicited electronic spam, but that can usually be controlled by anti-spam programmes. The spam that gets through is a minor irritant only requiring use of the delete button, but the more insidious unsolicited and unwanted arrival is the electronic virus. Discontented student hackers can sometimes infiltrate adult learning programme computer servers with the consequence that adult learners wherever in the world becoming infected too. An adult learner who is completing their studies part-time while maintaining a busy lifestyle, but is not a confident user of ICT and is removed from immediate technical expertise support, may lack the technical knowledge to protect their computer system so can lose data and, at the least, lose their motivation to continue when these technical issues strike.

Electronic plagiarism is a recent and unwelcome visitor to adult education programmes. When adult education was paper-based, copying of unacknowledged material was laborious, relatively simple to detect and consequently infrequent. The availability of the world's net-sourced literature in the home at the touch of a keystroke increases the temptation to plagiarise. The convenience of technology assisted searching followed by "copy and paste" also simplifies the process. Some adult learners remain unaware of the importance of acknowledging sources and will plagiarise innocently, others come from an education background where plagiarism is not considered as much of an issue as in most developed countries.

In pre-computer years, cheating was limited to unlawful strategies such as paying someone to write essays or copying essays from students studying in previous years, all dangerous and difficult to attempt. The net-based adult learner of today will receive unsolicited e-mail offering to provide bogus degrees, ready written essays for popular courses, and offers to provide custom-written assignments for a fee. Cheating has become easier and the pressure to acquire qualifications in contemporary society provides the motivation for some to cheat.

SOLUTIONS AND RECOMMENDATIONS

Issues are relatively simple to list, solutions and recommendations less so. One article is insufficient to address complex solutions to the host of adult education issues, controversies and problems that have occurred in the last two decades. Some issues as yet have no solutions, others have partial solutions; some have potential solutions that have yet to be tested, others have been solved. This section will address a selection of the issues raised in the previous section and introduce some newer forms of technology that are beginning to be used, or have potential for future use, in adult education.

Political Solutions

Political issues cannot usually be solved by adult educators. War, terrorism, protectionism and ultra-nationalism all pose threats to adult education, but also provide opportunities for more electronic delivery to those most affected by these issues. Potential students in countries vulnerable to such problems are not usually able to travel to other countries for their education so will seek options at home. International concerns are such that the United Nations General Assembly is holding a special session in 2009 to debate the crucial role of education in national emergencies and post-crisis situations. Home based education, whether for security, or nationalistic reasons, is an opportunity for domestic distance providers, or, where approved, international distance education providers, to establish programmes within the political environment of countries in crisis.

Web censorship is a threat more difficult to counter but it is the much maligned hackers who sometimes find unofficial electronic fixes for state censorship of the Web, that ultimately lead to easing of difficult to police Web restrictions. In the longer term, hunger for knowledge is a powerful motivator such that popular opinion can influence unpopular political policy. Adult educators would be advised to constantly look to take advantage of government policy shifts in broader technical areas that could have application in their own industry. Examples of policy shifts likely to increasingly occur in the future are technical measures to address digital divides of various kinds such as poverty, gender discrimination and unemployment.

Adult education workforce skill upgrade opportunities are likely outcomes from the global economic difficulties of 2009, either to keep those unemployed in constructive activity, or to develop new skills more appropriate to the more competitive business environment generated by the economic downturn. The good news for adult educators working internationally when the global economy recovery begins is that the internationalisation of education, technology and trade is an economically generated political force likely to continue in the longer term, and this political force should be seen as an opportunity by all providers of adult education. An example of this trend in the midst of the economic downturn is a major move by UNESCO, initiated by China, to promote multilinguism by developing an international cyber network for learning languages (UNESCO Institute for Statistics, 2009).

Economic Solutions

Transnational education is rapidly growing where economic drivers are encouraging technologically advanced countries such as Denmark to request tertiary students to include an international component within their tertiary education. Tertiary enrolments of students from less developed countries seeking education in middle income countries have increased by 77% in the past decade (UNESCO Institute for Statistics, 2005), many of those enrolling being adult learners. Globalisation will require more workers to have international experience, forcing adult learners to go off-shore using electronic technology to meet the employment requirements of the global order. Adult learners paying for their education themselves will be increasingly likely to Google the world in their efforts to source the cheapest and highest quality provider of distance education to meet their learning requirements.

Boom and bust economies can have a marked influence on adult education take up. While this article was being written, the credit crunch knocked trillions of dollars off the stock exchange and left old age pensioners bereft of their life savings. Dire predictions of declining numbers of tertiary students, particularly international students, were frequently heard in the latter part of 2008. From where I write in the southern hemisphere, we have begun semester one 2009 to find that both international and domestic student enrolments have increased. Shortage of money has deterred some but they have been replaced by greater numbers of students enrolling in tertiary programmes to improve their employability after leaving school, or to upgrade their qualifications in new areas if they have been made redundant.

The dotcom crash of the year 2000 and the more recent credit crunch have eroded public confidence in business. Some confidence has been lost by revelations of illegal activity by greedy entrepreneurs, and other by distrust of the "smoke and mirrors" technology systems that can mask signs of economic woe from the sight of investors. Many people have become suspicious of Web site promotional material, such as bogus qualifications, due to bitter experience, lack of user friendliness and lack of transparency. This applies as much to adult education as to business. Urban (2008) sees Web 2.0 technologies helping to improve consumer trust by facilitating user control and ownership of data. Adult educators can provide a friendly Web presence and authentication of their material via provision of transparent and authentic information sharing, thereby developing a trusting relationship that will endure over time (Dennis & Wisely, 2008).

Fisher and McKee (2008), commenting on reports indicating that since 1995, 25% of United States economic growth is the result of electronic network and information technologies at a cost of only 3% of GDP, suggest that cost benefits such as these are likely to continue in the future. When tertiary budgets are squeezed, cost effectiveness drives change. Despite the social and pedagogical advantages of electronic delivery of adult education that are evident to many academics, the economics of delivering more education to more students at what is perceived to be less cost is attractive to those in politics. Electronic delivery may also be perceived as good preparation for the 'real' world of work and hence become a desirable economic goal.

OECD surveys have established the importance of adult education for improved living standards and productivity. A 2005 report found that an equitable distribution of skills across the workforce had such a strong, positive impact on economic performance that it justified policies to address educational disadvantage for disadvantaged groups such as older adult learners. The pedagogical section below will address these solutions further.

Pedagogical Solutions

The UNESCO statistical report noted above states that much of the improvement in education participation across the globe can be attributed to increased participation in adult education. For example, in the countries surveyed, the proportion of 35–44 year olds with less than primary education has decreased from three quarters to half in eight years (UNESCO Institute for Statistics, 2005). Adult education via situated e-learning in the workplace is driven by economic factors but provides opportunities for adult educators to develop on-line pedagogies tailored to workplace needs and delivered in a manner sensitive to time and location constraints. Examples include greater use of formative assessment to increase feedback to learners struggling with new concepts and pedagogies or lacking in confidence. Continuous on-line assessment utilising electronic portfolios provides flexibility for students, limits the constraints of assessment fixed in time and place and assuages known issues for more mature learners such as exam anxiety. Generation X and Y adult learners can be encouraged into adult education by utilising their social networking skills and dispositions honed on Facebook, Twitter and the like. The developing cyberpedagogy or cybergogy will be based around collaborative learning models where learners construct their own learning in collaboration with other learners via various discussions, role playing and problem solving strategies (Luke, 2006) delivered on new and more creative software platforms such as Moodle.

Most adult learners who have access to the Internet are unlikely to use it purely for educative purposes. The Internet has become the entertainment forum for many. Witness the phenomenal growth of the social interaction sites already described, such as Facebook and Twitter. Futurists see the distinction between education and entertainment become increasingly difficult to define (Pauling, 2006), as in the virtual reality developments discussed later in this chapter.

Facial recognition technological developments (Mitchener, 2008) are likely to make on-line communication more personal and allow, for better or for worse, interpretation of emotions during discussions. More importantly, facial recognition would help solve cheating problem that blight many on-line programmes by answering the question: who is it that is responding to these questions? One concern the has already surfaced is that facial recognition has the potential to be misused by cyber stalkers looking for attractive targets in chat groups but, equally, facial recognition has the potential to make it more difficult for cyber stalkers to make out they are someone other than in real life. Face to face synchronous communication, such as freely downloadable with Skype, offers cheap communication for those with a computer and screen mounted camera. Little used by adult educators, technologies such as Skype improve interactivity, student confidence and help educators tailor the content they are delivering to the needs of their students.

Recent moves away from the hypertext language HTML that was used to develop the Web hold promise for adult educators. The semantic Web may not be fully developed until the end of the next decade (Warren, Davies, & Brown, 2008) but is a potential solution to some problems that adult educators experience, particularly when working across different cultures, languages and pedagogies. Differing interpretations of words and concepts can lead to misunderstandings that discriminate against learners working across cultures and languages. The previously quoted United Nations cyber linguistic initiative is one strategy that may assist in alleviating this problem.

It took 75 years for fixed line phones to reach 50% of consumers but only twenty years for most people in western countries to own a cellular phone. Internet uptake in the United Kingdom soared from 14% to 61% between 1999 and 2005 (Warren et al., 2008). New technologies, such as intuitive and collaborative Web 2.0 knowledge articulation processes, are showing even faster uptakes, at a pace never seen before (Warren et al., 2008). One particularly significant trend that can be expected to accelerate in the future is that of Web users increasingly designing their own content (Anderson & Stoneman, 2008), obvious examples being content sharing via blogs, shared knowledge creation on wikis or Wikipedia and the burgeoning plethora of social communication Web sites like Twitter, Facebook, MySpace, BeBo, Flickr, YouTube and the like.

Asynchronous electronic social communication networks have great potential for use in adult education. In a personal communication a colleague at another university explained that she had set up an alternative Web presence on Facebook and now gets more hits on Facebook than on the official university Web site. An adult learner in an ICT foundation class (preparation programme for entry to university for adults who did not attain university entrance qualifications while in compulsory schooling) that I was teaching responded to my suggestion that she e-mail to herself some work she had written in my class. Her response was: it is much easier to copy and paste to my BeBo page.

For many adult learners, Web-based social networks have become the repository for their tacit knowledge, personal knowledge they are willing to share (Marwick, 2001). When such knowledge becomes explicit via the Web site, it can be a rich, but as yet often little exploited, data source for learning communities within adult education programmes. Wikis, blogs and the like can exploit for educational purposes the Web networking and knowledge sharing characteristics of many of today's adult learners. Kings, Davies, Verril, Aral, Bryniolfsson, and Alstyne (2008) suggests that future knowledge management systems will build on Web 2.0 type knowledge articulation processes such as those mentioned above because they create a link between Web-based social recreational activity and shared learning.

Wikis became available on the Internet in 1994 but widespread uptake only began in the new millennium. The best known wiki is Wikipedia, now one of the most often quoted sources of information by students. Wikipedia's success comes from its open and interactive environment; anyone who has access to a Web browser can read it and add to it. The great attraction of wikis for adult educators is their use in collaborative learning models. Just as collaborative writing has made Wikipedia arguably the most used encyclopaedia of knowledge in the world, adult educators can create student groups where subtasks are delegated and the resultant work assembled electronically on the wiki. The resultant collaborative information resource is private to those who have access to the wiki allowing all those who take part to benefit from the collective research and expertise of the group.

Blogs differ from wikis as the information contained therein is available to any who can access the appropriate Web site. Blog authors document in reverse chronological order their musings in an informal manner and the blog so created, being public, can encourage input from others. Adult educators have been slow to grasp the potential of blogs because blogs have tended to be the domain of the young, particularly those in secondary schools. More recently, blogging has also becoming the domain of the not so young and this trend can be expected to continue as the younger generations enter adult education. The potential of the personal narrative contained in many blogs is an opportunity deserving of more attention in adult education. Adult educator hesitancy in using blogs relates to their open nature, others can input and move the blog away from the educational objective, or it can degenerate when interpersonal issues are introduced. Despite these disadvantages, blogs are very popular with many students and can provide rich chronological data in much the way that diaries once did, so should be considered by adult educators as another technological tool to improve learning.

Portfolios of student work are now popular at tertiary level and the e-portfolio has particular relevance for adult education. E-portfolios are compilations of student work assembled electronically, so they can include videos, graphic work and creative art genre as well as traditional text information. An e-portfolio is usually private to the student and their tutor, but could include blogs as a valid information source contributing to the e-portfolio.

Technological Solutions

Most of us eventually buy the latest technological device. Are there any adult educators who do not have a cellular phone, use a computer or access the Web? Only the computer existed two decades ago and for many of us, a PC was still too expensive and a laptop a dream. What is in store for us during the next decade?

Mitchener (2008) sees more seamless, automatic, synchronous and numerous network connections, developments we would all applaud. Specific technological developments likely to occur include improved voice recognition as is now available in exotic cars, wider use of improved touch screens as on the Apple iPhone and even technology that could include physical movement as a learning tool. Physical movement capable software is already available in interactive gaming systems such as the physical swings of golf clubs or baseball bats on the popular computer game Wii. Rapid increases in memory storage capacity utilising physically smaller componentry, particularly through use of nanotechnology, is likely to increase the physical portability of technological devices and hence access for distance learners.

Handheld mobile technology such as PDAs and mobile phones are increasingly merging into smartphones, always-connected Blackberrys and iPhones with their ready access to e-mail and Web on a handheld phone anywhere, anytime. Intelligent mobile devices allow lecturers and students to communicate asynchronously and cheaply by text or e-mail or synchronously by phone. Student to student and student to tutor text messaging (the correct term for text messaging is Short Messaging Service abbreviated on phones as SMS) to ask questions about coursework and share ideas, instant data recording while at work and recreation, capturing video clips for use in learning portfolios and using the in-built planner to keep track of assignment timelines are all examples of the technological applications currently in use by some adult educators (Dawson, 2007).

3G phones are common now, 4G phones with more seamless connectivity and roaming are most likely to be available within the next ten years (Dennis & Wisely, 2008). Improvements to batteries and greater use of intelligent alternative sources of electricity from sunlight, movement, sound and pressure changes are likely to create opportunities for adult education by improving access to information and communication in less developed countries and isolated areas.

The frustration, shared by teaching staff members and students, arising from slow downloads is a major barrier to the uptake of distance education. More information sharing is required, more documents include graphic material and Web sites that increasingly incorporate video clips all slow downloads. The touted answer to this problem has been increased bandwidth. In many countries broadband has become the rule rather than the exception and in this case Asian countries are outstripping their Western counterparts (Payne, 2008). Increased bandwidth capacity is quickly soaked up driving demand for even more bandwidth that exceeds the capacity of copper wire technology to deliver. Fibre optic networks are now common on many campuses but any component of the network in use that is not an optical network will slow downloads. Similarly, information entering and leaving network nodes is slowed. New intelligent network technology that bypasses unnecessary nodes can also be expected to increase speed (Payne, 2008). Adult educators can expect to see more complete optical systems installed in the next ten years, including interconnectivity across regional and national boundaries (Wittgreffe, Dames, Clark, & McDonald, 2008) that will, in turn, increase capacity to deliver more graphics-based and video based adult education programmes to more students.

Storage technology has increased incrementally in the last five years. Most of us now use a

$10 memory stick that can store everything that we have written in our lifetime. Memory sticks may soon have wireless capacity to enable them to talk to each other, allowing transfer of information anywhere, anytime from a small object around the neck, on a key ring or in a pocket, without being plugged into a computer (Pearson, 2008). With time pressures and transport problems driving increasing situated e-learning in the workplace instead of going to dedicated learning institutions, memory sticks that could communicate with each other would allow information transfer to occur over lunch or while working, without the need for a larger computer or smartphone.

Replacement of expensive, technically demanding, distance delivery software packages such as WebCT and Blackboard with cheap and easy to use technologies such as Moodle will further simplify and facilitate delivery of adult education. Many potential students avoid on-line courses because they consider themselves technologically illiterate or sign up with trepidation only when there is no other option available to them. Tertiary educators who teach their courses on-line have come to expect calls asking whether IT qualifications are required to join the course, or "I have not done this before" comments indicating lack of confidence. Easy to use software packages give new distance learners confidence, are less likely to crash at critical moments and are designed to increase student to student, teacher to student and student to teacher communication. They are also easier for adult educators to use for the first time.

Obtaining approval to purchase a new paper-based journal has become problematic in the author's university; new journals must be electronic journals. Variously described as E-libraries or digital libraries, virtual libraries are reality, or a partial reality, in many universities now. They provide an electronic interface between repositories of knowledge and learners individual needs that is more than the traditional index cards or electronic catalogues. Their unique feature is their ability to be searched using increasingly complex and inductive search engines to suit a learner's individual needs. In doing so they support the newer pedagogies where learners construct their own learning, the remaining limitations being the learner's technological literacy and the sophistication of the library search access (Brophy, 2006). Initially adopted to save expensive space needed for paper-based technology, virtual libraries are a boon for busy adult learners as they can completely obviate the need to attend a library in person. Journal and database searching is simplified and available from any keyboard, anywhere, anytime. Although electronic books are still not in vogue with many in adult education because they find reading a book on a screen odious, the increasing availability of electronic books combined with declining paper availability and cheapness, will force adoption. New electronic readers are becoming available that come closer to replicating the paper book. They still do not duplicate the physical page turning of a book, but can be read in bed or on the bus and are a great deal easier to transport in quantity.

Solutions to the cheating and plagiarism issues have centred around use of products such as Turnitin and MyDropBox, effectively large databases of written works that allow comparison of student text with that written previously. New pedagogical strategies such as portfolio assessment raise new issues for the detection of illegal activity that are beyond the scope of existing electronic detection methods. As always, a technological problem breeds a technological solution and new open architecture systems are being developed that can detect plagiarism in other media such as graphics and even the audio component of podcasts (Butakov & Scherbinin, 2009).

Cyberspace was a term coined by a science fiction author in 1984, but it soon become reality and was being discussed as a potential medium for adult education in the early 1990s (Boyd, 1993). Virtual games are now commonplace, but their use in adult education less so. Technology enabled virtual worlds formed by the merger of Google Earth and virtual reality programmes like *Second Life* offer the ability to inhabit a virtual world via avatars "that will be at best a virtual representation of planet earth and at worst, the frighteningly deep and dark spaces of collective human consciousness without the shackles of convention surrounding an evolved society!" (Dennis & Wisely, 2008, p. 139). Virtual reality provides unique opportunities for adult education based on personal choice and decision-making. Its potential advantages are that it happens in no fixed physical place and involves communities of learners interacting and collaborating to solve problems in ways not possible within the real world (Burbules, 2006).

Boyd (1993) saw application of virtual reality in adult education such as "gateways to other organisations' cyberspace worlds to provide observations of people at work, and apprenticeship-internship situations" (p. 245). Fifteen years on that prediction is already reality. One early example is use of virtual reality adapted to teach humanistic subjects such as history. Virtual Harlem is a collaborative learning environment where students can learn about the history of Harlem via virtual reality, giving the impression of being there (Sosnoski, Jones, Carter, McAllister, Moeller, & Mir, 2006). In 2009, virtual reality must still be regarded as experimental, expensive and of limited availability, so its current use in adult education is still limited.

This article began with a look at the technological past in adult education and there was mention of technology such as educational television that did not ever become mainstream. In contrast, strewn throughout the sections above are many examples of extremely rapid uptake of newer technology such as the Internet and its slightly slower, but nevertheless pervasive adaption for use in adult education. What of the future? Will we all be working as avatars in virtual reality scenarios?

FUTURE RESEARCH DIRECTIONS

This essay has highlighted many examples of the ever increasing speed of technical change, change that generates the most persistent and pervasive technological issue within adult education. The world's total knowledge doubles in ever shorter time frames and new products that have potential for application in adult education arrive regularly. How to keep up? Should we keep up? These questions beggar the real question, where is the research-based evidence in favour of improved pedagogy for each new technological tool?

Technological change can happen much more quickly than the time required to develop a research base rigorous enough to analyse the applicability of new technologies for improved educational outcomes. Good research takes time and it often takes even longer to become available in published form. By the time research into the veracity of a new technology is readily available, there is a newer technology. This places the adult educator in a difficult position. Students are often early adopters of new technology so look for courses utilising the latest technology, while lecturers tend to favour more conservative approaches. The moral high ground for the educator is to focus research on the pedagogy involved by posing the question, will it improve learning? Until that question is answered by sound, evidence-based research the adult educator is at risk of promoting a 90 day wonder that will go the way of educational television.

The role of the teacher is clearly changing in the increasingly cyber oriented world of adult education. Zao, Lei, and Conway (2006) see the traditional teachers' role as that of gatekeeper to knowledge, but the e-learning teachers' role as more akin to that of a designer of technological strategies and a learning facilitator rather than an instructor. But what will the adult educator working on a virtual reality learning model need to know and be able to do? The technical scientists are often generously funded to complete the technical research needed to make new technologies commercially viable because there is a potential economic return. Funding for pedagogically-based research into the application of new technology in adult education is often less readily available, as is adult educator's time to pursue the necessary research. In the course of writing this article, it has become clear that that there are a plethora of books devoted to the more abstract and theoretical issues within adult education but less devoted to applied research around the application of new technologies.

Timely technological support when applying new technology can be difficult to come by. Does this new, technically oriented environment require the e-learning adult educator to acquire new technological skills, should adult educators work collaboratively with technical experts, or can they depend on on-line support services to solve pedagogical and technical issues? Current experience with new technologies suggests that immediate support for the baby boomer generation adult educator is never on-site when required, and when the immediate problem is resolved another becomes apparent just after the technician has left the room, hung up the phone or terminated the link. The hope on the horizon is that the younger generation of more technologically savvy adult educators who have grown up with computers will fare better.

Pauling (2006) notes that Japanese researchers are working on hyper-reality models of learning, where reality and virtual reality blend at the whim of the learner and it becomes increasingly difficult to distinguish between what is real and what is virtual, such that it would be difficult to know if people are real or not, or even if they have human or artificial intelligence (Tiffen & Terashima, 2001). The new generations X, Y and Z adapt much more quickly, but how much more difficult will it be for all generations when they have to work with a completely new technical environment beyond their immediate experience, particularly if it becomes adopted as quickly as the Internet did? Future oriented research that attempts to define the knowledge, skills and dispositions required to link the pedagogical and technical requirements of future adult educators is not abundant but urgently needed.

Solutions and recommendations as outlined above are the personal views of the author. They are neither comprehensive nor inviolate but are intended to stimulate thought about an adult education future that becomes increasingly difficult to predict as the pace of technological change quickens. The overwhelming impression gained from the literature reviewed is that demand for adult education will continue to grow and the role of the adult educator and their students will continue to change with ever increasing momentum, due to societal changes and technological advances. For that we must be prepared as best we can.

CONCLUSION

The audience laughed when Maxwell Smart used a shoe phone in the 1970s television comedy series Get Smart. Does any reader of this article not have a mobile phone thirty years later? History tells us that many technological developments that were initially in the realm of the experimental laboratory have become pervasive. It also tells us that some have not. It remains to be seen whether the newer technologies described above are adopted as mainstream tools for adult education, whether those that are adopted last very long, and whether other technologies not envisaged above, arrive within the next ten years. What does not remain to be seen is that new technologies will arrive, and that some will become mainstream in adult education.

It seems likely that the trend of the last two decades to move away from paper-based provision of adult education to electronic provision will continue, as will the increasing prevalence of distance education delivery. History has shown us that predictions of the demise of the classroom teacher face to face with students, to be replaced with intelligent computers, did not happen in schools (Cuban, 2001), nor is it likely to happen in adult education. Some face to face delivery will continue. What did change in schools, and in adult education, was the mode of electronic delivery, the technical developments associated with electronic delivery and the pedagogy utilised via electronic delivery. History is our best predictive resource. Two decades of incredibly rapid technological change in adult education suggests that the future is more of the same.

REFERENCES

Anderson, B., & Stoneman, P. (2008). Predicting the socio-technical future (and other myths). In P. Warren, J. Davies, & D. Brown (Eds.), *ICT futures: Delivering pervasive, real-time and secure service* (pp. 3-16). Chichester, UK: John Wiley & Sons.

Augar, N., Raitman, R., & Zhou, W. (2006). Wikis: Collaborative virtual learning environments. In J. Weiss, J. Nolan, J. Hunsinger, & P. Trifonas (Eds.), *The international handbook of virtual learning environments (pt. 2)* (pp. 1251-1270). Dordrecht, The Netherlands: Springer.

Bates, T. (1993). Theory and practice in the use of technology in distance education. In D. Keegan (Ed.), *Theoretical principles of distance education* (pp. 213-233). New York: Routledge.

Berners-Lee, T., & Mark, F. (1999). *Weaving the web: Origins and future of the world wide web.* Stamford, UK: Orion Business.

Boyd, G. (1993). A theory of distance education for the cyberspace era. In D. Keegan (Ed.), *Theoretical principles of distance education* (pp. 213-233). New York: Routledge.

Brophy, P. (2006). The eLibrary and learning. In J. Weiss, J. Nolan, J. Hunsinger, & P. Trifonas (Eds.), *The international handbook of virtual learning environments (pt. 2)* (pp. 895-914). Dordrecht, The Netherlands: Springer.

Burbules, N. C. (2006). Rethinking the virtual. In J. Weiss, J. Nolan, J. Hunsinger, & P. Trifonas (Eds.), *The international handbook of virtual learning environments (pt. 1)* (pp. 37-58). Dordrecht, The Netherlands: Springer.

Butakov, S., & Scherbinin, V. (2009). The toolbox for local and global plagiarism. *Computers & Education, 52*, 781–788. doi:10.1016/j.compedu.2008.12.001

Cuban, L. (2001). *Oversold and underused: Computers in the classroom.* Cambridge, MA: Harvard University Press.

Dawson, D. (2007). *Handheld technologies for mobile learning.* London: Latimer Trend.

Dennis, R., & Wisely, D. (2008). Mobility and ICT. In P. Warren, J. Davies, & D. Brown (Eds.), *ICT futures: Delivering pervasive, real-time and secure service* (pp. 129-142). Chichester, UK: John Wiley & Sons.

Feenberg, A. (1993). Building a global network: The WBSI executive education experience. In L. Harasim (Ed.), *Global networks: Computers and international communication* (pp. 185-197). Cambridge, MA: MIT Press.

Fisher, M., & McKee, P. (2008). Flexible ICT infrastructure. In P. Warren, J. Davies, & D. Brown (Eds.), *ICT futures: Delivering pervasive, real-time and secure service* (pp. 67-78). Chichester, UK: John Wiley & Sons.

Gardner, N. (1989). The electronic campus: The first decade. *Higher Education Quarterly, 43*, 332–350. doi:10.1111/j.1468-2273.1989.tb01518.x

Halavais, A. C. (2006). Weblogs and collaborative web publishing as learning spaces. In J. Weiss, J. Nolan, J. Hunsinger, & P. Trifonas (Eds.), *The international handbook of virtual learning envi-*

ronments (pt. 2) (pp. 1215-1236). Dordrecht, The Netherlands: Springer.

Harasim, L. (2006). A history of e-learning: Shift happened. In J. Weiss, J. Nolan, J. Hunsinger, & P. Trifonas (Eds.), *The international handbook of virtual learning environments (pt. 1)* (pp. 59-94). Dordrecht, The Netherlands: Springer.

Hung, D., Chen, D. T., & Wong, A. F. L. (2006). An overview of virtual learning environments in the Asia-Pacific: Provisos, issues, and tensions. In J. Weiss, J. Nolan, J. Hunsinger, & P. Trifonas (Eds.), *The international handbook of virtual learning environments (pt. 1)* (pp. 699-722). Dordrecht, The Netherlands: Springer.

Isenberg, S. (2007). *Applying andragogical principles to internet learning.* New York: Cambria Press.

Johnson, J. (2003). *Distance education: The complete guide to design, delivery and improvements.* New York: Teachers College Press.

Jones, A., Kirkup, G., & Kirkwood, A. (1993). *Personal computers for distance education.* New York: St. Martin's Press.

Kings, N. J., Davies, J., Verrill, D., Aral, S., Bryniolfsson, E., & Alstyne, M. V. (2008). Social networks, social computing and knowledge management. In P. Warren, J. Davies, & D. Brown (Eds.), *ICT futures: Delivering pervasive, real-time and secure service* (pp. 17-26). Chichester, UK: John Wiley & Sons.

Kodama, M. (2008). *New knowledge creation through ICT dynamic capability.* Charlotte, NC: Information Age Publishing.

Leiner, B., Cerf, V. G., Clark, D. D., Kahn, R. E., Kleinrock, L., Lynch, D. C., et al. (2003). *A brief history of the internet.* Retrieved March 11, 2009, from http://www.isoc.org/internet/history/brief.shtml

Luke, C. (2006). Cyberpedagogy. In J. Weiss, J. Nolan, J. Hunsinger, & P. Trifonas (Eds.), *The international handbook of virtual learning environments (pt. 1)* (pp. 269-278). Dordrecht, The Netherlands: Springer.

Marwick, A. D. (2001). Knowledge management technology. *IBM Systems Journal, 40*(4), 814-830. Retrieved October 2, 2007, from http://www.research.ibm.com/journal/sj/404/marwik.html

McCarty, S., Ibrahim, B., Sedunov, B., & Sharma, R. (2006). Global online education. In J. Weiss, J. Nolan, J. Hunsinger, & P. Trifonas (Eds.), *The international handbook of virtual learning environments (pt. 1)* (pp. 723-788). Dordrecht, The Netherlands: Springer.

Mitchener, J. (2008). Device Futures. In P. Warren, J. Davies, & D. Brown (Eds.), *ICT futures: Delivering pervasive, real-time and secure service* (pp. 27-38). Chichester, UK: John Wiley & Sons.

Moore, M. G. (1995). American distance education. In F. Lockwood (Ed.), *Open and distance learning today* (pp. 32-41). London: Routledge.

O'Day, V. L., Ito, M., Adler, A., Linde, C., & Mynatt, E. D. (2006). Cemeteries, oak trees, and black and white cows: Newcomers' understandings of the networked world. In J. Weiss, J. Nolan, J. Hunsinger, & P. Trifonas (Eds.), *The international handbook of virtual learning environments (pt. 2)* (pp. 873-894). Dordrecht, The Netherlands: Springer.

OECD. (2005). *Promoting adult learning.* Retrieved March 14, 2009, from http://www.oecd.org/document/57/0,3343,en_2649_39263238_36675769_1_1_1_1,00.html

Olle, T. W. (2004). Eight significant events in the 50 year history of computing. In J. Impagliazzo & J. A. N. Lee (Eds.), *History of computing in education* (pp. 47-56). Dordrecht, The Netherlands: Kluwer.

Open University. (2009). *About the OU.* Retrieved March 11, 2009, from http://www.open.ac.uk/about/ou/p3.shtml

Pauling, B. (2006). Virtual learning environments in higher education "down under". In J. Weiss, J. Nolan, J. Hunsinger, & P. Trifonas (Eds.), *The international handbook of virtual learning environments (pt. 1)* (pp. 609-652). Dordrecht, The Netherlands: Springer.

Paulson, K. (2002). Reconfiguring faculty roles for virtual settings. *The Journal of Higher Education, 73*, 123–141. doi:10.1353/jhe.2002.0010

Payne, D. (2008). The future all optical network—why we need it and how we get there. In P. Warren, J. Davies, & D. Brown (Eds.), *ICT futures: Delivering pervasive, real-time and secure service* (pp. 93-114). Chichester, UK: John Wiley & Sons.

Pearson, I. (2008). Over the horizon. In P. Warren, J. Davies, & D. Brown (Eds.), *ICT futures: Delivering pervasive, real-time and secure service* (pp. 215-226). Chichester, UK: John Wiley & Sons.

Pole, T. (1968). *A history of adult schools* (3rd ed.). London: Woburn Press.

Pont, B., & Sweet, R. (2006). *ICT and learning: Supporting out-of-school youth and adults.* Paris: Organisation for Economic Cooperation and Development.

Putnam, R. (1995). Bowling alone: America's declining social capital. *Journal of Democracy, 6*, 65–78. doi:10.1353/jod.1995.0002

Riley, D. (2008). China to become world's largest internet market by users. Retrieved March 25, 2009, from http://www.techcrunch.com/2008/01/17/china-close-to-becoming-worlds-largest-internet-market-by-users

Roseberry, C. (n.d.). *What is the history of laptops?* Retrieved March 24, 2009, from http://mobileoffice.about.com/od/laptopstabletpcs/f/laptophistory.htm

Selwyn, N., Gorard, S., & Furlong, J. (2006). *Adult learning in the digital age.* Milton Park, UK: Routledge.

Sosnoski, J., Jones, S., Carter, B., McAllister, K., Moeller, R., & Mir, R. (2006). Virtual Harlem as a collaborative learning environment: A project of the University of Illinois at Chicago's electronic visualization Lab. In J. Weiss, J. Nolan, J. Hunsinger, & P. Trifonas (Eds.), *The international handbook of virtual learning environments (pt. 2)* (pp. 1289-1320). Dordrecht, The Netherlands: Springer.

Taylor, E. W. (2006). The greening of the adult education academy. In S. B. Merriam, B. C. Courtenay, & R. M. Cervero (Eds.), *Global issues and adult education: Perspectives from Latin America, Southern Africa, and the United States* (pp. 254-264). San Francisco: Jossey-Bass.

Tiffin, J., & Terashima, N. (2001). *Hyper-reality: Paradigm for the third millennium.* London: Routledge.

Tyack, D., & Cuban, L. (1995). *Tinkering towards utopia: A century of school reform.* Cambridge, MA: Harvard University Press.

UNESCO Institute for Statistics. (2005). *Educational trends in perspective.* Retrieved March 21, 2009, from http://www.uis.unesco.org/TEMPLATE/pdf/wei/WEI2005.pdf

UNESCO Institute for Statistics. (2009). *Expert meeting on cyber network for learning languages.* Retrieved March 21, 2009, from http://portal.unesco.org/en/ev.php-URL_ID=44836&URL_DO=DO_TOPIC&URL_SECTION=201.html

Urban, G. L. (2008). Online trust and customer power: The emergence of customer advocacy. In P. Warren, J. Davies, & D. Brown (Eds.), *ICT futures: Delivering pervasive, real-time and secure service* (pp. 39-54). Chichester, UK: John Wiley & Sons.

Warren, P., Davies, J., & Brown, D. (Eds.). (2008). *ICT futures: Delivering pervasive, real-time and secure service*. Chichester, UK: John Wiley & Sons.

Wittgreffe, J., Dames, M., Clark, J., & McDonald, J. (2008). End-to-end service level agreements for complex ICT solutions. In P. Warren, J. Davies, & D. Brown (Eds.), *ICT futures: Delivering pervasive, real-time and secure service* (pp. 115-128). Chichester, UK: John Wiley & Sons.

Zhao, Y., Lei, J., & Conway, P. F. (2006). A global perspective on political definitions of e-learning: Commonalities and differences in national educational technology strategy discourses. In J. Weiss, J. Nolan, J. Hunsinger, & P. Trifonas (Eds.), *The international handbook of virtual learning environments (pt. 1)* (pp. 673-698). Dordrecht, The Netherlands: Springer.

This work was previously published in the International Journal of Web-Based Learning and Teaching Technologies, Vol. 4, Issue 4, edited by E. M. W. Ng, N. Karacapilidis, and M. S. Raisinghani, pp. 82-99, copyright 2009 by IGI Publishing (an imprint of IGI Global).

Compilation of References

A philosophy of adult education (n.d.).

Adler, P. S., & Kwon, S. (2002). Social capital: Prospects for a new concept. *Academy of Management Review*, *27*(1), 17–40. doi:10.2307/4134367

Agosto, D. (2004). Girls and gaming: A summary of the research with implications for practice. *Teacher Librarian*, *31*(3), 8–14.

Ala-Mutka, K., Punie, Y., & Redecker, C. (2008). *ICT for learning, innovation and creativity.* European Commission, Joint Research Centre, Institute for Prospective Technological Studies. Retrieved 15 February, 2009, from http://ipts.jrc.ec.europa.eu

Allen, I. & Seaman, J. (November 2008). *Staying the course: Online education in the United States, 2008.* Needham, MA: Sloan Consortium. (http://www.sloan-c.org/publications/survey/pdf/staying_the_course.pdf).

Allen, I. E., & Seaman, J. (2003). *Sizing the opportunity: The quality and extent of online education in the United States.* Needham, MA: Sloan & Sloan Center for Online Education (SCOLE).

Allen, I. E., & Seaman, J. (2008). *Staying the course: Online education in the United States, 2008.* Needham, MA: The Sloan Consortium.

Allen, I. E., Seaman, J., & Garrett, R. (2007). *Blending in: The extent and promise of blended education in the United States.* Needham, MA: The Sloan Consortium.

Allen, I., & Seaman, J. (March, 2007). *Online nation: Five years of growth in online learning.* Needham, MA: Sloan Consortium. Retrieved April 22, 2009, from http://www.sloan-c.org/publications/survey/pdf/online_nation.pdf

Allen, I., & Seaman, J. (November, 2008). *Staying the Course.* Needham, MA: Sloan Consortium. Retrieved April 22, 2009, from http://www.sloanconsortium.org/publications/survey/pdf/staying_the_course.pdf

Alliance for Technology Access. (n.d.) Retrieved from http://www.ataccess.org

Allman, P. (1983). The nature and process of adult development. In M. Tight (Ed.), *Education for adults: Adult learning and education* (vol. 1, pp. 107-123). London: Croom Helm & The Open University.

Allman, P., & Mackie, K. J. (Eds.). (1983). *Towards a developmental theory of andragogy.* Nottingham, UK: The University of Nottingham, Department of Adult Education.

America.gov. (2004). *Increasing diversity predicted in U.S. population.* Retrieved March 12, 2009 from http://www.america.gov/st/washfile-english/2004/March/20040318124311CMretroP0.4814264.html

American Decades. (2001). *Minorities and women in the workplace.* Retrieved May 20, 2009, from http://www.encyclopedia.com/doc/1G2-3468302607.html

American Psychological Association. (1997). *Learner-centered psychological principles: A framework for school redesign and reform.* Retrieved April 20, 2009, http://www.apa.org/ed/lcp.html

Ames, C. (1992). Classrooms: Goals, structures and student motivations. *Journal of Educational Psychology*, *84*(3), 261–271. doi:10.1037/0022-0663.84.3.261

Amory, A. (1999). The use of computer games as an educational tool: identification of appropriate game types and game elements. *British Journal of Educational Technology, 30*, 311–321. doi:10.1111/1467-8535.00121

Anderson, A., McEwan, R., & Carletta, J. (2007). Virtual team meetings: An analysis of communication and context. *Computers in Human Behavior, 23*, 2558–2580. doi:10.1016/j.chb.2007.01.001

Anderson, B., & Stoneman, P. (2008). Predicting the socio-technical future (and other myths). In P. Warren, J. Davies, & D. Brown (Eds.), *ICT futures: Delivering pervasive, real-time and secure service* (pp. 3-16). Chichester, UK: John Wiley & Sons.

Anderson, L. W., & Krathwohl, D. R. (Eds.). (2001). *A taxonomy of learning, teaching, and assessment: A revision of Bloom's taxonomy of educational objectives*. New York: Longman.

Anderson, M. L., & Lindeman, E. C. (1927). *Education through experience: An interpretation of the methods of the academy of labor*, Frankfurt-am-Main, Germany, (Workers' Education Research Series, Monograph no. 1). New York: Workers Education Bureau Press, Inc.

Anonymous. (2006). *Minorities in the labor force: Workforce projections for 2010*. Retrieved May 5, 2009, from http://www.libraryindex.com/pages/2910/Minorities-in-Labor-Force-WORKFORCE-PROJECTIONS-2010.html

Antonocopoulou, E., Jarvis, P., Andersen, V., Elkjaer, B., & Hoyrup, S. (Eds.). *(2006)*. Learning, working and living. *London: Palgrave Macmillan*.

Apollo Group, Inc. (n.d.). Retrieved on March 23, 2009. from http://www.fundinguniverse.com/company-histories/Apollo-Group-Inc-Company-History.html

Apps, J. W. *(1988)*. Higher education in a learning society. Meeting new demands for education and training. *San Francisco: Jossey-Bass*.

Aragon, S. (Ed.). (2003). *Facilitating learning in online environments: New directions for adult and continuing education, vol. 100*. San Francisco: Jossey-Bass.

Assistive, T. A. P. (n.d.). Retrieved from http://www.resna.org/taproject/at/statecontacts.html

Athanasou, J. (2008). Career education. In L. M. English (Ed.), *International encyclopedia of adult education* (pp. 90-92). New York: Palgrave Mcmillan.

Augar, N., Raitman, R., & Zhou, W. (2006). Wikis: Collaborative virtual learning environments. In J. Weiss, J. Nolan, J. Hunsinger, & P. Trifonas (Eds.), *The international handbook of virtual learning environments (pt. 2)* (pp. 1251-1270). Dordrecht, The Netherlands: Springer.

Ausburn, L. J. (2004). Course design elements most valued by adult learners in blended online education environments: An American perspective. *Educational Media International, 41*(4), 327–337. doi:10.1080/0952398042000314820

Baden, C. (1998). *Adult learning in associations: Models for good practice*. New York: American Society of Association Executives.

Baltzer, H., Lazaros, E., & Flowers, J. C. (2007). Review of doctoral programs in technical education. *Journal of Industrial Teacher Education, 44*(2), 37–59.

Banas, E. J., & Emory, W. F. (1998). History and issues of distance learning. *Public Administration Quarterly, 22*(3), 365–383.

Bangkok, U. N. E. S. C. O. (n.d.). Information Literacy. *Communication and Information*. Retrieved March 15, 2009, from http://www.unescobkk.org/index.php?id=1897

Barab, S., Kling, R., & Gray, J. (2004). Designing for virtual communities in the service *of learning*. Cambridge, UK: Cambridge University Press.

Barr, R. B., & Tagg, J. (1995). From teaching to learning—a new paradigm for undergraduate education. *Change, 27*(6), 12–25.

Barrat-Esteve, J., Franquet-Sugrañes, T., Giménez-Costa, A., González-Bondia, A., Jaria i Manzano, J., Marquès i Banqué, M., et al. (2007). El diseño de una comunidad virtual como estrategia de adaptación del profesorado a los postulados docentes del EEES [The design of a virtual community as strategy to adopt teachers to the objectives of the European Higher Educational Space]. In D. García-San José (Ed.), *Innovación docente y calidad en la enseñanza de ciencias jurídicas en el espacio europeo de educación superior [Pedagogy innovation and quality of Law Science teaching in the European Higher Educational Space]* (pp. 171-200). Murcia, Spain: Ediciones Laborum.

Barrett, H. C. (2007). Researching electronic portfolios and learner engagement: The REFLECT initiative. *Journal of Adolescent & Adult Literacy, 50*(6), 436–449. doi:10.1598/JAAL.50.6.2

Barry, J. H. (1999). Lifelong learning in late modernity: The challenges to society, organizations, and individuals. *Adult Education Quarterly, 49*(2), 79–90. doi:10.1177/074171369904900201

Bash, L. (2003). *Adult learners in the academy.* Bolton, MA: Anker Publishing.

Basiel, A., Terrell, I., Revill, G., & Arnold, L., (2005). *Innovations in non-written forms of work based learning assessment.*

Bastable, S. B. (2003). *Nurse as educator: Principles of teaching and learning for nursing practice* (2nd ed.). Sudbury, MA: Jones & Bartlett.

Bates, A. W., & Poole, G. (2003). *Effective teaching with technology in higher education: Foundations for success.* San Francisco: Jossey-Bass.

Bates, T. (1993). Theory and practice in the use of technology in distance education. In D. Keegan (Ed.), *Theoretical principles of distance education* (pp. 213-233). New York: Routledge.

Baxter Magolda, M.B. (1992). *Knowing and reasoning in college.* San Francisco: Jossey-Bass.

BBC. (2007). *Skills pledge gauntlet to firms.* Retrieved March 27, 2009, from http://news.bbc.co.uk/1/hi/education/6751953.stm

Bee, H. L., & Bjorkland, B. J. (2004). *The journey of adulthood.* Upper Saddle River, NJ: Pearson.

Beguin, P. (2003). Design as a mutual learning process between users and designers. *Interacting with Computers, 15*(5), 709–730. doi:10.1016/S0953-5438(03)00060-2

Belenky, M.F., Clinchy, B.M., Goldberger, N.R., & Tarule, J.M. (1997). *Women's' ways of knowing* (10th anniversary edition). New York: Basic Books.

Benamati, J., & Lederer, A. (2001). Rapid information technology change, coping mechanisms, and the emerging technologies group. *Journal of Management Information Systems, 17*(4), 183–202.

Benbunan-Fich, R. (2002). Improving education and training with IT. *Communications of the ACM, 45*(6), 94–99. doi:10.1145/508448.508454

Berge, Z. (1995). Facilitating computer conferencing: Recommendations from the field. *Educational Technology, 35*(1) 22-30. Retrieved March 27, 2009, from http://comparative.edu.ru:9080/PortalWeb/document/show.action?document.id=15659

Berger, J. (2007). *Cultural components of technology and its implications for adult education.* Retrieved March 28, 2009, from http://www.oise.utoronto.ca/CASAE/cnf2007/Proceedings-2007/AERC%20CASAE%20Berger-2007.pdf

Berners-Lee, T., & Mark, F. (1999). *Weaving the web: Origins and future of the world wide web.* Stamford, UK: Orion Business.

Biggs, J. B. (2003). *Teaching for quality learning at university: what the student does* (2nd ed.). Buckingham, UK: Society for Research into Higher Education.

Billett, S. (2001). *Critiquing workplace learning discourses: Participation and continuity at work.* Retrieved March 20, 2009, from http://www.infed.org/archives/e-texts/billett_workplace_learning.htm

Billings, D. M., & Halstead, J. A. (2005). *Teaching in nursing: A guide for instructors* (2nd ed.). St. Louis, MO: Elsevier Saunders.

Billington, D. (2007). Seven characteristics of adult education. Retrieved March 25, 2009, from http://

meetingsnet.com/associationmeetings/mag/meetings_seven_characteristics_adult/

Billington, D. D. (1988). Ego development and adult education, (Doctoral Dissertation, The Fielding Institute). *Dissertation Abstracts International, 49*(7), University Microfilms no. 88–16, 275.

Billington, D. D. (2000). *Seven characteristics of highly effective adult learning programs*. Seattle: New Horizons. Retrieved June 3, 2009 from http://www.newhorizons.org

Blanchard, A., & Horan, T. (2000). Virtual communities and social capital. In E. L. Lesser (Ed.), *Knowledge and social capital: Foundations and applications* (pp. 159-178). Woburn, MA: Butterworth-Heinemann.

Blank, W., & Hernandez, V. (2008). Preparing CTE leaders online. *Techniques, January Issue*. Association of Career and Technical Education (ACTE).

Bleecker, J. (2006, May). *What's your social doing in my mobile? Design patterns for mobile social software*. Paper presented at the WWW2006 Workshop MobEA IV-Empowering the Mobile Web. Edinburgh, Scotland.

Bloom, B., Mesia, B., & Krathwohl, D. (1964). *Taxonomy of educational objectives*. New York: David McKay.

Bonk, C. J., Wisher, R. A., & Lee, J. Y. (2004). Moderating learner-centered e-learning: Problems and solutions, benefits and implications. In T. S. Roberts (Ed.), *Online collaborative learning: Theory and practice* (pp. 54-85). Hershey, PA: IGI Global.

Bork, A. (2001). Adult education, lifelong learning, and the future. *Campus-Wide Information Systems, 18*(5), 195–203. doi:10.1108/EUM0000000006266

Boucouvalas, M. (1999). Comparative thinking and the structures of adult cognition: An epistemologica and methodological challenge for comparative adult education. In J. Reischmann, A. Jelenc & M. Bron (Eds.), *Comparative adult education: The contributions of the international society for comparative adult education [ISCAE] to an emerging field of study*, (pp. 65-76). Ljubljana, Slovenia: Slovenian Institute for Adult Education and ISCAE.

Boud, D. (2000). Sustainable assessment: rethinking assessment for the learning society. *Studies in Continuing Education, 22*(2), 151–167. doi:10.1080/713695728

Boud, D., & Miller, N. (1996). Animating learning from experience. In D. Boud & N. Miller (Eds), *Working with experience* (pp. 3-13). London: Routledge.

Boud, D., Keogh, R., & Walker, D. (Eds.). (1985). *Reflection: Turning experience into learning*. London: Kogan Page.

Bourdieu, P. (1977). *Outline of a theory of practice*. New York: Cambridge University Press.

Bourdieu, P., & Wacquant, L. (1992). *An invitation to reflexive sociology*. Chicago, IL: University of Chicago Press.

Bourne, J., & Moore, J. (2004). *Elements of quality online education: Into the mainstream*. Needham, MA: Sloan Consortium.

Bower, B. (2001). Distance education: Facing the faculty challenge. *Journal of Distance Learning Administration, IV*(II). Retrieved February 25, 2009, from http://www.westga.edu/~distance/ojdla/summer42/bower42.html

Boyd, G. (1993). A theory of distance education for the cyberspace era. In D. Keegan (Ed.), *Theoretical principles of distance education* (pp. 213-233). New York: Routledge.

Boyer, E. (1990). *Scholarship reconsidered: Priorities for the professoriate*. Princeton, NJ: The Carnegie Foundation for the Advancement of Teaching.

Boyer, R. (2006). *Employment and decent work in the era of 'flexicurity'*. DESA Working Paper No. 32. United Nations, Department of Economic and Social Affairs, New York.

Brager, J., & Johnson, K. (1993). *Adult learning: New research on continuous learning in the business environment*. Atlanta, GA: American Society for Training and Development Annual Conference.

Bransford, J. D., Brown, A. L., & Cocking, R. R. (2000). *How people learn: Brain, mind, experience, and school*. Washington, DC: National Academy Press.

Bridges, E., & Hallinger, P. (1995). *Implementing problem based learning in leadership development*. Eugene, OR: Eric Clearinghouse on Educational Management.

Brockett, R. G. (1983, April). Self-directed learning and the hard-to-reach adult. *Lifelong Learning: An Omnibus of Practice and Research*, *6*(8), 16–18.

Brockett, R. G. (1984, February). Developing written learning materials: A proactive approach. *Lifelong Learning: An Omnibus of Practice and Research*, *7*(5)16–18, 28.

Brockett, R. G. (n.d.), *Humanism as an instructional paradigm*. Retrieved June 6, 2009, from http://www-distance.syr.edu/romiral&html

Brookfield, S. (1986). *Understanding and facilitating adult learning*. San Francisco: Jossey-Bass.

Brookfield, S. (1987). Developing critical thinkers. San Francisco: Jossey-Bass.

Brookfield, S. (2005). *The power of critical theory: liberating adult learning and teaching*. San Francisco: Jossey-Bass.

Brookfield, S. (2006). The skillful teacher. San Francisco, CA: John Wiley & Sons.

Brookfield, S. D. (2006). *The skillful teacher: On techniques, trust, and responsiveness in the classroom* (2nd ed.). San Francisco: Jossey-Bass.

Brookfield, S.D. (2006). *The skillful teacher (2nd edition)*. San Francisco: Jossey Bass.

Brophy, P. (2006). The eLibrary and learning. In J. Weiss, J. Nolan, J. Hunsinger, & P. Trifonas (Eds.), *The international handbook of virtual learning environments (pt. 2)* (pp. 895-914). Dordrecht, The Netherlands: Springer.

Brown, T. H. (2006). Beyond constructivism: Navigationism in the knowledge era. *Horizon*, *14*(3), 108–120. doi:10.1108/10748120610690681

Bruce, A., Feng, F., Nishizawaumiko, S., Palulis, P., Russel, B. D., & Worthing, C. (2003). Provoking signs: Un/canny moments as curriculum theorizing. *Educational Insights*, *8*(2), 1–20.

Bruckman, A. (1998). Community support for constructionist learning. *Computer Supported Cooperative Work: The Journal of Collaborative Computing*, *7*, 47–86. doi:10.1023/A:1008684120893

Bruner, J. (2002). *Making stories*. New York: Farrar, Straus and Giroux.

Burbules, N. C. (2006). Rethinking the virtual. In J. Weiss, J. Nolan, J. Hunsinger, & P. Trifonas (Eds.), *The international handbook of virtual learning environments (pt. 1)* (pp. 37-58). Dordrecht, The Netherlands: Springer.

Burbules, N. C. (2008). Tacit teaching. *Educational Philosophy and Theory*, *40*(5), 666–677. doi:10.1111/j.1469-5812.2008.00453.x

Burge, E. J. (2000). Editor's notes. In E. J. Burge (Ed.), *The strategic use of learning technologies: New directions for adult continuing education, no. 88* (pp. 1-5). San Francisco: Jossey-Bass.

Burge, L. (1988). Beyond andragogy: Some explorations for distance learning design. *Journal of Distance Education*, *3*(1), 5–23.

Butakov, S., & Scherbinin, V. (2009). The toolbox for local and global plagiarism. *Computers & Education*, *52*, 781–788. doi:10.1016/j.compedu.2008.12.001

Butcher, S. E. (2006, September). Narrative as a teaching strategy. *Journal of Correctional Education*, *57*(3), 195–208.

Butler, T., & Pinto-Zipp, G. (2006). Students' learning styles and their preferences for online instructional methods. *Journal of Educational Technology Systems*, *34*(2), 199–221. doi:10.2190/8UD2-BHFU-4PXV-7ALW

Candy, P. (1991). *Self-direction for lifelong learning: A comprehensive guide to theory and practice*. San Francisco: Jossey-Bass.

Carnevale, D. (2005). Government's request for data may delay Blackboard's purchase

Carr, P. B., & Ponton, M. K. (2003). The e-learning instructor. In Piskurich, G. *Preparing learners for e-learning* (pp. 139-154). San Francisco, CA: John Wiley & Sons

Carroll, J. M. (1990). *Learner characteristics: When working adults sit down to learn*. Retrieved May 4, 2009, from www.spsu.edu/htc/hughes/com

Cassidy, S. (2004). Learning studies: An overview of theories, models, and measures. *Educational Psychology, 24*(4), 419–444. doi:10.1080/0144341042000228834

Castells, M. (1997). *The rise of the network society*. London: Routledge.

Center for Online Learning. (2009). *Online course design: Bloom's taxonomy*. Statesboro, GA: Georgia Southern University. Retrieved on March 15, 2009, from http://academics.georgiasouthern.edu/col/id/bloom.php

Cercone, K. (2008). Characteristics of adult learners with implications for online learning design. *Advancement of Computing in Education Journal, 16*(2), 137–159.

Charlton-Laing, C., & Bailey, A. (2007, April). The effects of social capital on knowledge sharing within a virtual collaborative learning community. In *Proceedings of the 6th Annual ISOnEworld Conference*, Las Vegas, NV. Retrieved 15 February, 2009, from http://www.isoneworld.org

Chodacki, J. A. (2005). *The wisdom of the aging workforce: A commodity in crisis*. Unpublished doctoral dissertation, Colorado Technical University. Clark, J. F. (n.d.). *The role of cooperative education in the adult learning environment*. Retrieved March 20, 2009, from http://horizon.unc.edu/conferences/lc/papers/18.html

Christian, A. C. (1982). *A comparative study of the andragogical-pedagogical orientation of military and civilian personnel*. Unpublished doctoral dissertation, Oklahoma State University, Stillwater, OK.

Clark, B. (1983). *The higher education system*. Berkeley, CA: University of California Press.

Clark, B. (2002). *Growing up gifted: Developing the potential of children at home and at school*. Upper Saddle River, NJ: Merrill Prentice Hall.

Clark, D. (1999). *Andragogy*. Retrieved October 10, 2002, from http://www.nwlink.com/~donclark/hrd/history/history.html

Clark, M. C., & Rossiter, M. (2008). Narrative learning in adulthood. *New Directions for Adult and Continuing Education, 119*, 61–70. doi:10.1002/ace.306

Clayton-Pedersen, A. R., & O'Neill, N. (2005). Curricula designed to meet 21st-Century expectations. In D. Oblinger & J. Obligner (Eds.), *Educating the Net generation* (pp. 9.1-9.16). Educause. Retrieved February 15, 2009, from http://www.educause.edu/educatingthenetgen/5989?time=1236850547

Clement, D. (2004). *Welcome to retirement: Now back to work*. Retrieved March 10, 2009, from http://www.minneapolisfed.org/publications_papers/pub_display.cfm?id=1676

Clugh, G., Jones, A., McAndrew, P., & Scanlon, E. (2008). Informal learning with PDAs and smartphones. *Journal of Computer Assisted Learning, 24*, 359–371. doi:10.1111/j.1365-2729.2007.00268.x

Cochran-Smith, P. M., Feiman-Nemser, S., & McIntyre, D. J. (Eds.). (2008). *Handbook of research on teacher education: Enduring questions in changing contexts*. London: Routledge.

Coffield, F. (1996, November). *A tale of three little pigs: Building the learning society with straw*. Paper presented at the European Union Conference on Lifelong Learning, University of Newcastle upon Tyne, UK.

Coffield, F. (1997). Introduction and overview: Attempts to reclaim the concept of the learning society. *Journal of Education Policy, 12*(6), 449–455. doi:10.1080/0268093970120601

Coffield, F. (2000). *Differing visions of a learning society. Research findings Volume 1*. London: The Policy Press.

Cohen, D., & Prusak, L. (2001). *In good company. How social capital makes organizations work*. Boston: Harvard Business School Press.

Cohen, J. E. (2006). Goals of universal basic and secondary education. *Prospects, 36*(3), 247–269. doi:10.1007/s11125-006-0016-1

Coiro, J., Klein, R., & Walpole, S. (2006). Critically evaluating educational technologies for literacy learning: Current trends and new paradigms. In M. McKenna, L. Lobbo, R. Kieffer, & D. Reinking (Eds.), *International handbook of literacy and technology* (pp. 145-162). New York: Routledge.

Collins, A., Brown, J., & Newman, S. (1989). Cognitive apprenticeship: Teaching the crafts of reading, writing, and mathematics. In L. Resnick (Ed.), *Knowing, learning and instructing: Essays in honor of Robert Glaser* (pp.453-494). Hillsdale, NJ: Lawrence Erlbaum.

Collins, R. A., & Zacharakis, J. (2009). Impact of e-learning on adult education: A changing postmodern approach. In V. Wang (Ed.), *Handbook of research on E-learning applications for career and technical education: Technologies for vocational training,* (pp. 286-296). Hershey, PA: IGI Global.

Collins, R.A. (2006). Cognitive development of adult undergraduate students: Cohort and non-cohort settings. *Educational Considerations, 33(2),* 35-41.

Commission for Accelerated Programs. (n.d.) Accelerated Programs by institutions. Retrieved on March 23, 2009 from http://www.capnetwork.org/modules.php?op=modload&name=CAPDatabase&file=index&&letter=All&sortby=institutionname&.

Commission of the European Communities. (2006). *Towards common principles of flexicurity: More and better jobs through flexibility and security.* Retrieved February 15, 2009, from http://ec.europa.eu/employment_social/news/2007/jun/flexicurity_en.pdf

Compayre, G., & Payne, W. H. (1885). *The history of pedagogy.* Boston: J. S. Cushing & Co.

Conlon, T. (2002). Information mapping as support for learning and teaching. *Computers & Education, 106,* 6–14.

Conner, M. L. (1997). Andragogy + pedagogy. *Ageless Learner.* Retrieved October 22, 2007, from Internet

Conrad, D. (2008). Online learning. In L. M. English (Ed.), *International encyclopedia of adult education* (pp. 442-447). New York: Palgrave Macmillan.

Conrad, R. M., & Donaldson, J. A. (2004). *Engaging the online learner: Activities and resources for creative instruction.* San Francisco: Jossey-Bass.

Conrad, R., & Donaldson, J. (2004). *Engaging the online learner.* San Francisco, CA: John Wiley & Sons

Cooke, J. C. (1994). *Malcolm Shepherd Knowles, the father of American andragogy: A biographical study.* University of North Texas, Denton, TX, Unpublished Doctor of Philosophy Dissertation.

Cooper, C., Taft, L. B., & Thelen, M. (2004). Examining the role of technology in learning: An evaluation of online clinical conferencing. *Journal of Professional Nursing, 20*(3), 160–166. doi:10.1016/j.profnurs.2004.04.003

Cooper, M. K., & Henschke, J. A. (2003, November). *An update on andragogy: The international foundation for its research, theory and practice.* Paper presented at the Commission of Professors of Adult Education (CPAE) Conference, Detroit, MI.

Cornelius-White, J. (2007). Learner-centered instructors-student relationships are effective: A meta-analysis. *Review of Educational Research, 77*(1), 113. doi:10.3102/003465430298563

Cote, S., & Healy, T. (2001). *The well-being of nations. The role of human and social capital.* Organization for Economic Co-operation and Development, Paris.

Council of the European Union. (2001). *Report from the education council to the European Council: The concrete future objectives of education and training systems.* Retrieved 15 February, from http://ec.europa.eu/education/policies/2010/doc/concrete-future-objectives_en.pdf

Cox, T. (2008). Learning styles and students' attitudes toward the use of technology in higher and adult education classes. *Institute for Learning Styles Journal, 1*(Fall), 1-13. Retrieved February 13, 2009, from http://www.auburn.edu/~witteje/ilsrj/latestissue.htm

Cranton, P. (1994). *Understanding and promoting transformative learning.* San Francisco: Jossey-Bass.

Cranton, P. (2005). Learning styles. In L. English (Ed.), *International encyclopedia of adult education* (pp. 362-366). New York: Palgrave McMillan.

Cranton, P. (2006). *Understanding and promoting transformative learning*. San Francisco: John Wiley & Sons.

Cuban, L. (2001). *Oversold and underused: Computers in the classroom*. Cambridge, MA: Harvard University Press.

Dale, M., & Bell, J. (1999). *Informal learning in the workplace. DfEE Research Report 134*, London: Department for Education and Employment.

Daniel, B., McCalla, G., & Schwier, R. (2001, December). *A process model for building social capital in virtual learning communities*. Paper presented at the International Conference on Computers in Education (ICCE'02), Auckland, New Zealand.

Daniel, B., Schwier, R., & McCalla, G. (2003). Social capital in virtual learning communities and distributed communities of practice. *Canadian Journal of Learning and Technology, 29*(3), 113–139.

Daniel, G. (2007, October 9). Elearning in K-12 education. *WWWtools for Education*. Retrieved May 14, 2009, from http://www.getmail.com.au/wwwtools/viewpage.aspx?rid=37767

Daniels, P. W. (2004, Spring). Reflections on the "old" economy, "new" economy, and services. *Growth and Change, 35*(2), 115–138. doi:10.1111/j.0017-4815.2004.00242.x

Davenport, J. (1993). Is there any way out of the Andragogy mess? In M. Thorpe, R. Edwards, & A. Hanson (Eds.), *Culture and processes of adult learning* (pp. 109-117). London: Routledge.

Davenport, J. III. (1987). Is there a way out of the andragogy morass? *Lifelong Learning: An Omnibus of Practice and Research, 11*(3), 17–20.

Davidson, J. (2002). *You are not alone, says Jane Davidson*. Welsh Assembly Government. Retrieved March 27, 2009, from http://new.wales.gov.uk/news/archivepress/educationpress/edpress2002/748994/?lang=en

Dawson, D. (2007). *Handheld technologies for mobile learning*. London: Latimer Trend.

De Kanter, N. (2005). Gaming redefines interactivity for learning. *TechTrends, 49*(3), 26–31. doi:10.1007/BF02763644

Delahaye, B. L., Limerick, D. C., & Hearn, G. (1994). The relationship between andragogical and pedagogical orientations and the implications for adult learning. *Adult Education Quarterly, 44*(4), 187–200. doi:10.1177/074171369404400401

Delamarter, S. (2006). Strategic planning to enhance teaching and learning with technology. *Teaching Theology and Religion, 9*(1), 9–23. doi:10.1111/j.1467-9647.2006.00256.x

Dennis, R., & Wisely, D. (2008). Mobility and ICT. In P. Warren, J. Davies, & D. Brown (Eds.), *ICT futures: Delivering pervasive, real-time and secure service* (pp. 129-142). Chichester, UK: John Wiley & Sons.

Denzin, N. K., & Lincoln, Y. S. (2000). The discipline and practice of qualitative research. In N. K. Denzin & Y. S. Lincoln (Eds.), *Handbook of qualitative research* (2nd ed., pp. 1-28). Thousand Oaks, CA: SAGE Publications, Inc.

Derntl, M., & Motschnig-Pitrik, R. (2004, March 14-17). Patterns for blended, person-centered learning: Strategy, concepts, experiences, and evaluation. In *Proceedings of the 2004 ACM Symposium on Applied Computing*, Nicosia, Cyprus (pp. 916-923). ACM Publishing.

DeRocco, E. (2005). *Older Americans Act*. Speech by Assistant Secretary, Employment and Training Employment and Training Administration. Committee on Senate Health, Education, Labor and Pensions Subcommittee on Retirement Security and Aging. FDCH Congressional Testimony, May 17, 2005.

Deubel, P. (2006, Jan.). Game on. *T.H.E. Journal*, 30–41.

Dewar, T. (1999). *Adult learning principles (a selection)*. Retrieved October 22, 2009, from Internet

Dewey, J. (1986). How we think: A restatement of the relation of reflective thinking to the educative process. In J. A. Boydston (Ed.), *The latter works* (pp. 105-325).

Carbondale, IL: Southern Illinois University Press. (Original work published 1933)

Dholakia, U. M., Bagozzi, R., & Pearo, L. K. (2004). A social influence model of consumer participation in network- and small-group-based virtual communities. *International Journal of Research in Marketing, 21*(3), 241–263. doi:10.1016/j.ijresmar.2003.12.004

Diaz, D., & Cartnal, R. (1999). Students' learning styles in two classes: online distance learning and equivalent on-campus. *College Teaching, 47*(4), 130–135. doi:10.1080/87567559909595802

Dickinson, D. (1991). Creating the future: Perspectives on educational change. *Lifelong learning: A dream.* Retrieved March 30, 2009, from http://www.newhorizons.org/future/Creating_the_Future/crfut_knowles.html

Diekelmann, N., Schuster, R., & Nosek, C. (1998). *Creating new pedagogies at the millennium: The common experiences of University of Wisconsin-Madison instructors using distance education technologies* (commissioned final report to University System of Wisconsin no. 1). Madison, WI: University of Wisconsin.

Downing, K. (2001). Information technology education and health care: Constructivism in the 21st century. *Educational Studies, 27*(3), 229–235. doi:10.1080/03055690120076510

Drago, V. (2009). *How generations view the mobile Internet.* Boston: Forrester Research. Retrieved March 15, 2009, from http://www.forrester.com/Research/Document/Excerpt/0,7211,47296,00.html

Draper, J. A. (1998). The metamorphoses of andragogy. *The Canadian Journal for the Study of Adult Education, 12*(1), 3–26.

Drucker, P. F. (1994, November). The age of social transformation. *Atlantic Monthly, 274*(5), 53–80.

Du, H., & Wagner, C. (2005). Learning with weblogs: An empirical investigation. In *Proceedings of the 38th Annual Hawaii International Conference on System Sciences (HICSS'05),* Big Island, Hawaii (pp. 7). IEEE.

DuCharme-Hansen, B. A., & Dupin-Bryant, P. A. (2004). *Web-based distance education for adults.* Malabar, FL: Krieger Publishing.

Dunn, R., & Griggs, S. A. (Eds.). (2000). *Practical approaches to using learning styles in higher education.* Westport, CT: Bergin & Garvey.

Dunn, R., Honingsfeld, A., & Doolan, L. (2009, January/February). Impact of learning-style instructional strategies on students' achievement and attitudes: Perceptions of educators in diverse institutions. *Clearing House (Menasha, Wis.), 82*(3), 135–140. doi:10.3200/TCHS.82.3.135-140

Durrance, B. (1998). Some explicit thoughts on tacit learning. *Training & Development, 52*(12), 24–29.

Dziuban, C. D., Hartman, J. L., & Moskal, P. D. (2004). Blended learning. *EDUCAUSE Center for Applied Research . Research Bulletin (Sun Chiwawitthaya Thang Thale Phuket), 2004*(7).

East Lansing, MI: Michigan State University.

Edmondson, A., & Moingeon, B. (1998). From Organizational Learning to the Learning Organisation. *Management Learning, 29*(1), 5–20. doi:10.1177/1350507698291001

Educational Broadcasting Corporation. (2004). *What are cooperative and collaborative learning?* Retrieved March 25, 2009, from http://www.thirteen.org/edonline/concept2class/coopcollab/index.html

Eitington, J. E. (1989). *The winning trainer, instructor, facilitator, teacher, conference leader, etc.* (3rd ed.) Houston, TX: Gulf Publishing Company.

Elias, J. L. (1979). Critique: Andragogy revisited. *Adult Education, 29*(4), 252–256. doi:10.1177/074171367902900404

Elias, J. L., & Merriam, S. B. (2005). *Philosophical foundations of adult education.* Malabar, FL: Krieger Publishing Company.

Ellis, H. J. C. (c. 1993). *Andragogy in a web technologies course.* Hartford, CT: Rensselaer at Hartford, Department of Engineering and Science.

Ellis, R. (2003). *Task-based language learning and teaching*. Oxford, UK: Oxford University Press.

Ellison, N. B., Steinfield, C., & Lampe, C. (2007). The benefits of Facebook friends: Social capital and college students. Use of online social network sites. *Journal of Computer-Mediated Communication, 12*(4), 1143–1168. doi:10.1111/j.1083-6101.2007.00367.x

Enders, A. (2007). Rates of computer and Internet use: A comparison of urban and rural access by people with disabilities. *Ruralfacts*. Missoula, MT: University of Montana. Equal Access for Software and Information. (n.d.). Retrieved from http://www.rit.edu/~easi

Ertmer, P. A., Lehman, J., Park, S. H., Cramer, J., & Grove, K. (2003, March). Barriers to teachers' adoption and use of technology in problem-based learning. In *Proceedings of the Association for the Advancement of Computing in Education (AACE) Society for Information Technology and Teacher Education (SITE) International Conference*, Albuquerque, NM (pp. 1761-1766). Chesapeake, VA: AACE.

Eskridge, R. C. (1978). *The literary contributions of Malcolm Shepherd Knowles to the process of adult education*. St. Louis University, Missouri, Unpublished Doctor of Philosophy Dissertation.

European Commission. (2001, November). *Making a European area of lifelong learning a reality*. Retrieved February 15, 2009, from http://eur-lex.europa.eu/LexUriServ/LexUriServ.do?uri=COM:2001:0678:FIN:EN:PDF

European Commission. (2006, October). *Employment in Europe 2006 report*. Retrieved February 15, 2009, from http://ec.europa.eu/employment_social/employment_analysis/employ_2006_en.htm

European Commission. (2007, November). *Employment in Europe 2007 report*. Retrieved February 15, 2009, from http://ec.europa.eu/employment_social/employment_analysis/employ_2007_en.htm

European Commission. (2008). *The use of ICT to support innovation and lifelong learning for all - a report on progress*. Brussels, Belgium: Commission of the European Communities.

European Commission. (2008, December). *Eurobarometer 70*. Public opinion in the European Union. Retrieved February 1, 2009, from http://ec.europa.eu/public_opinion/standard_en.htm

Evans, C. (2007). The effectiveness of m-learning in the form of podcast revision lecturers in high education. *Computers & Education, 50*, 491–498. doi:10.1016/j.compedu.2007.09.016

Farmer, L. (2005). *Librarians, literacy and the promotion of gender equity*. Jefferson, NC: McFarland.

Farrell, G. M. (2001). *The changing faces of virtual education*. London: Commonwealth of Learning.

Federal Access Board. (n.d.). Retrieved from http://access-board.gov

Feenberg, A. (1993). Building a global network: The WBSI executive education experience. In L. Harasim (Ed.), *Global networks: Computers and international communication* (pp. 185-197). Cambridge, MA: MIT Press.

Fenwick, T. (Fall, 2008). Workplace learning: emerging trends and new perspectives in *New directions for adult and continuing education, 119*, 17-26.

Fenwick, T. J. (2000). *Experiential learning in adult Education: A comparative framework*. Retrieved March 27, 2009, from http://www.ualberta.ca/~tfenwick/ext/pubs/print/aeq.htm

Ferro, T. R. (1997). The linguistics of andragogy and its offspring. In J. Levine, (Ed.), *Proceedings of the Midwest research-to-practice conference in adult, continuing and community education* (pp. 29-34).

Ferry, B., Hedberg, J., & Harper, B. (1998). How do preservice teachers use concept maps to organise their curriculum knowledge? *Journal of Interactive Learning Research, 9*(1), 83–104.

Fidishun, D. (2000). *Andragogy and technology: Integrating adult learning theory as we teach with technology*. Retrieved on January 27, 2009, from http://frank.mtsu.edu/~itconf/proceed00/fidishun.htm

Field, J. (2006). *Lifelong learning and the new educational order.* Sterling, VA: Trentham Books.

Fischer, G. (2001). Lifelong learning and its support with new media. In N. J. Smelser & P. B. Baltes (Eds.), *International encyclopedia of social and behavioral sciences* (pp. 8836-8840). New York: Elsevier.

Fisher, M., & McKee, P. (2008). Flexible ICT infrastructure. In P. Warren, J. Davies, & D. Brown (Eds.), *ICT futures: Delivering pervasive, real-time and secure service* (pp. 67-78). Chichester, UK: John Wiley & Sons.

Fitzgerald, R., Taylor, R., & La Valle, I. (2003). *National Adult Learning Survey (NALS) 2002.* Nottingham, UK: Department for Education and Skills.

Flecknoe, M. (2002). How can ICT help us to improve education? *Innovations in Education and Teaching International, 39*(4), 271–279. doi:10.1080/13558000210161061

Fleming, N. (n.d.). *VARK: A guide to learning styles.* Retrieved March 16, 2009, from http://www.vark-learn.com/english/page.asp?p=categories

Flores, F. (1998). Information technology and the institution of identity. *Information Technology & People, 11*(4), 351–372. doi:10.1108/09593849810246156

Flowers, J. (2001). Online learning in technology education. *Journal of Technology Education, 13*(1), 17–30.

Flowers, J. (2005). The effect of online delivery on graduate enrollment. *Journal of Industrial Teacher Education, 42*(4), 7–24.

Flowers, J., & Baltzer, H. (2006a). Hiring technical education faculty: Vacancies, criteria, and attitudes toward online doctoral programs. *Journal of Industrial Teacher Education, 43*(3), 29–44.

Flowers, J., & Baltzer, H. (2006b). Perceived demand for online and hybrid doctoral programs in technical education. *Journal of Industrial Teacher Education, 43*(4), 39–56.

Fontana, D. (1981). *Psychology for teachers.* London: Macmillan/British Psychological Society.

Foster, A. (2008). Games and motivation to learn science: Personal identity, applicability, relevance and meaningfulness. *Journal of Interactive Learning Research, 19*(4), 597–614.

Fountain, J. (1997). Social capital: A key enabler of innovation in science and technology. In L. M. Branscomb & J. Keller (Eds.), *Investing in innovation: Toward a consensus strategy for federal technology policy* (pp. 84-111). Cambridge, MA: The MIT Press.

Fountain, J. E., & Atkinson, R. D. (1999, July). *Innovation, social capital and the New Economy: New federal policies to support collaborative research.* Progressive Policy Institute, Technology Policy Library. Retrieved January 15, 2009, from http://www.ppionline.org/ppi_ci.cfm?cp=1&knlgAreaID=140&subsecid=293&contentid=1371

Freire, P. (1970). *Pedagogy of the oppressed.* New York: Seabury Press.

Friedman, T. (2006). *The world is flat* (updated and expanded). New York: Farrar, Straus and Giroux. *G-7 Ministerial Conference on the Information Society: Cooperation on applications and testbeds.* (1995, January 12). Brussels. Retrieved March 15, 2009, from www.ifla.org/documents/infopol/intl/g7/g7-113qa.txt

Friedman, T. L. (2007). The *world is flat: A brief history of the twenty first century.* Picador, New York: Release 3.0.

Furter, P. (1971). Grandeur et misere de la pedagogie. University of Neuchatel. In E. Faure (Ed.), *Learning to be: The world of education today and tomorrow,* (p. 116). Paris: UNESCO.

Gardner, H. (1999). *Intelligence reframed: Multiple intelligences for the 21st century.* New York: Basic Books.

Gardner, N. (1989). The electronic campus: The first decade. *Higher Education Quarterly, 43,* 332–350. doi:10.1111/j.1468-2273.1989.tb01518.x

Gargiulo, T. L. (2009). *The top ten strategies for managers of mobile workers.* Retrieved April 10, 2009, from http://makingstories.net

Garner, S. (2005). *High-level colloquium on information literacy and lifelong learning*. Alexandria, Egypt: International Federal of Library Associations.

Gaytan, J., & McEwen, B. (2007). Effective online instructional and assessment strategies. *American Journal of Distance Education, 21*(3), 117–132. doi:10.1080/08923640701341653

Gee, J. (2007). *What video games have to teacher us about learning and literacy* (2nd ed.). Palgrave, UK: Macmillan.

Gehring, T. (2000). A compendium of material on the pedagogy-andragogy issue. *Journal of Continuing Education, 51*(1), 151–163.

Gillespie, M. (2005). Student-instructors connection: A place of possibility. *Journal of Advanced Nursing, 52*(2), 211–219. doi:10.1111/j.1365-2648.2005.03581.x

Giménez-Costa, A., & González-Bondia, A. (2007). Design of a wiki-based collaborative working strategy within the context of legal sciences. *European Journal of Legal Education, 4*(1), 105–114.

Glatthorn, A. A., Boschee, F., & Whitehead, B. M. (2006). *Curriculum leadership: Development and implementation*. Thousand Oaks, CA: SAGE Publications.

Gobet, F., Lane, P. C. R., Croker, S., Cheng, P. C.-H., Jones, G., & Oliver, I. (2001). Chunking mechanisms in human learning. *Trends in Cognitive Sciences, 5*, 236–243. doi:10.1016/S1364-6613(00)01662-4

Goleman, D. (1998). *Working with emotional intelligence*. New York: Bantam Books.

Goodman, P. S. (2002). *Technology enhanced learning: Opportunities for change*. Mahwah, NJ: Lawrence Erlbaum Associates.

Gorard, S., & Selwyn, N. (1999). Switching on the learning society? Questioning the role of technology in widening participation in lifelong learning. *Journal of Education Policy, 14*(5), 523–534. doi:10.1080/026809399286198

Grasha, A. (1996). *Teaching with style: A practical guide to enhancing learning by understanding teaching and learning styles*. Pittsburgh, PA: International Alliance of Teaching Scholars.

Green, J. (1998), *Andragogy: Teaching adults*. In B. Hoffman (Ed.), *Encyclopedia of educational technology*.

Greenberg, J., & Baron, R. (2002). *Behavior in organizations* (10th ed.). Englewood Cliffs, NJ: Prentice Hall.

Greene, G., & Kochbar-Bryand, C. (2003). *Pathways to successful transition for youth with disabilities*. Upper Saddle River, NJ: Merrill.

Greene, M. (1995). *Releasing the imagination*. San Francisco: Jossey-Bass.

Greene, M. (2001). *Variations on a blue guitar*. New York: Teachers College Press.

Gregorc, A. F. (1982). *An adult's guide to style*. Columbia, CT: Gregorc Associates, Inc.

Griffith, W. S. (1991). The impact of intellectual leadership. In J.M. Peters & P. Jarvis (Eds.), *Adult education: Evolution and achievements in a developing field of study* (pp. 97-120). San Francisco: Jossey-Bass.

Griswold, W. (2008). *Cultures and societies in a changing world* (3rd ed.). Thousand Oaks, CA: Pine Forge Press.

Grow, G. (1991). Teaching learners to be self-directed. *Adult Education Quarterly, 41(3)*, 125-149.

Hadley, H. N. (1975). *Development of an instrument to determine adult educator's orientation as andragogical and pedagogical*. Unpublished doctoral dissertation, Boston University School of Education, Boston, MA.

Halavais, A. C. (2006). Weblogs and collaborative web publishing as learning spaces. In J. Weiss, J. Nolan, J. Hunsinger, & P. Trifonas (Eds.), *The international handbook of virtual learning environments (pt. 2)* (pp. 1215-1236). Dordrecht, The Netherlands: Springer.

Halverson, R. (2005). What can K-12 school leaders learn from video games and gaming? *Innovate, 1*(6). Retrieved from http://www.innovateonline.info

Hamilton, M. (2006). Just do it: Literacies, everyday learning and the irrelevance of pedagogy. *Studies in the Education of Adults, 38*(2), 125–140.

Hamman, R. B. (1998). *The online/offline dichotomy: Debunking some myths about AOL users and the effects of their being online upon offline friendships and offline community.* Unpublished doctoral dissertation, University of Liverpool. Retrieved March 20, 2009, from http://www.cybersoc.com/mphil

Hanson, A. (1996). The search for a separate theory of adult learning: Does anyone really need andragogy? In R. Edwards, A. Hanson, & P. Raggatt (Eds.), *Adult learners, education and training 1* (pp. 99-108). London: Routledge and The Open University.

Harasim, L. (2006). A history of e-learning: Shift happened. In J. Weiss, J. Nolan, J. Hunsinger, & P. Trifonas (Eds.), *The international handbook of virtual learning environments (pt. 1)* (pp. 59-94). Dordrecht, The Netherlands: Springer.

Harrington, T., Staffo, M., & Wright, V. H. (2006). Faculty uses of and attitudes toward a course management system in improving instruction. *Journal of Interactive Online Learning, 5*(2), 178–190.

Harrison, D. (2009). *Engaging students in virtual learning.* Retrieved April 23, 2009, from http://campustechnology.com/Articles/2009/04/22/Engaging-Students-in-Virtual-Learning

Hars, A., & Ou, S. (2002). Working for free? Motivations for participating in open source projects. *International Journal of Electronic Commerce, 6*(3), 301–311.

Hartley, K., & Bendixen, L. D. (2001). Educational research in the Internet age: Examining the role of individual characteristics. *Educational Researcher, 30*(9), 22. doi:10.3102/0013189X030009022

Hartree, A. (1984). Malcolm Knowles's theory of andragogy: A critique. *International Journal of Lifelong Education, 3*, 203–210. doi:10.1080/0260137840030304

Havice, W. L., & Havice, P. A. (Eds.). (2005). *Distance and distributed learning environments: Perspectives and strategies: 54th yearbook of the Council on Technology Teacher Education.* New York: Glencoe McGraw-Hill.

Helmrich, E., & Neiburger, E. (2007). Video games as a service: Three years later. *VOYA, 30*(2), 113–115.

Henschke, J. A. (1973). *Malcolm S. Knowles: His contributions to the theory and practice of adult education.* Boston University, Unpublished Doctor of Education Dissertation. Retrieved June 3, 2009, from http://www.umsl.edu/~henschke

Henschke, J. A. (1987). Training teachers of adults. In C. Klevins (Ed.), *Materials and methods in adult and continuing education: International – illiteracy* (pp. 414-422). Los Angeles: Klevens Publications.

Henschke, J. A. (1989). Identifying appropriate adult educator practices: Beliefs, feelings and behaviors. In C. Jeffries, (Ed.), *Proceedings of the eighth annual Midwest research-to-practice conference in adult, continuing and community education* (pp. 89-95). St. Louis, MO: University of Missouri.

Henschke, J. A. (1995). Theory and practice on preparing human resource development professionals. In *Proceedings of Academy of Human Resource Development Research Conference* (pp. 1-11). St. Louis: University of Missouri.

Henschke, J. A. (1998b). Modeling the preparation of adult educators. *Adult Learning, 9*(3), 11–14.

Henschke, J. A. (1999). Historical antecedents shaping the terms performance and learning in human resource development: An exploratory study." In K. P. Kuchinke (Ed.), *Proceedings of the Academy of Human Resource Development Research Conference*, Alexandria, VA. (pp 611-619).

Henschke, J. A. (2000-ff.). *Andragogy.* Retrieved June 1, 2009, from http://www.umsl.edu/~henschke/andragogy/

Henschke, J., & Cooper, M. (2007a). Additions toward a thorough understanding of the international foundations of andragogy in HRD and Adult Education. An. Inst. de Ins. "G.Barit" din Cluj-Napoca, Series umanistica, tom. V, 2007, pp. 7-54. [This is the 2007 Yearbook of the Romanian Institute of Adult Education.]

Hernandez, V., Kirby, J., & McGee, S. (2004). *Competency assessment in distributed education.* Washington, DC: Association of Jesuit Colleges and Universities.

Hernández-Gantes, V. M., & Blank, W. (2009). *Teaching English language learners in career and technical education programs*. New York: Routledge.

Hernández-Pina, F., Martínez-Clares, P., Fonseca-Rosario, P., & Rubio-Espín, M. (2005). *Aprendizaje, competencias y rendimiento en educación superior* [*Learning, competences and performance in higher education*]. Madrid, Spain: La Muralla.

Higher Learning Commission (n.d.), Affiliated Institutions, University of Phoenix. Retrieved on March 23, 2009, from http://www.ncahlc.org/index.php?option=com_directory&Itemid=192&Action=ShowBasic&instid=1949

Hill, R. J. (2008). Troubling adult learning in the present time. *New Directions for Adult and Continuing Education, 119*, 83–92. doi:10.1002/ace.308

Hillier, Y. *(2005).* Reflective teaching in further and adult education *(2nd ed.). London: Continuum.*

Hirumi, A. (2002). A framework for analyzing, designing, and sequencing planned e-learning interactions. *The Quarterly Review of Distance Education, 3*(2), 141–160.

Hmelo-Silver, C. E. (2004). Problem-based learning: What and how do students learn? *Educational Psychology Review, 16*(3), 235–266. doi:10.1023/B:EDPR.0000034022.16470.f3

Hmelo-Silver, C. E., Duncan, R. G., & Chinn, C. A. (2007). Scaffolding and achievement in problem-based and inquiry learning: A response to Kirschner, Sweller, and Clark (2006). *Educational Psychologist, 42*(2), 99–107.

Hoare, C. (Ed.). (2006). *Handbook of adult development and learning*. New York: Oxford.

Hofer, B., & Pintrich, P. (1997). The development of epistemological theories: Beliefs about knowledge and knowing and their relation to learning. *Review of Educational Research, 67*(1), 88–140.

Hoffman, F. (1980*). How to teach grown-ups*. Calabasas, CA: Practical Management Associates, Inc.

Hofstede, G. (2001). *Culture's Consequence: Comparing values, behaviors, institutions and organizations across nations.* London: Sage Publication.

Holcomb, J. B., Dumire, R. D., Crommett, J. W., Stamateris, C. E., Fagert, M. A., & Cleveland, J. A. (2002). Evaluation of trauma team performance using an advanced human patient simulator for resuscitation training. *The Journal of Trauma Injury Infection and Critical Care, 52*(6), 1078. doi:10.1097/00005373-200206000-00009

Holmes, G., & Abington-Cooper, M. (2000). Pedagogy vs. andragogy: A false dichotomy? *The Journal of Technology Studies, 24*(2). Retrieved February 15, 2009, from http://scholar.lib.vt.edu/ejournals/JOTS/Summer-Fall-2000/holmes.html

Holvikivi, J. (2007). Learning styles in engineering education: the quest to improve didactic practices. *European Journal of Engineering Education, 32*(4), 401–408. doi:10.1080/03043790701332909

Hooks, B. (1994). *Theory as liberatory practice,* (from *Teaching to Transgress – as quoted by Kaminsky, Sherrie in "Comparing Pedagogy and Andragogy for Both Common and Dissimilar Meanings").* Retrieved June 4, 2009, from http://www.usm.maine.edu/~dlarson/kaminsky2.htm

Hopkins, L., & Thomas, J. (2002). *E-social capital: building community through electronic networks.* Retrieved 20 March, 2009, from http://www.sisr.net/publications/nd_hopkins_2.pdf

Horyp, S. (2006). Reflection in learning at work. In E. Antonocopoulou, P. Jarvis, V. Andersen, B. Elkjaer, & S. Hoyrup (Eds.), *Learning, working and living* (pp. 85-100). London: Palgrave Macmillan.

Houle, C. O. (1961). *The Inquiring Mind.* Madison, WI: University of Wisconsin Press.

Houle, C. O. (1992). *The literature of adult education: A bibliographic essay.* San Francisco: Jossey-Bass.

Houle, C. O. (1996). *The design of education* (2nd ed.). San Francisco: Jossey-Bass.

Howard, C., Schenk, K., & Discenza, R. (2003). *Distance Learning and university effectiveness: Changing educational paradigms for online learning*. Hershey, PA: IGI Global.

Huang, U. (2002). Toward constructivism for adult learners in online learning environments. *British Journal of Educational Technology, 33*(1), 27–37. doi:10.1111/1467-8535.00236

Hugo, J. (2003). *A comparison of and characteristics of educational multi-media*. Uganda: Naledi3Dfactory and UNE.

Hung, D., Chen, D. T., & Wong, A. F. L. (2006). An overview of virtual learning environments in the Asia-Pacific: Provisos, issues, and tensions. In J. Weiss, J. Nolan, J. Hunsinger, & P. Trifonas (Eds.), *The international handbook of virtual learning environments (pt. 1)* (pp. 699-722). Dordrecht, The Netherlands: Springer.

Hung, W. C., & Chao, C. A. (2007, May). Integrating advance organizers and multidimensional information display in electronic performance systems. *Innovations in Education and Teaching International, 44*(2), 181–198. doi:10.1080/14703290701240986

Hutchinson, N. (2001, June). Beyond ADA compliance: Redefining accessibility. *American Libraries*, 76–78.

Illeris, K. (2004). *Adult education and adult learning*. Copenhagen: Roskilde University Press/Malabar, FL: Krieger Publishing.

Illeris, K. (2004). *The three dimensions of learning*. Malabar, FL: Krieger.

Imel, S. (1989). Teaching adults: Is it different? *ERIC Digest, 82*(ED 305495).

Imel, S. (1998). *Technology and adult learning: Current perspectives*. Columbus, OH: ERIC Clearinghouse on Adult, Career and Vocational Education. (ERIC Document Reproduction Service No. 197).

Ingalls, J. D. (1972). *A trainers guide to andragogy*. Washington, DC: United State Department of Health, Education and Welfare.

Ingalls, J. D. (1976). *Human energy: The critical factor for individuals and organizations*. Reading, MA: Addison-Wesley Publishing Company.

Isenberg, S. (2007). *Applying andragogical principles to internet learning*. New York: Cambria Press.

Istance, D., Schuetze, H., & Schuller, T. (Eds.). (2002). *International perspectives on lifelong learning: Form recurrent education to the knowledge society*. Berkshire, UK: Open University Press.

Itin, C. M. (1999). Reasserting the philosophy of experiential education as a vehicle for change in the 21st century. *Journal of Experiential Education, 22*(2), 91–98.

James, W., & Blank, W. (1993). Review and critique of available learning style instruments for adults. *New Directions for Adult and Continuing Education, 59*. San Francisco: Jossey Bass.

James, W., & Maher, P. (2004). Understanding and using learning styles. In M.Galbraith (Ed.), *Adult Learning Methods: A guide for effective instruction*, (3rd Ed.) (pp. 119-139). Malabar, FL: Krieger Publishing.

Janicki, T., & Liegle, J. O. (2001). Development and evaluation of a framework for creating Web-based learning modules: A pedagogical and systems approach. *Journal of Asynchronous Learning Networks, 5*(1).

Jarvis, P. (1984). Andragogy: A sign of the times. *Studies in the Education of Adults, 16*, 32–38.

Jarvis, P. (2000). Globalisation, the learning society and comparative education. *Comparative Education, 36*(23), 343–355. doi:10.1080/713656613

Jarvis, P., & Parker, S. (Eds.). (2005). *Human learning: A holistic approach*. London: Routledge.

Jeong, A., & Lee, J. M. (2008). The effects of active versus reflective learning style on the processes of critical discourse in computer-supported collaborative argumentation. *British Journal of Educational Technology, 39*(4), 651–665. doi:10.1111/j.1467-8535.2007.00762.x

JISC & SCONUL. (2008). *Library Management Systems Study*. Sheffield, UK: Sero Consulting.

Jochems, W., von Merrienboer, J., & Koper, R. (2004). *Integrated e-learning: implications for pedagogy, technology and organization*. New York: RoutledgeFalmer

Johnson, D. W., & Johnson, F. (1997). *Joining together: Group theory and group skills* (6th ed.). Boston: Allyn & Bacon.

Johnson, D. W., Johnson, R. T., & Smith, K. A. (1991). *Cooperative learning: Increasing college faculty instructional productivity*. ASHE-ERIC Higher Education.

Johnson, D. W., Johnson, R., & Holubec, E. (1990). *Circles of learning: Cooperation in the classroom*. Edina, MN: Interaction Book Company.

Johnson, J. (2003). *Distance education: The complete guide to design, delivery and improvements*. New York: Teachers College Press.

Johnson, S. A., & Romanello, M. L. (2005). Generational diversity: Teaching and learning approaches. *Nurse Educator*, *30*(5), 212–216. doi:10.1097/00006223-200509000-00009

Johnson, S. D., & Benson, A. D. (2003). *Distance learning in postsecondary career and technical education*. St. Paul, MN: National Research Center for Career and Technical Education.

Jones, A., Kirkup, G., & Kirkwood, A. (1993). *Personal computers for distance education*. New York: St. Martin's Press.

Jones, S, Lang, G., Terrell, I., Thompson, K., Ramondt, L., & ULTRALAB associates (2001). *Establishing online communities for school leaders-an interim report*. Retrieved March 27, 2009, from http://www.ceilidhfolk.co.uk/bera2001th.pdf

Jorgensen, H. K. (1998), *Adult learning theories and religious education for seventh-Day Adventist college students: From theory to practice*. Presented for the 22nd Faith and Learning Seminar held at Seminar Schlossbogenhofen St. Peter Am Hart, Austria, August 9–21.

Kabuga, C. (1977). Why andragogy in developing countries? *Adult Education and Development: Journal for Adult Education in Africa, Asia, and Latin America*.

Kajee, L. (n.d.). *Making waves, not just surfing the net: ICT and learning in the ESL classroom*. Unpublished paper, University of the Witwatersrand, Johannesburg, South Africa. Kamansky, S. (n.d.). *Comparing pedagogy and andragogy for both common and dissimilar meanings*. Retrieved July 18, 2004, from http://www.usm.maine.edu/!dlarson/kaminsky2.htm

Kanuka, H. (2005). An exploration into facilitating higher levels of learning in a text-based Internet learning environment using diverse instructional strategies. *Journal of Computer-Mediated communication, 10*(3). Retrieved from http://jcmc.indiana.edu/vol10/issue3/kanuka.html

Kanungo, R. N., & Mendonca, M. (1996). Cultural Contingencies and Leadership in Developing Countries. In P.A.Banberger, M. Erez, & S.B. Bacharach, S.B. (Eds.), *Research in the Sociology of Organizations*, (vol. 14, pp. 263-295). Greenwich, CT: Jai Press.

Kapp, A. (1833). *Die andragogik ober bildung im mannlichen alter. Platons Erziehungslehre, als Padagogik fur die Einzelnen und als Staatspadagogik*. Germany: Minden und Leipzig.

Kasworm, C. D., & Londoner, C. A. (2000). Adult learning and technology. In A.L. Wilson & E. Hayes, (Ed.), *Handbook of adult and continuing education*, (pp.224-42). San Francisco, CA: John Wiley & Sons.

Kasworm, C.E., Polson, C.J., & Fishback, S.J. (2002). *Responding to adult learners in higher education*. Malabar, FL: Krieger Publishing.

Katz, R. N. (Ed.). (1999). *Dancing with the devil: Information technology and the new competition in higher education*. San Francisco: Jossey-Bass Higher and Adult Education Series.

Kayler, M., & Weller, K. (2007). Pedagogy, self-assessment, and online discussion groups. *Journal of Educational Technology & Society*, *10*(1), 136.

Keller, B., & Seifert, H. (2004). Flexicurity. The German trajectory. *European Review of Labor and Research*, *10*(2), 226–247.

Kellogg Commission (1999, September). *Returning to our roots: A learning society. Fourth Report*. Kellogg Commission on the Future of State and Land-Grant Universities.

Kennedy, G. E., Judd, T. S., Churchward, A., Gray, K., & Krause, K. L. (2008). First year students' experiences with technology: Are they really digital natives. *Australasian Journal of Educational Technology, 24*(1), 108–122.

Kenny, G., Pontin, D., & Moore, L. (2004). Negotiating socialisation: The journey of novice nurse academics into higher education. *Nurse Education Today, 24*(8), 629–637.

Kim, K., & Bonk, C. J. (2006). The future of online teaching and learning in higher education: The survey says… . *EDUCAUSE Quarterly, 29*(4).

King, K. P. (2005). *Bringing transformative learning to life*. Malabar, FL: Krieger Publishing Company.

King, K. P. (2008). Distance education. In L. M. English (Ed.), *International encyclopedia of adult education* (pp. 192-199). New York: Palgrave Macmillan.

King, P.M., & Kitchener, K.S. (1994). *Developing reflective judgment*. San Francisco: Jossey-Bass.

Kings, N. J., Davies, J., Verrill, D., Aral, S., Bryniolfsson, E., & Alstyne, M. V. (2008). Social networks, social computing and knowledge management. In P. Warren, J. Davies, & D. Brown (Eds.), *ICT futures: Delivering pervasive, real-time and secure service* (pp. 17-26). Chichester, UK: John Wiley & Sons.

Kirkpatrick, D. L. (1976). Evaluation of Training. In R.L. Craig. (Ed.) *Training & Development Handbook: A Guide to Human Resource Development* (2nd Ed.). New York: McGraw-Hill.

Kirkwood, A., & Price, L. (2005). Learners and learning in the 21st century: What do we know about students' attitudes towards and experiences of information and communication technologies that will help us design courses? *Studies in Higher Education, 30*(3), 257–274. doi:10.1080/03075070500095689

Kirschner, P. A., Sweller, J., & Clark, R. E. (2006). Why minimal guidance during instruction does not work: An analysis of the failure of constructivist, discovery, problem-based, experiential, and inquiry-based teaching. *Educational Psychologist, 41*(2), 75–86. doi:10.1207/s15326985ep4102_1

Knapp, L.G., Kelly-Reid, J.E., and Ginder, S.A. (2009). *Enrollment in postsecondary institutions, fall 2007; graduation rates, 2001 & 2004 cohorts; and financial statistics, fiscal year 2007* (NCES 2009-155). Washington, D. C.: National Center for Education Statistics, Institute of Education Sciences, U.S. Department of Education.

Knowles, M. (1989). *The making of an adult educator*. San Francisco, CA: Jossey-Bass.

Knowles, M. (1995). *Designs for Adult Learning*. Alexandria, VA: American Society for Training and Development.

Knowles, M. S. (1968a). Androgogy, not pedagogy. *Adult Leadership, 16*, 350–352.

Knowles, M. S. (1968b). How andragogy works in leadership training in the Girl Scouts. *Adult Leadership, 17*, 160–162.

Knowles, M. S. (1969). An experiment with group self-directed learning: The learning teaching team. In p. Runkel, R. Harrison, & M. Runkel (Eds.), *The Changing College Classroom*. San Francisco: Jossey-Bass.

Knowles, M. S. (1970). *The modern practice of adult education: Andragogy vs. Pedagogy*. New York: Association Press.

Knowles, M. S. (1972). The manager as educator. *Journal of Continuing Education and Training, 2*(2), 97–105.

Knowles, M. S. (1973). *The adult Learner: A neglected species*. Houston: Gulf Publishing Company.

Knowles, M. S. (1975). *Self-directed learning: A guide for learners and teachers*. New York: Association Press.

Knowles, M. S. (1980). *The modern practice of adult education: From pedagogy to andragogy* (2nd ed.). New York: Cambridge Books.

Knowles, M. S. (1980). *The modern practice of adult education: From andragogy to pedagogy*. Englewood Cliffs, NJ: Cambridge Adult Education.

Knowles, M. S. (1980). *The modern practice of adult education: From pedagogy to andragogy*, (Rev. ed.). New York: Cambridge Book Publishers.

Knowles, M. S. (1984). *Andragogy in action. Applying modern principles of adult Learning*. San Francisco: Jossey-Bass.

Knowles, M. S. (1984a). *The adult learner: A neglected species* (3rd ed.). Houston: Gulf Publishing Company.

Knowles, M. S. (1984b). *Andragogy in action: Applying modern principles of adult learning*. San Francisco: Jossey-Bass.

Knowles, M. S. (1989a). Adult learning: Theory & practice. In L. Nadler & A. Nadler (Eds.), *The handbook of human resource development* (2d ed.) (pp. 6.1 -- 6.23). New York: John Wiley & Sons.

Knowles, M. S. (1989b). *The making of an adult educator: An autobiographical journey*. San Francisco: Jossey-Bass Publishers.

Knowles, M. S. (1990). *The adult learner: A neglected species* (4th ed.). Houston, TX: Gulf Publishing Company.

Knowles, M. S. (1990). *The modern practice of adult education: From pedagogy to andragogy*. New York: Cambridge.

Knowles, M. S. (1991). *Lifelong learning: A dream*. Retrieved June 3, 2009, from http://www.newhorizons.org/future/Creating_the_Furure/crfut_knowles.html

Knowles, M. S. (1995). *Designs for adult learning: Practical resources, exercises, and course outlines from the father of adult learning*. Alexandria, VA: American Society for Training and Development.

Knowles, M. S. (1996). *Adult learning*. In R. L. Craig (Ed.), *ASTD training & development handbook: A guide to human resource development* (4th ed.) (pp. 254-265). New York: McGraw Hill.

Knowles, M. S., Holton, E. F., III, & Swanson, R. A. (1998). *The adult learner* (5th ed.). Houston: Gulf Publishing.

Knowles, M. S., Holton, E., & Swanson, A. (2005). *The adult learner* (6th ed.). Boston: Elsevier Butterworth Heinemann.

Knowles, M., Holton, E., & Swanson, R. (2005). *The adult learner*. Burlington, MA: Elsevier.

Knowles, M.S. (1969). *Higher adult education in the united states: The current picture, trends, and issues*. Washington, D. C.: Committee on Higher Adult Education, American Council on Education.

Knudson, R. S. (1980). An alternative approach to the andragogy/pedagogy issue. *Lifelong Learning, the Adult Years, 3*(8), 8–10.

Kodama, M. (2008). *New knowledge creation through ICT dynamic capability*. Charlotte, NC: Information Age Publishing.

Koehler, M. J., & Mishra, P. (2005a). Instructors learning technology by design. *Journal of Computing in Instructors Education, 21*(3), 94–102.

Koehler, M. J., & Mishra, P. (2005b). What happens when instructors design educational technology? The development of technological pedagogical content knowledge. *Journal of Educational Computing Research, 32*(2), 131–152. doi:10.2190/0EW7-01WB-BKHL-QDYV

Kolb, D. A. (1984). *Experiential learning: Experience as the source of learning and development*. Upper Saddle River, NJ: Prentice-Hall.

Kolekofski, K. E., & Heminger, A. R. (2003). Beliefs and attitudes affecting intentions to share information in an organizational setting. *Information & Management, 40*, 521–532. doi:10.1016/S0378-7206(02)00068-X

Kolko, B. E., Johnson, E., & Rose, E. (2007, July). *Mobile social software for the developing world*. Paper presented at the 2nd International Conference, OCSC 2007, Held as part of HCI International 2007, Beijing, China, (pp. 385-394).

Konana, P., & Balasubramanian, S. (2005). The Social–Economic–Psychological model of technology adoption and usage: an application to online investing . *Decision Support Systems, 39*(3), 505–524. doi:10.1016/j.dss.2003.12.003

Koper, R. (2004). Use of the semantic web to solve some basic problems in education. *Journal of Interactive Media in Education, 6*, 1–23.

Koper, R., & Olivier, B. (2004). Representing the learning design of units of learning. *Journal of Educational Technology & Society, 7*, 97–111.

Koper, R., & Tattersall, C. (2004). New directions for lifelong learning using network technologies. *British Journal of Educational Technology, 35*(6), 689–700. doi:10.1111/j.1467-8535.2004.00427.x

Kraemer, E. W. (2003). Developing the online learning environment: The pros and cons of using WebCT. *Information Technologies and Libraries, 22*(2), 87–92.

Krajinc, A. (1989). Andragogy. In C. J. Titmus (Ed.), *Lifelong education for adults: An international handbook* (pp. 19-21). Oxford, UK: Pergamon.

Kraut, R., Kiesler, S., Boneva, B., Cummings, J., Helgeson, V., & Crawford, A. (2002). Internet paradox revisited. *The Journal of Social Issues, 58*, 49–74. doi:10.1111/1540-4560.00248

Kreijns, K., Kirschner, P. A., Jochems, W., & Van Buuren, H. (2004). Determining sociability, social space, and social presence in (a) synchronous collaborative groups. *Cyber-psychology & Behavior: The Impact of the Internet . Multimedia and Virtual Reality on Behavior and Society, 7*(2), 155–172.

Krichen, J. P. (2004). *Online university administration: Impacts on instructors' management and course delivery.* Retrieved from http://www.decadeconsulting.com/decade/images/Jkrichen.pdf

Lagemann, E. C. (2002). *An elusive science: The troubling history of education research*. Chicago: University of Chicago Press.

Laiken, M. (2001). *Models of organizational learning: Paradoxes and best practices in the post industrial workplace.* Toronto: University of Toronto.

Landry, B. J. L., Mahesh, S., & Hartman, S. J. (2005, Spring). The impact of the pervasive information age on healthcare organizations. *Journal of Health and Human Services Administration, 27*(4), 444–464.

Laurillard, D. (1993). *Rethinking university teaching: A framework for the effective use of educational technology.* London: Routledge.

Lave, J., & Wenger, E. (1991). *Situated learning: Legitimate peripheral participation.* New York: Cambridge Press.

Lee, J., & Young, C. (2008). Middle level educators and online social gaming. In K. McFerrin, et al, (Eds.), *Proceedings of Society for Information Technology and Teacher Education International Conference 2008* (pp. 1726-1732). Chesapeake, VA: American Association of Computer Education.

Leiner, B., Cerf, V. G., Clark, D. D., Kahn, R. E., Kleinrock, L., Lynch, D. C., et al. (2003). *A brief history of the internet.* Retrieved March 11, 2009, from http://www.isoc.org/internet/history/brief.shtml

Li, C. (2007). *How consumers use social networks.* Boston: Forrester Research. Retrieved March 15, 2009, from http://www.forrester.com/Research/Document/Excerpt/0,7211,41626,00.html

Li, C., & Irby, B. (2008). An overview of online education: attractiveness, benefits, challenges, concerns and recommendations. *College Student Journal, 42*(2), 449–458.

Lieb, S. (1991). *Principles of adult learning.* Phoenix, AZ: Vision – South Mountain Community College. Retrieved May 26, 2009, from http://honolulu.hawaii.edu/intranet/committees/FacDevCom/guidebk/teachtip/adults-2.htm

Lincoln, Y. S., & Guba, E. G. (1985). *Naturalistic inquiry.* Newbury Park, CA: SAGE Publications, Inc.

Lindeman, E. C. (1926a). Andragogik: The method of teaching adults. *Workers' . Education, 4*, 38.

Lindeman, E. C. (1926b, 1961). *The meaning of adult education*. Montreal: Harvest House.

Livingstone, D. (2001). *Adults' information learning: Definitions, findings, gaps and future research*. Toronto: University of Toronto Centre for the Study of Education and Work.

Livingstone, D. W., & Sawchuk, P. H. (2005, Autumn). Hidden knowledge: Working-class capacity in the "knowledge-based economy." . *Studies in the Education of Adults*, *37*(2), 110–122.

London, J. (1973). Adult education for the 1970's: Promise or illusion? *Adult Education*, *24*(1), 60–70. doi:10.1177/074171367302400105

Long, H. B. (1991). Evolution of a formal knowledge base. In J.M. Peters & P. Jarvis (Eds.), *Adult education: volution and achievements in a develping field of study* (pp. 66-96). San Francisco: Jossey-Bass Publishers.

Lorenzetti, J. P. (2003). Thirty-two distance education trends. *Distance Education Report*, *7*(21), 1–6.

Lu, H., Jia, L., Gong, S., & Clark, B. (2007). The relationship of Kolb Learning Styles, online learning behaviors, and learning outcomes. *Educational Technology & Society*, *10*(4), 187–196.

Luke, C. (2006). Cyberpedagogy. In J. Weiss, J. Nolan, J. Hunsinger, & P. Trifonas (Eds.), *The international handbook of virtual learning environments (pt. I)* (pp. 269-278). Dordrecht, The Netherlands: Springer.

Lukow, J., & Ross, C. M. (2003). How learning styles affect student attitudes toward technology. *Schole: A Journal of Leisure Studies and Recreation Education*, *18*, 67-80.

Lumina Foundation (February 2009). *A stronger nation through higher education*. Retrieved March 7, 2009, from http://www.luminafoundation.org/publications/A_stronger_nation_through_higher_education.pdf

Lundberg, J., Castillo, D., & Dahmani, M. (2008). Do online students perform better than face-to-face students? Reflections and a short review of some empirical findings. *Revista de Universidad y Sociedad del Conocimiento*, *1*(5). Retrieved May 27, 2009, from http://www.uoc.edu/rusc/5/1/dt/eng/lundberg_castillo_dahmani.pdf

Luzón, M. J. (2009). Scholarly hyperwriting: The function of links in academic weblogs. *Journal of the American Society for Information Science and Technology*, *60*(1), 75–89. doi:10.1002/asi.20937

MacIntosh, J. (2003). Reworking professional nursing identity. *Western Journal of Nursing Research*, *25*(6), 725–741. doi:10.1177/0193945903252419

MacKenzie, D., & Wacjman, J. (Eds.). (1985). *The social shaping of technology*. London: Open University Press.

Maddux, C. D. (1994). The Internet: Educational prospects and problems. *Educational Technology*, *34*(9), 37–42.

Maehl, W. (2000). *Lifelong learning at its best: Innovative practices in adult credit programs*. San Francisco: Jossey-Bass Inc., Publishers.

Magjuka, R. J., Shi, M., & Bonk, C. J. (2005). Critical design and administrative issues in online education. *Online Journal of Distance Learning Administration*, *8*(4), Article 4. Retrieved April 28, 2009, from http://www.westga.edu/~distance/ojdla/winter84/magjuka84.htm

Mahmood, S. (2006). The employers' view on older adults as staff in early childhood education services. *Journal of Intergenerational Relationships*, *4*(3), 29–48. doi:10.1300/J194v04n03_03

Main, R. (2000). Leveraging technology for human performance improvement. In G. Piskurich, P. Becksi, & B. Hall (Eds.), *The ASTD handbook of training design and delivery* (pp. 453-472). New York: McGraw-Hill.

Malinen, A. (2000). *Towards the Essence of Adult Experiential Learning*, Jyväskylä, Finland: SoPHI Academic Press.

Maness, J. (2006). Library 2.0 theory: Web 2.0 and its implications for libraries. *Webology*, *3*(2).

Manner, J. (2005). Accommodating diverse learning styles with online course enhancements. *Journal of Interactive instruction . Development*, *17*(4), 19–21.

March, J., & Simon, H. A. (1958). *Organizations*. New York: Wiley.

Marsick, V. J., & Watkins, K. E. (1991). *Informal and incidental learning in the workplace*. London: Routledge.

Marsick, V., & Watkins, K. (1999). *Facilitating Learning Organizations*. Brookfield, VT: Gower.

Martinez, M. (2003). High attrition rates in e-Learning: Challenges, predictors, and solutions. *Learning Solutions e-Magazine*. Retrieved June 1, 2009, from http://www.elearningguild.com/articles/abstracts/index.cfm?action=viewonly2&id=5

Marwick, A. D. (2001). Knowledge management technology. *IBM Systems Journal, 40*(4), 814-830. Retrieved October 2, 2007, from http://www.research.ibm.com/journal/sj/404/marwik.html

Mazhindu, G. N. (1990). Contract learning reconsidered: A critical examination of the implications for application in nursing education. *Journal of Advanced Nursing, 15*, 101–109. doi:10.1111/j.1365-2648.1990.tb01678.x

McCarty, S., Ibrahim, B., Sedunov, B., & Sharma, R. (2006). Global online education. In J. Weiss, J. Nolan, J. Hunsinger, & P. Trifonas (Eds.), *The international handbook of virtual learning environments (pt. 1)* (pp. 723-788). Dordrecht, The Netherlands: Springer.

McClelland, J. (1994, February 13). Netsurfers. *The Observer.*

McCombs, B. L., & Lauer, P. A. (1997). Development and validation of the learner-centered battery: Self-assessment tools for teacher reflection and professional development. *Professional Educator, 20*(1), 1–21.

McCombs, B. L., & Vakili, D. (2005). A learner-centered framework for e-learning. *Teachers College Record, 107*(8), 1582–1600. doi:10.1111/j.1467-9620.2005.00534.x

McCormick, R., & Scrimshaw, P. (2001). Information and communications technology, knowledge and pedagogy. *Education Communication and Information, 1*(1), 2001.

McElroy, M. (2006). *The new knowledge management: Complexity, learning and sustainable innovation*. Boston: Elsevier Science.

McLoughlin, C., & Lee, M. J. W. (2007, December). Social software and participatory learning: Pedagogical choices with technology affordances in the Web 2.0 era. In *ICT: Providing choices for learners and learning. Proceedings ASCILITE,* (pp. 664-675), Singapore. Retrieved September 15, 2008, from http://www.ascilite.org.au/conferences/singapore07/procs/mcloughlin.pdf

McMahon, C., & Bruce, C. (2002). Information literacy needs of local staff in cross-cultural development projects. *Journal of International Development, 14*(1), 113–127. doi:10.1002/jid.864

McNally, M., Bannon, M., Greaney, J., Hickey, A., McDonnell, M., & Riordan, M. (2005, September). *The effects of a wireless on-line community network on social capital.* Paper presented at MobileHCI'05, Salzburg, Austria, (pp. 215-218).

McTighe, J., & Wiggins, G. (1999). *The understanding by design*. Alexandria, VA: Association for Supervision and Curriculum Development.

Merriam, S. B. (1999). The development of the discipline of adult education in the United States. *Andragogy Today: Interdisciplinary Journal of Adult and Continuing Education, 2*(3), 31–49.

Merriam, S. B. (2001a). Andragogy and self-directed learning: Pillars of adult learning theory. *New Directions for Adult and Continuing Education, 89*, 3–13. doi:10.1002/ace.3

Merriam, S. B. (Ed.). (2001b). *The new update on adult learning theory. New directions for adult and continuing education*. San Fransisco: Jossey-Bass.

Merriam, S. B. (Ed.). (2008). *Third update on adult learning theory: New directions for adult and continuing education, vol. 119*. San Francisco: Jossey-Bass.

Merriam, S. B., & Brockett, R. G. (2007). *The profession and practice of adult education: An introduction*. San Francisco: Jossey-Bass.

Merriam, S. B., & Cafarella, R. S. (1999). *Learning in adulthood: A comprehensive guide* (2nd ed.). San Francisco: Jossey-Bass.

Merriam, S. B., & Ntseane, G. (2008). Transformational learning in Botswana: How culture shapes the process. *Adult Education Quarterly*, *58*(3), 183–197. doi:10.1177/0741713608314087

Merriam, S. B., Caffarella, R. S., & Baumgartner, L. M. (2006). *Learning in adulthood: A comprehensive guide* (3rd ed.). San Francisco: Jossey Bass.

Merriam, S. B., Caffarella, R. S., & Baumgartner, L. M. (2007). *Learning in Adulthood: A Comprehensive Guide*. San Francisco: John Wiley & Sons Inc.

Meyers, S. A. (2008, Fall). Using transformative pedagogy when teaching online. *College Teaching*, *56*(4), 219–224. doi:10.3200/CTCH.56.4.219-224

Mezirow, J. (1981, Fall). A critical theory of adult learning and education. *Adult Education*, *32*(1), 3–24. doi:10.1177/074171368103200101

Mezirow, J. (1985). A critical theory of self-directed learning. In S. Brookfield (Ed.), *Self-directed learning: From theory to practice*: *New directions for continuing education, no. 25*. San Francisco: Jossey-Bass.

Mezirow, J. (1990). *Fostering critical reflection in adulthood: A guide to transformative and emancipatory learning*. San Francisco: Jossey-Bass.

Mezirow, J. (1991), *Transformative dimensions of adult learning* (pp. 198-201). San Francisco: Jossey Bass.

Mezirow, J. (1991). *Transformative dimensions of adult learning*. San Francisco: Jossey-Bass.

Mezirow, J. (1995). Transformation theory of adult learning. In E. W. Taylor (Ed.), *Transformative learning theory* (pp. 5-15), *New Directions for Adult and Continuing Education, 119* (Fall 2008). San Francisco: Jossey-Bass.

Mezirow, J. (1996). Contemporary paradigms of learning. *Adult Education Quarterly*, *46*, 158–172. doi:10.1177/074171369604600303

Mezirow, J. (Ed.). (2000). *Learning as transformation: Critical perspectives on a theory in progress*. San Francisco: Jossey-Bass.

Mezirow, J., & Associates. (2000). *Learning as transformation*. San Francisco: Jossey-Bass.

Miflin, B. (2004). Adult learning, self-directed learning and problem-based learning: Deconstructing the connections. *The entity from which ERIC acquires the content, including journal, organization, and conference names, or by means of online submission from the author. Teaching in Higher Education*, *9*(1), 43–53. doi:10.1080/1356251032000155821

Mihall, J., & Belletti, H. (1999). *Adult learning styles and training methods. Forget those 13,000 hours*. FDIC ADR.

Mikropoulos, T. A., & Strouboulis, V. (2004). Factors that influence presence in educational virtual environments. *Cyberpsychology & Behavior*, *7*(5), 582–591.

Miller, L. (2005). Using learning styles to evaluate computer-based instruction. *Computers in Human Behavior*, *21*(2), 287–306. doi:10.1016/j.chb.2004.02.011

Milligan, F. (1995). In defence of andragogy. *Nurse Education Today*, *15*, 22–27. doi:10.1016/S0260-6917(95)80074-3

Milligan, F. (1997). In defence of andragogy, Part 2: An educational process consistent with modern nursing aims. *Nurse Education Today*, *17*, 487–493. doi:10.1016/S0260-6917(97)80010-X

Milligan, F. (1999). Beyond the rhetoric of problem-based learning: Emancipatory limits and links with andragogy. *Nurse Education Today*, *19*, 548–555. doi:10.1054/nedt.1999.0368

MIT. (2005). Cell phone culture. *MIT communications*. Retrieved March 29, 2009, from http://web.mit.edu/comm-forum/forums/cell_phone_culture.htm

Mitchener, J. (2008). Device Futures. In P. Warren, J. Davies, & D. Brown (Eds.), *ICT futures: Delivering pervasive, real-time and secure service* (pp. 27-38). Chichester, UK: John Wiley & Sons.

Molyneux, E. (1986). Information technology education in industry. *Journal of Information Technology, 1*(2), 30–31. doi:10.1057/jit.1986.20

Moore, M. (1986). Self-directed learning and distance education. *Journal of Distance Education. "Revue de L'enseignmenta a Distance", 1-15.* Retrieved December 28, 2004, http://cade.athabascau.ca/voll.l/moore.html

Moore, M. G. (1995). American distance education. In F. Lockwood (Ed.), *Open and distance learning today* (pp. 32-41). London: Routledge.

Moreno, R. (2006). Learning in high-tech and multimedia environments. *Current Directions in Psychological Science, 15*(2), 63–67. doi:10.1111/j.0963-7214.2006.00408.x

Morrall, P. (1993, September-October). The beginning of the end of andragogy. *Senior Nurse, 13*(5), 42–44.

Mott, V. W. (2004). Book review: Learner-centered teaching: Five key changes to practice. *Adult Education Quarterly, 54*(3), 244–245. doi:10.1177/0741713604263058

Mott, V. W. (2008). Learner-derived curriculum development. In V. C. X. Wang (Ed.), *Curriculum development for adult learners in the global community volume I: Strategic approaches* (pp. 58-78). Malabar, FL: Krieger Publishing Company.

Mott, V. W. (2009). Evolution of adult education: Is our future in e-learning? In V. C. X. Wang (Ed.), *Handbook of research on e-learning applications for career and technical education: Technologies for technical training* (pp. 778-791). Hershey, PA: IGI Global.

Muller, L. H. (1992). *Progressivism and U. S. adult education: A critique of mainstream theory as embodied in the work of Malcolm Knowles.* New York: Teachers College, Columbia University.

Mumford, A. (1997). Action Learning as a Vehicle for Learning. In A. Mumford (Ed.) *Action Learning at Work.* Hampshire, UK: Gower.

Myers, I. B. (1993). *Gifts differing: Understanding personality type.* Palo Alto, CA: CPP Books.

Mynen, M. (C. 1997). *What andragogy means to me.* Retrieved December 3, 2003, from http://www.instructordiploma.com/ core/102%20b/victoria/mynen.htm.

Nadler, L., & Nadler, Z. (Eds.). (1989). *The handbook of human resource development* (2d ed.). New York: John Wiley & Sons.

Nahapiet, J., & Goshal, S. (1998). Social capital, intellectual capital, and the organizational advantage. *Academy of Management Review, 23*(2), 242–266. doi:10.2307/259373

National Center for Education Statistics. (2000). *Distance education at postsecondary education institutions: 1997-1998* (NCES Publication No. 2003-013). Washington, DC: U.S. Government Printing Office.

National Center for Education Statistics. (2002). *A profile of participation in distance education: 1999-2000* (NCES Publication No. 2003-154). Washington, DC: U.S. Government Printing Office.

National Center for Educational Statistics. (n.d.). International Comparisons in Education Glossary. Institute of Education Sciences, U.S. Department of Education, Washington, D.C. Retrieved on March 18, 2009, from http://nces.ed.gov/surveys/international/Intlindicators/glossary.asp#G

National Center of Dissemination of Disability Research. (n.d.). Retrieved from http://www.ncddr.org

National Rehabilitation Information Center. (n.d.). Retrieved from http://www.naric.com

Neal, A., & Winnipeg, M. (1995). Group apraxia: The phenomenology of acculturalism. *The Canadian Journal of Native Studies, 10*(2), 219–242.

Neihardt, J. G. (1979). *Black elk speaks: Being the life story of a holy man of the oglala sioux.* Lincoln, NE: University of Nebraska Press.

Newman, A. P. (1993). *Prison Literacy: Implications for Program and Assessment Policy.* Bloomington, IN: ERIC Clearinghouse on Reading and Communication Skills. ED 363 729 (pp. 49). Unpublished Doctor of Philosophy Dissertation.

Newman, M. (2006). *Teaching defiance*. San Francisco: Jossey-Bass.

NIACE. (2009). *Education promotes well-being – but over 25s excluded*. Retrieved April 4, 2009, from http://www.niace.org.uk/education-promotes-well-being–but-too-many-over-25-excluded

Nicholson, S. (2007). *The role of gaming in libraries: Taking the pulse*. Retrieved from http://boardgameswithscott.com/pulse2007.pdf

Nielsen, (2009). *Social networking's new global footprint*. Retrieved June 2, 2009, http://blog.nielsen.com/nielsenwire/nielsen-news/social-networking-new-global-footprint/

Nilson, L. B. (2003). *Teaching at its best*. San Francisco, CA: Anker Publishing.

Nilssen, A., & Greenberg, A. (July 2006). *The vital role of web conferencing in small and medium enterprises*. Live Oak, FL: Wainwright Research.

Nonaka, I. (1994). Dynamic theory of organizational knowledge creation. *Organization Science*, *5*(1), 14–37. doi:10.1287/orsc.5.1.14

Nonaka, I., & Takeuchi, H. (1995). *The knowledge creating company*. Cambridge, MA: Oxford University Press.

Nottingham Andragogy Group. (1983). Towards a developmental theory of andragogy. *Adults: Psychological and Educational Perspective, 9*. Nottingham, UK: University of Nottingham Department of Adult Education.

Novak, J. D. (2003). The promise of new ideas and new technology for improving teaching and learning. *Life Sciences Education*, *2*(2), 122–132.

O'Day, V. L., Ito, M., Adler, A., Linde, C., & Mynatt, E. D. (2006). Cemeteries, oak trees, and black and white cows: Newcomers' understandings of the networked world. In J. Weiss, J. Nolan, J. Hunsinger, & P. Trifonas (Eds.), *The international handbook of virtual learning environments (pt. 2)* (pp. 873-894). Dordrecht, The Netherlands: Springer.

O'Lawrence, H. (2006). The influences of distance learning on adult learners. *Techniques*, *81*(5), 47–49.

O'Lawrence, H. (2007). An overview of the influences of distance learning on adult learners. *Journal of Education and Human Development, 1*(1), 7. Retrieved March 12, 2009, from http://www.scientificjournals.org/journals2007/articles/1041.htm

Obama, B. (2006).*The audacity of hope*. Edinburgh, UK: Canongate.

Oblinger, D., & Oblinger, J. (2005). *Educating the net generation* (1st ed.). Retrieved from http://www.educause.edu/educatingthenetgen

Oblinger, D., & Oblinger, J. (2005). Is it age or IT: First steps toward understanding the net generation. In Oblinger, D. & Oblinger, J. (Eds.), *Educating the Net Generation, Educause*. Retrieved 15 February, 2009, from http://www.educause.edu/educatingthenetgen/5989?time=1236850547

OECD. (2000). Knowledge management in the learning society. *Education and skills*. OECD Publications Service, Paris.

OECD. (2004). OECD education. Retrieved 15 February, from http://www.oecd.org/document/7/0,3343,en_2649_39263238_33712135_1_1_1_1,00.html

OECD. (2005). *E-learning in tertiary education. Where do we stand?* Paris: Author.

OECD. (2005). *Promoting adult learning*. Retrieved March 14, 2009, from http://www.oecd.org/document/57/0,3343,en_2649_39263238_36675769_1_1_1_1,00.html

Olgren, C. H. (2000). Learning strategies for learning technologies. In E. J. Burge (Ed.), *The strategic use of learning technologies: New directions for adult continuing education, no. 88* (pp. 7-16). San Francisco: Jossey-Bass.

Olle, T. W. (2004). Eight significant events in the 50 year history of computing. In J. Impagliazzo & J. A. N. Lee (Eds.), *History of computing in education* (pp. 47-56). Dordrecht, The Netherlands: Kluwer.

Open University. (2009). *About the OU.* Retrieved March 11, 2009, from http://www.open.ac.uk/about/ou/p3.shtml

Osborn, S. (1999). *Andragogy.* Belgrade, Yugoslavia: Faculty of Philosophy. Retrieved May 23, 2009, from http://ifets.gmd.de/

Ovesni, K. (1999). *Andragogy as an integral part of educational sciences.* Belgrade, Yugoslavia: Faculty of Philosophy. Retrieved April 23, 2009, from http://ifets.gmd.de/

Ozuah, P. O. (2005). First, there was pedagogy and then came andragogy. *The Einstein Journal of Biology and Medicine; EJBM, 21,* 83–87.

Palloff, R. M., & Pratt, K. (1999). *Building learning communities in cyberspace.* San Francisco: Jossey-Bass.

Palloff, R. M., & Pratt, K. (2003). *The virtual student: A profile and guide to working with online learners.* San Francisco: Jossey-Bass.

Palloff, R., & Pratt, K. (1999). *Building learning communities in cyberspace.* San Francisco, CA: Jossey-Bass.

Paloff, R. M., & Pratt, K. (2001). *Lessons from the cyberspace classroom: The realities of online teaching.* San Francisco: Jossey-Bass.

Paradise, A. (2008, July). Informal learning: Overlooked or overhyped? *T+D,* 52-53.

Parker, J. (1992). *Employees pursuing technical baccalaureate degrees: Success factors.* NY: Teachers College/Columbia University.

Parker, J. (1996). Integrating technology into delivery methods for global technical education. *Compendium on uses of distance learning technologies in engineering education.* American Society for Engineering Education.

Parker, J. (2003). Transformative learning enhanced with technology. *Proceedings: transformative learning conference.* NY: Teachers College/Columbia University.

Parker, J., & Yiu, L. (2000). Action learning in cyberspace: a case example of a technology-supported laboratory management development program. *Compendium on uses of distance learning technologies in engineering education.* American Society for Engineering Education

Partlow, K. M., & Gibbs, W. J. (2003). Indicators of constructivist principles in Internet-based courses. *Journal of Computing in Higher Education, 14*(2), 68–97. doi:10.1007/BF02940939

Patterson, M. B. (2008). Learning disability prevalence and adult education program characteristics. *Learning Disabilities Research & Practice, 23*(1), 50–59. doi:10.1111/j.1540-5826.2007.00262.x

Patton, M. Q. (1990). *Qualitative evaluation and research methods,* (2nd ed.). Newbury Park, CA: SAGE Publications, Inc.

Pauling, B. (2006). Virtual learning environments in higher education "down under". In J. Weiss, J. Nolan, J. Hunsinger, & P. Trifonas (Eds.), *The international handbook of virtual learning environments (pt. 1)* (pp. 609-652). Dordrecht, The Netherlands: Springer.

Paulson, K. (2002). Reconfiguring faculty roles for virtual settings. *The Journal of Higher Education, 73,* 123–141. doi:10.1353/jhe.2002.0010

Payne, D. (2008). The future all optical network—why we need it and how we get there. In P. Warren, J. Davies, & D. Brown (Eds.), *ICT futures: Delivering pervasive, real-time and secure service* (pp. 93-114). Chichester, UK: John Wiley & Sons.

Pearson, I. (2008). Over the horizon. In P. Warren, J. Davies, & D. Brown (Eds.), *ICT futures: Delivering pervasive, real-time and secure service* (pp. 215-226). Chichester, UK: John Wiley & Sons.

Pelgrum, W. J., & Anderson, R. E. (Eds.). (1999). *ICT and the emerging paradigm for lifelong learning.* Amsterdam, The Netherlands: IEA.

Perkins, D. (1993). Teaching for understanding. *American Educator, 17*(3), 28–35.

Perry, W., Jr. (1999). *Forms of ethical and intellectual development in the college years: A scheme.* San Francisco: Jossey-Bass.

Peters, J. M., & Jarvis, P. (1991). *Adult education: Evolution and achievements in a developing field of study.* San Francisco: Jossey-Bass.

Pettitt, J. M. (2002). *Power relationships in two web-based courses.* Raleigh, NC: North Carolina State University. (ERIC Document Reproduction Service No. ED471832)

Phipps, R., & Merisotis, J. (1999). *What's the difference? A review of contemporary research on the effectiveness of distance learning in higher education.* Washington, DC: The Institute for Higher Education Policy.

Piskurich, G. (2006). *Rapid instructional design.* San Francisco, CA: John Wiley & Sons.

Piskurich, G. M. (Ed.). (2003). *Preparing learners for e-learning.* San Francisco: Jossey-Bass.

Planty, M., Hussar, W., Snyder, T., Provasnik, S., Kena, G., Dinkes, R., KewalRamani, A., and Kemp, J. (2008). *The condition of education 2008* (NCES 2008-031). Washington, D.C.: National Center for Education Statistics, Institute of Education Sciences, U.S. Department of Education.

Poggeler, F. (1994). Introduction – Trends of andragogical research in Europe. In P. Jarvis & F. Poggeler (Eds.), *Developments in the education of adults in Europe, 21*(9-15). Frankfurt am Main: Peter Lang, Studies in Pedagogy, Andragogy and Gerontology.

Pole, T. (1968). *A history of adult schools* (3rd ed.). London: Woburn Press.

Pont, B., & Sweet, R. (2006). *ICT and learning: Supporting out-of-school youth and adults.* Paris: Organisation for Economic Cooperation and Development.

Potts, D. (2005). Pedagogy, purpose and the second language learner in online communities. *Canadian Modern Language Review, 62*(1), 137–160.

Pratt, D. D. (1984). Andragogical assumptions: Some counter-intuitive logic. In *Proceedings of the Adult Education Research Conference*, (no. 25). Raleigh, NC: North Carolina State University.

Pratt, D. D. (1988, Spring). Andragogy as a relational construct. *Adult Education Quarterly, 38*(3), 160–172. doi:10.1177/0001848188038003004

Pratt, D. D. (1993, Spring). *Andragogy after twenty-five years.* In S. Merriam (Ed.), *New directions for adult and continuing education: An update on adult learning theory, 57*(15–24). San Francisco: Jossey-Bass.

Pratt, D. D. (1998). *Five perspectives on teaching in adult and higher education.* Melbourne, FL: Krieger Publishing.

Princeton University Wordnet (n.d.), Retrieved on March 7, 2009, from http://wordnetweb.princeton.edu/perl/webwn?s=adult%20education.

Prospects, (2007). *The UK's official graduate careers website.* Retrieved March 27, 2009, from http://www.prospects.ac.uk/p/types_of_job/adult_education_lecturer_job_description.jsp

Putnam, R. (1995). Bowling alone: America's declining social capital. *Journal of Democracy, 6*, 65–78. doi:10.1353/jod.1995.0002

Putnam, R. D. (1995). Bowling alone: America's declining social capital. *Journal of Democracy, 6*, 65–78. doi:10.1353/jod.1995.0002

Puzziferro, M., & Shelton, K. (2008). A model for developing high-quality online courses: Integrating a systems approach with learning theory. *Journal of Asynchronous Learning Environment Learning Networks, 12*(3). Retrieved on February 15, 2009, from http://sloanconsortium.org/node/1409

Quinsee, S., & Hurst, J. (2005). *Blurring the boundaries? Supporting students and staff within an online learning environment* (ERIC Document Reproduction Service No. ED494786). Retrieved on April 28, 2009, from http://www.eric.ed.gov/ERICWebPortal/Home.portal?_nfpb=true&_pageLabel=basic&Clearme=true

Qvotrup, L. (2006). *Knowledge, education and learning. E-learning in the knowledge society.* Frederiksberg, Denmark: Samfudsliteratur Roskilde Universitets Forlag.

Rachal, J. (2000). *Effectiveness of andragogy.* Concurrent session presentation. American Association for Adult and Continuing Education Conference, Providence, RI, November, 2000.

Rafaeli, S., Ravid, G., & Soroka, V. (2004). De-lurking in virtual communities: A social communication network approach to measuring the effects of social and cultural capital. In *Proceedings of the 37th Annual Hawaii International Conference on System Sciences (HICSS'04)-* (Track 7-Vol. 7), Big Island, Hawaii.

Ramachandran, N. (2006). New paths at work. *U.S. News & World Report, 3/20/2006, 140*(10), 46-48.

Ravens, R. (1982). *The Origin and Growth of Action Learning.* London: Chartwell Bratt.

Reichgelt, H., Lunt, B., Ashford, T., Phelps, A., Slazinski, E., & Willis, C. (2004). A comparison of baccalaureate programs in information technology with baccalaureate programs in computer science and information systems. *Journal of Information Technology Education, 3*, 19–34.

Reischmann, J. (1999). Adult education in Germany: Roots, status, mainstreams, changes. *Andragogy Today: Interdisciplinary Journal of Adult and Continuing Education, 2*(3), 1–29.

Resnick, P. (2002). Beyond bowling together: Socio technical capital. In J. M. Carroll (Ed), *HCI in the New Millennium* (pp. 247-272). Reading, MA: Addison-Wesley.

Retrieved March 28, 2009, from http://209.85.229.132/search?q=cache:syDJ2FC_ROAJ:www.mdx.ac.uk/wbl/research/research_docs/Basiel-WBL2005.pdf+Lydia+Arnold&cd=17&hl=en&ct=clnk&gl=uk

Reyes, A., & Zarama, A. (1998). The process of embodying distinctions. A re-construction of the process of learning. *Cybernetics & Human Knowing, 5*(3), 19–33.

Reynard, R. (2009). *Can we gauge technology's impact on learning outcomes?* Retrieved April 23, 2009, from http://campustechnology.com/Articles/2009/03/25/Does-Technology-Improve-Learning

Reynolds, K. C. (1997, March). *The name assigned to the document by the author. This field may also contain sub-titles, series names, and report numbers. Postsecondary education in cohort groups: Does familiarity breed learning?* Additional information about the document that does not fit in any of the other fields; not used after 2004. Paper presented at the Annual Meeting of the American Educational Research Association, Chicago.

Rheingold, H. (1993). *The virtual community.* Reading, MA: Addison-Wesley. Retrieved January 6, 2009, from http://www.rheingold.com/vc/book/intro.html/

Richardson, W. (2009). *Blogs, wikis, podcasts, and other powerful web tools for classrooms.* Thousand Oaks, CA: Corwin Press.

Rickman, J., & Grudzinski, M. (2000). Student expectations of information technology use in the classroom. *EDUCAUSE Quarterly, 23*(1), 24–30.

Riddel, S., Baron, S., & Wilson, A. (2001). *The learning society and people with learning difficulties.* Bristol, UK: The Policy Press Publishing.

Rieber, L., & Noah, D. (2008). Games, simulations, and visual metaphors in education: Antagonism between enjoyment and learning. *Educational Media International, 45*(2), 77–92. doi:10.1080/09523980802107096

Riley, D. (2008). China to become world's largest internet market by users. Retrieved March 25, 2009, from http://www.techcrunch.com/2008/01/17/china-close-to-becoming-worlds-largest-internet-market-by-users

Robb, W. M. (1990). *Can South African andragogics improve understanding between Anglo-American and Continental European adult educationists?* In *Toward 1992 – Education of Adults in the New Europe. Proceedings of the 20th SCUTREA* Conference (pp. 71-77), West Sheffield, UK.

Robinson, R. D. (1995). *Helping adults learn and change.* West Bend, WI: Omnibook.

Roblyer, M., & Doering, A. (2009). *Integrating educational technology into teaching* (5th ed.). Boston: Allyn & Bacon.

Rogers, A. (2002). *Teaching adults* (3rd ed.). London: Open University Press.

Roschelle, J. (1999). Transitioning to professional practice: A Deweyan view of five analyses of problem-based learning. *Discourse Processes: A Multidisicplinary Journal, 27*(2), 231-240.

Roseberry, C. (n.d.). *What is the history of laptops?* Retrieved March 24, 2009, from http://mobileoffice.about.com/od/laptopstabletpcs/f/laptophistory.htm

Rosen, R., et al. (2000). *Global literacies.* New York: Simon and Schuster.

Rosenstock-Huessy, E. (1925). *Andragogy – 1925*, Retrieved October 26, 2005, from Internet

Ross, B. E. (1987). Integrating Andragogy with Current Research on Teaching Effectiveness. In *Proceedings of the Lifelong Learning Research Conference* (pp. 29–33). College Park, MD: University of Maryland.

Ross-Gordon, J. & Brown-Haywood, F. (2000). Keys to college success as seen through the eyes of african american adult students. *Journal of Continuing Higher Education, 48(3),* 14-23.

Rostad, S. (1998). *Nordic Folk Academy Socrates project entitled 'The public and the library'.* Nordic Council of Ministers, St. Strandstraede 18, DK-1225 Copenhagen K, Denmark. Retrieved June 1, 2009, from http://x-stream.fortunecity.com/melrose/81/sweden.htm

Rovai, A. P. (2001). Building classroom community at a distance: A case study. *Educational Technology Research and Development Journal, 49*(4), 33–48. doi:10.1007/BF02504946

Russell, A., & Thompson, K. (2002). *Talking heads, It's progress, transfer to Wales and Scotland and relevance to the Republic of Ireland.* Presented to ITTE at Trinity College Dublin July 2002. Retrieved March 27, 2009, from http://www.ceilidhfolk.co.uk/paper2002.pdf

Russo, T., & Benson, S. (2005). Learning with invisible others: Perceptions of online presence and their relationship to cognitive and affective learning. *Educational Technology & Society, 8*(1), 54–62.

Rutenbeck, J. (2000). The 5 great challenges of the digital age. *Netconnet,* (Fall), 30-33.

Ryan, R. C. (2000). Student assessment comparison of lecture and online construction equipment and methods classes. *T.H.E. Journal, 27*(6), 76–83.

Saba, V. K. (2001). Nursing informatics: Yesterday, today and tomorrow. *International Nursing Review, 48*(3), 177–187. doi:10.1046/j.1466-7657.2001.00064.x

Salmon, G. (2000). *E-moderating: The key to teaching and learning online*. London: Kogan Page.

Sander, L. (February 2009). Colleges woo adults who have some credits but no degree. *Chronicle of Higher Education, 54(23)*, A29.

Sandman, L. R., Reischmann, J., & Kim, Y. S. (2007). Emerging adult educators' experiences in an international on-line forum. *Convergence, 40*(1/2), 25–40.

Saner, R., & Yiu, L. (1994). European And Asian Resistance to the Use of the American Case Method in Management Training: Possible Cultural and Systemic Incongruencies. *International Journal of Human Resource Management, 5*(4), 953–976.

Sangrá, A. (2002). A new learning model for the information and knowledge society: The case of the Universitat Oberta de Catalunya (UOC). *The International Review of Research in Open and Distance Learning, 2(2).* Retrieved March 31, 2009, from http://www.irrodl.org/index.php/irrodl/article/view/55/114

Sangrá, A., & González-Sanmamed, M. (2004b). El profesorado universitario y las TIC: Redefinir roles y competencias [University teachers and the ICTs: Redefining roles and competences]. In A. Sangrá & M. González-Sanmamed (Eds.), *La transformación de las universidades a través de las TIC: Discursos y practices* [*University changes through ICTs: Discourses and practices*] (pp. 79-80). Barcelona: UOC.

Sangrá, A., & González-Sanmamed, M. (Eds.). (2004a). *La transformación de las universidades a través de las TIC: discursos y prácticas* [*University changes through ICTs: discourses and practices*]. Barcelona, Spain: UOC.

Savicevic, D. (1991). Modern conceptions of andragogy: A European framework. *Studies in the Education of Adults, 23*(3), 179–201.

Savicevic, D. (1999a). Adult education: From practice to theory building. In F. Poggeler (Ed.), *Studies in pedagogy, andragogy, and gerontagogy,* (pp. 1-275). Frankfurt am Main: Peter Lang.

Savicevic, D. (1999b). Understanding andragogy in Europe and America: Comparing and contrasting. In J. Reischmann, Z. Jelenc, & M. Bron (Eds.), *Comparative adult education 1998: The contribution of ISCAE to an emerging field of study* (pp. 97-119). Bamburg, Germany: ISCAE Proceedings.

Sawchuk, P. H. (2003). *Adult learning and technology in working-class life.* New York: Cambridge University Press.

Schaffert, S., Bischof, D., Bürger, T., Gruber, A., Hilzensauer, W., & Schaffert, S. (2006, June 11-14). *Learning with semantic wikis.* Paper presented at the 1st Workshop on From Wiki to Semantics, 3rd Annual European Semantic Web Conference (ESWC), Budva, Montenegro. Retrieved April 29, 2009, from http://www.salzburgresearch.at/research/gfx/semantic_wiki_elearning.pdf

Schatzki, T. R., Knorr-Cetina, K., & Von Savigny, E. (Eds.). (2001). *The practice turn in contemporary theory.* London: Routledge.

Schlenker, B. (2008). Conversation 2.0. *c>training,* 45(7), 32.

Schmidt, E. K., & Gallegos, A. (2001). Distance learning: Issues and concerns of distance learners. *Journal of Industrial Technology, 17*(3). Retrieved on February 22, 2009, from http://nait.org/jit/Articles/schmidt041801.pdf

Schoech, D., & Helton, D. (2002). Qualitative and quantitative analysis of a course taught via classroom and internet chatroom. *Qualitative Social Work, 1*(1), 111–124. doi:10.1177/147332500200100174 8

Schon, D. A. (1983). *The reflective practitioner.* New York: Basic Books.

Schön, D. A. (1987). *Educating the reflective practitioner. Toward a new design for teaching and learning of professions.* San Francisco: Jossey-Bass.

Schultz, T. W. (1961). Investment in human capital. *The American Economic Review, 51*(1), 1–17.

Scotland, L. T. (2008). *Online Communities.* Retrieved March 27, 2009, from http://www.ltscotland.org.uk/onlinecommunities/login.asp

SCUTREA. (1992). *Changing culture and adult learning.* Papers from the SCUTREA Annual Conference (22nd, Canterbury, England, United Kingdom, July 8-10, 1992). Retrieved March 30, 2009, from http://www.eric.ed.gov:80/ERICWebPortal/custom/portlets/recordDetails/detailmini.jsp?_nfpb=true&_&ERICExtSearch_SearchValue_0=ED358290&ERICExtSearch_SearchType_0=no&accno=ED358290

Searle, J. (1995). *The construction of social reality.* New York: Penguin Books.

Secundo, G., Elia, G., & Taurino, C. (2006). A process-oriented and technology-based model of virtual communities of practices: Evidence from a case study in Higher Education, Paper presented at the IV International Conference on Multimedia and ICTs in Education (m-ICTE2006), Seville, Spain. In *Current Developments in Technology-Assisted Education,* (pp. 1032-1036).

Selwyn, N., Gorard, S., & Forlong, J. (2006). *Adult learning in the digital age: Information technology and the learning society.* New York: Routledge.

Senge, P. M. (2006). *The Fifth Discipline: the Art and Practice of the Learning Organization.* New York: Doubleday Currency.

Shananhan, P. (1992). Towards a knowledge democracy? University adult education, information technology and unemployed persons. *Studies in the Education of Adults, 24*(1), 57–68.

Siemens, G. (2004). *Connectivism: A learning theory for the digital age.* Retrieved September 15, 2008, from http://www.elearnspace.org/Articles/connectivism.htm

Simpson, C., & Du, Y. (2004). Effects of learning styles and class participation on students' enjoyments level in distributed learning environments. *Journal of Education for Library and Information Science*, *45*(2), 123–136.

Simpson, E. (2005). Evolution in the classroom: what teachers need to know about the video game generation. *TechTrends*, *49*(5), 17–22. doi:10.1007/BF02763685

Simpson, J. A. (1964). Andragogy. *Adult Education*, *37*(4), 186–194.

Skinner, B. F. (1968). *The technology of teaching*. New York: Appleton-Century-Crofts.

Sloan-C. (2009). *NASULGC-Sloan national commission on online learning benchmarking study: Preliminary findings*. Retrieved on March 3, 2009, from http://www.sloan-c.org/publications/survey/nasulgc_prelim

Smick, D. M. (2008). *The world is curved: Hidden dangers to the global economy*. New York: Penguin Group.

Smith, M. C., & Smith, T. J. (2008). Low-education adults' participation in informal learning activities: Relationships with selected demographic characteristics. *Adult Basic Education and Literacy Journal*, *2*(2), 67–73.

Smith, M. K. (1996). Andragogy: The history and current use of the term plus an annotated Bibliography. In *The Encyclopedia of Informal Education*. Retrieved April 12, 2009, from http://www.infed.org/lifelonglearning/b-andra.htm

Snyder, T. & Hoffman, C. (1991, February). *Digest of educational statistics 1990.* (NCES 91-660). Washington, D.C.: Office of Educational Research and Improvement, U.S. Department of Education.

Snyder, T. (2009). *Mini-Digest of Education Statistics, 2008* (NCES 2009-021). Washington, D.C.: National Center for Education Statistics, Institute of Education Sciences, U.S. Department of Education.

Sorohan, E. G. (1993). We do, therefore we learn. *Training & Development*, *47*, 47–48, 50, 52–55.

Sosnoski, J., Jones, S., Carter, B., McAllister, K., Moeller, R., & Mir, R. (2006). Virtual Harlem as a collaborative learning environment: A project of the University of Illinois at Chicago's electronic visualization Lab. In J. Weiss, J. Nolan, J. Hunsinger, & P. Trifonas (Eds.), *The international handbook of virtual learning environments (pt. 2)* (pp. 1289-1320). Dordrecht, The Netherlands: Springer.

Spira, J., & Fientuch, J. (2005). *The cost of not paying attention: How interruptions impact knowledge worker productivity.* New York: Basex.

Squire, K. (2006). From content to context: Videogames as designed experience. *Educational Researcher*, *35*(8), 19–29. doi:10.3102/0013189X035008019

State Higher Education Executive Officers (SHEEO). (2008, September-October). Second to none in attainment, discovery, and innovation: The national agenda for higher education. *Change: The Magazine of Higher Learning*. Retrieved March 7, 2009, from http://www.changemag.org/Archives/Back%20Issues/September-October%20 2008/full-second-to-none.html.

Stehr, N. (1994). *Knowledge societies. The Transformation of labor, property and knowledge in contemporary society*. London: Sage

Sternberg, R. J., & Horvath, J. (Eds.). (1999). *Tacit knowledge in professional practice: Researcher and practitioner perspectives*. Mahwah, NJ: Erlbaum.

Sternberg, R. J., & Wagner, R. K. (Eds.). (1986). *Practical intelligence*. Cambridge, UK: Cambridge University Press

Stilborne, L., & Williams, L. (1996). *Meeting the needs of adult learners in developing courses for the Internet*. Retrieved on January 15, 2009, from https://www.isoc.org/inet96/proceedings/c4/ca_2.htm

Streumer, J. N. (2006). *Work Related Learning*. New York: Springer.

Suanmali, C. (1981). *The core concepts of andragogy*. Doctoral Dissertation, Columbia University Teachers College, New York City, Dissertation Abstracts International, University Microfilms no. 8207343.

Symonds, W. C. (2005). America the uneducated. *Business Week, 11/21/2005*, (3960).

Tait, A., & Mills, R. (1999). *The convergence between conventional and distance education.* London: Routledge.

Task Force on Distance Education and Training in Professional Psychology American Psychological Association. (2002). *Principals of good practice in distance education and their application to professional education and training in psychology.* Washington, DC: American Psychological Association, Task Force on Distance Education.

Taylor, E. W. (2006). The greening of the adult education academy. In S. B. Merriam, B. C. Courtenay, & R. M. Cervero (Eds.), *Global issues and adult education: Perspectives from Latin America, Southern Africa, and the United States* (pp. 254-264). San Francisco: Jossey-Bass.

Taylor, E. W. (2007). An update of transformative a critical review of the empirical research (1999-2005). *International Journal of Lifelong Education, 26*(2), 173–191. doi:10.1080/02601370701219475

Taylor, E. W. (2008). Transformative learning theory. *New Directions for Adult and Continuing Education, 119*, 5–15. doi:10.1002/ace.301

Taylor, E. W. (Fall 2008). Transformative learning theory in New directions for adult and continuing education no. 119 p. 5-15.

Taylor, K. (2006). Autonomy and self-directed learning: A developmental journey. In C. Hoare (Ed.), *Handbook of adult development and learning.* New York: Oxford.

Taylor, K., Marienau, C., & Fiddler, M. (2000). *Developing adult learners: Strategies for teachers and trainers.* San Francisco: Jossey-Bass.

Taylor, M. (1986). Learning for self-direction in the classroom: The pattern of a transition process. *Studies in Higher Education, 11*(1), 1986.

Taylor, M., King, J., Pinsent-Johnson, C., & Lothian, T. (2003). Collaborative practices in adult literacy programs. *Adult Basic Education, 13*(2), 81–99.

Tennant, M. (1996). *Psychology and adult learning.* London: Routledge.

Terrell, S., & Dringus, L. (1999). An investigation of the effect of learning style on student success in an online learning environment. *Journal of Educational Technology Systems, 28*(3), 231–236.

Thistlethwaite, L. (1996). *Five levels of cooperative learning activities for adult learners.* Retrieved March 15, 2009, from http://aeonline.coe.utk.edu/PDFramework/Instructional%20Approaches/Cooperative.pdf

Thomas, L., & Knezek, D. (1995). *Technology literacy for the nation and for its citizens.* Retrieved April 28, 2009, from http://www.iste.org/AM/PrinterTemplate.cfm?Section=Technology_Literacy

Thompson, M. M., & McGrath, J. W. (1999). Using LNs to support a complete educational experience. *Journal of Asynchronous Learning Environment Learning Networks, 3*(2). Retrieved on March 17, 2009, from http://www.sloan-c.org/publications/jaln/v3n2/v3n2_thompson.asp

Thorpe, Dr. E. (1999). *Andragogy and technology.* Dissertations and Theses: A&I database, Publication No. AAT 3194155.

Tiffin, J. (2003). *Virtual Reality.* Retrieved April 1, 2009, from http://www.guardian.co.uk/education/2003/aug/06/highereducation.uk3

Tiffin, J., & Terashima, N. (2001). *Hyper-reality: Paradigm for the third millennium.* London: Routledge.

Toossi, M. (2002). A century of change: The U.S. labor force, 1950–2050. *Monthly Labor Review*, (pp. 15-28). Retrieved May 20, 2009, from http://www.bls.gov/opub/mlr/2002/05/art2full.pdf

Tough, A. (1967). *Learning without a teacher.* Toronto: Institute for Studies in Education.

Tough, A. (1979). *The adult's learning project.* Toronto: Institute for Studies in Education.

Tremblay, E. (2009). *Six strategies for helping the adult distance learner succeed.* Retrieved March 25, 2009, from http://www.lib.unb.ca/Texts/Teaching/bin/get4.cgi?directory=SEP99/&filename=tremblay.html

Tsao, J., Takahashi, K., Olusesu, J., & Jain, S. (2006). Transformative learning. In M. Orey (Ed.), *Emerging perspectives on learning, teaching, and technology*. Retrieved March 10, 2009, from http://projects.coe.uga.edu/epltt

Tyack, D., & Cuban, L. (1995). *Tinkering towards utopia: A century of school reform*. Cambridge, MA: Harvard University Press.

Tyler, R. W. (1950). *Basic principles of curriculum and instruction*. Chicago: University of Chicago Press.

Tynjala, P., & Hakkinen, P. (2005). E-learning at work: Theoretical underpinnings and pedagogical challenges. *Journal of Workplace Learning*, *17*(5/6), 318–336. doi:10.1108/13665620510606742

Umbrell, C. (2006). *Generational health and safety: Five generations, one workplace*. Retrieved March 27, 2009, from http://www.aiha.org/Content/AccessInfo/synergist/synergistsampleart1.htm

UNESCO Institute for Statistics. (2005). *Educational trends in perspective*. Retrieved March 21, 2009, from http://www.uis.unesco.org/TEMPLATE/pdf/wei/WEI2005.pdf

UNESCO Institute for Statistics. (2009). *Expert meeting on cyber network for learning languages*. Retrieved March 21, 2009, from http://portal.unesco.org/en/ev.php-URL_ID=44836&URL_DO=DO_TOPIC&URL_SECTION=201.html

United Nations. (2003). *Declaration of principles. Building the information society: A global challenge in the new millennium*. The Hague: United Nations.

United Nations. (2006). *World information society report*. Paris: United Nations.

United States Department of Education. (2004). *Toward a golden age in American education*. Washington, DC: U. S. Department of Education. Retrieved May 14, 2009, from http://www.ed.gov/about/offices/os/technology/plan/2004/index.html

United States Department of Labor. (1991). *Secretary's Commission on Achieving Necessary Skills (SCANS)*. Washington, DC: Government Printing Office.

University of Phoenix (n.d.). Retrieved March 23, 2009, from http://www.phoenix.edu/about_us/about_university_of_phoenix.aspx

Urban, G. L. (2008). Online trust and customer power: The emergence of customer advocacy. In P. Warren, J. Davies, & D. Brown (Eds.), *ICT futures: Delivering pervasive, real-time and secure service* (pp. 39-54). Chichester, UK: John Wiley & Sons.

van der Spek, J., I. Mulder, de Poot, H., & moelaert, F. (2002). *A Comparative Study on Social Capital in Communities in Three Sectors*. Presented to the Research workshop on social capital and IT, held on 27-28 May 2002. https://doc.telin.nl/dscgi/ds.py/Get/File-23047/social_capital_gigacscw_final.pdf

VanGent, B. (1996). Andragogy. In A. C. Tuijnman (Ed.), *The international encyclopedia of adult education and training* (pp. 114-117). Oxford, UK: Pergamon.

Varela, F., Thompson, E., & Rosch, E. (Eds.). (1993). *The embodied mind*. Cambridge, MA: MIT Press.

Verduin, J. R., & Clark, T. (1991). *Distance Education: The foundations of effective practice*. San Francisco: Jossey-Bass.

Vischeck (for color blindness). (n.d.). Retrieved from http://www.vischeck.com/index.shtml

Von Forrester, H. (1984). *Observing systems*. Salinas, CA: Intersystems Publications.

Vossen, G., & Hagemann, S. (2007). *Unleashing Web 2.0 from concepts to creativity*. Burlington, MA: Morgan Kaufmann Publishers.

Vygotsky, L. (1978). *Mind in society*. (M. Cole, Trans). Cambridge, MA: Harvard University Press.

Wahlstrom, C., Williams, B., & Shea, P. (2003). *The successful distance learning learner*. Belmont, CA: Wadsworth.

Wang, V. C. X. (2007). Chinese knowledge transmitters or western learning facilitators adult teaching methods compared. In K. P. King & V. C. X. Wang (Eds.), *Comparative adult education around the globe* (pp. 113-1370). Hangzhou, China: Zhejiang University Press.

Wang, V. C. X. (2007-2008). Chinese knowledge transmitters or western learning facilitators adult teaching methods compared. *Perspectives: The New York Journal of Adult Learning, 6*(2), 15–40.

Wang, V. C. X. (2008). *Facilitating adult learning: A comprehensive guide for successful instruction.* Boston: Pearson Education.

Wang, V. C. X., & King, K. P. (2006). Understanding Mezirow's theory of reflectivity from Confucian perspectives: A model and perspective. *Radical Pedagogy, 8*(1), 1–17.

Wang, V. C. X., & King, K. P. (2007). Confucius and Mezirow—understanding Mezirow's theory of reflectivity from Confucian perspectives: A model and perspective. In K. P. King & V. C. X. Wang (Eds.), *Comparative adult education around the globe* (pp. 253-275). Hangzhou, China: Zhejiang University Press.

Warren, C. (1989). Andragogy and N. F. S. Grundtvig: A critical Link. *Adult Education Quarterly, 39*(4), 211–223. doi:10.1177/0001848189039004003

Warren, P., Davies, J., & Brown, D. (Eds.). (2008). *ICT futures: Delivering pervasive, real-time and secure service.* Chichester, UK: John Wiley & Sons.

Wartenberg, A. D. (1994). *Andragogy and whole language.* Paper presented at the Annual Meeting of the Deleware Valley Reading Association, Merion, PA, 3/15/94. ERIC Documentation Reproduction Service No. ED 365958.

Watson, D. (2001). Pedagogy before technology: Rethinking the relationship between ICT and teaching. *Education and Information Technologies, 6*(4), 266.

Watson, G. (1960-1961). What do we know about learning? *Teachers College Record,* 253–257.

Watson, G. (Ed.). (1967). *Concepts for social change.* Washington, DC: National Training Laboratories Institute for Applied Behavioral Science, NEA.

WebCT. *Chronicle of Higher Education, 52*(16), A29. Retrieved January, 22, 2009, from http://chronicle.com/weekly/v52/i16/16a02901.htm

Webster, F. (1995). *Theories of the information society.* London: Routledge.

Webster, F. (2002). *Theories of the information society,* (2nd ed.). London: Routledge.

Webster, R., & Sudweeks, F. (2006). *Teaching for e-learning in the knowledge society: Promoting conceptual change in academics' approaches to teaching.* Current Developments in Technology-Assisted Education. Retrieved January 10, 2009, from http://www.formatex.org/micte2006/pdf/631-635.pdf

Webster's Encyclopedic Unabridged Dictionary of the English Language – Updated Revised Deluxe Edition. (1996). New York: Random House Value Publishing, Inc.

Webster's New Collegiate Dictionary. (1975). Springfield, MA: G. & C. Merriam Company.

Weimer, M. (2002). *Learner centered teaching* (1st ed.). San Francisco: Jossey-Bass.

Weinfan, L., & Davis, P. (2004). *Challenges in virtual communication: Videoconferencing, audioconferencing, and computer-mediated communications.* Santa Monica, CA: RAND Corporation.

Wellman, B., & Wortley, S. (1990). Different strokes from different folks. *American Journal of Sociology, 96*(3), 558–588. doi:10.1086/229572

Wellman, B., Salaff, J., Dimitrova, D., Garton, L., Gulia, M., & Haythornthwaite, C. (1996). Computer networks as social networks: Collaborative work, telework and virtual community. *Annual Review of Sociology, 22,* 213–238. doi:10.1146/annurev.soc.22.1.213

Welton, M. R. (1995). *In defense of lifeworld.* Albany, NY: SUNY Press.

Wenger, E. (1998). *Communities of practice: learning, meaning and identity*. Cambridge, UK: Cambridge University Press.

West, A. (2006). *Personalised learning: The limits to individualism*. Retrieved April 1, 2009, from http://www.nec.ac.uk/info/category-browse?usca_p=t&category_id=5480

Westat, K., & Creighton, S. (2000). *Participation in adult education in the United States: 1998-1999*. Washington, DC: U. S. Department of Education.

White, B. A., & Bridwell, C. (2004). Distance learning techniques. In Galbraith, M. (Ed.) *Adult learning methods: a guide for effective instruction*. (pp. 273-288). Malabar, FL: Krieger

Wikipedia, (2009). *Wiki*. Retrieved May 5, 2009. from http://en.wikipedia.org/wiki/Wikis

Wilhelm, A. (2004). *Digital nation: Toward an inclusive information society*. Cambridge, MA: MIT Press.

Wilson, B. (2002). A study of actors promoting success in computer science including gender differences. *Computer Science Education*, *12*, 141–164. doi:10.1076/csed.12.1.141.8211

Winter, R. (2003). *Alternative to the essay*. Retrieved April 1, 2009, from http://www.guardian.co.uk/education/2003/jun/10/highereducation.uk

Wittgreffe, J., Dames, M., Clark, J., & McDonald, J. (2008). End-to-end service level agreements for complex ICT solutions. In P. Warren, J. Davies, & D. Brown (Eds.), *ICT futures: Delivering pervasive, real-time and secure service* (pp. 115-128). Chichester, UK: John Wiley & Sons.

Wlodkowski, R. J. (2008). *Enhancing adult motivation to learn: A comprehensive guide for teaching all adults (3rd edition)*. San Francisco: Jossey Bass.

Woods, H. (1998). *Andragogy: The act, process, or art of imparting knowledge and skill to adults*. Retrieved October 23, 2007, from http://www.survival.com/gogy.htm

World Bank. (2003). *Constructing knowledge societies: New challenges for tertiary education*. Washington, DC: Author.

Yang, B. (2003). Toward a holistic theory of knowledge and adult learning. *Human Resource Development Review*, *2*(2), 106–129. doi:10.1177/1534484303002002002

Yiu, L., & Parker, J. (2005) Cyber action learning and virtual project teams for leadership and management development. In R.L. Jacobs & A.M. Osman-Gani(Ed.), *Workplace training & learning: cases from cross-cultural perspectives*, (pp. 1-14). NY: Pearson/Prentice Hall.

Young, G. (1985). Andragogy and pedagogy: Two ways of accompaniment. *Adult Education Quarterly*, *35*(3), 160–167. doi:10.1177/0001848185035003005

Young, M. F. D. (1998). *The curriculum of the future. From the "new sociology of education" to a critical theory of learning*. London: Falmer Press.

Zemke, R., & Zemke, S. (1981). Thirty things we know for sure about adult learning. In P. G. Jones (Ed.), *Adult learning in your classroom*, (pp. 115-118). Minneapolis: Lakewood Publications.

Zemke, R., & Zemke, S. (1996). *Adult learning: What do we know for sure*? In D. Zielinski (Ed.), *The new training library: Adult learning in your classroom* (pp. 71-74). Minneapolis: Lakewood Books.

Zhao, Y., Lei, J., & Conway, P. F. (2006). A global perspective on political definitions of e-learning: Commonalities and differences in national educational technology strategy discourses. In J. Weiss, J. Nolan, J. Hunsinger, & P. Trifonas (Eds.), *The international handbook of virtual learning environments (pt. I)* (pp. 673-698). Dordrecht, The Netherlands: Springer.

Ziemlewski, J. (2009, February). Chemical engineering progress. *Bulletin of the American Institute of Chemical Engineers*.

Žiljak, T. (2005). Lifelong learning policies in the European Union and Cro

Zirkle, C. (2002). Identification of distance education barriers for trade and industrial teacher education. *Journal of Industrial Teacher Education*, *40*(1), 20–44.

Zirkle, C. (2002). Identification of distance education barriers for trade and industrial teacher education. *Journal of Industrial Education, 40*(1), 20–44.

Zmeyov, S. I. (1994). Perspectives of adult education in Russia. In P. Jarvis & F. Poggeler (Eds.), *Developments in the education of adults in Europe* (pp. 35–42). Bern, Switzerland: Peter Lang.

Zmeyov, S. I. (1998). Andragogy: Origins, developments and trends. *International Review of Education, 44*(1), 103–108. doi:10.1023/A:1003107931006

About the Contributors

Victor C. X. Wang, Ed.D., an associate professor, joined the faculty at California State University, Long Beach (CSULB) in 2002 and has been the credential coordinator of Career and Technical Education and adult education since 2005. Dr. Wang's research and writing activities have focused on workforce education, the foundations of adult education, adult teaching and learning, training, transformative learning, cultural issues in vocational and adult education, distance education, human performance technology and curriculum development. He has published well over 100 journal articles, book chapters and books during his seven years at CSULB and has been a reviewer for five national and international journals. Currently he serves as the editor in chief of the International Journal of Adult Vocational Education and Technology. He has won many academic achievement awards from universities in China and in the United States, including the Distinguished Faculty Scholarly & Creative Achievement Award in 2009. Dr. Wang taught extensively as a professor in Chinese universities prior to coming to study and work in the United States in 1997. He has taught adult learners English as a second language, Chinese, computer technology, vocational and adult education courses, research methods, administrative leadership, human resource management and curriculum development for the past 20 years in university settings. Two of the books he has written and edited have been adopted as required textbooks by major universities in the United States, and in China. In addition, numerous universities worldwide including Howard University, Princeton University, Yale University, University of Chicago, Cornell University, UC-Berkeley and Rice University have cataloged his books and journal articles.

* * *

Manuel Ahedo, since 2006 he has been Associate Professor in Sociology in the University Rovira i Virgili (Catalonia – Spain), where he is a member of the Research Group in Social and Organizational Analysis, and a member of the GID (Group of Pedagogical Innovation) of the Faculty of Law Sciences of the same University. He is Bachelor (5 year- Licenciatura) in History in 1988 by the University of Deusto in Spain; Bachelor (5 year- Licenciatura) in Sociology in 1997 by the UNED (Spain's National Distance University). He made an MSc in Science and Technology Studies by the University of Edinburg (Scotland, United Kingdom) in 1998. In 2002 he obtained his PhD degree in Sociology in the University of the Basque Country (Spain). His main areas of interest are comparative social sciences, with a major focus on comparative economic and educational sociology, mainly at the European Union level. Currently he is interested in the organizational and institutional factors in comparative socio-learning systems.

Royce Ann Collins, Ph.D. is an Assistant Professor of Adult Education in the Department of Educational Leadership at Kansas State University. She has 17 years experience in administration of higher education for adult learners with expertise in faculty development and adult learning.

Teresa Torres-Coronas has a bachelor's degree in economics (Barcelona University) and a PhD in management (Rovira i Virgili University). She won first prize in the 2000 edition of EADA related management research. She is the author of the book Valuing Brands (Ediciones Gestión 2000, Spain), co-author of the book Retrieve Your Creativity (Septem Ediciones, Spain), and co-editor of the books Changing the way you teach: Creative tools for management education (Septem Ediciones, Spain), e-HRM: Managing knowledge people (Idea Group, USA), Higher creativity for virtual teams: Developing platforms for co-creation (Information Science Reference) and, The Encyclopedia of HRIS: Challenges in e-HRM (Information Science Reference). She is author of many articles and conference papers about intangible management, management education, and applied creativity and IT. She is management professor at the Universitat Rovira i Virgili. She is one of the researchers of the ELIS group: E-government for Local Integration with Sustainability (Hull University). She is an active member of the Management Education and Development Division (Academy of Management) and the Information Resources Management Association (IRMA).

Jeremy Dickerson is an assistant professor in the Department of Business and Information Technologies Education in the College of Education at East Carolina University. Jeremy received his doctoral degree in technology education with a minor in training and development from North Carolina State University and has over 10 years experience working in various higher education settings as a professor, private educational consultant, computing coordinator and information technology manager. Jeremy is a member of the National Business Education Association, the International Society for Business Education and the International Technology Education Association.

Lesley Farmer, Currently a Professor at California State University Long Beach, Dr. Lesley Farmer been coordinating their Librarianship program since 1999. She also taught and served as the external examiner for the University of Hong Kong's library science program, as well as worked as a library professional in K-12 school, as well public, special and academic libraries. Dr. Farmer earned her M.S. in Library Science at the University of North Carolina Chapel Hill, and received her doctorate in Adult Education from Temple University. She serves as the International Association for School Librarianship Vice President for Association Relations, helped edit their newsletter, and was selected for their research award. She edits the International Association of Library Association School Libraries Section Newsletter, and chaired the Education Division of Special Library Association. She has chaired the International Education SIG and the Gender Studies SIG for the Association of Library and Information Science Educators, and serves as treasurer for the Alpha Chapter of Phi Beta Delta (honor society for international scholars). Dr. Farmer presents regularly at national and international professional conferences. She has edited library journals, written twenty-four books and over a hundred articles and chapters; the most current books are titled Teen Girls and Technology (Teachers College Press, 2008) and Your School Library (Libraries Unlimited, 2009). Her research interests include information literacy, collaboration, assessment, and gendered educational technology.

Annette Greer, Ph.D. is Co-Director of the Office of Interdisciplinary Health Sciences Education, Assistant Clinical Professor for Public Health, and Visiting Instructor for Adult Education and the Honors Program at East Carolina University. She has been a presenter for several years for the Think In: A Teaching With Technology Showcase, UNC-CAUSE, and UNC-TLT conferences focusing on learner-centered use of technology in teaching. She has also presented at the Technologic Innovations in Nursing Education conference. Dr. Greer's research interests include learner-centered education, use of technology in education, inter-professional education, faculty development for online environments, technology as caring, and art as reflection in end of life care. Dr. Greer has additional degrees in agriculture and also has particular interest in women's health as it relates to pesticide use, rural health, and adolescent risk behaviors. She is investigator or co-investigator of service-learning and community services grants funded from K.B. Reynolds, Golden Leaf Foundation, Duke Endowment, and NC Humanities Council. Her publications focus on inter-professional education, service-learning. learner-centered pedagogy, innovation in pedagogy, and the use of technology.

John A. Henschke, Ed.D. studied with Malcolm S. Knowles at Boston University (BU). He wrote his doctoral dissertation at BU on Malcolm's contribution to the theory and practice of adult education up through 1972. John recently retired after 39 years with University of Missouri – Associate Professor of Adult Education in the College of Education at the University of Missouri-St. Louis; and, Continuing Education Specialist in the East Central Region of the University of Missouri Extension. He is now a Faculty Member of the Doctoral Program and Graduate Research, Lindenwood University, School of Education, St. Charles, MO 63301; E-Mail: JHenschke@lindenwood.edu; Phone: 636-949-4590 [Work]; Phone: 314-651-9897 [Cell]. Andragogy Website: http://www.umsl.edu/~henschke

Victor M. Hernandez-Gantes received an M.S. in Agricultural Education with concentration in International Agricultural Development, and a Ph.D. in Educational Research and Evaluation from Virginia Tech. He has served as Associate Researcher at the Center on Education and Work, University of Wisconsin-Madison, as Associate Professor at Florida State, and as Senior Educational Researcher in the Center for Educational Technologies (CET)—a center sponsored by NASA—at Wheeling Jesuit University. He currently leads the doctoral program in Career and Workforce Education at the University of South Florida. Over the years he has collaborated with organizations and faculty at a number of universities nationally and internationally. This synergistic collaboration has resulted in a number of research and demonstration projects in the areas of professional development, vocational and technical education, and the integration of mathematics and career education supported by the U.S. Department of Education, National Center for Research in Vocational Education, and NASA. He has published numerous articles on the impact of programs designed to connect school- and work-based learning on student learning and career development. His most recent publication is a book entitled Teaching ELLs in CTE Programs (with B. Blank), published by Routledge.

John Hope, Ph.D., his background is teaching in New Zealand primary, intermediate and secondary schools. He left school teaching after some years as the principal of New Zealand's largest primary school, a school featuring nationally recognised programmes for gifted students and an international reputation for use of ICT. Later in his career John became a school inspector and curriculum writer and was seconded to the University of Auckland as Director Primary Teacher Education to establish initial teacher education programmes. Following successful establishment of teacher education programmes, other University of Auckland appointments followed, including Director of the University of Auckland Principals Centre, and Associate Dean (International) positions in two faculties. He currently directs several overseas twinning degree programmes, coordinates all international activity within the Faculty of Education and has university-wide international responsibilities. Teaching and supervision interest include pedagogical applications of ICT in learning, educational leadership and gifted education. Research activity includes the same topics, but also includes research into education for international settings.

Eric Kisling has his B.S. in Commerce & Business Administration from the University of Alabama, Tuscaloosa, Alabama. He earned his M.S. and Ph.D. in Instructional Systems Technology from Indiana University, Bloomington, Indiana. Dr. Kisling is an Assistant Professor in the Business and Information Technologies Education Department at East Carolina University, Greenville, NC. Dr. Kisling teaches face-to-face and online undergraduate courses in Information Technology and Business Education. His research explores the implementation of socio-technical systems methodologies in online courses, understanding the quality of work life (QWL) of both students and teachers in face-to-face and online courses in traditional, undergraduate education, the use of androgogy in information technology classrooms, virtual environments in education, freeware and open source solutions, e-waste, and Web 2.0 technologies.

Geraint Lang is a principal lecturer in the Faculty of Education at Anglia Ruskin University in the United Kingdom. He first worked for the university's learning technology research centre, Ultralab from 2000 until 2006. He was part of the team that developed and ran the then DfES (the UK government's Education Department) pilot online community for head teachers, *Talking Heads*. Between 2002 and 2003 Geraint, a fluent Welsh speaker, was seconded to the Welsh Assembly Government to assist in setting up a similar bilingual online project (called *Pen-i-Ben*) for newly qualified head teachers and their mentors throughout Wales. In 2005 he joined the Ultraversity learning facilitation team, tutoring on Anglia Ruskin's wholly online BA (Hons) Learning, Technology Research degree course. Mature students from a variety of workplace backgrounds utilise technology for learning in order to study collaboratively online from locations throughout the world. Geraint's involvement in the application of technology for learning has focused his research interests in the area of continuous professional development through facilitated online communities. In recent years he has also been able to draw upon his previous experience developing video records of achievement for young people with special educational needs by working on two educational animation developments with the BBC.

James B. Martin, Ph.D. is the Associate Dean of Academics for the Army's Command and General Staff College at Ft. Leavenworth, Kansas. His career educating adults began 17 years ago and has encompassed work at adult-focused programs at small liberal arts colleges and working with the Army and other services in educating senior officers. His areas of research currently include faculty development and assessment.

George R. Maughan, Ed.D., is currently Professor and Director of the PhD in Technology Management Program at Indiana State University. He received his doctorate from West Virginia University. He has taught and conducted research on the topics of technology studies, technology transfer and management, training, and communication systems in higher education for more than 26 years at West Virginia University and Indiana University before joining the faculty at Indiana State University in 2003. For

16 years, Dr. Maughan was President of Training Consultants, Inc., a management consulting firm that focused on human resource and training issues for organizations such as U.S. Department of Energy, Saab Cars USA, Dominion Transmission Corporation (natural gas), Monsanto, National Drinking Water Clearinghouse, and General Electric. In addition, he has served as consultant for the U.S. Agency for International Development, the U.S. Information Agency, and the Asian Development Bank in India and Sri Lanka. Both domestic and international consulting projects involved strategic planning and trouble-shooting of workforce performance issues in technological organizations. He began his career teaching Junior High School. Dr. Maughan has published books, journal articles and made numerous professional presentations throughout his career. His current research interests include: technological literacy, cognitive processes of master technicians, training for development in 3rd world countries, and technology transfer and management.

Vivian W. Mott, Ph.D. is Professor and Chair of the Counselor and Adult Education Department in the College of Education at East Carolina University in Greenville, North Carolina. She earned her Ph.D. from the University of Georgia and her B.S. and M.S. in Education from the University of Tennessee. She also holds graduate certificates in Gerontology, Women's Studies, and Ethnic Studies. She is a Cyril O. Houle/Kellogg Research Scholar, Salzburg Fellow, recipient of ACHE Exemplary Professional Contributions Award, the NCAEA Gruman Award for Lifelong Service to Adult and Continuing Education, East Carolina University's Women of Distinction Award, and other teaching and research awards. Dr. Mott's research interests focus on the development of professional expertise, multicultural issues, and ethics in education and business. In particular, her research and program development in areas of mentoring and professional development have included Native American women, higher education faculty, multinational corporations, public school teachers, and retired women. Her publications include numerous journal articles and 15 book chapters; she is co-editor of two books, Organization of Adult and Continuing Education (1995), and Charting a Course for Continuing Professional Education: Reframing Professional Practice (New Directions, No. 86, 2000). Her work has been published in Adult Education Quarterly, Continuing Studies in Education, Journal of Transformative Education, and the New Directions on Adult and Continuing Education series. Dr. Mott is founder and owner of Wilson Mott & Associates, a consulting and management firm specializing in human resource management and organizational culture, with business/industry and governmental clients throughout North America.

Davison Mupinga, Ph.D. completed his doctoral work in career and technical education from Louisiana State University and is currently an Associate Professor in Career and Technical Education in the department of Teaching, Learning and Curriculum Studies at Kent State University. Dr. Mupinga has taught a variety of courses in career and technical education, human resource development, technology education, and instructional technology. Over the years, he has conducted new teacher certification workshops, train-the-trainer programs, and occupational safety training programs. His research focuses on career and technical teacher education and international vocational education. He has published numerous research articles in a number of refereed and practitioner journals and presented at national and international conferences on career and technical education, human resource development and instructional technology. Dr. Mupinga's most recent research is on integrating technology into instruction, specifically, examining the impact of internet tools on learning. Dr. Mupinga is a member of the Association of Career and Technical Education, and the International Vocational Education and Training Association; and currently, he is the Editor of the International Journal of Vocational Education and Training.

Mario Arias Oliva, has a PhD in Management from Rovira Rovira i Virgili University. His PhD research was about Virtual Organizations. He took courses at Erasmus Universiteit Rótterdam as well as MBA courses at Rotterdam School of Management (Holland). He is professor at Rovira i Virgili University in the management area. Dr. Arias also collaborates with the Center for Computing and Social Responsibility, De Montfort University (UK) where he is an international research associate since (2002). He has conducted several research projects, including "Self-employment analysis in Spain" (Edited by the Spanish Economic Ministry) and The Relationship between Training Consultancy Organizational Design and Strategy:The Effects on Quality and Performance of Training Services (Edited by the Spanish Union "Unión General de Trabajadores, UGT"). Mario Arias has been invited speaker to several MBA programs, seminars, courses and international conferences.

Judith Parker has earned a doctorate, Ed.D. degree, and an M.S. degree in Adult and Continuing Education from Teachers College/Columbia University in New York, an M.S. degree in physics from Purdue University in Indiana, and a B.S. degree in physics and mathematics from Notre Dame College in Ohio. Dr. Parker has over 20 years experience in leadership positions within business organizations emerging into the global market and has been instrumental in leading them toward becoming global learning organizations. She has worked extensively with technical managers and technical employees in Asia and Europe in leadership education and training and technical employee skill development. Dr. Parker's academic experience includes teaching adult learning and leadership theory and practice, staff development and training, and organizational development, in graduate programs at Teachers College/ Columbia University and St. Mary's University of Minnesota using totally on-line format, totally classroom format and blended delivery. She also teaches college physics and astronomy at Muhlenberg College in Pennsylvania. She has presented numerous papers at conferences globally including the Academy of Management, American Association of Physics Teachers, American Society of Training and Development, College Industry Education Conference, Quality and Productivity Management Association, Business and Multimedia Conference in Ireland, Lisbon 2000 European Conference on ODL Networking for Quality Learning, and World Open Learning for Business Conferences in the UK. She has authored numerous articles in publications including the "Compendium on Uses of Distance Learning Technologies in Engineering Education" and the "Journal of the International Association for Continuing Engineering Education" and book chapters including "Cyber Action Learning and Virtual Project Teams for Leadership and Management Development" with L. Yiu in the book Workplace Training and Learning: A Cross-Cultural Perspective and the chapter "The Online Adult Learner: Profiles and Practices" in Handbook of Research on E-Learning Applications for Career and Technical Education by edited by Victor Wang. She has been elected a Fellow of the American Association for the Advancement of Science, and has received the American Association of Physics Teachers Innovative Teaching Award and the Park College Educational Partnership Award.

Steven W. Schmidt is Assistant Professor of Adult Education at East Carolina University in Greenville, North Carolina. He holds PhD and M.S. degrees in Adult Education from the University of Wisconsin – Milwaukee, and a Bachelor of Business Administration degree from the University of Wisconsin – Whitewater. Prior to joining the faculty of East Carolina University, Schmidt spent 18 years working in the Fortune 500, primarily in the areas of employee training and development. His research interests include workplace learning, cultural competence in the workplace, and online learning.

M. Arántzazu Vidal-Blasco, has a bachelor's degree in economics (Barcelona University) and a Ph.D. in accounting (Rovira i Virgili University). She is professor at the Universitat Rovira i Virgili. She is working in several research projects about e-learning and higher education and she is also doing research on intellectual capital management in non-profit organizations.

Index

D

E

F

M

N

O

P

R

S